SOCIOLOGY for
CANADIANS

IMAGES OF SOCIETY

SECOND EDITION

‖▌ EX LIBRIS ▪

_____

_____

SOCIOLOGY for CANADIANS

IMAGES OF SOCIETY
SECOND EDITION

ALEXANDER HIMELFARB
Department of Justice
Ottawa

C. JAMES RICHARDSON
Department of Sociology
University of New Brunswick

McGraw-Hill Ryerson Limited

Toronto   Montreal   New York   Auckland   Bogotá
Caracas   Lisbon   London   Madrid   Mexico
Milan   New Delhi   Paris   San Juan
Singapore   Sydney   Tokyo

SOCIOLOGY for CANADIANS

IMAGES OF SOCIETY
SECOND EDITION

1 2 3 4 5 6 7 8 9 10 ML 0 9 8 7 6 5 4 3 2 1

∞ Printed and bound in Canada using acid-free paper.

Care has been taken to trace ownership of copyright material contained in this text. The publishers will gladly take any information that will enable them to rectify any reference or credit in subsequent editions.

Canadian Cataloguing in Publication Data
Himelfarb, Alexander, date
Sociology for Canadians

2nd ed.
Includes bibliographical references.
ISBN 0-07-549310-1

1. Sociology. 2. Canada—Social conditions.
I. Richardson, C. James, 1941–   . II. Title.

HM51.H56 1991   301   C90-094908-2

Photograph Credits
Pages 3, 94, 145, 270, 311, 344 (both), & 370: Dick Hemingway.
Page 33: Steve Soloman.
Pages 113 (PA 150432), 182 (PA 154119), 209 (PA 93924), & 403 (PA 152504): National Archives of Canada.
Page 241: Canadian Wildlife Service, Environment Canada.
Page 65: Ministry of Industry and Tourism.

CONTENTS

CHAPTER 2 DOING SOCIOLOGY

PART TWO BASIC CONCEPTS AND PROCESSES

CHAPTER 3 CULTURE

CHAPTER 4   SOCIAL STRUCTURE

CHAPTER 5   SOCIALIZATION AND INTERACTION

CHAPTER 6   THE CHANGING FAMILY

CHAPTER 7   DEVIANCE, CONTROL, AND CHANGE

PART THREE PERSPECTIVES ON CANADA

CHAPTER 8 DEMOGRAPHIC PERSPECTIVES

PART FOUR   INEQUALITY IN CANADA

CHAPTER 11   SOCIAL INEQUALITY

xv

CHAPTER 12   EDUCATIONAL INEQUALITY

CHAPTER 13   ETHNIC INEQUALITY

PART FIVE CONCLUSION

CHAPTER 14 DIMENSIONS OF SOCIAL CHANGE

PREFACE

The first edition of this text, *People, Power and Process*, was written a decade ago. As sociologists who did their graduate work in the late 1960s and early 1970s, we had witnessed and been part of the cultural and social upheaval of that period. We had been excited and enthused by the accompanying upheaval in sociology as mainstream American functionalist sociology was attacked, in turn by Marxist sociologists, by those committed to interpretive approaches and by Canadian nationalists. We were keen to write a book that would incorporate all of these changes. Naturally, that first book very much reflected these events and debates and, in particular, the concern with the fate of Canadian society. This was the issue that was predominant in the first really genuine attempt to create a Canadian sociology distinct from the American approaches we had all been required to learn.

In 1982 we revised and enlarged the book, largely in response to suggestions by professors, who had used the text in the classroom, and by our students, and partly as a result of our own dissatisfaction with our first attempt at writing a textbook. We think that the result was an improvement though we saw our second attempt not as a new book but as a respectable and needed revision. Our publishers chose to give the 1982 book a new title and to keep the earlier work in print. But, nevertheless, the 1982 edition continued to be informed by and to discuss issues which were receding further into the past: though still important, these were now more properly seen as part of the history of the discipline of sociology.

This edition retains the basic theoretical approach and most of the organization of our first two efforts. In both we were concerned with how to convey to students the link between the sociology of everyday life and the larger and sometimes less obvious issues of social structure. In coming to grips with that problem, our mentors, then as now, are through their writings, Berger and Luckmann and C. Wright Mills, sociologists who, in our view, have come closest to welding the micro and macro into a unified perspective. In this, as in previous editions, we have tried, as much as possible, to view interpersonal relations within a larger structural context and tried to focus on how people make sense of and effect change within these social structures.

Moreover, this edition of the book retains the initial premise that we did not want to write a book about Canadian society but, rather, an introduction to sociology which, unlike introductory textbooks of the time, would have relevance to Canadian students. We are still presenting a book which draws upon the rich social-psychological literature of American sociology and the ever-growing body of literature taught in Canadian society courses and, given the now large number of Canadian introductory textbooks on the market, we assume in most introductory courses as well.

So, there are a number of continuities between this edition and our previous books. But, inevitably, there were many examples and references to then current events which are now dated. For example, while in the long run we do face an energy crisis and the ecological dangers of burning fossil fuels grow more and more urgent, we simply cannot take for granted that these are issues of concern to most students. Nor, to use a related example, can we in 1988 write about Alberta in the way we could in the early 1980s. Much of this revision, then, is an updating to make the book more relevant to today's students, and, of course, to take advantage of more recent data.

There are, however, at least two reasons other than mere face lifting for this revision. The first is what we noted above, that some of the issues and debates which informed our first book are now history, and some of what seemed like great break-throughs at the time have not come to fruition or have not had all that much impact on how sociologists go about their business. Thus, we write this edition from a different vantage point than we did in 1978 or even in 1982.

The second reason is that, in recent years, we have seen considerable rethinking among Canadian sociologists about a whole lot of issues that seemed almost universal truths a decade ago. We have had to rethink much of what we "knew" about ethnic inequality. We have had to revise many of the earlier pronouncements about the nature of power and inequality in Canada and the way in which capitalism developed in this country. While dependency theory has not been abandoned completely, some of what we described in the earlier editions now seems to most sociologists as simplistic and parochial, based on incomplete evidence or dubious assumptions.

Some of this rethinking made its way into *Sociology for Canadians* but here it is dealt with more explicitly and, we think, more clearly. One result is that there is now a separate chapter on the development and state of Canadian sociology; in earlier editions this had been subsumed within a more general discussion of political culture and ideology. This was an addition aided considerably by the publication in 1985 of the "State of the Art" issue of the *Canadian Review of Sociology and Anthropology* and, in the following year by Bob Brym's extended piece in *Current Sociology* on anglophone Canadian sociology now, with the collaboration of Bonnie Fox, extended into book form (Brym and Fox, 1989).

Sociology in Canada, as elsewhere, is in the process of being transformed by feminist scholarship and perspectives. Superficially, this means a change in language and this text does conform to recent guidelines about sexist language and suggestions of how to avoid the more subtle manifestations of sexism in what one writes and says. At a more crucial level, feminist critiques have made all social scientists more sensitive to the fact that men and women have often inhabited different but equally important social worlds — something that did not emerge very clearly, if at all, in earlier theory and research. And, with that sensitivity, has come recognition that much of our sociology, while purporting to be about people, has really been about men, their lives, their work, their social mobility and so on. And, insofar as women have been studied, they were so from a male perspective. We do not claim this edition fully incorporates a feminist perspective, partly because it remains the product of two men and partly because that perspective is only now making its way fully into most of the areas of sociological theory and research that we are describing in this introduction to sociology. But, it has been informed by that perspective and is, in important ways and at various levels, a different book than we wrote in the past. The dominant perspective in Canadian sociology in the 1970s became dependency theory; in the 1980s it was feminism.

Unlike the previous edition, the book is divided into four rather than five parts. Part One introduces the fundamental debates, controversies and assumptions about human nature and society and how these have created and shaped sociological perspectives and ways of doing research. Part Two again concentrates on concepts, approaches and processes that describe and explain the relationship and tension between the individual and society, between everyday life and social structure. However, several changes have been made to this part.

First, in the previous editions, we chose to introduce students to the sociology of marriage and family within an explicit focus on processes of change and in the context of the discussions in the preceding thirteen chapters. This has surprised many users of the text who have come to expect family to be introduced early on in an introductory textbook. While we remain convinced that one can best grasp the nature of debates about social change when it is grounded in a familiar and substantive area such as family and kinship, the chapter now follows the discussion of socialization and interaction. Continuing controversies about the relationship between economic change and family change have meant that an important focus of this chapter remains the issue of social change. Second, the discussion of political culture and ideology, which formed part of what was formerly Chapter 8, "Political Culture and Sociology," has now been incorporated into Chapter 3, "Culture." Finally, we have felt increasing dissatisfaction with the discussion in Chapter 13, "Collective Behaviour and Social Protest," and now attempt to deal with some of these issues in the context of the discussion of deviant behaviour and social control.

Part Three brings all of the discussion of Parts One and Two to bear on Canadian society, its demography, its sociology and its economy. As mentioned earlier, Canadian sociology now occupies a separate chapter and is given a more extended treatment than in previous editions. Another change is that while this remains a dual as opposed to a multi-authored text, Dr. Ab Currie, a specialist in the area, has provided extensive materials on demography and a discussion which introduces you to how demographers think about their society. As with the previous edition, Part Four focuses explicitly on dimensions of inequality — class, sexual, educational and ethnic inequalities — in Canadian society. It is in these chapters, particularly, that much of the recent research and rethinking in sociology are most clearly reflected. The final chapter serves as a summary of these issues by focussing on people's responses to inequality and collective attempts to change society.

At the request of those who had used earlier editions, more teaching materials are included. New to this edition are chapter "Overviews." These are not intended as substitutes for reading the chapters but as guidelines to reading the chapter, what issues to look for and what questions you should be asking and be able to answer or think about when you have finished the chapter. Another addition is a glossary of "Key Concepts" at the end of the text. Again, memorizing these is not the same as reading the chapter and learning about the concept in the context of the discussion. But, they may be useful as study aids and ways to alert you to what we believe are the important issues. All chapters once again end with "Suggestions for Further Reading." Each list is meant to be suggestive rather than exhaustive, particularly since we mention no journal articles and have included only those books we think suitable for students just beginning to study sociology.

On a more personal note, this edition of the text has been a long time in the writing partly because the authors, once members of the same sociology department, have, for a number of years, been physically separated. As professional and domestic commitments have mounted, it has been nearly impossible to do the kind of collaborative writing we both enjoyed through the first two books. But, partly, the long delay reflects a certain friendly interpersonal tension between the two authors. One has remained committed to Canadian academic sociology and has been influenced by the new directions in the discipline. The other has chosen perhaps another kind of sociology, in the public service, and has been concerned with issues of public policy. Out of the unfortunately limited exchange between the authors has, we hope, emerged a joint commitment to ask how Canadian sociology matters to Canadians.

A decade after writing our first preface, we continue to owe much to the influence of Leo Zakuta, now retired, and the late Rex Lucas, both of whom, at various points, were our teachers at the University of Toronto. Many others have provided ideas and encouragement. Richardson would, in particular, single out Bob Brym, Jennie Hornosty and Larry Wisniewski, all of whom, in different ways, have kept him sane. Himelfarb gives similar thanks to John Evans, Frum Himelfarb and C. P. Nuttall for much the same reasons. As ever, we owe a special but different appreciation to our children and wives. Frum Himelfarb and Jennie Hornosty are, themselves, academics and, as we acknowledge above, both made important intellectual contributions to the writing. But, Alex thanks Frum and Jim thanks Jennie for much more. Our children may not have helped in the writing but we are better sociologists because of them. Himelfarb thanks David, Nomi and Jordan; Richardson, Jason, Justin, Michael and Rebecca.

SOCIOLOGY for CANADIANS

IMAGES OF SOCIETY
SECOND EDITION

PART
O N E

PERSPECTIVES AND METHODS

CHAPTER 1

SOCIOLOGICAL PERSPECTIVES

OVERVIEW

INTRODUCTION

CONTEMPORARY SOCIOLOGY: POPULAR IMAGES

SOURCES OF CONTROVERSY

THE SOCIOLOGICAL TRADITION

BASIC ASSUMPTIONS

THOMAS HOBBES

JEAN JACQUES ROUSSEAU

THE DEVELOPMENT OF SOCIOLOGY

AUGUST COMTE

EMILE DURKHEIM

KARL MARX

MAX WEBER

SOCIOLOGY IN NORTH AMERICA

THE ACTION/BEHAVIOUR CONTROVERSY: WEBER AND DURKHEIM

SOCIAL STRUCTURE: SUBJECTIVE AND OBJECTIVE

PRIVATE TROUBLES AND PUBLIC ISSUES

CONTEMPORARY PERSPECTIVES ON SOCIAL STRUCTURE

THE ORDER MODEL

THE CONFLICT APPROACH

THE SYMBOLIC INTERACTION APPROACH

DEBATES WITHOUT RESOLUTION

APPROACH OF THIS TEXT

SUGGESTIONS FOR FURTHER READING

OVERVIEW

This chapter introduces you to the discipline of sociology, to some sense of how sociology developed, to the great thinkers who shaped that development, and, most important, to how sociologists carve out a particular subject area for study and analysis. You should, by the end of this chapter, know what it is that sociologists study, the importance of perspectives in helping them define their subject matter, and the crucial controversies and debates that ensure that sociology will continue to grow and evolve.

While you will have certain common-sense assumptions about sociology, you are asked to put these aside. You will be presented with some of the crucial names in the development of sociology — August Comte, Emile Durkheim, Max Weber, Karl Marx, and George Mead — but you will not be expected to know the richness and texture of their work. For that, you will have to read their classic writings. In this chapter you are only expected to understand how each contributed to carrying out the distinctive discipline of sociology and contributed to the current perspectives in the discipline.

You will also be introduced to three major perspectives: order, conflict, and symbolic interactionism; these will reappear throughout the text. In this chapter, it is important that you come to understand how the philosophical assumptions sociologists make about human nature shape the questions they ask and the answers they produce.

This chapter will allow you an opportunity to explore and, perhaps, rediscover your own assumptions about human nature because sooner or later, as a sociologist or a citizen, you will have to make some value choices and commitments.

▌ INTRODUCTION

Some time back, J. O'Neill described sociology as the skin trade. This is to say that sociology is about people and their relationships. Of course, people have, in some way, always thought about the nature of humans, about themselves and their relationships. In fact, that is part of what makes sociology so difficult. You begin this course with many theories and assumptions about social life, about "how to win friends and influence people," about how to beat the system, and even about large issues, such as freedom and democracy and the dangers of socialism. Many of these ideas you have inherited from your parents and from the society in which you live. Some of these ideas you've picked up in everyday life because they seem to you to have worked. They are just common sense, you would say.

In teaching our classes, we invariably find some students who ask whether they are still entitled to their opinions on matters of social life. Where do their opinions stand against those of sociologists, they ask. The answer lies in the difference between how sociologists think about the social world and how we all think about it in our everyday lives. Certainly, sociology is about ideas. It is also about observations. Most important, it is about the link between ideas and observations and how the scientific method can help us to a fuller understanding of the society in which we live, an understanding that may extend beyond and even challenge our common-sense theories. This is why the role of science in sociology has been a major preoccupation of the theories we will be discussing in this chapter.

Sociology also differs from everyday thinking because it forces us to transcend our immediate experiences. This is true in two ways. First, it forces us to think about the quality of evidence we are using in deriving our conclusions. Think how often you have been involved in some argument in which your opponent offers the coup de grâce: I had a cousin who tried it and it worked. How can you answer? The sociologist's preoccupation with systematic observation asks always to look at the quality of evidence for a conclusion. Second, sociology has defined a subject matter that forces us to think about everyday life in new ways. Think how often you explain your experiences in terms of villains, victims, and fools, individual characteristics, and stereotypes reflecting some prejudice about what *all* women, Jews, blacks, English Canadians, French Canadians, or aboriginal Canadians are like. Our fear of crime in some areas of the city is simply because of "those people." That person was successful because of his/ her special qualities or because he/she is a villain, and that other one was a failure because he/she was a fool or she is a woman.

Sociologists ask us to think about these issues in a very different way. They ask us to suspend our judgments for a moment and ask how the economic system or the education system or even the family structure can help us understand these people and their behaviour. The discipline of sociology is, finally, about the relationship between people and the society in which they live. It examines, through systematic observations, theories about how social forces shape human behaviour.

We will, therefore, often encounter sociological questions that we would not otherwise have thought to ask. For example, sociologists care about accounting for the rise of capitalism or the role of Canada in the world economy. In many ways being a sociologist means understanding the relationships between what may appear to be remote historical and theoretical issues and the preoccupations of our everyday lives.

CONTEMPORARY SOCIOLOGY: POPULAR IMAGES

Some years ago Peter Berger (1963) wrote that sociology had not yet permeated the public consciousness. There were, he regretted, no jokes about sociologists. People did not know enough about sociologists even to joke about them. All this has changed. If the jokes and barbs on public affairs shows, in situation comedies, and in the popular press are any indication, sociology is coming of age. If this is true it means that as you read this book you carry certain images, probably stereotypical images, of what sociologists do and how they do it.

Certainly these stereotypes and the bad press sociology has been receiving are based on real problems in the discipline. Much in the study of sociology does seem incomprehensible, badly written, and sometimes irrelevant to more pressing concerns. When it is easy to understand, it seems little more than common sense. Moreover, many would argue that when sociologists are not stating the trivial or creating gobbledygook, they are confusing us with statistics. However much merit there may be in these accusations, it may be too early to confess our sins. We certainly don't wish to discourage you before you begin what we think is an exciting discipline. Let us look more closely at each of these images of sociology and the extent to which each is an exaggeration and a distortion.

As we said, many people seem to view sociologists as mainly manipulators of statistics, as "number crunchers." And many seem to feel that the use of statistics is somehow inappropriate in the study of human behaviour, that statistics miss what is important about people's behaviour—that "no good can come of it."

First, sociology has many varied research techniques, not all of them statistical. Indeed, many sociologists studiously ignore statistical analysis. Sociology has its humanists and artists, and many view sociology, ideally, as some combination of art and science.

Nevertheless, some social statistics are likely to be found in almost any substantial piece of sociology; nor is this altogether a bad idea. Our common-sense perceptions tell us that the times are changing: rates of mental illness are soaring, patterns of sexual behaviour have, for better or worse, dramatically changed, rates of homicide and other crimes of violence are on the upswing, and families are much smaller than in the past. Careful statistical analysis, however, may reveal that the nature and direction of the change is not as we perceive.

Robert Merton (1961) describes how many an amateur sociologist has tried to account for the supposedly increased rates of mental illness in North America. However, because of the careful statistical analysis carried out by some professional sociologists, we now know that the rates of mental illness are probably no higher today than they have been for the last hundred years. In other words, our amateur sociologist might well be explaining something that does not exist. At the least, statistics are useful to help us describe what it is we are trying to explain.

This is not to say that some sociologists do not suffer from "quantophrenia," a slavish devotion to statistics. Some sociologists may be so preoccupied with research techniques that they lose sight of the substance of sociology. Certainly there are a number of important sociological questions that do not lend themselves to statistical analysis. There is something discomfiting, about asking people to assess their happiness on a scale of one to ten, to attach some number to their sense of self or their spiritual commitments.

This is not to say that such issues are not of central interest to the sociologist, but rather that the concern with quantification may lead to a spurious or misleading precision. A sociology based purely on statistical analysis would indeed be sterile but, for the most part, this is not the direction of sociology. Sociologists do not try to count everything. They learn by living with the groups they are studying, by talking to people, by studying historical documents. As sociologists continue to have at their disposal more sophisticated statistical techniques, in conjunction with other "softer" methods, they are more able to assemble systematic data for analysis.

Another common view of the sociologist is that of the jargon monger who invents unnecessary, usually ugly, words to complicate, mystify, and impress. When social science researchers explain how system components "simultaneously interface and impact upon one another through a feedback loop," they may impress; they certainly mystify. They may simply be saying that things are related to one another in complicated ways. On the other hand, they may not be. Here jargon is getting in the way of communication. Very often everyday words would do nicely, but not always.

Sociologists do have a technical language. Sociology provides a way of viewing the social world that is different from other social sciences and different from how we view the world in everyday life. It "sees" different things and it must sometimes invent words to describe what it sees. Also, as with any discipline, sociology requires a technical language to facilitate precise communication so that when several sociologists use the same words we can trust that they mean more or less the same things.

Again, however, the accusation has some merit; no doubt some sociology, perhaps much sociology, is jargon filled, and this can become a problem when some versions of sociology become incomprehensible even to other sociologists. In this text we try to avoid jargon and technical language as much as possible, but the latter cannot be entirely avoided. One must distinguish between jargon and technical language; to learn a discipline one must learn its language.

What seems to upset the critics of sociology most, however, is their belief that sociology is attempting the impossible in trying to find regularities or uniformities in human behaviour, and that what sociologists are doing is dangerous because it puts people "in boxes," dehumanizing them. Sociological knowledge, the argument goes, is dangerous to society because it is the resource "through which men can be molded to fit a new and obnoxious social order" (Merton, 1974:15).

There is an obvious inconsistency here. If it were true that sociology was destined to fail in its search for patterns or uniformities in human behaviour, it is difficult to see how it could be a danger to anyone. You can't have it both ways. One cannot argue both that the sociologist's attempt to predict human behaviour is doomed to failure because people are far too complex and unpredictable, and that the sociologist's attempts to predict human behaviour are dangerous because the knowledge produced may be used to manipulate and control people. The real questions here must be separated and will be dealt with throughout the text. First, what are the limits to sociology? How much can it ever hope to know? How much can it ever hope to predict? And, second, how must sociology be used and for whose ends?

This brings us to a related accusation that the findings of sociologists are trivial, that sociologists spend thousands of dollars to find out what everyone already knows or what journalists and film-makers seem able to find out more effectively and at much less cost. Part of the reason for this accusation rests in the fact that there seems to be an unfortunately long filtering process before sociological findings reach the public. And certainly sociology does sometimes confirm what we already know.

In fact, however, sociologists are more likely to upset rather than to confirm popular or common-sense notions. Peter Berger (1963) calls this the "debunking theme" in sociology. Many undergraduate students find sociology helpful not only in understanding society and others, but in understanding themselves. At the same time, many find that sociology can be upsetting as one after another of their beliefs is challenged or held up for investigation. Do the poor commit the bulk of crimes? How much upward mobility is there in Canada? Are Canadians witnessing the breakdown of the family? You may find that what you "know" about these things and the answers you find in this text are different. Even if it turns out that you were right about what is happening, you may find that you had not thought out or recognized the implications. Here sociology can contribute.

Basic to sociology is the notion of *unintended consequences*, that as people engage in social relationships their behaviour produces consequences that were not the intent of those relationships. For example, intensified punishment of criminals may produce more crime rather than inhibit it. Organizations that attempt to bring back into line such "deviants" as drug users, alcoholics, and fat people may often make it harder for these people ever to think of themselves as normal. Behaviour that seems sensible in the short run may prove disastrous in the long run. Growing recognition of the importance of these unintended consequences has led to a demand for the services of sociologists in such fields as law, social work, medicine, education, city planning, business and labour, to name a few.

This is not to say that journalists and artists do not contribute valuable insights about human behaviour and society. On the contrary, journalistic writers and "pop sociologists," such as Hunter Thompson, Morton Hunt, Tom Wolfe, Philip Slater, Alvin Toffler, Vance Packard, June Callwood, and Susan Crean have the knack of homing in on what are the important social issues to most people in their society. Indeed, they reach a far wider audience than do academic sociologists and are therefore likely to have much greater impact.

Also, because they are less constrained by the rules of the sociological method, their analyses of social problems and social institutions are often more direct and hard hitting than conventional sociology. Jessica Mitford's (1977) analysis of American "death institutions," in particular the undertaking industry, is one of the most interesting and penetrating studies available on the topic.

Social scientists occasionally do choose to present their work in a novelistic or discursive way, often with moving and impressive results. For example, Elliot Leyton's book, *Dying Hard*, tells us, without the aid of statistical tables or social science theory, a good deal about what we all ought to know about the world of Canadian miners. In a graphic description of how miners must learn to live with the prospect of "miner's disease" and the slow death that inevitably follows, Leyton teaches us all a good deal about the relationship between the individual and the mining industry (and capitalism more generally). Unquestionably, the artist provides countless insights for the sociologist.

However, it is important to keep in mind the distinction between these kinds of work and conventional sociology and to understand the distinctive role of sociological research. First, it is more difficult to replicate journalistic and artistic accounts and to tell what information was left out. Good sociological research, like good science generally, points out the "deviant" cases and indicates what hypotheses and hunches were not confirmed. Ideally, good sociological research involves a search for negative cases, which the journalist or artist may ignore because they spoil the thrust of the argument.

Second, as we shall explore more fully in the next few chapters, journalists, artists, and the public generally may not share the sociological emphasis on social structure —

the larger context that frames our actions. As will become evident, things that seem personally alarming, such as unemployment among young people, may also be social problems, the result of structural change in Canadian society.

But, there is another more subtle issue that we are only beginning to understand. Sociology, certainly in Canada, is dominated by the generation of the 1960s. Their concerns, their preoccupations, may not be the same as yours. Many are only now coming to realize the potential of the new information technology. Sociologists in Canada rely very heavily on the power of the written word, books and professional articles which may communicate inadequately to a generation raised on VCRs, video cameras and personal computers linked to vast networks of information banks and fellow users. It may well be that sociologists will have to confront directly the question of how to communicate effectively to an audience which counts in bits and bytes. Certainly, it will be interesting to watch the new generation of sociologists reappraise the obsessions and techniques of the dominant sociologists of the day. But, sociology, like art, is judged on its ability to capture what is enduring about the human condition.

SOURCES OF CONTROVERSY

We have described some of the controversies that rage about sociology and within sociology. One could be dismayed at the amount of disagreement within the field. We shall argue that these controversies might better be viewed positively, as necessary for the advancement of any science.

These controversies are not new. They have their roots in debates that precede sociology as a discipline, and in long-standing conflicts about human nature and the relationship of the individual to society. Indeed, as we shall describe briefly in the next few pages, sociology grew up in the context of this and other fundamental debates.

THE SOCIOLOGICAL TRADITION

One of the features that distinguishes humans from other species is that they do indeed reflect upon themselves and their relationship to the larger community. These concerns — sociological issues — are by no means new. But typically, explanations of the social world, as of the natural world, have been couched in the language of religion, magic, and the spirits. This has meant that for long periods of time what we now conceive as important sociological concerns were then treated as heresy — one does not question that which is a product of the gods. We might say that while it is universal that people seek explanations, what is more unique to our times is where and how we look for the answers and the lack of certitude with which we accept these answers. Quite simply, sociology is one way of explaining ourselves to ourselves. To understand this way of knowing demands that we understand how sociology broke with more traditional explanations.

Sociology has its roots in the eighteenth century and, in particular, the intellectually and socially exciting period prior to the French Revolution — the Enlightenment. Historians refer to the eighteenth century as the Enlightenment to emphasize the dramatic break from what seems largely to have been centuries of darkness, the long period from the fall of the Roman Empire given over to superstition and ignorance. A variety of forces seemed to come together in the Enlightenment, ideas and assumptions that were crucial to the development of the sociological perspective.

During this time, social and political philosophers were much taken by advances in the physical sciences in the preceding century, above all, those of Sir Isaac Newton. Newton had almost single-handedly created a revolution in scientific thought. His laws demonstrated that reason and observation could be — indeed must be — united. Newton supposedly "discovered" the law of gravitation when he saw an apple fall from a tree. What is significant here is not that he had access to this simple observation; many people had seen many apples fall. Newton, however, came up with the idea (however such thinkers come up with such ideas) that the same force that pulled the apple might also be the force that held the moon in its orbit around the earth; he looked for the pattern in his observations. Unlike many thinkers before him, Newton did not stop here, but tested his ideas with more observations. His calculations confirmed what he had imagined. To look for the pattern in observations and to test the theory we build with more observations is the essence of the **scientific method**.

In the heady climate of the eighteenth century, it was a small step to recognize that the scientific method of Newton's physics could be generalized and used to understand social phenomena as well as physical phenomena (Zeitlin, 1968:7). Basil Willey (1962:13), a British professor of English, sums it up this way: *When Newton bound together in one dazzling synthesis the great and the little, the stars in their courses and the fall of an apple, a thankful generation, at once scientific and pious, could explain with its spokesman, Alexander Pope: Nature and Nature's laws lay hid in night: God said, "Let Newton be!" and all was light!* Such "light," it was soon recognized, might be applied to the social world as well.

BASIC ASSUMPTIONS

The implications of the scientific method coincided with two other changes in basic assumptions about the individual and society: (1) the notion that society was not divinely constructed but was constructed by people and therefore could be changed — what we refer to as **secularization**; and (2) the idea that societies could be improved, that they "progress" and could be made Utopian. There was, in other words, a growing sense that just as science could progress, so could there be moral and social progress. This optimistic view, though seriously shaken by two world wars, by the Holocaust, and by a growing ambivalence about the benefits of a technological society, is still very central to the sociological perspective.

But almost from its beginning sociology has been divided into two deeply opposed perspectives, what are usually referred to as *order* or *conflict* theories. These are in turn based on two radically different assumptions about "human nature." We use the word "assumption" because neither view of human nature can really be tested or proved in a scientific way. As with the question of whether Heaven exists or not, human nature lies outside the realm of science — it is what we call a metaphysical question. The essential question asked is whether people are inherently good or inherently evil. As we shall see, it turns out to make a lot of difference which of these two positions one takes.

Throughout most of Western civilization, the assumption that human beings are inherently evil has predominated. From the Judeo-Christian perspective the human is a fallen creature who, though redeemable to some extent, can never attain perfection. However, as social philosophers began to contemplate the origin of society, they also began to contemplate what people might be like without all the trappings of society. What would people be like in "a state of nature"?

THOMAS HOBBES

One famous and influential answer to the preceding question came from Thomas Hobbes

(1588–1679) who, in his great work *Leviathan*, pessimistically maintained that without society, life would be solitary, poor, nasty, and brutish. He started from the assumption that people are basically egotistical, selfish, antagonistic, and hostile to one another, that there would be a "war of all against all" if there were no state to keep people in check and make them conform.

In modified forms, the Hobbesian "solution" to the problem of order has permeated —some would say dominated—the sociological tradition even to the present and has made sociology essentially a conservative tradition. It shows itself, for example, in Edmund Burke's (1729–1797) condemnation of the French Revolution, the classic conservative response to violent upheaval (Burke, 1790). People, Burke argued, need the traditions of the church and of the aristocracy. To do away with these through revolution is to invite anarchy and the breakdown of civilization. Similarly, Auguste Comte (1798–1857), often called the "father of sociology," believed that while change was possible and while society could be perfected, order and progress must go hand in hand (Comte, 1843). And, as we shall see, Emile Durkheim (1859–1917), another early and very influential sociologist, also viewed society as essential to people's well-being. When social constraints are insufficient, when order breaks down, people may, according to Durkheim, be more prone to commit suicide.

Following the work of Durkheim, more recent theory of crime and deviance (see Chapter 7) begins with the idea that these are an outcome of social disorganization and breakdown. It emerges also in the belief that children in the family and in the school require "structure," rigid schedules, set tasks and assignments, stern parents and teachers (see Chapters 5 and 12). Ask yourselves what you think of free schools, liberalized drug laws, the roles of parental discipline and of the police. Your answers will be shaped in large part by your assumptions about

humans, by whether you believe they must be constrained or freed from constraints. In its most pessimistic versions the order perspective becomes *reactionary*; it denies that society can be improved at all. In its more optimistic forms we have conservatism: things can be improved, but we must always move cautiously and carefully.

I JEAN JACQUES ROUSSEAU

Jean Jacques Rousseau (1712–1778) is perhaps the most famous and influential spokesman for the opposite view of human nature. In Rousseau's hypothetical "state of nature," people are, if anything, intrinsically good. If they seem to be corrupt and evil and greedy, the blame rests not on something innate in people but on society. In this view society, for the most part, represses rather than sustains people. This sentiment is most clearly captured in Rousseau's famous phrase that opens *The Social Contract* (1762): "Man is born free; and everywhere he is in chains." For Rousseau, the "state of nature" is not a condition of selfishness, hostility, and misery but of freedom and great happiness. The evils of life are a direct consequence of society and the state, laws and institutions. In nature people are free to create and to enjoy life and this freedom.

In *The Social Contract*, Rousseau moves on to the question of how people can gain freedom in organized society. Not surprisingly, perhaps, his discussion is rather fuzzy and confusing. Rousseau advances the notion of a community, a unity greater than the sum total of the individuals who compose it. Inherent individual rights would be transferred to the community as a whole, but individuals would not lose their rights as individuals because they comprise the community and share equally in its rights.

Rousseau imagined a "community" that shares common ideals, shares a culture as well as rights, and that, as it takes control of its own destiny, comes to express "the common will." Rulers and governments are simply

ply servants who must execute the general will; if they do not they must be overthrown. In short, Rousseau believed that because people are basically good, a better society is possible, a society directed at enhancing individual freedom and fulfillment.

We mention Rousseau not because he played a large part in the growth of the sociological tradition but because he was one of the first thinkers to delineate the social and political implications of assuming that we are born noble. Just as a conservative view of society can be traced to Thomas Hobbes, so a more liberal, even radical, view of society can be traced back to Rousseau. For Rousseau the evils in society were the consequences of society. To realize their potential, people would have to overthrow the social order that limited them and deprived them of their humanity. For Hobbes, like Burke and Durkheim, the social order is what protected us from ourselves, our antisocial and self-destructive nature.

This cleavage between the perspectives of order (Hobbes) and conflict (Rousseau) persists today. But neither Hobbes nor Rousseau made any claims to being scientific or empirical in their approach. Before we examine the recent versions of this cleavage between conflict and order, we should briefly describe those early sociologists who contributed most to the development of a more scientific approach to the question of order and conflict.

THE DEVELOPMENT OF SOCIOLOGY

Most discussions of the development of sociology are really attempts to trace the development of a particular kind of sociology — *positivist sociology*. "Positivism," as a philosophy of science, argues that the only things scientists should ask about are questions that can be answered with observable, that is,

empirical data. Just how much positivism is good for sociology, just how much this philosophy has led sociologists to undervalue or even stifle intuition are questions to which we shall return. For now we shall simply trace the most powerful influence in contemporary sociology — the development of positivism.

AUGUSTE COMTE

As we mentioned previously, most sociologists recognize Auguste Comte as the true "father of sociology," whatever this might mean. Comte did coin the term "sociology," a new discipline that he thought of as a reform science. Comte shared with Hobbes a concern with the need for order and structure. Writing just after the French Revolution, which seemed to give impetus to a particular brand of conservatism, Comte was concerned with how societies might progress more slowly and cautiously and thereby avoid the chaos, terror, and excesses that seemed to accompany revolutionary change. For Comte, progress must be achieved through the formulation of universal scientific laws of society. Using the methods of the other sciences — observation, experimentation and comparison — a new science, a "mother science," must emerge to study society as a whole, as a being in itself.

To Comte society was more powerful than the individual; society and its fundamental unit, the family, shaped the individual. To understand people, then, one had to understand the working of society, its persistence and change. This notion of the primacy of social groupings is obviously the *raison d'être* of sociology. Although Comte's notion of a reform science did not develop much beyond the hope for a better age, he did a good deal to carve out a new scientific discipline.

EMILE DURKHEIM

The sociologist who did most to give some flesh to Comte's hope for a mother science was another French sociologist named Emile

Durkheim, born, as it would happen, one year after Comte's death. We do not know the extent of Comte's influence on Durkheim, but Durkheim did concern himself with the same problem — the development of the scientific or positivistic study of society as a being in itself, as an "organism." Durkheim viewed society as based on and held together by interdependence, collective beliefs, and ritual. What he wished to do was to study the social world in the same way that physicists and chemists study the natural world. In his own words, we must treat social facts as things that stand outside any one person and that can be studied in their own right.

His first major work, *The Division of Labour in Society* (1893), described the changes in societies as they moved from simple to more complex. Simple societies are held together by common beliefs and common values, what Durkheim called **mechanical solidarity**. Complex society is held together by interdependence; with greater specialization of labour people come to depend on others for the production of goods and services: *organic solidarity*.

Organic solidarity, however, remained a future state, one that could only be brought about through the conscious intervention of those who possessed a scientific understanding of the social order and who could then assess what is "normal" and what is "pathological." His major concern was with how moral order might be maintained in the France of his day, a society in transition from feudalism to industrialism and capitalism. In his later work, *The Elementary Forms of Religious Life* (1919), Durkheim analysed the role of religion, and particularly religious ritual, in promoting social solidarity.

We can see that what Rousseau (and, as we shall see, Karl Marx) saw as constraining the individual, Durkheim saw as necessary for human well-being. This view is perhaps clearest in his most enduring study, *Suicide* (1897). In this work, in particular, Durkheim's view of human nature emerges: society shapes individuals and protects them from their "natural state," from their antisocial and destructive "instincts."

Durkheim's *Suicide* and *The Rules of the Sociological Method* (1895) are the works that probably have most profoundly influenced the course of sociology. In the latter work he describes the procedures that he then used in his examination of suicide. Because *Suicide* remains an excellent example of the application of positivism in social science research, it deserves a more detailed description.

Suppose you heard that one of your friends had committed suicide. After your initial shock you would no doubt wonder why. Why would anyone commit suicide? No doubt you would think in individual terms. You would probably think of circumstances that might have created intense unhappiness. Perhaps your friend's business went bankrupt or perhaps he or she failed university or college or lost a loved one. The common-sense notion seems to be that suicides can be explained in terms of personal tragedy, and obviously such factors do constitute part of the explanation.

At the same time, however, much that is interesting and important is left out by these psychological explanations. If we examine suicide rates (that is, the number of suicides per 1000 population), we find that certain categories of people are more likely to commit suicide than others. For example, men are more likely to do so than women, Christians more than Jews, city folk more than country folk, single people more than married people. Nor does it seem that happiness can be the only factor operating. Durkheim set himself the task of accounting for these differences in rates of suicide.

In this study, Durkheim was concerned with demonstrating the importance and value of a purely sociological perspective. He therefore placed his emphasis on social or group factors. Durkheim did not simply go out and collect suicide data; he began with a hunch about what he would find. His hunch, his "theory" of suicide, was that too much or too little integration into social groups would produce high suicide rates. Once he started collecting his data to test his theory, he decided that no one explanation would explain all suicides. There were, he concluded, different types of suicides.

According to Durkheim's initial theory, then, too little or too much social integration leads to higher than normal rates of suicide. The first two types of suicide, *altruistic* and *egoistic*, are distinguished on the basis of the extent to which individuals are integrated into social groups. Suicide is described as altruistic if it occurs because people have over-identified with their group. Suicide is said to be egoistic if it is the result of an individual's lack of identification or lack of ties to his or her group. What Durkheim needed to test his ideas were suicide statistics for groups that had either very high or very low levels of solidarity or cohesion.

Durkheim's tests for his notion of altruistic suicide are a good example of his technique. If Durkheim was right, he should have found a high suicide rate for people in a situation in which their commitment to the group was excessively strong. The military provides an obvious example in that the value of the military group is always placed above that of the individual. Indeed, Durkheim found that in every European country suicide rates were higher for the military than they were for civilians.

Now this does not constitute very strong proof of Durkheim's ideas. A number of alternative explanations could be offered. Perhaps those in the military suffer more hardships. Perhaps they are unhappier, more fearful. If these alternative explanations were valid, we would expect enlisted men, who obviously suffer more hardships than officers, to be more prone to suicide. If this were the case, it would cast doubt on Durkheim's explanation. Durkheim found the opposite — officers had a higher suicide rate. The longer a man had been in the army, the more likely he was to commit suicide. Volunteer soldiers were more prone to suicide than those who had been drafted. Re-enlisted men were more prone than those who were in the army for the first time. Durkheim concluded that his idea was supported by the evidence. Those most attached to the army were more prone to suicide. Similar high rates of suicide are found in Japan and other cultures that place more importance on the group than on the individual. In such groups the significance of life declines and the individuals might be provoked to suicide in situations that would not motivate others to do so.

Egoistic suicide is the other side of the coin. According to Durkheim, intimate group ties, emotional attachment to close (primary) groups, give individuals necessary support during times of stress and give meaning to individual goals. We would expect, and Durkheim found, higher rates of suicide for single people than married people, for childless couples than for families with children. Again, evidence seems to support Durkheim's theory.

Durkheim also used the notion of egoistic suicide to account for the differences in suicide rates among various religions. Protestantism emphasizes the individual, self-reliance and self-control. The individual supposedly has a direct relationship with God. Roman Catholicism places more emphasis on ritual, which provides strong group support, and an organized group authority. In addition, while Roman Catholics can depend on the Church for redemption if they have sinned, Protestants cannot. As we would expect from all this, Protestants have higher rate of suicide than Roman Catholics.

Jews provide a particularly good test of egoistic suicide. Although nineteenth-century European Jews supposedly had higher rates of mental illness than Roman Catholics or Protestants, they had a lower rate of suicide than either. Durkheim argues that this was the result of a higher degree of social solidarity in Jewish family life and of being a minority. Similarly, when Protestants were a minority, they too showed lower suicide rates.

Durkheim's third type of suicide he called *anomic*. In Durkheim's view people are most content when their everyday behaviour is governed by clear and meaningful goals. When people lack these goals their lives become meaningless and suicide becomes more likely. In certain situations — a rapid change in society or in an individual's position in society—goals are destroyed and the result is a condition of anomie — normlessness. Durkheim found, for example, that suicide rates were influenced by the business cycle. No one is surprised to learn that suicide rates rise in time of severe economic depression. What is more striking is that prosperity also produces more suicides. During times of sudden prosperity, people can supposedly no longer be certain about which goals to strive for. They become confused because suddenly anything seems possible — there are no ceilings to their ambitions. If individuals have achieved their old goals easily they must create new ones and, according to Durkheim, the result is an endless upward spiral in search of the impossible—and perhaps suicide. Suicide, particularly anomic suicide, was for Durkheim an extreme symptom of the pathological condition of the society of his time. It was one example of the social disorganization that occurs when societies are in transition between two moral orders, that of mechanical solidarity and organic solidarity — in Durkheim's time, between feudal and industrial society.

Durkheim's work on suicide has been subjected to many methodological and theoretical critiques (e.g., Douglas, 1967). Indeed, if we continued to read *Suicide* as a source of information and a thorough explanation of rates of suicide, we would have to count it as a rather minor contribution. His work remains important not because of what it tells us about suicide but because it has provided us with a model of the sociological perspective.

Durkheim has influenced sociological thinking for at least three reasons. First, he attempts to show that the feelings and actions of people are not solely psychological but are derived at least partially from social forces "outside" any one individual; feelings, including the desire to commit suicide, thus are affected by variations in the way society is organized. Second, by emphasizing the social, Durkheim attempted to carve out a distinct subject matter for sociology, one which could not be reduced to the psychological or biological. Finally, by maintaining the view that "social facts may be regarded as things" that can be studied as natural objects, Durkheim did much to create a positivist sociology — one which, like the natural sciences, is based on reason and observations and on the systematic collection of data. Durkheim, then, has had a greater influence on the direction of sociology than any social thinker other than Karl Marx.

KARL MARX

Although most people know at least something about Karl Marx because of his contributions to political ideology and his role in the development of communism, what is frequently overlooked is that he also has a very important place in the development of sociology. Marx was born in Germany in 1818. There he studied philosophy and journalism and later, in Paris and Brussels, economics. He did his most important writing in London where he moved to escape hostility aroused by his political views and activities. Like Durkheim, Marx was attempting to understand the nature, workings, and human implications of the industrial revolution and the rise of capitalism.

Unlike Durkheim, Marx follows more or less directly in the tradition of Rousseau rather than Hobbes. But unlike Rousseau, Marx never claimed that there ever had existed a primordial stage of history when people were actually free and happy. He did state, however, that precapitalist societies were characterized by more cooperative, less competitive, social relationships.

In Marx's view, human fulfillment is found primarily in work.

Far from being a sacrifice of one's time . . . truly human or "productive activity" is the mediating link between humanity and nature. It is through spontaneous, conscious, and creative labor that individuals express, realize, and develop their peculiarly human potentialities (Archibald, 1978:34–35).

Also, in Marx's conception of human nature, we are not the antisocial creatures painted by Hobbes but rather are essentially social. Work inevitably involves humans in cooperative relationships with others. However, society, particularly capitalist society, has distanced and alienated humankind from their essence. Those who must sell their labour for a wage by working for others become machine-like cogs in a complex division of labour; they become alienated from the all-important productive activity, the products of that activity, their fellow workers, and themselves. They come to feel powerless and meaningless. Marx was confident, however, that the workers would finally revolt against the owners and after a brief period in which they took power the state would slip away and people would finally find their fulfillment in spontaneous and creative work.

At the core of his theory is the idea that the economic base of a society, the mode of production, determines the "social, political, and spiritual processes of life." In other words, the way people earn their living profoundly affects how they think and how they relate to others and the very shape of the society and its culture. Although influenced by Georg Hegel, an idealist German philosopher, Marx was not an idealist but a materialist. This is evident in his famous phrase "It is not the consciousness of men that determines their existence but on the contrary, their social existence determines their consciousness" (Feuer, 1959:43). That is, he did not see ideas or values as the moving force in history but rather what people do, particularly in the production of material goods, as determining all else.

What people do, their production activity, determines their attitudes. Thus workers are different from owners. According to Marx, the very fact that some people own wealth and capital — the means of production — "forces" them to think in certain ways, to hold the world views that uphold the existing order, be it feudalism or capitalism. Moreover, they will attempt to impose these world views on others and make them the only conceivable reality. This is possible because those who possess the wealth of a society also possess control of the major agencies of socialization — the schools, the media, the church. Whereas Durkheim emphasized the positive contributions of religion in creating social solidarity and social integration, Marx saw most religion as ideological, an "opiate" that not only blinded people to the real nature of their condition but that also inhibited them from trying to change their miserable situation. According to Marx, people are blinded when they believe that either it was God's will that some should be poor and oppressed or one must endure privation now in order to find happiness in the next world.

For Marx social history is the history of class struggle. He defines classes as those who share the same position in the production process. In capitalist societies this means owners and workers, the **bourgeoisie** and the **proletariat**. Marx believed that class conflict existed in all spheres of society and that this conflict would lead to the inevitable overthrow of the capitalist economy; the conflict would lead to greater class awareness, class consciousness, and ultimately revolution. Marx's theory of social change was evolutionary. Society changes as the means of production change, and these changes occur through progressive stages. The final stage is communism in which there is no individual ownership and private property is abolished. With no more property distinctions, class distinctions and class conflict would disappear.

Marx believed that while these changes are inevitable, people are not totally passive observers. One could, as did Marx himself, seek through the use of a scientific study of society to understand how societies are organized and, most importantly, how they change. In this way, Marx hoped the social scientist could perhaps speed up evolution or at least act as a "midwife" to social change—make smoother the transitions which, like birth, are inevitable.

In later chapters we will have more to say about Marx; why for instance his predictions about the fall of capitalism have not been fulfilled and how his analysis helps us to understand social inequalities. In any case, his emphasis on how a society makes its living, its economic institutions, and how economy is related to other aspects of society has been highly influential.

Marx certainly could not be described as a positivist. In fact, he rejected the idea that scientists could ever be entirely neutral. He believed that if they pretended to be neutral they were lying, perhaps to themselves and perhaps to others. For Marx, all sciences had to be explicitly committed to the betterment of humankind, and the human sciences had to make those commitments explicit. But he was not a mere ideologue. In his concern with the careful gathering of empirical data for studying if and how the mode of production in a society was related to the organization of that society, he also contributed to the development of sociology.

❙ MAX WEBER

By the turn of the century, Germany had produced a number of social thinkers who shared a concern with liberalizing German society while at the same time responding to orthodox Marxism. The most influential of these was Max Weber (1864–1920). As will become evident, Weber shared a great deal with his contemporary, Emile Durkheim, and more explicitly with Karl Marx. But his theories opened up a rather different approach, which became particularly important in North America. Like the others we have discussed, Weber was concerned with applying scientific methods. In this context he argued for the development of sociology as a *value-free* discipline. By this Weber meant that, while sociologists and historians must study people's values and how these values influence their behaviour, they cannot judge these values and decide whether they are true or not. Certainly sociologists have values to which they may be strongly committed. This was definitely true of Weber himself. And these values no doubt direct sociologists to ask certain kinds of questions of the social world; the sociologists' values will usually define their area of investigation. However, the sociologist's analysis, according to Weber, must adhere to the value-neutral rules of the scientific method.

At the same time, Weber rejected the narrow positivism of theorists like Durkheim. He did not believe that social life could be studied in the same way as inanimate objects. Unlike the other social theorists we have discussed, Weber gave a central place to empathy, intuition, and individual motives. According to Weber, in order to understand patterns of behaviour, sociologists had first to gain a subjective understanding—an understanding of how people themselves view their own behaviour.

This kind of understanding, what Weber called *Verstehen* (literally, "understanding"), and what later sociologists call taking the role of the other, cannot be achieved through observation alone. Somehow the sociologist must imaginatively get into the heads of the people he or she is studying to see the world through their eyes. But *Verstehen* means more than this. In order to build general laws, the sociologist must proceed to put this concrete understanding into the larger social context. Subjective understanding is not enough; sociologists must also gain causal understanding of patterns of behaviour, causes that are outside and beyond the individuals themselves. So while Weber emphasized individual motives, he shared with Durkheim and Marx the belief that these motives were socially derived.

Weber countered Marxist theory not by opposing it but by modifying it. With his analysis of historical and comparative data, Weber tried to show that religious or cultural ideas are not simply the result of, or dependent upon, economic factors. He argued instead that "ideas become effective forces in history" (Weber, 1958:90). His theory about the rise of capitalism in Europe illustrates this notion. Earlier, Marx had argued that capitalism emerged from technological developments of the industrial revolution and from the wealth that early expeditions to the New World brought back to Europe — from materialistic factors. Weber maintained that while such materialistic factors were no doubt important and were necessary conditions for the rise of capitalism, they were not sufficient explanations; we also need to take into account ideas and beliefs that make capitalism possible. He tried to show, for example, that there was a "reciprocal causality" between the economic system of capitalism and the ideas of Calvinism.

According to Weber, the "spirit" of capitalism was a combination of the values of hard work, thrift, asceticism, and the willingness to pour profits into new investments and expansion. He went on to argue that the roots of this "spirit" could be found in Puritan Protestant sects of which Calvinism was the prime example. He demonstrated that modern capitalism first arose where these sects were strongest and that in other societies that he studied — ancient Judaism, China, and India — modern capitalism did not arise because these values were absent. In his analysis, he rejected what had been taken for granted among most economists: that economic behaviour was governed by purely rational motives. The capitalist activities of Protestants were supposedly motivated by a sense of religious duty and by anxiety over eternal salvation.

In this belief system human activity "only has meaning in relation to God's purposes," yet these purposes cannot be comprehended by humans without His having revealed them, and He may choose not to do so! God chooses only a few people for eternal grace, and the choice has already been made, such that one cannot affect it, nor is there even any way of discovering whether one is in fact among the chosen! (Archibald, 1978:69–70)

Thus members of the Protestant sect are left to their own resources to face their destiny, a lonely and unenviable position. According to Weber, their way of coping with their position was a constant attempt to prove to themselves and others, through worldly success, that they were among the chosen, hence the relationship between the spirit of capitalism and the Protestant ethic.

Weber was one of the most complex and far-ranging of the early sociologists. Throughout this text you will encounter, for example, his theories of power, stratification, and bureaucracy. For now it is enough to say that Weber's emphasis on historical and comparative analysis and on *Verstehen*, that is, understanding people's actions through the meanings they attach to their own and others' behaviour, remain important concerns in the discipline.

SOCIOLOGY IN NORTH AMERICA

We have been talking about European sociologists and thinkers. Indeed most of those we now think of as classical sociologists were European. At the beginning of the twentieth century, when people such as Durkheim and Weber were developing sociology, there was no sociology in Canada. However, a somewhat different kind of sociology was developing in the United States.

In Europe sociology emerged partially in response to the need to understand the implications of the rise of capitalism and industrialism and the demise of feudalism. And most of these thinkers who we now think of as sociologists were trained in and drew upon philosophy. In the United States, however, sociology developed along quite different lines. As an outgrowth of the social gospel movement, its emphasis was much more on immediate, social problems and was often indistinguishable from social work.

For European sociologists, the focus was the whole of society: how is it changing? why does it change? what will be its fate? For the most part, early American sociologists seemed to take their society for granted and to assume that their system was the best one possible. The problems needing research, then, were such things as how to integrate into American society the vast waves of immigrants coming into the country; how to deal with the supposed disorder caused by the equally massive movements of people from farms to cities; how to deal with crime, alcoholism, and mental illness. In a sense, European sociology was largely about the collective good and healthy societies, and American sociology was about individual happiness and fulfillment, a reflection of the American brand of liberalism (Brym, 1986).

Not surprisingly, then, sociology in the United States in the late nineteenth and early twentieth centuries followed more in the tradition of Weber's *Verstehen* than in the more rigidly positivistic approaches exemplified by Durkheim.

Durkheim's influence came somewhat later in the history of American sociology, at a time when social scientists felt that the most pressing questions—urbanization, industrialization, immigration, and the disorder supposedly resulting from these processes — could best be handled by Durkheim's conservative emphasis on social order and integration. These two traditions, essentially conservative and liberal sociology, have dominated in America. Marx, with his emphasis on conflict, change and the consequences of inequality was, if he existed at all, the straw man, whose name was raised only to be

rejected in the same breath. Early American sociology was characterized by a kind of optimism that made Marx's approach and predictions seem irrelevant or dangerously divisive.

Later, particularly in the 1960s when a variety of forms of conflict in America could no longer be ignored, American sociologists increasingly turned to Marx's insights in order to understand what was occurring in their society. For the most part, the development of Canadian sociology paralleled the development of American sociology. Sociology in Canada is the focus of a later chapter. As we shall see, the way in which Canada itself has developed meant that Marx's work had an earlier and more receptive audience among Canadian academics.

THE ACTION/ BEHAVIOUR CONTROVERSY: WEBER AND DURKHEIM

The classic sociologists have left us a legacy of debates and controversies that continue to characterize and divide the field of sociology. Indeed, these various theorists are considered classic because they have managed to capture at least one side of what are fundamental debates. One of these debates, which we have just discussed, stems from the opposing assumptions about human nature that we have traced back to Hobbes and Rousseau. For sociologists, one of the most important debates is what might be termed the action/behaviour controversy as reflected particularly in the works of Durkheim and Weber.

The question here centres around the dilemma of the individual and the society. Weber was concerned with action, subjectively meaningful behaviour; he emphasized how people use what is inside their heads to shape their own behaviour. Durkheim, on the other hand, was not really concerned with action, but with how behaviour is shaped by external constraints. It seems safe to say that the Durkheimian view has been seen as the most purely sociological perspective. In one form or another, the notion that society is more powerful than the individual is the core of sociology. It may be this very fact that gives such credibility to the image of sociology as dehumanizing or anti-individual.

This is precisely the criticism of contemporary sociology that lies at the heart of Dennis Wrong's now classic phrase "the oversocialized conception of man." By this, Wrong (1961), a fairly contemporary American sociologist, was saying that however much sociology must focus on society, it cannot let the individual disappear. Individuals, he argues, are indeed constrained, moulded, and shaped by their society, but they are more than this. What this "more" may be is a source of considerable debate in itself, but whatever it is, it cannot be ignored. There is always some theory of individual motivation implicit or explicit in any theory of society.

The most central question seems to be, do we view the social world as outside of people, independent of them, or are social phenomena only inside people's minds? As we hope will be apparent by the end of this book, these two views are not really opposite or contradictory. On the one hand society does stand outside of us, limiting our actions and making us act in predictable and patterned ways. On the other hand the social world is, at the same time, a subjectively shared world. By this we do not mean that you can wish away the social world any more than you can wish away winter. But the social world may no longer affect your decisions, your actions. If, in fact, people achieve a state in which the external world no longer constrains them, this may often mean the same as "madness," unless of course they can convince enough people to go along with their individual version of the world. If so, they have created a counterculture, a social movement, perhaps a new cult or religion.

SOCIAL STRUCTURE: SUBJECTIVE AND OBJECTIVE

Indeed the issue of madness serves as a useful illumination of the subjective and objective dimensions of social structure. One can subjectively liberate oneself from the structural constraints of a particular society, step outside the patterns as it were. It is in this sense that the existential psychiatrist R. D. Laing has described the "mad" as "prophets of a new order." The crucial point, however, is that while the "mad" are supposedly subjectively "liberating" themselves, they are, after all, designated as mad and treated as such. In other words, they experience directly the weight of social structure, even at the same time as they subjectively free themselves from it. All of us experience the weight of social structure in our everyday lives. In the words of C. Wright Mills, one of the few early American sociologists influenced by Marx:

When a society is industrialized, a peasant becomes a worker; a feudal lord is liquidated or becomes a businessman. When classes rise or fall, a man is employed or unemployed; when the rate of investment goes up or down, a man takes new heart or goes broke. When wars happen, an insurance salesman becomes a rocket launcher; a store clerk, a radar man; a wife lives alone; a child grows up without a father. Neither the life of an individual nor the history of a society can be understood without understanding both (1959:3).

Indeed most of us have at least episodically felt trapped. Things seem to have been laid out for us. There seem to be limits to how much we can ever hope to accomplish. Things seem to happen to us that shape our lives — events, circumstances, the workings of vast impersonal forces seem more powerful than us. Some of the problems we encounter, some of our troubles, seem to have no solution within our control. In essence we have described the subjective experience of social structure. Thus, ***social structure*** is defined as those patterns of social relationships into which we are born, which have existed before us and which we "know" will persist after our deaths.

Most of the time social structure appears to us as something real and outside of us in almost the same way that the walls and corridors of a building limit and direct our physical movements. The very fact that these patterns have had such a long history may lead us to view them as somehow independent of human activities; that is, as if they had some life of their own. They may indeed seem overwhelming and unchangeable. Social structure, in part, constrains us through the sheer weight of custom and tradition. As Karl Marx puts it, "The past weighs like a nightmare on the living."

At best, in our everyday lives, we have only the vaguest notion of what these structures are. This is something we do not think about in our day-to-day relationships; for us, these day-to-day relationships are the paramount reality. Our awareness of the social world is bounded by the social scenes in which we live. The vividness of our face-to-face interactions, our close-up scenes—in the family, at school, and at work—blind us to the context that frames these scenes. And just as we recognize, in our everyday lives, that we may be "in a rut," we recognize that we may be having trouble seeing beyond our own experience, seeing outside the rut. Part of the weight of structure stems from our bounded awareness.

PRIVATE TROUBLES AND PUBLIC ISSUES

Our resolution of the action debate is heavily influenced by C. Wright Mills's (1959) distinction between **private troubles** and **public issues**, what we believe to be a particularly insightful attempt to understand the complex relationship between the individual and society. We all know what personal problems are — problems of finding a job, getting along

with a mate, living within our income. Public issues, on the other hand, are more difficult to understand and articulate. We all know about and may engage in debates about increasing unemployment, rising divorce rates, and inflation. We find it harder, however, to talk about these issues in relation to our everyday lives.

The ability to draw the link between the personal sphere and the public sphere is, for Mills, the sociological imagination. Public issues transcend our immediate environment, our personal *milieu*; they deal with the way in which many such personal *milieux*, society as a whole, are structured. For example, when one man is unemployed, that is his private trouble. We must look to his character, his background, his skills, to understand and deal with the problem. However, when many are unemployed, that represents a structural problem and therefore a public issue. High unemployment rates raise questions not of the character and skill of all these individuals but of the structure of opportunities in society.

Even when unemployment rates soar, when unemployment has clearly become a public issue, the people who are unemployed are likely to worry not about the opportunity structure but rather about problems in their own *milieu* — how can they get other jobs, how can they feed themselves and their families, what are they going to do? In fact, in our society, it may be part and parcel of the ideology that people are encouraged to see problems as personal troubles. And most important, this focus leads them to blame themselves, to define the problem as some shortcoming in character or skill. They may look to their immediate *milieu* and perhaps locate the problem in their family. It is the task of sociology, according to Mills, to help people make the distinction between private troubles and public issues in their own lives.

This, we might add, has been at least one of the tasks of the sociology of women. For example, Connelly and Christiansen-Ruffman, two Halifax sociologists, explicitly studied women's consciousness of their problems in terms of public issues or private troubles. They used both formal interview data for 223 women from other studies and intensive interviews with a subsample of 25 women. According to their data, not all women are conscious of personal troubles as public issues. Among those who are, however, only a minority are able to link their own private troubles to the structural problems, the public issues, of being a woman in contemporary society. Apparently, a number of women, especially housewives isolated in their homes, see their unhappiness as something that is their own fault:

[These women] recognize their private troubles and are miserable, dissatisfied wives and mothers. They are obviously upset with their situation but do not see it resulting from their position as women. Their dissatisfaction is, therefore, usually couched in more personal terms. They often have little recognition of the structurally inequitable position of women in society and the personal interpretation usually given their problem by friends and doctors does not generally lead to such recognition (1977:170–171).

Therefore, in seeking solutions to personal problems, it may be necessary to look beyond the personal *milieux* to the larger structural issues.

Mills felt that sociologists must be able to shift back and forth from the individual to the societal level. They must understand the history and structure of the society and the social psychology of the individuals they are studying, and they must be able to link the two. As we said, Mills referred to this analytic ability to relate individual problems to public issues as the "sociological imagination." According to Mills, sociology could help people understand their personal problems in social terms by relating the individual and the social. In short, sociologists must attend to both the objective and subjective dimensions of social structure, to both how people shape their actions and how they themselves are shaped.

CONTEMPORARY PERSPECTIVES ON SOCIAL STRUCTURE

To understand this larger social reality we must first ask how the components of a society are connected to one another. There are three models, often thought to be competing models, that sociologists use to answer this question.

These models can be traced to the influence of Durkheim, Marx, and Weber. Following very much from Durkheim, the **order perspective** model views society as a *system* — emphasizing the integration of the parts and the role of values in holding the parts together.

The second model, the **conflict approach**, draws heavily from the work of Marx and his emphasis on social structure. It sees social structure in terms of layers, emphasizing inequality, and sees society as held together by force and manipulation used by those on the top layer. The third model, drawing from the work of Weber and early American sociologists, views society as **symbolic interaction**, as built up or constructed as people fit their lines of action to one another. The order model helps us draw the "blueprint" of society and, like any blueprint, it will exaggerate how harmoniously the parts connect; it is the plan, not the product. The conflict model tells us how the blueprint was created and, through focusing on contradictions within the plan, how it might be changed. Finally, the interaction model tells us how, in using the plan, people modify and elaborate upon it. In this sense, society is not the plan or even simply the result of the plan but is built up out of the actions of people.

Some writers have argued that the number of different and competing ways of "doing" sociology reflects the discipline's lack of a single unifying *paradigm* or strategy (Kuhn, 1962). Sociology does lack the kind of paradigm taken for granted in the natural and physical sciences that rely on the time-honoured techniques of the laboratory. Sociologists must rely more heavily on *perspectives*, theoretical models of the world that guide their research activity, observations, and analysis. As there are no "free-floating" intellectuals, the perspectives sociologists adopt and their approach will reflect their own interests, the groups in which they are or have been a member, and their own personal and emotional needs. Nor are these approaches or perspectives subject to proof in the way that sociological theories must be. Perspectives can only be evaluated in terms of how useful they are in producing good social theory.

THE ORDER MODEL

For a long time in the United States, sociology was dominated by assumptions that America was a unique and exciting experiment in democracy. Things were good, and the question was: What makes the society so good and how do we keep it that way? In this context, the order model, particularly a perspective called **structural functionalism**, dominated sociology (Gouldner, 1970). And, despite the challenge to the perspective in the 1960s and 1970s, its influence has persisted. While few sociologists today would call themselves structural functionalists, many rely on the concepts and methods of this approach.

Although not to the same extent, the influence of this perspective has also been felt in Canada. In Chapter 12, for example, we describe John Porter's (1968) functional approach to the role of educational institutions in Canada. The influence of this approach is also apparent in Rex Lucas's (1971) analysis of one-industry communities. In fact, whatever their approach, most Canadian sociologists have had to come to grips with structural-functionalism, and particularly its foremost American spokesman, Talcott Parsons.

When, for example, Emile Durkheim described how religion can serve to help integrate society, his approach was functionalist. His primary concern was how various aspects of society helped to hold that society together. This is the essence of functionalist analysis. Functionalists look at structured or patterned aspects of societies as necessary parts of a social system; they ask how a change in one part (for example, education) influences other parts (for example, social stratification) and how such changes influence the social system as a whole (for example, society). Their emphasis is on how each part contributes to the adjustment of the social system or its subsystems.

We can perhaps make this clearer by analogy. Think, for instance, about a car engine that has been taken apart and strewn randomly about a garage floor. We can study each of the parts—carburetor, heads, valves, pistons, etc.—separately. We can even try to classify the parts, impose some sort of "taxonomic order" to these bits of metal. But we may also want to understand the carburetor, not as a thing, but as a part having an integral function in relation to other parts (the fuel pump, the ignition system, and so on) and as part of the total engine *as a system*. In short, we may be less interested in the actual components and more interested in what goes on between them as they contribute to the thing called an engine. Of course, much the same is true for the "parts" — the institutions — of society.

The particular feature of functionalism is that it directs us to think about a total system and to view aspects of that system in relationship to the system. As the engine analogy suggests, the whole is greater than the sum of its parts. Put the parts together in the proper way and we have an entity, an engine, which is something greater than all of the parts taken separately; it is a system of interactions and interrelationships, and from a functionalist perspective so is society.

Clearly, when we are dealing with complex societies it is difficult, except in the most general way, to talk about the whole thing at once. The result is that most of the time most sociologists are concentrating on understanding one aspect of the society. To use our analogy once more: some mechanics become carburetor specialists or experts on ignition systems. But it is still necessary for them to think of these as part of the engine system affected by other parts of that system. To lose track of this is to engage in what C. Wright Mills (1959) called "abstracted empiricism" — research carried on without a guiding theory.

A particularly influential spokesman for structural functionalism was the American sociologist, Talcott Parsons. More so than most of his predecessors, Parsons was heavily influenced by European sociologists, in particular Weber and Durkheim. According to Parsons (1951), every social system has certain needs that must be met. He describes these in terms of four general problems every system must solve:

Adaptation: All systems must develop ways to handle and adjust to circumstances that bring about change.
Goal attainment: All systems must set goals for their members, provide means for achieving these goals, and provide means to motivate the members to strive for these goals.
Integration: All systems must develop ways to ensure harmony among the parts of a system.
Pattern maintenance and tension management: All systems must have ways of transmitting established patterns of behaviour and ways of reducing strains in the system.

Parsons proceeds to look at the parts of the system in terms of how they contribute to the fulfillment of one or another of these needs. We can see, for example, how the family contributes to pattern maintenance and tension management. The school, too, contributes to pattern maintenance and, to the extent that it is able to "cool out" failures, to tension management.

The way in which Parsons poses these problems is to put them at a very general and abstract level. He explicitly means them to be functional problems that all societies, groups, personalities, even organisms must solve if they are to survive in their environment.

Robert K. Merton (1968), a contemporary of Parsons, has tried to develop a paradigm — a recipe — by which the functionalist perspective can be used to analyse concrete social phenomena such as social mobility, deviance, role behaviour, the nature of groups, prejudice, and so on. He distinguishes among *functions*, which contribute to the adaptation of the systems, *nonfunctions*, which have no appreciable effect on the system, and *dysfunctions*, which contribute to the disintegration of the system.

Because of their concern with what holds society together, most functionalists have given little attention to dysfunctions, nor, of course, are nonfunctions of much interest to them. Functional analysis, then, is generally the analysis of "positive" consequences. Merton also distinguishes between **manifest** and **latent functions**. Manifest functions are those consequences that are intended and recognized by the people being studied; latent functions are those consequences that are unintended and/or unrecognized by them. Not surprisingly, most functionalists concentrate on latent functions, those functions that people do not already know about.

One of the most interesting examples of functional analysis is Herbert Gans's (1972) treatment of poverty in America. It is particularly interesting because it is a work of irony and sarcasm; it follows the paradigm and yet at the same time manages intentionally to convey some of its deficiencies. The theme of his study is that poverty performs important functions for society and various groups within society; that is why it persists. For example, poverty ensures that the dirty work will get done. Who else but the poor would take on those jobs that most of us find disgusting or demeaning? The poor provide a market for inferior or unwanted goods and services — day-old bread, second-hand clothing, run-down housing, inept lawyers and doctors. The poor provide the rest of us with feelings of superiority, perhaps charity, and the welcome notion that, for us, things could be worse. Poverty creates a whole range of middle-class occupations — social work, philanthropy, and so on — which could not otherwise exist as they do. Poverty perhaps helps motivate the rest of us to try to strive for conventional goals, since the poor are so often held up as examples of what happens to people who are lazy or otherwise inferior.

These few examples should illustrate Gans's intent. Unquestionably, poverty is manifestly dysfunctional for the poor and, as we discuss in Chapter 11, for society as a whole in many ways. However, when trying to assess the *net balance of consequences*, we must ask, "functional for whom?" What is functional for some is dysfunctional for others. This may lead to conflict, and the most powerful group will prevail. But functionalists tend to emphasize, perhaps overemphasize, consensus and integration and to ignore conflict and power. That is, functionalists tend to discuss how institutions are functional for society as a whole. They assume that society is held together by consensus, common values, and can thus be treated as a unity. Clearly they often ignore that any society is characterized by competing or conflicting interests. What is functional for one group may well be dysfunctional for another.

By the late 1960s, there was mounting dissatisfaction with the traditionally dominant perspectives in sociology, particularly structural functionalism, to the extent that some sociologists spoke of there being two or more kinds of sociology. Wilson (1970) wrote of a *new* paradigm; Dawe (1970) spoke of "two sociologies."

Events of the last two decades have dramatized the question of how to treat inequality and conflict in sociological theory and research. In the United States, images of unrest and conflict have long since replaced the more benign and complacent views that were possible before the experience of the 1960s. Conceptions of the role of America abroad have also undergone a massive redefinition, bolstered, no doubt, by the emergence of Third World political and economic thought and action.

Within Canada, too, this perspective was found inadequate to cope with issues of rising national consciousness, the facts of American cultural and economic imperialism, the progressive alienation of Quebec, the dialectic of hinterland and metropolis, the persistence of inequality. Obviously the functionalists' stress on value-consensus is well placed. How could a society exist without substantial agreement about what ends are desirable and important? But whose values? Which groups have the power to enforce their definitions on others? Are dissidents, those who do not share the dominant values, simply to be seen as deviants? Conflict theory, which has often arisen in opposition to functionalism, deals with many of these neglected issues.

THE CONFLICT APPROACH

One of the first sociologists to criticize the work of Talcott Parsons was a European sociologist, Ralf Dahrendorf. Writing a few years before the conflict of the 1960s, Dahrendorf (1959) argued that the functionalists' emphasis on harmony and consensus treats society as though it were a Utopia, free of conflict and force or coercion. He argues for a more balanced picture, one that recognizes that societies must have some stability, consensus, and order, if people are to live together, but recognizes as well that conflict is everywhere in society and that people do not always conform because they want to but are sometimes forced to conform.

Following and modifying the works of Karl Marx, Dahrendorf views conflict as a natural part of any society, as a natural response to coercion and injustice, and as an important mechanism of social change. While functionalism emphasizes *legitimate authority* to which people give their willing allegiance and obedience, the conflict approach emphasizes *power*, the ability of some groups to make others do their bidding. Society is divided by the different interests of the different groups or classes within it; it is held together by the coercion of the powerless by the powerful. The powerful have a *vested interest* in maintaining their power; the powerless have a vested interest in gaining power. From this perspective conflict is not surprising. Rather, it is the absence of conflict that would be surprising and require explanation.

The conflict approach can be used to examine those situations in which some group challenges established authority (see Chapter 14) or those situations in which the powerful group controls or constrains the others. The empirical work may range from studies of collective violence or the rise of social movements to the study of the manipulative uses of the mass media or the conservative influence of the schools.

Structural functionalists have often claimed that theirs is a value-neutral perspective, that it could be used for conservative or radical ends. We agree with critics such as Dahrendorf that it has an inevitable conservative basis. Its very language directs us to some issues and away from others, to legitimate authority and away from power and force, to consensus and away from conflict. The conflict approach, perhaps because it has so often arisen in opposition to functionalism, lays fewer claims to value-neutrality. Its concern has been much more explicitly with vested interests and the processes by which these are perpetuated and protected. It has, therefore, been less reluctant to advocate change of systems as compared to change within systems and, in effect, to put its values on the line.

The conflict approach contains many different and sometimes competing theories. In its vulgar forms, it focuses on good guys and bad guys, on how the rich get richer at the expense of the poor and powerless. It sides with the poor and sometimes tries to make society appear a parable of good and evil. In its more sophisticated form, it focuses on the system of production, capitalism in particular, and how the system, and people's relationship to it, shape our lives. We will be returning to these issues repeatedly in this book. The conflict approach has very much informed our view of Canadian society.

However, this perspective also has problems. In its analysis of power structures and conflicting interests it has, like functionalism, tended to ignore people's everyday activities, to ignore that society is built up by the meaningful activities of people. These are the issues addressed by the perspective of symbolic interactionism.

THE SYMBOLIC INTERACTION APPROACH

We have already discussed Max Weber's notion of *Verstehen*, or understanding. A very similar view developed among American sociologists at about the same time as Weber. For example, Charles Horton Cooley (1864–1929) developed the notion of *sympathetic introspection*, putting oneself in another's position as a technique for applying sociology. W. I. Thomas (1863–1947) emphasized the importance of people's **definitions of the situation** in determining their behaviour. In the words of the Italian playwright Pirandello, "right you are, if you think you are"; people act on the basis of what they believe to be real. Thomas also helped develop the technique of participant observation whereby the sociologist learns about a group by observing it and by actually participating in its life.

Of particular importance was George Herbert Mead's (1863–1931) notion of **role-taking** to describe the social act, a process in which two or more people take one another into account, imagine one another's intentions, and thus guide their own behaviour. He was moving away from the notion that any kind of structure or social system made people what they were. In his view, people are not simply products of vast and immutable social forces. Rather, people do things and think things in their everyday lives that change the social world, often in unpredictable ways. He was not, of course, saying that people were not constrained by social structure. Rather, he viewed those structures as necessary for human interaction and as much a product of human interaction as a constraint to it. His was an extremely optimistic view that saw, even in conflict, the opportunity for people to work things out and, therefore, to become better through their interaction with others.

Symbolic interactionism is very much the product of the University of Chicago, particularly through the work of George Herbert Mead and his students, among them Herbert Blumer. Because many of Canada's early sociologists were trained at the University of Chicago, it has had a powerful influence on the discipline here.

Central to this perspective is the theory of the development of self (see Chapter 5). Children become human and are socialized by interacting with other humans. They learn and internalize the perspectives of others, including how they imagine others see them. The perspectives of others are incorporated into their selves and self-concepts. Social interaction is possible because of shared symbols; because we can communicate shared meanings through language, we are able imaginatively to take other people's positions, take their roles and view ourselves as these others view us.

When people interact, each tries to understand the other's perspective. Each tries to "read" the gestures, both verbal and nonverbal, of others to try to figure out what they are thinking and what their intentions are. People, then, do not simply react to gestures,

they interpret them. This interpretation process occurs through an internal conversation, a conversation the individual has with himself or herself based on his or her reservoir of past experience. We respond not to the objective features of the situation but to our own interpretations, our *definition of the situation*. Interaction is a process of negotiation as those interacting try to define the situation, decide which rules or norms apply to such a situation, and constantly adapt to and modify one another's behaviour accordingly.

Symbolic interactionists have made important contributions to our understanding of the fluid and meaningful nature of interaction. People do not react to stimuli in some automatic robot-like fashion; they attach meanings to situations and act on the basis of those meanings.

There are many examples of symbolic interactionist studies in Canada, particularly in the area of deviance. Perhaps the most fascinating example, however, is Rex Lucas's (1969) study of the behaviour of coal miners during a mine disaster. Lucas was part of a team, which included psychiatrists and psychologists, who went to a Canadian community after it had suffered a major mine disaster. The team wished to study responses to disaster. As part of the research design, miners who had been rescued were interviewed and were asked to reconstruct as faithfully as possible what had happened while they were trapped. Two separate groups had been trapped; six men had been trapped for over eight days and twelve men for over six.

Lucas shows how both groups behaved differently. In the group of six, there was virtually no way to escape close observation by the others. There was high *visibility* in this group. The men in this group were concerned about how such expressive behaviour as crying, praying, and singing might affect them and the group as a whole. They were worried, for example, that crying might be contagious and that such behaviour would threaten their self-concept. Lucas shows how the men tried to control one another's behaviour and how they tried to exert self-control. In the group of twelve, where visibility was not so high, there was more tolerance for expressive behaviour.

Lucas also shows how the behaviour of all the miners changed as their definitions of the situation changed. For the first three days, the miners believed that their predicament was only temporary. All their activity was based on their belief that there was a way out or that they would soon be rescued. After about three days, their definitions changed and so did their behaviour. No longer convinced that they would be saved, or that there was a way to escape, their concern became survival. The objective situation had not changed, only their definition of the situation.

In perhaps the most intriguing part of the book, Lucas describes how the miners came to drink their own urine. They had no water left and had exhausted all alternatives. One miner, in a joking and tentative manner, offered the suggestion that perhaps they would have to drink their own urine. Gradually the miners worked out new definitions of urine drinking—others had done it or worse in similar situations; anyone would do it; they were "forced" to do it if they were to survive; and, finally, it was quite a natural thing to do in the circumstances. Even after the group had redefined urine drinking, each miner had to convince himself, through an internal conversation, that it was an acceptable thing to do. Finally, all the miners did drink their urine, acting on the basis of their definition of the situation.

In all, Lucas provides us with an excellent example of how symbolic interactionism can provide rich insights into human behaviour. Nor does he succumb to some of the pitfalls of symbolic interactionism. Lucas begins his study with an account of the context of the interaction he studied, the community, its structure, and culture. Unfortunately most symbolic interactionists tend to ignore these larger issues. Too often they fail to relate the interaction to its social context. As well, like functionalism, symbolic interactionism is unable to account for power except through a similar assumption of value and norm consensus. In their optimism about the constructive potential of negotiation, they fail to come to grips with the reality that negotiations do not start off even.

DEBATES WITHOUT RESOLUTION

We have described some of the controversies and conflict that seem to characterize sociology. Some have suggested that the intense disagreements among sociologists are reason for concern and dismay. We would suggest, rather, that these controversies might better be viewed positively, as necessary for the advancement of any discipline. Perhaps by now we have alienated you, the reader. You may be saying that it is somehow inappropriate that you are more, rather than less, confused having gone to the trouble of reading this chapter. Enough preamble, enough teasing: What are the right answers? What is human nature? Order or conflict? Individual or society? Positivism or *Verstehen*?

First, the bad news. This text, your course, your university degree will not resolve these issues for you. The classic sociologists are classics because they knew the questions and provided *an* answer, not *the* answer. Nor should it be surprising that, in studying humans and the structures they build, we might have to wear a variety of lenses, none of which captures the whole reality. Throughout the text, you will be invited to try on these lenses, to try out how much they allow you to see and how much they blind you to.

Perhaps now you are asking, is all this not hopelessly relative — isn't one perspective, one set of assumptions, as good as another?

The answer in this text is no. Certainly different questions demand different approaches, and many sociologists use a combination of approaches or alternate approaches. But finally one must make choices.

All the classic sociologists recognized this. They all made choices, for better or for worse, because they were all somehow concerned with the societies in which they lived and how these might be made better. And, of course, this meant that they had to make value choices; they had to engage themselves in ideological debates. They were engaged in their societies.

There is an obvious temptation to avoid ideological debates and simply to go out into the world and gather data. Many contemporary researchers, and perhaps many of you, would say, enough theorizing, enough moral philosophy, let's get on with it. In fact, much of the sociology you will come across will seem divorced from these kinds of theoretical and ideological discussions. Many research articles seem simply to report things as they are. Others seem merely to be devoted to developing and refining a variety of research techniques that lead to ever greater quantification and more sophisticated data manipulation. C. Wright Mills (1959) has described this kind of sociology as "abstracted empiricism," a sociology that evades confrontation with the various dilemmas and issues we have discussed by simply ignoring them.

These "abstracted empiricists" have argued that sociology must be undertaken for its own sake, that it should produce knowledge that people can use however they see fit. Sociologists, they argue, should stay out of the question of how this knowledge should be used because concern about the uses of their knowledge might distort their research and analysis. This fact-gathering approach, which tries to ignore the "big issues," is neither possible nor desirable. Such an approach represents a loss of the sociological imagination, is untrue to its founders, and is unfair to the people it studies.

APPROACH OF THIS TEXT

Our own approach is very much shaped by Mills's thinking and by his keen awareness of the real dangers in the pretense to value neutrality. His work serves to remind us all that sociological knowledge does have consequences for people and their lives, it does get used, and sociologists had better face up to that reality. We believe that sociology can help people to understand themselves and their problems and thus act as a liberating influence on people in much the same way as art and literature. At the same time, it can provide the scientific basis for societal reform. Indeed, we will go so far as to say that if sociologists do not consciously make this part of their agenda, they will fall prey to the very structures they are studying; that is, their work will end by upholding the system in which they work, however repressive it may be, and all of this under the guise of neutral science.

To put this more simply, perhaps we cannot escape the fact that it matters which questions sociologists ask and how they go about seeking answers. It matters, for example, whether the sociologist asks how is it that things are working so well, or how is it that things are working so badly; whether conflict is seen as endemic or an aberration; whether inequality is seen as a strain in, or a fundamental feature of, the system.

If there is any good news, then, it is that this textbook represents a choice. To capture adequately Canadian society, we see no alternative but to adopt a conflict perspective and thereby to focus on power and inequality. In our view, the debate about the individual and society has to a large extent been insightfully handled by C. Wright Mills's notion of private and public issues. But we also believe that it is important to recognize people's active role in creating their social world and therefore their capacity for creating new social worlds.

Certainly the individual is a social product,

but this represents only one side of the picture. Somehow we must get at how individuals experience these social constraints and how they modify and recreate them in everyday life. We believe this is the particular strength of symbolic interactionism that serves to illumine our everyday lives — for most of us, most of the time, our only reality. This perspective, while stressing values and norms, emphasizes their ambiguity. It directs us to consider how norms are emergent from interaction rather than from social institutions, negotiated rather than fixed.

Conflict theory and symbolic interaction theory represent for us opposite sides of the central paradox of social life: people are both products and producers of social structure. Throughout this book, we shall examine what people believe about their world and, at the same time, try not to exclude from our discussion the things that limit their freedom of action.

At the same time we do not believe that one has to make a choice between scientific and *Verstehen* sociology. There are limits to and room for both. Nor do we accept the notion that the search for a scientific sociology is inevitably conservative. While we feel that scientific sociologists are mistaken in their attempts to remain neutral in the face of ideological and value debates, we are unable to condemn scientific sociology out of hand. We believe that the productions of the scientific method are as potentially radical in their implications as they are conservative. In other words, while the questions we ask are ultimately ideological, that is, value laden, data emerging from the systematic application of the scientific method are not inherently biased one way or the other, or at least they need not be. The results of the careful use of statistical analyses equally with those of good qualitative analyses are what people make of them; they are as capable of transforming the social structure as they are of upholding the most oppressive forms of social inequality.

The orientation of the authors of this book is both humanistic and radical. We believe that sociology can provide its students with a new way of looking at the world that makes it difficult for them to say, "I have no choice" or "Things couldn't be any other way." Such "bad faith" is replaced by a new awareness of alternatives and possibilities — sociology becomes, in effect, liberating. As well, the analysis of social inequality and power may discourage the personalization or privatization of interests or problems. It is in this sense that we would use the term "false consciousness"—a lack of awareness of collective interests. Sociology, by linking personal problems and public issues, can provide the privatized student with a public sense. By its very nature, sociology must profoundly change those who become committed to it.

All of this — debates, controversies, our suggested resolutions — may, at this point in your introduction to sociology, strike you as "pretty heavy stuff," as intimidating and perhaps irrelevant to your interests. We have raised these issues because they are fundamental concerns, not only of sociology, but of all the disciplines that you will encounter during your university career. There is no choice but to try to grapple with and to understand them.

At the same time, we do have one final piece of good news: while the findings of sociological research may have important consequences for society and for those we study, sociology is also fun.

Sociology has, at times, the same excitement and intrigue as a mystery story; once you've started, it is, as they say, "hard to put down." One reason is that the subject matter —people and their relationships—is ever fascinating, ever novel. Moreover, as we hope you will discover, in "doing sociology," there is something exciting and compelling in using our imagination, our experience, and our technical skills to try to solve or to gain insight into that which we find puzzling and unknown.

III SUGGESTIONS FOR FURTHER READING

For those interested in gaining a fuller appreciation of the development of sociology and its social and philosophical roots, Robert A. Nisbet's *The Sociological Tradition* (1967) provides an excellent introduction. Other useful sources include Raymond Aaron's *Main Currents in Sociological Thought*, Vols. 1 & 2 (1965); Lewis A. Coser's *Masters of Sociological Thought* (1981); Anthony Giddens's *Capitalism and Modern Social Theory* (1971); and Randall Collins's and Michael Makowsky's *The Discovery of Society* (1978).

Collins and Makowsky also provide a useful introduction to contemporary perspectives and issues. Somewhat more advanced introductions to contemporary theorizing are William Skidmore's *Theoretical Thinking in Sociology* (1977); and Percy S. Cohen's *Modern Social Theory* (1968). Later on in the course you might also want to read Peter Berger's *Invitation to Sociology* (1963).

In our view, to understand social structure you can do no better than C. Wright Mills's *The Sociological Imagination* (1959). An excellent collection of his articles is *Power, Politics and People* (1967). An interesting textbook that uses Mills's insights and perspective is *Character and Social Structure* (1953), by H. H. Gerth and C. W. Mills.

To get the flavour of sociology, glance through some of the academic journals. The two major English Canadian journals are the *Canadian Review of Sociology and Anthropology* and *The Canadian Journal of Sociology*. Most Francophone sociologists publish in *Recherches sociographiques* and *Sociologie et sociétés*. The most important American journals are the *American Sociological Review* and the *American Journal of Sociology*. British sociologists publish in the *British Journal of Sociology*, *The Sociological Review*, and *Sociology*.

CHAPTER 2

DOING SOCIOLOGY

OVERVIEW

INTRODUCTION

SOCIOLOGY AND THE SCIENTIFIC METHOD

THEORY AND OBSERVATION
THE CLASSICAL EXPERIMENTAL DESIGN
QUASI-EXPERIMENTAL DESIGNS

THE PROBLEMS IN OBSERVING PEOPLE

OBJECTIVE AND SUBJECTIVE APPROACHES TO OBSERVATION

UNOBTRUSIVE MEASURES
SURVEY RESEARCH
STATISTICS AND SOCIAL RESEARCH
QUESTIONNAIRES
INTERVIEWS
LIMITATIONS OF SURVEY RESEARCH

ATTITUDES AND BEHAVIOUR

DEFINITIONS AND MEANINGS

PARTICIPANT OBSERVATION

COMPLETE OBSERVATION
OBSERVER AS PARTICIPANT
PARTICIPANT AS OBSERVER
COMPLETE PARTICIPANT
INFILTRATION

ETHNOMETHODOLOGY

SOCIOLOGIST AS PARTISAN
APPLIED SOCIOLOGY
VALUES AND PRAXIS

SUGGESTIONS FOR FURTHER READING

OVERVIEW

This chapter does not teach you the nuts and bolts of doing sociological research. For that you will have to go to one or more of the texts on methods in social research mentioned at the end of this chapter. And, no doubt, you will have to take one or more courses in social research methods before embarking on an actual research project. Our aim in this chapter is more modest, but in some ways more complex. We want, here, to introduce you to some of the issues involved in doing research in the social as opposed to the natural sciences and to give you some appreciation of why knowledge of the social world is, in many ways, more difficult to acquire than knowledge of the physical world.

Two major differences between, say, physics and sociology, are, first, that as we study or observe people they may, unlike rocks or molecules, change their behaviour simply as a result of our studying them. And, second, since people, unlike rocks can change their minds, they may, once they hear about our theories and predictions, change their behaviour and, in effect, make our predictions, if not our theories, essentially incorrect. Much of this chapter, then, is devoted to showing how sociologists have tried to find ways to study human behaviour and, at the same time, overcome these two basic problems.

Nevertheless, despite the fact that the social world is very different than the physical world and is more difficult to study, we want you to appreciate that social scientists do conduct research using the same fundamental approaches as natural scientists. They are equally committed to the scientific method and, wherever possible, use research designs that approximate or are analogous to the classical experimental model.

Frequently, in practice, this has meant the use of samples and survey research and, in turn, statistical analyses of one kind or another. In this chapter, you will be introduced to the logic of sampling, to various kinds of survey research, and to some basic aspects of statistics. You won't leave this chapter knowing how to do survey research or calculate various statistics. But, you should know enough to be able to read a report or article on social research and not be completely dismayed by the fact that it contains numbers and tables.

Of equal importance is that we try to point out some of the difficulties with survey research and statistical analysis and to start you thinking critically about the material you will be reading in the next few years. A good deal of the chapter discusses alternatives that sociologists have developed to counteract problems with such objective approaches as interviews and questionnaires. We will be introducing you to approaches that have used various forms of direct observation of people in their natural settings.

Whatever the kind of research, there remains the question of the role of the researcher when he or she is carrying out a study and reaching conclusions that may have a direct impact on people's lives. This is especially apparent when researchers are engaged in what is called "applied research," that is, research that is not simply testing a theory or trying to build knowledge but is, rather, expected to produce results that allow the sponsors of the research to make decisions about whether to retain a program or develop new legislation and new programs. As you will learn, this is often a difficult situation for the researcher who is committed to the norms of science and who is informed by the kinds of sociological insights we have discussed in Chapter 1.

Finally, we will briefly consider the fact that not all who consider themselves sociologists do work that falls into or conforms exactly with the more conventional ways of "doing sociology." Those who call themselves ethnomethodologists challenge many taken-for-granted assumptions that make it possible to think of sociology as a science. Ethnomethodology is a complicated field, and we will give you only a partial and very incomplete taste of that perspective. Of more general importance is the theme of some sociologists who believe that, however difficult it is to study human behaviour, we have one advantage over natural scientists. We are people studying people, and this means we can, to some extent, draw upon our own experience to build theories and test the theories of others.

▮ INTRODUCTION

In practical, perhaps simplistic terms, the most saleable resource sociologists have to offer is their command of the tools of empirical research. Outside of academic sociology, this is indeed what sociologists sell, and we see the results in public opinion polls, market research, operations research, and program evaluation. Thus, to some, sociology is very much a technical enterprise in which shop talk consists of issues of research design, sampling, reliability, and validity. For these practitioners a good sociological education is very much a professional education, emphasizing statistics and their use, the latest computer programs, and developments in methodology. And for these sociologists "the classics" mean something very different from what you have previously read in Chapter 1.

The view of research methods in this chapter is quite different on two levels. First, we shall try to show that methodological questions cannot be divorced from the kinds of theoretical concerns and debates discussed in the first chapter, and, rather, must be subservient to them. Second, we shall try to show the dangers, and perhaps moral failure, of treating sociology as merely a technical/professional discipline that does not attend to the debates in moral philosophy.

This chapter does not provide you with a recipe for doing sociological research; it is not a technical primer. It does three things. First, it shows you how sociologists have attempted, in their research techniques, to deal with the issues raised by the problem of social knowledge. Second, it is intended to make you more critical and skeptical of the findings you encounter of the productions of social science. And, third, it seeks to make you more comfortable with methodology and statistics.

▮ SOCIOLOGY AND THE SCIENTIFIC METHOD

"Is sociology a science?" is one of the truly boring questions that begins many introductions to sociology. The answer in this text, as in the others, is yes in a variety of ways. First, as you read in Chapter 1, one of the major threads in the tradition of sociology has been the optimism that the tools and approach of the natural sciences can be applied to the social world. Second, it is probably fair to say that contemporary sociologists, even those who abhor the scientific emphases of much recent sociology, all work within the classical scientific research design. Unquestionably, there are debates about how best to achieve this, how rigidly to adhere to it, how much is gained or lost by it. Nevertheless, whether explicitly or only in the background, the scientific method is there. What is the scientific method?

First, it is a set of norms, more simply, a set of rules for finding things out. One such rule, and perhaps the most obvious, is honesty. This is not so trite as it might at first appear. It means that, unlike many popular writers, we cannot allow ourselves to ignore the negative cases, the findings that spoil our arguments, disturb our prose, or reduce the news value of our findings. This may mean that researchers must engage in a deliberate search for negative cases as a demonstration to themselves and their audience that they gave their ideas a thorough test. And honesty also means a detailed accounting of the techniques used, the obstacles encountered, and the technical and substantial deficiencies of which the researchers themselves are aware.

A second norm is what Greer (1967) has called the norm of publicity. Simply, this means that the productions of sociology, like any other science, must be made public. In part, this reflects an ideological rather than a methodological concern; the norm seeks to assure access for all, rather than for a powerful few, to the fruits of science. But publication is also a methodological issue since by publicizing their work researchers leave themselves open to refutation (sometimes ridicule) and the possibility that their conclusions will be put to the test by others. Publishing is not simply something professors do in order to get promoted. It is a larger norm of the scientific enterprise. It is in this context as well that one must understand how dangerous and destructive to the growth of science is the attempt by any agency or institution to suppress the findings of research.

THEORY AND OBSERVATION

It may also seem obvious and perhaps trite, in the context of the twentieth century, to point out that an important part of the scientific method is the combination of reason and observation. Yet this is a relatively new way of doing things, one which we can trace back to the Enlightenment and the rise of science. Really, this means little more than that theory and observation go hand in hand. It is not enough to think we are right, we must eventually test whether we are right. Not surprisingly there is some degree of controversy about how best to go about achieving this union. Again, the debate is between the objective or positivistic sociologists and the subjective or more humanistic sociologists.

Positivistic sociologists try, essentially, to emulate the hard sciences. They have adopted the **hypothetico-deductive method** exemplified by Durkheim's theory of suicide, whereby hypotheses (tentative generalizations) are deduced from theory (hunches about how things are related) and are tested by precise quantifiable data. They are very concerned with precision and are likely to make use of official statistics, large-scale surveys using mailed questionnaires, and so on.

At the other end of the continuum we have the more humanistic sociologists who argue that many important social issues do not lend themselves easily to quantification. They make the most of the fact that they live in the social world that they are studying; they can empathize, drawing on their own experience, to a greater extent than most other scientists can in their respective disciplines. These sociologists use methods such as participant observation, content analysis of documents, and case studies.

In a sense, Glaser and Strauss (1967) offer a compromise position. They argue that sociologists have spent too much time testing theories, many of which may be outdated or irrelevant. The generation of new theory is at least as important as the process of verification; some version of the humanistic approach may be most appropriate for generating new theories, while the more positivistic approach may be best suited for verification.

For Glaser and Strauss, then, new theories are generated through a process of exploration; that is, research is undertaken without specific hypotheses. Positivists insist that their research begins with specific hypotheses; they must deduce from some theory a tentative statement of how two or more concepts will be related (for example, the higher one's educational attainment, the more likely one is to vote in a particular way), and they must provide the operations for measuring these concepts and testing the relationship. Glaser and Strauss feel that the generation of new theory requires that hypotheses and concepts emerge from the research experience itself— the resultant theory they refer to as grounded theory, that is, grounded in the empirical world. Through a process of constant comparison of different research settings, more general theories can be developed. The process of moving from specific observations to general theory is called induction (see Figure 2.1). In any case, sociology is probably best viewed as some combination of humanism and positivism.

There is room in sociology for a hard scientific approach and a more artistic or humanistic approach, for insight and imagination as well as precision and accuracy. As you encounter examples of sociology that rely on one approach or another or some combination, you should be careful not to judge them by the wrong standards but rather be sure you know where they fit.

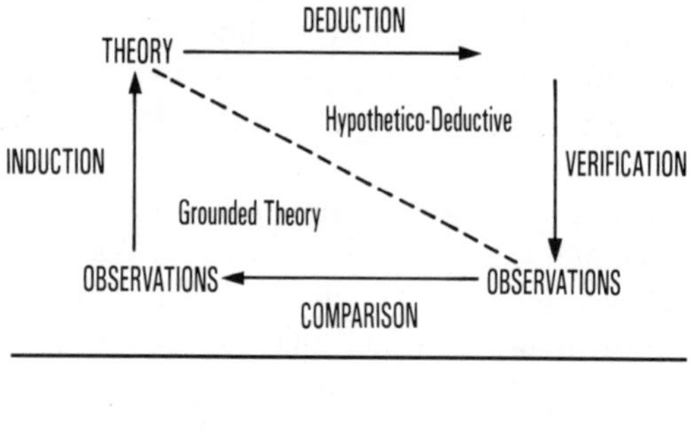

To return to our original question, sociology is in some sense a science, but it is also a kind of scholarship, an art form, and for the very best sociologists it is a combination of all of these.

THE CLASSICAL EXPERIMENTAL DESIGN

Having said that, it appears that what tips sociology in the direction of being a scientific rather than a humanistic discipline is that the general commitment to the norms of the scientific method usually (though not always) means an equal commitment to developing research designs that are at least analogous to those of the natural sciences. As we shall see, this is seldom possible in practice, but in the back of most sociologists' minds, when they develop a research project, is the ideal of the *controlled experiment* or, as it is usually called, the **classical experimental design**. It is this model that best and most precisely allows us to describe relationships between variables and, ultimately, to determine, perhaps, the causes of human behaviour. Moreover, explicitly or implicitly, the validity and usefulness of findings that emerge from sociological research will be judged in terms of this particular model.

Figure 2.2 shows the basic features of this research design. The model can most easily be illustrated by experiments in medical research where animals, such as rats, are the subjects. Suppose that a scientist wishes to test a new drug or treatment that he or she hopes will cure certain kinds of cancer. In ways that we probably do not want to think about, a group of rats are made cancerous. Innocent

---

FIGURE 2.1

THE SCIENTIFIC METHOD

FIGURE 2.2

CLASSICAL EXPERIMENTAL DESIGN

EXPERIMENTAL GROUP	Before measure (Time 1)	Introduce test factor	After measure (Time 2)
CONTROL GROUP	Before measure (Time 3)	Do not introduce test factor	After measure (Time 4)

Time 2 − Time 1 = Difference 1
Time 4 − Time 3 = Difference 2
Difference 1 − Difference 2 = Effects due to test factor

---

and unsuspecting rats are *randomly* placed in an *experimental* or a *control* group. That is, our now cancerous rats have an equal probability of being assigned to one of the two groups (an easy way would be to flip a coin each time a rat came out of the cage—heads you live, tails you die).

The idea underlying randomization is that prior to the introduction of the test factor (the new drug or treatment) the two groups should be interchangeable. This is called *prior randomization*. Simply, rats in the experimental group are given the new drug (at Time 1 when both groups of rats have a cancer); those in the control group receive nothing. (When humans are the subjects, the control group members sometimes receive a placebo since people sometimes have the tendency to get well simply because they think they have received medication.) At Time 2, a second set of measures or observations is made of both groups of rats. If fewer rats in the experimental group are cancerous than in the control group, we can conclude that the *independent variable*, the drug or treatment, brought about the difference.

Upon reflection, you will realize that, in many respects, the classical experimental model simply reflects what should be our common-sense queries about any report of research findings. If we are told that a new diversion program that deals with juvenile

delinquents reduces recidivism (committing a subsequent crime) we should immediately ask: compared to what or when. Further, we would want to know how youths were chosen for the new program. Were those chosen convicted of fairly minor offences or did they come from what authorities regard as "good" homes? Clearly, if youths were not randomly chosen to take part in the program, we cannot conclude that diversion (the independent variable) reduces recidivism (the dependent variable). Youth on diversion may not have committed another crime no matter what the nature of the intervention.

Except in the controlled setting of the social psychologist's laboratory, most sociological research is unable to actualize the precision and simplicity of the classical experimental design. It remains, rather, a kind of analogy rather than a reality. Figure 2.3 shows a simplified version of this design. In any research, we would, of course, like to have data for all four cells of the figure. But, frequently, there are no "before" measures available. Or, even more problematic, there is no adequate control group. Such problems are especially likely when the researcher cannot design the study from scratch but must work with what already exists. This is usually the case usually in applied research.

FIGURE 2.3

SIMPLIFIED CLASSICAL RESEARCH DESIGN

	BEFORE	AFTER
EXPERIMENTAL GROUP	Cell A	Cell B
COMPARISON OR CONTROL GROUP	Cell C	Cell D

For example, some years ago your authors were asked to carry out evaluations of experimental family-court projects — unified family-court demonstration projects. Those funding the projects wanted to know whether they are more efficient, less costly, more humane, and less adversarial than traditional approaches for dealing with family problems. We were asked, then, to test the hypothesis that unification causes certain changes in the way family law is administered. Clearly, to test that hypothesis, we needed information in each city where there was a unified family court prior to unification (Cell A) and in a comparable city where no demonstration project was planned (Cell C). Then, of course, we needed "after" measures of the same things once the unified family courts had been in operation long enough to be running smoothly (Cells B and D). But, the evaluation research did not begin until after the projects were underway so that, aside from relying on people's memories of how things had been, it was not feasible to collect "before" data.

Similar difficulties arose with respect to developing and using control groups for each of the four projects. Aside from the practical problems of duplicating the research in other cities, we could not be sure whether we could find comparable cities. Are, for example, Saskatoon and Regina or Fredericton and Saint John, proposed experimental and control settings, respectively, sufficiently alike to be used in this way? Is there another city in Canada like Hamilton? Is there another city in the world like St. John's, Newfoundland? The result was that, as with much research, we could only collect information about one time and one research setting (Cell B) so that the research was, in the end, mainly descriptive. This was valuable information for some purposes, but we could not test the basic hypothesis of the evaluation.

Given enough money and time, it is possible that in evaluating the unified family courts, we could have developed a research design that came fairly close to approximating the classical experimental design. But, we also have experience of situations where a control group does not exist, is too small, or is unique in its characteristics. For instance, in evaluating criminal legal aid in New Bruns-

wick, we wanted, naturally, to compare the situations and outcomes of clients who used the legal aid service with those who hired a private lawyer. To our dismay, we learned that virtually all those charged with an offence that could lead to imprisonment were represented by a legal aid lawyer. The few who did use private lawyers were charged with quite different kinds of offences — embezzlement, real estate frauds, influence peddling, and trafficking in drugs. They were, in other words, a different clientele from those charged with break and enter, rape, assault, robbery and other nefarious crimes. So, the obvious question as to whether legal aid delivers the same standard of legal representation and produces the same kind of outcomes as representation by private lawyers was difficult to answer. Again, the most we could do was to compare our findings with those from other legal aid evaluations and use generally accepted standards of what constitutes good legal representation in a criminal court.

A crucial component of the controlled experiment is that subjects must be randomly assigned to the two groups and are, therefore, at the outset of the experiment, indistinguishable. With rats, monkey, or mice this is, usually, easy enough to do. Obsessive positivists do try to experiment with rats or pigeons and then to generalize to the human condition. Unless you believe that the difference between rats and humans is not very great, these studies have only limited utility and can capture only a narrow dimension of what it means to be human. Some social psychologists and sociologists have experimented with people, but this almost always means lying to the subjects of the experiments or exploiting some vulnerable group.

In natural or real-life settings, we cannot, even in the interests of science, ethically, and often legally, deny people a public service or, on the other hand, require that they accept it. To use another example from our own research, one of us recently carried out a study that compares divorcing couples who have used a court-based divorce and separation mediation service with those who have used a purely legal or adversarial process to resolve their marital and familial problems and disputes. The best research design would have been one that, on a purely random basis, allocated half of the couples to mediation and half to the purely legal process. However, we could not force people to go the mediation route nor could we tell people that, because this was a research project, they must go to lawyers and depend on the court process.

The problem that this raises is one that is generally present in natural settings: the problem of self-selectivity or, as it is sometimes called, *self-selection*. Those who choose mediation may not be the same as those who choose to fight things out with the help of lawyers. It is likely that those who feel very bitter and hostile to one another will not be very receptive to using a mediator. In turn, those willing to negotiate and compromise and who turn to a mediator might have reached an amicable settlement even if the service did not exist. Prior randomization is, in this instance, at least possible in principle. But, in most sociological research, even if there were no legal and ethical problems and subjects were willing, it would still be impossible for the researcher to decide or have a say in who goes into which of the two groups.

Research on the effects of divorce on children is a good illustration of this latter problem. For obvious reasons, there has been a good deal of interest and concern about what impact a divorce has upon the children caught up in marital disputes. Always a traumatic experience for everyone, it has been argued that children of divorced families are more likely to be truant and delinquent, to have poorer school performance, and to experience more regression (e.g., bed wetting) than children of intact families. Research that has looked at this problem has produced rather inconclusive and sometimes contradictory results. The problem, of course, is that

researchers cannot decide, beforehand, which children get "assigned" to divorcing families and which to intact families. Nor, as it happens, can we simply compare children from the two groups and conclude that if, say, delinquency is higher among children of divorced families than intact families this is necessarily a result of divorce.

It may well be true: the break-up of their parents' marriage may cause children to do all sorts of things. But, because the two groups we are comparing are not interchangeable, we can never know for certain that other causal factors are not at work. That is, families where a divorce occurs are, for the most part, probably quite different than families where a divorce does not occur. Children in the former may have experienced much higher levels of marital discord than those in the latter. Indeed, where children have lived with a great deal of strife and, perhaps, violence, divorce may, in fact, have the opposite effect; it may be beneficial to some children. Moreover, since following divorce or separation most children live with their mothers and since female-headed single-parent families are usually poor, the detrimental effects we observe may be a result of poverty rather than divorce.

QUASI-EXPERIMENTAL DESIGN

How, then, can we sort out what is the effect of divorce on children? The most common, though by no means fully satisfactory, method is to *control* for certain factors. While we cannot make the two groups of children completely interchangeable, we can divide them up into groups so that it is possible to compare subgroups of children of divorced and nondivorced families that are similar in most respects. For example, as some researchers have tried to do, we can control for level of martial discord. Simply, we divide the group of children from divorced families into two groups—those who have experienced a high level of marital discord and those who have experienced low or little marital discord. We do the same for children from intact families.

Leaving aside the question of how to measure "marital discord," if there is little difference in rates of juvenile delinquency between children of divorced and intact families with similar family experience, we would have to conclude that divorce per se appears to have little or no effect on whether children become delinquent. Rather, the causal factor seems to be "marital discord." Of course, had the findings showed the opposite result, so that after controlling for marital discord there were still differences in rates of delinquency between children of divorced and intact families, the researcher would be in a stronger position to conclude that divorce is a cause of delinquency.

Undoubtedly, in this example, the researcher would also want to introduce some further controls, such as level of income of the children's families, which parent has custody of the child, and so on. Indeed, using some statistical techniques, the main limit to the number of controls is the researcher's imagination and the number of measures (questions) it is possible to put to respondents.

Can we, at this point, state conclusively the effects of divorce on children? The answer unfortunately is no. No matter how far the breakdown is carried, without an experimental design and, therefore, prior randomization, we can never know for certain whether some other unmeasured factor is, in fact, the causal factor. Nor is the situation as simple as all that. Even if we could somehow duplicate in sociological research the classical experimental design, it is not at all clear that sociology would suddenly begin to have the precision of physics or chemistry.

Here we must introduce a caution, one that applies to all reports about research findings in the social sciences. We have said that the task of social sciences is to develop theories that allow us to predict, and perhaps change, human behaviour. However, we really cannot, even with the best of research designs, say that poverty, for example, *causes* juvenile delinquency, or poor school performance, or anything else. What we can say is that children who grow up in poverty are *likely* to do worse in school, and are at higher risk of becoming delinquent than children who grow up in affluence. That is, some impoverished children do well in school and many do not become juvenile delinquents.

A particularly apt illustration of this is Christopher Jencks's American research on why some people achieve a high status occupation and others do not. Everyone "knows" that it helps to choose parents who are affluent, intelligent, and white. Attending the "right" schools and universities also helps, as does being born male. Yet, when Jencks and his research associates put these and many other factors into the computer, it turned out that even all these statistics about an individual only helped predict his or her occupational achievement about half of the time. As Jencks points out, there is, on average, as much difference between brothers raised in the same family as between blacks and whites in the United States. He concludes that other, largely unmeasurable things, like chance, luck, and personality are also responsible for determining who does and who does not achieve occupational success.

If there is one area in sociology that has been well researched, it is occupational achievement and social mobility. Should we, given these kinds of conclusions, despair of social research? If you expect definitive answers, then the answer is probably yes. But, we would also ask you to consider how it would be, if these researchers, using their sophisticated statistical techniques, could have predicted exactly what would be the eventual occupational status of every child. If so, our social world would be the deterministic one envisioned and satirized in Aldous Huxley's *Brave New World*.

We are, in other words, introducing you to a central paradox of social science. Social scientists develop theories and do research as if the social world were deterministic. But, they are, it seems, at the same time, committed to the belief that people possess *will*. Not only is there a paradox here but also a certain irony: it is quite possible that through their research social scientists will develop a fairly strong theory that allows for predictions, but people, hearing about the theory and the predictions, will change their behaviour in order to avoid the dire prediction. This has sometimes been referred to as the problem of the *suicidal prophecy* as compared with the *self-fulfilling prophecy* (see, for example, our discussion in Chapter 10 where we discuss why some of Karl Marx's predictions about the future of capitalism have not been fulfilled). So, one of the vexing things about studying and theorizing about people is that, unlike rocks or molecules, people are seldom passive. Not only might they change their behaviour when they know we are observing them, they may also do so when they hear about our theories.

If all of that were not enough, there are some researchers, who claim to be sociologists, who would deny that the ideal research model is, in fact, the classical experimental model. In particular, one stream of feminist sociology denies that the kinds of research models sociologists (predominantly male) have traditionally adopted are, in fact, the way the field should develop. They do not accept that traditional research, based on the notion of causality, can adequately address the key questions of the discipline. This book is written by two male sociologists. It is quite probable that our maleness does blind us to other approaches, other ways of seeing the world. Certainly, we are unable to conceive of social research that is not based in notions of comparison and, ultimately, some notion of causality.

In trying to come to grips with these issues, philosophers and social scientists have battled about "free will" and "determinism." Philosophers have sometimes been angry at social scientists because, in looking for deterministic relationships, they seem to deny the existence of free will. Sociologists have pointed to the consistency of the relationship they have found between, say social class and education, and have asked if humans are truly free. Research, in the end, is really based on what might be called "soft determinism." We know that the social world impinges upon us and constrains us in many ways. Research describes the limits to our freedom and, at its very best, provides some sense of how to reduce those limits. Here, as we find ourselves about to enter the realm of philosophy and epistemology and other things we barely understand, we end this cautionary tale only to begin an equally perplexing discussion: how *do* we study people and social relationships between people?

THE PROBLEMS IN OBSERVING PEOPLE

The enduring methodological debate in sociology can be characterized in a variety of ways: objective versus subjective; humanistic versus positivistic; normative versus interpretative. In a sense all of this comes down to one basic questions: can people be studied in the same way, using the same techniques, as things? However they answer this question, whichever side they take, sociologists are likely to agree that people and their societies are complex and therefore difficult to study. For some, the complexity of the social world is seen only as matter of degree different from the physical world. For others, the difference is more fundamental.

Think, for example, of observing the outcome of combining certain chemicals in a laboratory. The problems you encounter are technical: questions of the precision of measurement and the accuracy of observation. Now think of observing an interaction between two people or trying to explain why people commit crimes. So much of what we have to observe is not directly observable. We cannot see intentions, beliefs, and the sentiments that accompany action. Nor can we be sure that the people we are observing see their behaviour as we do. Just think how often in everyday life we misinterpret each other's gestures. How often do we do so unknowingly? Moreover, consider how often we may intentionally change our behaviour when we know we are being watched, especially by an outsider.

Finally, then, whichever position one adopts, sociologists will find it inescapable, whether they like to admit it or not, that they will always have to ask: what does this mean? "The hardest data rest on the softest foundations."

OBJECTIVE AND SUBJECTIVE APPROACHES TO OBSERVATION

Few sociologists would disagree that these kinds of data—the subjective worlds of those we study—present very difficult methodological problems to the researcher. Some would hold that we must somehow ignore them, study perhaps only that which can be directly measured. This was essentially Emile Durkheim's argument in treating social facts as things. Those who adopt this position hold that this is the only way in which sociology can be objective and scientific. Unquestionably, this interpretation of sociology has great appeal. Who, for instance, isn't tempted by the desire to simplify, to find once and for all answers to why people behave as they do? There is also something reassuring and convincing about tables of statistics and studies that deal with "cold, hard facts," rather than the subjective perception of the artist's world of emotions, intentions, and beliefs. However

tempting this approach may be, many sociologists argue not only that it leaves out what is most important about humans, but also that its objectivity is a fallacy. Like it or not, we have to enter into the minds of the people we study.

This position was clearly articulated by the early American sociologist, Charles Horton Cooley, and is clearly reminiscent of Max Weber's emphasis on *Verstehen*. Cooley (1926) pointed out that we can't treat social knowledge as identical to physical knowledge. In Cooley's words, "social life is lived chiefly in the imagination." In other words, one cannot learn about social life simply by observing behaviour, one must also get at people's thinking processes—how they think and feel about what they are doing. According to Cooley, sociologists are in a uniquely advantageous position: they have access to their own thinking processes, to their own feelings, and therefore, through a process of sympathy and introspection, can empathize with the people they are studying. Thus for Cooley, "objective" research techniques, whereby sociologist stand back from their subjects, must be complemented by "subjective" research techniques whereby sociologists become involved with their subjects. Cooley was taking the subjective position in this long-standing debate.

Those who favour objective techniques often decry the lack of rigour, precision, and representativeness of more subjective, that is, qualitative studies. "Objective sociologists" are prepared to ignore Cooley's injunction either because they feel people's "inner workings" can never be known with any precision or because they feel that these inner workings are relatively unimportant in determining people's behaviour. They are often prepared to assume that there is a similarity between observer and observed, that their subjects think and feel about a situation pretty much as they themselves think and feel about it. In many instances, they are probably correct. Where sociologists are raised and socialized in the same culture and milieu as the people they study, it is, perhaps, safe to assume that values, definitions, and meanings will be more or less similar. However, the further afield they go, the more likely it is that such will not be the case. Anthropologists studying other cultures are extremely aware of the need to see things not from their own viewpoint but from the perspective of those they study, since the two may be quite far apart. But, the need is probably as great when one is studying members of a subculture or different social class within one's own society. Much of the sociology of deviance, for example, has developed out of the attempt by sociologists to move from objective to subjective approaches. We discuss this more fully in Chapter 7.

Objective sociologists have been concerned primarily with developing techniques that could produce reliable and reproducible findings; that is, two researchers using the same technique in the same situation should produce the same data. In this context, we can understand their concern with measurement and quantification. Ideally, they are trying to limit the influence of sociologists' subjective perceptions, what they think they see. This is not to say that they are ever so naive as to claim that they have achieved this goal; it remains an ideal.

Perhaps the most difficult problem sociologists, and scientists generally, confront is that their mere presence may change the social situation in ways they may never fully fathom. A particularly interesting example is provided by Allan King's documentary film on the family, *A Married Couple*. In this film, King secured the permission of a couple to film their daily lives, their interaction together and with their child. King produced an absorbing and, at the same time, perplexing film. What we see is moving and apparently true to life. But, the audience must inevitably ask, how much is "real," how much is acting for the camera, and how much are these lives changed by the presence of the

observers? The "married couple" ended up getting a divorce: would they have if the film had never been made? We can only speculate. This is precisely the problem confronted by sociologists doing research: how much of what they observe is "natural" or "true to life" and how much is the consequence of their own research activity? What can the sociologist do about this problem?

UNOBTRUSIVE MEASURES

One approach is to avoid people altogether. Many objective sociologists have tried to minimize the observer's influence by developing techniques that cannot affect the people being studied. Webb and his associates (1966) refer to such techniques as unobtrusive measures. Some of these are rather amusing (if not distasteful). For example, Webb suggests that if you want to know something of the lifestyle and status of people in a neighbourhood, you might simply go through people's garbage. In fact, this technique has been used with apparent success by journalists, biographers, and, apparently, credit assessors.

The paper shredder now so much a part of every government department surely represents the recognition of just how much "garbage" can teach us. Webb also suggests that rather than ask people which exhibit in a museum they like best, measure the wear on floor tiles.

Obviously such techniques are limited in how much they can tell us, nor can they always be easily applied. But a more conventional and frequently used unobtrusive technique is the analysis of historical documents —letters, diaries, newspaper accounts, etc.— often prepared for nonsociological purposes. For example, through the analysis of a variety of historical documents, William Acheson (1972 and 1973) was able to draw a picture of the social backgrounds and value orientation of Canada's industrial elite in the nineteenth century. This historical work has provided the basis for much of the contemporary analysis of the Canadian corporate elite. Also, Harold Innis and S. D. Clark, who contributed much to the growth of sociology in Canada, made extensive use of historical materials.

Similarly, census material, though in some instances initially collected obtrusively, can tell us a great deal about the social composition and changes in any population. Clearly, such methods cannot be employed as easily if we wish to know about contemporary behaviour or attitudes in a systematic way.

SURVEY RESEARCH

In the minds of many, sociology is most closely associated with **survey research**. Certainly this is a technique heavily used by sociologists. As the name implies, it involves a survey of a relatively large number of people. It makes use of sampling that allows for representativeness of the population being studied. This is because, by definition, a **random sample** is one in which everyone in the population has an equal chance or probability of entering into the sample. While we could, in principle, survey the whole population, we have learned, as sampling procedures and statistical techniques improve, that it is unnecessary and inefficient to do so. With careful procedures, we can use a sample to represent the entire population.

We encounter the results of such sampling all the time. When we hear that three out of four dentists recommend a certain kind of chewing gum or that seven out of ten doctors believe that a certain kind of soap keeps you feeling fresher, we are being told the results of a survey of a selected few of the population. Obviously, how carefully and honestly this sample was selected is seldom mentioned in these kinds of statements. How many doctors were surveyed? How do we know that they are representative of all doctors in Canada? Is there any reason to believe that they are a unique sample? Indeed, one may often wonder how many samples were taken before the

"right" answers were found. Sociological studies that use sampling techniques will consciously address these issues with greater or lesser degrees of success; as a reader, you will likely know the size, nature, and biases in their sample and will be better able to assess the probable accuracy of the findings. This requires that you have some rudimentary knowledge of the ways data are presented and analyzed.

STATISTICS AND SOCIAL RESEARCH

Many of our students claim that they are interested in sociological research but, at the same time, admit that they are frightened and intimated by the very notion of statistics and numbers. We can sympathize with some of those fears: some research reports and articles do present and use statistical analyses and techniques that *are* daunting to all but the most mathematically sophisticated. We cannot, in this brief chapter, provide the kind of mathematical knowledge that might allay your fears or, for that matter, even hope to give you a kind of "cookbook" knowledge of statistics that will allow you to steer your way through some of the more complex studies. However, we can, perhaps, offer you some perspective on the matter by asking what are the purposes of statistics and statistical analyses. Statisticians distinguish between two basic kinds of statistical analyses — **descriptive statistics** and **inferential statistics**. Each involves different goals or purposes.

The need for descriptive statistics arises from the obvious problem that most of us are unable to retain a large number of pieces of information in our heads. We need some way, some set of measures, which summarizes and distills information and allows us to make comparisons with other groups. For example, after a mid-term exam had been returned, you would, no doubt, be rather impatient if the professor simply called out *all* the scores for the entire class. You would prefer that he or she give you the *average* or mean grade for the test or quiz. You would want a single statistic that both describes the whole class and, at the same time, gives you some comparison of your grade with others in the class.

Two other useful statistics are the *median* and the *mode*. The median is the score that, in effect, divides the scores of the class in half: 50 percent of the class had scores below the median score and 50 percent had scores above the median. The mode is the most common score: for example, most people got 60 percent on the exam.

As you ponder some more, you might also ask for the *range* of scores — the spread of grades—to determine whether it was an easy or hard test. You may want to know what *percentage* of the class failed the test or what percentage got A's. And, if you are wondering whether you chose the "right" section of the course, you may want to compare both the average grade and the percentage of failures with those in other sections.

So familiar are we with percentages that it may not have occurred to you that they have anything to do with statistics. They are, however, the most commonly used statistic because they provide a way of standardizing different whole numbers. If 15 students in your class of 135 failed the test and 27 in your friend's class of 165 failed, which did better? Without reducing these figures to percentages (11.1 percent and 16.4 percent, respectively), it is not immediately apparent which class had the largest *proportion* of failures.

Often things we would like to know about a group or a society cannot be reduced to averages. If, for example, your professor had used letter grades rather than numbers, the most you could do is develop *frequency distributions*. That is, you could ask for the number and percentage of students in the class who received an A or a B, and so on. Again, this would allow you to put your grade into some sort of perspective relative to others in the class and to compare your class with others.

In sum, measures of *central tendency* (mean, median, mode), percentages, ratios, and frequency distributions are all examples of descriptive statistics. All are ways of summarizing and describing in more simple and meaningful ways larger amounts of information about a group or a society. As our example is meant to suggest, they are also common-sense techniques that we all use in everyday life but, until now, may not have dignified with the term descriptive statistics.

A somewhat less basic descriptive statistic you may encounter in your reading is what is called a **measure of association** or *correlation coefficient*. As we have seen, one of the goals of social science research is to test hypotheses. A hypothesis predicts a relationship between two variables. Again, we are all familiar with relationships. For instance, there is a close, though not perfect, relationship (correlation) between age (one variable) and height (a second variable) of children. Although we are generally able, by looking at a child, to guess his or her age, we are not always correct. When wrong, we probably say something to the effect that the child is tall or short for his or her age. The reason we are sometimes wrong is, of course, because the correlation is not perfect. In fact, as with most biological aspects of humans, the correlation is about 0.80. This means, for reasons we won't go into here, that you will be right about 64 percent of the time in guessing a child's age from knowing his or her height or vice versa. A correlation coefficient of 1.00 means that there is a perfect positive relationship between two variables. A correlation coefficient of 0.00 means there is absolutely no relationship. And, of course, some things are inversely related so that as the value of one goes up the other goes down. A perfect negative relationship would have a correlation coefficient of -1.00.

To illustrate briefly, consider a researcher carrying out some research to test which of the old clichès is correct: "absence makes the heart grow fonder" or "absence sets the heart to wander." We won't worry here about how one might design such a study or how we might measure such a variable as "fondness." But, assuming it could be done, the researcher would calculate a correlation between length of absence and degree of fondness. He or she would then report that the correlation between absence and fondness is, say, 0.60 or, if the alternative version of the cliché turns out to be correct, that the correlation is -0.60: the greater the absence from the partner, the less the fondness for the partner. Or, of course, it is possible that there is no or very little relationship between absence and fondness, in which case the correlation would be zero or very close to zero. Correlations simply describe the degree and direction of the relationship between two variables.

The need in social research for what are called *inferential statistics* emerges from the fact that most research is based on samples rather than on the whole population. But few researchers are content simply to describe what they found in their sample. They would like to generalize what they have learned to the whole population from which the sample was drawn. They would like to make inferences, hence inferential statistics. As we mentioned earlier, survey research almost always makes use of sampling because, as long as the sample is drawn properly and is a random sample, it can be used to represent the larger group (population) at considerable savings in time and cost. However, there is always a possibility that through bad luck, the researcher has drawn an unrepresentative sample.

How could this occur? Statisticians begin with the notion of probability. If you flip a coin many times, you would expect an equal number of heads and tails since, of course, the probability of getting a head or a tail is 50 percent (unless the coin is loaded). But, if you flip a coin only ten times, it is quite within the range of probability that you will get more heads than tails. Similarly, if one were to draw an infinite number of samples from the same population, some samples would consist of all

males or all females or all rich people and so on. Inferential statistics are simply ways of determining the probability that what one finds in a sample could have been due to chance.

You are most likely to come across inferential statistics when two groups of subjects are being compared. Suppose, for example, that a researcher, using a random sample of college students, finds that male students are more likely than female students to read the sports pages of the newspaper. Using a statistical test, he or she might report that the difference between men and women is *statistically significant*. That is, what the test shows is that the probability that the difference between the two groups is due to chance is extremely low. Or, to put it another way, there is a very high probability that what has been found in the sample is true for the whole population from which the sample was drawn.

Note that we are talking about probabilities not certainties. There is always some possibility that the differences observed in the sample are, in fact, due to chance and are not true at all. In sociology, a finding is considered statistically significant if there is less than a 5 percent probability that it is due to chance. Sociologists, in other words, are generally prepared to be wrong one time in twenty. Medical researchers, on the other hand, in determining the effects of a new drug, for example, are usually not prepared to be wrong that often and consider a difference statistically significant only if there is less than a 1 percent probability that the finding is due to chance. The reason, of course, is that medical findings may have immediate consequences whereas, usually, sociologists are testing hypotheses that are not likely to be put so immediately into practice and to have quite such drastic consequences if the findings turn out to be incorrect.

In sum, all that a statistically significant result tells us is that there is a high probability that what we have observed in our random sample can be generalized to the population or group from which it was drawn. Or, to put it another way, had we studied the whole group, the findings would be very similar to what we found in the random sample, But, statistically significant results are not necessarily *substantially* significant or important. The way in which tests of statistical significance work is that the larger the sample, the more likely it is that any difference between, say, men and women (or any other comparison) will turn out to be statistically significant. For example, some years ago, Peter Blau and Otis Dudley Duncan collected data on a sample of some twenty thousand Americans in their study of occupation mobility in the United States. As they correctly point out, even a difference of 1 or 2 percent between, say, blacks and white, would be statistically significant. But, one would hardly want to make any kind of policy decision on the basis of that small a difference.

Unfortunately, researchers are sometimes rather sloppy in how they report their findings and simply report that there was a significant difference between two or more groups in their sample. As a reader, you may well interpret this to mean an important difference, which it may or may not be. Inferential statistics won't tell us anything about whether a finding is important; to repeat, all they tell us is the probability that we can generalize the findings or results to the population.

An example might clarify what we are attempting to convey here. Some years ago, one of us served as an external examiner for an M.A. thesis in which the candidate had compared the test scores (at age twelve) of a sample of children who had started school early with students who had started later. He found that those who had started early had, on average, lower test scores than those who had started school later. As he pointed out, the differences he measured are statistically significant. Unfortunately, he also took this to mean substantially significant and discussed

at length, in his thesis, the policy implications of his findings. But, the actual differences between the younger children and the older children were relatively small. In other words, there was a difference, most likely, but the difference probably did not matter very much.

QUESTIONNAIRES

Survey research involves the use of either a questionnaire or an interview schedule. Strictly speaking, questionnaires are research instruments that are self-administered. In doing research on students, for instance, self-administered questionnaires work well because the researcher can hand out the questionnaire during class time and can usually be present to answer any questions that might arise. Obviously, mail questionnaires are also self-administered questionnaires. These are especially likely to be used when the sample of people being studied is far flung geographically or when funds are very limited. Their main advantage is that they provide a relatively cheap and quick method of collecting a good deal of data.

There are, however, several problems. First, response rates to mail questionnaires are often as low as 40 percent and probably, even with follow-up letters, seldom go much above 70 percent. Second, questions asked must be highly structured and close-ended; there is little opportunity for exploratory questions or elaborate answers. Finally, the interviewer is not present to evaluate the commitment the respondent has to the questionnaire as a whole or to answer or elaborate on questions that the respondent has about specific questions and about the goals of the research project. Nor can the researcher "probe," that is, ask follow-up questions about limited or ambiguous answers.

No doubt you all have, at one time or another, received a questionnaire in the mail that you intended to fill in but never got around to it. And if you did fill it in, were you not disappointed at how little it captured of what you really thought and what you would have liked to say? Or perhaps you hastily checked off the boxes but could scarcely remember what you had said shortly after mailing it back.

▌ INTERVIEWS

For these reasons, most survey researchers probably prefer to be present to conduct the interview. But to do so is also to enter into a role relationship that in turn will influence the nature of the responses. We can expect, for example, that factors such as the age, sex, and ethnicity of the interviewer will affect not only the probability of getting the interview but also how people go about answering questions about, say, sexual behaviour. Their answers may not be the same if given to a male rather than a female interviewer, or a priest rather than a psychologist. Could you be as honest about those feelings you know you should not have about some minority if a member of that minority were interviewing you? Like participant-observation, interviewing as a research technique is highly dependent on the skill of the interviewer and is as much art as it is science. In contrast, self-administered questionnaires are dependent on the skills of the researcher who constructs the research instrument.

Of course when the project is a large-scale study, one that is based on a large sample and that therefore makes considerable use of what Roth (1974) calls "hired-hand research," many of these same problems arise. That is, if there are a number of interviewers out in the field or if the field work has simply been contracted out to a survey research firm, the actual researchers may be as remote from the data collection process as if they had sent out a mail questionnaire. Even if they do conduct some of the interviewing themselves, they will still have to pretest the interview schedule very carefully and eventually create fairly structured and close-ended questions. Not only does this cut down on the amount of coding at the end of the field work, it also helps to reduce some of the variation in interviewing techniques among those hired to carry out the interviews; all can then ask precisely the same question and in most cases code the answer using the pre-established logical or possible answers to the question.

Interviewing as a research technique is not, however, confined to large-scale studies of only random samples of the population. Frequently the researcher simply has a list of topics that he or she plans to cover in the interview. The exact wording of the questions is left unspecified, to be put in a way and in an order that seems most appropriate at the time of the interview. Questions are followed up with other related and unanticipated questions that seem relevant and interesting. This approach is especially useful for exploratory research and for intensive interviews — what have come to be called "in-depth" interviews. Though unstructured interviewing is more likely to generate abundant case material, it is best suited to small-scale studies where there is only one interviewer. As we might expect, because the questions are not set out in a formal manner, such research is hard to replicate.

Ideally, most researchers would like to be able to generalize their findings, to be able to say that their sample is representative of some universal application: all secondary-school teachers in Manitoba, all teenagers in Canada, all firms with sales under $2.5 million, and so forth. Often, however, it is not possible to put together a random sample of the population we wish to study because no one knows its size or the exact location of its members. The most obvious examples come from studies of deviance. For instance, since we don't know the exact size of the homosexual population in Canada, it is impossible to give every homosexual an equal probability of showing up in our sample. This does not coincide with the definition of randomness.

Any group we choose is a nonrandom sample, one which we can never be sure is representative of all homosexuals. In fact most researchers interested in deviant subcultures have used some variation of the technique called "snowballing" or "chain interviewing." This was partly the method used by Jean Veevers (1973) to interview voluntarily childless couples in Canada. The numbers and whereabouts of such couples is, of course, unknown. Her only recourse was to start with couples she already knew with the anticipation that they would know other couples who would put her in touch with still others. Of course, as useful as this technique may be, we must always keep in mind that findings of nonrandom surveying cannot be generalized beyond the group studied and must always be viewed with caution.

LIMITATIONS OF SURVEY RESEARCH

The sample survey is a very common and reasonably efficient method of collecting information on characteristics and attitudes of the people — the population — we wish to study. One particular advantage of survey research is that by the time the final research instrument is constructed, most things asked of people have become close-ended questions; respondents are given a list of responses and need only choose the one most appropriate to their situation. From there it is a very easy step to code these data in a form that can be processed by computers. Thus, survey data can easily be summarized, analyzed, manipulated, and stored in data banks for later use by other researchers. Because of this, however, some have questioned whether in effect the tail was beginning to wag the dog; are we perhaps forcing and delimiting our data so that it will fit into our programs and meet the various assumptions that sophisticated statistical techniques require?

However, the most fundamental criticisms of survey research emerge from the objectiv-ity-subjectivity controversy, from the basic problem raised by Cooley, that social knowledge and physical knowledge are not identical and cannot be studied in the same way. So, despite its efficiency, survey research has a number of limitations.

Try answering the questions in Figure 2.4. Most of you will find that you can indeed answer them. Let's say that you answered "television" for the first question. What have we learned from your answer? That you trust what you learn on TV most? That you make most frequent use of television? That you don't care about the news at all but you happen to come across it while waiting for "Dallas" to come on? Which of these did you mean and how are we, the researchers, going to know? Say that you answered "strongly agree" for the next question. Do you? Do you know what the plight is? Have you thought much about this before or does it play any part in your everyday thinking at all? Again, what does your answer tell us? Finally, say that you answered "60" to the last question. How do you define grocery shopping? How accurately do you believe you are able to recall such behaviours? Do you trust your own answer? On another day would you answer the same for any of these questions as you did today?

FIGURE 2.4
SAMPLE SURVEY QUESTIONS

1. What is your major source of news:
   (a) Radio (b) Television (c) Newspaper
   (d) Magazines (e) Other

2. To what extent do you agree or disagree with the following statement:
       The plight of native women in Canada is one of Canada's most serious social problems.
   (a) Strongly agree (b) Agree (c) Don't know
   (d) Disagree (e) Strongly disagree

3. How often have you gone shopping for groceries over the past twelve months?
   (a) 40 + times (b) 60 + times (c) 80 + times
   (d) 100 + times

ATTITUDES AND BEHAVIOUR

A major problem is that attitudes and behaviour are not always synonymous. There is, in other words, often a discrepancy between what people say they do or will do and what they actually do. For example, when people are asked if they wear seat belts when driving, a large majority say they do. Yet in one test (near Chicago), the investigators found that when drivers were stopped at a checkpoint, only about 40 percent were in fact wearing their belts. When people are asked about neighbours, many say that they really don't have much to do with them, that they "don't like to be in each other's pockets." But observation of the neighbourhood shows that there is a good deal of interaction; that, in fact, people are constantly in and out of each other's houses (Young and Willmott, 1973).

Does this mean that people are lying to the interviewer? Probably not. What is more likely is that people are talking about what they think is the ideal norm, what they wish they did, or what they think the interviewer thinks is the "correct" or proper answer. For instance, many believe that they ought to use seat belts or show respect for a neighbour's privacy. We might add that when faced with actual social situations, hypothetical predictions based on ideal norms about how to act in that situation may, for a variety of reasons, go by the board. This is nicely illustrated by studies of prejudice and discrimination. Bartenders who claim that they won't serve a black because they work in what is, in effect, an all-white bar often do so when confronted with a black customer. They do so for the simple reason that it avoids a scene or confrontation. Conversely, many who claim that they are not prejudiced turn out to be so in specific circumstances—not accepting easily the fact that one's own son or daughter is planning a mixed marriage, for example.

Coxon and Jones (1978) have suggested that we face very similar problems when we ask people to undertake the very boring job of ranking, in terms of prestige or social standing, upward of two hundred occupations. These authors speculate that people may "react in one way to an occupation title that is encountered in the middle of a long and rather abstract task, but in quite another way when they meet someone whose job is covered by that same occupational title" (p. 31).

Obviously there will be many instances where people will simply lie or deny any knowledge of the subject. Door-to-door research will not, for instance, tell us very much about who practises tax evasion or who in the population supplements his or her income by selling stolen car parts. Thus, much that is of sociological interest simply cannot be asked in survey research because people have good reasons for denial or concealment. Either the activity is illegal or shameful or people do not have sufficient trust in the interviewer or aren't sure how information on, say, income will be used later.

One of the authors of this book (Richardson, 1977) found in doing intensive interviewing of mobile people that once they had accepted the researcher into the home, most of these people were prepared to reveal all sorts of intimate information about themselves, whether it was relevant to mobility or not. But, when these same people were asked even basic information—occupation and residence—about their friends and relatives, they became very tense and suspicious. They became even more alarmed and anxious when they were asked whether it would be possible to contact their fathers and administer a similar interview with them. Many refused outright. Some said that they would have to think about it but apparently never did. Others who did agree often warned that their fathers were old and crotchety and might not be very good respondents (in fact this was very seldom the case).

We do not know the exact reason for this

reaction. Perhaps people felt that while they had nothing to hide, they were less sure of others and were not about to take the chance of introducing a relatively unknown interviewer to their friends and relatives. Perhaps they were concerned about getting caught in an unintentional lie — they feared two versions of the same story. To a considerable extent, an intensive interview is a conversation, in this case one that in effect asked people to tell their story. When we do this in everyday life, perhaps on a plane trip with a stranger, we do so knowing that our story, how we describe ourselves, will not be scrutinized later.

DEFINITIONS AND MEANINGS

A further limitation of survey research is that the categories, the issues, and concepts that are being introduced to people we are interviewing may or may not have the same meaning or the same importance to them as they do to the sociologist. This has been especially obvious in studies of deviance. For example, studies of people who apparently engage in homosexual behaviour, who might objectively be categorized as homosexual, often find that they themselves do not so categorize their behaviour. Some deny the label of deviant or disagree that what they do is really homosexual activity. Studies of social stratification and social mobility have also focused on the problem of whether subjective views about the class structure correspond at all to our objective measures — categories which derive perhaps from Marx.

Martin (1854), for example, after exploring the relationship between subjective and objective determinants of social status and social class, was led to ask whether terms like upper, middle, and working class had the same significance for all who used them. Did

they, in other words, share substantially the same mental map of the social scene? His conclusion was that there is only limited congruence between objective and subjective classes, a finding also borne out in a famous study by Elizabeth Bott. As she concludes: *Our data suggest, on the contrary, that people disagree profoundly in their views on class, so much that we sometimes wonder if they were talking about the same society. Our conclusion is that in certain important respects they are not . . . but . . . live in different worlds; they have different jobs, different neighbours, and different family trees. Each bases his ideas of class on his own experience, so that it is hardly surprising that each had a different conception of the class structure as a whole (1971: 169–60).*

Similarly, Richardson (1977) questioned whether social mobility means the same thing to most people as it does to sociologists; how closely do personal definitions of mobility correspond to the conventional or objective measures of mobility? For sociologists, social mobility means the movement of people from one social class to another, status mobility as well as economic mobility. However, only a tiny minority of respondents shared this definition. For most, status mobility was either not considered or viewed as unimportant. For them, mobility meant economic mobility, a better-paying job, a bigger car, a better house, and so on.

Also, as our earlier illustration suggests, a good deal of the time people may not be very aware of what they "really" do and don't do and how often. It is not, in some instances, a particular desire to stretch the truth, or to please the interviewer, or to talk about what ought to be. Instead, it is a simple question of not knowing. Think, for example, how you would answer such questions as, "How many times have you gone to the store" or "How many people did you 'interact' with in the past week?" It may be that the best answer people can give to certain kinds of questions may not, in fact, be a very accurate measure of their actual behaviour. Moreover, people may simply not be able to articulate exactly why they do something. Think how often you ask yourself why you have acted in a particular way. How well do we know ourselves?

Finally, people may not even have heard or thought about the issues, the categories, the concepts that we introduce in the interview situation. For instance, to ask people their position on the status rights of Indian women or their views on the Meech Lake Accord, assume that they have a position on these issues and that they know these are issues. Similarly, Lorna Marsden (1972) points out that to ask people what ought to be the population policy for Canada assumes far more technical and demographical knowledge than most of us have.

In asking people whether they thought they had been socially mobile, it was sometimes difficult to avoid explaining to people what the concept means; many people had never heard of the term, even though objectively they had "experienced" upward or downward mobility (Richardson, 1977). Even with very careful and intensive "piloting" of our interview schedule and with well-trained interviewers, there is a real risk that we are going to "educate" our respondents about the very thing we are trying to learn about.

PARTICIPANT OBSERVATION

To overcome some of these problems, many sociologists have advocated some variation of the technique known as ***participant observation***. In Becker's (1958: 652) words, "the participant observer gathers data by partici-

pating in the daily life of the group or organization he studies either openly in the role of researcher or covertly in some disguised role, observing things that happen, listening to what is said, and questioning people over some length of time." Participant observation as a research technique has been especially advocated by symbolic interactionists who believe that as researchers we can't remain aloof and act as "objective" observers of human action and behaviour. It is necessary to enter into "real-life" situations. We must try to catch the process of interpretation through which people construct their actions. We must, in other words, find ways to take the role of those we are studying, see the world from the standpoint of the actor, and come to share his or her definition of the situation (Blumer, 1969). Participant observation seems to provide the most effective technique for fulfilling these objectives.

As Becker's definition suggests, participant observation can, in fact, range along a continuum from complete observation to complete participation. As Figure 2-5 shows, the main difference centres around the amount of role involvement that the researcher has in the group he is studying. In most cases, the researcher is faced with the difficult task of managing two roles simultaneously, one as a member of the group and one as a scientist observing the group, recording what happens and eventually trying to make systematic sociological sense of these observations and experiences. But, as we move closer toward the complete participant end of the continuum, another element, that of concealment, perhaps "infiltration," is also involved.

FIGURE 2.5

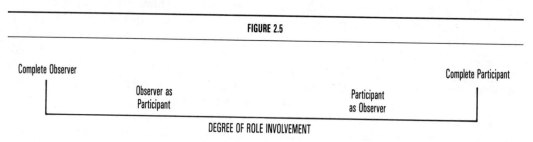

DEGREE OF ROLE INVOLVEMENT

COMPLETE OBSERVATION

We can find in existing sociological research examples of all four of these positions plus some which fall in between. Probably the most extreme example of pure or complete observation is work done by social psychologists using two-way mirrors. The hope is that "subjects" will not even be aware that they are, in fact, being observed. These are, of course, laboratory studies. In natural settings, it is seldom possible for the observer to be "invisible." Perhaps one of the best-known studies very near the "complete observer" end of the continuum is one usually referred to as the "Bank Wiring Room." This research was part of the Hawthorne studies carried out by Roesthlisberger and Dickson in the 1930s. A detailed analysis of this study was later incorporated into George Homans's study, *The Human Group* (1980).

Fourteen men were taken out of a large department of an electric company and put in a room by themselves. These men assembled, soldered, and inspected banks of terminals used in telephone exchanges. An observer was placed in the back corner of the room as "a disinterested spectator." In an attempt to minimize his effect on the group, he was give a number of rules to follow. While he should remain on friendly terms with the men and not set himself apart from the group, he was not to give any orders, enter into any arguments, thrust himself into or infiltrate any conversations, or seem eager or anxious to hear and see what the men said or did. Finally, he was not to violate any confidence or give any information to supervisors and managers. In short, he was to be as unobtrusive as a piece of furniture.

Was he successful in this "role"? Homans concluded that he was, that he had very little effect on the behaviour of the group. But in the final analysis, we are in the same position as we are in considering Alan King's documentary film of a family. We have no way of knowing whether the same people would have behaved the same or differently if they were not under observation.

In most situations, even if one wanted to do so, it is extremely difficult to remain in the "role" of observer. In fact, as Blumer (1969) suggests, it is incorrect to do so since all the researcher ends up doing is practising "the worst kind of subjectivism." That is, the observer fills in the process of interpretation with his or her own surmises, his or her own interpretations, rather than trying to catch that process as it is experienced by the members of the group.

Complete observation, then, suffers from many of the same limitations as does survey research: The aloof and "objective" researcher can never be sure that what he or she "sees" is what the people he or she is studying "see," that the meaning he or she gives to basic concepts is the meaning others give to these same concepts.

OBSERVER AS PARTICIPANT

Anthropologists long ago abandoned the nineteenth-century pretence that useful research could be done by remaining solely in the role of observer. Undoubtedly one of the most sensitive and insightful accounts of the dilemmas and uncertainties associated with the position of observer as participant is Elenore Bowen's (1954) anthropological novel, *Return to Laughter*. Bowen describes the obstacles she met in studying a distinctly foreign culture. Learning the language of the group, crucial and difficult as this is, represents only the first step. She also had to work out a role acceptable to the community or tribe that would also allow her to carry on as a scientist. Somehow she had to maintain the thin balance between impartiality, avoiding taking sides in quarrels, and the need to be intimate with people, to be part of the action. She had to reconcile her human inclination to give medical aid when possible with the scientific need to get on with her research.

Many of these same dilemmas are also

described in William Whyte's classic sociological study of a Boston slum, *Street Corner Society* (1955). Like Bowen, he also found it difficult not to become "over-involved," and had to decide when and when not to interfere; for example, whether or not to lend money to members of the gang. Whyte's study also shows how crucial it is for the researcher to have the cooperation of at least one member of the group or community. In Whyte's case, "Doc," leader of the "Norton Street gang," was not only a key informant, but also vouched for Whyte to the community: as Doc's friend, he could be trusted.

PARTICIPANT AS OBSERVER

Some of the best research in the participant-observation tradition has come from researchers who first of all were participants, active members in the group, and who then decided that the group or community should also be studied systematically. They tapped their own predicament, their own experience of the human condition. The obvious advantage of this participant-as-observer approach is that the researcher already has a vested interest in the group or is at least interested in the group's activity.

Ned Polsky (1969) became interested in the subculture of pool rooms and the role of hustlers precisely because from the age of thirteen onward he frequented pool rooms and, as an adult, played an average of more than six hours a week in various rooms.

Similarly, one of the authors joined Weight Watchers to lose weight. As he became more familiar with Weight Watchers, he requested permission of the group to make it an object of study. Thus, he moved from participant to participant-observer. His own predicament, his own experience, enabled him to empathize with fat people, how they viewed this common stigma, and what it felt like to lose this stigma. He could also extrapolate beyond the group and recognize that many of the same sociological processes at work in Weight

Watchers are also found in other self-help groups, indeed in any group that offers people some sort of physical or psychic renewal (Himelfarb, 1975).

COMPLETE PARTICIPANT

At the other extreme end of the continuum — complete participant — we can perhaps distinguish two aspects: retrospective analysis and infiltration. Clearly there are many situations and many groups that we have experienced solely as participants. Only in retrospect do these experiences seem worth re-analyzing and rethinking. Often we are simply working outward from our own personal experience. We begin to wonder whether our family life or our educational experience was unique or typical. Thus, it is probably a rare sociologist who does not at least illustrate his lectures, books, and articles by retrospective analysis of his own experiences of social life. Gouldner (1970) suggests that it is, indeed, these prior experiences that make a given theory intuitively convincing or unconvincing. Hunches, hypotheses, the very questions we ask as sociologists emerge from the background assumptions that we all carry with us and that derive from our own store of social knowledge.

In a sense, you have probably been doing something very much like sociological research for most of your lives. You've participated in groups, with friends and family, and from time to time have no doubt looked back, reappraised, and analyzed what was really taking place. You've sometimes sat in a café or on a bus and from a distance observed others, made guesses about who they were, imputed motives to them, and even made up stories about them though, of course, you were not very confident that your guesses were right.

Probably you have also been engaged in heated debates with friends and family as to why particular people behaved as they did or, more generally, why certain changes are occurring in society. Finally, there are a few people, your intimates, whom you feel confident you know more fully and richly than any social scientist could hope to, and this knowledge often provides you with the basis for your notions about how people and certain categories of people think and behave. Let us assure you that what you have learned as an everyday researcher will be valuable to you as a not-so-everyday sociologist. Such analysis is not only inescapable, it is also what enriches and creates social theory.

It is these kinds of experiences that sociologists are intentionally seeking when they become part of the social group they wish to study. When this is done through "infiltration," we have the clearest example of trying to recapture the natural experience.

I INFILTRATION

"Infiltration," on the other hand, raises a number of ethical issues. By infiltration we mean the attempt by the researcher to pass as a genuine participating member of a group in order to observe unobtrusively. Given what we have said about the possible effect of the observer on what he or she is observing, it is perhaps understandable that many researchers have wanted to conceal their observer role, to act as if they were solely members of the group. Certainly, much of what we know about, say, deviance in the work world could not have been obtained had the researcher revealed his or her "real" purpose in belonging to the work group. For example, one sociologist, while a summer employee in hotels, was able to see how the "fiddle" was worked against hotel owners and customers and was able to show some sociological reasons for its persistence. It is difficult to see how, as a genuine participant observer, he would have had access to this "inside" information (Marx, 1983).

Much the same could be said for the study by Laud Humphreys of homosexuals, *The Tea Room Trade*. However, this study raised considerable controversy and led to demands that his Ph.D. degree be revoked. Humphreys

first played the role of "voyeur" and look-out in a public toilet. This gave him an opportunity to observe behaviour without anyone being aware that he was an observer. As the men left, he also recorded the licence plate numbers of their cars. Several months later he interviewed them in their homes, ostensibly as part of another study. At this time he made no mention that he had encountered them in the "tea room." They apparently didn't remember or recognize him. It is probable that as an "infiltrator" Humphreys's presence had a very minimal effect on that which he wanted to study.

Nevertheless, the consensus is that Humphreys overstepped the bounds of ethical responsibility and respect for privacy. As a result of this and other similar studies, various sociological associations have developed professional codes of ethics. Generally these require researchers to reveal their observer roles and to request permission of those they study before using or publishing the research findings. In addition, people who are subjects should be given a reasonable amount of information as to the nature of the research, how the information revealed will be used, and who else will have access to the data.

Does this place ethical considerations before science? Perhaps. But in most instances it is not at all clear that much the same information couldn't have been obtained without "infiltration." Ned Polsky (1969), besides his studies of poolroom subcultures, has also done similar research on professional criminals. He argues that there really is no need for concealment and recommends rather that the researcher be honest about his intentions and not pretend to be what he is not. In his view, criminal subcultures are not all that different from other groups one might choose to study. Both require that the researcher develop trust. Both require the cooperation of an insider who will vouch for the researcher's integrity. Both depend on snowballing, i.e., building up a sample from one's initial contacts.

We might also note that in infiltrating some groups, it is problematic whether the researcher can escape "contaminating" what he or she hopes to observe. Festinger and an associate (1956) wanted to study a cult that claimed to be in touch with creatures from outer space who were to visit earth on a particular day. The researchers posed as "believers," as legitimate members of the group. But we may well ask what effect the presence of two educated men, professors, had on a group of largely lower-middle-class people. Couldn't their very presence be seen as validation of the group's beliefs? Festinger points out that they tried to remain "neutral" members, but even a noncommittal "hmm" is likely in such situations to be interpreted positively or negatively.

All of these approaches to sociological research are attempts to come to grips with the complexity and difficulty of studying and making sense of human behaviour. Despite the obvious differences between survey research and participant observation, both approaches share the belief that sociology can be in some sense scientific, that we can develop theories and test them systematically in a manner fundamentally the same as in the natural sciences. These sociologists have not, in other words, despaired of the possibility of a sociology that can help us understand human behaviour.

ETHNOMETHODOLOGY

In the past few pages, we have been trying to show you how the techniques of social science are both consistent with and different from the techniques of everyday life. The basis of the difference is that social scientific techniques are an attempt to systematically increase the plausibility level of what we know about any particular group and to define more carefully and precisely how far we can generalize what we know. The question remains: How do we know we know?

This question has formed the basis for the development of a perspective, perhaps more about than within sociology. This perspective, called by its practitioners, **ethnomethodology**, has provided a critique of the assumptions that underlie sociological methods and, in particular, participant observation. Ethnomethodologists ask what is obviously a crucial question: Can an observer ever know what the people he is studying are thinking in any situation? Do not the sociologists, like everyone, impute meanings to others based on their own experiences and interests?

The ethnomethodologists, like symbolic interactionists, agree that meanings are central to the understanding of human behaviour. Unlike symbolic interactionists, however, ethnomethodologists are not willing to assume that sociologists can take the role of the other; instead, they argue, sociologists construct roles and impute them to the people they are studying. It is this constructing and imputing of roles and meanings, what ethnomethodologists sometimes refer to as accounting procedures, that these theorists make the focus of their study. They take what people say, not necessarily as reflections of internalized values but as attempts to make the world appear rational and orderly to themselves and others. Talk, then, can be studied in itself, not for what it says about the content of people's thoughts about the world, but for what we can learn about the techniques or rules people use to account for themselves and the world. With this emphasis, ethnomethodologists do not try to become involved with the people they are studying but try, rather, to maintain some detachment.

Harold Garfinkel (1967), for example, devised an experiment in which a number of undergraduates were told that they were to try out and evaluate a new counselling technique. They were to go into a room alone and, through a device in the wall, speak to a counsellor, ask him questions that could be answered with a yes or a no, then speak into a tape recorder about what they had learned from the answer. The counsellor and students would not see each other. The students, however, had been misled or duped. The counsellor was not at all a counsellor but a "stooge," a research assistant; his responses were based on a prepared list of random yes's and no's, so that the questions the students asked were irrelevant as far as the counsellor's responses were concerned.

Despite the randomness of the answers, the students were able to make "sense" of them, give "meaning" to them; some even claimed to have learned from the experience. "Answers" that they could not easily "understand" they assumed would become clear sooner or later. In any case, the ethnomethodologist used the data produced in this experiment not to learn about the students' lives, but to understand how people in general impose order on chaos.

There are obvious ethical questions raised by such techniques, as well. Having been deceived, many students may have felt embittered by the experience. Although they had given their consent to participate in the experiment, they did not, by necessity, know what the experiment was. They had given their consent to participate in a different experiment. Perhaps this kind of trickery, although necessary for scientific purposes, shows a disregard for people and their rights to choose and would make many sociologists, including us, hesitate to employ such a technique no matter how productive it might prove to be.

Ethnomethodologists have a rather ambiguous position in sociology quite apart from these ethical considerations. In part, this may be because they have made their work unnecessarily difficult to understand. In part, too, it may be that ethnomethodologists keep asking questions that have no answers but seem, nevertheless, to undermine much of the work in the behavioural sciences. Many sociologists might even suggest that they not be included in this chapter. Certainly, our brief discussion does not do them justice (and we shall return to their work in Chapter 5), but we do treat them, however briefly, as a reminder that more conventional research methodologies are compromises with, not solutions to, the problems of social knowledge.

SOCIOLOGIST AS PARTISAN

Not only are researchers faced with the difficulty of choosing a methodology to study the world, they must also resolve the question of why they want to know and how they will use this knowledge. Just what is the sociologist's responsibility to the people he or she is studying? Howard Becker (1967) demonstrated one position when he asked, "Whose side are we on?" His statement reflects the position of a number of sociologists in the 1960s who seemed to identify with the "underdogs." But it is not entirely clear what taking their side meant beyond trying to see the world through their eyes and trying to present their perspective to the public as legitimate. In other words, this work seemed essentially a call for understanding and tolerance. And we believe these to be worthwhile aims indeed.

However, radical sociologists have voiced their dissatisfaction with this position because it does not explicitly point to the structured conditions of power and inequality that must be changed if the position of the underdog is to be improved. This raises what may be the central issue: if underdogs perceive their problems in terms of there immediate *milieu* or perhaps don't even see themselves as having any particular problems, does the sociologist "educate" them? Does the sociologist try to remedy "false consciousness"? Similarly, when people do perceive their troubles in terms of public issues, should the sociologist become their advocate, using his or her resources to help them achieve their aims?

Peter Berger (1963) warns that sociology is not for everyone because inevitably it upsets apple carts and many will suffer as a result of the new questions they come to ask. At the very least, we can take Berger's warning that it is a considerable responsibility to impose or even offer one's viewpoint to others. There is also the danger that the sociologist is simply replacing the views of those being studied with his or her own view of reality. But to recognize these dangers is not to abrogate our responsibility to the people we are studying; it is only to understand that the exercise of this responsibility must be performed with care and empathy.

We argue throughout the text that the sociological perspective can be viewed as a resource for developing a critical understanding of society and for understanding one's position in society. Sociologists do have a resource that they can offer those who wish to change their condition. It is difficult to imagine that a sociologist who has become involved in the lives of others could leave with no concern about helping. One way in which he or she can help and still respect the subjective world of these others is to learn from them what their problems, frustrations, and dilemmas are and to place this information within a sociological perspective; in other words, to return to the people their own definitions of what is wrong in a way that makes it easier for them to see how to effect social change (see Bodemann, 1978).

APPLIED SOCIOLOGY

On the surface, this is not so very different a position from that of the "applied sociologists," many of whom claim to take a value-neutral stance. They argue that their job is to answer the questions put to them by their employers and to provide the best means to achieve their employers' goals. Those who buy this research are usually large corporations or the state. The stand of value-neutrality generally translates into what is perhaps an unwitting defence of the status quo. That is, the resource of sociology is provided for those who have a vested interest in preserving the system. Even the applied sociologist

who offers radical solutions, who challenges the goals of his or her employers, will have no control over how his or her information is being used. In any case, he or she is not likely to be hired very often.

For example, if an evaluation of an experimental program turns in completely negative results, those who hired the social evaluator are not likely to abandon the program or implement his or her more moderate suggestions. If evaluators wish to have some impact, their recommendations must be framed within the system of goals and programs (Weiss, 1972:115). It may be that applied sociologists, those directly involved in policy formulation and program evaluation, are least effective in creating the kinds of changes that might be most important in terms of humanistic values.

To take one example, head-start programs, along the lines of "Sesame Street," were inspired by the work of a number of sociologists intent on affecting social policy. Unquestionably, such programs have much merit but, as we see in Chapter 12, they do not appreciably affect the structured inequalities that so drastically curtail the life chances of those to whom the program were directed.

Increasingly, sociologists are finding themselves in something of a moral bind. Those committed to large-scale research often have to turn to funding agencies, public or private, that have their own hidden or even explicit agendas and that may impose very serious constraints on the research enterprise. Further, the researcher may have very little influence on how his or her research is interpreted and used and in extreme cases whether it is even made public. Given the growth of evaluation research, especially for the government, many of you may find yourselves doing precisely this kind of research. All of this has meant that most research involves wrestling with one's conscience, making decisions as to how far one is willing to compromise, how many risks one is willing to take and, most important, where one's commitments lie.

VALUES AND PRAXIS

It is in this sense we can appreciate Berger's (1971) insistence that sociologists remain unaligned, nonpartisan. Only in this way, he argues, can the sociologist maintain a constance vigilance over the consequences of any human actions, of any group, that threaten human freedom and dignity. He is asking if, as the fortunes of groups change, sociologists may not find that the meaning of their partisanship also changes. To take the extreme example, in a successful revolution in which the dominated become dominant, do the revolutionary sociologists now become the guardians of the new order? Will their partisanship limit their ability to maintain a critical consciousness and to defend the values that led to their original partisanship? What happens if the oppressed become the oppressors? The way out of this dilemma of whether the sociologist should be partisan ultimately centres around partisanship to values rather than to groups.

The dilemma confronting sociologists is not whether they should be committed to values or attempt to be value-neutral; we believe sociologists must be committed to humanistic values, such as human dignity, equality, and freedom, however difficult these are to articulate and to define. This is what we think of as praxis — theorizing as a way of life as we seek to understand these values for ourselves and therefore for our discipline, in all our interactions and relationships, and in our search through popular and classic literature and, in the bodies of knowledge that comprise the humanities.

To John O'Neill, writing out of the tradition of phenomenology and Marxism, theorizing as a state of mind and way of life allows us to move beyond the confining circle of our own cultural worlds, to imagine uncharted futures, and leads us "to care for what is desperate in the human condition and the times through which it passes" (1972:236).

Armed with an explicit ethical position rather than the pretence to value-neutrality, the sociologists can afford, perhaps are even obliged, to surrender to the setting of their research. Only in this way can they learn the desires and frustrations, the obstacles and hardships in the lives of the people they are studying. They can learn of the constraints that prevent people from realizing their condition while at the same time they can avoid these constraints in their own perceptions. By ignoring values and by pretending that we have done away with their influence or by ignoring the subjective worlds of those we study, we make ourselves vulnerable to being "cultural dopes" who ask only the conventional questions or "paternalistic do-gooders" who enter the field thinking we already have the answers.

SUGGESTIONS FOR FURTHER READING

Because at least one course in research methods is required of all students specializing in one of the social sciences, there is a seemingly endless number of basic texts that attempt to introduce students to the issues and practicalities of doing social research. Most provide adequate and usually detailed introductions to the research enterprise and are, for the most part, meant to be referred to rather than read from cover to cover. Typical of these are Earl Babbie's *The Practice of Social Research* (1989) and Mark Abrahamson's *Social Research Methods* (1988). A more lively approach can be found in B. Erickson's and T. Nosanchuk's *Understanding Data* (1979). More recent

Canadian books are Peter Li's *Social Research Methods* (1985) and Winston Jackson's *Research Methods* (1988). Some years ago, Paul Lazarsfeld et al. edited a collection entitled *Continuities in the Language of Social Research* (1972), which contains some of the seminal articles on quantitative research. An excellent though demanding critique of social science research methods is Stanley Lieberson's *Making it Count* (1985). The appendix to William Whyte's *Street Corner Society* (1955) remains a classic introduction to the problems of doing field research and participant observation. W. B. Shaffir's, R. A. Stebbins's and A. Turowetz's edited collection *Fieldwork Experience* (1980) will give you a good sense of the advantages and disadvantages of participant observation as does Sandra Kirby's and Kate McKenna's *Experience, Research, Social Change: Methods from the Margins* (1989). And some of the articles in Marcia Millman's and Rosabeth Moss Kanter's edited collection *Another Voice: Feminist Perspectives on Social Life and Social Science* (1975) provide a powerful critique of field work and community studies. More recently, Ruth Bleir's edited collection, *Feminist Approaches to Science* (1986) takes this critique further by examining the assumptions underlying the scientific method from a feminist perspective. Dorothy Smith's *The Everyday World as Problematic: A Feminist Sociology* (1987) and *The Conceptual Practice of Power: A Feminist Sociology of Knowledge* (1990) are highly influential examinations of feminist methodology. Since part of the reason for learning about methodology is to evaluate the research of others, we strongly recommend Paul C. Stern's *Evaluating Social Science Research* (1985). Some of the now-classic edited collections that describe and give examples of ethnomethodological studies include David Sudnow's *Studies in Social Interaction* (1972) and Hans Dreitzel's *Recent Sociology*, vol. 2 (1970). A good discussion of both methodological ideals and the reality of actual research practice is Abraham Kaplan's *The Conduct of Inquiry* (1964). Many of the issues on the sociologist as partisan, discussed in J. David Colfax's and Jack L. Roach's edited collection, *Radical Sociology* (1971), remain as relevant today as when they were first introduced.

PART
TWO

BASIC CONCEPTS AND PROCESSES

CHAPTER 3

CULTURE

OVERVIEW

This chapter introduces the basic tool of anthropologists, the concept of culture. However elusive it may be to define what it means to be a Canadian, it means something, and what that is we often only recognize in opposition, that is in contrast to how other people live their lives. The basic components of culture are introduced to provide a better understanding of how our shared symbols, the language or languages we learn, and the values and knowledge we are exposed to, shape us in ways of which we are often unaware.

The focus of this chapter is Canadian culture, what it is, what it was, and how it is changing. It should be clear by the end of the chapter that talking about the culture of a complex modern society is far more difficult than describing the cultures of simpler societies of the past. The issue of Canadian culture is a complex one, and students will want to consider how the cultures of all societies are changing as information about different societies becomes more readily available and as technological change seems to outpace our ability to harness that technology for the greater good. Canadian students will want to consider how Canadian culture has been shaped, in part, by its two founding groups, the French and the English, in part by its native past, in part, by its multicultural, mosaic tradition; and, in part, by its proximity to the United States.

In this chapter, you will learn the meanings of culture as a concept and some of the dimensions of Canadian culture as part of everyday life. You should have some understanding of how you may be, in part, a product of this culture and what this might mean about your attitudes and values on a variety of issues. And, finally, you should have some sense of how culture reflects some of the material realities of society, though this is dealt with far more extensively in later chapters of this text.

Because of the importance of the relationship between culture and structure, much of this chapter is devoted to the notions of ideology and political culture. What we think about how our society and its political institutions operate and, in whose interests they operate, will lead us either to approve and uphold the current structures of power and inequality or to question and oppose them. These ideologies will shape not only our political behaviour but our attitudes and actions toward a variety of social problems and issues we encounter in our everyday lives.

INTRODUCTION

About thirty years ago, an American anthropologist wrote the following description of a culture he had been studying, the Narcirema.

The Narcirema have an almost pathological horror of and fascination with the mouth, the condition of which is believed to have a supernatural influence on all social relationships. Were it not for the rituals of the mouth, they believe that their teeth would fall out, their gums bleed and their lovers reject them. . . . The daily body ritual performed by everyone includes a mouth rite . . . which strikes the uninitiated stranger as revolting. . . . The ritual consists of inserting a small bundle of hog hairs into the mouth along with certain magical powders and then moving the bundle in a highly formalized series of gestures. In addition to the private mouth rite, the people seek out a holy mouth-man once or twice a year. These practitioners have an impressive set of paraphernalia, consisting of a variety of augers, awls, probes and prods. The use of these objects in the exorcism of the evils of the mouth involves almost unbelievable ritual torture of the client (Miner, 1956:506).

Both authors have at one time or another read this and similar passages to their introductory sociology classes. For years student reactions seemed fairly uniform, some giggling at the bizarre customs and a good deal of open laughter, and perhaps a sense of foolishness when they were told that Miner's work is, in fact, a satire on the North American concern about oral hygiene and our relationship with the dentist and the bathroom. We've stopped using these excerpts in the classroom for a variety of reasons. Students don't laugh so much any more; they don't seem to find the satire very funny. And many guess what Miner is getting at quite early on. This strikes us as a significant lesson about culture.

CULTURE AND ETHNOCENTRISM

A rather simplistic interpretation, perhaps, of Miner's story is that we should stop thinking of other cultural behaviours as more bizarre or less natural than our own. If we reflect about our own way of life, rather than simply taking it for granted, we will no doubt conclude that it too is quite bizarre, sometimes inexplicable and often apparently arbitrary. For many of you, there is nothing new and startling about this moral. In one way or another all of us have come to accept the notion that there is more than one way to do things; that indeed our way of doing things may not even be the best. In an earlier edition of this text we loosely described culture in these terms:

*Culture consists of systems of ideals and ideas — **ideal culture** — way of thinking and plans or recipes for behaving in any group of people, specifically those systems of ideas which are passed on from generation to generation.*

*Anthropologists have also used the term to include the products and application of these systems of thought, that is, the tools and artifacts of the group — **material culture**. Sociologists, however, usually maintain the distinction between ideal culture and material culture.*

People do not usually think of the systems of ideas passed from generation to generation in their own group as cultures; rather, most of us think of these ideas as truth, reality, the best or even the only ways of thinking and behaving. People forget that the way they choose their spouse, raise their children, do their work, and so on are all part of a long cultural tradition. Most people think of these activities as somehow natural. On the other hand, the traits of other cultures are often seen as unnatural. It is bizarre to worship many gods; to have more than one wife or husband; to marry, through a formal arrange-

*ment, someone you have never met. These are puerile, weird, or amusing cultural traits. It is only right and natural to worship one god, to have one mate, and to marry for love. This way of thinking—judging other groups from the standards of our own culture—is called **ethnocentrism**. Most groups exhibit some degree of ethnocentrism, or more simply, most people hold the prejudice that their way of life is the best (1979:43).*

CULTURE SHOCK

To some extent it is still true that many of our cultural notions are taken for granted, that we are still ethnocentric to some degree. But it seems plain that this description applied more to us when we, the authors, were students than it applies to you. You have heard of the anthropological descriptions of the varieties of ways people go about handling or solving the problems of geography and climate. We do not think it unfair to say that anthropology is not as newsworthy as it was even twenty years ago. In the past, when we went overseas to learn about different cultures firsthand, we often experienced *culture shock*, the feeling of unreality, confusion, and anxiety that accompanies the realization that the ways of thinking and acting that we have always taken for grated are simply no longer appropriate. For many of us, the confrontation with new ways of life produced a very uncomfortable sense of the fragility of right and wrong, of the arbitrariness of our social reality. It is our impression that students today are less easily shocked; they have been exposed to many often conflicting beliefs and varieties of lifestyles and seem less shocked than confused. A discussion of culture today must be framed differently than in the past; indeed, culture means something different.

In the past, culture had an almost tangible reality that was apparent in the way it constrained people's lives and choices.

Anthropologists could study culture much as Durkheim recommended: as a thing. What anthropologists said about culture, not only foreign cultures but our own, was novel because we had taken for granted our own way of life; we had lived it rather than reflected on it. It is this very feature of culture — its taken-for-grantedness — that gives it much of its power to constrain and limit us. Only the outsider, the stranger, could understand a people's way of life as culture; for the people who lived that culture it just *was*. Today we are far less certain about what to value, about right and wrong, and about any one way of life. Culture is less taken for granted.

THE TYRANNY OF FREEDOM

To the extent that reflection about culture is no longer restricted to satirists, strangers, or social scientists, culture seems to be losing its hold. The conservative says we are becoming uprooted; the liberal says we are becoming more free; and the radical says we are alienated—the sickness of our culture reflects the sickness of our society.

What does this mean in our everyday lives? How many of you who are women feel you must get married and have children? To what extent does the religion of your parents provide you with a ready-made set of answers with which you are comfortable? How many of you know what your career or job will be with the same degree of confidence as the blacksmith's son of the past? It would appear evident that you have a greater degree of freedom in the choices you make. In one sense this is unarguably true, but don't be misled because, in another sense, it means that as you are subjectively freed, you will encounter different kinds of limits to your freedom. As women become subjectively freed to have a career, they increasingly discover the objective obstacles to achieving their goals.

Even given this, we obviously are faced with the necessity of making a number of choices: whether to get married, whether to have children and when, how to define career success, and so on. Most of us, or at least many of us, are having trouble finding the standards or guidelines to aid us in making these choices. Today when someone says "Whichever choice I make it's always the wrong one," he or she is saying something about the "tyranny of freedom." Nor is it surprising that many look back, with some degree of envy, at pastoral images of a simpler and surer time. In the confusion, in looking for answers, we return to our culture, which is essentially our only resource, since it provides the only *common stock of knowledge* to understand and judge ourselves and our fellows.

In the past, culture found expression in our every thought and action, even in our most private moments. How and what we ate, whom and how we loved, even what we daydreamed, were influenced by the culture in to which we were born.

But even as the cultural hold is weakening, we are limited by the ideas and knowledge available to us. While the genius, the artist, the revolutionary, for that matter all of us, add our own unique qualities to our activities, we must work with cultural tools — cultural notions of truth, beauty, and goodness. We are all inescapably part of a long cultural tradition and we are able only on occasion to transcend it. What is the difference between past and present culture? The influence is probably no less pervasive. Rather, the difference resides in the fact that we are no longer so committed to our cultural notions of truth, beauty, goodness, and meaning. Culture provides for us our more or less common stock of knowledge but as we have learned more about people in other places and as societies have become more complex and diversified,

this knowledge also has become more varied, complex, and fluid. It is simply no longer so clear what is the "true" and "right" path.

This is not to say that there were not costs associated with the seemingly more certain and unitary culture of the past. There are individual and social costs in an unquestioning commitment to one's culture. A number of studies have shown that those people who are most ethnocentric are also usually least flexible. Not only are they intolerant of other cultures, they tend to be intolerant of change and often find it difficult to cope with novel or ambiguous situations. There is little appreciation or room for human diversity; the line between normalcy and deviance is sharply drawn. One of the goals of a liberal arts education surely is to broaden our perspectives, to make us sufficiently flexible to be able to view new and different ideas with more tolerance or at least more objectivity.

CULTURAL RELATIVISM

Sociology and anthropology have often been referred to as the "relativizing" disciplines that make everything seem right and nothing wrong. Many sociologists are *cultural relativists*; they argue that all cultures are equally worthwhile and that one should not judge other cultures on the basis of one's own culture. These sociologists have been concerned with avoiding the easy pitfall of disparaging other cultures, especially in comparison to their own. They have, for example, criticized Westerners' attempts to help modernize underdeveloped nations. They have felt that so-called modernization failed to respect the cultural integrity of these societies and therefore was likely to have unanticipated and disastrous consequences.

Many other sociologists are dissatisfied with this stance; indeed, the issue of cultural relativism poses an important dilemma for sociology. Today, many find extreme cultural relativism unsatisfying. They argue that if sociologists are going to have some input in social policy or, more generally, if they are to contribute to making society better, they must make some informed, though by no means certain, decisions about what changes would be best for whatever society or institutions they are studying.

At a personal level as well, many of us find extreme forms of relativism, however convenient and useful, ultimately unsatisfying. We say "convenient" because today, apparently, almost any behaviour can be justified by reference to some culture, somewhere. It's all too easy to take advantage of the opportunities our expanded knowledge of other cultures provides. We ourselves have on occasion "used" the norms and customs of other cultures to justify our various peccadilloes and gaucheries, from burping in a restaurant to perhaps more serious breaches of etiquette. More generally, it occurred to us, it may be a characteristic of our age that we are prepared to justify almost any behaviour on the basis that sometime, somewhere, the behaviour is treated as normal.

We do not mean to trivialize what is a very important issue because in some very real sense, we believe, most of us long for the kind of commitment that we seem to have lost. We feel we must be committed to something, but what? The hope of liberal scholars has been that our commitments will somehow come out of the very kinds of reflections about culture we have been discussing. Some anthropologists have made the search for cultural universals, for a new basis of moral commitment, the raison d'être of their work. And a number of sociologists have demanded that sociology develop a set of criteria, including normative standards, for passing judgments and making choices.

VALUE-COMMITTED SOCIOLOGY

A number of writers, such as Alvin Gouldner (1970), Ivan Illich (1970), André Gunder Frank (1969) and Daniel Bell (1978), insist that sociologists must develop and commit themselves to a set of standards for evaluating not only other cultures but their own. In essence they are arguing that evaluations (and recommendations based on such evaluations) are not only desirable, they are virtually inevitable and therefore must be made explicit. Part of this task involves uncovering the unstated and often unrecognized background assumptions — world views that guide the sociological endeavour itself. For some, such as Alvin Gouldner (1970), this has meant we must develop what he called a "reflexive sociology."

The historical mission of a Reflexive Sociology . . . would be to transform the sociologist, to penetrate deeply into his daily life and work, enriching them with new sensitivities, and to raise the sociologists's self-awareness to a new historical level (1970:489–490).

According to Gouldner, such a sociology would have to be radical because it would recognize that knowledge of the world cannot be advanced apart from sociologists' knowledge of themselves and their position in the social world or apart from their efforts to change these; radical because it seeks to transform as well as to know the alien world outside the sociologist as well as the alien world inside him or her.

The question here is obviously not one solely within sociology or the social sciences. Ideally, much of the time you will be spending at university, inside and outside the classroom, will be a search for commitments and ways of making them meaningful and real in your behaviour. What we have been suggesting is that this is a lot harder to do now than it was in the past. All of this holding up our culture for examination, all of this reflection can lead to anomie, a kind of normlessness. Yet it remains, paradoxically, that only by challenging our taken-for-granted assumptions can we be at all confident that we are anything more than "cultural dopes" acting out other people's choices and not making our own choices at all. In the following pages we shall look more closely at the elements of culture, particularly symbols and values.

THE COMPONENTS OF CULTURE

In 1953, Jean Bruller, writing under the name of Vercors, wrote a best-selling novel in which an anthropological expedition discovers a group of strange creatures, Tropi, who seem to be something more than animals but less than human. In a fictional trial, theologians, biologists, and social scientists offer their testimony about whether the Tropi are human. In so doing, they must come to grips with the age-old question—what is human? The Tropi are lovable and apparently loving; they seem curious; they use tools and are able to make a wide variety of sounds and gestures. They at least seem to have a society. What must we know about the Tropi before we can classify them as either people-like apes or ape-like people?

Humans do not always come off well in comparison to animals. There are animals with greater speed, greater strength. Humans, however, can think abstractly. They can devise ways to control or live better in their environment; they can originate ideas, share them with other members of their group, and transmit them to future generations. The mechanism for sharing and transmitting ideas is symbols. "Man's capacity to form symbols and words which represent phenomena of his external and internal worlds is his most distinguishing characteristic" (Meuller, 1973:19). Humans are symbol users.

As sociologists, if we could not penetrate the language of the Tropi, that is, if we could not know that they used symbols, we would have to testify that they were not human. This is essentially the problem that we face when we impute to animals — for that matter to babies — human-like thoughts and sentiments. Both may, in their behaviour, appear to exhibit affection or guilt, for example, but unless we share a common universe of symbols, language in other words, we cannot know whether they are even capable of such emotions.

SYMBOLS

Symbols are any objects to which people have attached some shared value and meaning. The Canadian flag, the fleur-de-lis, or a wave of the hand all have more or less shared meaning to people in our society. Clearly, these symbols are arbitrary. A wink or a whistle is a symbol that North American society recognizes and that conveys a particular meaning. Whether received with appreciation or disgust, the recipient knows what was intended. But we also find that these same gestures may mean nothing or something quite different in other cultures. There is no reason why, for example, money must be represented by bills and coins as we know them. But once the symbol has been created, used, and, particularly, passed down from generation to generation, it takes on a reality of its own and may in fact become sacred.

LANGUAGE

The most important system of symbols for humans is language. Language is also perhaps the most difficult of the symbols to subject to analysis. All of us depend upon language in virtually every aspect of our daily lives. Nevertheless, this dependence is taken for granted, in large part because of its pervasiveness.

Part of the complexity in studying language stems from the fact that it embodies cumulative human experience. Language, in effect, gives us a sense of what Berger and Luckmann (1967) call historicity, a sense that there has been a past, a past that somehow belongs to us. In earlier societies, the job of communicating and transmitting knowledge about the past rested largely with elders who informally passed on various beliefs, myths, and superstitions through stories, wise sayings, rhymes, and so on. This oral tradition is part of every society including our own—for example, the myth of Santa Claus — and is generally referred to as folklore. But today knowledge is being increasingly produced and transmitted by "knowledge specialists" or "experts."

As societies became literate, as they moved from an oral to a written tradition, the nature of knowledge changed. For the first time people were able to scrutinize, reread, and compare written documents. Their standards of evaluating knowledge therefore changed. No longer as free to create an imaginative, mythological history, literate societies made a greater attempt to distinguish fact and fiction. Nevertheless, part of the task of historians, our knowledge experts, is to integrate past events into the culture. As they impose order on past events, they in effect create history and create for us a heritage of dramas, heroes, and villains. Samuel Butler makes this point well in his unfair but witty description of historians:

It has been said that although God cannot alter the past, historians can; it is perhaps because they can be useful to Him in this respect that He tolerates their existence.

The English conquest of New France in 1763 is a historical fact, but what we know about the conquest, the battles, and its heroes will depend on which text we have read and particularly on whether the test was written by a French Canadian or an English Canadian. The Royal Commission on Bilingualism and Biculturalism (1968) devoted a good deal of attention to the way history was presented in Canada. The commission found that, typically, historical events were depicted very differently by the English- and French-Canadian texts.

In fact the two versions of Canadian history were often irreconcilable. Canada has a dual history and, as Richert (1974) shows, that duality is reflected in the attitudes of French-

and English-Canadian students. For example, when students were asked which figures in history they most admired as heroes, English Canadians most often chose English heroes and, almost without exception, French Canadians chose French heroes. While history may often be an integrating or binding force in a nation, by providing the people with a rich heritage of which they can be proud, this obviously need not always be the case. Rather, it appears that history in Canada may well be a divisive factor, one that may retard social and cultural integration (Richert, 1974:162).

In any case it is language that provides us our link to the past. It is also through language that we can imagine the future and indeed influence the future by passing on our ideas. Language, then, gives us a place in the flow of history; it conveys to us that the world existed before us and will exist after us. Over a century ago, Marx and Engels wrote that "language, like consciousness, only arises from the need, the necessity, of intercourse with other men" (Feuer, 1963:251). Human existence depends on language. At the same time, the ideas embedded in the language we learn shape our view of the world. One has no choice but to learn the language and therefore the ideas of the group into which one is born.

LANGUAGE AND THOUGHT

An intriguing question is whether we are able to think abstractly because of language or whether we have language because we are able to think. There is substantial controversy about just how much language determines our thought processes. According to one view, language provides us with the labels (names), categories, and concepts that enable us to think about the world in the first place.

This is the view, for example, proposed by Benjamin Whorf (1956) in what has been termed the Whorf-Sapir hypothesis.

Essentially the argument states that without language there can be no meaning. The labels or names that the child learns direct the selection process, that is, direct the child to perceive only certain aspects of the environment; the child will not recognize what he or she has no name for. As well, language provides the categories through which people come to conceptualize their world, think about it, and therefore experience it; language forms our experience of the world. This does not mean that at some level we cannot experience some aspect of the world not contained in our language, but rather that we do not retain these experiences.

Whorf and Sapir, anthropologists and linguists, believed that the structure of the language of a people determined the whole of their culture. They derived much of their theory from a study of the Hopi, a peaceful and nonaggressive Indian tribe. The Hopi language, unlike our language, virtually ignores verb-noun differences. For example, rather than saying "the women is leaving us," they would more likely say something equivalent to "leaving." Sentences in English, on the other hand, almost invariably portray something or somebody doing some action. In other words, English is a more active language that, according to Whorf's argument, is reflected in our concern with controlling nature and other people rather than simply accepting "life as it is," as do the Hopi.

One could speculate that a similar deterministic relationship exists between the Inuit language and Inuit culture. The Inuit language contains no word to express the first person pronoun. So rather than say, "I am hungry," the Inuit would say, "Somebody is hungry." Perhaps this is reflected in the greater appreciation of the community, of the collective rather than of the individual.

Opposing this thesis is the perspective of structuralism, developed with particular force and clarity by the French anthropologist, Claude Lévi-Strauss. He describes his main thesis in *The Elementary Structure of Kinship*: Every new-born child comes equipped, in the form of adumbrated mental structures, with all the means available to humankind to define its relations to the world in general, and its relations to others (1969:93).

For Lévi-Strauss, infants' thoughts represent the "common denominator" of all thought and all cultures. If there are differences between Inuit and Hopi, or between Russians and Mexicans, these are the results of what are ultimately similar kinds of responses to different kinds of ecological circumstances. Lévi-Strauss would not argue with Whorf's and Sapir's emphasis on the importance of language in transforming human thought; all would agree that it is language that distinguishes us from lower animals. Lévi-Strauss, however, disputes the deterministic relationship proposed in the Whorf-Sapir hypothesis. When children learn a language they learn to select among their mental structures, emphasizing some and rejecting others. And while language does indeed allow people to communicate with one another, it also means that "the unlimited possibilities available to the child are irremediably lost."

As a partial illustration of this, consider that babies are born with the capacity to make the necessary sounds of every langauge in the world. Yet at a later point we find it difficult, if not impossible, to duplicate the sounds of certain languages. In learning to speak our own language correctly, we must, in effect, suppress some potential sounds and develop others.

Language, then, represents specialization. Structural linguists have proposed similar hypotheses. While Lévi-Strauss is concerned with understanding culture and particularly its elementary structures, structural linguists, notably Noam Chomsky, have been interested in how all language is ultimately similar because it is the outcome of basic and universal cognitive processes. For structural linguists, languages are "superficially" dissimilar but identical at the level of "deep structure" because people of all cultures think in the same basic way.

It is difficult, perhaps impossible, to determine which of these hypotheses is correct, whether language determines our thought or thought determines language. Perhaps Whorf and Sapir are right about content and Chomsky about linguistic structures. What is clear is that all agree that language mediates our thought processes, guides our perceptions, and allows us to establish relationships with the past, with others in our present, with the future, and even with eternity in symbolizations of our gods and other worlds.

LANGUAGE AND FREEDOM

As will be evident in Chapter 5, symbolic interactionists often portray language as liberating. As children acquire language, they become progressively freer from their biological natures, their "instincts." They become more able to express themselves, to externalize their internal states, and to manipulate the behaviour of others around them. And because language contains accumulated past experience, people are able to profit from this experience and are liberated from the necessity of creating new techniques to handle each situation they encounter. They have the benefit of knowing how previous generations learned to control their environment and to cope with problems of geography and climate.

On the other hand, and this is particularly evident in the work of Sapir and Whorf, language is seen as constraining an individual's freedom. In a sense, the child becomes the heir to the linguistic stereotypes of generations. Another way of putting this is that we are heirs to what C. Wright Mills calls a "vocabulary of motives" through which we "understand" our own and others' behaviour.

In our society, for example, we learn to distinguish between madness and sanity, mental health and mental illness. The latter term has provided us with a residual category that we use to account for the apparently inexplicable. Thomas Szasz (1960; 1961), the social psychiatrist, has described how the term "mental illness" has been expanded to cover an increasing range of behaviours, until finally it is now used to describe virtually any behaviour that is unconventional. However, in earlier periods, people were constrained by a different vocabulary of motives. In the medieval period, for example, people usually accounted for bizarre behaviour in terms of possession by the devil. In later periods people were more likely to think in terms of "moral" and "immoral" behaviour.

. . . what formerly was thought of morally is in our time thought of esthetically or psychiatrically. Whereas formerly maidens and ladies spoke of "wicked" men and of "good" and "bad" conduct, today they speak of "decent" and "indecent" conduct or of "neurotic" and "stable" persons (Gerth and Mills, 1953:123).

Today the notion of mental illness seems to have brought with it a widespread intolerance of the unconventional and seems to threaten our appreciation for human diversity. Our perception of others, then, is filtered through the linguistic symbols we have learned.

A more obvious example of what we mean by a linguistic stereotype is in the area of prejudice and discrimination. Once we have acquired language, we are able to learn about and think about categories of objects and people beyond our immediate perception. For example, we can come to love or hate categories of people we have never met. These sentiments do not emerge from our own direct experience of the people in question but are "inherited" prejudices. For example, many people who are not aware of ever having met a Jew will often feel that they know what Jews are like and indeed this "knowledge" may prove highly resistant to change.

Some who have not met Jews may still learn what it means to be "jewed down" in financial transaction. People may learn prejudicial definitions without ever being aware of what they have learned.

Over the past few years, we have heard many complaints and jokes about the feminist attack on our language. Many have treated as trivial women's concerns to eliminate the consistent sexist bias in English. But ask yourself what kind of prejudicial assumptions are smuggled into our thinking when we use terms such as "mankind" or even manpower. Are we saying that there is a certain primacy in maleness or that the work world is a male preserve? The de-sexing of language may be an important step toward the elimination of sexual stereotypes.

Even our conception of what constitutes a social problem is determined in part by the language we have learned. An excellent example is provided in I. A. Richards's study of Chinese culture and language at the time of Mencius. The Chinese word for "aged" makes no distinction between age in the chronological sense and the ethical pattern of behaviour — deference and reverence — thought due the old. In Mencius's period, people could not think about whether they ought to treat the old with reverence; they did not "discuss or treat as open to discussion the rightness of paying respect to age as age" (Richards, in Mills, 1967:436) or, in the words of C. Wright Mills, "their language would not allow a definition of the problem" (pp. 436–437). While what to do about old people constitutes a social problem in our society, it could not in theirs because their language could not encompass the idea.

STOCK OF KNOWLEDGE

It should be clear by now that as we learn the language of our group we are also learning the implicit rules and evaluations of our group. As Kenneth Burke puts it:

The names of things and operations smuggle in connotations of good and bad — a noun tends to carry with it an invisible adjective and a verb an invisible adverb (Burke, 1965:224).

In other words, as we are learning language we are learning much more — the social texture and context of life. What we are also learning is the stock of knowledge that has been created in the past and that includes everything that the members of the groups "know" about every aspect of the world.

To describe what we are learning as knowledge rather than as beliefs implies a transformation process; ideas undergo a process Berger and Luckmann (1967) refer to as "objectification." They explain that when people create an agreed upon way of handling something in the environment, they are likely to recognize that their solution is arbitrary; it is simply a convention. But when they pass on this convention to new members of the group, new-born children, for example, the convention is translated into the reality. What was simply a way of handling a problem becomes *the* way such problems are handled.

For example, let us imagine that a man and woman on an island decide that their breakfast each day would, for reasons of convenience and taste, consist of fish. Their children would learn that breakfast means fish; people eat fish for breakfast. Indeed, to eat eggs for breakfast might for these children not only seem bizarre, it may in fact seem revolting.

Convention becomes objective knowledge about reality. Very often in transmitting a convention to their children, parents feel called upon to justify it, to make sense of it, perhaps to make it appear as the right and sensible way of doing things. According to Berger and Luckmann, one way of doing this is to explain what was simply a convention as being ordained by some supernatural being, a commandment of a god or gods. Eating fish for breakfast may become incorporated into the common stock of knowledge not only as a piece of information but also as something sacred and inviolate. If this becomes the case, people are unwilling or unable to imagine alternatives.

How we think is in large part determined by how previous generations have thought. Language obviously captures the dialectic of people as creators and people as products because, at the same time, it is language that allows us to form relationships with others and therefore to engage in collective action. Language makes us part of the group, but it is also the resource we use for thinking of ways to change the structure or organization of the group.

We might add that an understanding of the fundamental constraints inherent in language is a first step toward transcending these constraints. No doubt the wish to transcend the constraints in our language is implicit in the emphasis of liberal education on learning other languages. Perhaps from the perspectives of these other languages, we can come to learn the limitations built into our own. In fact, language constraints may be more potent for North Americans who very often speak and think in only one language than for Europeans who more often have learned several. In some fundamental sense, Europeans may be more cosmopolitan, less prone to ethnocentrism, than North Americans.

VALUES

People are symbol users; they are also moral creatures. Very seldom do we think or talk in purely descriptive terms. We are almost always evaluating. When we describe someone as a heavy drinker we are doing more than simply describing a behaviour pattern. We are also saying something like "isn't that just terrible"; or "isn't that just fine"—depending on our values. When we describe someone as mentally ill, we are not simply describing him or her, we are also evaluating the person. However much the psychiatrist insists on the neutrality of the concept — its scientific status — it is pejorative. People are moral creatures likely to praise or condemn other people's customs and behaviour.

It you were asked to describe what makes French Canadians and English Canadians different, you would probably answer in evaluative terms rather than describe actual differences. Popular or stereotypical notions hold that Francophones are more animated than Anglophones and have a greater joie de vivre. Certainly, as Pierre Berton (1975) has noted, the American version of French Canadians, as conveyed through Hollywood films, portrays them as "happy-go-lucky and high living," which probably, from an Anglophone perspective, implies that they are childlike and irresponsible. What the Anglophone thinks of as sensible and businesslike is probably seen by the Francophone as cold and calculating. These characterizations are for the most part myths; they do not hold up under close scrutiny. However, they may tell us something about the groups' projected values; that is, how they like to talk and think about themselves. What we are trying to illustrate here is that people make evaluations, but they do so on the basis of shared notions of what ought to be; people judge behaviour on the basis of values they have learned.

We use values as rough guidelines for planning our course of action and probably more frequently for judging the actions of others. When we say people are moral creatures we mean that they make moral judgments, not necessarily that they behave morally. Values provide the basis for judgments. The relatively new language of "guilt-free sex," "being nonjudgmental" — and the apparent abhorrence of value judgments underline the confusion about which values we should be committed to. To the extent a group is committed to the same values, it is said to have a distinct identity.

IDEOLOGY

This latter function of values, that they help us to explain and justify what is happening to us and to society more generally, is of particular importance. The pre-eminent sociological question is, "How is social order possible?"

Why does society not fragment into a variety of warring groups? As we described in the first chapter, the conflict perspective has emphasized force or the threat of force; powerful groups in society by definition have a virtual monopoly on force and are thereby able to exact compliance to their wishes. Superficially, at least, most of us are likely to find that explanation implausible. We do not live in a kind of military dictatorship where we are constantly confronted with the symbols of force. For example, part of the horror many people experienced after the invocation of the War Measures Act in 1970, and particularly the subsequent image of machine-gun-carrying soldiers in the streets of a Canadian city, may have been because it served as a reminder of the important role of force. Nevertheless, brute force can only be a temporary basis for compliance; it is an unstable basis for order. A society based solely on force would have to be a society in which "Big Brother" really could watch all of our actions and tap all of our thoughts. Most of the time force is not called into play because we more or less willingly cooperate in maintaining social order.

This, of course, raises the question why, in the face of inequality, force can be left in reserve. Perhaps the most important and certainly most influential answer comes from Karl Marx. For Marx, certain ideas and cultural beliefs are of more consequence because they serve to justify the position of the privileged class—landowners in feudal times, capitalists when he was writing in the nineteenth century. He believed that only those in the owner class had the leisure time to develop ideas and, most important, the power and resources to communicate them to others. As Parkin puts it:

Marx's claim that the ideas of the ruling class are, in every age, the ruling ideas rests upon the fact that those who control the major agencies of socialization typically occupy privileged class positions. As a consequence, their definition of social reality, and their moral judgments, are far

more likely to be blessed with the stamp of public legitimacy than are the social and moral constructs of those in subordinate class positions (1971:42).

Most sociologists have followed Marx's notion of ideology as a world view or belief system that corresponds to the interests and concerns of ruling classes and powerful groups in a society. At times ideologies are simply rationalizations for the existing state of affairs. Religious beliefs may be ideological because they, in effect, reconcile people to their low position in society, to their poverty. This is nicely illustrated in a verse from a nineteenth-century Anglican hymn, "All Things Bright and Beautiful." It reminds parishioners that the inequality between lord and serf is part of God's plan and must therefore be accepted:

The rich man in his castle
The poor man at his gate
He made them high and lowly
And ordered their estate
All things bright and beautiful.

A number of European sociologists have emphasized the ways in which the economic elite have used the media to manipulate symbols, to convince members of society that all is serene and as it should be (see Ossenberg, 1971:165–168). This is hardly surprising since the owners of the media are also members of the economic elite. Such a view of the media often seems to portray "media barons" fairly successfully "brainwashing the masses." Certainly, as Elkin (1971) and others have demonstrated (e.g., Caldwell, 1978), the English press has at times blatantly manipulated its somewhat captive audience by its misleading reporting of political events in Quebec.

However, for the most part, media influences probably operate much more subtly than in the case of Quebec. No doubt the media offers a limited perspective, but these limits do not always reflect a deliberate attempt to manipulate public consciousness; they may often simply reflect the limited perspective of those who control the media. As media control becomes concentrated in the hands of a few, it should not be surprising that the media present one consistent and conservative point of view.

In response to the model of media as manipulative, a number of sociologists, particularly American sociologists, maintain that the media simply reflect societal views. But whose views? It seems clear that the media ask certain kinds of questions, make selections about what is important and what is not, report events as if they had no history, no social context, all within a framework that assumes that if a problem does exist it can be resolved within the system. Perhaps the most fundamental limitation of the perspective presented through the media is that only certain kinds of futures can be imagined; essentially their perceptions of "what is" frame their notions of "what might be." Whether deliberately manipulative or not, this certainly coincides with the ideology, with the world view, of the economic elite.

So, while ideologies are often simply rationalizations — justifications or apologies — they are much more, as Marx was fully aware. Perhaps, then, it is more useful to view ideology as a set of limits to consciousness rather than simply a set of justifications. Martin Shaw, for example, describes ideologies in just these terms:

Ideology . . . is not apology, although it may and often does entail it. Ideologies are world-views which, despite their partial and possibly critical insights, prevent us from understanding the society in which we live and the possibility of changing it. They are world-views which correspond to the standpoints of classes and social groups whose interests in the existing social system and incapacity to change it make it impossible for them to see it as a whole (1972:33–34).

The way ideology works can indeed be quite subtle. Just think of some of your aesthetic values. You may like McDonald's hamburgers, paintings on velvet, plastic fruit, artificial flowers, and colonial-style furniture, or what have you but you may at the same time "know" that you are "wrong" to like these things—that these represent bad taste. So you don't admit to reading Harlequin Romances, *Mad Magazine*, or enjoying country and western music. You "know" that knowledge of the impressionists, Mozart, opera and ballet are somehow more worthy, somehow more valuable. Many of us are embarrassed by the gap between our personal tastes and our sense of the aesthetic values and judge ourselves accordingly. We feel guilty about watching television rather than reading a "good" book and sometimes feel compelled to lie about which programs we are watching. Quite simply, we have bought an elite version of culture on the basis of which we disparage our own and ourselves. Just at what point an elite culture is simply a way of excluding some behaviours by deeming them less worthwhile and at what point it represents a critical assessment based on the intrinsic worth of the behaviour is never very clear. Is there, in other words, some absolute standard by which to judge a novel, a painting, or a film, or are we uncritically accepting the personal tastes and values of the more powerful?

POLITICAL CULTURE

WHY IDEOLOGY?

Ideologies direct us to "see" some things and of course blind us to other things. What this means is that the ideas we bring with us, whether taken-for-granted or explicit, will shape our understanding of the world. The problem, as always, is that people are attached to different ideas and values, different and often conflicting beliefs about what is and ought to be, what we celebrate as progress, and what we bemoan as decline. In her book, *Ideological Perspectives in Canada*, Pat Marchak, a sociologist at the University of British Columbia, introduces ideology as follows:

Social reality doesn't appear to us directly. It is revealed to our understanding through a screen of assumptions, beliefs, explanations, values, and unexamined knowledge. Together, these elements of the screen comprise an ideology, and the ideology directs our attention to some realities but not to others; interprets what our senses transmit but in terms of what is already accepted as truth. An ideology grows with us from childhood. Some parts of it are deliberately transmitted by parents, schools, the media, and the other institutions of our society. Other parts are more casually conveyed through example: the unspoken assumptions and attitudes of those around us. If a complete ideology is subjected to close scrutiny it can seldom meet the test of consistency. It provides explanations which are not logically connected to one another, permits the holding of values which are not congruent. Even so, it provides some dominant themes, some rules of thumb, some central beliefs that guide our actions and our perceptions in our habitual rounds of activity (1981:1).

DOMINANT IDEOLOGY AS CONVENTIONAL WISDOM

One characteristic that distinguishes complex from simple societies is that no single ideology will represent a full consensus. Rather, we must think in terms of a dominant ideology and a number of competing or counter-ideologies. If, for example, one was to characterize Canadian political culture as essentially liberal, we would not be capturing all Canadians and their beliefs. We would be trying, rather, to detect some dominant threads. We would be describing Canada's *conventional wisdom*, but this does not mean that Canadians, even those who share the dominant ideology, are equally committed to it. And, of course, many Canadians will identify themselves in terms of their rejection of the conventional wisdom; there will inevitably exist any number of alternative competing ideologies.

When we describe Canada's dominant ideology or conventional wisdom we should, presumably, be describing what most of you believe. But this is why we talk of "conventional wisdom"; we may not know that we believe in any particular ideology. Very often beliefs may appear to us as unassailable facts, or what any sensible person knows, or what any "right-thinking" Canadian understands; or our beliefs may be so taken-for-granted that we have never held them up for reflection and inspection.

For some of you, though probably few, the "Canadian ideology" we describe in this chapter will capture your deepest political commitments — the issues you care about, the problems you see, and the solutions you are willing to fight for. Fore more of you, the dominant ideology captures not so much your commitments as your taken-for-granted world. Of course, some of you will have commitments that oppose the conventional wisdom, that offer a different perspective on our society. We shall return to the issue of alternative and counter-ideologies. For now, we simply point out that even those who oppose the conventional are unquestionably influenced by it, even if only through their knowledge of what is conventional and how they, themselves, are not.

THE MEANING OF IDEOLOGY

What of those who claim to have no ideology? We have asked our students on occasion whether they had or were committed to some ideology. This is an ambiguous and perhaps a strange question but it often produces surprising answers. Some have answered "yes" and have described their ideologies with one of the traditional labels: liberal, conservative, socialist or, more broadly, right wing or left wing.

We find, however, that these labels mean very different things to different students. Sometimes labels such as liberal or conservative seem to mean a commitment to a Canadian political party supposedly reflecting one of these ideological positions. Sometimes the labels mean an intuitive or gut-level commitment to some core value the particular ideology seems to represent — civil liberties, distributive justice, tradition, and order. Rarely do the ideological labels indicate a full-blown world view. In fact, many, with apparent pride, give credence to Daniel Bell's (1962) contention that we are living at the end of ideology, as they claim that no ideology can grab their commitment and that they formulate their opinions on an issue-by-issue basis; no single overriding moral or value principle serves as the basis of the positions they take on such issues as abortion, capital punishment, narcotics legislation and the like.

All of these students have an ideology, though for most of them the ideology is *implicit*. For example, commitment to a political party probably indicates a belief that the democratic political process works, that social change must proceed through institutionalized means and so on. An issue-by-issue approach probably indicates a rejection of utopian thinking and a taken-for-granted belief that the system itself need not, or cannot, be fundamentally altered. As you read this chapter, you may wish to ferret out, make explicit and articulate, your own assumptions and ideologies.

How might you do this? Let us give you a simple example out of our own classroom experience. One of us confronted a class of "Canadian Society" students almost all of whom claimed to be ideology-free. He then proceeded to ask their views on a variety of specific issues, for example, narcotics legislation. Should there be such legislation? Do we need narcotic laws? Some answered that this was a foolish question. "Surely," they said, "this is precisely the role of the state, to pro-

tect us, even from ourselves." Think back to Chapter 1. Are you not reminded of Hobbes's egocentric, acquisitive beast and his "Leviathan" keeping order? Perhaps what we are seeing in the students' answers is an implicit ideology based on certain assumptions about humans and their relationship to the state. Whether or not the students have a full-blown ideology, they do have certain basic assumptions. And, to the extent that these assumptions remain implicit and are taken-for-granted, they limit them more than they know.

Other students expressed more ambivalence about narcotics legislation. One argued that it was necessary to protect children, but that adults should have the right to exert responsibility for their lives, and that, in any case, there are dangers in too much state intrusion. Here we have rather different assumptions. Because people are basically good, they must be protected *from* and not only *by* the state; their goodness must be preserved. In short, one need not look too hard to find the Hobbes/Rousseau "debate" in the ideological commitments of Canadians, even of those who deny ideological commitment or, for that matter, any knowledge of Hobbes or Rousseau.

At the same time, however, there is a sense in which the phrase "the end of ideology" rings true. There is no question that specific ideologies, well-articulated visions of utopia, are very much alive in academia. But what about most Canadians? In our everyday interactions with students there seems to be a disenchantment with utopian images or with the belief that the struggle is worth the effort. They seem to be saying that perhaps people can "fight city hall," but "city hall can't fight the corporation." To quote one of our students, "The corporations have it locked up."

We remain unconvinced, however, that utopian images have died. Rather, the sense of futility, powerlessness — the various forms of alienation — probably better reflect not a loss of utopian ideals but a loss of hope that there are means for achieving these ideals. Utopias no longer direct our aspirations and actions; they are treated in the realm of fantasy or wishful thinking. Any maybe, too, we are disenchanted with what we take to be the failures of traditional ideologies, and so, ideally, we search for new answers or, more frequently and more sadly, "we don't think about politics much."

David Bell and Lorne Tepperman conclude their analysis of Canadian political cultures in much the same terms:

The enthusiasms that first greeted Diefenbaker in 1958, and the wave of "Trudeaumania" a decade later, understandably subsided when neither man turned out to be the knight in shining armour voters expected. Increasingly, enthusiasm turned to apathy, apathy to cynicism.

Politics, as the working out of visions of a better world, have almost disappeared from the national scene in Canada. We find instead politics as administration and a mere balancing of selfish interests. National unity cannot be created out of such flimsy stuff (1970:250).

ALTERNATIVE AND COUNTER-IDEOLOGIES

Finally, a few of you will deny that you are either conventional or cynical, that instead you are committed to an alternative ideology. Probably, however, your alternative is infused with and constrained by the conventional wisdom.

Societies can be distinguished by how much ideological leeway they provide, that is, by the extent to which they tolerate open departures from the conventional wisdom. In this respect, Canadians generally think of Canada as quite open. Nevertheless, the notion of alternative ideologies implies *permissable departures* from the dominant mode; it's acceptable to be "socialistic" in Canada, to be "sympathetic to the ideals" of Marxism, but it's probably unacceptable, outside of academia, to be a committed Marxist,

Communist, Fascist, or neo-Nazi. In short, when we describe the Canadian ideology, Canada's political culture, we are not describing one unified ideology but rather the range of permissibility in what Canadians can believe without being seen as on the lunatic or dangerously subversive fringe.

On this fringe are the true counter-ideologies that *threaten* convention, that propose a very different kind of Canada. Perhaps, to your dismay, you will often find these counter-ideologies quite alive in your various social science courses. Perhaps only here will you find a vigorous commitment to radical perspectives on Canadian society. But outside the university, for the present at least, it seems safe to say that the conflict of ideologies in Canada is relatively muted and poses no real threat to the structure of Canadian society. Communists and revolutionaries are still seen, in Canada, as on the lunatic fringe or as now outdated by social and political change. And this will mean that ideological disputes will lack the heat, the fervour that similar discussions in, say, Nicaragua promise. In the Third world and now, in a different way, in Eastern Europe, the ideological conflicts are unquestionably bringing with them radical consequences and fundamental change.

CANADIAN IDEOLOGY

In describing Canadian ideology we will be using familiar terms — liberal, conservative, socialist. Perhaps the biggest problem with these terms is that they are so familiar. For many of us they are strongly evocative, even if we might find it difficult to specify their content. Liberal, for example, evokes wishy-washyness; conservative evokes stodgyness; and socialist evokes naivety. These images often constrain our understanding. Further, in any heated political exchange it soon becomes evident that such designations as liberal or conservative can mean very different things to different people. Do liberals believe in medicare or is that a socialist cause? Can even a conservative believe in medicare? Added to this confusion are the various upper-case ideologies—big "L" liberalism, for example—supposedly represented by the political parties that carry these labels. Virtually every industrialized nation has its "Liberal," "Conservative," and "Socialist" (Labour) parties whose platforms and politics seem to reflect very different interpretations of these words.

We can talk about ideologies at two levels. First, we can describe them in some artificial pure form much as we find reflected in the classical writings of John Stuart Mill, Edmund Burke, and Karl Marx. Second, we must understand ideology in the context of the particular social and historical conditions of the society we are examining. So just as Mill, Burke, and Marx must be understood within the context of eighteenth and nineteenth century social change, so, too, must Canadian ideology be understood within the context of the unique features of Canadian society.

Quite simply, liberalism, or any of these ideologies, does not mean one thing once and for all time; political ideologies are not disembodied idea systems existing independent of people, without a historical and structural context.

Nor, as the historian Hartz (1964) maintained, can we understand Canadian ideologies simply by tracing which fragment of the spectrum of Old World ideologies the original settlers of French Canada and English Canada brought with them. Certainly they will have brought ideologies with them, ideologies that reflected their position and experience in Europe. However, these ideologies will have changed to reflect the facts of Canadian life — its late development, its regional disparities, its hostile climate and geography, its changing patterns of immigration, and its changing occupational structure.

Moreover, it would be misleading to imagine that only one ideology was important to the "New World." And as always in the competition of ideologies, we must ask which

groups had the most resources to make their ideology the dominant one. In the conflict of ideologies, even the dominant ideology will have been transformed; the dominant ideology can never exist in "pure form," "uncontaminated" by competing systems of ideas. Gad Horowitz makes this very point:

The three components of the English-Canadian political culture have not developed in isolation from one another; each has developed in interaction with the others. Our toryism and our socialism have been moderated by liberalism. But by the same token, our liberalism has been rendered "impure," in American terms, through its contacts with toryism and socialism. If English-Canadian liberalism is less individualistic, less ardently populistic-democratic, more inclined to state intervention in the economy, and more tolerant of "feudal survivals" such as monarchy, this is due to the uninterrupted influence of toryism upon liberalism, an influence wielded in and through the conflict between the two. If English-Canadian liberalism has tended since the depression to merge at its leftist edge with the democratic socialism of the CCF-NDP, this is due to the influence which socialism has exerted upon liberalism, in and through the conflict with them (1966:47).

THE DOMINANT IDEOLOGY: CANADIAN LIBERALISM

Most social scientists would agree with Marchak that the dominant ideology in Canada has become the liberal ideology as it has always been in the United States.

The liberal ideology assumes that each child may choose his or her way of life, determine his or her own future, arrange his or her itinerary, that all are equal in this opportunity. The liberal ideology rests on the premise that the individual is more important than the society and that the society does not have the right to limit an individual's freedom to pursue happiness as he or she chooses to define it (1981:16).

In other words, from a liberal perspective or ideology, the just society is not one of equality of condition, one where resources are distributed more or less equally, but one in which there is alleged to be *equality of opportunity*: people, it is believed, should have the equal right, regardless of ethnicity, sex, or family background, etc., to rise in the social hierarchy, to compete for scarce resources—power, prestige, and money. Marchak shows, even by this limited definition of "equality," that is, equality of opportunity, that we fall far short of the ideal. So, of course, does the United States. We will look further at this in the second half of the text.

In addition, liberalism places considerable emphasis on individual fulfillment even if this is at the expense of others. Robin Mathews argues that

the human product, in human terms, of the liberal ideology is the Robber Baron of free enterprise—and the cop-out hippie/yippie of the so-called counter culture. The liberal ideology supports all manifestations of liberal anarchist individualism, whether that of the rich free enterpriser who manipulates the community for his own profit or the so-called disengaged rejector of community who denies it (1973:214).

The liberal ideology espouses what C. B. MacPherson (1962) calls *possessive individualism*. Rather than collectivism, the emphasis is on freedom to rise (and fall) in the class and status hierarchy. Generally, it has also taken for granted the efficiency and "rightness" of free enterprise over public enterprise and of private property over collective property. Indeed any other form of social and economic organization may be seen as inconceivable.

What does this mean in everyday life? It means, for example, that the answers parents provide children, teachers provide students, clergy provide their congregations, the answers we find in the media, and our conventional wisdom are those of individual rights, individual freedoms, and the importance of self and self-betterment.

Consider, for a moment, the television programs all of us watch and the commercials in which they are sandwiched. Much has been written about the effects of violence on television and of the potential for cynicism as children come to realize that the TV commercials they watch make unrealistic promises about their products. Much has been written and said of the essential mindlessness and triviality of our media. Such concerns are often justified. But these kinds of criticisms ignore or understate the ideological content of much of our television fare. Ralph Miliband, a British social scientist, points out that

the mass media . . . can and do contribute to the fostering of a climate of conformity, not by the total suppression of dissent, but by the presentation of views which fall outside the consensus as curious heresies or, even more effectively, by treating them as irrelevant eccentricities, which serious and reasonable people may dismiss as of no consequence. This is very "functional" (1969:213).

From "Dallas" to "Another World," from "Cosby" to "L. A. Law," we learn that every problem is an individual one, to be solved through one's own efforts, through the transformation of self, never through collective action that might transform the system.

It is, of course, not a coincidence that liberalism is the characteristic ideology of capitalist societies. It supports capitalism, serves to justify it as a system. And those who benefit most from the system, the owners and controllers, are very likely to embrace an ideology that justifies and solidifies their privileged position. Further, their ability to control public information and public agencies of socialization means that the most readily available ideas and answers are *their* ideas and answers. It is in this sense that liberalism is the dominant, though not the only, ideology in Canada.

But it is a distinctly Canadian liberalism, one that is, paradoxically, more conservative and more socialist than American liberalism. As we have become more closely affiliated with the United States and more distant from Britain, the American version of liberalism has all too often come to be the standard by which we judge ourselves. We would be better to understand our ideology in terms of our own history and the history in Canada of both conservatism and socialism.

THE IDEOLOGY OF THE PAST: CANADIAN CONSERVATISM

Canadian society has often been depicted as conservative in its traditions and politics. We can see this conservatism in our reluctance to change, our caution, our desire to maintain "what is best of our past," in the uneasy and slow acceptance of a new flag, our own anthem, a patriated constitution, or constitutional change. More significantly, we can see Canadian conservatism in our quiet acceptance of inequality of opportunity. This, in essence, is the main thrust of John Porter's (1965) important study of class and power, *The Vertical Mosaic*. Canada, in Porter's view, emerges as ethnically fragmented, inegalitarian, an immobile society with an almost caste like elite. Rather than the vigour and innovation of the American melting pot ideology, we settled for a mosaic ideology, one which left the British (specifically English and Scots) at the top of the Canadian social hierarchy and other ethnic groups somewhere below. Canada appeared to be "behind" not only the United States but also perhaps other liberal capitalist democracies in Europe. Porter's study concluded that we have

a long way to go to become in any sense a thoroughgoing democracy. . . . Even into the 1960s Canadian education systems have yet to become democratized through to the university level. The possibilities for upward mobility are reduced and, at the same time, shortage of highly trained people for the new occupational structure continue. In this respect Canada is behind twentieth-century democracy elsewhere (1965:557–58).

George Grant has understood our conservatism, in part at least, as our attempt to maintain an identity distinct from the United States. In his book, *Lament for a Nation*

(1965), Grant describes how Canadians sought to maintain an identity separate from America through what he calls our "Conservative Nationalism." It was this which linked most Canadians, and which even linked English Canada to French Canada. What was in Ontario stuffy and stodgy Presbyterianism was, in Quebec, repressive and archaic Catholicism —two Canadian versions of conservatism.

Others have agreed with Grant. John Porter (1967:56), for instance, has argued that "English and French Canadians are more alike in their conservatism, traditionalism, religiosity, authoritarianism, and elitist values than the spokesmen of either group are prepared to admit." He goes so far as to ask if Francophone and Anglophone cultures are not simply "subcultural variants" of a single culture in which the core values are conservative. S. D. Clark (1968:236) has also argued that we clung to these traditions because they made us different from the more "open" and "liberal" climate of American society.

Until recently, the dominant ideology in Quebec was unquestionably the ideology of conservatism, which defined Quebec primarily as the bearer of a culture; the task of the Québécois was to preserve the symbols and values handed down by their ancestors. Gerald Fortin, a sociologist from Laval, has described the traditional values these Québécois wished to preserve and to pass on to their descendants.

[This ideology of conservatism extols] the merits of the French language, the Catholic religion, the spiritual culture, the national history, rural life, and the family: it warns of the dangers of English imperialism, industrialization, urbanization and the means of mass communication. . . . (Rioux, 1973:269).

More recently, for many Québécois, as for most Canadians, the emphasis has shifted; conservatism no longer provides satisfactory answers. Québécois no longer see Quebec as primarily a cultural unit but more typically as a modern industrial society that must become the master of its own political and economic destiny. This change in ideology is discussed more fully in Chapter 13.

THE COUNTER IDEOLOGY: CANADIAN SOCIALISM

Socialism, too, has a long history in Canada, though one far more erratic and far more on the fringe than either liberalism or conservatism (Penner, 1977). In part we can understand this erratic history as an outcome of the threat socialism has, episodically, posed or been seen to pose to the structure of Canadian society, to the existent distribution of resources. And when this threat has been considered greatest, Canadians have witnessed their own brand of McCarthyism in, for example, the purging of socialists and Marxists from unions and even from the CCF. Another reason for the erratic history of socialism in Canada no doubt rests with the inevitable strength, the victory, so to speak, of democratic liberalism. From our liberal ideology we come to see socialism as a threat; it is thought to stand for the loss of individualism, of personal freedoms that have seemingly become sacred.

Conservatism finds its utopia in the past, in a nostalgia for what has been or might be lost. Socialism, on the other hand, is based on a future utopia, one that represents a radical break from the present social arrangements. But just what this utopia might look like is not entirely clear. Although Marx left us with the most thorough critique of capitalism available, he did not provide us with the same kind of clear and detailed blueprint of the socialist utopia. It is in this sense that some theorists characterize socialist revolutions as experimental. It is in this sense too, perhaps, that women and those committed to ethnic culture might wonder what the socialist revolution might give to them and what their position would be.

But, of course, socialism does provide a world view. It dictates a class analysis of society, a view of social change as the product of class struggle, a belief that capitalism inevitably serves the interests of those who own or control the means of production and that

decisions affecting all of us in our everyday lives are made by a very few. And, finally, socialism directs us to a commitment to the working class, those who must sell their labour to the capitalists and who are relatively powerless to take control of their fate. Socialism implies a commitment to the interest of the working class because of the belief that, for them, capitalism means exploitation and in relative, if not absolute, terms increasing misery. At a gut level socialism often means abhorrence of inequality and a belief that things could be otherwise.

On these issues, those who would call themselves socialists, perhaps even communists, would not disagree. But what distinguishes socialism most from liberalism and conservatism is its future utopianism, and this also exposes it to sharp internal conflicts. We can find, uncomfortably juxtaposed, visions of world socialism and national socialism, visions of gradual transformation and rapid social change, visions of reform and revolution. These uncomfortable juxtapositions are no more evident than in the history of the CCF/NDP. We have seen the CCF/NDP move to the right and thereby lose the commitment of some of its members, and we have seen attempts to move it to the left, as in the Waffle movement, to the chagrin of others of its members. And we have seen it change its course from a broadly based social movement committed to education and grass-roots social change to become a political party committed to electoral success. Marchak nicely captures the ideological development of the NDP:

[It] begins with a cry of despair at the conditions of the Depression. It softens to a whimper with the onset of the War and becomes a relatively polite request for reform before the War is over (1981:115).

Socialism in the NDP has been a liberal socialism; except for brief outbursts it has been muted. Insofar as it may be said to offer a utopian image, it is a "modest utopia," one that apparently requires no radical break from our present structures. It reflects the current mistrust most of us have for utopian promises. At the same time, socialism has had its influence on the Canadian version of liberalism. And it is perhaps this influence that truly distinguishes Canadian ideology from American.

Canadians have been far more accepting of governmental control to protect the public from free enterprise. Such modern public institutions as Ontario Hydro, the CNR, the CBC, Air Canada, the Canada Council are distinctly Canadian. When a government seeks to "privatize" these institutions — sell them off, it typically does so, as we have seen, with great care and typically against strong opposition. In many respects, then, we have what John Meisel (1977) calls a public enterprise rather than a free-enterprise system. Various manifestations of the welfare state — medicare, social security, regional development and other social innovations — have been implemented far more quickly and easily in Canada than in the United States.

CURRENT DIRECTIONS

In sum, the dominant ideology in Canada and the United States has been some variant of liberalism, whatever else might be mixed in. But Canadian liberalism is different from the American version. It focuses less exclusively on individual rights and freedoms and allows more room for collective rights and public enterprise. The irony, of course, is that in judging ourselves by the standards of American liberal ideology and in worrying about "catching up" with the United States, we sell ourselves short. We remain slaves to colonial thought patterns. Herschel Hardin argues that

Canada, in its essentials, is a public enterprise country, always has been, and probably always will be. Americans have, or at least had, a genius for private enterprise; Canadians have a genius for public enterprise. As long as we describe Canada in terms of the American model, we will continue to see ourselves as second-rate Americans, not being Americans at all (1974:140).

A number of sociologists would argue that these differences have grown smaller, that Canadian liberalism increasingly and inevitably looks like the American parent with its emphasis on individual rights and freedoms. But to the extent that ideology is meant to convince most of us that things are going fairly well, to quieten our despair, liberalism seems to have been a failing ideology. To many Canadians, liberal solutions were seen to aggravate the problems. No liberal reforms, no specific bits of legislation, no new social programs seemed to alter radically the worst features of our everyday lives, our growing insecurity in the job market, our sense of powerlessness. For many Canadians this has meant the search for new ways of thinking about their society.

Sometimes it seems that the most powerful human influence for change right now in Canada is a neoconservatism; in its extreme, it is our own version of the *moral majority*, or more accurately, a vocal and committed minority organizing and fighting for reactionary change, a return to what is probably the false pastoral picture of large happy families, free of sin, unexposed to pornography, homosexuality, and heresy (Richards, 1981). Some neoconservatives, unlike most liberals, are willing to see dramatic government intervention, through legislation and law enforcement, as an important means to achieving a better society.

Another version of neoconservatism is concerned less with social values than with fiscal and economic matters, free market, private enterprise, small government, balanced budgets, free trade, which, ironically, parallel the classic or pure form of nineteenth-century liberalism.

CULTURE CHANGE

The sociologist's emphasis on ideology rather than culture represents not merely a semantic difference from most anthropological works but rather serves to emphasize that some groups are more powerful and are able to achieve dominance for their culture — to make theirs the culture of the society. But it is wrong to assume that cultures—ideologies—are so monolithic or powerful that they do not change. Built into any culture at a variety of levels is change.

SOURCES OF CULTURAL CHANGE

While the major source of cultural change within societies is the conflict of competing ideologies, there are a number of other sources of change that we shall examine first. One perspective emphasizes the importance of *technology* in determining culture change. Sociologists distinguish between ideal culture and material culture. Televisions and typewriters, cars and snowmobiles, knives and forks, machines and computers are all examples of the material culture. Material culture is what makes its way into museums; archaeology is partly about reconstructing ideal cultures from the remains of past material cultures. Material culture includes the technology and material things used by any group to control its environment; it is how the knowledge of a culture is put into practice to achieve the goals of that culture. Technology, however, is not simply the product of culture; according to some perspectives, it is also the producer of culture.

TECHNOLOGY AND CULTURE

One example of such a theory, made particularly relevant by Alvin Toffler's notion of "future shock," is William Ogburn's (1922) version of technological determinism. Ogburn argues that technological change always outpaces cultural change; there is, in his terms, "cultural lag." Cultures change as people try to catch up with the new technology and, because they do not catch up, cultures are always changing.

What are the implications of the computer revolution? Is technology changing how we do our work and how we relate to others and even how we think? Has our culture caught up?

This is not to say that we can see technology as a force in itself that is somehow self-perpetuating. This would ignore what conflict theorists emphasize: that certain groups control technology and direct it in ways they believe will most benefit them. Very often these groups believe that what benefits them also benefits society. This is the idea behind many businessmen's apparent belief that profit means progress, that if business is healthy, society is healthy. In any case, the conflict theorists stress that it is the powerful groups in society that direct technology in their perceived self-interest.

Nevertheless, we can understand the notion, implicit in the work of Ogburn and Toffler, that technology seems to have a life of its own, independent of any groups. Whatever the powerful may have intended, technology has quite apparently had far-reaching unintended consequences. Who could have imagined the consequences for every aspect of our lives of the mass-produced automobile? Ironically, decisions made for short-term gain may have disastrous long-term implications for everybody, including the powerful groups who made the initial decisions. Dumping chemical wastes into the Great Lakes may have seemed economically advantageous in the short run. In the longer run, of course, we are collectively faced with the massive and expensive task of cleaning up the lakes. This is not to say that those who did most of the polluting will foot the bill or be held accountable for their actions. Perhaps the crucial point is that the exploitation of arable land and the polluting of our water and air cannot, in the long run, be in anyone's best interests.

Once technology is created and set in motion, it does indeed take on a life of its own and moves us speedily closer to what Michael Harrington refers to as the "accidental century." In this phrase, Harrington has captured an important notion: even if we accept the view that the powerful use and control technology in their own best interest, we must also recognize that technology has gone beyond their control.

Each new invention, like the automobile, television, nuclear power, space rockets, was a triumph of human intelligence. But the totality of these inventions, with all their revolutionary consequences, was an increasingly puzzling, even mysterious, society. As the parts became more ingenious and minutely calibrated, the whole became more irrational to those who had unwittingly fabricated it. The legend of one of Goya's Caprichos etchings — *The Dream of Reason Produces Monsters* — seemed as much social science as surrealism (Harrington, 1966:29).

At the same time, Harrington recognizes that the direction of technology is based on the decisions of the powerful and, if we are to bring technology back into control, we must uncover the human power behind it. In other words, the unintended but increasingly well-recognized consequences of technology pose a crucial question for liberal democracies. It seems evident that no longer can individualistic or private goals determine the direction of technology. Its impact on all of us demands public intervention; we must give priority to collective survival and this must inevitably mean public intervention in the affairs of individuals. The complexity of technology requires the restructuring of human values. Because of this, public intervention can be viewed quite apart from radical ideology. In these terms it no longer makes much sense to worry about "creeping socialism." The concern might be better viewed in terms of creating an ideology of survival.

The technological argument emphasizes how material forces — climate, geography, and the technological attempts to deal with them — shape the culture of any people. But in focusing on the material, there is the danger that we may lose sight of how people in their everyday interactions influence, however minutely, the shape of culture. Sociologists refer to as *action* those behaviours that are guided by cultural prescriptions. The way in which cultural values are transmitted into norms that guide behaviour — the process of institutionalization — is described in the following chapter. But at this point it is important to emphasize that just as a house is different from and more than its blueprint, so is action different from the cultural "blueprint" for action. People act upon, modify, elaborate, recreate, and even invent; culture provides the base but does not determine the outcome. Indeed, the way that these inventions and elaborations, these recreations and creations of culture become *routinized*, justified, and integrated into culture is the other side of institutionalization. Institutionalization describes the reciprocal process whereby culture shapes action and patterned behaviour affects culture. The examination of human action and interaction as we describe it in Chapter 5 is the study of people's creation of culture even while they are bound by it. As mentioned at the beginning of this chapter, cultures are historical products. In talking about human culture, we are breaking in at one point of this production process and talking about the "product." Interaction focuses on the process itself. But this means more than simply the interactions of our daily lives, and our interpersonal relations; a dominant culture is shaped primarily in the interaction between groups, in the interaction between different and competing cultures.

CULTURE AND CONFLICT

Particularly in this context, the concepts of counterculture, subculture, "shadow" culture, and so forth, become important. However dominant the controlling culture is, it is never the sole set of ideas in any complex society.

In a variety of ways, groups within society will try to preserve their own subcultures: they may attempt to isolate themselves from the influence of other groups, as in the case of the Hutterites in Western Canada; they may "go underground," such as the homosexual subculture centred around the gay bar; or they may try to achieve the even more difficult task of maintaining their own symbols and values and at the same time developing some commitment to the dominant culture — the situation for most immigrant groups; and finally, they may confront the dominant culture in an attempt to provide either an alternative, as many believe was the case for communal living, or a replacement — revolution.

We might view these various patterns, shown in Figure 3.1, as a series of adaptations to the dominant culture. The two extreme cases, 1 and 6, provide the most obvious examples of culture change. In the first case, the subculture is swallowed up by the dominant culture and ceases to exist. In the latter case it is the dominant culture that is changed, either because, in whole or part, the "revolution" was successful, or at least because the dominant culture had to confront the challenge and adapt to it. Even when the challenge is met with force, and the revolution is unsuccessful, "representatives" of the dominant culture will eventually have to use the cultural symbols to justify the use of force and explain the revolution. Indeed the fact that the threat was overcome will probably become part of the culture, even institutionalized as a national holiday, a day of celebration. As we have seen, a cynical view of the historian's task contends that he or she integrates such events into the culture, preserving in his or her account some sense of the heroic defeat of villainous forces.

When we turn to the other attempts at adaptation to culture contact in Figure 3.1, the implications for change may be less obvious. One would think that isolation, for example, would protect the subculture while at the same time making it unlikely that it will influence the dominant culture. In fact complete cultural isolation is impossible, and such subcultures as Hutterites must be constantly vigilant against the inevitable intrusions and seductions of the lifestyles of the dominant culture (Peter, 1976). And, however negatively those within the dominant culture view the Hutterites, they at least know that it exists as an alternative. The Hutterite values, to some extent, enter the common stock of knowledge.

FIGURE 3.1

ADAPTATIONS TO CONTACT WITH DOMINANT CULTURE

CULTURE CONTACT WITHIN SOCIETY

Nature of contact	Goal
1. Assimilation	Surrender to dominant culture
2. Isolation	Subculture preservation
3. Underground	Self-preservation
4. Dual commitment	Structural assimilation without behavioural assimilation
5. Counter-culture	Provide cultural alternatives
6. Contra-culture	Displace or radically alter the dominant culture

---

Clearly this mutual influence becomes much more apparent when we talk about counter-cultures and underground cultures. Both are typically seen as threats and are directly challenged by the dominant culture; their survival is always precarious. At the same time, counter-cultures invite members of "straight" society to experience counter-institutions — free universities, communes, encounter sessions. However short-lived these institutions or people's involvement in them, it is unlikely that once having experienced these alternatives, one can reenter "straight" society quite so straight. There seems also to be a certain attraction, a romantic appreciation of the "low-life" underground cultures. Indeed a so-called "night on the town" may involve, perhaps vicariously, a visit to what W. E. Mann (1970) calls the "underside" of a city.

In a sense it could be argued that underground cultures are useful to conventional society in that they provide a safety valve for the kind of behaviour and experience deemed dangerous to dominant values but that no one supposes can ever be eradicated. But as people move back and forth between the cultures, they transport cultural items; some of our most colourful and apt expressions originated in the gay bar, the jazz club, and the poolroom (Polsky, 1969).

Finally, as we shall see in detail in Chapter 13, it is impossible to maintain dual commitment without sacrificing either opportunities in conventional society (structural assimilation) or ethnic differences in behaviour (behavioural assimilation). In fact as the dominant or host culture and these alternate cultures come in contact, they must inevitably influence one another. Clearly the host culture is not static and will be affected by its subcultures, counter-cultures, and its various immigrant groups. But these changes are minor when compared to the extinction or gradual dissolution that is the fate of most competing or alternative cultures.

CULTURAL DIFFUSION

Much the same processes occur between societies as within. At the most obvious level we are all aware of the process of cultural diffusion—a process that becomes more and more inevitable as, in Marshall McLuhan's terms, the world becomes a "global village." No culture can remain insular and therefore distinct. There is a danger, however, in considering diffusion as the harmonious borrowing and lending of cultural traits and habits. Certainly this does occur and, at some level, countries of the world may share more and more cul-

tural traits. However, the process is not one of simple exchange, nor is it necessarily a purely accidental process. As one speaks of dominant cultures within a society, one might by analogy describe the world powers as dominant cultures in the international sphere. Certainly dominant cultures, in these terms, do pick up cultural items from other cultures — international cooking, fashions, and folk art, for example; however, what the dominant culture passes on — whole technologies, for instance — will obviously involve these weaker societies in a much more fundamental cultural change.

For example, it was generally hoped that as Third World nations incorporated the technology of industrialization, they would experience not only a drop in death rates but also a decline in birth rates. Improved standards of health and hygiene did indeed bring with them a decline in infant mortality, and therefore death rates more generally, but not the anticipated decline in birth rates. What we seem to be witnessing in these societies, in exaggerated form, is the kind of cultural lag and future shock we have discussed previously.

Population explosion in the underdeveloped world underscores the kind of dilemmas culture contact entails. It seems that a society cannot adopt a part of the package, say medical technology, without adopting pretty much the whole package — westernization. And this inevitably involves massive and probably painful change in the fabric of that culture. It also seems that dominant cultures take for granted that they do have solutions to Third World problems without much consideration for the long-term consequences. They may even define these problems in their own cultural terms. Perhaps we can characterize the standard argument as "if these nations want to get ahead, they will simply have to give up their culture, forget about their useless traditions, in essence, westernize." With increasing recognition of the dangers inherent in such a view, some theorists have sought ways in which Third World nations might benefit from Western technology without incurring such dramatic social and cultural costs. For example, some have suggested some form of "intermediate technology" that provides certain benefits but ideally poses fewer problems of cultural adaptation, people may not have to become Westerners overnight to benefit from some of the technological resources.

CULTURAL IMPERIALISM

Marxist theorists are more likely to view the contact between dominant powers and other cultures in terms of imperialism. From this perspective, when a dominant culture directly contacts one of these other cultures it is always in a situation of exploitation. There is a clear parallel in what happens between societies with what happens within societies. As we have seen, the dominant culture in a society is at least in part an ideology of justifications. Similarly, those who are concerned with the nature and consequences of imperialism seek to understand not only the exploitation of one nation by another but also the ideology of imperialism that seeks to justify it.

Perhaps the archetype of imperialistic relationships is South Africa. Whites entered South Africa principally to exploit its resources, including the labour resources, and they arrived with a more advanced technology for both exploiting resources and exacting compliance. As with all such relationships, the white ideology defined white dominance in terms of exchange between unequal partners. While the whites might have profited economically and otherwise, they have supposedly brought culture to the "uncultured," civilization to the "uncivilized," and salvation to the "heathen." Furthermore, the ideology maintains that what the whites are taking does not deprive the host culture that was unable to benefit from the resources without white intervention. To put all of this much more simply, the ideology of imperialism is often some form of racism. Very often the host

culture will come to believe in its own "inferiority" and will internalize the racist ideology, and when this occurs the exploitative relationship is stabilized. In other words, when the host culture incorporates the beliefs of the dominant culture, that is, develops a *colonial mentality*, it adopts as standards of self-evaluation the values of the foreign power. However, just as we described the persistence of subcultures and counter-cultures within societies, pockets of resentment and antagonism inevitably persist. Imperialism, then, necessarily involves some interplay between legitimation through ideology and force.

Finally, as we shall examine in more detail in later chapters, Marxist theorists maintain that the underdevelopment of Third World countries should not be attributed solely to their unwillingness or inability to adapt their culture to technological innovations. Rather it is in the dominant powers' best interests to keep these nations in some stage of under- or arrested development.

CONCLUSION

Culture is ideas, ideas about what is and what ought to be. These more or less shared ideas pervade every aspect of our lives, but, like the air we breathe, we rely on culture without thinking much about it. To the extent that we take cultural ideas for granted, treat rules and values unreflectively, and accept prepackaged knowledge, we are constrained by our culture. Sociology can liberate our thinking by holding these ideas up to examination, by making explicit that which is taken for granted and by studying and often debunking common-sense knowledge.

At the same time, a complex society inevitably means some degree of culture conflict and change, particularly as urbanization brings more and more people from different backgrounds into close proximity and as people are inundated with media images of different lifestyles and new possibilities. Understanding culture and culture change is recognizing that cultures are historical phenomena, the products of past conflicts, and that they reflect the achieved dominance of some groups over others.

We have described people as choice makers. They may, however, assume that there are no choices, that the ways they have learned are the only ways, or they may believe that there are so many choices that there is no one right choice. Many sociologists seem to believe that the latter is becoming increasingly the case in Western society.

Some see it in highly negative terms and describe individuals in our society as alienated from each other; others see it more positively and describe man and woman as protean, able to move from one social world to another with relative ease, to enjoy a fuller and broader range of experiences. But the ideas one has and the choices one makes can only be understood in the context of the structure of opportunities for realizing one's ideas and actualizing one's choices, that is, the social structure.

III SUGGESTIONS FOR FURTHER READING

Aside from the readings mentioned in the chapter, we can think of no better introduction to the concept of culture and the difficulties of understanding a new culture than Elenore Smith Bowen's fictionalized account of her field experiences among the Tiv of Northern Nigeria, *Return to Laughter* (1964). Edward Hall's *The Hidden Dimension* (1966) and his earlier *The Silent Language* (1959) are very readable analyses of how various societies use non-verbal aspects of culture such as time and space. One of the most comprehensive surveys of "theories of culture" is anthropologist Marvin Harris's *The Rise of Anthropological Theory* (1968). Harris is also a proponent of a "materialistic" explanation of what he calls the riddles of culture. This theory is most provocatively set out in his collection of essays entitled *Cows, Pigs, Wars and Witches* (1974) and more formally in *Cultural Materialism* (1980). An examination of the changing meaning of culture in modern capitalist society is provided in Daniel Bell's *The Cultural Contradictions of Capitalism* (1978).

A number of now classic works have explored the relationship of technology to culture. Lewis Mumford's *Technics and Civilization* (1934), Margaret Mead's *Cultural Patterns and Technical Change* (1955) and Jaques Ellul's *The Technical Society* (1967) are among the more readable. An influential book of the 1970s which explores the impact of both technological and social change is Alvin Toffler's *Future Shock* (1970). An example of the highly controversial work of Marshall McLuhan, describing the relationship of communication and culture is his *Understanding Media: The Extensions of Man* (1965). Robert Persig's *Zen and the Art of Motorcycle Maintenance* (1975) deals with many of the same issues using a semi-biographical approach.

Studies which have explored aspects of Canadian culture include Horace Miner's *St. Denis* (1939), John Seeley's and others' *Crestwood Heights* (1956), S. D. Clark's *Church and Sect in Canada* (1948), *The Developing Canadian Community* (1968) and *Canadian Society in Historical Perspective* (1976), John Porter's *The Measure of Canadian Society* (1979), an important section of S. M. Lipset's *The First New Nation: The United States in Historical Perspective* (1963) and Pat Marchak's *Ideological Perspectives on Canada* (1988). A useful introduction to and critique of Canadian studies is R. Brym's and Bonnie Fox's *From Culture to Power: The Sociology of English Canada* (1989). A number of classic sociological essays on Canadian culture can be found in James Curtis's and Lorne Tepperman's edited collection, *Images of Canada: The Sociological Tradition* (1990).

CHAPTER 4

SOCIAL STRUCTURE

OVERVIEW

INTRODUCTION

THE MEANING OF SOCIAL STRUCTURE

IMAGES OF SOCIETY

THE BLUEPRINT: STRUCTURAL FUNCTIONALISM
THE GENESIS: CONFLICT APPROACH
THE EXPERIENCE: INTERACTION APPROACH

SOCIETY AS SYSTEM

SYSTEM NEEDS
INSTITUTIONAL NEEDS
INSTITUTIONAL ORDERS
FUNCTIONAL ALTERNATIVES

INSTITUTIONS

FORMS OF SOCIAL ORGANIZATION

THE NATURE OF GROUPS
COLLECTIVIZATION AND GROUP FORMATION
PRIMARY AND SECONDARY GROUPS
SIMPLE AND COMPLEX SOCIETIES

CHANGE: THE ORDER APPROACH

PATTERN VARIABLES

SOCIETY AS STRUCTURE

CONCLUSION

SUGGESTIONS FOR FURTHER READING

OVERVIEW

This chapter introduces you to the foremost concept of sociology: social structure. The structured relationships that characterize a society and the individual's position in those relationships shape individuals far more than do individuals shape these structures. This is the fundamental and often unsettling premise of sociology.

As you should recall from Chapter 1, some sociologists see a certain harmony between human needs and the social structures in which they meet these needs. In this view, social structures are inevitable and reflect the cumulative rationalist of generations of people sorting out how best to live together. Other sociologists emphasize the burden social structures impose on individuals and see these structures as the result of a history of conflict and class struggle. In the former view, social structure is largely social institutions meeting human needs; in the latter view, social structure is layers of social inequality defining people's opportunities and life chances.

By the end of the chapter, then, you should understand the major meanings of social structure, the importance of this concept to sociology, and the ways both order and conflict theory help us to understand what it means to be social beings who, in order to survive, must live our lives with others.

You should also know something of how our social relationships, and how social structure, have changed as our society has evolved and continues to evolve. For most classical sociologists, the major sociological questions have been how particular structures develop and change and what the impact of these changes on the quality of human life is.

INTRODUCTION

In one way or another, the basic tool for every sociologist is the concept of social structure. What makes sociology unique, different, for example, from history, or psychology, or even most social psychology, is its appreciation of social structure. Even sociologists who study intimate face-to-face interactions or the life-styles of particular groups understand that what they are studying is constrained and shaped by social structure. The need for a distinctive Canadian sociology stems precisely from this reality: to understand the Canadian family, or Canadian ethnic groups, or deviance in Canada, one must understand Canadian society—the Canadian structures.

Those who are generally referred to as macrosociologists study the structures themselves and in a very real sense, then, provide the framework for the sociologists who focus on specific institutions or groups. In later chapters we will describe the major currents in Canadian sociology that seek to describe the genesis and development of Canadian society and the fundamental structures of inequality. In this chapter we will describe the general meaning of social structure and, in so doing, address the basic sociological question: How, and to what extent, are our beliefs and behaviours shaped by the social structures in which we live?

No doubt many of you will be able to recall your school days of cliques and outsiders, of winners and losers. These cliques were real and could shape your experience of school, your opportunities, and even your sense of worth. While being on the outside often meant a certain kind of pain, being on the inside meant having to conform to rules not of your own making. These "small" structures we know all too well. But, they are embedded in and reflect larger structures less visible to us. When you worry about employment opportunities after graduation and, at the same time, you know that some of your peers

"have it made," you are beginning to recognize that we live within structures of opportunity and constraint. When you realize that, however uncomfortable computers make you, you had better "cotton on" because that's where the opportunities are, you are saying something about social structure. Even when you cut your hair, or buy a tie, or a special outfit before a job interview, you are responding to the power structure, the structure of inequality in which we live.

Sometimes we get angry at the pressures, because of our sense of injustice, or at ourselves because we have "sold out." Sometimes we feel powerless and become fatalistic, accepting that the structures are just too big to fight or change. But most of the time, we just live obliviously within them, doing the best we can within limits we take for granted and, in doing so, we help maintain those very structures.

Sociology forces us to look squarely at these structures, how they develop and how they impinge upon our lives. Within classical sociology, much as within art, there have been three major moral themes in the approach to social structure: the conservative approach has generally asked how people might best be shaped or helped to fit into the structures and to maintain them; a more radical approach has asked how structures might be changed to accommodate people and their needs for autonomy and creativity; and the existential (or academic) approach has simply described the structures, the gap between human needs and social reality, and despaired.

THE MEANING OF SOCIAL STRUCTURE

The idea of social structure suggests that human behaviour is patterned, repetitive, and to some extent predictable. These patterns constitute the structure of opportunities (and limitations) that we must all confront. To get the sense of social structure, we can start by thinking about an opposite and hypothetical situation, one in which there is no social organization, no shared culture or language. What we do have is an organism—one which gets hungry, thirsty, cold, and sexually aroused. "It" wants something and it goes after it. To get what it wants, it might very well act aggressively, smashing its way through to its objective: food, warmth, sexual gratification. In other words it could "run amuck," oblivious to things around it, unmindful of consequences, unaware of rules and of abstract norms about property, decorum, and deference.

Such a view of human beings, that this is what they are *really* like, is very close to that of William Golding, especially in his novel, *Lord of the Flies*. In this novel, children on a deserted island, accidentally placed outside the constraints and norms of civilization, revert to savagery, bestiality, and egoism. There is literally "a war of all against all" on Golding's fictional island.

Of course, such a picture of humanity is difficult if not impossible to conceive. There is, first of all, the obvious problem that the human organism is born helpless, undeveloped and unable to fend for itself. This means that even to survive there must be some regularized forms of social activity. But even aside from the biological necessity, the notion of people in a presocietal state is a sociological absurdity. We are always dealing with people as socialized organisms—this is by definition what is meant by "human." We are dealing with people who have personalities and who therefore require affection, stimulation, praise, and so on. Children raised in isolation or by animals — so-called feral children — either are not "human" or, what is more likely, were partially socialized before being abandoned. Even Golding's children began to develop a social structure, however primitive and myth filled, that was related to their earlier socialization.

IMAGES OF SOCIETY

While the sociologist's version may look pale in contrast to the novelist's in capturing the meaning of structure in our everyday lives, sociologists have been particularly successful in depicting the broad picture and the connections that the artists may miss; that is, in providing us with images of society. As we saw in the first chapter, we can distinguish three major images or perspectives: structural functionalism, conflict, and interaction.

THE BLUEPRINT: STRUCTURAL FUNCTIONALISM

Imagine that you have the power to create from scratch a system of interacting humans that worked in a relatively orderly fashion—suppose you were a god of sorts. What kind of blueprint would you draw? First of all, as we have mentioned, it would depend on what kind of people you populated your system with. Are they blank slates upon which almost anything could be printed? Are they basically good, wanting to be sociable and cooperative? For argument's sake, let us suppose that you set yourself the most difficult challenge: you've populated your world with greedy and acquisitive people (actually we don't know why you've done this and, as will become evident throughout the text, the image of humans as evil has been one of sociology's most limiting assumptions).

You have your challenge, what is the blueprint? Somehow you have to teach these people to value the same things. You have to teach them the most efficient and least harmful ways of achieving these things. You have to develop mechanisms by which new members are taught the rules and the goals. Perhaps the safest way of achieving all of this would be to have prewritten parts, much as in a play, that showed people how to fit together their lines of action and that included as many relevant stage directions as you could imagine. In short, you would have to set limits on individual discretion: first, by ensuring that all members are taught the values and way of life, teaching what sociologists call *socialization*; second, by making sure that those who best exemplify the values are able to exert influence on the rest, what sociologists call *leadership* and *authority*; and finally, by creating a set of inducements for good performances and a set of punishments for bad ones, what sociologists call *social control*. Supposedly, the best actors become directors and, to protect themselves from those who do not carry their load, they create boards of censors and reviewers (for example, police and psychiatrists). Now we have something of a self-perpetuating system or a blueprint.

You've drawn the blueprint. This blueprint is what we think of as the contribution of structural functionalists. Sociologists, not surprisingly, are not satisfied with such a depiction of the genesis of social structure. However useful we may find this blueprint, many sociologists, informed by Karl Marx, have argued that, without knowing how the blueprint was created, we are likely to idealize it, to miss its distortions, the ways in which it doesn't work, even the contradictions built into it, and thereby miss the processes of change.

THE GENESIS: CONFLICT APPROACH

Those who view society as structure emphasize what the structural functionalist theorists miss. The conflict perspective is historical, seeking to understand how people, rather than gods, have built up the system and passed it on.

If you think of the blueprint we have just created, the conflict approach does not deny that there are prewritten scripts that allow us to fit our lines of action together or directors who keep the flow of action smooth. Rather, they ask who wrote the script because they know that the script serves some interests better than others and that the ability or power to write the script was no doubt achieved through conflict among groups with different interests. While conflict theorists would never dispute that we need some sort of script to get through life, they also recognize that the content of that script is always shaped through struggle and therefore always serves the interests of the most powerful.

This perspective is based on an understanding of the importance of survival in history. At the simplest level, people must eat, must somehow produce for themselves a subsistence. Different ways of producing subsistence produce different types of relationships among people. With greater division of labour, greater relations of inequality inevitably emerge. The conflict approach, then, focuses on the different forms the inequality takes and the ways in which one's position within these layers of inequality shapes one's destiny. This perspective highlights contradiction and conflict rather than consensus and harmony. Societies are shaped by the mode of production. Societies must be analyzed in terms of the classes created by this mode of production and the struggles among these classes. And people must be understood as products of their class position, while, at the same time, they are the producers of history.

If you pursue a course in sociology and read more widely in the field, you will soon discover that what we have presented, the blueprint and the genesis, are usually taken to be competing perspectives, a fundamental schism in sociology. Indeed they do represent a schism. Structural-functionalism is a perfectly natural perspective to the conservatives who value order, who pretty much like what they see, and who are at best cautious about change. The conflict approach helps those who might be called "radical" articulate and understand their anger and sense of injustice at the contradictions and inequalities that are the focus of their demands for change.

To become a sociologist, you will have to come to grips with your ideological commitments. But for now this is not what we intend that you take from our discussion. Rather, we encourage you to learn the blueprint as a useful way of describing the patterns and relationships that characterize society during its periods of stability and to learn the conflict approach as an explanation for how all of this came about and for how and why it is all likely to change.

THE EXPERIENCE: INTERACTION APPROACH

Perhaps you are asking yourself just what this has to do with you and how you live your everyday life. Sure, you might say, I can see how my class background may have influenced what I believe and what I have become, but I am different from others in my social class; I do things differently and I change. No doubt you recognize that you have certain parts to play that are the same parts others play: daughter, student, friend; but you play these differently, sometimes rewriting the parts or virtually writing the parts from scratch. Again we confront the difficulty that sociology may often miss what we experience most keenly in our everyday lives.

But there is yet another image of society that strives to provide some of the richness and insights we find in novels. The interaction approach views society as built up and maintained through people's everyday actions as they try to fit these actions to the actions of others. The focus here is on how we interpret the world that is given to us, its culture and structure, how we rewrite our parts and act in terms of our own interpretations, and how, through our actions and interpretations, we all reshape our society.

The interaction perspective is the focus of the following chapter. But for now let us consider how this perspective enters into the debate between conservatives and radicals. Practitioners who take this perspective are often likely to find themselves in a state of disrepute. First, interactionism smacks of liberalism with its attention to self and the individual and with its optimism. Second, it often seems to be trivial, telling us more than we want to know about our mundane interactions.

While we will pursue these issues again, we can take this opportunity to emphasize once more that the interaction perspective is a crucial dimension of the *sociological* perspective. It allows us to see most vividly how larger structures impinge upon us and set limits to our freedom, and to understand what this does to us, not only objectively but subjectively, and finally it focuses on how these subjective experiences provide for us a mainspring for action. Within the limits imposed by culture and structure, we think about and act upon the world, and, often in our thoughts and sometimes in our actions, we transcend these limits. Neither the blueprint nor the structure perspective changes the fact that we often act in unpredictable ways.

At the outset of this book we indicated that our approach is a combination of the conflict and interaction approaches. The central questions, for us, are the roles of power and inequality in creating the blueprint and the ways in which people actualize and modify it in their everyday lives. We believe, with Gerth and Mills (1953), that these two approaches allow us to link personal troubles and public issues.

As we will discuss later in the text, there is a danger in sociology, as in any intellectual discipline, for that matter, of becoming so wedded to a single theory or perspective that we not only divide the world into heretics and believers, but we also simplify the always complex and often, thankfully, unpredictable human world. It should come as no surprise that to understand the objective and subjective sides of human relationships, we may have to look through many different perspectives. Thus, we cannot blind ourselves to the utility, for heuristic purposes, of pretending that we can "stop" society at some point and describe it as an entity, a system with no history, a blueprint in which people are merely rule followers. Many of the concepts that now define conventional sociology and that are used to some degree, although somewhat differently, by all sociologists, emerged from structural functionalism and continue to be useful to understanding social life.

SOCIETY AS SYSTEM

SYSTEM NEEDS

If you think again about playing god and constructing a system, your starting point will probably be to ask what does any system need to survive. No sociologist would dispute that societies must meet certain basic needs — biological, economic, and social — if they are to survive at all. Simply, all societies must reproduce themselves, they must make arrangements to care for infants, to teach them the language and culture, and to turn them into functioning adults who will also reproduce and care for their young.

There must also be some sort of economy: people have to be fed, clothed, and sheltered, and goods and services must be produced and distributed to members of the society. Arrangements also have to be made to cope with physical and mental illness and injuries. There must be some provision for organizing "legitimate violence," either to keep members in line or to ward off external enemies. Finally, all societies, all groups, must face the crucial problem of providing their members with values that motivate them to carry out various activities required for social survival and that provide a rationale for the existing social structure. Somehow the various activities of the members must be organized and coordinated; some degree of social order is necessary if the many societal tasks are to be performed at all.

INSTITUTIONAL ORDERS

In setting out these various prerequisites, we are in effect describing the major parts or **institutional orders** of a social structure. An institutional order consists of all those activities within a social structure that have a similar function. We can speak of a kinship order, a religious order, an economic order, a political order, a military order, an educational order, a health and welfare order, and so on. In a complex industrial society, such as Canada, these various orders appear fairly clearly separated and distinct from one another and may be further subdivided into specific institutions. In simple societies these orders may be less "visible" because they are overlapped and fused together. The medicine man may, for instance, also be the spiritual leader and, in some instances, the political and military leader as well. As Gerth and Mills point out:

We may isolate one aspect of a society from another for the sake of analysis, but we have to realize that often, as in the peasant village and the garrison state, the analytical isolation is not experienced; life is an inseparable fusion (1953:27)

As we shall see later in this chapter, religious and/or kinship values may, in many societies, permeate all social relationships, all social orders, whether the activity in question is essentially economic, political, educational, or medical in nature.

This, of course, fails to consider the question raised by Marx, and conflict theorists generally, of whether the economic institutions are not the substructure — the basis — for the shape and order of all other institutions. While order theorists, such as structural functionalists, have tried to examine how all of these institutional orders fit together to keep a society going, conflict theorists examine how institutional orders, religion, education, and communications are shaped by and reflect the economic order and therefore the economic interests of the few.

FUNCTIONAL ALTERNATIVES

There is a danger in assuming that some feature of a society that serves a function, that is, that meets one of these needs, cannot be changed. Part of the *sociological imagination* is to conceive alternative ways in which needs may be met. While societal needs set parameters to the ways in which societies can be constructed, they do not, of course, mean that no change is possible.

One of the main arguments set forth by conservatives is that if something exists, we remove it at our peril. There may, to the conservative, be dire consequences for social order and social integration if we try to remove or reform a particular institution. This, for example, was at the heart of Edmund Burke's critique of the French Revolution: the aristocracy and the church served important functions. To destroy them was also to invite chaos and anarchy. In fact, the "Reign of Terror" that followed the revolution proved Burke to be right in at least the short run.

But what conservatives often forget is that there are functional *alternatives*, or, as the old saying has it, there is more than one way to skin a cat. Certainly the church, however corrupt it had become, did have an integrating function in that it provided people with a sense of meaning and purpose. But other institutions, especially those connected with science and education, were to some extent supplanting the church, and the state and secular ideologies became the focus of loyalty. Similarly, many of the traditional and necessary functions of the family have, in contemporary society, been parcelled out to other institutions (the educational system, for example) without necessarily destroying society in the process.

INSTITUTIONS

Institution is used in two ways. First, it is meant to capture regular and patterned behaviour designed to achieve some goal. In other words, in any society there are patterned and regularized ways of gaining success, sexual gratification, and so forth. In fact, institutions have even developed around how we handle death. For example, Peter Marris (1978) has described how the institution of mourning provides clear-cut and supposedly beneficial ways of handling the death of people close to us. Mourning not only allows us to express our grief but, as an institution, it gives us guidelines as to when it is appropriate to resume normal life. Without such guidelines we might feel inhibited from putting an end to our grief and ever again enjoying ourselves.

The second use of the term institution captures, at a common-sense level, that complex sets of relationships can literally be found within buildings. Prisons, universities, and corporations are institutions in both common-sense and sociological terms. Further, functionalist theorists typically group institutions together into what we have already described as institutional orders in terms of which societal needs they meet and which functional prerequisites they fill. As we shall see later in this chapter, when sociologists attempt to describe the kinds of changes that have accompanied industrialization, they are in part describing ways in which institutional orders and their relationships change.

Institutions seem to be two things. First, they are the human equivalent of instincts. They guide and channel behaviour in more or less predetermined and predictable ways. This implies that institutions are the result of *cumulative rationality* — generations of people's best attempts to achieve goals. Second, institutions meet the basic needs of society and keep it operating without undue friction, conflict, or disruption.

It is no doubt difficult to get a sense of what institutionalization means in human terms; it seems detached from our everyday lives. Within this concept, there is an implicit view of human biography. We are born into a set of patterns, the family, which ensures that we are socialized and which regularizes the ways in which this occurs. We leave the family and enter the patterned set of relationships we call education, which extends the socialization process and provides us with special skills to enter the regularized and ordered world of work. If we have been successfully socialized, we fit into these patterns and can take our place. Even our leisure, our "free time," is institutionalized. The conflict we may have with our boss about wages and working conditions is institutionalized. Our sexual activity, our romantic relationships, the raising of our own children, and ultimately our deaths occur within institutions. The corridors have been built and we walk through them.

However, we must still ask ourselves about how these corridors were constructed in the past and how they are changed in our everyday interaction or, more dramatically, through conflict and revolution.

The structural functionalists' treatment of institutions has typically ignored that different groups have had different inputs historically in creating these institutions and that possibly what exists works best, not in some objective or functionally necessary sense, or for society as a whole, but for the more powerful groups in society.

FORMS OF SOCIAL ORGANIZATION

THE NATURE OF GROUPS

If pressed, most people would probably distinguish between sociologists and psychologists by saying that the latter study individuals and the former study groups. We hope by now that this will seem something of an oversimplification. Essentially, sociology is about the social action of individuals, groups, organizations, and societies. But this distinction does contain elements of truth; many sociologists have started their work by viewing groups as

building blocks of society in much the same way that cells are the basic unit of all living organisms. To understand how societies work, the argument goes, we have to start with groups and work upward to organizations and eventually whole societies. This, for example, was the approach used by George Homans (1950) in *The Human Group*. Homans first tried to show that groups — whether at work, in the community or in an isolated tribe — have a very similar social structure. He then tried, somewhat less successfully, to show that what is true for small groups is true for larger collectives, such as organizations and communities. Sociologists have been especially interested in both the nature and the internal structure of groups and the kinds of groups that can be found in modern society.

While the general idea of a group may seem fairly straightforward and obvious, it is, like many concepts, more elusive the more we try to pin it down. According to Robert Merton (1968), "the concept of group refers to a number of people who interact with one another in accord with established patterns." Others have tried to narrow this broad definition by referring to *small groups* as

a plurality of individuals (two or more) who are in contact with one another, who take one another into account and who are aware of some significant commonality (Olmstead, 1959:21).

In terms of this definition, a role relationship is also a group, one that has only two people. In practice, however, a small group usually means a number of people who have established and shared interaction patterns and who define themselves as members of the group and who are so defined by others.

George Simmel, a German sociologist, showed that something qualitative happens when we go from a two-person group, a *dyad*, to a three-person group, a *triad*. In a dyad, if one person breaks off interaction, by going to sleep, for instance, the group ceases, at least temporarily. In a triad, interaction continues even when one member is "out of play." Also, in a triad, two can "gang up" on a third, one member can play the other two off against one another, or act as intermediary, strategies that children, indeed all family members, seem very adept at using. Who, for instance, cannot recall the feeling that parents were in league? Who has not at one time or another practised "divide and conquer" in order to surmount what in combination would have been a resounding no? It is perhaps for this reason that a baby represents one crisis point in marriage and family life.

Triads, then, introduce the problem of *role conflict* as we try to be two different "people" at the same time. A familiar example of this often happens when we bring two of our friends together who have never met. We like them both, but as a threesome the situation is sometimes awkward and we cannot explain why. At other times we meet a friend's friend and wonder what one sees in the other. It may be that we are accustomed to taking the lead in one role relationship but tend to follow in the second relationship. In the triadic situation we cannot be both leader and follower at the same time.

▌ COLLECTIVIZATION AND GROUP FORMATION

Often people use the term group to refer to any collection of people whether or not they interact with one another or even take each other into account. For example, we are likely to talk about the various ethnic "groups" that make up Canadian society. We read in a newspaper that a large "group" of people turned out to welcome home a winning football team. Strictly speaking, of course, these are not groups in the way we have just defined them, but **aggregates** and **collectivities**, respectively. An aggregate is a grouping of people on the basis of some status characteristic, such as age, sex, amount of education, type of residence, ethnic origin, religion, and so on. An aggregate is a social category that

may in fact have been somewhat arbitrarily created by a social scientist, as is often the case with income groupings or occupational divisions. A collectivity, on the other hand, is simply a large number of people who have at least some values and norms in common but who do not interact with one another in any sustained and patterned fashion.

Both aggregates and collectivities always have the potential for group formation. In collectivities, ongoing and patterned interaction is likely to emerge simply because there are norms and values in common. Commuters on a bus are not a group but a collectivity. However, let the bus become stranded in a snowstorm for a few hours and a group is likely to form. Indeed, the coming together of strangers in the face of some emergency or disaster is a very common theme in movies and novels. Erving Goffman (1961a:7-14) has suggested that, when people come together casually or unexpectedly, "focused gatherings" is a better term to use than group, since group implies sustained and continuing activity.

Of equal interest is the process by which aggregates come to be collectivities and, perhaps, groups in the full sense of the word. What seems to occur is that under some conditions people become, or are made aware, that they share a situation or interests with others. For example, although sociologists are fond of creating categories, it is unlikely that anyone could have imagined that divorced fathers might start to view themselves as a "class" with shared interests and to arrange to further those interests as fathers' rights. It also seems unlikely they ever thought of themselves in quite that way in the past, until a few showed many that they were neither unique nor alone. A "private trouble" became a "public issue."

Consciousness or awareness that some objective status or situation is shared with others is often the starting point for collective behaviour. Because people in aggregates have shared interests, they can potentially be mobilized in defence of these interests. The most famous discussion of this process is Karl Marx's distinction between a *class in itself* and a *class for itself*. Marx argued that it was easy enough to distinguish two main classes—capitalists (bourgeoisie) who own the means of production and workers (proletariat) who sell their labour. But as long as workers remained unaware of their objective situation, they were simply members of an objective category, a class "in itself." Without awareness, not much change could be expected.

For Marx, however, modern workers were potentially a revolutionary force in society. Instead of being scattered and isolated from one another, as were peasants in the previous era, workers under capitalism were increasingly concentrated in large factories. They were beginning to develop trade unions and to interact politically with one another. Workers were on the verge of becoming consciously aware of their shared objective situation and of their shared interests. Workers were in the process of becoming a class "for itself," in short, a group.

In the 1970s the idea of "consciousness raising" became part of everyday language. It was especially common at the height of the women's liberation movement. As the study by Connelly and Christiansen-Ruffman (1977) showed, consciousness-raising groups were explicitly formed to bring women to a subjective awareness of their shared objective situation.

Just as early Marxists hoped that class consciousness would eventually transcend national boundaries and unite workers everywhere, so it was hoped that feminism would transcend class and regional boundaries, that the status category of woman would be transformed into a "sisterhood." We examine social movements in Chapter 14. In Chapter 13 we shall see how ethnicity has come to be perceived as the symbolic focal point for asserting and defending collective interests; how at times ethnic categories become genuinely ethnic groups.

PRIMARY AND SECONDARY GROUPS

Clearly, groups vary in size, in duration, in the degree to which norms and rules are routinized. One of the main distinctions between types of groups is whether the group is essentially a *primary group* or a *secondary group*. The term "primary group" and our appreciation of their importance come from the work of Charles Horton Cooley. He suggests certain groups, such as the family, are primary

. . . in the sense that they give the individual his earliest and completest experience of social unity, and also in the sense that they do not change in the same degree as more elaborate relations . . . (1909:26)

We usually think of primary groups as being relatively small, involving warm, intimate ties and spontaneous interpersonal relations. Ideally, primary groups are ends in themselves rather than means to other ends. That is, we enjoy interaction and activity within a primary group for its own sake, not simply because we want to get something done. In Simmel's terms, there is pleasure in sociability. Also, in primary groups our relationships with others tend to be more all inclusive, to involve our "total personality." We are not acting solely in terms of one of our statuses, but in terms of our "real selves."

Besides the family, friendship groups, gangs, and often workers are examples of primary groups. Primary groups provide us with the basic link between self or personality and society. They provide the context in which we are first socialized, made into social beings, and they are, throughout life, the main way in which our identity, our sense of who we are, is sustained, maintained, and sometimes transformed. It is within the primary group that we experience love, compassion, intimacy, care, and caring. But it is also within primary groups that we are most likely to experience hatred, jealousy, sibling rivalry, and rejection, the emotional pain that is the flip side of happiness and security.

Secondary groups can be defined roughly as the opposite of what we have just said about primary groups. Relationships among members are expected to be cool, impersonal, and perhaps contractual. Typically, we are not expected to involve our whole personality, our whole self, but a "segment" of our self, in secondary group relations. Finally, secondary groups are seen as means to other ends rather than ends in themselves; people do not come together for the sake of "getting together," but because they want to accomplish some special task. Professional associations, committees, and shareholders' meetings are examples of secondary groups.

As these definitions suggest, the crucial difference between primary and secondary is not to be found in the nature of the group as such, but in the kind of social relationships that are supposed to occur in various social situations. The culture, in other words, tells us how, ideally, we ought to behave toward others in particular situations. At the same time we must remember that no relationship is totally primary or totally secondary. Modern marriage, based as it is on love and companionship, probably comes as close as any to being primary. But even the most intimate and encompassing marriage will still be some distance from completely primary. We are likely, for instance, to show a somewhat different side of our personality to other people than to our mate. There are things about ourselves that we may reveal to strangers but not to our spouse.

A clear example of a secondary relationship is perhaps that between a customer and a cashier in a supermarket: the whole interaction sequence may be performed with only a simple phrase about the total bill being spoken. We will probably not remember what the cashier looked like and will not be able to place him if we see him in a different social setting. But even this relationship may become more primary. If we shop at the same store again and again, the cashier may become separated from his cash register in our minds. He may become someone we

"know," a name and a "personality." Primary and secondary represent the extremes, what are often called "polar opposites" on a continuum of social relationships.

Modern western societies are unique in the kind of primary relationships and secondary relationships that co-exist and overlap one another. We move from the intimate and enveloping environment of the family to the more cool and unemotional setting of formal organizations or bureaucracies: school, university, the business firm. We learn to relate differently to those we think of as friends and relatives, those who are acquaintances and those who are strangers.

SIMPLE AND COMPLEX SOCIETIES

As we have seen, sociology grew out of the massive changes occurring in the eighteenth and nineteenth centuries. Robert Nisbet (1967) has argued that virtually all of the classical sociologists were trying to understand two revolutions, the French Revolution and the Industrial Revolution, different kinds of revolutions that nevertheless had enormous impact on social relations and on the nature of social structure or organization. Alvin Toffler, you will recall, maintains that Western society has been caught for the past 300 years in a "firestorm of change" and that the rate of change is ever accelerating. We face the prospect of future shock — culture shock in our own society.

Looking backward, it appears to us now that the two revolutions brought about changes that were in fact "evolutions" rather than "revolutions," that the change was rather slow in coming. Nisbet argues, however, that it did not appear so to those caught up in the change. As he says:

To intellectuals of that age, radical and conservative alike, the changes were of almost millennial abruptness. Contrast between present and past seemed stark — terrifying or intoxicating, depending upon one's relation to the old order and to the forces at work on it (1967:22).

As is so often the case, the human side of these changes emerges most clearly and dramatically in art, literature, and poetry. W. B. Yeats, the Irish poet and playwright, captures in his remarkable poem "The Second Coming" (1915), images that the social theorists were also attempting more prosaically to articulate. As he puts it:

Things fall apart; the centre cannot hold;
Mere anarchy is loosed upon the world,

It seemed for most social theorists that the bonds that had held society together for so long had given way to a new order, one that was ever-changing, unstable and "normless." Societies, it was argued, had been organized around the values of community, kinship, religion, traditional hierarchy, and authority. The social integration and social organization of the past had given way to social disorganization or *anomic* society; a situation in which the traditional social constraints had been replaced by the totally new social order of a mass society: urbane, industrialized, scientific, rational, and secular.

Particularly at the end of the nineteenth century sociologists became convinced that something qualitatively different was occurring as societies became more complex. All seemed to have in mind a contrast between simple societies and complex societies. While most recognized that no society is completely one or the other, they did feel that the general direction of change was from the primary relations of peasant society, village and parish, to the secondary relations and associations of urban, industrial, and bureaucratic society.

We can perhaps understand what these theorists had in mind by contrasting small-town or rural life with big-city life. Chances are that many of you have first-hand experience of small traditional communities in which seemingly everyone is either related to everyone else, or at least everyone knows a good deal about others and about their past. Nicknames acquired in youth may stick with people throughout their lives. Statuses and labels may also be difficult if not impossible to lose as long as one remains in that community. For example, Mr. Jones may still be known as the "younger Jones boy, the wild one," well into his old age. The man who delivers the mail is not simply the letter carrier, Mr. Johnson. He is Al Johnson, who married Ida Williams, your third cousin who had a son, Bill, who moved to Alberta, and is doing something on the pipeline, and who has a daughter who is supposed to be "very bright." And so it goes—a way of life that centred on kinship and community, one that in varying degrees has been the typical way of life for most people throughout most of the world throughout most of history. The contrast, of course, is the city.

In a very famous paper called "Urbanism as a Way of Life," Louis Wirth, an American sociologist, described life in the city this way:

Characteristically, urbanites meet one another in highly segmental roles. They are, to be sure, dependent upon more people for the satisfactions of their life-needs than are rural people and thus are associated with a greater number of organized groups, but they are less dependent on particular persons, and their dependence on others is confined to a highly fictionalized aspect of the others' round of activity. This is essentially what is meant by saying that the city is characterized by secondary rather than primary contacts. The contacts of the city may indeed be face-to-face, but they are nevertheless impersonal, superficial, transitory, and segmental. The reserve, the indifference, and the blasé outlook which urbanites manifest in their relationships may thus be regarded as devices for immunizing themselves against the personal claims and expectations of others (1938:12).

Thus, one important difference in social organization has centred around the dichotomy between rural and urban. This was a peculiarly American perspective, particularly the view of the "Chicago School" of sociology. It grew out of what was most obvious to these sociologists; that internal migration (urbanization) from the farm to the city and immigration from Europe were creating fundamental changes in the American city. In contrast to the rural life, cities seemed filled with wickedness and decadence. As Carl

Sandburg said of Chicago: "They tell me you are wicked and I believe them, for I have seen your/Painted women under the gas lamps/ Luring the farm boys."

In Europe sociologists were attempting to contrast the traditional and the modern by use of dichotomies. Perhaps the most famous of these was formulated by Ferdinand Toennies, a German sociologist, who spoke of transition from *Gemeinschaft* to *Gesselschaft* — from community to society (or association). Emile Durkheim, focusing on the degree and scale of division of labour, spoke in terms of *mechanical* societies versus *organic* societies. Max Weber, writing at about the same time as Durkheim, argued that authority had

moved from *traditional* to *rational-legal*. Robert Redfield wrote about two types of society, the *folk* society and the *urban* society. Like the proverbial seven blind men touching and then trying to describe an elephant as a wall, as a tree trunk, as a snake, and so on, so various theorists were trying to present various aspects of what was perceived as a massive change in the way people relate to one another. Figure 4.1 shows these various dichotomies and the particular aspect of social structure each was considering.

What all of the classic theorists were responding to was what they felt was not only loss of community and kinship but also loss of religion, which seemed at some level to be

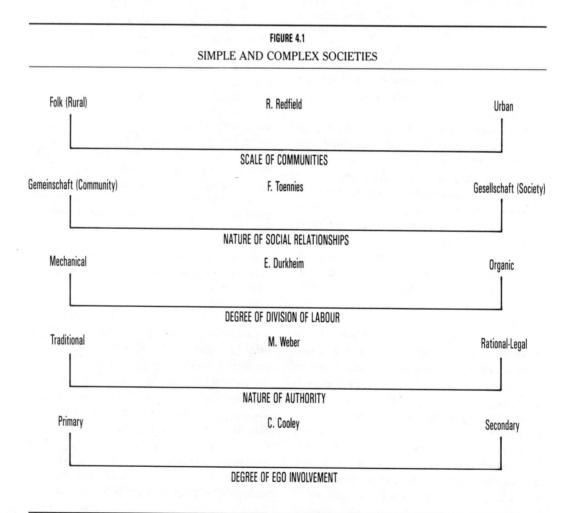

FIGURE 4.1

SIMPLE AND COMPLEX SOCIETIES

Folk (Rural)   R. Redfield   Urban

SCALE OF COMMUNITIES

Gemeinschaft (Community)   F. Toennies   Gesellschaft (Society)

NATURE OF SOCIAL RELATIONSHIPS

Mechanical   E. Durkheim   Organic

DEGREE OF DIVISION OF LABOUR

Traditional   M. Weber   Rational-Legal

NATURE OF AUTHORITY

Primary   C. Cooley   Secondary

DEGREE OF EGO INVOLVEMENT

the glue that held relationships together. So modernization meant in part a *secularization* of relationships. The feudal society persisted so long partly because the traditional relationships were culturally defined in terms of *sacred* rites and obligations.

Social bonds, then, were not simply between people but also with God — hence the strength of oaths, of fealty, and of allegiance. To break these was to sin, to break one's word with God. Clearly, fealty long ago disappeared but the sacred has until very recently been apparent in marriage. Many still believe that marriage vows are sacred vows that cannot be broken. It is at the same time apparent that while the marriage ceremony may still exhibit many of the trappings of the sacred, it has become essentially a civil ceremony to legalize a contractual relationship. Today people are even willing to talk about drawing up marriage contracts, perhaps even on a renewable basis. Secularization means that violating the vows is a legal matter, not a sin.

CHANGE: THE ORDER APPROACH

While we have suggested that the order approach cannot account adequately for change, theorists have had to confront these kinds of dramatic changes. They have had to describe and account for modernization. Although they use the language of the conservative, they have managed to isolate some of the central dimensions of these changes. In their view, these changes are system adaptations. When one thing changes — industrialization — other things in the system must also change. And, not surprisingly, the order theorist (or structural functionalist) will describe the major changes in positive terms, as functional adaptations. So, instead of talking about the alienation of the individual in mass society, they are likely to speak of the functional necessity of impersonality and personal detachment and of secularization. Moreover, these changes — loss of community, decline of kinship and religion, depersonalization in mass society — appear to just happen in this approach; there is little appreciation of the role of real people and powerful elites in determining the direction of these changes. Indeed, many twentieth-century theorists seem to have lost sight of what was the impetus of much of the nineteenth-century theorizing: the deep concern and fear about the direction of future society. The early theorists asked whether these changes were inevitable and, if so, what could be done to mitigate their consequences. Even if their answers were usually pessimistic, they did pose the questions.

PATTERN VARIABLES

One of the most famous contemporary attempts to describe these changes is Talcott Parsons's *pattern variables*. Parsons, too, thinks in terms of dichotomies. He argues that any role relationship or society as a whole can be described in terms of some combination of the pattern variables. These pattern variables are described in terms of two polar opposites:

1. *Affectivity-affective neutrality* concerns the amount of emotion or affect that is appropriate in a given interaction situation. Should a great deal or little affect be expressed?
2. *Diffuseness-specificity* denotes the issue of how far-reaching obligations in an interaction situation are to be. Should the obligations be narrow and specific or should they be extensive and diffuse?
3. *Universalism-particularism* points to the problem of whether evaluation and judgment of others in an interaction situation is to employ standardized and agreed-upon criteria or subjective standards. Should evaluation be performed in terms of objective, universalistic

criteria or in terms of more subjective, particularistic standards?

4. **Achievement-ascription** *deals with the issue of how to assess an actor, whether in terms of performance or on the basis of inborn qualities, such as sex, age, race, and family status. Should an actor treat another on the basis of achievements or ascriptive qualities that are unrelated to performance?*

5. **Self-collectivity** *denotes the extent to which action is to be oriented to self-interest and individual goals or to group interests and goals. Should an actor consider his personal or self-related goals over those of the group or larger collectivity in which he is involved? (Turner, 1974:36)*

These opposites represent dilemmas of choice and, according to Parsons, every system can be characterized in terms of the solutions it provides to each of these dilemmas. But of more importance, Parson believed that as societies industrialize they must change in particular ways: the system requires fundamental changes in values and orientations to achieve efficiency, perhaps even to survive. Basically what Parsons is arguing is that in industrialized societies, the kinds of relationships based on kinship are no longer appropriate or functional. Rather, what is supposedly needed now are the kinds of values associated with bureaucracy.

In a complex society the child must supposedly learn to integrate the perspectives of a variety of groups; she must also learn to distinguish among kinds of relationships. In simple societies most, if not all, of a person's social life is lived within the context of kinship. Community and kinship are almost synonymous. In complex societies part of our life is lived within the family, but we also participate in other institutions. In moving from family to school and work, we are also confronted with different kinds of social relationships and different patterns that supposedly represent the "best" ways of handling such relationships. The pattern variables provide one way of describing these different kinds of patterns and of summarizing the dichotomies we have discussed above.

Perhaps the easiest way to illustrate the pattern variables is to look at the university as an institution. According to the institutional blueprint, students are admitted not on the basis of personal characteristics (ugly, obnoxious, etc.), family background (rich, poor, etc.), or social characteristics (sex, colour, religion, etc.), but on the basis of general rules that supposedly apply to all people in the same way and are based on performance or achievement in the past (high school grades). Moreover, students are to be evaluated in these same terms, that is, on the basis of general rules regarding performance. Also, the student/professor relationship is expected to be a "professional" relationship, with limited emotional involvement and specified focus of interest. In other words, it is expected to be a relationship restricted to the institutional sphere of the university. All this presumably provides the most efficient way of selecting, educating, and evaluating students.

In the family, on the other hand, members are in fact expected to treat each other with warmth and with concern for each individual as a "total person." Nor should performance or lack of it affect the quality of the relationship. In the family, one should be responsive to individual differences and use subjective standards of evaluations. We would not expect to be called upon to justify, in terms of some general rule, why we love the people in our family.

Parsons is arguing that complex societies must be characterized by universalism, affective neutrality, achievement and specificity, whereas relationships in simple societies have been characterized by the polar opposites. These changes, for Parsons, were functionally necessary. When we look at social stratification in Chapter 11, however, we shall suggest that, while ideals may have shifted in these ways, there is a wide gap between these ideals and what actually happens to people. While industrial societies are supposed to be characterized by universalism and achievement, they remain particularistic and ascriptive. All we are saying is that sex, colour, family background still matter even while ideals may be shifting; we are more than some distance from full equality of opportunity.

The gap between the ideals and the reality can easily be demonstrated empirically. More important, there may be theoretical reasons why the gap can never be bridged. No doubt the functionalists recognize that universalism and achievement (equality of opportunity) have not arrived and that discrimination persists. However, their belief that universalism and achievement are functionally necessary leads them to view inequality of opportunity as a "strain" in the system, a residue of the past, that is in the process of being overcome (see Collins, 1971).

Alternatively, as we are stressing throughout this book, the persistence of ascription and particularism (inequality of opportunity) may be explained by the fact that we live in a layered or stratified society, one in which groups with different amounts of power are in conflict with one another. We shall look at the relationship between industrialism and capitalism in Chapter 10.

SOCIETY AS STRUCTURE

At this point we shall give less attention to the conflict perspective because it receives so much attention in the rest of the book. The conflict approach centres our attention on the layers of inequality in society. In every known society, there are some "who get most of what there is to get" and who therefore constitute an elite of sorts. The power base of this elite varies in terms of the dominant mode of production in the society. In any case, society is shaped in large part by the conflict between this elite trying to maintain its position, and other groups tying to improve theirs. Of course the elite have an advantageous position in this conflict and are able to exact compliance and solidify their position. As Harold Laswell (1950) suggests, they do this through

gaining control of the important societal tools: violence, symbols, practices, and goods.

While dominant groups may temporarily use violence to maintain their position and influence others, and while force may never be too far below the surface in any social system, it cannot be the basis of social structure. However, by controlling the symbol producing institutions, dominant groups are able to make dominant their culture, or better, their ideology, to justify their position and therefore "structure" the inequalities. Further, in their control of the production and distribution of goods, they are controlling the sanctions, the inducements and punishments that underpin these structures. Inequality becomes most fully institutionalized and clearly structured when it is formalized into a set of rules and laws and legal procedures for enforcement. The political system creates these "practices" and the legal system and agencies of enforcement provide the last lines of defence against opposition to the structures.

The ability of the dominant group to maintain these structures and to impose its culture is always problematic to some degree. Competing interest groups arise and, as we have shown, coalesce into groups offering alternative or competing ideologies. Revolutions do occur, as well as the more frequent minor insurrections. Even when these do occur, the elite must accommodate itself to the pressures and even anticipate them. It is for these reasons that Karl Marx viewed history as conflict and change.

CONCLUSION

There is a sense, at the level of experience, that none of this is new to you. You've read about it in novels, you've seen it in films, and you've experienced it in your solitary moments of reflection about the social pressures that block your aspirations. You know it through your anger at those who have power over you and your discomfort for those you know are worse off than you. You are experiencing it when you realize that you hate what you are doing, but know that you will continue to do it, and when you feel intimidated in the presence of your "betters" and superior in the presence of your "inferiors." This is the subjective side of social structure.

The order approach and the structure approach are attempts to provide a broader perspective in which to understand these isolated experiences. They can help you understand that you have been made by history, by the society in which you are born, by your social class, and by your social groupings.

The order approach describes the machine: the structure approach tells us how the machine was built, how it is fuelled, and the faults in it that are likely to make it break down. But neither the system analogy nor the structure approach helps us understand how people in their everyday lives view social structure; we know something of how they are more or less constrained by it, but not of how they handle and modify it. This is the goal of interaction approaches to social structure. In the next chapter, we examine how people learn these structures through socialization and modify them through a continuous process of interaction.

▌▌▌ SUGGESTIONS FOR FURTHER READING

Probably the best all-around demonstration of structural functionalism at work is the various essays by Robert K. Merton in his *Social Theory and Social Structure* (1968). Another readable collection that also views social structure and role theory from a functionalist approach is W. J. Goode's *Explorations in Social Theory* (1973). Michael Banton's *Roles* (1965) provides a useful introduction to role theory. For a slightly satirical critique of role theory, indeed of sociology generally, see Stanislav Andreski's *Social Sciences as Sorcery* (1974). An excellent but more difficult critique of system perspectives on role theory is Aaron Circourel's article, "Basic and Normative Rules in the Negotiation of Status and Role" (1970).

A basic book on the nature of groups is Michael Olmstead's *The Small Group* (1959). Another is W. J. H. Sprott's *Human Groups* (1958). And, of course, George Homans's *The Human Group* (1950) remains one of the most important statements on group structure. Finally, we urge you read Rex Lucas's *Men in Crisis* (1969), one of the finest studies, pulling together data on real-life groups with research on laboratory groups.

Robert Nisbet (1967), whom we mentioned in Chapter 1, is also a very good source for a depiction of modernization and its impact on sociology. See also his *Social Change and History* (1969). For a highly readable, but conservative, reaction to these changes, we suggest José Ortega y Gasset's *Revolt of the Masses* (1932).

Throughout the second half of the book we shall be suggesting readings within the conflict approach. Aside from the Mills reading, some easy and valuable introductions are: Harold Laswell's *Politics: Who Gets What, When, How* (1950); Charles Anderson's *Political Economy of Social class* (1974); Frank Parkin's *Class Inequality and Political Order* (1971); Pat Marchak's *Ideological Perspectives on Canada* (1988); Peter Archibald's *Social Psychology as Political Economy* (1978) and Richard Sennett's and Jonathan Cobb's *The Hidden Injuries of Class* (1972).

CHAPTER 5

SOCIALIZATION AND INTERACTION

OVERVIEW

INTRODUCTION

SOCIALIZATION

LIMITS TO SOCIALIZATION
DEVELOPMENT OF SELF
MEAD'S THEORY OF DEVELOPMENT OF SELF
ROLE LEARNING
ROLE AND SELF
MORAL DEVELOPMENT
REFERENCE GROUPS AND SOCIALIZATION
HUMAN NATURE AND SOCIALIZATION

APPROACHES TO INTERACTION

NORMS AND INTERACTION
SYMBOLIC INTERACTIONISM
THE DRAMATURGICAL MODEL: PEOPLE AS ACTORS
THE GAME MODEL: PEOPLE AS PLAYERS
THE EXCHANGE MODEL: PEOPLE AS PROFIT SEEKERS
THE ETHNOMETHODOLOGICAL MODEL: PEOPLE AS EXPLAINERS

CONCLUSION

SUGGESTIONS FOR FURTHER READING

OVERVIEW

This chapter tries to bring down to the level of interaction, the concepts of social structure and culture. You are introduced to the concept of socialization, that is, to how individuals acquire the cultural values, knowledge, and rules necessary for them to interact competently with others in their society. You are asked to consider the extent to which childhood and ongoing socialization mould us into purely social animals who are little more than the sum total of the roles we have learned or the extent to which each individual preserves something unique—not social—that defies prediction and can never be captured by a sociological theory.

You are introduced in this chapter to those who have helped us to understand childhood socialization—C. H. Cooley, G. H. Mead, J. Piaget, and L. Kohlberg—all of whom recognized the active part that children play in their own socialization and that socialization is never complete.

You are also introduced to the major models used by sociologists to analyze everyday or face-to-face social interactions. Symbolic interactionism, dramaturgy, game theory, exchange theory, and ethnomethodology are more than simply tools to analyze how people fit their actions together in every day life. Each also asks fundamental philosophical and moral questions about what humans have become in the face of the social structures in which they live. In this chapter, you will be exposed to models of interaction that variously categorize people as actors concerned about the impressions they are making on others, game players competing to win in each interaction, bargainers looking to ensure that they come out with some profit, and frightened and fragile people trying to make some sense of it all. And you will be able to consider just how much of your reality these models are able to capture.

▌ INTRODUCTION

Ultimately sociologists are, or should be, concerned with discovering how culture and structure permeate our everyday lives, how they shape and are shaped by our interactions with others. Conceptually, sociologists have viewed **role** as the link between social structure and culture and the individual. For the sociologist, then, we all play social roles.

In a sense, the concept of social role simply describes how people step into patterned expectations that constrain how they behave. You are well aware that when you are being a "friend" you are behaving quite differently than when you are being a son or a daughter or a father or a mother. You no doubt have also experienced the sense of sacrifice involved in playing a role well. You have not always wanted to behave like a good friend or son or daughter, but you have held yourself in check and given something up in the process. And, sometimes too, you have not lived up to these expectations and have experienced the social consequences of failure to meet role expectations.

These insights are not, of course, unique to sociology. Artists have always been preoccupied with the human costs of living in society, with the costs of being engulfed in a role to the extent that one loses oneself, or of being outside of all social roles and having no self. The *Diary of a Mad Housewife* and *The Outsider*, though very different, are both about the costs of living outside society and thus about social roles.

The philosophical and sociological question that runs through this chapter, then, concerns the tension between "individual" and "role." How do we maintain self in interaction with others? In part this is also a question of the extent to which we simply act out the role, playing our part in the social structure and reading the lines as culturally written—life as classical drama. At the other extreme, life is more like Monty Python or Second City, where we make up the lines as we go. Yet still another way of asking the question is whether we, individually, are the sum total, the product, of our social roles, or whether each of us brings some dimension, a self, that insulates us from simply being a social product.

These are difficult questions, but they are not only the questions of philosophers, sociologists, and artists. When you ask yourself who you are and where you are going, when your life strikes you as absurd, when your obligations are overbearing, when parents feel guilt in those moments when they hate their children, or when adolescents feel pressured to do what they feel is immoral—all of these questions amount to, in very real terms, a search for self in the face of social obligations and expectations of other people's making.

Social role, then, can be defined as the patterned expectations and obligations or social norms that adhere to the different positions in the social structure. While resources and, therefore, a certain power or absence of power come with each position, so too do the expectations and obligations we call social role. Parents, bosses, prime ministers all have certain prerequisites and rights that come with their positions; they are also constrained by role obligations and expectations. Everybody pays a price.

There is an ironic flip side to role. While conflict theorists have emphasized the "costs," the alienation of the idividual from the role he or she plays, order theorists emphasize how roles are essential for interaction. Think of how strange and awkward you feel when you enter someone else's world, when you don't know the rules, when you don't know what role to play. Symbolic interactionists study role with a recognition that it is both necessary and constraining but that people also have the capacity to affect the roles they play and, in fitting their lines of action into those of others, to modify the structures in which they live. This chapter focuses on this approach to role, on how role is acquired through socialization and modified in the course of interaction.

SOCIALIZATION

Anyone who has had prolonged contact with young children has no doubt been stung, physically and psychically, in any number of unexpected ways. One soon discovers that, unlike most adult acquaintances, children cannot be trusted. They are unpredictable; they may, for no reason we can understand, poke us in the eye or tell us we are fat. Our adult friends are more predictable because they have acquired the culture, the symbols, norms, values, and beliefs of our society. They have, in other words, been *socialized.*

Socialization is the interactive process whereby people acquire and internalize the culture of a group. We say "interactive process" because socialization requires interaction with already socialized people. It presupposes society. It is through such interaction that the child becomes human in a social sense, and it is through such continued interaction that we are all socialized throughout our lives.

LIMITS TO SOCIALIZATION

Many sociologists, and certainly functionalists, have viewed child or **primary socialization** as the process whereby the child learns to want or even to need to conform to social rules. According to this view, children *internalize* social norms, that is, make them part of their personality; they carry society around in their heads and follow social rules in almost every situation.

A similar and usually complementary view emphasizes how children learn to value or to need social approval from others, particularly those they like and respect. In either case, socialization is seen to produce conformists. Predictably, such a view encounters problems when trying to account for the many instances in which people violate rules, even rules that they have "internalized." The chapter on deviant behaviour deals with these issues.

We should, therefore, begin the discussion of socialization with some cautions. First of all, while we are all socialized, we are probably never *fully* socialized; we are, after all, biological beings born with differing capacities and drives. While all sociologists will emphasize the social, they will, as we saw in Chapter 1, approach it in different ways, depending on their basic or background assumptions about human nature. For some, other drives or motives — materialism or sex — seem as important wellsprings of social action as our need to conform, to gain social acceptance (Wrong, 1961).

A second caution to keep in mind is that, while we talk about how the child learns to conform to rules, we must always ask whose rules. Certainly we all do learn to conform to rules to some degree, but we do not all learn to conform to the same rules. Much of the chapter on deviant behaviour discusses the aspect of how some groups attempt and succeed in enforcing their standards on others. We see that we may often conform because we must.

Infants are born into a ready-made world that will shape them far more than they shape it. If we are born in Canada, for example, we will inevitably share certain features with others who were also born and raised in Canada. However, we are not all exposed to the same aspects of Canadian culture. It will make a considerable difference, for example, if one is born in New Brunswick or in "Upper Canada." These regional differences are made more complex by internal subcultures along ethnic, religious, and class lines. The family unit itself does more than simply relay the larger culture to the newborn. It also selects aspects of social reality, modifies and interprets the culture for the child. It presents the world outside as a social *milieu* to be feared or trusted. Indeed, the family must be treated as a social system in itself. The socialization of the child will be different in a single-parent family; it will differ from large families to small ones; it will differ for the first born, the second born, and so on.

Obviously, there are many sources of heterogeneity in socialization. These differences will influence what and how much the child learns about the social world and, in turn, will influence the child's life chances. To take one example, Basil Bernstein (1961), a British sociolinguist, has demonstrated that the linguistic backgrounds of working-class children can account in good part for these children's poor school performance. Working-class parents use a restricted or limited language code that makes it difficult for their children to become sensitive to differences in interpretation and nuance of meaning; they often seem to confuse the word for an object with the object itself; that is, they do not learn about language as a tool or resource.

Middle-class parents will more likely use an elaborated language code that allows their children to be more sensitive to the possibility that different people will interpret the "same" thing in different ways. If Bernstein is correct, this would obviously mean that, for the most part, middle-class socialization experience gives children a distinct advantage when they enter schools that are also largely middle class.

Finally, even if we have been socialized, have learned the rules, and are seeking approval from those around us, conformity is still an accomplishment. Just think of the countless times that you have miscued, committed a social blunder, made a fool of yourself. Successful socialization is often defined in terms of how well individuals "fit" into their social group, how well they can interact with others. However, the rules one learns are only guidelines for behaviour, and it is not always clear which rules to apply when. Interacting with other people always involves some effort, thought, and negotiation. It is in this sense that socialization never quits. Nevertheless, it is during childhood, through the process of primary socialization, that we become human. It is in this stage that the child develops interactive skills, particularly through his development of a self-concept.

DEVELOPMENT OF SELF

Although much has been written about the psychological processes involved in primary socialization, little is known for certain. Obviously we cannot "get into the heads" of the children going through this process, certainly not in the early stages. Many of the sociologists who have specialized in this area have based their theories on observation of their own or a small number of children. Nevertheless, however difficult to test, this work has been extremely important in helping us to understand social interaction more generally.

Many psychologists and social psychologists agree that the key aspect of primary socialization is the child's development of *self*. Initially, the child is apparently unable to distinguish himself or herself from the rest of the world; it is all one. Much of the first year or so of the child's development is spent in learning that there is a world out there and, often painfully, the rough shape and feel of that world. As the psychologist James Mark Baldwin argued, the child learns first the "not-I" before becoming conscious of himself or herself as an "I" (in McCall and Simmons, 1978:205). Gradually the child learns that he or she is distinct from the rest of the world, including other people. As children engage in what is largely a trial-and-error exploration of the world, they soon discover, for example, that it feels rather different to strike oneself than to strike ones mother.

One of the early and influential contributions toward understanding development of self is Charles Horton Cooley's theory of "looking-glass self." Children are obviously dependent on the others around them for all forms of comfort. According to Cooley, children become keen observers of these others and soon discover that they can influence them, that certain actions bring attention or food or anger. They learn that they have the power to influence others.

A girl six months old will attempt in the most

evident and deliberate manner to attract attention to herself, to set going by her actions some of those movements of other persons that she has appropriated. She has tasted the joy of being a cause of exerting social power, and wishes more of it. She will tug at her mother's skirts, wriggle, gurgle, stretch out her arms, etc., all the time watching for the hopeful effect (1902:197).

The child soon learns to do different things and be different people for others. The child becomes deeply concerned about how these others view him or her. Thoreau wrote that it take two to speak the truth, one to speak and one to listen. This "need" for an audience to tell us that what we speak is true, that our accomplishments are worthwhile, that we are beautiful, good, or otherwise is the essence of Cooley's "looking-glass self." We see ourselves through the eyes of others; we imagine how others see us, how they judge us, and this reflected image evokes some self-feeling, such as pride or shame.

Cooley pointed out that not everyone's judgment is equally important. Some people are more *significant* than others. According to Cooley we find our most significant "mirrors" in primary groups (groups in which we have intimate face-to-face interaction). In early life the family is our most important looking glass. The child's self-image at this time is typically rudimentary. Children are learning what their parents expect, and they are able to see and evaluate themselves in terms of these expectations. But as the child becomes immersed in the world outside the home, plays with other children, and meets other adults, the sense of self quickly becomes more rich and complex.

MEAD'S THEORY OF DEVELOPMENT OF SELF

The most compelling and most complete account of the self-development process was provided by George Herbert Mead (1934), whose work is clearly influenced by Cooley's formulations. For Mead, as for Cooley, self and

other are inseparable concepts; self and society are bound together. Mead describes how the child gradually comes to acquire a self as he or she begins to learn and use language. Mead agreed with Cooley that what distinguished human socialization from animal learning was the ability of humans to shift perspectives, to see the world from another's vantage point. This is only possible when we learn language, symbols that mean much the same to others as they do to us. Mead's most important contribution is perhaps just this — his understanding of the importance of the symbolic process. Animals respond to one another on the basis of natural *signs* rather than significant (meaningful) symbols.

Imagine, for example, that someone reaches his or her hand out to you and in the upturned palm there is something you want. You do not simply respond to the stimulus; you interpret the gesture. You imagine what is in the other person's mind; you imagine his or her *intentions*.

In Mead's terms, for humans, as opposed to animals, the gesture stands for the completed act. Humans interpret the intentions of others before they themselves act. This is the basis of the symbolic interactionist perspective, which we shall discuss later on. For now, we are interested in how the child learns this interpretive process. Children may at first grab what is in the upturned hand, but they soon learn not to.

For Mead, the process occurs through three stages of increasing complexity. In the first stage, the *preparatory stage*, children simply imitate the actions of those around them. A son may, for example, like his father, "read" the newspaper, though he cannot yet read. In this stage he is engaging in actions that he does not really understand. Nevertheless, he is learning a good deal about the relationship between his actions and the actions of others toward him. In the second stage, children begin to *play* the roles of others. They may, for example, play at being parent and scold themselves for being naughty.

Children can do this as they acquire language because it is through language that they are able to think of themselves abstractly and respond to themselves as others do. It is in this stage then that the child is learning *to take the role of the other.*

Through actually playing out the roles of mother, father, others, and so on, children are learning to take on roles, learning to imagine how others see a particular situation and, most important, learning to respond to themselves as others would. Each child comes to ask, "Am I being bad, naughty?" It is through such role taking that one develops a self-concept and learns to exert self-control in terms of the imagined expectations of others. During the play stage, however, the child's role-taking is unorganized; the child takes one role at a time, one after another. Because the young child has no single organized standpoint from which to view himself or herself, he or she has no organized conception of self.

In the final stage, the *game* stage, children learn to take a number of roles simultaneously, to see themselves from a generalized standpoint. Mead uses the example here of a baseball game. To play the game, the child must imagine the expectations of all the others in the game simultaneously and must develop a composite, generalized set of expectations of all the others in the game. Mead referred to this as the development of the **generalized other**, or the learning of group norms. In this stage, then, the child no longer thinks of himself or herself only in relation to particular *significant* others, but also in relation to the *generalized* other, his or her synthesis of the group or community as a whole. The child has now learned to think in terms of a set of standards — group norms — that he or she can apply consistently across a wide variety of situations. This marks the development of self; children can now respond to, control, and organize their own behaviour.

ROLE LEARNING

As children play at certain roles, they are learning not only about themselves and how they are seen by others but also about roles that they may play in the future. They are engaged in a process of **anticipatory socialization**. They are playing at roles that one day they will play for real. They are learning what is expected of mothers, fathers, teachers, older brothers and sisters, men and women, as well as a host of other roles — detective, firefighter, astronaut — that they are less likely to play as an adult.

When parents buy their daughters dolls, cooking sets, and makeup kits, they are encouraging them to practice certain roles. As parents tell their children stories, relate myths, encourage daughters to help in the kitchen and sons in the garage, they are providing their children with a particular set of resources and direction for their early role rehearsal. And although children are usually given a good deal of leeway in their play, parents will generally attempt to "correct" the child who is consistently practising the "wrong" roles. Even today, many parents who are pleased to see their sons rehearsing roles traditionally female, playing with dolls for example, find that the son often meets with ridicule when he goes into the outside world.

From the time of the child's birth, parents and others place the child in a number of roles. For a long time the child is unaware of these ascribed roles. Immediately, for example, a male child is given a male name, dressed in male clothing and encouraged to participate in "male activities." He is also ascribed roles on the basis of his parents' religion and class standing. These ascribed roles, and particularly the sex roles, come to be taken for granted by the child and form the backdrop for all other role learning. The female child learns that only certain kinds of play and games are deemed appropriate for her. While her brother pretends to be a football player, she may pretend to be the cheerleader; while a young boy pretends to be an engineer, the young girl may pretend to be a nurse or teacher.

One of your authors recently observed a group of five and six year olds who were "graduating" from their kindergarten class. While it is likely that there were differing degrees of understanding of a graduation ceremony, it was apparently an event to be taken very seriously. As a result of the rehearsals, all knew how to make the entry, how to position themselves on stage, and how to come forward to receive their "diploma." The girls came in their prettiest party dresses while the boys were dressed neatly but informally. To the consternation of some parents, but not all, dangling from the cardboard graduation hats were pink ribbons for the girls and blue ribbons for the boys. Having received their "diplomas," the children remained lined up on the stage to sing some songs for the audience. It was of interest, at least sociologically, that between numbers, all of the boys, seemingly spontaneously and individually (since it was hard to see one another and look forward at the same time) began to use their diplomas as telescopes to scan the audience and their parents. The girls, on the other hand, retained their decorum until the end of the ceremony.

As far as we know, children do not naturally assume "appropriate" sex roles, what are generally referred to as gender roles. There is, in other words, nothing in our biology to make five-year old boys more prone than five year old girls to pretend their diploma is a telescope. Yet, many in other disciplines will argue that there is a biological base to the different roles boys and girls come to play. And this view is very much in evidence in common-sense thinking about females and males. Even among liberated

parents who express their frustration as their daughter insists that she wants to be a nurse and not a doctor, there lingers a degree of uncertainty of how much is nature and how much is nurture in the acquisition of sex roles.

The sociological view is that gender is learned through socialization. Children *learn* through both subtle and not so subtle ways to walk and talk and dress in certain ways. There is, for example, pressure for little boys, while still toddlers, to have their hair cut and to wear a limited range of colors or be labelled by outsiders as a "she." Similarly, little girls are decked out in dresses and stockings for birthday parties, thus limiting the play activities possible to them compared to boys at the same party.

At the more subtle level is some evidence that, from birth, boy and girl babies are treated differently such that boys receive more physical interaction and play of a rougher nature while girls receive more verbal interaction. But, we do not know what impact this has on the development of gender roles. Boys, it seems, are generally slower to learn to talk and to become toilet trained while girls are generally more "sociable" and "helpful." But, sorting out what is biological and what is sociological is no easy task. We do not, for example, know to what extent parents behave differently because of the biological differences in development and behaviour of their infants and toddlers. Do parents "knowing" that girls train earlier than boys have higher expectations of the former than the latter and effectively create a self-fulfilling prophecy? Or, do little girls actually develop the necessary muscles for control earlier than little boys? And, more generally, how is gender socialiation, social learning generally, affected by the birth order of children and the sexual mix of siblings? This is indeed a murky area and, as the example suggests, is made even more so by parents not having a completely independent role in the socialization process: children early on will be affected by the role models presented on television and what others outside of the family define as appropriate sex-role behaviour.

What is certain is that our sex role becomes a core feature of our self and a taken-for-granted basis for our actions. Others respond to the children (and adults) in terms of their sex role performances. Children modify their performance in terms of these reactions and, as we have said, come to see themselves as these others see them. The sociological perspective does not so much deny that there is a biological reality as it emphasizes, gives primacy to, the human capacity, indeed the human right to move beyond biology and anatomy and to choose our own destiny. We may be born something but we are made or make ourselves social. The biological "facts" with which we are born may be, but should not be, used to constrain us. In any case, some of these "facts" have been exposed as myth in anthropological and femininist literature and others may be irrelevant in a technological society where biological differences provide inadequate explanations of the continuing sexual segregation and patterns of inequality in the labour force.

ROLE AND SELF

Clearly, role and self are closely related. Some of the roles we learn, though not all, will become an important part of our self-concept and will influence much of our adult behaviour. Just how this early role learning influences our adult role performances is quite variable.

Perhaps the two most important dimensions of early role learning for later life are the range of roles to which we are exposed and the extent to which they become incorporated as part of our selves. Some children will have been exposed to a wide variety of role performances, and the knowledge acquired through this exposure becomes a valuable resource for anticipating and accommodating a wide variety of situations in later life. Socialization, then, is in part about the acquisition of knowledge.

Some children will be actively encouraged to play out a wide repertoire of roles that then may become part of their self-concept, while others may be restricted and constrained in the roles they are allowed to play and therefore internalize. Perhaps most important in whether and how we internalize the roles we play as children is the sense we get from those around us of our adequacy or competence. Some children learn to think of themselves as inadequate — as stupid and inferior. The world becomes a place to be feared and mistrusted. Thus, the early role learning of some children may create obstacles for them that make it hard later to take on some adult roles. They may develop unreasonably low expectations that make them reluctant to assume new and demanding ventures (see Atkinson and McLellan, 1948; and Hoffman, 1972). On the other hand, some children's early experiences may lead them to develop unreasonably high expectations that make it almost inevitable that they come to see themselves as failures. Early socialization then can influence in later life our desire or even our willingness to achieve.

MORAL DEVELOPMENT

Child socialization describes the gradual process whereby children overcome their initial egocentrism. The young child "is at first enclosed in his own point of view and sees all things from within it" (Lindesmith and Strauss 1968:258). As children acquire language, they participate in a wider range of social relationships and, as we have shown, begin to take on other people's perspectives. This aspect of socialization has received its greatest emphasis and most meticulous description in the works of the Swiss psychologist Jean Piaget (1948; 1952; 1954).

Although Piaget does not explicitly use the term role, nor does he fully appreciate the role of language acquisition, his detailed study of working-class children in Geneva lends a good deal of support to the sociological work we have described. His emphasis has been on the expanding cognitive ability of the child, on how the child develops increasingly more sophisticated understanding of the physical and social world. One area in particular in which his work complements that of Mead's is his treatment of moral development.

Piaget describes the development of children's moral judgments as they move from egocentric to relativistic standards. According to Piaget, the child up to the age of four or five is a *moral absolutist*; right is right and wrong is wrong and those who do wrong must be punished regardless of the circumstances. Later, up to the age of about nine or ten, the child comes to realize that moral rules do not possess the same kind of reality as the physical world; they are a product of the group into which the child is born. The child realizes this as he or she gains some sense of the varied perspectives of others (similar to Mead's "generalized other"). Finally, children become *moral relativists*; they come to see rules as somewhat flexible and some rule violations, under mitigating circumstances, as forgivable. A number of other studies lend support to Piaget's findings (see Brown, 1965).

There is more question, however, about Piaget's explanation for these findings. Piaget argues that absolutism in the young child was the result of the authoritarian parent-child relationship, a relationship based primarily on punishment and reward in one direction. The child's view becomes more relativistic and general as he or she comes to participate in more egalitarian and cooperative relationships, particularly with peers. This explanation probably underemphasizes the importance of the child's increasing language and role-taking skills, quite apart from the nature of the realtionships he or she is in.

Nevertheless, Piaget has been used by a number of educators to justify their pleas for more "freedom," less authoritarianism and structure in the school setting (see Nyquist and Hawes, 1972).

Piaget has also inspired a good deal of research on moral development, and a particularly interesting example is provided by Lawrence Kohlberg (1963; 1964). Kohlberg's cross-cultural study of children's moral judgment seems to show the influence of both Piaget and Mead. The study consisted of asking children, varying in age from seven to seventeen, a series of questions that contained some moral dilemma. He asked, for example, whether it would be right to steal under the following circumstances:

A woman is near death. Doctors believed that one particular drug might save her, and this drug was available at the local drugstore. But the druggist was charging very much for the drug, and the woman's husband could only collect half the price. He told the druggist about his wife's condition and asked him to lower his price or allow him to pay the rest later, but the druggist refused. The man finally broke in and stole the drug. Should he have done this?

On the basis of the children's answers to this and similar questions, Kohlberg distinguished three levels of moral judgment, each level divided into two stages. These levels and stages represent increasing complexity and relativism similar to Piaget's findings.

Kohlberg calls his three levels *preconventional, conventional,* and *postconventional*. In each of these levels, the child is often "well-behaved," responsive to the cultural notions of good and bad, but in each level the basis of conformity varies. At the preconventional level, the children are concerned with the rewards and punishments their actions bring. In stage one, children are primarily concerned with avoiding punishment; this is how they judge good and bad. For example, their answer to the moral dilemma posed might be, "The man should not steal the drug because his mother will be mad and punish him." In stage two, children become more concerned about rewards for their actions. They might answer in this stage that indeed the man should steal because he needs his wife to cook for him.

The second level, the conventional level, involves a concern with living up to the expectations of, and gaining the approval of, significant others. In the first stage of this level, children are concerned with gaining the approval of others. They wish to be viewed as good or nice. They might answer the experimental question in terms of how others would react to the husband, whether he would be seen as bad for stealing. In the second stage children are characterized by a "law-and-order" orientation. They have learned respect for authority, and rules are seen as inflexible and a matter of duty. The child might answer simply that the man should not steal "because it is against the law."

The final level, the postconventional level, represents the most sophisticated moral judgments; children are developing moral values and principles. In the first stage, children are concerned about general community standards and procedures for evaluating behaviour. They might answer the question in terms of what is best for the community as a whole and might consider means of legally changing the laws so that the man might be able to get the drugs he needs. The child is concerned about law and order but is willing to consider changes to the order in terms of some general principles. At the second stage children are most concerned with personal conscience. At this stage they have developed some universal ethical principle and recognize that these are self-chosen principles that require a good deal of reflection and deliberation before a moral decision can be made in any given situation.

The stages of moral development are presented as follows:

— 1. Obey rules to avoid punishment.
— 2. Conform to obtain rewards, have favours returned, and so on.
— 3. Conform to avoid disapproval, dislike by others.

— 4. Conform to avoid censure by legitimate authorities and resultant guilt.
— 5. Conform to maintain the respect of the impartial spectator juding the terms of community welfare.
— 6. Conform to avoid self-condemnation. (Kohlberg, 1970)

REFERENCE GROUPS AND SOCIALIZATION

One of Kohlberg's major contributions was his recognition that not all people achieved the "highest" levels of moral development; children could become "stuck" at lower levels. He believed that conflict, having one's beliefs challenged, allowed one to see new possibilities. In modern society, where we are at least exposed to a wide variety of different groups with different beliefs and standards, we are more open to such conflicts than in the past. *In modern mass societies people may assume perspectives of groups in which they are not recognized members, sometimes of groups in which they have never participated directly and sometimes of groups that do not exist at all (Shibutani, 1955:569).*

What this means is that constructing lines of action becomes increasingly complex as we come to use the standards of our own groups and the groups to which we aspire, and as we continue to encounter groups that use different standards to evaluate our behaviour. These *reference groups* provide us with different perspectives we must sort through and choose from. Exposure to conflicting beliefs is essential for moral development. Mead, too, believed that individuals achieved their highest level of humanity when they could continue to develop their own personal syntheses of the conflicting expectations and interpretations they encountered.

In the 1960s a number of sociologists argued that too few of us were achieving this level, that too many of us were unreflective conformists. Perhaps the changes in content and patterns of socialization are also contributing to changes in moral development.

Most sociologists agree that the socialization process, both its form and its content, is changing rapidly in contemporary society. One argument is that these changes are leading to a greater permissiveness in the range of roles children are allowed to play. Bronfenbrenner (1970), for example, points to a number of changes in the family structure, many of which result in less parental attention and supervision for children. Certainly, in our society both parents may work (often because they must), and the family unit is less likely to include other adults to take the parents' place. Increasing numbers of children, it seems, are being raised in single-parent families, and parents, particularly middle-class parents, seem to be spending more time away from their children. All of this may mean that socialization by the nuclear family will be supplemented by new alternatives, not only day-care centres, but also informal neighbourhood co-operatives. Perhaps men, old people, and the child's peers will become increasingly influential in the child's socialization (Symposium, 1973). Already the school has become very important in child socialization since much of any teacher's time is devoted to teaching children to value education, to become "good citizens" and to conform to a large array of rules which may have little to do with education *per se*. These issues are treated much more fully in Chapter 12. On the other hand, some sociologists point out that despite these changes, the small family size in contemporary society means that parents have more rather than less time with their children.

The change in the experience of childhood in the 1980s is perhaps one of the most important concerns confronting academics and politicians in the development of social policy. As parents we have both watched our children confronting choices and dilemmas that we were able to escape until adulthood. We have heard our young children ask us whether there would be war, indeed whether they would have a future. We have wondered whether to warn our children about the dan-ger of talking to strangers because, as concerned as we have been, we have worried about the distrust, paranoia, and loss of innocence all of this entails. As parents, we have worried about how to prepare our children for a future we barely understand while still allowing them to be children. Sometimes we take small comfort from the realization that our children are influenced less by us than we sometimes hoped and sometimes feared. They are exposed to much more and they bring something of themselves to every interaction.

People are not solely the rules and roles they have internalized. They are more than the internalized perceptions and expectations of others. What this "more" is necessarily involves us in some discussion of human nature.

HUMAN NATURE AND SOCIALIZATION

In his discussion of the social self, Mead distinguishes between two aspects of self: the *I* and the *me*. Mead does not see them as two entities, but rather as two modes of interacting with or relating to people. The child's behaviour is dominated by the "I" — the impulsive tendencies of the individual. As the child is socialized, his or her behaviour is increasingly influenced by the "me" — the internalized meanings and expectations, the standards of the group. According to Mead, the "I" and the "me" complement one another — the "I" initiates actions and gives impulse, while the "me" gives direction to the impulse. The "I" and "me," taken together, constitute the self-process. While the balance between "I" and "me" may vary from individual to individual and from culture to culture, all socialized humans have both. Action is based on a "conversation," or at least interplay, between the two.

This view of self has important implications for understanding human behaviour. The "me" is the part of self that represents the social roles the individual has internalized.

This is the rule-following, conforming aspect of the individual. The "I," on the other hand, thinks beyond social roles to possible futures beyond what has been learned. For Mead, it is what allows us to defy socialization. It is the spontaneous, creative aspect of self. For example, the "I" may tell students to complain to professors that their classes are boring or that they do not devote enough attention to their students. The "me" will act as something of a critic of this line of action, cautioning the student to consider the consequences. How will the teacher and others in the class react? What will parents and friends think if the complainer fails the course? And how will all this make the student feel? The "me" helps us understand the stability and predictability of much of our behaviour. The "I" allows us to recognize, at the same time, the human spontaneity and creativity we also find.

Mead, then, gives us a view of the individual and society in which the individual does not completely disappear. Self cannot exist apart from society. Only through interaction with others do children gain the resources to think about themselves and their relationship to the world. But society is not simply poured into our heads. We are shaped by the social world into which we are born, but we also act upon that world and help to shape it. With the resources we learn, we are able to imagine futures we have not learned, and we may act upon these images.

Mead's distinction between the "I" and the "me" is often compared to Freud's discussion of the "id" and the "ego." The comparison, however, is not a very apt one. According to Freud, the "id" is the impulsive part of a person's personality, the part which must be brought under control by socialization. The "id," however, unlike the "I," is antagonistic to the social; it is a bundle of sexual and aggressive drives that must be brought under control if society is to exist. Freud's view is clearly much more pessimistic than Mead's. The former's view of human nature implies that children are unwilling participants in their own socialization, that they resist it. Socialization involves the *repression* of

children's natural tendencies and this is achieved only with the greatest pain. The socialized human has learned to *sublimate* these natural drives of sex and aggression into social pursuits that do not threaten society. To be human means to live in an unnatural and therefore potentially explosive state; Freud did not have much hope that the situation could be otherwise.

Obviously the assumptions we make about human nature will influence not only our theories of socialization but also our views about how best to socialize children. Those who view people as essentially bad will emphasize the importance of supervision and discipline. Those who view people as essentially good will advocate greater permissiveness, less supervision. Obviously the assumptions that parents make will greatly influence the child's socialization. Mead's position, that people are neither inherently good nor inherently evil, falls somewhere in between. According to this view, supervision and discipline are necessary for the development of the "me," and the freedom to engage in unsupervised play is important for the development of the "I." Mead emphasized neither the individual nor society, but social interaction — how people take one another into account, take each other's role, respond to one another's gestures and intentions, and thereby influence one another. Thus people are essentially symbol users. Mead has been influential in encouraging sociologists to examine the process of social interaction and has "fathered" a sociological approach to interaction — *symbolic interactionism.*

APPROACHES TO INTERACTION

NORMS AND INTERACTION

One of the things in our environment or situation that we have to take into account and interpret is other people. Imagine a blind date organized by a third party who tells you nothing about the person at all. Likely, things will be awkward at first. Before you can really interact you have to get to know one another. There may be some long pauses, perhaps because of shyness, but maybe because you have no idea what to talk about. But at the same time, you are not out on a date with an alien intelligence. Chances are you share a language in common and are both Canadians. You can estimate pretty quickly whether he or she is younger, older, or about the same age as yourself. Finally, the situation in which you find yourself is a relatively well-defined one — it is a date, not a job interview nor a business engagement. Not only is it a date, but it is a *first* date, and a blind one to boot.

In short, while it may be a very trying, perhaps even disastrous experience, you do start out with some idea of how to act in this situation. It is not, in other words, completely unstructured. You can, as it were, call on the culture for help. Vague as they may be in actual practice, there are cultural norms about how to act with someone of the opposite sex. There are norms about how to act with someone your own age compared to someone older or younger. There are also norms about how to behave on dates generally and about blind dates specifically.

At the same time, neither of you is a programed robot nor a stage actor with memorized scripts from which you know exactly what to expect from the other person and what the final outcome will be, as shown in Figure 5.1.

FIGURE 5.1

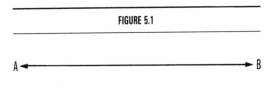

Rather, you are improvising and estimating as you go along, This turns out to be true for all social situations and social interaction. What seems to occur is that whenever we encounter another person, we are

immediately posing a number of questions: Who and what is this other person relative to me? Who and what am I relative to him or her? What do I want from this encounter? What does this person think I want? What does he or she want? What does he or she think I think he or she wants? What sort of situation is this anyway? Does the other person agree with what I think this situation is? We could go on. To make things even more complicated, we must remember that the other person is asking exactly the same kinds of questions. Interaction even between two people is a complex business of estimating and negotiating, as shown by Figure 5.2. Interaction is, it seems, a never-ending series of estimates, of trying to see the situation from at least two points of view — our own and the other person's.

FIGURE 5.2

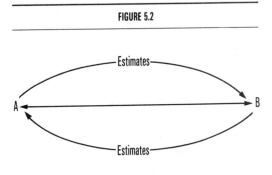

Faced with these questions and complications, we might well ask how social interaction ever gets started. Why are we not suspended or paralyzed, afraid to act at all? Or, once started, how can we speak about social order, patterned social activity and relationships? Part of the answer is that despite a great deal of ambiguity, the questions we ask in social situations are structured questions. There is a common stock of knowledge to which we can make recourse; it is a safe assumption that a good deal of the time others will also make recourse to this same knowledge. Most important, people tend to routinize interaction so that even though each interactional situation is in some ways unique, it is also in some ways patterned, and these newly created patterns may enter the common stock of knowledge. Otherwise, as Peter McHugh (1968:26) points out, "No one would be able to get out of bed and dressed in the morning; rather he would think until bedtime of every alternative procedure and potential happenstance."

A more formal way to put this is to say that all social behaviour involves *norms*. Social order and social action are possible because of two related factors: (1) the culture provides us with values which are translated into norms which, in turn, become the rules which govern interaction; and (2) to some degree, at least, social actors share a common culture and therefore a common value system. For example, a cultural value may be that it is wrong for women to be promiscuous. Translated into a norm, this may mean that one should be cautious about entering into a sexual relationship. Translated into a more specific rule, this may mean that one should not go to bed with a man on a first date, especially a blind date. The hope is that there will be some agreement about this value, that the other person (in this case, the man) will not only have knowledge of this value but will believe in it as well.

There is a chance, however, that in this specific case the man has learned a somewhat different set of values. While the culture may say that women should not appear "too easy and willing," it may, in contradiction, say that men should get as much sexual experience as possible and that they should be aggressive in heterosexual relationships. The culture may, in fact, have a double standard: one set of norms for women and another for men. This may or may not mean conflict in the relationship. For instance, one outcome may be that the woman, actually desiring to make love, feels constrained by the norms not to do so. Similarly, perhaps the man, though desiring the woman, does not agree with the double standard. Perhaps he believes that all people ought to wait until they are married, or perhaps he believes that this is what the woman believes. Nevertheless, he may still

feel that he ought to conform to the norms of the double standard, to make a try, because *she* might accept (and expect) the double standard. She expects him to make a pass; he realizes that he is expected to; she says no. He expects her to say no, and so it goes.

As we can see, even a relatively simple encounter turns out to be highly complicated, the outcome far from certain. In varying degrees all social relationships contain elements of *Mad* magazine's "Spy vs. Spy" series. This provides one reason why we cannot view social interaction as ever completely structured or totally predictable. Another reason is that norms and rules may become modified through interaction and as circumstances seem to demand. As we have seen in Lucas's study of the mine disaster, new norms can be created in interaction.

Nevertheless, in every situation we bring with us a norm and some idea of how to use it. Though rule governed, we are also rule users. The game of chess, for instance, provides us with rules, some specific, some very general, which we must interpret and try to use given our definition of how the game is going. At the same time, we are far from free to make any move we want. Faced with a more powerful opponent than ourselves, a wrong move may have very objective consequences: we lose our queen and must resign; we are checkmated. As it is with chess, so it is with social life. Social norms also constrain us and, in many instances, to violate them is to invite disaster — imprisonment, death, ostracism, poverty, scorn, and ridicule. Social behaviour is, in its essence, an effort to conform to rules and norms. Attempts to live up to them and efforts of others to make us conform are what make situations social.

Arguably, it is as difficult to understand the complexities of face-to-face interaction as it is to understand whole societies. And just as there are several competing models for viewing society, there have emerged several models for viewing interaction. The dominant and most influential model derives from the work of George Herbert Mead.

SYMBOLIC INTERACTIONISM

Howard Becker (1964) has distinguished three major uses in the social sciences of the term interaction. At the simplest level, interaction is viewed as the reciprocal influence of individuals. According to this view, interaction is the virtually automatic response of individuals to stimuli. No sharp distinction is drawn between human interaction and the communication of gestures that characterizes animal interaction; interaction is equated with *stimulus-response*. We shall return to this use of the term in our discussion of exchange theory. The second view defines human interaction as **symbolic interaction**. This view stresses the difference between human and animal behaviour. For humans, symbolization transforms interaction. Because of symbolization, individuals do not respond directly to one another, to stimuli, but to their own interpretations of others. Interaction is mediated by symbols, particularly linguistic symbols; stimuli are never directly apprehended by the interactors. In this use of the term, interaction is equated with communication, and communication always means interpretation. This is related to the third use of the term. Interaction describes the *internal dialogue* people engage in, communication not only with others but with themselves. This third use of the term equates interaction with the self-other process, that is, the process of making indications to oneself about the social world in terms of what one thinks others think.

It is these last two uses of the term that are central to the symbolic interactionist perspective. As we mentioned in Chapter 1, symbolic interactionism is one of the dominant perspectives in North American sociology. This is due primarily to the work of Herbert Blumer (1969a), whose writings have served to keep alive the ideas of George Herbert Mead and to illustrate their implications for sociology. Blumer describes symbolic interactionism in terms of three basic premises:

— 1. People act toward things on the basis of the meanings that the things have for them.
— 2. The meaning of such things is derived from, or arises out of, the social interaction that one has with one's fellows.
— 3. These meanings are handled in, and modified through, an interpretative process used by the person in dealing with the things he or she encounters (1969a:2).

The first premise simply restates what we have been saying all along about the importance of symbolic interaction; people do not respond to stimuli but to the meaning those "stimuli" have for them. Blumer notes that, while few social scientists would argue with this premise, they persist nevertheless in underplaying meaning. Human behaviour is treated too often, according to Blumer, as simply the product of internal (psychological) factors — attitudes, unconscious and conscious motives, and the like — or of external forces — roles, rules, social pressures, and the like. In order to understand human behaviour, Blumer argues, we must give prior attention to how people themselves define these internal and external "forces." It is on the basis of these meanings that people act.

The second premise states that meanings are a social product, a product of social interaction. "The meaning of a thing for a person grows out of the ways in which other persons act toward the person with regard to the thing" (Blumer, 1969a:4). A central aspect of the process of interaction, according to this view, is the creation of shared meanings. This definitional process was particularly well illustrated in Lucas's study of the trapped miners. The emphasis here is clearly on interaction, not the individual.

The third premise is perhaps the one that most clearly distinguishes symbolic interactionism from other perspectives in sociology and social psychology. Here Blumer is emphasizing the fluid nature of interaction. People do not simply apply the meanings they have acquired in some automatic way; because they have selves, they are able to engage in an internal dialogue in which they make indications to themselves and point out what is meaningful. People do not merely apply meanings; rather they handle them, select among them, and modify them in terms of the perceived demands of the situation. The use of meanings is an interpretative process.

What is meant by an interpretative process? Consider, for example, tying up a dog that has never been tied up before. Chances are that the dog will resist in response to the *stimulus* of the rope. But what happens if we tie up some people? One response, of course, is simply to resist. But suppose that this is explained to them as part of a game, or for their own reasons they interpret this as a game. Or if they are on a ship on a rough sea, they believe (interpret) that they are being tied up for their own safety. In these cases they will not likely resist; they will respond to their *interpretations*, not simply to the stimulus of the rope. This process of interpretation is the focus of studies in symbolic interactionism.

No doubt the central concept of symbolic interactionism is "definition of the situation" (see Stebbins, 1967). At the simplest level, what this means is that we must place people, objects, and ourselves into meaningful categories in any situation before we are able to formulate a plan of action. In any situation we must socially place the others we are interacting with, attach an *identity* to them, and at the same time we must establish our own personal identity.

As Foote (1951) has pointed out, our own situational identity, who we are in any situation, is not automatically given but is always more or less problematic. For example, how would you define the situation if, while dining out, you found that you were being waited on by a close friend? Does the situation call for the kinds of actions appropriate between friends or those that we think define the waiter/customer relationship? Who is it you are interacting with and who are you in this situation? Does one leave a larger tip or per-

haps no tip at all? Chances are that whatever you do will involve some degree of embarrassment because of the identity ambiguity. A good deal of symbolic interactionist research examines how people *negotiate* definitations, and particularly identities, in problematical situations.

The most seductive aspect of Mead's version of symbolic interactionism is its optimism about the relationship between the individual and society. There is a harmony, supposedly, between self and other. Self is created, but never consumed, by the social. Only because they have been socialized by other humans can individuals be choice makers, self-determined actors rather than slaves to biology. People, essentially social, can communicate with other people through shared symbols and fit their actions together to build structures that maximally benefit all. Ultimately, people can remake their "nature" through this interaction. A dose of optimism is no doubt a healthy thing.

But we know, as depicted in Chapter 4, that even if we are choice makers, often we seem to have no choices; that even if we are symbol users, we often find ourselves unable to express ourselves, to make others understand or to understand them; that even if we are social, we are also more and, because of this, we often experience the costs of living in society, not just the rewards.

A John Wyndham character, from the perspective of a science-fictional society which is overcoming these difficulties, gives us a "backward look" at our own world. From this perspective we are the backward "old people."

They [the old people] were only ingenious half-humans, little better than savages; all living shut off from one another, with only clumsy words to link them. Often they were shut off still more by different languages, and different beliefs. Some of them could think individually, but they had to remain individuals. Emotions they could sometimes share, but they could not think collectively. When their conditions were primitive they could get along all right, as the animals can; but the more complex they made their world, the less capable they were of dealing with it. They had no means of consensus. They learnt to co-operate constructively in small units; but only destructively in large units. They aspired greedily, and then refused to face the responsibilities they had created. They created vast problems, and then buried their heads in the sands of idle faith. There was, you see, no real communication, no understanding between them. They could, at their best, be near-sublime animals, but no more.

Pretty depressing stuff but also an indication that there is something undeniably naïve about Meadian optimism. There are costs to living in society, and those sociologists interested in examining our everyday lives have developed increasingly cynical images of human nature, at least as it has come to be shaped by contemporary society. Even those influenced by Mead, dramaturgists and game theorists, for example, offer us images of humans that might be said to describe us as "near sublime animals, but no more." These images offer us many insights about our everyday lives. Ultimately, however, you will want to understand more of how the particular kind of society we live in shapes our nature and perhaps, too, how our natures might yet again be remade. This is the focus of the second half of the book. At this point let us examine how much these contemporary images illumine our experience, our everyday lives. As you think about each model, think too about the deeper controversies we introduced at the beginning of this chapter. Ask not simply, Is this who we are? but also, Must we be so? How might we become something more? Can we achieve this something more individually, through self-improvement, or must we change the social structures that have shaped our natures?

One particular brand of symbolic interactionism, dramaturgy, uses the analogy of the theatre to help us understand people's attempts to control the definition of the situation.

THE DRAMATURGICAL MODEL: PEOPLE AS ACTORS

The **dramaturgical model** views social life in terms of actors performing for audiences, wearing masks, using props and, finally, reading the reviews. The analogy is really not to classical theatre's rigidly followed scripts (as in conventional role theory), but to improvised theatre where the actors work out the script as they go.

To the role theorist, the archetypical role is that seen in ritual or classic drama, in which every line and gesture of every actor is rigidly specified in the sacred script. In our view, the archetypical role is more nearly that seen in improvised theatre, such as is provided by the Second City Troupe, which performs extemporaneously with only the broad outline of the sketches and of the characters assumed (McCall and Simmons, 1978:7).

Much of the inspiration for this perspective comes from the work of Cooley. He believed that a dramatic turning point in children's socialization is their realization that they can to some extent control the conduct of others. Initially the children's attempts to "impress" others are obviously just that; the children have not learned to be subtle. As adults, we learn to hide the fact that what we are trying to do is impress others, to affect how they view us. We learn to do so without appearing to do so. This has been the point of departure for much of the work of Erving Goffman, who has done most to develop the dramaturgical model.

According to this view, whatever the situation, we are trying to convey a particular impression of who we are. In other words, much of our interaction is devoted to *impression management*. Goffman describes the "stage-craft" and "stage-management" techniques we all use in everyday life.

Think, for example, of what you go through when you invite someone to dinner.

You set the stage, the scenery, perhaps by making it cleaner and more tidy for your guest. You create a scene of a neat, clean home in which a neat, clean person might live. You select some props to display who you are. You might, for example, put away your *Mad Magazine* and *Playboy* and put out *Saturday Night* and that book on Cézanne. You push the television into the corner of the room and place a carefully chosen record on the stereo. You have other props you can manipulate. What self do you wish to display? Pork and beans? An exotic curry? Or an elegant steak tartare? Or an affluent tenderloin? And how will you dress? As Gregory Stone argues, our clothes and our appearance, generally, are crucial props in staking out an identity. "By appearance, a person *announces* his identity, shows his values, *expresses* his mood, or *proposes* his attitude" (Stone, 1962:101). And, finally, you will adopt some style for your dinner party — friendly and informal, formal and more distant, or warm and romantic.

In all of this you are the actor, getting ready to perform for an audience and then, for better or worse, playing out the drama. And, of course, the guest, too, is an actor performing for you, the audience. What each of you sees in the actual encounter is only a small part of all the behaviour that went into the performance. If you are a good actor, your audience will not see the inner performance as you wonder whether the meal is a disaster or as you are struck by an inability to make small talk. In fact, each of us takes great pains to keep from view the rehearsals, preparations, and dirty work that go into our performance.

Goffman distinguishes, as in the theatre, two regions of performance: the *back region* and the *front region*. In the back region, outside of the view of the audience, you can, to some extent, drop your front. Here, you prepare your performance, rehearse, and check that your appearance is suitable for the front region. In the backstage of kitchens, bathrooms, and bedrooms, we do the dirty work that we hope remains invisible to the audience we keep in our living and dining rooms.

We may, in this behind-the-scenes work, enlist the aid of others whom we make part of our team of mutual cooperation. We call upon members of the family or neighbours to help in our preparations and to forgive the blemishes we haven't yet covered. With the arrival of the audience, we expect them to come together as a team, and so family bickering stops at the sound of the doorbell, and each member is expected to keep to himself or herself information about back-stage region behaviour and to contribute to the performance. Every parent has suffered embarrassment at the hands of children who are too honest and, in effect, become bad team players.

The performance is given in the front region. Crucial to this performance, to our success in impression management, is information control. At the same time as we seek to give certain information about ourselves, we withhold other information. We schedule our performances so that outsiders cannot observe a performance not intended for them. We may not want our guest to enter the kitchen, or look in our medicine chest, or open our closets. We may wish to make sure children are well out of the way. Information "leaks" can spoil our performance and are a continual source of embarrassment in everyday life.

Clearly, actors do not have complete control over their performances or, more precisely, over how others respond to their performances. As Goffman puts it, not only do we *give expressions*, we also *give off expressions*. People do not simply observe what we knowingly present to them, they also observe and judge us on the basis of unintended gestures, "nervous mannerisms," such as trembling knees, sweaty palms, blushing, slips of the tongue and so on. In fact, as people have learned to be somewhat cynical, they may use the expressions given off, thought to be beyond the control of the performer, to judge the sincerity of the performance. The audience will often check the fit between expressions given, thought to represent the performance, and expressions given off, thought to represent the person behind the mask, the "real" meaning of the performance.

In short, as we give a performance, claiming and staking out an identity, there is no guarantee that the identity we are claiming will be validated by our audience. We have all, at one time or another, received bad reviews. Our identity may be discredited because the audience may decide we are "phonies," that we do not have the credentials — the *content* — to justify our identity claim. Or, our identity might be discredited because the audience views our performance as inept. We do not have the *style*. This is nicely illustrated by the audience response to two people playing the role of professor. One, Thorstein Veblen, was the author of the witty and insightful work, *The Theory of the Leisure Class*. Because of this book, Veblen attracted large crowds of students to his lectures. Unfortunately, students found him to be a bad and boring lecturer. The result, according to one of his students, was that his course would begin with 250 to 300 students and would end with only 1 or 2 persistent ones. Veblen was high on "content," extremely low on "style." Indeed, had it not been for the written evidence of his intellect, he would likely have been declared incompetent.

We can compare this case with "MacDonald," a psychology professor at Lakehead University in the mid-1960s. MacDonald was well liked by both students and colleagues. One of the authors of this book, during a visit to the nearby teacher's college where MacDonald also taught a course, was told that he was one of the best teachers that Lakehead had ever sent over. Then, to everyone's horror, it was learned that MacDonald was an imposter; he had assumed the identity and credentials of another person, someone who had graduated from a university in the southern United States. The point is that the "per-

former" was discredited not because he was found to be "incompetent," but because, by sheer accident, the *real* MacDonald discovered and pointed out the fraud. Whereas Veblen had content, but no style, the imposter had style but, from the point of view of formal training, lacked content.

In other words, our identities may be discredited in terms of our performances rather than in terms of what we *really* are. For example, in one of his works, Goffman (1963) describes how people who possess some *stigma* — for example, a physical deformity, "personal problems" thought to lead to behaviour such as alcoholism or mental illness, or membership in a particular religion or race — may find that their identity as normal human beings is challenged.

Goffman is often criticized for developing too cynical a model of humans and interaction. To talk about people as actors seems to imply that they are always playing parts, not themselves. All the language seems to imply pretence, phoniness, and calculated manipulation. There seem to be two elements to this criticism. First, many people infer from the model the view of people as anxiety-ridden, sweaty-palmed actors concerned only about how they are coming across to others, which does not jibe with their own experience. Second, there seems to be some concern that dramaturgy implies that we are insincere in our everyday relationships. These criticisms, however, do an injustice to the model.

Goffman and others who use the perspective do not imagine that we are necessarily preoccupied with our own performances. This may be the case in some rare circumstances, such as a first date or a job interview, but for the most part we are able to take for granted our performances and those of others. From our socialization as children we have been taught how to perform for audiences and to change our performances as the audiences change. None of this is new to us. As well, we give most of our performances over and over again until they become routine and require little thought. We tend to become aware of our performances only when they have been challenged, when our identity has been discredited, or when we are confronted with an ambiguous situation.

Goffman emphasizes that most of the time our performances are not discredited, that typically, people give one another the benefit of the doubt. We assume that people are who they present themselves to be unless proved otherwise. As socialized adults we learn that tact requires us to avert our eyes or pretend not to notice those social gaffes that could discredit an actor's performance. Interaction may be precarious but it works because most of the time we support each other in our mutual performances — though we may remember most vividly those instances where our audience let us down and our identity was discredited.

Furthermore, the dramaturgical model does not imply that actors are insincere. According to this model, actors are sincere if they believe in their own performance and they are insincere if they do not. A further analogy, then, might be the "method actor." Perhaps the sincere performer, like the method actor, is the one who cannot perform a role unless he or she believes it. These are the situations when self and role fit together. Nevertheless, Goffman recognizes that we are often called upon in everyday life to perform roles that we find distasteful or that lack congruence with our self-concept. In these situations, actors may exhibit *role distance*, giving expressions to others and perhaps to themselves to convey that they do not really mean what they are doing.

Finally, Goffman himself warns his readers that the language of the stage is simply a device, a rhetoric, a way of helping us to understand what we find so difficult to understand — our own interaction. The dramaturgical model is an analogy: scaffolding, and "scaffolds, after all, are to build other things with and should be erected with an eye to taking them down" (Goffman, 1951:254).

It is important to emphasize again, however, that this perspective that views people as negotiators of identities does not capture all aspects of human behaviour, nor necessarily the most important aspects. If people were simply the negotiators of identities, the actors, the wearers of masks (and different masks for different audiences), they would be rather empty. They would be much like one of T.S. Eliot's "Hollow Men," who asks:

Let me also wear
Such deliberate disguises
Rat's coat, crowskin, crossed staves
In a field
Behaving as the wind behaves

Goffman's dramaturgical approach seems to work best when we are considering what he calls "brief encounters" — secondary relationships — between sales person and customer, waiter and customer, professional and client. It is less useful when we are examining the sustained interaction of a primary relationship. No doubt, as Eric Berne (1964), the father of transactional analysis, has argued, people play games in even the most intimate of relationships and put on fronts and hold back information, but in a more limited and restricted manner than is possible in brief encounters. For example, while husbands and wives may perform for one another, they are also a team, constructing a shared definition of reality; they are often engaged as team members along with the rest of the family to present a particular performance, a particular definition of the situation to "outsiders" (Berger and Kellner, 1964). In other words, when people are "backstage," does it make any sense to talk about an "audience" for their "performance"? Goffman does not very adequately capture the kind of interaction that we think of in everyday life as intimacy.

But perhaps this is Goffman's message: that in contemporary society our creative energies are being consumed by our efforts to package ourselves in acceptable ways, to fit ourselves to social demands, even when we find these personally distasteful. Perhaps when we rush back to our families and our intimate groups to relax and be our "real selves," we no longer know how. Still worse, as Kurt Vonnegut warns us, perhaps we simply become who we have pretended to be for so much of our time.

Goffman's is a perspective that understands the power of the social. You may often find his work upsetting because it seems to diminish us all to mere actors. At the same time, you will recognize yourself, especially in those situations where the "weight of social opinion" seems to give you no choice except to play out a particular role. Think of the times when you have "become" somebody you yourself despise because you wish to please or appease someone with power over you. Of course, we are not *mere* actors, but this image of contemporary humans must certainly capture a part of us we all know. That we are more is evidenced by the very fact that we often hate ourselves most when we recognize the truth of Goffman's image.

What else are we? What else have we become in the face of the social structures confronting us? Another image views people less as actors than as game-players competing for prizes, needing therefore not only to win but also to defeat the competition.

THE GAME MODEL: PEOPLE AS PLAYERS

As we have mentioned, Mead recognized the importance of games in child socialization. Through games, children learn to read the cues offered to them by others, to take the roles of others, and to fit their lines of action with the actions of others. A number of sociologists and social psychologists have followed this lead and have argued that games provide an apt analogy for social interaction more generally. They use games as a perspective for looking at social interaction. If we define games as those interactions in which

one party is seeking some end at the expense of another party, but bound by some agreed-upon rules, the comparison between games and a good deal of social interaction seems apparent. In a game, the payoff or outcome depends not only upon one's own performance but also upon the performances of others in the game, upon the performances of one's opponents. Because of this, we must try to imagine beforehand what our opponents are going to do. In other words, we must take the other's role before we form our own line of action. Similarly, in everyday interaction, our behaviour depends upon the behaviour of others, and we must try to imagine the intentions of others, what others are going to do, before we act. As well, both in games and in everyday interaction, the behaviour of all the participants is bound by a set of rules, agreed-upon norms, for "playing the game."

We might distinguish two types of rules: *constitutive rules* are the rules without which the game (or interaction) could not be played at all; *preferred rules* are the rules that describe how the game is usually played and the expectations about how players will play. Constitutive rules describe the taken-for-granted roles that form the basis of the game; in poker, for example, the number of cards that are necessary, the notion of following in order, the idea that people will not look at one another's cards, and so on. Preferred rules are the rules that describe the etiquette and style of play. Similarly, in interaction there are some rules that, if violated, disrupt interaction entirely and other rules that simply indicate preferred styles and manners in interactions.

If, for example, you were constantly to ask people what they meant when they offered conventional messages such as "How are you?" you would no doubt be violating a constitutive rule and disrupting interaction (Garfinkel, 1967; Cicourel, 1964). People take for granted that when they ask us how we are, we will understand the question, just as in poker the players will assume that the others in the game will wait their turn, and so on. In interaction there are also a number of rules that direct us in how to answer such conventional questions. For example, we are not expected to tell someone about all of our ailments and physical difficulties when they ask us, "How are you?" This, however, is a preferred rule as its violation would not likely disrupt interaction entirely.

Finally, both games and social interaction are "probabilistic"; we can never be certain that our action will bring about the required response in others, though the odds are probably much easier to work out in game situations. Much of our gaming behaviour is the plotting and devising of strategies to maximize the probability that we will be successful in bringing about the desired response in our opponents (Brittan, 1973).

A number of laboratory studies have devised game situations in order to study the kinds of strategies people employ. The classic laboratory game involves three (and sometimes more) subjects who are asked to play a board game for some reward, for example, points that can later be converted into money. The object of the game, much like Parcheesi, is to move around the board before one's opponents. Each participant moves his or her gamepiece a number of spaces, depending on the roll of the dice. Unlike Parcheesi, however, all participants move their gamepiece on each roll. The reason that they do not all finish at the same time, in a tie, is that each is assigned a different "weight" or value at the beginning of the game. For example, one might be given a "three" and the other two "two" each. What this means in the game is that the "three" would move the gamepiece three times the roll of the dice, while each "two" would move twice the roll of the dice.

The outcome of the game is obviously predetermined by the experimenter; those with the highest "weights" will always win. However, the experimenter encourages the participants to form coalitions to alter the predetermined outcome. The experimenter explains that any two participants can unite and form a team. Say a "three" and a "two" formed such a coalition. Each member of the coalition would move the piece the roll of the dice multiplied by the combined total of their two scores, in this case five times the roll of the dice. They would win the game and somehow divide the spoils. In the example we have given, any coalition would win: "three" and either one of the "twos" or both "twos."

The experimenter is interested in examining what kinds of coalitions the players will form in order to change the predetermined results of the game. Clearly, each "two" would lose if he or she did not form some coalition with one of the other two players. The players in these experimental games will usually bargain with one another to decide which coalition will be most effective in winning, and they will bargain about how to divide the spoils once the game has been won. For example, a "three" coalescing with a "two" might ask for a greater share of the winnings.

A number of conclusions have been drawn from this experiment and many variations of it. People will usually try to form a coalition in which the power difference is in their favour, that is, in which they have more "weight" than the others in the coalition. If this is impossible, they will try to avoid situations in which the power difference is too great. They will try to maintain some "minimal power" (Caplow, 1956). In other words, the players are trying not only to win the game but also to have some dominance over their partners. As well, it seems that the players will form the smallest coalition necessary to win the game (Gamson, 1961); they will try to form a winning coalition that nonetheless does not mean that they have to divide the pie in too many ways.

Of course, the forming of coalitions is only one of the many possible game strategies employed either in games or in everyday life. One central feature of most game strategies is "concealment." In games, it is important to conceal our strategies, our techniques, our plots from our opponents. Success usually depends on concealing such information, perhaps even upon misleading our opponent deliberately. Again we can find many analogies in everyday life.

Obviously the game model depicts humans as primarily calculating and manipulative. In everyday life we are quite willing to look at some interactions in these terms. Many of us seem to view politics as primarily a "game." *Politicians are seen as being engaged in a deadly pastime of moving strategic pieces so that they place their opponents at a disadvantage. Strategic advantage is obtained by playing the game in as economical and calculating a manner as possible (rational efficiency). The players who can amass the greatest number of pieces (indoctrinated supporters, resources, offices, etc.) can be considered to be in a position of relative strength vis-à-vis the other players (Brittan, 1973:129).*

Most of us, however, are reluctant to apply such a model to our own interaction or to the interaction of those close to us. Nevertheless, surely you can find a number of analogies in "the family game," "the dating game," "the course-assignment game," and so on. In families, for example, one often finds children forming coalitions to stand against their parents, plotting together in the "back stage," and concealing their strategies from their parents. They develop techniques to gain certain ends, money, or special privileges, and more generally to gain greater autonomy, greater control over their parents and therefore their lives. Similarly, parents will often form coalitions "against" their children, devising strategies to get the child to go to bed at "bedtime" or "to behave" in front of visitors in order to gain more control over their children's behaviour.

The gaming perspective can be useful in helping us understand the struggle for power and control in social interaction. Implicit in this perspective is the notion that cooperative solutions can be demonstrated to be more advantageous than individualistic solutions though a number of experiments have shown that people do not typically make the "rational" or "logical" decision.

As with dramaturgy, it would be dangerous to take this analogy too seriously. It does not capture all aspects of social interaction. Not all interaction can be characterized as the participants' attempts to maximize their own ends, nor is all interaction strategic in the sense of games, nor is it necessarily premised on concealment. Just think, for example, of the importance you attach to your friendships, or certain friendships, in which you are able to disclose some of the most secret and private features of yourself. This is the essence of the psychotherapeutic relationship and perhaps one of the reasons that it is so initially painful and highly emotionally charged and ultimately valued by the participants. In fact, we often seem to find great release in those encounters with strangers on a bus or a plane for example in which we use the episodic and transitory nature of our interaction, the fact that we are not likely to see these people again, to "bare our souls." Such interaction is not very well captured by the game perspective.

There are perhaps even more important differences between game situations and everyday life. In everyday life we are less likely to be as sure of the rules of interaction as we are of the rules of a game. Indeed, in everyday interaction two "players" may well be playing different games with different rules. In everyday interaction rule violation is probably much more frequent than it is in game situations. In a game the rules apply in the same way to all the participants. In everyday life the rules are selectively applied and enforced, and some people have more power in creating, applying, and enforcing these rules (see Chapter 7). Finally, games are a matter of fun and enjoyment and, while much of our interaction is intrinsically pleasurable to us (Simmel, 1964), not all of our interactions are voluntarily entered into, and most of them, whether pleasurable or not, affect our lives in ways that games cannot replicate.

In the game perspective we have "people as players" seeking to maximize their ends through strategy and bargaining. The cynicism reaches its peak in a third image of humans: as calculating "exchange machines." Gone completely is the optimism of Mead's symbolic interactionism where people's future lies in their ability to create harmonious relationships. This image—exchange theory—presents people who know no altruism, who are driven by internal forces (motives), who are acquisitive and self-seeking. Exchange theorists seem to be arguing that this is precisely what we are, always have been, and always will be. They too, like Mead, have been guilty of ignoring the extent to which our "nature" is produced by the social structures in which we live. Nevertheless, their perspective has perhaps captured something of what we have become.

THE EXCHANGE MODEL: PEOPLE AS PROFIT SEEKERS

Although there are a number of versions of the **exchange model** in social psychology and sociology, we shall focus on the works of George Homans (1958; 1961) who did most to bring exchange principles to the attention of sociologists. His work represents a substantial departure from the principles of symbolic interactionism. Homans has been concerned with the development of deductive theory— a set of general principles that would allow sociologists to predict human behaviour in a wide variety of situations. While sociologists look to historical, structural, or cultural factors to explain human behaviour, Homans insists that the most general explanatory principles can be drawn through focusing on individual motivation. Homans, drawing his principles primarily from B. F. Skinner's highly influential behaviouristic psychology and from elementary economics, intends his exchange theory to apply to "all" human interaction.

The guiding idea is that people behave in a way to maximize rewards and minimize costs. This does not mean that people are simply concerned with gaining immediate gratification. People's behaviour, according to this perspective, is governed by *enlightened self-interest*; they seek only to make some profit in any interaction (Homans, 1961:79). Of course, the basic ideas of exchange theory have existed for a long time, as Homans himself points out, both in the work of early social thinkers and in our common-sense view of motivation. What Homans has tried to do is to present these ideas in an explicit and systematic way so they can be subjected to some testing. At the same time, he tried to develop a model of humans that people could recognize in terms of their everyday experience.

— 1. If, in the past, a particular stimulus has accompanied rewards for an individual's behaviour, the more similar later stimuli are to these early ones, the more likely the individual is to perform the same or similar activity.

— 2. The more often a person's activity is rewarded, the more often he or she will perform that activity.

— 3. The more valuable the reward an individual receives, the more often he or she will perform the activity so rewarded.

— 4. The more often an individual has in the recent past received a rewarding activity from another, the less valuable any further unit of that reward becomes to that individual.

— 5. If an individual's expectations of the rewards and costs of his activity are not met, if he or she feels the exchange has not been "fair," he or she will become angry and behave aggressively. (1961:53– 75).

The first three principles derive directly from the psychological work of Skinner. The first axiom describes the learning theory principle of *generalization*. Take, for example, coaches in hockey. When the combination of players that they have used in the game produces a victory, their activities in that situation have been rewarded. In the next game we may find that coaches try to use exactly the same players; that is, they perform the same activities, seeking the same reward. Some coaches have been known to wear the same clothing that they wore the last time their team achieved a victory. If the situations are the same, people will behave in ways that "worked" in the past.

The second proposition is basic to learning or reinforcement theory. This proposition simply states that people will continually perform activities that have met with rewards in the past; the more often the activity has been rewarded, the more frequently people will engage in that activity. If studying hard has consistently brought students good marks, they will more often study harder than those who have tried and failed.

The third proposition recognizes that there is substantial variation in what people find rewarding. Rewards are *variables*. Some people may value highly the reward of good marks, others may not. The more valuable the reward, the more likely it is to produce reward-seeking behaviour.

The fourth proposition derives from both reinforcement theory and elementary economics. It introduces the notion of *satiation*: people can get too much of a good thing. At the simplest level this means that food is not as valued a reward to a well-fed person as to a hungry one. More generally it means that after a time rewards will decrease in value. If you eat steak every day, steak will lose some of its value as a reward. In elementary economics, this is known as the principle of *marginal utility*. The value individuals attach to any commodity depends on how much of that commodity they already possess. The value that they attach to any reward depends on their past history, how much and how often they have been rewarded in the past.

In the fifth proposition, Homans introduces a new concept, essentially an elaboration of Skinner's work: the concept of *distributive*

justice. Skinner observed that when pigeons do not receive their expected rewards, they exhibit behaviour that seems to reveal anger and frustration. Homans argues that people will respond in much the same way, but, being more sophisticated than pigeons, they make some calculation before they exhibit anger or frustration. They weigh the "cost" of the activity against the rewards they have received and thereby determine whether the "net reward" or profit was fair and just. In other words, when people receive punishment when they expect rewards, or assess the rewards as insufficient repayment for their investment (other rewards they have sacrificed), they will become angry and behave aggressively (see Turner, 1974:235–237). This is the core of exchange theory. Before we examine its failings, we shall briefly illustrate how it is applied to explain interaction.

Homans has used these ideas to analyze the interaction in a federal law-enforcement agency (first reported in Blau, 1955). These agents had the task of making prosecution decisions about legal cases and, as with most legal matters, their task entailed a good deal of ambiguity. Although official bureaucratic policy forbade consultation among agents, this became a routine practice. There was general agreement among the workers about who were the most and the least-skilled among them. Typically, workers would ask the more skilled among them for advice about their cases. The rewards these less-skilled workers received were obvious: help with their work, social support and training from respected workers. But the more-skilled workers also received rewards in the exchange.

When friends help us move, we often offer them a good deal of beer in exchange. Similarly, the less-skilled workers might offer to buy the more-skilled ones a "free" lunch. But more often and more important,, what they gave to those who offered help were respect and social esteem. Put simply, if you ask someone for help, and you do not do this in a deferential manner, and you do not show proper respect and gratitude afterwards, you are not likely to receive help from this person again. Homans characterizes interaction among law-enforcement officers as this kind of social exchange.

In the agency, the demands made on the time of the more-skilled workers affected their own work — their sense of distributive justice was violated. In turn, they raised the price for the help they gave; they demanded more deference, more gratitude, more respect. According to Homans, they also raised the price because they were becoming satiated with the reward of self-esteem from their colleagues. Since the less skilled workers were often unwilling to pay the price — the costs were too great — they asked these experts for help less and less often.

The most interesting and potentially fruitful application of exchange principles is Peter Blau's (1964) analysis of *power*. Blau defines power as the ability of an individual (or group) to extract compliance in an exchange relationship. According to the exchange perspective, people *allow* others to influence them because it is in their best interest to do so. Power is tied to the notion of dependence. If people cannot, or believe they cannot, get something that they "need" from any other source, they will continue to interact with the source of these rewards even if the costs seem great and the exchange unfair. To put it another way, those who possess a highly valued and scarce resource have power over those who feel they need the resource. When this resource is something that gets used up or constantly needs replenishing — money, food, sex, for example—power is at its greatest. People will incur high costs to get these rewards. But according to exchange theory, power is never absolute. There is usually some other source for the reward, and, if people realize this, they will shop around for the source that exacts the lowest costs. This does not mean that the power relationship is eliminated but rather that the power is constrained. Even if no other source of the

reward seems to be available, those in the weak position are still likely to have some power, though considerably less, over those in the stronger position. In the exchange perspective power is always to some degree reciprocal.

Let us take the example of the student/ professor relationship. The professor has power over the students in that he or she controls something the students "need" — grades. To some extent the professor can exact compliance from the students — influence them to sit through the lectures, do assignments, write exams—even if the costs are great. However, the students can drop out, switch courses or, most subtly, try to work it so that the professor comes to value their respect and goodwill and thereby comes to be careful about what he or she demands. The students in this situation have at least some influence.

Exchange theory obviously has a good deal of face validity when we think of many of our everyday-life situations. When we give someone a gift, it seems generally the case that we expect to receive in return a gift of similar or equal value. When we have been invited to dinner, we will often think in terms of "owing" a dinner invitation in return. When people fail to meet our exchange expectations, we may hesitate to trust them in future interactions.

Nevertheless, despite its obvious appeal, exchange theory has a far more limited applicability than Homans intended and is also fraught with conceptual problems. First of all, exchange theory is probably not very useful for handling situations involving force or coercion. Exchange does not seem to enter the picture when we have been *forced* to engage in some activity; our calculations of costs and rewards are certainly less relevant. As Blau (1964) himself has recognized, exchange principles do not seem to apply very well in situations in which people are acting out of fear. When people are acting, say, out of a fear of eternal damnation, or of losing their jobs, or of arrest, they may well be calculating costs, but there is no exchange. It would appear that game theory's work on coalition formation and other versions of symbolic interactionism would be more useful in these situations. When people are acting on the basis of fear, they are imagining the responses of others, viewing themselves as objects and controlling their behaviour in terms of these symbols.

Furthermore, the exchange assumption of "the essential ubiquity of the hedonistic calculus" may also limit the range of situations for which it can be applied (Brittan, 1973). When people give an anonymous donation to charity or, more generally, when they behave altruistically, are they simply seeking to maximize their own self-interest? One might certainly answer that they are behaving generously so that they will feel good about themselves, but to say that this is simply a particular example of exchange-reward is to stretch the term beyond reason. Again, we would argue that symbolic interactionism and its emphasis on the reflexive nature of self offer a more useful perspective. People care what others think of them and how others' perceptions make them feel about themselves, but they also care about how *they* feel about *themselves*.

Although, in a sense, we could view almost anything as a reward or exchange relationship, the theory becomes circular or what scientists call tautological; it explains everything and therefore nothing. To say that somebody willingly undergoes pain in a relationship because he or she finds the pain or other aspects of the relationship rewarding is, in the end, not very instructive. To say that every act of sacrifice or heroism or evil was a result of some exchange, some reward, fails to give us much insight into the fundamental questions of human behaviour. In these terms, it seems clear that exchange theory would benefit from a closer alliance with symbolic interactionism (see Singlemann, 1972).

Exchange theory must be stretched too far to capture many of our most important experiences: our fears and confusions, our bursts of generosity, our commitments to failing causes. Again, "profit seeker" may be some part of who we have become, but it is not the whole story. Yet another image of who we are focuses on some of the fears and confusions, specifically our fear of the unknown and especially our fear of meaninglessness and chaos. Ethnomethodology, drawing on Mead and on phenomenological philosophers (e.g., Alfred Shutz, 1964), gives us "people as explainers."

THE ETHNOMETHODOLOGICAL MODEL: PEOPLE AS EXPLAINERS

Superficially, at least, ethnomethodology seems in many ways similar to symbolic interactionism. Norman K. Denzin (1969) has gone so far as to argue that they are sufficiently similar to be quite easily synthesized. Both are interested primarily in the negotiation of symbols in everyday interaction. Denzin, however, failed to recognize the full extent of ethnomethodology's departure from conventional perspectives. Symbolic interactionism, like all sociological perspectives, views interaction in the context of society; symbolic interactionism seeks to explain how people fit their lines of action together and pattern their interactions on the basis of more or less shared meanings. Symbolic interactionists assume that these patterns exist, and they seek to account for them.

Ethnomethodologists, on the other hand, refuse to make this assumption. They do not assume that social order exists "out there." They ask a rather different question: how do people, including sociologists, produce and maintain for one another the *presumption* that the social world is real and orderly (Garfinkel, 1967)? In other words, they ask how people plan and explain their behaviour to themselves and others in the process of interaction; how they make their behaviour and the behaviour of others *appear* rational and orderly.

For the ethnomethodologist, consensus or agreement in interaction does not refer to the actual meshing or fitting together of meaning, but to the interactants' *belief* that this has been accomplished. When you say to your friend that you love the colour blue, or hate communism, or believe in God, your friend may have no notion of what you really mean by any of these words. Your friend, in fact, may mean very different things when he or she says love, or hate, or blue, or communism, or God. It may even be that as hard as you try, you could never really know (or know that you know) each other's interpretations. And yet, you somehow think that you are communicating not only in a way that is sensible to you but in a way that is sensible to others. You may even come to believe that you see the world in the same way as your friend, thus confirming that the world is an orderly and sensible place.

Ethnomethodologists wonder how this is possible. According to this view, social order or, more accurately, a *sense* of social order, is created and maintained in interaction.

The ethnomethodologist's goal, then, is to uncover the methods people use to make sense of the world and to make the world appear sensible to themselves and others with whom they are interacting.

In fact, the cement that holds society together may not be the values, norms, common definitions, exchange payoffs, role bargains, interest coalitions, and the like of current social theory, but people's explicit and implicit "methods" for creating the presumption of a social order (Turner, 1974:322).

Ethnomethodology, then, is the study of people's accounting procedures, the methods people use for making the world visibly rational and orderly for themselves and those they are interacting with. Ultimately, ethnomethodologists hope to uncover the rules whereby people construct these accounts. However, these rules are difficult to study because they are implicit. One of the ways that ethnomethodologists have tried to overcome this problem is by the technique of "disruption" (Garfinkel, 1967:37). The general idea is to start with the commonplace, familiar scenes, and to make trouble, to force the "subjects" to make explicit what they usually take for granted. For example, Harold Garfinkel, the major proponent of ethnomethodology, asks his students to perform an assignment in which, in their everyday interaction with others, they ask for clarification of the meanings of commonplace remarks that they would be expected to understand. One student provided Garfinkel with the following report:

On Friday night, my husband and I were watching television. My husband remarked that he was tired.

Wife: *How are your tired? Physically, mentally, or just bored?*

Husband: *I don't know. I guess physically, mainly.*

Wife: *You mean that your muscles ache or your bones?*

Husband: *Don't be so technical.*
         (After more watching.)

Husband: *All these old movies have the same kind of old iron bedstead in them.*

Wife: *What do you mean: Do you mean all old movies or some of them, or just the ones we have seen?*

Husband: *What's the matter with you? You know what I mean.*

Wife: *I wish you would be more specific.*

Husband: *You know what I mean! Drop dead!*

This and similar experiments provide ethnomethodologists with a good deal of their material for theorizing. In this particular example the husband obviously *assumed* consensus; he assumed that he and his wife were using shared meanings, that they understood one another. In everyday life, we are always saying only a fraction of what we mean, and we assume that others can fill in the rest. In this case, when the wife challenged this assumption, the husband became indignant. No doubt he assumed that she was doing this strange thing deliberately. In this and similar experiments, people try to *normalize* the situation and try to make it appear sensible. The husband will, for example, impute motives to his wife to account for her bizarre behaviour. Perhaps she is teasing him because she is angry. Perhaps she is tired or drunk. Perhaps she is going mad. Perhaps with more information everything will soon come clear. We use these techniques in everyday life as we are continually imputing motives to others and ourselves in order to make sense of behaviour (Blum and McHugh, 1971). Children, on the other hand, may be more willing than adults to tolerate highly "unstructured" situations. This is the thrust of John Holt's (1964; 1967; 1969) various books on the socialization and education of children.

It is also of significance that people who find themselves in ethnomethodological experiments typically react with such vehemence. In the example cited, the husband was not simply confronted with an awkward or annoying situation; he was confronted with a threatening one. When our assumption of shared meanings, of consensus, is challenged, we realize how difficult communication really is. We realize how imprecise and problematic our use of language is. We realize the precariousness and fragility of "social order."

Thus far, ethnomethodologists have done little more than demonstrate that such interpretative rules as we have described do exist. The problems that they will encounter in developing an adequate methodology to uncover these rules and a general theory of these rules are substantial. This is particularly the case since these interpretative rules may well be situation specific, created anew in each interaction situation. In any case, ethnomethodologists have provided sociologists with new questions and have contributed to conventional perspectives on interaction in their description of accounts and people's attempts to normalize the apparently abnormal (see Scott and Lyman, 1968).

But, finally, ethnomethodology will, and can, never be more than a provocative footnote to sociology. It is ultimately too frightening for sustained contemplation. It is the road to madness to wonder if, or assume that, there is no order out there, that there is no meaning, that we are really not communicating, that we are solitary beings creating solitary realities in an absurd world. We cannot believe this. We are sociologists because we do not believe this and, as sociologists, we are the people the ethnomethodologists study

when they look to uncover the order and meaning of it all.

CONCLUSION

We have described a perhaps confusing number of images of humans and of interaction. All of these images are simply perspectives with which to view interaction; none is complete, and none is entirely wrong. People are actors, game players, bargainers, explainers of the world, and much more. People sometimes follow rules in a relatively unthinking way; they sometimes use rules to guide their interaction; and they sometimes use rules to account for interaction. All of these perspectives emphasize in one way or another people's active and creative roles in shaping their world.

But these perspectives do not tell us how social structures shape our nature. How does living in Canada, an economically dependent capitalist country, make us what we are? How does the structure act back on us in different ways, depending on our social class, or on the province in which we live, or on our sex? These are the issues of the chapters which follow.

Nevertheless, it is our belief that symbolic interactionism in particular is important because an understanding of how people view the world and how they act in terms of their own perceptions helps us link micro and macro, "the private and the public, the innermost acts of the individual with the widest kinds of sociohistorical phenomena" (Gerth and Mills, 1963:xvi).

The contemporary images, what we have called the "cynical images," perhaps capture the private sphere too well. They may help us understand the costs of living in a liberal capitalist society in much the way of a novel; that is, in a way that you should honestly test against your own experience. These images may tell us what it means to live in a culture that makes it difficult to fulfill what the psychologist Erik Erickson has called our *needs* for intimacy, for *generativity* (commitment to future generations), and finally, for integrity.

III SUGGESTIONS FOR FURTHER READING

An excellent introduction to the area of socialization is Alfred Lindesmith et al., *Social Psychology* (1977). Jerome Manis and Bernard Meltzer have compiled collections of readings that include the classic work of Mead and Cooley as well as the work of more recent symbolic interactionists and ethnomethodologists, *Symbolic Interaction: A Reader in Social Psychology* (1967, 1972, and 1983). Useful sources on child socialization include Frederick Elkin's and Gerald Handel's *The Child and Society* (1984), Elia Zureik's and Robert Pike's two-volume collection of articles, *Socialization and Values in Canadian Society* (1969), and David Goslin's *Handbook of Socialization Theory and Research* (1969). Phillippe Arie's *Centuries of Childhood* (1962) and Anthony Synnott's article "Little Angels, Little Devils: A Sociology of Children", *CRSA* (1983) give excellent accounts of changing perspectives on childhood and, in turn, socialization. Secondary socialization is examined in several articles in Jack Haas's and William Shaffir's *Shaping Identity in Canadian Society* (1978) and in Howard Becker's well-known study of socialization into the medical profession, *Boys in White* (1961).

There is now a large and growing literature on socialization into sex roles. A now classic work is Eleanor Maccoby's and Carol Jacklin's *The Psychology of Sex Differences* (1974). More recent Canadian works include Marlene Mackie's *Exploring Gender Relations* (1982) and Esther Greenglass's *A World of Difference: Gender Roles in Perspective* (1983). Jo Freeman's edited collection, *Women: A Feminist Perspective*, contains a number of articles on gender socialization.

Erving Goffman's *Presentation of Self in Everyday Life* (1959) remains the most compelling introduction to dramaturgical sociology. You might also wish to look at his *Asylums* (1961), *Stigma* (1963), *Behaviour in Public Places* (1963) and *Frame Analysis* (1974), in which he shows the influence of ethnomethodology. Kenneth Burke has also been important in the development of dramaturgical sociology. See his *A Grammar of Motives* (1969). Peter Blau's *Exchange and Power* (1964) is no doubt the best and most readable statement on exchange. It is hard to suggest any reading that provides a clear statement of ethnomethodology. You can, however, get the flavour of this approach by reading Harold Garfinkel's lengthy analysis of "Agnes" in his *Studies in Ethnomethodology* (1967). Finally, for approaches to interaction not discussed in this chapter, see Edwin Hollander's and Raymond Hunt's collection, *Current Perspectives in Social Psychology* (1971).

THE CHANGING FAMILY

OVERVIEW

In the previous three chapters, you have considered how sociologists think about society and social relationships. You have been introduced to some of the fundamental concepts: culture, symbols, social knowledge, values, ideology, structure, institutions and institutionalization, small groups, aggregates and classes, roles, socialization and role learning, role playing and symbolic interaction. These are the essential elements of the sociological perspective. They are the major tools you will use to understand the relationship between society and the individual.

In this chapter, you will see how these concepts become concrete in an examination of the family, how changes in culture and social structure effect changes in the family, how the family can be viewed as a society in microcosm, how it is in this social unit that we experience most directly the impact of social change.

Most students will expect, in such a chapter, a good deal of detail on family relationships, patterns of child rearing, sexual behaviour, and, on the darker side, incest, violence and family breakdown. You will find some information on all of these in the chapter, but the focus is on larger social issues—on how social and economic change have affected the family, family roles and, in particular, the roles of mother, wife and woman in society. It is in this context that we look at Canadian patterns of marriage, of family life, of divorce and of remarriage.

It will be important for you to try to move beyond your personal and emotional understanding of the family so that you can link your experience to these issues of culture and social structure. You should also take out of this chapter some sense how these family changes act back upon society so that the family can be viewed as both an instrument and a product of social change.

To take one example, when you think of divorce, you probably often think of the particular characteristics of the family in dissolution—was there violence, was there extramarital sex, another man or woman, or was it a bad marriage to begin with. This chapter leads you to ask some new questions: such as how the phenomenon of divorce is linked to changing patterns of sexual inequality, to increasing participation of women in the labour force, to secularism and individualism and, at another level, to the rise of industrial capitalism.

The family is a slippery concept. In common-sense and scientific terms it is used to mean many different things. Perhaps, in some ways, the diversity of meanings and definitions, the variety of relationships which at least some would call family, the greater ambiguity and the wider choice about family life, are the most important changes you should be trying to understand. Many who are reading this book will soon make, or are in the process of making, these decisions about when and if to marry, when and if to have children, and whether to stay married. As you are making these decisions and wondering about what is right, morally or personally, you might think back to what we have been discussing in the previous chapters about how these are new kinds of choices, new kinds of decisions and these new views and questions about family and family life represent fundamental changes in the culture and structure of our society.

▎INTRODUCTION

The chapters you have read all deal with important aspects of the sociological perspective. Many of you, however, may feel that these chapters are rather abstract and have not touched your *private lives*. No doubt you recognized that you somehow learned a culture that sets you apart from some people, allows you to interact effectively with other people and, in some ways, limits you. You probably recognize that you do feel some constraints depending on who you are interacting with, that you are different when at school than when at leisure, in a large group than in a smaller one or, yet again, with just one other person. But you might feel that none of this captures the totality of being human nor even the most important parts, those parts that are revealed in your most intimate relations, particularly in the family.

However outmoded the terms, dating and courtship probably grab much of your emotional commitment. And among your most trying decisions will probably be those about marriage and family. In short, family seems to be regarded as a special and private realm. But as we pointed out in Chapter I, we believe that the primary task of sociology is to link the private and the public, to understand, for example, the relationship between the family and broader sociohistorical processes. While it may seem remote to ask questions about how, say, the rise of capitalism and industrialism has influenced family life, we shall argue instead that this is at the very heart of the matter.

At the same time, what occurs within the family is not an automatic response to these forces. Throughout this book we emphasize and illustrate the sociological paradox that people are not only created and constrained by society, they are also creators able, within certain limits, to effect social change and to interpret in novel and unanticipated ways those large-scale changes which often seem

simply to be happening to them. As with all institutions, the contemporary family is "the product of human agency, not of abstract social 'forces'" (Lasch, 1979:xx).

To make this more understandable, we would ask that you look again at our discussion in Chapter 4 of the shift from simple to complex societies. There we described the shift from social structure based solely on traditional bonds of kinship and community to modern urban, secular society based more on secondary relationships centred around a market economy. The rise of capitalism and industrialism were seen as transforming the family. From this perspective, the family was an institution which had things happen to it.

Yet, what social historians have demonstrated is that people were not passive agents in these changes. Some welcomed the opportunity to flee to the cities and the factories from the constraints of small communities and the burdens of supporting their kin. And, alternatively, some resisted the forces of modernization by continuing to maintain kinship because it was in their interests to do so: capitalism freed people from obligations but also brought about new layers of vulnerability which, paradoxically, caused many to turn more to kin than in the past.

Many of the changes in the family sociologists have been predicting for decades—the demise of the nuclear family, the development of alternative family forms — have not followed inexorably from the forces of industrialization and capitalism. Traditional notions of the "ideal family" have shown a remarkable persistence. As Ferdinand Mount (1980) maintains, the family has always been a "subversive institution" in the sense that it has resisted efforts of church and state to control marriage, fertility and divorce. And, at the same time, it has also resisted change. Of course, the family is changing nevertheless, but not in some automatic homogeneous fashion. The change has been one of conflict and strain as some welcomed and some resisted it, some benefited and some lost.

DESCRIBING THE FAMILY

PROBLEMS IN STUDYING THE FAMILY

Paradoxically, the family is the institution we know most intimately and yet least well. We know what is happening in our own home, our own marriage, but we have only fragmentary and uncertain knowledge of what goes on elsewhere. As you will discover, if you haven't already, we seldom know what even our best friends' marriages are *really* like and we are often surprised when what seemed the perfect couple separate or get a divorce. Nor do we have a clearcut notion of what is a "normal" marriage.

This is nicely illustrated by a British study of sex and marriage by Geoffrey Gorer (1969). He found that the frequency of sexual intercourse among married people ranged from twice daily down to once or twice a month with the median being about twice a week. Yet at least three-quarters of the respondents in his survey thought of themselves as "about average." Nor was there consistency among those who thought that they departed from the norm; some who had sexual intercourse quite frequently, thought of themselves as below average, some who had sex very infrequently viewed themselves as above average.

Gorer's study demonstrates that it is not as difficult as we once imagined to obtain information even about something as intimate as sexual behaviour. Indeed, it looks as if once the researcher has been accepted inside the home very little is regarded as private information. But, Gorer's study shares with most studies of family and marriage the fact that his research techniques allow him only to report on attitudes and statements about behaviour but not on the behaviour itself.

What we are suggesting here is that sociologists, for the most part, have not been as successful as novelists and film makers in penetrating the interior of the family and in capturing the largely unexplored territory which we both "know" and do not know. The reason, of course, is that more than other aspects of social life, contemporary marriage and family life are almost exclusively "backstage" behaviour so that much of what we do within the family is "private and unrehearsed," not intended for an audience. We seldom "display our dirty linen in public," but seek rather to present to outsiders an image or performance which conforms as much as possible to our concept of the ideal and normal family.

Another obstacle in studying the family is that we are likely to find it difficult to move beyond our values and emotional commitments. It is within our families that most of us experience, for better or for worse, our most human attachments. Our attitudes about our parents, our children, our siblings and our mates are often filled with contradictions, confusion and passion. It is little wonder that these relationships are at the heart of psychology and the study of child development and socialization.

When sociologists discuss "institutions," the bundle of norms and roles described in Chapter 4, they use the family as the example *par excellence*. For most people, the loss of a parent or child or mate is a double loss: the loss of the individual and the disruption to the institution. Because these institutions do touch us so deeply, because family does matter in ways that most institutions do not, change in the family is felt more profoundly, more directly.

Because we all look at the family and how it is changing from the vantage of our own personal and social interests, we more often try to *evaluate* rather than *understand*. Because of the immediacy of the family, we rarely try to link our experiences to larger social issues. We react to change with anger, hurt, or relief. Those who resist change look for villains — women's liberation or permissive sexuality or, more immediately, selfish spouses, preoccupied parents and spoiled children, all signs of spiritual decay. And, those who welcome the change, look to heroes — feminism, sexual and other forms of human liberation.

The authors, in writing this chapter, were forced to examine their own values about family and family change. In this process, we came to recognize the necessity of warning the reader that, to the extent that we cannot escape our own prejudices, it is important to keep in mind that the chapter was written by two males, both in families with children. As much as we believe that enduring relationships among adults and raising children fill some fundamental human needs, we cannot pretend to understand fully the position of women in the family or the impact of impoverishment on families. No doubt, this chapter, like the discipline of family sociology, is infused with values.

Probably, the best we, as anyone studying the family, can hope to do is to try to stick to empirical statements (on average people marry somewhat later than twenty years ago; the divorce rate has risen steadily over the past two decades, people, on average, have 1.7 children) and avoid statements which use such value-laden terms as "evolution," "adaptation," "progress," "decline," "success" and "failure." In other words, before we can speak of progress we have to specify where it is we want to go; before we speak of decline we have to make clear why we believe the past to have been better than the present.

WHAT IS A FAMILY?

As with many concepts in sociology, while we have a common-sense idea of what a family is, we also have considerable difficulty in creating one definition. Indeed, as Emily Nett (1988) has recently pointed out, "family" is about as multi-purpose a noun (or adjective) as can be encountered in the English language. Historically, a family included biologically related members, employees, apprentices and servants. Philippe Aries's (1962) account of the development of family life suggests that this was especially the case in medieval society. But even as late as 1851, the British census defined the family in terms which few of us would accept today:

. . . as persons under one head; who is the occupier of the house, the householder, master, husband or father; while the other members of the family are, the wife, children, servants, relatives, visitors and persons constantly or accidently in the house (quoted in Katz, 1975:229).

Cross-culturally we also run into problems. In most societies, husbands and wives and children live together either in a separate dwelling or in the home of one set of parents. But there are a number of well-known exceptions; the Nayar of Northern India and the Israeli *kibbutz* in its early stages, for example, seemed in their lack of family structure to break every anthropological rule or generalization. Moreover, there are, as Fallers (1965) points out, cultures where people "fictionalize" a biological kinship. At the death of senior generations, people join the household of distant kin and biologically unrelated persons and begin to address and treat them as "parents" and "siblings." Perhaps this is not so different from the many times we "adopt" aunts and uncles in an apparent attempt to invent an extended family.

Something of the complexity of reaching a definition of the "normal" Canadian family is reflected in Figure 8.1, which describes what Statistics Canada thinks of as the census family.

While such a definition seems to cover a number of situations, in present Canadian society, there remains debate about what other kinds of "familial life styles" or "relationships" may also be regarded as a family. Are same-sex partners living together, perhaps with children from a previous marriage, a family? Debates about what is and is not a family are not simply academic because what

FIGURE 6.1

THE CANADIAN CENSUS FAMILY

The Canadian census family definition, which has been in use since the 1941 Census, defines a family as consisting of a husband and wife, with or without never married children, or a parent with one or more children who have never married, living together in the same dwelling. Adopted children and step-children are counted as own children, as are guardianship children under 21 years of age. Once a child is married, he or she ceases to be considered a part of the parents' family for census purposes, even though living in the same household. Such married children when living with husband or wife, and/ or children, constitute a second family unit within the same household. All unmarried sons and daughters living at home, regardless of age, are considered by definition, as members of families . . . the census family concept used in the Canadian census can refer to all the following diverse groups: (a) a young divorcee who rears one or more children in a flat in her parents' household; (b) a young widower living in a rented home who has been left to bring up one or more children alone, due to the death of his spouse; (c) a newlywed couple who have just set up housekeeping in a few rooms in their parents' home, or in an apartment of their own; (d) a young couple who reside with a number of their young children (but with no others, related or non-related) in a home of their own in the suburbs; (e) an elderly couple, residing in a flat or an apartment because their children have grown and live elsewhere with their own young families.

SOURCE: S. Wargon, "Using Census Data for Research on the Family in Canada." *Journal of Comparative Family Studies*, 3, 1 (Spring 1972): P. 150, 158.

is and is not defined as a family may have economic and social implications for those living in such arrangements. For example, people who live in a common law relationship, while recognized as a family for census purposes, may not be eligible for the same tax deductions as married couples, and rights to property acquired during the "marriage" differ from province to province if the relation-

ship ends. Also, there is presently a legal debate as to whether same-sex partners have the same rights as heterosexual couples.

We are not going to provide you with a single definition of the family. What you should recognize, rather, is that there are many definitions, reflecting current debates about lifestyle and morality. Official definitions of the family, the definitions that underlie and social programs, are being challenged and changed as feminists, gay rights activists and anti-poverty groups reveal how restrictive and unjust these definitions have been. At the same time, other movements are strongly resisting such changes because of the importance they attach to the traditional breadwinner family of husband, wife and offspring. As Margrit Eichler (1988) describes, when the United States held a "White House Conference on Families" in 1980, the pro-family movement took great exception to the use of the plural "families." In the view of these fundamentalist Christians, the family is a divinely sanctioned institution and to talk of the other forms the family takes in modern society is to pose a direct threat to *the* family, the patriarchal family of the Judeo-Christian tradition.

Whatever your position, you are being exposed to increasingly varied arrangements of people who claim for themselves the status of family. Fundamentalists may wish to uphold the notion of the traditional patriarchal family with a single breadwinner supporting a wife and children, but, as sociologists, we must recognize that the reality in Canadian society, as in other Western societies, is increasing numbers of one parent families, female-headed families, dual income and dual career families, intentionally childless families and remarriage families and a broad range of ethnic variations. The study of family has become the study of social change and diversity.

We have said that the family has changed and is changing. Perhaps the most profound change is subjective. As we described in our discussions of culture and social structure, as with other aspects of society, the family has lost its taken-for-granted status and some of its ability to constrain us. The taken-for-granted assumption that children will grow up, get married and have their own children no longer holds. The notion that when we marry it will be for life and for better and for worse no longer holds. The clear prescriptions and expectations for how various members ought to behave have been replaced by debates about family roles. The family, to use a sociological term, has become deinstitutionalized in the sense that there are fewer constraints on family-type behaviour (Beaujot, 1988:308).

This is not to suggest that you do not know what is and is not a family. For the most part, you operate with some common-sense notion of the concept of family and it is out of this notion that sociological and, to some extent, legal definitions emerge. You distinguish between kin, those tied to you by blood and marriage, and others who are not. You distinguish between close family of birth and the family you marry into and you generally give special status to the family with whom you share residence. Moreover, you understand that when people say they are going to visit family, or that they want a large family, or that they have decided not to have a family, or that their family was originally Irish, they are using the term in different ways, all of which capture some dimensions of the concept. Clearly, family means many different things. But, the very fact that we ask the question "what is a family" reflects a growing self-consciousness about family and family relationships.

Two points should be evident from this discussion. First, it has been increasingly difficult to come up with a definition of the family that could do justice to all of its meanings and the diversity of arrangements that we now refer to as family. And, second, any definition of the family will be based on some notion of what is right and proper. And, most of us are less sure of what is right and proper than were previous generations. The complexity of

these issues and the multiplicity of ways families and kinship groupings have been organized in various cultures has produced a large, technical vocabulary to try to capture change and diversity in family forms.

FAMILY, KINSHIP AND SOCIETY

As we discussed in Chapter 4, for most of the classical sociologists, the rise of industrialism and capitalism meant a fundamental change in social structure and social relationships. Underlying their various descriptions of social change (mechanical — organic, community — society, traditional authority — legal rational authority, folk — urban) was the common belief that modernization was undermining, if not totally destroying, **kinship** and perhaps the family itself.

However, later functionalists, most notably Parsons (1954), Parsons and Bales (1955) and Goode (1956), provided a more positive interpretation of changes in family and kinship. They argued that the family has been evolving in response to the demands of industrial and capitalist society. In this view, the family was not disintegrating, as many feared; it was merely changing and adapting. The extended kinship structure was "evolving" into the *relatively* isolated and independent **nuclear family**. It was an adaptation because the nuclear family "fits" better into industrial and bureaucratic society and, as described later in this chapter, comes to have specialized functions.

For sociologist committed to a functional perspective, this image of change in the family was a compelling illustration of how change in one part of the social system requires change and adaptation in another part of the system. They could, on the one hand, argue that when people are not so completely locked into a kinship structure, they are freer to move where work exists or in response to the demands of their existing job. If they have no formal obligations to kin outside the nuclear family then upward social mobility is easier; they need not take a whole lot of relatives with them as they make their upward climb.

On the other hand, functionalists accepted the view of the classical sociologists that modernization means a change not only in social structure but also values. Because capitalism is based on profit maximization which, in turn, means rationality and efficiency, there is little room for sentimental or traditional ties and commitments. Ideally, family-type relationships ought not to enter into business and bureaucracy. We are supposed to be hired and promoted because we have demonstrated ability and competence to do the job. As W.J. Goode (1963:108) summarizes it: "The extended family system with its standards of ascription, particularism and diffuseness is ideally not permitted to interfere with the efficient functioning of a modern enterprise." The decline of kinship is, then, functional to both the individual and to the society.

Critiques of the functionalist perspective have come from at least two directions. First, recent research by social historians strongly suggests that the functionalist characterization of change is based on a false and, perhaps, romantic notion of the family of the past and an exaggeration of the extent to which industrial capitalism came to depend upon relationships based on economic efficiency rather than traditional kinship ties. Second, both historical and sociological research suggests that, under some circumstances, the bonds of kinship may be more important in contemporary society than the functionalist view allows. Some further aspects of both of these critiques are described in the following paragraphs.

ROMANTIC MYTHS ABOUT THE FAMILY

While we all have a feeling that families and family life have changed, it is less evident what these changes actually are. Only recently have social historians devoted attention to the pre-industrial family. Their research calls into question the conventional wisdom held by most people, sociologists included.

What this research has shown is how much our debates about change in the family are based on myth, guesswork, and nostalgia. Most of us seem to carry around a vision of the golden family of the past which was filled with material help and support, warmth and security and a strength which overcame virtually any economic hardship or threat. In contrast, our own families must, inevitably, look weak and fragile. This ideal, often reiterated in bad novels, movies and television, has probably never existed except as an ideal.

Before we talk about how the family has changed, we have to develop a more realistic picture of the family of the past. Commonsense tells us that the families of the past had more often to confront the early death of a parent or the more frequent death of newborn children. We know, too, that many families had to face the harsh struggle for survival which allowed little space for romantic conceptions of childhood and adolescence. By and large people married because it was economically rational to do so and they had children in the hope that they would shortly be workers and would eventually support their parents in their later years.

Recent historical research has dispelled the myth of the two or three generation extended family living in the same household. The careful work by Peter Laslett (1967 and 1972), a British historian, and his colleagues, in what is known as the Cambridge Group, suggests that large and complex families were never, in Europe at least, in the majority. Rather, in the countries studied so far, about three-quarters of households were small, consisting of husband and wife and their children. Similarly, American research shows that there has never been an era in American society when two or three generations were residing in the same household (Hareven, 1982). Canadian data are, at present, extremely limited. Emily Nett concludes, however, that

the type of household in which most Canadians resided, from the time of settlement in Acadia,

New France, New England and later Upper Canada was the nuclear or 'simple' family household. This was the case regardless of geographical locale or whether the residence were backwoods, settled farm, village, or urban. If kin were nearby, people did not live as long as at present. The issue of whether to take on and to support elder kin rarely arose (Nett, 1981:242).

Perhaps the ideal in the past, too, was the large extended family under one roof. But Michael Katz (1975) points out, as with cultural ideals in general, most people simply lacked the resources to actualize their notions of the ideal family. In part, then, our image of the large extended family of the past may be an accurate reflection of the family life of the rich, the only people who could afford to house and feed so many. In general, Katz's research suggests that the richer people were, the larger the household that they maintained.

At the same time, as the 1851 definition of a household which we quoted earlier should suggest, the composition of the household in pre-industrial and early industrial periods differed considerably from that of today. While such households were not, ordinarily, filled with numbers of extended kin, they did include strangers: apprentices, servants, boarders and lodgers. As Hareven (1982) points out, the tendency of families to include strangers suggests that rather than a private retreat, the family was conceived by most as a relatively open institution and as the site of an array of functions. Many households were, then, both workplaces and residences. And, as Emily Nett concludes, Canadian families prior to this century were more "malleable" in that they contracted and expanded to include both kin and strangers as economic circumstances required.

What all of this should suggest is the importance of social class, of poverty and inequality, in shaping family structure, family relationships, and the power and situation of various family members. Families past or present have had to develop strategies to cope with the uncertainties of the economy and the

insecurities of the marketplace. In any historical period we can find instances where two or more generations shared the same residence but we also find this was not a matter of choice but the result of unemployment or shortage of low cost housing (Nett, 1981).

So, as we look backward and try to describe previous family forms, we must ask which family are we talking about? In the 19th century, for example, working-class children were viewed by their parents as breadwinners and by capitalists as a source of cheap labour. At the same time, in middle and upper class families, children were viewed as innocents in need of nurture and protection. In the middle classes, the home was idealized as a refuge whereas in the lower classes the ravages of capitalism all but destroyed family life. Which family of the past are we talking about when we speak of social change? And, are we comparing the "family of the past" with the "typical" present-day family in a middle class suburb or with the present-day family on social assistance living in one or two room hovels along the roads of Atlantic Canada or struggling to find affordable accommodation in Toronto's overheated real estate and rental market?

Perhaps the most important contribution of this historical research is that it allows us to see that what we assume to be unique to our time—the tensions, the crises, the dilemmas we experience—are enduring, ongoing and possibly inescapable aspects of family life. And what does appear to be changing has been a long time in the making.

While we talk of the process of industrialization as a "revolution" it is obvious that the growth of capitalism and industrialism did not occur over night. Chad Gaffield (1984:22) points out that both involved several transitional stages which affected different regions and industries at different times. It would be unfair to suggest that functionalists were not aware of the transitional nature of the social changes they were considering. But, particularly in their analysis of the declining importance of kinship and its functional necessity, there is a lack of historical accuracy and appreciation of the complexity of the changes they were studying.

One criticism of the functionalist argument is that it is based on a depiction of a family form that never was. The second criticism is that kinship did not lose its importance with the rise of capitalism and industrialism and may, in fact, have become more crucial to people's survival during these momentous changes.

KINSHIP AS RESOURCE

In the 1950s and 1960s a number of sociological studies showed that the family still matters very much in industrial capitalist societies. In what many regard as a classic study, Young and Willmott (1957) used an anthropological approach to show that in Bethnal Green, a working-class district in London, people were very closely linked into a kinship structure and were extremely reluctant to move from the area for that reason.

As they show, with the rise of capitalism and the greater vulnerability which that brought about, both women and men came to rely more on their kin. Women did so because, as we describe later in this Chapter and in Chapter 10, Capitalism and Industrialism, they were now more dependent on their husbands' uncertain wages. Men, too, faced the vulnerability which comes from having to sell one's labour in an impersonal labour market and often depended on family connections to find a job. Since Young and Wilmott, a large number of studies in Britain and North America have produced similar conclusions (Adams, 1970).

Indeed, the role of women as "kin keepers" and the particular importance of kinship to them seems in Quebec to be very similar to the British pattern. Philip Garigue (1957), for example, writing about the same time as Young and Willmott, found that, in Montreal, wives are the ones who kept tabs on the lives not only of their own relatives, but also of their husband's relatives. Similarly, Colette Moreux indicates that at least in the 1960s Quebec nuclear families were embedded in a kinship structure.

Some people in Saint Pierre seem to be spatially surrounded by their kindred, living in a street which bears their name and which an ancestor had acquired so that his numerous children might live there. They may have a sister-in-law living above them, another across the street, their parents on their right, and a brother a little further away . . . . Contacts among relatives are usually frequent and often almost obligatory: so are the quarrels and related tensions. But, the ideal, which most people try to practice, is that quarrels must be patched up and that kin groups must be united at least vis-a-vis non kin, which almost automatically means strangers (1971:128).

Studies in Toronto, Hamilton, Manitoba and Newfoundland were able to show conclusively that these kinds of kinship ties were not restricted to Quebec but could be found among Canadians of various ethnic backgrounds and in different regions of the country (Piddington, 1961; Pineo, 1969; Boissevain, 1970; Irving, 1972; Martin-Matthews, 1976). Tamera Hareven, though writing about the United States, reaches conclusions which are probably true of Canada and most other industrial societies. She points out that

Preindustrial family patterns and values were carried over into the industrial system, providing important continuities between rural and urban industrial life. Rather than being a passive victim, the family was an active agent in the process of industrialization. Families migrated in groups to industrial centers, recruiting workers into the factory system, and often several family members continued to work in the same place. Migration to industrial communities did not break up traditional kinship ties. Rather, families used these ties to facilitate their own transitions into industrial life. . . . While rural/urban or overseas migration temporarily depleted kinship groups, networks were gradually reconstructed in the new location through chain migration (1982: 76-77).

Most of what we know about the role of kinship in industrial society comes from studies of working-class or ethnic communities. It is not surprising that, for those new to a country or who lack economic resources, kinship would continue to be an important resource. With the exception of *Crestwood Heights*, a study done in the 1950s by Seeley and his associates, we know very little about the kinship structure of Canadian middle-class families. This classic study provides strong support for the functionalist arguments. One of their most striking findings was how isolated from kin were these upper-middle class families.

As these sociologists were highly committed to the functionalist perspective, it may be that they were not asking the right questions. Studies in Britain and the United States have shown that in the middle class, as well as in the working class, relatives play a very important role in helping young couples get started (Bell, 1968; Firth and others, 1969). However, what Sussman (1953) called the "help pattern" does not necessarily take the form of finding jobs for young people; it is more directly economic help, often disguised as gifts, "loans" to buy houses and so on (Bell, 1968).

Litwak (1960), who studied the effect of mobility on kinship in the United States, suggested many years ago that the appropriate term to describe modern kinship is *modified extended family*. He points out that "institutional segregation" makes it possible for people to be upwardly mobile and still keep in contact with kin. By this he simply means that we are able to see relatives one day — what Goode (1964) calls "ascriptive" friends — and friends and acquaintances the next day. Who, for instance, has not at one time or another explained to a friend that "I'm busy Sunday, we have relatives coming." The unspoken implication is that no one would willingly choose to spend a day with someone else's relatives if it could be avoided.

There is the possibility, then, that we are able to move fairly readily between family-type relationships and the more impersonal and "objective" relationships which are supposed to characterize business and bureaucracy. Colin Bell (1968) concluded, from his study of middle-class families in Wales, that the two types of relationships can and do coexist; while kinship may be extremely important to people's social and emotional needs, they may, at the same time, be committed to the kinds of norms of business and bureaucracy we have described in Chapter 4, Social Structure.

At this point, the debate between the functionalists and their critics begins to look like a non-debate. We know that the family has changed in some ways. Whether we describe the new norm as a relatively isolated nuclear family or a modified extended family, we know that certain choices are now available to family members, choices that would have been inconceivable even a couple of generations back. Though there are fairly definite and unambiguous commitments between members within the nuclear family, how we should act, what we owe and can expect from other relatives, including our parents (and our grown-up children), is much less clear and far more open to negotiation, circumstances and, ultimately, choice.

Whether we call upon our family members for help, whether we rely upon them for support, whether we restrict our sexual behaviour to our marital partners are now, at least to some extent, matters of choice rather than issues of law or necessity. Morgan (1975) argues that we have a certain amount of leeway about whether to use the kinship structure either to seek help or to pass our benefits to others. If we have been successful financially, for instance, we do not have any clear cut obligations to help out our unemployed brother-in-law or, to reverse the situation, any "legal" right to ask a wealthy brother-in-law for a job. But we often do so.

To the extent that the poor have fewer choices, generally, to the extent that they are more vulnerable, kinship probably remains a valuable resource. One might speculate that the working-class or poor family has changed the least. For the rest, it is probably a matter of degree. It is likely that people will *use* the kinship structure whenever it is to their benefit to do so. For those at the bottom of the class structure, with little in the way of resources at their command, kinship itself is a resource which offers the possibility of mutual aid and exchanges and provides a measure of security against the uncertainties of the labour market. For those more favorably placed, extended family ties are important means of maintaining and enhancing high status. For most of us, family does matter and it is really a question of circumstance whether it matters only socially and emotionally or also economically.

THE FAMILY MATTERS

While the economic benefits of belonging to a family may vary, few would dispute that family matters to us individually. The previous chapter on socialization showed how most of us are, at least in part, shaped by our families. And, as much as we may resent it, the members of our family often continue to exert influence on us long after our childhood. Perhaps the more usual question sociologists have asked is how family matters to society.

Again, how sociologists have answered this question has varied with the perspective of the sociologist. Functionalists have tried to capture how the family serves to contribute to the survival of society and how the functions of the family have changed as societies have changed. Marxists, feminists, and other conflict theorists have focused instead on inequalities within and among families, how the family has been perverted so as to serve the needs of capitalist society and those who benefit most from it.

THE FUNCTIONALISTS

An important assumption of functionalist sociologists and anthropologists is that if the family is a universal institution it must serve some universal functions. What those who are speaking in terms of functions are saying, essentially, is that all societies must somehow cope with their present survival and their biological and social continuity. Somehow, people must be clothed, fed and sheltered; births need to be legitimated; infants and children require regular care and attention; and the culture has to be transmitted to the next generation.

Biological imperatives enter into the picture as well, restricting the range of social arrangements that we can imagine. It takes a male and female to bring about reproduction but women have babies. And those babies are not like little fish which arrive in the world ready to fend for themselves. Humans are born helpless, take a long time to mature and require a good deal of sustained affection and stimulation if they are to be socialized into human beings, all of which suggests some sort of stable relationship such as the family. Also, the fact that there are about as many men as women in the world probably creates considerable pressure towards monogamy and makes polygamy the outcome of unusual circumstances or extreme inequality.

As we discussed, the nuclear family has seemed to many social scientists as universal because many of the functional requirements of society appear everywhere to be fulfilled by it. Kingsley Davis (1948) lists as universal family functions *reproduction, maintenance, placement and socialization*. George Murdock argued that the nuclear family was basic and universal because it most adequately coped with all of the biological and social imperatives making survival possible:

In the nuclear family or its constituent relationships we thus see assembled four functions fundamental to human social life—the sexual, the economic, the reproductive and the educational. Without provision for the first and third, society would become extinct; for the second, life itself would cease; for the fourth, culture would come to an end. The immense social utility of the nuclear family and the basic reason for its universality thus begin to emerge in strong relief (1940:10).

Such a statement leant a kind of solidity to the family, a sense that it is inviolate and cannot be changed. Yet one of the ways in which to view changes in the family is in terms of changes in its functions. William J. Goode, a functionalist theorist who has contributed greatly to our understanding family and society, has suggested that these basic functions should not necessarily be seen as universals fixed for all time but as "variables." The functions of the family, he argued, have more or less importance depending on the type of society, the position of the family within given societies and, as feminists would argue, how we view men's and women's roles.

The class position of the family may have a significant effect on how much attention is paid to legitimacy. Higher status families have more in the way of property and status to pass on to their children than do those at or near the bottom of the class structure and will usually demand greater conformity to the norms of legitimacy. (Though much favoured over the legitimate son, Tom Jones, the "bastard," was not in line to inherit his father's estate.) Likewise, when most positions in a society are *ascribed*, "illegitimate" children pose a considerable threat to the social order since no one knows exactly how to treat them and what rights and obligations accrue to them. In contrast, when status is based at least partly (or ideally) on achievement criteria, the legitimating function may be relatively unimportant. For example, recent family law reform in some Canadian provinces has done away with the concept of illegitimacy entirely; children are children and that is the end of the matter.

Scientific and technological change may also have an effect on the sexual and reproductive functions of the family. For instance, modern contraceptive devices (coupled with changing attitudes about women as property) reduce the need to confine sexual activity within marriage. Even the reproductive function could in principle be divorced from the family. Artificial insemination is a reality and

we are, at the moment, caught up in the legal, moral and social implications of reproductive technologies. This is not to suggest that test tube babies are either desirable or inevitable, but rather that we cannot assume that the family as we know it is the only possible alternative.

At a more prosaic level, it is apparent that many of the family's traditional functions and tasks have, with the development of industrial society, been split away from the family and "parcelled" out to other institutions. Functionalists viewed this as a specific example of a more general process of specialization and differentiation which occurs as societies undergo modernization. The most obvious illustration of this process is education, which now is almost entirely the responsibility of the state. But we can add to this a long list of activities once carried out within the family and the kinship structure. Compared to, say, the pioneer family, food production, much of food preparation, part of child care and recreation are carried out by other specialized agencies and institutions. It is in this sense that we can speak of the family as moving from *production* unit to *consumption* unit; the paid work of family members takes place outside the home and is largely invisible to other members so that the major ties among family members come to centre around leisure and the planning of consumption rather than work.

MODERN FUNCTIONS

At the same time, functionalists such as Talcott Parsons and Neil Smelser argued that we should not assume the modern family is an institution with little to do. Certainly, suggested Parsons, it is true that the family has lost some of its functions but this does not signify its demise or that it has become a useless survival from a bygone era. Rather, it has in his view become specialized in socialization and the emotional support of adult members.

The kind of argument Parsons proposes is that "proper" socialization is necessary for the development of "healthy personalities." As discussed in the previous chapter a variety of studies have shown, for example, that infants receiving good physical care but insufficient cuddling, love, fondling and stimulation by a parent or some substitute can "waste away," even die. Similarly, many researchers have tried to demonstrate a link between delinquency and a lack of love and security during childhood; that is, "inadequate socialization" supposedly produces "unhealthy personalities." This is a murky area indeed given how little we know about what "ideal" socialization would look like and how immersed in moral and value judgement any discussion of "healthy" and "unhealthy" personalities must be.

According to Parsons, the other major function of the modern family is that it acts as a refuge from the pressures of the work world. In a society where many relationships are secondary and where status and self-respect depend on what one achieves (or fails to achieve), the nuclear family is a key primary group where one is a taken-for-granted member, where relationships are warm and affectionate and ends in themselves rather than means to other ends. At home, people can ideally be "themselves," free to recharge their emotional batteries for yet another encounter with the cold, impersonal world of work and bureaucracy. To a great extent, what is supposed to occur in the small private world of the modern family mirrors what occurs societally in traditional or tribal societies—we are taken as we are and can seldom improve or lower our ascribed status through our achievements or failures.

Parsons was, of course, a conservative. For him, the father provided the link between the private world of the family and the relationships of industrial society. The father protected the family from the outside and the mother nurtured it from within. Children needed both for security and comfort, on the one hand, and preparations for the outside world, on the other. One need not accept Parsons's views to appreciate how well he has captured the cultural image of the family that dominated post-war thinking in Canada and the United States. This is what people thought families should be. And, certainly, in the early years of this century, one of the hard fought battles by both the union movement and early feminists was to compel capitalists to pay the "family wage," a wage which would allow women to stay home and look after their husbands and children.

Few would disagree that this family form did serve well to cushion some from the alienation of work in capitalist society and prepare children to take on roles on the outside. Clearly, the family, as Parsons understood it, was functional. What Parsons missed in his analysis was, first, relatively few families ever looked much like his ideal description and second, his model of the functional family meant women had a secondary role both within the family and in society generally.

The model seems to be the American family and the middle-class American family in particular. Parsons ignores, for example, rural families and upper-class and lower-class (especially black) families, which add up to a large body of exceptions within American society alone. Indeed, it often seems that for functionalists, lower-class families, where men have low-paid and low-status work and women are forced by economic circumstances to work outside the home, either are ignored or are viewed as perhaps dangerous "anomalies."

The second problem with Parsons's analysis is that, while he recognized that the sexual division of labour within the modern family could produce strains for both men and women, his emphasis on the benefits or even inevitability of this sexual division of labour may have blinded him to the heavy costs on women of the so-called model family, costs which contributed to the rise of feminism in the 1960s and 1970s.

Most feminists would likely agree that Parsons's depiction of the sexual division of labour and of functions is historically accurate. But, feminist perspectives criticize the language of functionalism and of sex roles because it implies that this dichotomy is somehow "natural" and therefore fixed for all time. Feminists argue instead that with different or equal socialization experiences, both men and women are capable of taking on the socioemotional role and of nurturing children. And, or course, most would argue that both men and women can and should be engaged in work outside the home.

THE MARXIST/FEMINIST APPROACH

Dorothy Smith, over a series of books and articles, has argued that the problem with the functional analysis of the family is not that it is inaccurate but that it is ideological—that it takes for granted rather than challenges the kind of society in which we live and the patriarchal relationships within the family. That is, any list of functions of the family is at least partly a value statement about what the family ought to be and what, ideally, it should do. Yet, if as Smith suggests, we substitute capitalism for "industrialization," then we can begin to ask new questions. We can begin to look at the way in which the modern family is functional in maintaining and upholding a system of class inequality and in exploiting both men and women. The same functions, then, take on a very different cast when viewed from a Marxist perspective:

. . . the home is a place where people are stored when they are not at work, where they are maintained and serviced, fed and cleaned, where they are psychologically repaired and the injuries of the daily routine and tensions generated on the job made good, and where the next generation of employees is produced and trained for their future occupational roles (1973:22).

Smith is not suggesting that the family does not perform certain functions in modern society. She is, rather, asking in whose benefit are these functions or tasks performed? The total society? Family members? Her answer is that the family largely serves the interests of capitalist society; although it was almost demolished during the early stages of capitalism, the family persisted because it seemed to offer a refuge in the face of the ravages of the industrial revolution and the rise of capitalism.

The interests it serves, then, are not, as the functionalists maintain, values of the total society, but of those who benefit from capitalism, the ruling class. Smith argues that the family does not really provide a sanctuary from the consequences of capitalism since its very structure and internal relationships are shaped by the relative success of its members, particularly men, in the labour market. But, as a feminist, it is not surprising that she has focused specifically on the situation of women. She describes their position in the family as essentially a double bind. They are asked to uphold the external moral order which demands that men be "productive" members of society while women in effect stay home to tend the husbands' needs.

THE FAMILY MATTERS FOR WHOM?

At this point in our discussion you may feel somewhat confused — and with good reason because these discussions of the functions of the family contain within them several levels of confusion and controversies which are central to the enduring debate we have described in Chapter I, between functionalist and conflict theorists. As we have just seen, while social historians have show that functionalists probably underestimated the complexities of social change generally and family change specifically, no one denies that the family matters. A fundamental difference between functionalists and Marxists is not about the importance of the family for capitalism and industrialism but whether the functions the family serves are in the best interests of society generally.

At the risk of some simplification we can say that functionalists view the family and its functions as contributing to the integration of industrial society and as helping family members to fit into that society. Marxists, conflict theorists, view the family as an institution which has been bent in ways which serve capitalism and, as we shall see in later chapters, the interests of the few.

There is, however, another level of confusion: are we talking about whether family matters for the society or for the individual? As we have seen, functionalists felt that the changes taking place within the family were simply responses to the demands of capitalism and industrialism for individualism rather than allegiance to kinship and community. But, there is a kind of sexist myopia in this analysis. It is assumed that men are the only ones to be involved in the labour force or to become capitalists. Feminist theory and research has, in forcing a rethinking of the family, forced us to focus on how the changing functions and structure of the family have had different consequences for men and for women.

WOMEN AND THE FAMILY

THE PRE-CAPITALIST FAMILY

Earlier, we noted that social historians have provided us with new insights into the family of the past and dispelled many of the myths surrounding it. At the same time, the attempt of this more recent social history, to understand the past from the perspective of the less powerful members of society, has had the important spin-off that we now know much more about the role of women within the family and in the economy generally and how this has changed.

Much of this work has also taken place within a Marxist perspective and has led both

to a further criticism of functionalism and to new questions about and explanations of women's unequal position within the family and capitalism. This historical research has focused on how changes in the mode of production and the nature of work have led to change in the family and the position of women within it and the larger society.

According to this work, before the industrial revolution and capitalism the family had become so developed it was a closely integrated unit. This was because the family was often the unit of production, with the crucial division of labour being between members of the family who worked at different tasks, largely agricultural, later "cottage" industries.

Essentially, the pre-capitalist and pre-industrial family was patriarchal. That is, it was presided over by the husband who legally and often in practice was the undisputed master. But though women and children were punished harshly and often beaten, they were also crucial to the operation of the farm. Women were often able to earn more from their work than could their husbands. As Young and Willmott point out:

It was probably the exceptional wife who was not beaten by her husband, sometimes brutally; and her love, if she had any, was often alloyed with fear of her master. But when so much depended on the person to whom God had joined him, it would have been cutting his own throat to antagonize her too much (1973:67).

As long as the family was the basic unit of production, women were part of the economy; their labour in the household was not simply housework, it was what Marxists call *productive labour*. That is, what was produced within the household contributed to the Gross National Product and at a later point also to the profits of the capitalists.

THE CAPITALIST FAMILY

Gradually, from the beginnings of the nineteenth century, the family lost its economic functions to industry much as it would later lose some of its educational ones to the school. As we shall see in later chapters, capitalist development involves, among other things, the centralization of production in factories. This in turn had important consequences for relationships between family members. As E. P. Thompson, the historian, puts it:

Each stage in industrial differentiation and specialization struck also at the family economy, disturbing customary relations between man and wife, parents and children and differentiating more sharply between "work" and "life" . . . The family was roughly torn apart each morning by the factory bell (1963:416).

Of particular importance in the family of capitalism was that the situation of women in the working class worsened appreciably. Unless they were working outside the home, which was only possible in certain localities and industries, they were now no longer part of the economy. Whereas in the pre-capitalist family, women had some control over their economic situation, with the growth of industrial capitalism, they became dependent upon their husbands and much more under their power. No longer could women produce food and clothing for themselves and their children; they now required cash for these things and yet, the husband's wage was viewed as his to be spent as he saw fit.

As early as 1851, Mayhew, a British social researcher, wrote about the lot of costermongers' (street merchants') wives.

The costermongers strongly resemble the North American Indians in their conduct to their wives. They can understand that it is the duty of the women to contribute to the happiness of the man but cannot feel there is a reciprocal duty from the man to the woman. The wife is considered as an inexpensive servant and the disobedience of a wish is punished by blows . . . Often, when the man is in one of his drunken fits—which sometimes lasts two or three days continuously—she must by her sole exertion find food for herself, and him too. To live in peace with him there must be no murmuring, no tiring under work, no fancied cause for jealousy—for if there be, she is either beaten into submission or cast adrift to begin life again—as another's leavings (quoted in Young and Willmott, 1973:76).

We cannot, of course, be totally without sympathy for the predicament of men during this long period, to the kinds of forces which apparently drove people to drink, to violence and to selfishness. While as *wage earners* men may have been all-powerful within the home, their work worlds were often abysmal. And after long days in a factory, down a coal mine or on the streets selling, the pub was probably far more congenial than the squalor of a nineteenth century working-class home.

As Zaretsky (1976:29) argues, "male supremacy (patriarchy), which long antedated capitalism, became an institutional part of the capitalist system of production." One indication of this is that, as in most patriarchal societies, the company of men was now felt to be more desirable than that of women and children, thus creating even greater separation between home, work and leisure. (One need only visit the Italian or Portugese sections of Toronto to see this still in operation—cafes and bars are almost exclusively filled with men. Similarly, in Quebec, taverns, until the introduction of *brasseries*, were legally restricted to men.)

Even where men were more humane to their wives and children, they were still faced with low-paid and irregular employment, squalid living conditions and the constant threat of the poorhouse, which could fragment and eventually destroy families as successfully as the "factory bell." Capitalism and the rise of industry created new forms of vulnerability for men as well as for women and their children.

CONSEQUENCES FOR WOMEN

But many would argue that the changes for women caused by the rise of capitalism were more momentous than they were for men. For women the rise of industrial capitalism had several consequences. The first is that extended kinship relations became female-centred rather than male-centred. When husbands could not be relied upon to provide economic security, either because they were spending most of the income on alcohol and tobacco or because they were unemployed, women began to build an informal organization with other women in their own defence and in the defence of their children. It was, as Young and Willmott put it, "an informal women's trade union" composed of strong ties between mother and daughter and at times sister and sister.

Although nominally patriarchal, under capitalism the family became in effect *matrilocal*. That is, after marriage, daughters brought their husbands home to live until suitable accommodation could be found in close proximity. Mothers provided their daughters with security, knowledge and practical assistance. Frequently, they freed daughters from child rearing and made it possible for them to work outside the home. In turn, as mothers grew old the flow of services was reversed and they looked to daughters to support and care for them in their old age. Something of this is caught in the old rhyme:

A son is a son till he takes a wife,
A daughter's a daughter for the rest of her life.

Young and Willmott are describing a family form typical in Britain up until about the 1950s, one which is insightfully caught in the cartoon strip *Andy Capp*. But this same "union of women" has also been found in other societies where the position of women is particularly weak. This pattern was imported into English Canada by the nineteenth and early twentieth century British immigrants and developed independently in Quebec. There is also independent evidence in Canada and the United States that the capitalist family and its effect on the situation of women was very similar to what developed in Britain.

A second consequence was the emergence of social movements designed to improve the situation of women. Universal suffrage is what we remember most about the feminist movement of the early decades of this century. But equally, if not more, significant was the strong link between this movement and the temperance movement. Women such as Nellie McClung were less concerned with equal pay, child care and sexual inequality — issues central to Women's Liberation in the 1960s and 1970s — than they were with getting legislation passed that would give women some control over their own destiny, some protection for themselves and their children, some say over how their husband's pay cheque was spent (Roberts, 1976). For example beer parlours, at least in the Prairie Provinces, were forced to close over the supper hour, presumably so that men would remain sober enough to remember that they had better take home the pay cheque before it all went in one evening (see Gray, 1970).

A third consequence of changes within the capitalist family and the nature of work was the creation of the base for gender-based occupational segregation and inequality. So entrenched were the role and status of women within the family, that when women did enter the labour force, the occupations available to them were those consistent with their familial roles — maid or seamstress, nurse or teacher, and later social worker.

While we can understand occupational segregation in cultural terms, that is in terms of perceptions held about and often by women, this does not provide a complete explanation of occupational inequality. Why has "women's work" been lower paid and why have working women, in whatever jobs, been paid less than men doing the same or equivalent work? Part of the answer may be that women's work was culturally less valued or was seen as only marginal to the "real" work world as it was so often an extension of the unpaid labour done in the home.

Marxists provide an explanation based on the structure of capitalist society. They argue that, in the capitalist system, the wage paid to men was viewed as family income. Any money paid to women, then, was treated as "pin money," a bonus or at best a *second* income. This allowed women to be treated as a "reserve army of labour," prepared to fill in as necessary, take on a range of often menial tasks and expect and accept relatively little remuneration.

It is important to emphasize that women in all stages of family evolution have played a crucial role in family strategies for survival. In special circumstances, when husbands are ill, when women are widowed, when there is a special need for resources, or in enduring conditions of poverty, women have worked inside and outside the home. And their work has contributed to the household economy. In capitalist society, that contribution has been little recognized and less rewarded. There is, however, a growing body of research that demonstrates women's contribution to household income. This has been shown more tangibly, for example, in changing divorce legislation that gives formal recognition to the wife's contribution to household income and assets.

A fourth and major consequence of capitalism was that to the extent that women were able to remain at home and "be provided for" by their husbands, they became isolated from the world of work as defined in a capitalist society. Productive labour was that which happened outside of the home and which made profits for the capitalists. Domestic labour, work within the home, again from the point of view of the capitalist, becomes unproductive labour. However necessary this kind of labour actually is, being "just a housewife" brought with it economic dependence and low social standing relative to wage earning males.

Some have argued that housewives may be compared to a class which has not become "aware of itself" or conscious of its objective interests. Isolated and separate from one another, housewives begin to view their problems—boredom and dissatisfaction, depression and low self-esteem, fear to try anything new and feelings of uselessness—as "private" troubles rather than "public" issues (Conelly and Christian-Ruffman, 1976; Oakley, 1974).

Especially in the middle class, then, having to say that one is "just a housewife" is indeed problematic. It is not likely to make one the centre of attention at a cocktail party, for instance, but more crucially, the housewife role is one which seems purposely built to undermine the confidence of those who practice it. Morgan notes the following about this role:

The job is unpaid and carried out in relative isolation from others, with the exception of children who may be defined as "getting in the way." With a split between home and work we get a loss of an objective standard by which to measure oneself and one's actions. Status is not a fixed thing, a static evaluation, but an ongoing accomplishment. Where there are relatively few others who are in a position to evaluate one's work and activity, one's status and identity becomes much less certain (1975:141–142).

Some of what we have just described may strike you as simply an image of the "bad old past." Surely, you may be thinking, this brief account of the family, the situation of women and children as capitalism developed may have been true for your grandparents but not for your parents and will certainly not apply to you. If a man, you probably anticipate being involved in parenting and imagine that your wife will be in the labour force. If a woman, you anticipate, take for granted, that, like your husband, you will have a career. And, because you will probably follow the norm and have only one or two children (1.7 if you want to be perfectly average), you are aware that even if you do choose to reject day care and to stay at home while your children are babies, this will probably be only a temporary disruption of your work life outside the home. And, you anticipate that your husband will also be involved in the raising of the children and will be equally involved in other domestic duties. In other words, we guess that you have expectations of marriage and family life based on greater equality and symmetry of marital roles.

THE SYMMETRICAL FAMILY

In tracing the development of family and marriage under various stages of capitalism, this was precisely the argument advanced by Young and Willmott (1973). They argued that the capitalist family is in the process of moving into a third stage, what they referred to as the **symmetrical family**. By "symmetrical," they are drawing attention, first, to the fact that, inside marriage, the roles of men and women are becoming less segregated. Women are more likely to be in the labour force; men are more likely than in the past to "help out" around the home, doing work which was traditionally woman's work — changing diapers, washing dishes, cooking and so on.

Second, as they argue, family life has become more "privatized." That is, both men and women have turned inward to the conjugal family so that relatives and work friends count for less, immediate family members count for more. Young and Willmott argue that now there is much greater emphasis on companionship in modern marriage, a much greater emphasis on spending leisure time together and in planning and making purchases for the home jointly. They do not, of course, argue that total symmetry of roles has been accomplished but that there are economic, cultural and demographic forces pushing the family in this direction:

By the next century society will have moved from (a) one demanding job for the wife and one for the husband, through (b) two demanding jobs for the wife and one for the husband to (c) two demanding jobs for the wife and two for the husband. The symmetry will be complete. Instead of two jobs there will be four (Young and Willmott, 1973:278).

However, many would argue that this is a too sanguine picture of the modern family and a too optimistic prognosis of its future and of the role and situation of women in marriage and family. No doubt, as Young and Willmott and others have argued, there are, compared to the past, certainly what might be called "strains" towards greater equality, greater symmetry within modern marriages. At the same time, patterns of mate selection tend to undermine these changes and perpetuate traditional inequalities within the family.

It is, for example, still viewed as problematic by many Canadians if men marry women older than themselves. And, related to this, is the cultural ideal that women should not have a higher income, a better education and more upward mobility potentials than their husbands, all of which tips the balance of power towards men. We do not know whether these are conscious factors in mate selection. But, they are social facts which we must take into account because they do shape relations within the family. Generally, men marry women who are younger and who earn less than themselves. The combination of relative youth and/or lower qualifications means that the wife's contribution to family income rarely exceeds 50 percent of the husband's contribution. Women, by and large, are "junior partners" in the marriage and this means that their role within the family is likely to be subordinate to their husbands'.

There is the old problem of assessing whether the glass is half empty or half full: should we congratulate ourselves on the progress we have made towards equality, or should we be concerned with the distance we have yet to go before we reach real sexual equality? Feminists have generally taken the second view and have pointed out that sociologists of the family (who in the past were usually male) have exaggerated the advances women have made within and without the family, economically, legally and socially. They are more likely to point to the unequal strains that marriage and child rearing place on women, how women's position within the family is essentially subservient and what a good "deal" men get from marriage (Eichler, 1988).

Nor is the situation of working wives without problems. Research that has looked at what people *actually* do, rather than at what they say they do (as in the Young and Willmott study), shows that the egalitarian or symmetrical family is an overly optimistic concept. For instance, two Canadian studies, one on the east coast, one on the west coast, which have used time diaries, come up with the unexpected finding that when women go out to work, men's work and leisure time show very little change (Meissner and others, 1975; Clark and Harvey, 1976). Rather, what seems to happen is that men go on much as they did when their wifes were at home, whereas women's work increases dramatically.

Overall, the amount of time spent on housework declines somewhat but men do not take on extra jobs around the house. They continue to do the same stereotyped jobs — washing the car, mowing the lawn, shovelling snow — that they have "always" done, while women simply work much harder within and outside the home. And even when men do take on extra jobs around the house, this is usually in the form of "helping out": doing the dishes, putting the children to bed once in a while, reading them a story, cooking the odd meal. Rarely, it seems, do husbands take equal responsibility for planning the week's menu, setting up dental appointments for the children, redecorating the living room and so forth. We seem, in other words, to be stuck at the second of Young and Willmott's stages of two-jobs-for-the-wife and one-for-the-husband pattern.

In sum, while men are quite obviously more family oriented than in the past, more involved with child care and the running and maintenance of the home, we have some way to go before it can be said that the typical marriage is in fact a symmetrical marriage. Nevertheless, the concept of symmetrical family may be becoming a standard against which married partners judge themselves, the increasingly accepted ideal. This slow process to greater equality and less segregation provides the context for understanding con-temporary patterns of marriage and divorce in Canada.

CANADIAN PATTERNS: MARRIAGE, DIVORCE, REMARRIAGE

LOVE AND MARRIAGE

One song tells us that love and marriage go together like a horse and carriage. But there is another song in another musical, *Fiddler on the Roof*, in which, after several decades of marriage, Tevye asks his wife, "Do you love me?" She evades his question and counters by reciting the many ways in which she has fulfilled the many duties that make up the role of the good Jewish wife. For her, as for most people in the world, love, or the lack of love, is irrelevant. What counts and what are grounds for complaint (or satisfaction) are how well each marriage partner has lived up to the role obligations that tradition has ordained.

According to Hugo Beigel (1952), love has gone through three phases in Western societies, the courtly love of the twelfth and thirteenth centuries, its revival in the eighteenth and nineteenth centuries, and finally the "romantic love complex" of the twentieth century. But only in this last phase has it anything to do with marriage.

We are all familiar with cartoons showing the lady in the tower bidding farewell to her brave knight who is about to ride off to battle, her "favour" tucked carefully in the sleeve of his armour. But as Beigel points out, both are in fact married—to other people. It could not have been otherwise since their parents would have chosen their marriage partners perhaps even before they were born. Nor was an "affair" in the offing. Like adolescent or puppy love (at least until recently), courtly love was based on celibacy, perhaps frustration and certainly idealization of the other partner. Men in the upper classes married in order to produce heirs, could and did rape peasant girls as they rode off to the crusades or other battles and could put certain women on "pedestals." Beigel suggests that when love reemerged in the eighteenth and nineteenth centuries it was no longer celibate and idealistic. But while sex and love had become intermingled, the love object was seldom, if ever, one's spouse — it was still someone else's. Hence the rise of "lovers" and "mistresses."

The third stage is one with which we are thoroughly familiar: the rise of what is usually called the ***romantic love complex***. Richard Udry (1974:137) describes it as the myth that "for every girl there is a boy; when they know each other they will fall in love, experience bliss and live together happily ever after." Ralph Linton, an anthropologist, pointed out many years ago that American culture is unique in that it has attempted to capitalize on and make as the basis of marriage selection that which is in most cultures viewed as aberrant, irrational and undesirable—romantic love (Linton, 1936:175). Linton could, of course, quite easily have included Canada, the country wherein *Harlequin* romances originate, in his generalization.

Are we any longer ready to accept the romantic images of Harlequin Romances and Hollywood film makers? Or, has the questioning about the family and family relationships helped to debunk or at least to make us wary of the notion of romantic love? When we talk about marriage for love, we are not talking about people's motives. The motives or reasons for marrying one person or another are always complex decisions shaped by many factors, social, economic, and personal. Romantic love is ideological in that it emphasizes personal choice; it sets certain criteria for mate selection (for example, virginal and sexually attractive women) and it allows us to explain to ourselves and others, our choices.

We are now probably less naive about the extent to which our choice of partners is free from social influences such as religion and ethnic and class background. And, it is no longer as legitimate to judge women in terms of their previous sexual background and present attractiveness. The old symbols of romance—dates, flowers and candies—were tied to sexual inequality, and songs such as "Diamonds are a Girl's Best Friend" spoke to women's dependancy and vulnerability. All of these images have become increasingly intolerable to most Canadians. Perhaps with greater sexual equality, we have to redefine our notions of love and perhaps, too, the symbols of love — that must become symbols based on equality.

As women become less dependent on men, in fact their competitors, perhaps marriage, with or without romantic love, becomes again a question of partnerships and alliances where it makes sense to talk about marriage contracts and to formalize the distribution of family assets should the marriage fail. Marriage is apparently moving from institution, through love to companionship and perhaps contract.

In our view, this represents an important change that sociologists, including ourselves, only dimly understand. It is of course perfectly possible that, as with most sociologists, we have for too long been out of the "dating and mating game" to appreciate the present-day subtleties and complexities of how young people do get together and marry. But, we have asked our students to comment on the now dated literature on dating and mate selection and there is consensus that the formalized rituals of dating, going steady, "pinning" and engagement probably no longer exist for most young Canadians. In their place are such concepts as "hanging out together" (platonic) and "Seeing a lot of each other" (apparently not platonic). Early sexual activity, living together, testing relationships and delaying marriage until after such tests, are all — relatively speaking — new phenomena that have not been subject to the same kind of investigation as were earlier patterns of dating and mate selection. Much remains to be learned about the emotional and social dimensions of "courtship and marriage" in contemporary Canada.

OUT-MARRIAGE, IN-MARRIAGE

Why do attitudes differ so dramatically between our Western culture and others, past and present? William Goode (1959) has suggested that the answer is to be found in the degree of importance that marriage has for the society and the kinship structure. Marriage, according to Levi-Strauss (1956:65), is an effective means of forming alliances with potential enemies. As he says, in many tribal societies, "one either marries out or gets killed out." The same principle was at work when even as yet unborn children of one European monarch were promised in marriage to the children of another, thereby turning possible war into an alliance.

More generally, suggests Goode, who marries whom can be disregarded and left to romantic attraction only when there is no property, power or titles to be passed through the kinship structure. Normally, he points out, "both mate choice and love are too important to be left to children." In other words, it is only when parents or society have little to gain or lose by the union that marriage selection is "unrestricted" and not arranged by the parents on behalf of the children.

Throughout most of history love relationships have been seen as potentially disruptive to stratification systems and to the existing social order, based as it is on strong racial, ethnic, and religious ties that define who is out-group, who is in-group. Increasingly, however, the importance of family as the formal unit of stratification is, for most segments of society, declining.

Farmers and ranchers who typically pass on their property to sons are a notable exception. They have some interest in whom their sons choose as marriage partners. The "right" marriage may sometimes mean a consolidation of two properties into one; the "wrong" marriage may mean that if a divorce occurs the wife will, under most marital property acts in Canada, be legally entitled to half of the assets, thus diminishing the family property.

For similar reasons, those at the top of the class structure who have considerable wealth, status, and power to pass on may be very concerned about who comes into the family. But the vast majority of people have neither wealth nor power to preserve, nor alliances to maintain and consolidate. So, suggests Goode, the precise nature of the marriage union is not so crucial as it was in earlier periods or in other societies.

Of course, marriage is never totally unrestricted. Our "field of eligibles" never includes everyone in the society. All societies, including our own, have formal and informal rules about **exogamy**—what group we must marry outside of — and **endogamy** — what out-groups are ineligible as sources of marriage partners. An exogamous rule is that it is illegal to marry anyone within our own kinship structure such as brothers, sisters, grandparents, an aunt, an uncle and so on. These, by law, are declared *incestuous* marriages even when there is no "blood" relationship between the two people. Endogamous rules, formal or informal, also limit our choice of marriage partners. Tradition in India, for example, prohibited marriage outside one's caste and, historically, it was illegal in most parts of the United States for blacks and whites to inter-marry.

In Canadian society there are few formalized rules about endogamy. Theoretically, we are free to marry virtually anyone who is outside our kinship network. In practice, there is obviously considerable pressure from family and community for us to marry someone within our religious group, our community, our social class, our ethnic community and so on.

There is, then, a tendency in Canada, as elsewhere, towards *homogamy* — marriage to someone roughly the same background and religion as ourselves. While most of us want to marry for love and most probably do so, marriage patterns suggest that other factors come into play, making falling in love less random and unpredictable than our myths and assumptions sometimes led us to believe. It seems that while people want to marry for love, the field of eligible mates and love partners is seriously curtailed by personal choice, family influences, and beliefs about the consequences for marriages of too much difference in backgrounds. People, consciously or unconsciously, may avoid situations where they run the risk of falling in love with the "wrong sort of person."

Something of this process is caught in the statement, "I want to marry for love, but why can't I fall in love with someone who is rich?" The implication is that there are a lot of potential partners, so that who we fall in love with depends on whom we are exposed to. Parents who move to a better district or who encourage their children to belong to a religious youth group are in effect acting on this assumption, trying to stack the cards in favour of a "love match" that is also a "socially acceptable" match.

CHOOSING MARRIAGE

Whether based on a desire for love, or on more "practical" considerations, most contemporary Canadians marry. But, while the marriage rate generally rose over the first half of this century and people progressively married at a younger age, a rather dramatic change began to occur in the late 1960s. Table 6.1 contains a number of pieces of information about the present Canadian family. It is evident that while, in 1965, most (95 percent) people married, this figure has fallen to 86 percent. And, the age at which both men and women marry has increased.

In earlier editions of this text we suggested that the very high rates of marriage and the age at which people marry, gave Canada very much the look of a "married up" society and that single people formed a much smaller minority of the population today than at any time in the past. We would still have to cling to that same conclusion but with less tenacity than ten years ago. Men, we suspect, still want to marry, because consciously or unconsciously, they recognize that it is in their best interests to do so. Women, again consciously or unconsciously, appear to recognize the costs marriage may have for them and some

TABLE 6.1

INDICATORS OF FAMILY-RELATED DEMOGRAPHIC CHANGES, CANADA, 1965 AND 1985.

	1965	1985
Divorce		
Percent of marital dissolutions due to		
—divorce	11	42
—death of a spouse	89	58
Nuptiality		
Median age at first marriage		
—women	21.2	23.7
—men	23.7	25.6
Proportion of adults expected to marry	95	86
Percent of 18-29 who have ever been in common-law unions		23*
Fertility		
Total fertily rate (average births per woman)	3.1	1.7
Median age of women at first birth	22.9	25.4

*1884
Source: R. Beaujot, "The Family in Crisis," *Canadian Journal of Sociology* 13(3) (1988:306).

resist it. And, though most in the end do marry, Table 6.1 suggests that they have fewer children and do so later in their life.

Nevertheless, most people do marry or form common-law relationships and will probably continue to do so in the future. Except in big cities, those who do not marry find few institutional alternatives still intact that would substitute for family life. And when they turn to former friends, now married, they are likely to feel left out and find that there is little space in the intimate and insular environment except perhaps for other married couples. Later, the birth of children excludes even further the single person from the institutions and lifestyles of the "married up" society.

Are new patterns of marriage evolving? Certainly the demographic conditions have changed. People live longer; consequently marriage "for life" is a longer term proposition. Children will probably move away while their parents are still quite young but, at the same time, longer life expectancies will mean they may have obligations to parents until they themselves are quite old.

Not only have the demographics of marriage and family life changed, so too have the social and cultural conditions. It is probably true that the shift from institution to companionship means that fewer Canadians are marrying with the same sense of certainty or fatalism as in the past. Ask yourself, for example, what one should do in a marriage that is not working. When do we know that a marriage is not working? Is divorce a solution even for families with children? Certainly your answers to such questions are very different than they would have been in the nineteenth century.

A liberal ideology has allowed us to view self-fulfillment, the pursuit of individual projects, as both legitimate and worthy goals. When we think of rights, we think not of rights of the family but of individual rights, of rights of wives, of husbands, and of children. The family must not interfere with these rights and individual pursuits. When it does we are jus-

tified in escaping. The stigma of divorce is disappearing; we no longer feel the need to see one partner judged guilty in the break-up; and a generation or more of children is learning that it is quite normal for Mother and Father to live in different houses and to have different spouses. A new concern for children's rights, for developing new forms of custody relationships, for developing new methods of mediation and conciliation to make divorce easier and less painful all might be seen to reflect our taken-for-granted acceptance of the legitimacy of divorce as a solution.

But think of the irony. We have described how capitalism is a system marked by new forms and layers of vulnerability. We learn to package and sell ourselves in the marketplace. We measure ourselves and are measured by our occupational and material attainments and these are, for most of us, outside our control. Many of us feel alienated in our work. Many of us feel insecure and afraid. And the marriage rates in Canada would indicate that many of us hope to find love, meaning, a sense of security and wholeness in the intimacy of our families.

Does our liberal ideology make this impossible? Can each of us make our personal projects our first priority and still find all of this in family life? We might ask, as well, how often we blame the persistent insecurities, our depressions and dissatisfactions on our families rather than on the social structures or ourselves. The family, then, seems to have become many different things: a temporary refuge, a medium for self-fulfillment, a source of meaning, a scapegoat for our failures. And the family cannot be all of these things (see Himelfarb, Lazar and Richardson, 1980). Perhaps, too, as we move away from the notions of romantic love, our expectations about marriage may be, to some extent, more realistic. And, if true, this may not be altogether bad.

Some sociologists have argued that the high expectations people have of marriage put a very heavy strain on the social fabric. Ernest van den Haag points out that:

Marriage was to cement the family by tying people together "till death do us part" in the face of the fickleness of their emotions ... Marriage differed from a love affair inasmuch as it continued regardless of love. Cupid shoots his arrows without rhyme or reason. But marriage is a deliberate rational act, a public institution making the family independent of Cupid's whims ....

Instead of saying "till death do us part" we might say "till we get bored with each other"; and instead of "forsaking all others", "till someone better comes along." Clearly, if the couple intend to stay "married" only as long as they want to, they only pretend to be married; they are having an affair with legal trimmings (1974:141).

Van den Haag advocates that for romantic love, we substitute affection, a sentiment which comes not from the "chemistry" of a first encounter, but which emerges over time as people live and work together. Those who have studied "successful" and "unsuccessful" marriages lend support to this view. In the place of enduring love, intimacy and sexual attraction, they are forced to speak of processes of "disenchantment," "disengagement" and "corrosion." Pineo (1961), for example, argues that the free selection of mates means that the couple begins marriage with a maximum of love and compatibility. The result is that they have nowhere to go but down. So, some degree of disenchantment may be an almost inevitable outcome of modern marriages. Marriages that do survive and that seem "healthy" are those in which people have somewhat lower expectations. They do not define "a good marriage as an intimate, intense, emotional relationship but rather as a practical, friendly, but business-like way of arranging their lives" (Skolnick, 1973:215).

None of this tell us which marriages will succeed, which will fail. Sociology is probably weakest in its understanding of human intimacy and the passions of love and hate, intimate indifference and sometimes physical violence that can characterize sexual relations. How some can stay together in apparently destructive relationships and others drift apart from what appears to be a mutually healthy relationship is rarely, if ever, understood.

THE FAMILY IN CRISIS

Many critics of marriage and family have begun to look at the consequences of the modern family for all members, women certainly, but men and children as well. Richard Sennett (1970), for example, speaks of the "brutality of the modern family." He contrasts life at the turn of the century (in the United States) with modern suburban life. He suggests that while what we have described as the capitalist family was often poverty stricken, it had a richer social life. People lived in over-crowded, often squalid slums but they, at any rate, were in close contact with one another. There were "escape valves" in the form of clubs, bars, coffee shops, relatives and the street itself. People had to come into contact with a lot of other people simply to get by at all.

Of course, not all of these contacts were necessarily idyllic; one has only to read Mordecai Richler's accounts of growing up on St. Urbain Street in Montreal to realize conflict with neighbours, rent agents, and storekeepers was endemic. But whether relationships between people were based on conflict or harmony there was, nevertheless, contact with people of various ages, ethnicities, religions and temperaments. Sennett contrasts this with the situation of the average suburban nuclear family that is insular, isolated and segregated from the greater part of society.

Moreover, the symmetrical family ideal is premised on equality that forces men and women for the first time in history to be "friends" together and with their children. Conflict, which is inevitable, is no longer acceptable. There is what Sennett calls a "guilt over conflict syndrome": one should not argue in front of the children; spats between husband and wife become grounds for divorce. For Sennett, the real "brutality" of the family lies in its insularity and *privatization*: people outside the family, including relatives (especially old people), cease to be real, to be individuals to whom we owe sympathy or obligation.

The conviction that a family is the whole social arena in a microcosm stifles parents and children both in an obvious and in a subtle way. Clearly, no bond of four or five people represents the full spectrum of attitudes and human traits to be found in the wider society. The family as a world of its own can therefore become highly exclusive . . . It is a short step from concentrating on one's own home affairs to sanctioning terrible repressions of disturbance from below: if the poor are silenced, then there need be no intrusions on the "meaningful" circle of one's own life, the intimate relationships between Pop, Mom and the kids (1970:33).

Is this an exaggerated, perhaps unduly pessimistic view of the modern family? We would like to think so but there is growing evidence that the family has its dark side as well as its "happy family" mode. Novelists and dramatists, too, often depict how family members conspire, consciously or unconsciously, to drive another member insane or how couples remain together through bonds of hate rather than of love. As Morgan (1975:103) concludes, art and social science are in accord that family life is two-edged: "one edge is warm, protective and fiercely loyal while the other edge is destructive, narrow and ultimately violent."

Violence in the family is not new. It is probably not even increasing, though we do not know this for sure. Family violence — against wives, children, or grandparents — is, however, now recognized in all its brutality. It is not new but it is no longer tolerable. Those who in the course of their professional work deal with children are now required to report suspected cases of child abuse. Police in Canada no longer treat wife assault as a private matter. It is necessarily treated as a crime. But, only as women are fully equal to men and are free from economic dependancy will it be possible to break the vicious cycle of violence that generations of wives have endured.

However much violence there may have been in the past, contemporary family violence has been made visible to all of us and we have come to see it as an important social problem. Steinmetz and Strauss (1974:50), who have studied violence in the family, conclude that "violence seems as typical of family relationships as love."

Various studies indicate that the "battered baby syndrome," once thought to be limited to broken and disreputable families, is probably the monopoly of no single type of family. Rather, battering, physical, and sexual abuse and neglect seem to be the product of three or more generations of what culturally may be thought of as normal parent-child relationships. "The battering parent is the battered child grown up" (Van Stolk, 1970), a view at least partly shared by others who have more recently studied the parents of battered children (Lenton, 1990).

Naturally not all families generate or accentuate violence. But even without these, the nuclear family has appeared to many to be in a state of crisis. Generally, it seems no longer capable of encompassing the intense individualism, the concern with personal happiness and projects, that characterize contemporary capitalist society and which were once limited to men but now apply equally to both sexes.

In Chapter 8, we will see that it has often been possible to link demographic changes such as age at marriage, marriage, and fertility rates to economic changes such as depressions and periods of economic prosperity. And earlier, we suggested that the Canadian family has experienced a number of demographic changes. But, some of these changes, notably a lower marriage rate and a birth rate well below replacement levels, began only in the mid-1960s, a period of relative economic stability.

As Roderic Beaujot (1988:308) has recently noted, the rather abrupt changes in the demography and structure of families after 1965 (See Table 6.1) seem to be a result of a fundamental change in the very "logic of family life." In the mid-1960s, people, he argues, began to feel less constrained by external or traditional norms. Women, in effect, became as men had been for a considerable time, part of the "me" generation: women, too, began to put their own interests above those of family and either rejected marriage entirely or drastically reduced their fertility.

For Beaujot, a demographer, the crisis is not in the family *per se* but "between the interests of women on the one hand and the reproduction of society on the other hand." As we have described, marriage and child rearing impose greater costs for women than for men and until these inequalities change, until, as Young and Willmott optimistically anticipated, men and women both have two jobs, one inside the home and one outside, it is safe to say that the present-day nuclear family is in something of a crisis. And, this has led to greater fragility of marital relationships.

SEPARATION AND DIVORCE

Not long ago, textbooks on the sociology of marriage and family devoted only a short chapter to divorce and a few paragraphs to remarriage families. More recently, with the exception of family violence and child abuse, no other family issue has captured as much attention as marriage breakdown and its consequences. Certainly, popular perceptions of the divorce rate often exaggerate the extent of marriage breakdown in Canadian society. But there is no doubt that divorce is a sufficiently pervasive and, perhaps, normative aspect of family life as to cause us to change our attitudes about it and its consequences.

Two or three decades ago, divorce was most often seen as disastrous—a singular and unusual event that undermined and destroyed the family and family relationships. Children of divorce were depicted as "products of broken homes," victims to be pitied. However, in the 1970s a more positive view of divorce as a possible solution rather than the problem emerged. The Law Reform Commission of Canada (1975), for example, suggested that divorce is not necessarily destructive of family life. Since many divorcees remarry, divorce may, at times, offer a constructive solution to marital conflict.

Similarly, Ann Marie Ambert (1980:10) began her Canadian study by depicting divorce "as a normal process with specific tasks to be mastered, recognizable stress to be dealt with and satisfaction and goals to be sought for." And many researchers concerned about children in divorce came to the conclusion that often times such children are better off living in a divorced family than in an unhappy, perhaps violent, intact family environment.

However common divorce may be statistically, it is probably never a normative or routine event to those involved. Studies of divorce and marriage breakdown generally show that the reality is almost invariably some degree of trauma and disruption for all family members. It seems to matter little who initiated the divorce; both spouses find their lives disrupted and both are likely to experience a variety of conflicting emotions ranging from feelings of rejection, anger and bitterness to ambivalent relief that an unhappy situation has ended (Cherlin, 1978). And, since small children, more than anyone else, live their lives in the circumscribed world of the family, changes in its patterns or structures have, in the short run at least, momentous impact on their lives. They are caught up in a series of life changes not of their devising, over which they have little control and from which, often, they have little to gain. Yet, these changes strike at the very core of their world (Richardson, 1988).

As well, divorce and the family patterns that develop from it have consequences that go beyond the immediate family. The breakdown of marriage brings about an obvious change in family structure but also a restructuring and reorganizing of family ties and kinship relations. It shatters taken-for-granted notions of what is meant by a family and how, as a small group, a family relates to other families and the community. Divorce, rather than ending the family and family relationships, creates a diversity of family forms and more complex family relationships; for many family members it also means impoverishment. As we have said, family matters, but so does divorce.

Until recently, Canadians could congratulate themselves that, as with some other social problems, we were better off than the United States. But, as Table 6.2 shows, our divorce rate, until the early 1980s, about half the American rate and considerably below that of all but four industrial countries is now higher than all but four countries and close to that of the United States.

In other words, the Canadian divorce rate rose more quickly in recent years than it did in other societies. (Figure 6.2). There was a particularly large jump following the first uniform Canadian divorce legislation, *The Divorce Act, 1968*. In the year preceding this legislation, the rate was 54.8 per 100 000 people. In the year following the legislation, the rate rose to 124.2 per 100 000 people and contrary to expectations at the time, it continued to rise to a peak of 285.9 per 100 000 in 1982. By 1985, the rate had fallen to 244.4 per 100 000. But, since 1986, when new divorce legislation came into force in Canada, there has, again, been a sharp increase (308.8 and 339.5 per 100 000 population in 1986 and 1987 respectively). Because couples now need to be separated for one rather than three years, this increase was anticipated but was expected to be only a short term increase. However, preliminary estimates for 1987 and the first part of 1988 suggest that the divorce rate may once more be on the rise (Richardson, 1989).

To put these rates into more concrete and, perhaps, human terms, a divorce rate of 340 per 100 000 population means that, in 1987, approximately 90 000 Canadian marriages were ended by divorce. Or, to put it another way, demographers at Statistics Canada, using the 1983 — 84 divorce rates, estimated that about 28 percent of marriages will end in divorce. Clearly, if divorce rates continue to rise so will the proportion of marriages likely to end in divorce.

In about half of divorces, the couple divorcing has children. And, like their married counterparts, they have, on average, 1.7 of them. Annually, at these current rates of divorce, some 65 000 children in Canada will become "children of divorce." If we add to this figure marriages which break up but where there is no divorce and only some form of separation, over 100 000 children are affected annually by the break up of their parents' marriage.

There are several reasons to anticipate that divorce rates will continue at present or higher levels. One is the *secularization* of society generally. At the simplest level this means

---

TABLE 6.2

COMPARATIVE DIVORCE RATES FOR CANADA AND COUNTRIES WITH HIGHER DIVORCE RATES IN 1986

COUNTRY	YEAR	DIVORCE PER 1000 MARRIAGES	YEAR	DIVORCE PER 1000 MARRIAGES
CANADA	1984	286.6	1986	445.3
Denmark	1983	548.1	1986	472.3
England &	1983	426.1	1985	461.0
Wales	1983	555.6	1986	482.9
Sweden	1983	482.4	1986	482.9
United				
States				

Sources: Statistics Canada, *Vital Statistics*, Vol II: *Marriages and Divorces*, 1984, table 23: Statistics Canada, *Marriages and Divorces*, *Vital Statistics*, Shelf Tables, table 22.

FIGURE 6.1

DIVORCE RATES PER 100,000 POPULATION, CANADA, 1967–1987

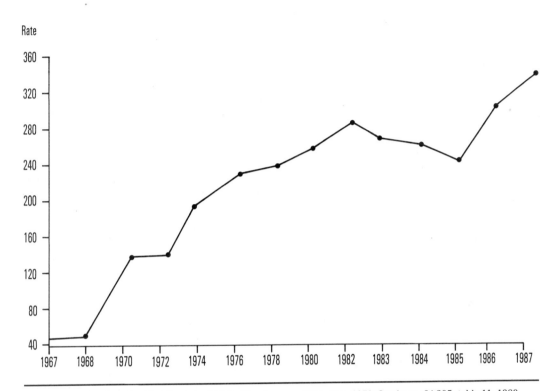

Sources: Statistics Canada, *Vital Statistics*, Vol. II: *Marriages and Divorces, 1979*; Catalogue 84-205, table 11; 1980, table 11; 1982 and 1985, table 10. Rates for 1986 and 1987 were obtained from special runs for the Department of Justice, Canada.

that marriage vows once regarded as sacred come more and more to look like secular contracts. And like any contract, they can be terminated by failure of one party to live up to its terms or by mutual consent of both parties. For many people God is no longer a third party to the marriage contract.

Second, as people begin to see that divorce does not necessarily ruin their friends financially and emotionally, it become more feasible to imagine it as a possibility for themselves. Thomas Cottle, for instance, argues that divorce affects more than the partners involved:

That a growing percentage of marriages end in divorce has caused many couples to look upon

their own marriages as far more frail, precarious and strained than they ever recognized. Like microbes carrying vicious illness, the threat of divorce is in the air, and a not insignificant number of families now huddle together waiting for the disease to reach them. Equally important, as the nature of family life generally becomes more publicly discussed, the sacredness of marriage, and more particularly the marriage bond, is eroded, and marriage, in many people's eyes, becomes just another one of life's everyday institutions (1980:43).

A third reason for expecting divorce rates to remain high is that as more and more married women participate in the labour force, they are, to some extent freed from their former dependancy on their husbands. As we describe in later chapters, women on average earn much less than men and are often segregated into low-paid jobs, which means that as single parents they will often be living in poverty. But, the fact that there is a labour market for women (and social assistance) means that they do have an alternative. A relatively low income or poverty is often preferable to living in an unhappy and perhaps violent marriage. And, where there was alcoholism and unemployment or sporadic employment by the husband, the low income provided by social assistance or work in the marginal work world may be compensated by predictability of income and greater control and mastery of their economic fate (Richardson, 1987).

FAMILY LAW REFORM

The first uniform divorce legislation in Canada came into force only in 1968. It introduced a number of "fault" grounds for divorce of which adultery and physical and mental cruelty were the ones most commonly used. In addition was the concept of "marriage breakdown" which could be demonstrated in a number of ways but most commonly used has been separation for three years. From its implementation the *Divorce Act, 1968*, was viewed by many as a compromise piece of legislation which, in the end, pleased neither those opposed to divorce or those who wished to make things easier for couples whose marriage has ended. The long waiting period placed undue hardship on people or forced them to invent grounds if they wished a more speedy divorce but, in the end, did not deter people from ending their marriage. The legislation, in other words, did not seem in tune with changing conceptions and realities of family life, marriage and divorce.

Nevertheless, it was not until 1985 that new legislation was passed. And, in the compromises its drafters were once again forced to make, we see illustrated much of the debate about the family, what Berger and Berger

(1983) describe as the "war over the family." Pro-family groups were opposed to any legislation which, in their view, further undermines the sanctity of the patriarchal family and, at the very least, urged that, for moral reasons, the notion of fault be retained. Fathers' rights groups, concerned about what they perceive to be the bias of family courts in favour of women, argued forcibly for a "presumption" of joint custody of children.

Various groups concerned with the status of women opposed the notion of joint custody, unless requested by both parents and urged that the legislation not be based on an illusion of equality but recognizes the disadvantaged position of women in the wider society and economy. And, still others hoped that the new legislation would make divorce easier and less painful and would recognize that there is little the state can do to buttress failed marriages.

The *Divorce Act, 1985*, replaces the concept of fault with that of marriage breakdown. But, there is an element of compromise since marriage breakdown can be demonstrated not only by separation (now for only one year) but also by adultery or mental and physical cruelty. As with most provincial legislation, the divorce legislation is written in gender neutral language: it talks about spouses and parents not husbands and wives, mothers and fathers. Either parent, then, can be granted custody of the children and could request child and spousal support from the other parent.

While the *Act* does not preclude the possibility of joint custody, it does not make this a preference and instead stresses custody and access arrangements which, when it is in their best interests to do so, give children maximum access to both of their parents.

The new divorce legislation does away with the concept of alimony, that by the very fact of having been married, a woman is entitled to support after divorce. Rather both spouses are expected to become economically self-sufficient and support that is granted is expected to be short term and to have as one of its objectives, the promotion of economic independence (for example, to enable a woman to upgrade her qualifications before entering or reentering the labour force). At the same time, as Status of Women's groups had urged, the legislation recognizes that older women who had remained in the home to look after husbands and children may have difficulty entering the labour force and should not be penalized for what was, presumably, a joint decision.

Finally, one of the objectives of the legislation is to reduce the adversarial nature of divorce — what has come to be called "Kramer vs. Kramer" disputes over child custody — and the associated costs. While mandatory mediation of such disputes was rejected, lawyers are required to advise their clients of the availability of divorce mediation services in their particular communities and that mediation may be a better and less costly way to settle intractable disputes than fighting it out in front of a judge. Procedural changes such as divorce without a formal hearing and joint divorce applications are further attempts to reduce the adversarial nature of the divorce process.

DIVORCE OUTCOMES

It is too early yet to tell whether the new divorce legislation will have much impact on either the outcomes or the process of divorce. But, research prior to the *Divorce Act, 1985*, suggests that, despite changes in attitudes about divorce and about the roles of men and women with respect to parenting, the outcomes of divorce remained much the same in recent years. About 48 percent of divorces involve one or more children and in about 71 percent of these divorces, sole custody is granted to the mother. In such cases, access or visitation rights are almost always granted to the father.

In recent years we have heard a great deal about bitter custody disputes and the inequality fathers face when they attempt to maintain contact with their children following divorce. While judges are required to make their decision based on "the best interests of the child" principle, fathers' rights groups maintain that what this means in practice is that children, especially those in their "tender years," are seen usually as better off with their mother. The above statistic simply bolsters their case that in custody disputes, the odds are stacked against fathers.

However, the reality is somewhat different than these groups portray. First, in only a tiny minority of divorces (probably less than five percent) is custody contested in court. In the tiny minority of cases where men do contest custody, they are "successful" about 40 percent of the time (Richardson, 1988). But, in general, there is little evidence to suggest that men want custody of their children in the sense of taking on the role of primary caregiver. And, one of the more intractable problems is that often men do not live up to their parenting obligations or do so unpredictably.

If there has been a change in post-divorce relations and arrangements, it is that joint custody appears to be more common than in the past. We qualify this because, prior to the *Divorce Act, 1985*, this category did not exist so that there were no reliable statistics on its incidence in Canada, only estimates. Recent research indicates that about 13 percent of custody awards are now joint custody awards and that in half of these there is joint parenting in the sense that the children spend roughly equal amounts of time in two households (Richardson, 1990).

From the point of view of children and their adjustment to the separation or divorce of their parents, joint custody — shared parenting — seems to be a positive development and a sensible arrangement for many divorcing families. Studies that have examined the effects of divorce on children have generally found that an important factor, in their adjustment to the break up of their family, is the continuing contact with both parents, which joint custody seems to offer (Wallerstein and Kelly, 1980). But, shared parenting requires a considerable amount of time, money and energy, things that most people do not have or are unwilling to expend. This seems especially so for men, who as Weitzman (1985) found, generally want less not more contact with their children.

Whether by consent or by court order, most children of divorce end up living with their mothers. And the consequence of this is that these children live, at least for a time, in female headed single parent families whose incomes usually put them below the poverty line. In what is perhaps the most widely quoted study, Lenore Weitzman (1985) concludes that, in the United States, divorced men experience, on average, a 42 percent increase in their standard of living while divorced women and their children experience a 73 percent decline.

While we do not have such compelling statistics for Canada, recent research does show that 58 percent of divorced women and their children have incomes below the poverty line compared to about 10 percent of men after divorce or separation (Richardson, 1988). This is mainly because men rarely have custody of the children of the marriage but are, on average, required to pay only about 18 percent of their gross income in child support. All of this assumes that men actually pay the support of their children as agreed to or ordered by the court. The reality is that many men, probably a majority, start out making the payments but eventually do so very sporadically or not at all. Marriage and family fall especially heavily upon women, but so it seems does divorce.

DIVORCE AND CHANGING FAMILY FORMS

As we have suggested, divorce does not necessarily end familial relationships but complicates them in ways we are only beginning to understand. But the family structures that divorce brings about — single parent and remarriage families — are not new. Historically oriented demographers inform us that the likelihood that, for example, children will experience family dissolution and living in a single parent or a remarriage family probably hasn't changed much over the last 150 years.

What has, of course, changed is the cause: what resulted in the past from the death of one parent is now caused by the break up of the parents' marriage; it is quite clearly very different for children to know that they live in a single parent family because their mother or father is dead than to do so knowing that one of their parents, usually the father, is alive but only partially involved or not involved at all in their lives.

There are also difficulties where one or both parents have remarried after divorce rather than as a result of the death of one of the parents. As with single parent families, remarriage is not a new phenomenon. According to Statistics Canada, about 29 percent of marriages in the 1980s were remarriages. But as with marital dissolution, the pattern has shifted from remarriage following widowhood to remarriage following divorce, with the result that (as of 1983) in slightly over 90 percent of remarriages, either one or both parties had been divorced. Overall, it seems that within five years of divorce, about half of men and 40 percent of women will remarry. People, in other words, are not necessarily opposed to marriage *per se* but to their *specific* marriage (Richardson, 1990).

Divorce and remarriage complicate, and in confusing ways, expand kinship relations and the kinship universe that the child perceives. This is because many of those who divorce and remarry will have children from the previous marriage and many will have more from the second marriage. While these children will be half-siblings, they will have quite different perceptions of their family structure and of their kinship universe. To the extent that they remain in contact with both parents, children of the first marriage will experience two family structures and probably two sets of rules and expectations. Those of the second marriage will have experience of only one family and only a partial knowledge of their brothers' and sisters' more complicated world; and, if both parents remarry then the children of the first marriage might, in effect, have four separate sets of relatives and relationships. Thus, many of the taken-for-granted assumptions about what is a family and who is and is not a family member may differ considerably, depending on which child and which member of these "reconstituted families" we ask (Gross, 1985).

These are issues we are only beginning to research and to understand. As with the divorce process itself, there is evidence to suggest that people, including children, do adjust to these more complicated structures and perhaps come to take them for granted. For children, especially those who have been living with their mothers, remarriage may mean that they no longer are living below the poverty line, but, when fathers paying support have new families, the first children may suffer (Mossman, 1985). Much of the research on remarriage families suggests that adults are satisfied with their second marriage and think it far superior to their first one. There is consensus that the most damaging situation for children is a home torn by habitual and sometimes violent conflict. The happier marital situation of the custodial parent may, then, have positive spin-offs for the children.

CONCLUSION

Later in the book you will be introduced to the impact of feminist theory and research on the development of Canadian sociology, generally. In this chapter you have seen something of how a sociology based on feminism has, as one influential book put it, brought about a "rethinking of the family" (Thorne and Yalom, 1982). First, feminist theory and research has challenged what Margrit Eichler (1988) refers to as the "monolithic bias" in family literature — the notion that there is only one family form and that variations are deviations. Second, feminism has undermined the view of family structures as "natural" and as based immutably on biology. Third, a feminist sociology, when wedded to Marxism, provides a powerful critique of the

functionalist emphasis on the family functions and family roles that are now seen as ideological in the sense discussed in Chapter 3.

Finally, more concretely, feminist research has shown us more clearly how families, family structures and family changes are experienced differently by women and men and, perhaps, girls and boys. This research, for example, shows that ideals of motherhood and mother love, of the sanctity and privacy of the family, often mask inequality and blind us to the extent men's interests have, under capitalism, dominated women's interests. And, more generally, this research allows us to see that capitalism, with its emphasis on individualism and a separation of home and work, has different consequences for women than for men.

Marxists and feminists have helped all of us to rethink our own attitudes about family and our roles within family. Women have, increasingly, come to recognize the double bind, the exploitation, the constraints, that they have had to accept to receive the kinds of benefits of family life that functionalists talk about. It has, no doubt, been more difficult for men to rethink their position, given that the costs seem less and the benefits greater. Nevertheless, men, too have begun to ask how much they have given up, or missed out on, by leaving child rearing to their wives and by judging themselves on the basis of their ability to protect and feed their family. The Marxist and particularly feminist critiques have not only sought to understand family change, they have contributed to the evolution of the family.

Notwithstanding the critiques and crises we have described, it remains that most people choose marriage because they are seeking intimacy, secure trusting relationships, a sense of meaning in their human interactions and a refuge from the stress and hypocrisy of their interactions with strangers, those they have power over and those who have power over them. And, as we have described, when these needs are not met, many also divorce and either choose to redirect their needs or, if more optimistic, to try again.

III SUGGESTIONS FOR FURTHER READING

Given the importance of the family for society and the individual, it is understandable that all of the social sciences have been concerned with aspects of family, marriage, kinship and child rearing. This in itself has produced an immense body of theoretical and applied literature and more popular "how to do it" books ranging from Alex Comfort's *The Joy of Sex* to Benjamin Spock's *Baby and Child Care*

Among the many American textbooks on the *sociology* of the family, we particularly recommend Arlene Skolnick's *The Intimate Environment* (1987) now in its fourth edition and Bert N. Adams's *The Family*: A Sociological Interpretation (1975). Two excellent British textbooks are D. H. Morgan's *Social Theory and the Family* (1975) and C. C. Harris's *The Family in Industrial Society* (1988)

Until recently research on the Canadian family has for the most part appeared in articles rather than books or textbooks. S. Parvez Wakil's *Marriage, Family and Society 1293(1975)* and K. Ishwaran's *The Canadian Family* (1976) provide edited collections of some of the earlier articles on family and marriage in Canada, as does K. Ishwaran's *Canadian Families: Ethnic Variations* (1980) and his *Marriage and Divorce in Canada* (1983). Two multiauthored textbooks are Maureen Baker's *The Family: Changing Trends in Canada* (1984) and K. Anderson et al.'s *Family Matters* (1988). There is a television series produced by TVOntario which this latter text is meant to supplement. Margrit Eichler's *Families in Canada Today*, second edition (1988), is both an excellent text and an important contribution to a feminist perspective on the family. Emily Nett's *Canadian Families: Past and Present* (1988) provides a basic and somewhat more conservative introduction to the Canadian family.

Family violence in Canada is examined in a number of articles in Mary Alice Bayer Gammon's *Violence in Canada* (1978). Linda Macleod's *Battered but Not Beaten: Preventing Wife Abuse in Canada* (1987) is a recent and controversial study of one aspect of this violence and the two volume report *Sexual Offences Against Children* (1984) provides a thorough examination of another aspect of "the dark side" of family life. Howard Irving's *Divorce Mediation* (1980), his edited collection, *Family Law: An Interdisciplinary Perspective* (1981) N. Bala's and Kenneth Clark's *The Childhood the Law* (1981) and C. J. Richardson's *Court-based Divorce Mediation in Four Canadian Cities* (1988) will give you some sense of changing perspectives in family law in Canada. Important American books on divorce are Kenneth Kressel's *The Divorce Process* (1985), Lenore Weitzman's influential *The Divorce Revolution* (1985) and the much-quoted *Surviving the Breakup* (1980) by J. Wallerstein and J. Kelly.

Aside from Philippe Aries's *Centuries of Childhood* (1962), the work which has done most to spur interest in the history and development of the family is Peter Laslett's *The World We Have Lost* (1965). The work he has stimulated is represented in a volume he has edited, *Household and Family in Past Time* (1972), and in Michael Anderson's historical work on kinship, *Family Structure in Nineteenth Century Lancashire* (1971). A particularly interesting and provocative history of the family is Lawrence Stone's *The Family, Sex and Marriage in England 1500-1800* (1979) as is E. Shorter's, *The Making of the Modern Family* (1970). Michael Katz's *The People of Hamilton Canada West* (1975) is not only of obvious relevance to Canadian students but is also an excellent book. A classic functionalist work on family change under industrialization is William J. Goode's *World Revolution and Family Patterns* (1963). As is apparent, a major influence on our thinking about family and change is Michael Young's and Peter Willmott's *The Symmetrical Family* (1973). You might also want to read their earlier books, *Family and Kinship in East London* (1957), and *Family and Class in a London Suburb* (1960). These are now generally regarded as works that had a profound influence on the development of British sociology and on family and community research generally. Eli Zaretsky's *Capitalism, the Family and Personal Life* (1976) is an excellent and readable analysis of the effects of capitalism on family life from a Marsixt perspective, an account that nicely complements and extends Dorothy Smith's article which we cite in this chapter, as does Christopher Lasch's *Haven in a Heartless World* (1979). J. Dickinson's and B. Russell's edited collection *Family, Economy and State* (1986) examines a number of aspects of the family under capitalism both in Canada and elsewhere.

There is, as we might expect, a large and ever growing literature on women and the family. A good starting point is S. J. Wilson's *Women, the Family and the Economy* (1986) and B. Thorne and M. Yalom (eds) *Rethinking the Family* (1982). Two influential books on the housewife role were Ann Oakley's *The Sociology of Housework* (1974) and H. Z. Lopata's *Occupation Housewife* (1971). More recent Canadian work in this area are M. Luxton's *More than A Labour of Love* (1980) and M. Luxton's and H. Rosenberg's *Through the Kitchen Window* (1986). More general aspects of women, work and family and the domestic labour debate can be found in B. Fox's edited collection, *Hidden in the Household* (1980) and R. Hamilton's and M. Barret's edited work, *The Politics of Diversity* (1986).

CHAPTER 7

DEVIANCE, CONTROL, AND CHANGE

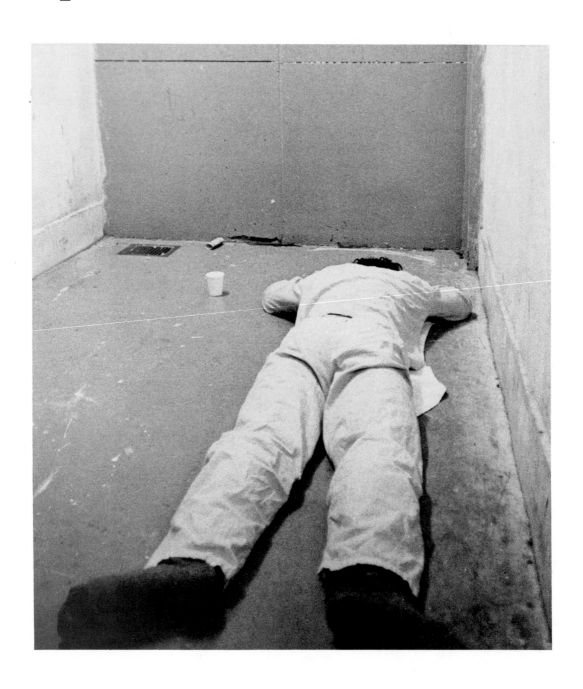

OVERVIEW

INTRODUCTION

DEVIANCE, CRIME, AND PUNISHMENT
EARLY THEORIES
EARLY APPROACHES

THE DEVIANT BEHAVIOUR PERSPECTIVE

ANOMIE AND SOCIAL STRUCTURE
DIFFERENTIAL ASSOCIATION
OPPORTUNITY THEORIES
THE LIMITS OF DEVIANT BEHAVIOUR THEORY

THE LABELLING PERSPECTIVE

CREATING DEVIANCE
VICTIMLESS CRIMES
CREATING DEVIANTS
THE DEVIANTS' PERSPECTIVE

DEVIANT CAREERS

CRIME AND DELINQUENCY

CRIMES AGAINST PERSON
CRIMES AGAINST PROPERTY
JUVENILE DELINQUENCY

DIVERSION: THE SAGA OF A LIBERAL REFORM

CRIME AND DELINQUENCY: SUMMARY

SUMMARY AND CONCLUSION

SUGGESTIONS FOR FURTHER READING

OVERVIEW

In this chapter, you should discover the ambiguity of the concept of "deviance," and how sociological definitions have evolved over time. You should understand the conservative origins of criminology and the gradual evolution of the sociology of deviance, which in its more recent versions emphasizes the ideological and political dimensions of crime and deviance. Perhaps most important is recognizing the dangers in drawing too sharp a line between "normal" and "deviant," "sane" and "insane," "deviance" and "dissent."

After reading this chapter, you should be able to contrast the way deviant behaviour theorists such as Merton and Sutherland try to explain deviance in terms of socialization and opportunities with the way labelling theorists such as Becker and Lemert try to explain why certain behaviours (and people) are labelled deviant in the first place and the role of power and conflict in this process—and you should understand some of the limits of both approaches.

Also, you should have some appreciation of crime and delinquency in Canada and how these are an expression of Canadian social structure. In this context, you should be able to explain some of the unanticipated consequences of liberal reforms in criminal justice, such as the emphasis on diversion or changes to sexual assault legislation.

Finally, this chapter should help you understand how the study of deviance is simply one way of gaining a better understanding of the normal tensions between individual and society and the ubiquitous conflicts between those who make the rules and those who do not.

INTRODUCTION

DEVIANCE, CRIME AND PUNISHMENT

The last three chapters have shown why people conform to institutionalized standards of behaviour. One view is that they internalize these standards of behaviour which guide their actions. It is impossible to imagine interaction without such standards. At the same time, however, which of us has never felt an impulse to do something we "knew" to be wrong? It should be no surprise that sociologists have given a good deal of attention to those who act on these "deviant" impulses: people who steal, kill or eat too much, for example. If, as we have said, social control is largely self-control, why is it that the mechanisms of self-control are not sufficient to keep these people "in line"?

Some sociologists seem to find these "deviants" rather a nuisance, a tiresome exception to otherwise quite neat theories of "ordered interaction." Perhaps, they argue, something went wrong in their socialization or maybe they were subjected to some unusual social pressures; the implication seems to be that there is something wrong either with these deviant people or with their immediate environment.

Some sociologists, on the other hand, seem to find great delight in studying and theorizing about deviants. To them deviants are a nice illustration of the paradox of human nature—that we are determined but also free. These theorists are not surprised that people often do unusual things. In fact they seem to expect it. They are more interested in what happens to the deviant. Why are some deviants selected for special treatment? How are they affected by this treatment, be it informal social control — ridicule, rejection — or the more elaborate formal social control—arrest, prosecution, and incarceration?

Both perspectives, the focus of deviants and the focus on social control, have produced theories and empirical data that have enhanced our understanding, not only of deviant behaviour, but of behaviour more generally.

EARLY THEORIES

The first systematic attempts to understand nonconformity were largely motivated by fear of criminals and deviants. There is a certain unsettling moral absolutism in most early criminology. The law was seen to capture what was moral and good and those who violated the law were, by definition, evil. Early criminology, then, looked for the sources of evil. Criminology grew rapidly as a discipline in late nineteenth and early twentieth centuries, in large part, because it addressed a persistent human preoccupation: what nature of person could do these evil things and how can we predict and control this evil.

The notion that some people actually choose to do evil, and that these people are in most other respects just like us, is perhaps one of the more frightening thoughts for those living in contemporary society. Thus, any criminologist who offers some hope that these criminals differ fundamentally from us and that they can be diagnosed and dealt with has always had an audience.

EARLY APPROACHES

Cesare Lombroso, writing at the turn of the century, was one of the early proponents of a "type of people" theory of deviance or, more accurately, criminality. For Lombroso, not only were criminals born rather than made, but they could be recognized because they carried physical stigmata, outward signs of their depravity. With calipers in hand, Lombroso measured the jaws, foreheads, and the set and distance between eyes of criminals and so-called non-criminals and convinced himself and most others of his day that not only did criminals look different from other folk, thieves looked different from murderers. You could quickly spot the criminal and put him away. Some sense of the attractiveness of this approach is that even today, most cartoons depict convicts using stereotypes which mirror Lombroso's so-called empirical findings. Students and followers of Lombroso's view tried to replicate, refine or elaborate his work with predictably inconclusive results. Nevertheless, the notion that people who do bad things are fundamentally different from normal people has a continual and unquestionably comforting influence in criminology and popular conceptions of crime and deviance.

These early approaches to crime and deviance were infused with a sense of good and evil. Crime was evil and committed by evil people. Geoffrey Pearson captures well the language of nineteenth century thinking about the criminal classes:

Sewage and drains were guiding metaphors for those who depicted the deviance of this time. "Foul wretches" and "moral filth" lay heaped in "stagnant pools" about the streets. When they moved, they were seen to "ooze" in a great "tide." The population was "slime" which gathered in ghettos which were described as "poisoned wells," "canker-worms," "sinks of inequity" and "plague-spots." Their houses were described as "cesspits," and their way of life was a "moral miasma" . . . the city "reeked" of vice: the "scum" and the "dregs" of society was a "moral debris" . . . . The words "pustule," "fever," and "wart" came readily to hand describing the moral condition of the labouring and dangerous classes (1975: 161).

In this passage, Pearson seems to be equating the labouring class and the criminal (dangerous) class. In fact, he is acknowledging the confusion of the times. It was during this period that social thinkers merged the notions of urban poverty and criminality in a way that was to dominate conceptions of crime and deviance to the present. But perhaps more important, this confusion reflects the greatest fear of that period, that the chaos, the "senseless" violence of the criminal classes, would spread to the "respectable" labouring class.

In later chapters, you will find that industrial capitalism meant the creation of new classes, new antagonisms, new conflicts and new fears. The early work that came later to dominate North American sociology reflected the fears of the "new aristocracy." To these early conservative writers, the behaviour of the poor was irrational and dangerous. Certainly, it represented a threat to the "rationality," the logic of the newly emerging order and a threat to those who most benefited from it.

This is the context in which we must understand twentieth century attempts to build theories of deviance. Sociologists have tried to throw off the moral and political language of these early works, to cast off the images of pathology and sickness, and have tried instead to develop "scientific" theories of deviance, as a "normal" part of any society.

THE DEVIANT BEHAVIOUR PERSPECTIVE

In the 1930s American sociologists began to move away from the notion that deviants and nondeviants were two different types of people. Most sociologists rejected the earlier theories which held that deviants were biologically or psychologically defective. Moreover, in attempting to develop social theories of deviant behaviour, they rejected the earlier notion that some acts were inherently improper or wrong — inherently deviant — as judged from some absolute moral standard such as the law. What is considered deviant changes over time and varies from place to place.

Not surprisingly, these sociologists defined deviance in sociological terms: the violation of a social norm, rule-breaking. In later writing, R. K. Merton said that **deviance** "refers to conduct that departs significantly from the norms set for people in their social statuses.

It must be related to the norms that are socially defined as appropriate and morally binding for people occupying various statuses" (Merton, 1968: 723–724). In other words, what is deviant for a woman, say initiating sexual contact, may not be deviant for a man. What is deviant for an adolescent, drinking alcoholic beverages, for example, may not be deviant for an adult. While the use of morphine might be considered appropriate behaviour for the "sick role," it is otherwise viewed as deviant behaviour.

In their efforts to move away from biological and psychological theories, some sociologists may have gone overboard in their emphasis on the social. Dennis Wrong (1961), you will recall, has accused sociologists of developing "an oversocialized conception of man"; once individuals have internalized the norms and values of their society, they become purely social "cultural dopes" (Garfinkel, 1967), incapable of independent creative action. They are a rule-followers *par excellence*. Moreover, order theorists have emphasized the consensus about norms and values that exists in most societies. Thus we have a picture of the members of the society not only following rules but also following pretty much the same rules. Now we have a problem — where do deviants come from?

For American sociologists, in the early decade of the twentieth century, the answer to this question seemed apparent. America was a society undergoing rapid social change and the sociologists of the day, many of whom had been clergymen and social workers, were concerned about the consequences for families and individuals of these changes. They were witnessing the rapid move of people from rural America to cities, increases in immigration and the growth of slums in huge cities, such as we now know them.

For many American sociologists these changes were bringing with them *social disorganization* as manifested in a wide range of social problems such as alcoholism, mental illness, crime and deviance, generally. In the University of Chicago, in particular, sociologists developed new techniques for studying urban crime, most of which were directed at locating the problem so that social reforms might ameliorate the worst conditions of city life.

While the impetus was, in large part, humane liberal reform, this work was often cast in the language of moral absolutism and a biblical notion of right and wrong. Little attention was given to the possibility that the structure of American society might be creating "social disorganization." Rather, the focus was on how to preserve what was best in American society, much as Durkheim sought to preserve the society of his day in the fact of the changes he was witnessing. It is out of this tradition that emerged two of the dominant theories — anomie theory and differential association.

ANOMIE AND SOCIAL STRUCTURE

Robert K. Merton (1939) provided one solution which for a long time dominated the field. Drawing on the work of Durkheim (1897), Merton developed the *theory of anomie*. It holds essentially that the social structure can exert pressure on some social groups to commit deviant acts.

He argued that all societies teach their members cultural goals and the means appropriate to achieving these goals. Some groups, however, may not have access to the legitimate means to achieve the goals they have learned to value. It should be obvious that in North America some groups — non-whites, the poor — are in a disadvantaged position in the competition for the scarce and desirable resources — power, prestige and particularly money. They are likely, for example, to encounter discrimination in the educational and occupational structures, the institutionalized means of acquiring power, prestige and money. This conflict or gap between cultural goals and institutionalized means leads to anomie, a state in which norms lose their power to regulate behaviour. The strain of anomie can lead to a search for new, often illicit, means of achieving "success."

Merton, for example, was struck by the disproportionately high rate of crime among the lower classes. Much of this crime, goes the argument, can be understood as an example of innovation, the attempt to achieve conventional success in unconventional ways (theft). Innovation is particularly common in North America, where greater emphasis is placed on the importance of economic success than on the legitimate routes to success. It does not matter so much how you get there as long as you get there. Merton suggest that there may be a grudging admiration for those who cheat their way to the top. To some extent the "con-artist" may be an American folk hero. While the innovation of new means to success may be a common response to anomie, it is not the only response.

Some people may give up or lower their desire to achieve goals, but continue to abide "almost compulsively" by the rules. Conformity may become an end in itself, a response Merton calls ritualism. An example might be the officious and nitpicking bureaucrat — the "bureaucratic virtuoso," for whom the rules of the game are more important than winning.

Merton suggests two other possible adaptations to anomie besides innovation and ritualism. Retreatism occurs when individuals reject both the goals they once held and the means for achieving these goals. They withdraw from the game. The skid row alcoholic and the drug addict are often cited as examples. Rebellion occurs when people not only reject their old goals and means, but also substitute new goals and means, a new value system. Revolutionaries and political activists are in this sense rebels.

Tepperman has suggested that Merton's typology of the range of adaptations to thwarted aspirations can be useful for understanding Canadian society.

There is in Canada as in other industrial societies, a bad fit between culturally induced aspirations — such as the predominant aspirations for high status jobs that are in short supply — and the potential for realizing these aspirations in socially approved ways. There are various adaptations to the sense of failure and frustration felt on being denied one's goals. The frequency with which one or another adaptation is selected varies from society to society, and varies over time. An individual may even try many adaptations in his lifetime. The denial of aspirations and the attendant sense of failure are widespread in Canadian society and may continue as such into the foreseeable future. In this respect, failure and the psychological and social adaptations to it represent a major problem in our society (1975:200).

DIFFERENTIAL ASSOCIATION

For Merton, deviants are "normal" members of society; they have internalized the appropriate norms and values. They have become deviant because of the pressures exerted by the social structure. This view, however, represents only one of the streams of the deviant behaviour perspective. Edwin Sutherland (1939) offers a different solution to the "problem of deviance" with his theory of **differential association**. Like Merton, Sutherland focuses on the process of socialization. Unlike Merton, Sutherland emphasizes the differences in norms and values among the various subgroups in society.

For Sutherland, deviants, like the rest of us, are rule-followers. They are simply following the rules of their own group. Deviant behaviour is learned in the same way as any other behaviour. All of us are exposed to patterns of behaviour and definitions both which favour law violation and which discourage it. What determines if one engages in deviant behaviour is the balance between deviant and conventional contacts. In short, we learn deviant behaviour from the people around us, primarily through interaction in close, intimate groups.

In light of this, it should be no surprise that many researchers have come to see the prison as a place of higher education for criminals. More generally, Sutherland's theory would predict a higher rate of crime in urban rather than rural society. The city is characterized by diversity, with many different subcultures and different ways of life. Urban life also involves a good deal of geographic mobility. The diversity and mobility of urban societies are likely to create more possibilities for pro-criminal associations — contacts which encourage law violation.

OPPORTUNITY THEORIES

Several theorists have explicitly attempted to bring Merton's and Sutherland's theories together. Cloward and Ohlin (1960), for example, have argued that in order to understand why any group is likely to turn to crime we must ask about the availability of both legitimate opportunities and access to legitimate means and illegitimate opportunities, for example, the availability of criminal role models.

This emphasis on opportunity is well-placed. The desire or felt need to commit a deviant or criminal act is not enough in itself. One must also have the opportunity — the ways and means.

It would be extremely difficult, if not impossible, to embezzle if one were not strategically located in a work system, perhaps as a bookkeeper or purchasing agent. A would-be confidence man needs confidence and salesmanship, just as those who would engrave counterfeit plates need artistic ability. A successful "society" jewel thief would obviously need "society" contacts and a degree of savoir faire. To "crack" a safe takes skill, and one can hardly steal atomic secrets if one has no access to such secrets. Similarly, an unknowledgeable middle-class housewife who wished to "sample" marijuana might have to pass up the experiment since she might not know where to obtain the "pot" (Bryant, 1974:8).

To become a deviant one must learn the appropriate attitudes and skills, one must have the opportunity to act on these attitudes and use these skills, and one must learn to recognize these opportunities. The fact that different groups have different opportunities is certainly a large part of the explanation of why different groups engage in different kinds of deviant and criminal acts.

THE LIMITS OF DEVIANT BEHAVIOUR THEORY

The "deviant behaviour" approach is the perspective that has dominated the study of deviance in North America. Researchers have been concerned, for example, with documenting and explaining the high rates of crime, or at least certain kinds of crime, among the poor, Native people, blacks and other oppressed social groups. With this increasing research has come a corresponding increase in the awareness of just how complicated deviance is.

Deviance is an extremely slippery concept. What in one context is deviant is, in another, conformity. In a complex society with a variety of reference groups, with more than one set of institutions, people may indeed not be out of step but, as Thoreau put it, merely marching to a different drummer.

Recently a number of sociologists have suggested that the search for the causes of deviance may have taken sociology in the wrong direction or at least that there are other equally important questions. Surely everyone has done something, at one time or another, that can be termed deviant. Most children, for example, know the guilty pleasures of eating candy stolen from the counter or bought with money from mother's purse. As well, most have known the shame of being found out. Perhaps such behaviour is "polygenetic," and has many different causes, which can never be captured by a single theory of deviance causation (Lemert, 1972). There are, however, other important questions that sociologists might ask about deviant behaviour.

THE LABELLING PERSPECTIVE

In the 1960s and the 1970s, along with the emergence of the youth movement with its New Left politics and counter-culture values, and perhaps as part of all this, a variety of approaches arose against the portrayal of deviance as senseless and irrational. The challenges came from diverse sources, but what unified them was a sympathy with the participants and a demand that their motives be understood, that their perspective be appreciated. These sociologists emphasized the political dimensions of deviance. As Horowitz and Liebowitz write:

The traditional distinction between social problems and the political system is becoming obsolete. Behaviour which in the past was perceived as social deviance is now assuming well-defined ideological and organizational contours, while political marginals are adopting a deviant lifestyle. This merger of social deviance and marginality creates a new style of politics, based on strategies that are traditionally considered illegitimate. The result of this trend is estimated to be an increase in the use of violence as a political tactic, and the development of a revolutionary potential among the expanding ranks of deviant sub-groups (1968:280).

Certainly this means that campus demonstrations, urban race riots and violent labour disputes are to be viewed as rational, goal-directed and purposive. But this approach also insists that deviants be accorded political status. This is reflected, for example, by Taylor, Walton and Young (1973) in their statement that juvenile delinquents are actually engaged in the redistribution of property. As well, vandalism comes to be seen as an inarticulate attempt to fight injustice and to right wrongs (Pearson, 1975:97). Ian Taylor (1971) makes a similar case for soccer hooliganism. What these writers are saying is what Karl Marx predicted — that the early collective actions of the revolutionary working class would be primitive, directed at the "wrong enemies."

According to this argument, criminal and deviant behaviour should also be viewed as inarticulate or primitive political action. The "appreciative approach" of the 1960s and 1970s has been an important corrective to the taken-for-granted assumptions which had dominated the field. These sociologists were less likely to see change as "traumatic"; they sympathized with those who sought social change, and they, therefore, turned upside-down the area of deviance, seeing it not only as a sign of human diversity but also as political protest. In the words of Stanley Cohen:

There is much talk of alienation, dropping out, disaffiliation and youth on the streets. There is confusion about the line beyond which "stealing" becomes "looting," "hooliganism" becomes "rioting," "vandalism" becomes "sabotage." When do "reckless maniacs" become "freedom fighters"? Are the everyday encounters between the police and urban slum youth throughout the world somehow stripped of their political significance if what is happening is not defined as a "riot" or "disturbance"? (1973:120)

Out of this approach emerged a number of critical perspectives on crime and deviance, most of which drew upon the most influential approach called labelling theory. The *labelling perspective* was developed primarily by Edwin Lemert (1951), Howard Becker (1963) and Edwin Schur (1971). For labelling theorists, deviance is a matter of social definition, and "deviant behaviour is behaviour so labelled" (Becker, 1962). In formulating "new" questions about deviance, labelling theorists have drawn on both conflict theory and symbolic interactionism.

CREATING DEVIANCE

The cornerstone of this perspective is skepticism. The sociologists must not take for granted and must question society's labelling of certain forms of behaviour as deviant. Societies, or more precisely powerful groups within society, create deviance by creating and enforcing rules. Here we can see labelling theory's debt to conflict theory.

To say that society creates its deviance and its

social problems is not to say "it's all in the mind" and that some nasty people are going around creating deviance out of nothing. . . . But it does mean that the making of rules and the sanctioning of people who break these rules are as much a part of deviance as the action itself . . . . So, whenever we see terms such as deviance and social problem, we must ask: "Says who?" (Cohen, 1971: 17).

We must ask who has the power to designate certain acts as deviant and how do they achieve this.

Howard Becker, for example, studied the development of anti-marijuana legislation in the United States. He points out that anti-marijuana laws were passed without any consultation with marijuana users—those best able to provide "expert testimony." He concludes that the most significant pressure to criminalize marijuana smoking came from narcotics agents themselves. They had a *vested interest* in expanding their jurisdiction. In a similar study, Shirley Cook (1969) traces the development of Canadian narcotics legislation. She describes the conflict between Chinese immigrant groups and English-speaking Canadians and the power of English-speaking Canadians to legislate their morality.

Becker has coined the term *moral entrepreneur* to describe those individuals or groups who attempt to *criminalize* behaviour which they feel threatens their way of life and their morality (Schur, 1965). Conventional wisdom has it that law reflects the moral climate of the community. But which constituents do legislators listen to? Some may be louder than others. For example, psychiatrists are among the most powerful moral entrepreneurs. Not only do they define the conditions under which a person should be regarded as insane, certainly a most consequential label, but they also influence legislators in deciding which acts should be viewed as criminal (Vaz, 1976).

Once some behaviour is made illegal it may also come to be seen by most people as immoral (Henshel and Henshel, 1973:59–65). Law, then, serves a symbolic function; it designates certain behaviours morally inferior.

VICTIMLESS CRIMES

The area which best illustrates this conflict of values is what some sociologists refer to as *victimless crimes*. Prostitution, homosexuality and marijuana use, for example, are forms of deviance in which the participants are willing, no one is directly injured and those involved are unlikely to bring complaints. These acts are criminalized because some people, not directly involved, do not approve. Similar arguments have been raised regarding abortion, narcotics use and many other "crimes," which, if not precisely victimless, are at least consensual in that all participants in the "criminal act" are participating out of choice.

The labelling perspective allows us to examine the consequences of criminalizing such acts. What are the consequences, for example, of the criminalization of drug use? Edwin Schur (1965) has attempted to demonstrate that the narcotics laws have "made things worse." Because of the high risks involved in the manufacture, importation and distribution of narcotics, these drugs are scarce and the price is high. Drugs become an attractive commodity to organized crime. The addict feels forced to engage in other crimes to support his or her other habit. Narcotics legislation has aggravated the narcotics problem and, according to this view, has compounded the difficulties in law enforcement.

The addict is also edged out of the conventional society. The need for secrecy, the fear of reprisal and the need for illegal contacts all encourage addicts to restrict their interaction to those who are also engaged in prohibited activities. Obviously the prohibition of certain activities will change the way in which those activities are carried out. Whatever one's moral position is on these activities, the questions raised by labelling theory serve as an illustration of the potential of the perspective for challenging the legal structure (Henshel and Henshel, 1973:65).

The question of whose rules define deviance inevitably involves an examination of economic and political power, issues which are discussed at length in future chapters. For now it is enough to indicate that in very many ways, men make the rules for women; whites make the rules for nonwhites; the middle class make the rules for the poor; and so it goes.

. . . much of what is considered deviant in society (e.g., types of mental illness, prostitution, abortion, drug addiction, vagrancy, etc.) represents little more than the special brand of morality of the prevailing power holders in the society (Vaz, 1976:46).

▌ CREATING DEVIANTS

At another level of analysis, labelling theorists also ask who has defined the deviant "the one to whom that label has been successfully applied." The point is that rules are enforced selectively. Certain groups in our society — police and psychiatrists — play a key role in social control; they are the "master labellers." A good deal of empirical evidence has been collected on how they decide who is "criminal' or "mentally ill."

These decisions are influenced by a number of factors, the most important of which seems to be the social position of the "deviant." Werthman and Piliavin (1967), for example, have found that police in a San Francisco ghetto operate on the basis of stereotypical criteria in deciding which teenagers are "delinquent enough" to be arrested. What does the boy look like, how is he dressed, what is his family background, what is his attitude during interrogation?

The central conclusion of this and numerous other studies is that *political criteria* play an important part in police decisions. The "good pinch" is an arrest that is politically all right, that does not meet with community disapproval. This is best achieved when there is a good deal of consensus that the crime involved is serious (sexual crimes, for example), and when the "criminal" is already seen as disreputable.

Perhaps the disproportionately high rate of crime among the poor or native people, for example, can best be understood in terms of the social organization of social control. That is, official crime statistics may tell us more about the ideologies which support official social control and the activities of agents of social control than they do about criminal behaviour.

In Canada, for example, native people are consistently over-represented in the penal system. Does this mean that they are more likely to engage in crime or that they are more likely to get arrested and incarcerated? We are not suggesting that the police are going around arresting native people whether or not they break the law. What we are saying is that if two boys, one native Canadian, the other European, break the same law the native Canadian is more likely to be arrested, convicted and sentenced to prison.

Just how much the police are influenced by political criteria is open to question. First of all, it is well to point out that the majority of the police officer's time is not spent in crime detection or apprehending criminals, but in other aspects of police work such as traffic control and public assistance. Beyond this, criminologists and sociologists do not agree on just how or why the police, as representatives of the criminal justice system, are more likely to detain or arrest the poor than the privileged.

Augustine Brannigan (1984:94) describes two dominant metaphors of how the criminal justice systems operate. One metaphor views the criminal justice system as a funnel:

. . . only a portion of all crimes will be noticed by the public or the victim. Of these, only a portion will be reported to the police. Of these, only a portion will result in an arrest. Of these only a portion will be prosecuted. And of these, only a portion will be convicted. Consequently, the size of a cohort dwindles the further along in the process it gets.

Sociologists who work within this metaphor appear to be making two assumptions: first, that the people who end up in jail were guilty of a crime; and second, that only a small proportion of guilty people end up in jail. Most of these sociologists argue that the criminal law and the criminal justice system are designed to address particular kinds of crimes and particular kinds of offenders, specifically street crimes committed by the poor.

Brannigan suggests that there are two problems with this metaphor. He argues first that not all of those who end up being processed through all the stages of the criminal justice system are in fact guilty (though most probably are) and second, that the criminal justice system is not so much directed *against* the poor as *for* the rest.

Brannigan prefers the metaphor of a net, the criminal justice system net that can catch more or less and different kinds of crimes and criminals, depending upon what one is fishing for. The net is not directed against poor people, per se, but rather the rest are better able to escape it.

What this means is that those people who are arrested and go to jail are, by and large, quite guilty of their crimes, but they are not the only elements of society engaged in serious, harmful behaviour, nor are they the only elements of society to be engaged in serious criminal cases as a result of that behaviour. They are, nonetheless, overrepresented in the cohorts that receive the most punitive treatment by the criminal justice system.

In any case, part of the reason that the powerless groups are more likely to be arrested can be found in the actions of the ordinary citizen. An excellent example is provided by David Stymeist (1975) in his study of "Crow Lake," the name of a fictitious town in Northern Ontario. In Crow Lake, as elsewhere in Canada, native people are frequently arrested and almost always for public drunkenness (see Table 6.2). Stymeist describes how the police routinely park outside of the Crow Lake Hotel, the town's largest tavern, around closing time, waiting for "arrests." The patron, who may be a friend or a steady customer, is asked if he wishes them (the police) to call a cab. The white customers are often picked up at the rear entrance and driven home unseen by the police. Native people are not accorded this kind of treatment and must leave by the

front entrance where they are often picked up by the police.

Despite the debate among criminologists, it seems evident that police, like most of the rest of us, will have learned and incorporated cultural stereotypes, and these stereotypes will influence how they treat people in various social positions in their day-to-day activities (see Thornton, 1975). Indeed, Jock Young (1971), a British sociologist, argues that the police are more vulnerable than most of us to the stereotypes presented in the mass media because they are isolated from the rest of the community and have few friends outside of the police. Accounts by blacks in cities in Canada, the United States and Britain would indicate that they are more likely to be stopped at night by police for routine checks and are therefore at much greater risk of being arrested for offences such as impaired driving or illegal possession.

Another example of selective labelling is provided by Edmund Vaz (1965) who interviewed a number of middle-class Canadian high school boys to find out how many of them had committed delinquent acts. While very many of them admitted that they had performed such acts, very rarely had they been labelled as delinquent.

These studies, called self-report studies, have a rather controversial history in sociology. From the results of such studies, usually on juveniles, some sociologists have concluded that middle and lower-class youth are about equally likely to commit criminal acts and thus the high rates of lower-class crime must simply reflect the greater likelihood that they will be labelled. Other sociologists have pointed out that middle class and lower-class youth seem to break different kinds of laws; lower-class youth committing more serious infractions. They conclude that the higher rates of lower-class crime are a reflection of the behaviour of the lower-class youth rather than the behaviour of the labellers.

No doubt, both views contain a truth. Labelling theorists force us to view "becoming deviant" as an interactive process. As we indicated earlier, it takes two to label, to arrive at a social definition of an act. In the interaction between say, a young offender, for example, who is native or poor and a police officer who is an official agent of the system of social control, a public servant, the cards are stacked against the young offender. The label of deviant is negotiated through an unequal negotiation process.

Labelling theory makes us aware that not all those who have broken a rule are labelled deviant; nor can we assume that all those who have been labelled deviant have broken a rule. What "deviants" do have in common is that they have been negatively labelled and such negative labels — crook, nut, fool — can exert a powerful influence on their lives.

THE DEVIANTS' PERSPECTIVE

Labelling theorists, drawing on symbolic interactionism, have focused on the interaction between the labeller and the "deviant." To examine this interaction it is important to know how deviants view themselves and their actions. A good example of an attempt to get at the "inner lives" of deviants is Humphreys's (1970) study of *tearoom trade*, male homosexual behaviour in public washrooms. Humphreys found great variation in how the men who engaged in such homosexual behaviour defined themselves and their actions. We can use his data to develop a typology of deviants. One of his most interesting findings was that not all of the men who engaged in such homosexual behaviour saw themselves as homosexuals. Some seemed to be saying that while homosexuality is deviant, the label does not apply to them. They claimed that the tearoom provided them with a source of quick impersonal sex; they went for the orgasm, not the company. (Because they did not get involved with their tearoom partners, this kind of sex did not threaten their family lives.) They might be termed the "falsely accused."

On the other hand, some of the men claimed there is nothing wrong with homosexuality in general. Homosexuality, they claimed, is a perfectly natural act. These men were generally immersed in a homosexual subculture with values different from those of conventional society. Some homosexuals may actively invite the label, "come out of the closet," in an attempt to change societal values. Others may be more concerned with leading a "normal homosexual" life among other homosexuals (see also Sawchuck, 1974). The former groups might be termed "dissidents," the latter "subcultural deviants." Subcultural deviants are isolated or isolate themselves from conventional labels.

Of course many of the tearoom participants believed both that homosexuality was immoral and that they were homosexuals. Except for their limited tearoom contact, they generally avoided other homosexuals, in "gay bars," for example, and consequently had not learned to justify or rationalize their behaviour. Unlike the former categories, they were likely to feel guilt and self hatred. They are the "pure deviants."

In short, the people being labelled may disagree with the labellers. There may be a conflict of values (for example, the social desirability of homosexual behaviour) or *definitions* (for example, the applicability of the label "homosexual"). Looking through the deviants' eyes, we can distinguish the types of deviants listed in Figure 7.1.

The dissident and the subcultural deviant, immersed as they are in a deviant subculture, are less vulnerable to the negative reactions of others than are those deviants who are still attempting to maintain a commitment to conventional norms and values.

DEVIANT CAREERS

Labelling of individuals as deviant seems to have a self-fulfilling effect.
Indignation, punishment and segregation from the community might mark the person out in a

FIGURE 7-1

THE DEVIANT'S PERSPECTIVE

		VALUE CONFLICT	
		Behaviour Is Deviant	Behaviour Is Not Deviant
DEFINITIONAL CONFLICT	Label Is Accepted	PURE DEVIANT	ACTIVE DISSIDENT
	Label Is Not Accepted	FALSELY ACCUSED	SUBCULTURAL DEVIANT

special way, and together with others in a similar position, he might eventually act in ways that resemble society's stereotypes of him (Cohen, 1971:17).

The negative label often denotes a **master status**. The individual comes to be seen as first and foremost a deviant. He or she is seen in a completely new light. When the labelling is public, the "deviant" becomes a symbol — the dramatization of evil, a reminder of the importance of the rules and the consequences of violating them.

The general principle at work is a simple one: when others decide that a person is non grata, dangerous, untrustworthy, or morally repugnant, they do something to him, often unpleasant, which is not done to other people. This may take shape in hurtful rejections and humiliations in interpersonal contacts, or it may be formal action to bring him under controls which curtail his freedom (Lemert, 1972: 68).

Imagine that you have discovered that your male friend is a homosexual. Initially this is rather a shock, but soon you begin to "recall" certain of his past behaviours which "should" have made his homosexuality obvious to you. In retrospect, you say that you can certainly find a number of instances which "fit" and now everything he does seems to confirm his homosexuality. In short, our perception becomes selective. In reacting to the deviant, the social audience engages in a process of *retrospective interpretation* on the basis of common-sense stereotypes.

Often these reactions will have a profound effect on how deviants view themselves. This will be the case particularly when most of the people the deviants encounter respond to them and their behaviour in similar ways. The deviants may feel degraded by the reactions of others. They may feel a dramatic loss of status and dignity. Even the deviants who believe they have been falsely accused may begin to experience self-doubt and guilt. Often they incorporate the negative labels into their self-conceptions. Once actors have developed deviant self-concepts, they are well on the path to a deviant way of life, or what Lemert calls *secondary deviation*. The deviants may find that they have limited alternatives in choice of friends, occupation and so on. At this point, they may begin to seek out the only people they believe can give them the support and understanding they need — other deviants.

It is also of interest that societies have rather elaborate rituals and "ceremonies" to mark the *status passage* (Glaser and Strauss, 1971) from citizen to convict, from sane to insane, from normal to deviant, but virtually no public statement of the reversal (Garfinkel, 1956; Goffman, 1961; Gusfield, 1971). Public flogging and now "trial by the press" make the public aware that justice has been served and the guilty have been punished. And in the process, the accused is transformed. However, there are no comparable statements from the press when a convict is released from prison. Perhaps, as Durkheim argued, punishment is more an example to others — one way in which the collective conscience is shored up — than deterrence, rehabilitation or retribution. Certainly, crown prosecutors and judges are often concerned that a particular sentence be viewed as a "message to the community" that certain behaviours will not be tolerated.

As the outcasts come to restrict their associations to other "deviants," they may learn to justify their behaviour, to neutralize their feelings of guilt and even to redefine the activity in positive terms. The labellers — conventional society — may become the "outsiders": corrupt, hypocritical, square, what have you.

These learned justifications may not only allow further participation in the deviant activity, they may even encourage it. So, for example, fat becomes beautiful, "a sign or result of character, spirit, love of life, or some other rare and desirable quality" (Himelfarb and Evans, 1974:231). Membership in the organized deviant group — subcultural deviance — is the final stage in the *deviant career*. At this point, the *process of becoming deviant* may be virtually irreversible. People become deviant because they have been labelled deviant.

On the other hand, some organized deviant groups, the Gay Liberation Front, for example, have taken an active part in trying to change public definitions and social policy. At this point, whether their actions are seen as political protest in the form of dissidence, or deviance, depends on the ideology of those doing the labelling. In any case, it would appear that deviance might in fact be seen as a source of important social change. Some groups have a vested interest in maintaining the status quo, others in changing their society, and so we return to the initial question of the labelling theorists: which groups have the power to enforce their values on others?

Labelling theory has, in fact, had a profound impact on social policies and social programs. On one level, we can see the impact in the greater care shown by special services for the mentally handicapped and physically disabled and the labels used to describe their clients. The new labels such as "special people" recognize that these may have special needs but seek to avoid the damaging effects of negative labels.

At another level, we can also see the impact in legislation. In Canada, this is, perhaps best illustrated in the new sexual assault legislation.

Prior to this legislation, courts did not treat rape as simply a case of assault. Rather, it seems that the rape victim was asked to demonstrate that she had behaved in a sexually "moral" and "proper" way; rape was defined in large part in terms of what role the victim played or was perceived to have played. Further, it seemed that to the courts only certain kinds of women could be raped. Lorenne Clark and Debra Lewis (1977) analysed rape cases for several years—those which came to trial, those reported but not tried and the many which were never reported officially. They found that the police decision to pursue a rape case was largely based on their perception of the victim. Police were apparently less likely to put forward a case for prosecution, for example, if the victim lived alone or if she had been drinking, or if she was from the lower class.

Clark and Lewis did not blame the police for these decisions because, as they observed, the police were in a "structural bind." On the one hand, they get into trouble if their arrests consistently fail to produce convictions. On the other hand, they were often frustrated because many of the cases they "knew" to be rapes were unlikely to produce convictions. They knew that successful cases usually demanded that the victim be middle class, "morally upright" and living "under the protection" of parents or husband.

Clark and Lewis concluded from their research that women were viewed by the courts as property and rape was not assault but a crime against the property of men.

Men have defined rape as a sexual offence because it is an attack on their sexual property. One of the worst consequences of this definition is that it leaves no harm to be punished unless a "valuable" woman is physically damaged by the rape attack. If no economic harm is done, or if this harm is very minimal, there appears to be no theoretical basis for treating rape as a legal offence or for punishing the rapist. The rapist commits a wrongful act because he damages or "steals" another's property; his crime is sexual because the property stolen is sexual. But when the victim does not belong to somebody else, or does not possess qualities which make her potentially valuable, then her rape cannot be perceived as wrong (1977:160).

In 1973, the new sexual assault provisions to the Criminal Code sought to ensure that the female victim of sexual assault was no longer treated as though she, herself, was on trial and that her sexual life would not be open to scrutiny. The testimony of victims of sexual assault was now considered sufficient evidence and did not need to be corroborated by evidence of penetration, torn clothing or witnesses to the assault. Moreover, the rule of "recent complaint," that a credible victim would have set up a "hue and cry" at the first available opportunity, was abolished. This latter change was in recognition that victims, initially afraid or ashamed, may need time to decide to report the offence to the police.

For the first time, wives were afforded explicit protection against sexual assault by their husbands. The fundamental change in the legislation, mainly away from rape to sexual assault, recognized that what was at issue was a brutal and violent attack rather than an act of sexuality. And, this way of viewing the crime also gave recognition that men could be the victims of sexual assault. By helping us to recognize how the previous rape offences reflected, in large part, men's assumptions about women, and how the implementation of this legislation allowed men to make the rules for women, labelling theory has contributed to major social reform.

At the same time, research that has attempted to evaluate this particular reform suggests that there are often unanticipated consequences, positive and negative. No doubt victims of sexual assault are treated better by police, by crown prosecutors and by the courts. But, many defence lawyers are concerned that some of the basic safeguards provided by the traditional adversarial processes and rules of evidence are undermined by this legislation: it is now much more difficult to mount a defence than in other kinds of criminal offences. And since most victims of sexual assault who report at all do so very soon after the incident, crown prosecutors are frustrated that they cannot introduce "recent complaint" as evidence of the victim's sincerity. Finally, many are concerned that replacement of "rape" by the concept of "sexual assault" is to trivialize the offence. Judges, in their sentencing, generally recognize the difference between what we know as rape and other forms of sexual assault, but what is reported to the public is that someone was charged with sexual assault.

. . .

Before we leave labelling theory it is important to emphasize that labelling, that is, categorizing others, is a fundamental feature of how people think about the world. Labelling theorists simply encourage us to examine the labels we use, to question what we may have taken for granted, to ask how the labels emerged and what are the consequences of their use. They also encourage us to question and even challenge the prevailing legal system

CRIME AND DELINQUENCY

Just as deviance varies from society to society and time to time, so too does criminal behaviour. To take one example, in traditional Inuit society acts become criminal only when they threaten the survival of the community, not when they threaten an individual. In virtually every modern society, however, those actions which are thought to involve "some serious violations of person and property" are held to be criminal (Hagan, 1977:20). Of course, just exactly what constitutes such "serious violations" is not always clear. Groups will define this differently and, as we have shown, interest groups will often compete to get their definitions enacted into law.

Behaviour defined as criminal falls into three broad categories. We have already described the category of *victimless crimes*. Laws against drug use, pornography, many forms of sexual deviation and so on are supposedly enacted to protect us from ourselves (see Goode, 1973:121–124). It seems likely that the pressure groups do not feel the need for such protection themselves but for the mass of people "less able" to manage their own affairs. And as we have suggested, underlying this paternalism are the concerns of powerful groups with maintaining the status quo, protecting vested interests and preserving their own lifestyle by legally enforcing their morality.

‖ CRIMES AGAINST PERSON

However, when most of us discuss and worry about increasing crime we are thinking about *crimes against person* and *against property*. Certainly no crime captures the public imagination like murder even though, as we can see in Figure 6.2, Canada is a relatively nonviolent country, particularly in comparison to the United States. Indeed Canada is a less criminal nation in general.

Few would quibble with the notion that murder and other forms of violence against people must be dealt with as crimes. However, given that most murders occur in the home among intimates, it is unlikely that greater vigilance or the expansion of the police force would make much difference.

Nevertheless, the fear of crimes of violence and violent criminals, the fear of being mugged, assaulted or worse, is apparently growing to dramatic heights in Canada. As D. J. Baum points out, these fears have little to do with the Canadian reality.

Day after day, Canadians, both rich and poor, place curfews on themselves. They limit and intimidate their children by instilling fear of violence from unknown criminals. They restrict their own freedom to travel and meet others. They create and heighten the very feelings that led many of their parents and grandparents to leave their native land and seek Canada as a home. They do all this out of fear . . . Yet how curious it is . . . those whom they fear are generally not violent. They commit crimes against property without acts of violence . . . (1979:2).

However rare in Canada, the sexual murderer, the killer of children, the killers of police officers, shape our perceptions of crime. Through the lurid and dramatic media coverage of these rare but horrifying events, through the fictional accounts of violence in American television programs, our fear of crime may become disproportionate to the actual risk of violent criminal victimization. In Canada, violent crime has been a relatively steady seven percent of all crimes though our attitudes about crime control and punishment seem fuelled more by this seven percent than by the majority of often more trivial and opportunistic crimes against property.

Historical accounts of violence in Canada (e.g., Bercuson and Knafla, 1979) raise some question about whether we are truly living in a more violent age. What may be happening is that we are living in an age of growing intolerance of violence, that our definition for unacceptable violence is far broader than in the past. Perhaps, today, we are less likely to see the barroom brawl or the street corner fight as a minor community problem.

Perhaps, too, violence within the family is coming to be recognized as a public issue rather than a private trouble. It is no longer tolerable that parents may beat their children or that husbands abuse and exploit their wives.

Much of the violence of the past has been kept invisible, within the ghetto or the family home. With the increasing visibility of violence, it becomes more threatening to us all and our values and attitudes to crime and punishment are transformed. Known cases of child abuse and child sexual assault are on the increase though the actual incidence may not have changed.

There is another side to this growing fear of violence. In the late 1960s, Alex Gigeroff created a good deal of controversy by arguing that every criminal act was an interaction between offender and victim and that guilt had to be apportioned between the two. At a time when the victims movement was gaining steam and demanding better treatment at the hands of police and courts, the idea that victims participated in their own victimization was not a welcome one. Certainly this idea can be dangerous and easily overstated such that victims are made to feel guilty because of the behaviour of others.

Nevertheless, Gigeroff has captured something of how our fear of criminal victimization at least, in part, reflects our belief that we have rights, rights to move freely and without constraint, rights to walk alone at night unmolested, perhaps even rights to leave our children unattended to play. And, with this growing commitment to this sense of individual rights, comes a growing intolerance for the behaviour of others that constrains those rights.

CRIMES AGAINST PROPERTY

Certainly more court and police time is taken up with *crimes against property* — theft, shoplifting, vandalism and so on, than with violent crimes or crimes against the person. Indeed most of the laws in the Criminal Code are in one way or another concerned with the protection of property. In a society such as ours, where we are all bombarded by campaigns encouraging us to buy, to own, to accumulate material possessions, it is not surprising that those "who have" are preoccupied with the concern that those "who have not" will simply take. It is in this context that

we can understand the pressures on agencies of law enforcement to come down hard on what may be trivial crimes of property.

Not all crimes against property are likely to be handled by the criminal justice system. Public pressures on the police are generally for them to handle what have been termed "crimes in the street" rather than "crimes in the suite" (Goff and Reasons, 1980). Individual *white collar criminals*, embezzlers, for example, are less likely to be processed as criminals than are vandals or car thieves. In part, this is because of the relative invisibility of these crimes to the public and therefore the lack of public pressure for their control. In part, too, this is because the larger corporations are able to handle these crimes and the costs of these crimes internally and through the use of internal disciplinary mechanisms including firing employees. Often, such informal crime control is seen as preferable as the corporation avoids the loss of public confidence by keeping these infractions private.

Many of the most serious white collar or corporate crimes are simply too complex and difficult to detect for the police. As well, the line between legal and criminal is difficult to draw and culpability difficult to assign when a corporation deliberately sets out to ignore statutes prohibiting certain corporate behaviour. Polluters, price-fixers, and tax evaders may be breaking the law but are rarely designated as deviant. They may often see their behaviour as a legitimate part of the business enterprise, and legal intervention as state intrusion into private affairs.

JUVENILE DELINQUENCY

Criminal justice processes emerge clearly when we examine juvenile delinquency in Canada. Canada passed its first juvenile delinquency act in 1908. While there is some debate about the direction of influence between Canada and the United States regarding approaches to the legislation on juvenile delinquency, both American and Canadian legislation appear to have had a similar development and certainly have been closely connected (Hagan and Leon, 1977).

An excellent text on the development of juvenile delinquency legislation in America is Anthony Platt's *The Child Savers* (1969). According to Platt, feminists at the turn of the century provided the impetus for special juvenile delinquency legislation. He points out that these feminists did not challenge basic structures or assumptions, as contemporary feminists have done, but were primarily concerned with extending the woman's role outside the home and with reforming society, particularly in such areas as the education and treatment of children outside the home. Many were particularly concerned with the predicament and future of lower-class youth who, of course, were the most likely to come into contact with the courts. The "child-saving movement" clearly reinforced, rather than challenged, dominant values revolving around motherhood and the role of women.

In any case, this movement was able to influence legislation and to create and occupy a range of court-related treatment occupations — counsellors, court workers, social workers. The central theme of this new approach to juvenile delinquency, a theme objected to by many law enforcement officers, was that juvenile delinquents should be treated not punished. In Canada a similar movement (or movements) emphasizing separation of juvenile and adult offenders and treatment and probation for juveniles, rather than punishment, had similar success (Hagan and Leon, 1977).

Under the Juvenile Delinquents Act of 1908 (revised 1929), a child was considered to be delinquent if he or she violated any provision of the Criminal Code, provincial statutes or municipal by-laws. But the definition of juvenile delinquency was much broader than that of adult criminality. The definition of a juvenile delinquent also included any youth "who is guilty of sexual immorality or any similar form of vice, or who

is liable, by reason of any other act, to be committed to an industrial school or juvenile reformatory under the provision of any Dominion or provincial statute." It is difficult to imagine any youth who could not have been sentenced under the broad terms of this Act.

We have already described the influence of political criteria on police decisions to arrest. This may be no less true of the sentencing activities of judges. For example, as Tepperman argues:

Judges tend to come from a particular social stratum: they are well-educated and relatively prosperous besides generally having professional, social, and political attachments to the elite. Their sentencing patterns often reflect the concerns of any prosperous person for life and property when dealing with poor people, especially during a period of social discontent like the Depression. The judiciary has a political and not only rational-intellectual activity in which written rules and community standards are applied to information about behaviours. Like the others engaged in maintaining order, judges tend to support the status quo. Some evidence shows that judges are selected because they are in sympathy with the ruling class (1977:85).

Clearly judges had a particularly high degree of discretion in the handling of juvenile cases. This discretion was legitimated in terms of **individualized justice** and in the name of treatment. Recently, in Canada, a sentencing commission examined the philosophy and purposes of sentencing and published its findings and recommendations. The response to these recommendations may also serve as a response to the current lack of a comprehensive philosophy of the purposes of sentencing. In the meantime, debates continue about the extent to which sentences should reflect the particular needs of offenders or more abstract notions of justice. While Canada also lacks comprehensive court statistics that would tell us about current patterns of sentencing, debates flourish about how much disparity there is in sentencing and whether this is necessarily a problem.

The old juvenile delinquency legislation encouraged disparity by promoting individualized justice — sentences designed to meet the particular needs of particular offenders. But what did this mean for the juvenile who came in contact with the juvenile court? For one thing, the juvenile who saw the variability in court decisions in convictions and sentencing, often developed a "sense of injustice" which further alienated him from conventional society (Matza, 1964).

This sense of injustice was likely to be enhanced because delinquents in Canada were not guaranteed the same degree of protection against the court, for example, in their rights to legal counsel, as were adult criminals. Further, the juvenile accused, say, of "joy riding," would no doubt come to recognize the contradictions built into a system which continually encouraged him to evaluate himself in terms of whether he had a car and the type of car he owned and at the same time punished him for "borrowing" a car for a while. In fact, the great bulk of juvenile crimes by males involve cars.

As well, the emphasis on "treatment" in juvenile justice may be misleading. First of all "treatment" may often mean little more than incarceration, "doing time" in an understaffed reformatory or training school. More important, however, there is a good deal of question about whether the treatment programs that were offered worked (Hagan, 1977: 182ff).

Indeed Matza (1964) points out that social workers are often the ones who teach the juveniles how to justify their delinquency as they explain to them that they are not really accountable for their actions, that the delinquency is not really their fault but rather a result of their poverty, their broken homes, their alcoholic parents or what have you. All of these factors — the growing sense of injustice, the learned justifications and of course the official public labelling of the juvenile as delinquent — probably encourage rather than discourage further delinquent activity (see Vaz, 1976:167–169).

In response to just such concerns the Law Reform Commission drafted new legislation and proposed alternative approaches to juvenile delinquency which suggested a growing awareness of the problems in the organization of juvenile justice. Out of this work emerged the *Young Offenders Act*, proclaimed into legislation in 1983 and amended in 1986. This *Act* not only provided the juvenile with more legal protection but also emphasized the juvenile's accountability for his or her actions. This represents an attempt to bring the juvenile justice system closer to the adversary relationship of the adult criminal system.

At the same time there has been growing emphasis on finding alternatives to incarceration and compulsory treatment not only for juveniles but for all offenders. The Law Reform Commission has described the basic elements of a program of **diversion** which would minimize or even eliminate the contact offenders have with the justice system.

Many, though certainly not all, offences could be dealt with informally within the community; some charges might simply be dropped; and many cases could be settled out of court. Often alternatives to incarceration could be found. It is not clear exactly where to draw the line, that is, which crimes might be handled by such diversion, but what we have described as victimless crimes and many of the offences of young offenders may be the places to start. In essence, a policy of diversion or nonintervention argues that, whenever possible, leave deviants and criminals alone (Hagan, 1977:196).

DIVERSION: THE SAGA OF A LIBERAL REFORM

The notion of pretrial diversion, now well established in the United States and gaining acceptance in Canada, was very much a product of the liberal optimism of the sixties. The proponents' aims were noble:

they wanted to save accused offenders from the indignities of pretrial detention, from the stigma of a criminal conviction and from the debilitating effects of a jail sentence (Potter, 1981:8).

They wanted to make the prison a sentence of last resort. Prisons, it was understood, were a breeding ground for crime, a training school for criminals, dehumanizing and alienating. If young offenders, first-time offenders and nonserious offenders could be given counselling or job placement *within the community*, they would escape the worst consequences of criminal justice processing and would have a far greater chance for rehabilitation. This was the argument.

The reality has been less rosy. While it is too early yet to draw firm conclusions about diversion programs, we have become increasingly aware of their limitations, of how often the original aims have been distorted by judges trying to clear their dockets, by prosecutors trying to find a way to deal with weak cases, by defence lawyers who have little commitment to weak or powerless clients, whatever the merits of their case (Potter, 1981).

How can this happen? K. E. Renner, a Dalhousie psychology professor, argues that the diversion programs being developed in Canada have lost the original image of diversion as a significantly new way of thinking about criminal justice, as a way of reducing the authority and intrusion of the criminal justice process. Rather, diversion has become *yet another reform which adjusts the mechanics of the process, but leaves unaddressed the very problems which created the need for diversion in the first place (Renner, 1979:1-2).*
Diversion has become part of the problem according to this argument.

Imagine that you are a prosecutor who "knows" some young offender is guilty but you lack the evidence to be confident of a conviction. You may see in "diversion" a way of imposing sanctions on the offender without the risks of a trial. We say "impose sanctions" because typically diversion programs have not simply "left offenders alone" but rather

have promised those accused of an offence that they would not face a trial if they were to perform some community service, make restitution or submit to treatment; that is, diversion has often become punitive. It has also become a mechanism that allows the criminal justice system to cast its net more widely, to capture in it those who might otherwise have gone free.

Imagine, too, for a moment, that you are a young, first-time "offender" approached with such an offer. And suppose you were not guilty of the offence. Might you not agree to participate in such a program if you knew this meant that you could avoid a trial, something most of us no doubt would find embarrassing and intimidating. And, of course, a trial poses some risk even to the "innocent." Many, no doubt, would forego their right to a hearing to minimize their contact with the apparatus of the criminal justice system.

As practiced in Canada diversion has apparently become mere tinkering. Some radical theorists have gone further to suggest that the concept of diversion and the programs it has spawned distract our attention from the need for more fundamental reform of the criminal justice system. We are, the radical argument goes, sending these people back into the same so-called communities, the same layers of inequality and vulnerability, that brought them to the attention of the police in the first place. An emphasis on diversion diverts us from necessary social, economic and political reforms. In other words, diversion focuses its solution on the individual when the real problem is one of social structure (see, for example, Morton and West, 1977). No doubt there is merit to this view. The real problems do reside elsewhere and diversion does not seem to be providing the hoped for results.

But the work of radical sociologists and their critiques may often make almost any social action seem a rather hopeless business. What are we to do? Reforms that look good on paper seem in the end to be corrupted and compromised beyond recognition. Are we to wait for some sort of revolutionary change that will solve or at least address the real problem? Should we only work towards such long-term ends? Is there no place for liberal reform? Many sociologists spend a good deal of their time and emotional energy trying to sort out just such issues.

We shall treat these questions more directly in Chapter 9 and again in Chapter 14. For now let us say that we believe there is an important place for "liberal" reform within a radical perspective. Perhaps it is important to humanize our institutions *within* the system at the same time as we try to make more fundamental changes of the system. Perhaps only in this way can we hope to provide something of a blueprint for the "new order."

Getting back to diversion, we would argue that even though "leaving criminals and deviants alone" does not solve the basic problems, it remains a worthwhile goal. Adult diversion programs, "fines options programs," which allow convicted offenders to work off some of their fine rather than go to prison, post-conviction diversion—all still more or less in the experimental stage — do point to worth-while directions for reform.

About 40 percent of the Canadian prison population are in prison because they have been unwilling or unable to pay court-imposed fines. The original sentencing judge has decided that they do not belong in jail or prison but they end up there. Diversion of some sort is better. Fewer than 20 percent of those in prison have been convicted of crimes of violence. What of the other 80 percent? Some sort of diversion would probably be better for many of them. The costs of incarceration continue to climb in a time of restraint. There may be better ways to spend this money.

Diversion undoubtedly creates new problems. Denial of due process, "informal justice," may create a wider criminal justice net. Compulsory treatment as a "diversion" alternative may pose even greater threats to our individual liberties than imprisonment. But diversion remains a worthwhile goal. These qualifications simply remind us that the reform struggle is not easily won nor ever complete.

Diversion programs *can* be set up in such a way that the due process of the accused is protected (Potter, 1981 and Renner, 1979). Safeguards can be provided for those "in need of treatment" (Himelfarb and Lazar, 1981). Even if the fundamental problems are not solved, the consequences can be softened.

But such an approach demands that we be both clear-headed and hard-headed. We must know what we want and can expect from such reforms as diversion. Do we mean diversion to be another kind of attempt at rehabilitation of the supposedly wayward, or do we mean it as a way of making the justice system more humane and responsive without jeopardizing the individual's dignity as a responsible actor? Perhaps those charged with a criminal offence "have a right not to fit in, not to be perfect, not to be 'rehabilitated'"; and perhaps it is best to allow them to plead their case or, whenever possible, if the risk is not too great, to leave them alone (see Potter, 1981).

CRIME AND DELINQUENCY: SUMMARY

We should reiterate that official labelling or, more generally, official social control activities, are not *the causes* of delinquent or criminal behaviour. It is hard to argue with the thesis that poverty and obstacles to mobility produce unusual pressures to commit certain criminal acts.

However, it is probably true that we cannot provide a general theory of the causes of deviance or crime; different kinds of deviant and criminal behaviour probably require different kinds of explanations. What we have tried to show, however, is that a general understanding of deviance and crime requires an examination of how rules are made, applied and enforced—the activities of social control. As we have shown, the weight of law falls more heavily on some groups than others.

Powerful groups have more say in creating the rules and laws for the rest of us. Police and the courts do, at least to some degree, apply these laws selectively. Some groups are more likely than others to get arrested, to get convicted or to get committed for mental treatment. Public labelling, incarceration and "treatment" may serve to alienate, or at least further alienate, many people from conventional society. And this alienation may, for many, lead to commitment to a professional criminal career.

Finally, as Vaz (1976:169) cautions us:

Those groups and agencies responsible for the control and prevention of deviance are themselves likely to break rules in the course of their duties. Neither formal nor informal control agents are special kinds of people, nor are they immune to the forces and processes operating to produce deviance in society. Therefore, we should not be surprised when we hear of the cruelty of parents towards their children, of the viciousness of prison guards and the staffs of correctional institutions towards their inmates, or of the immorality of priests. Nor should we be shocked to learn about corruption among our law enforcement agencies, that inspectors and politicians as well as judges can be bribed, that cheating, malingering, favouritism and wickedness are found among the institutions designed to watch over us. As Albert K. Cohen suggests " . . . we have travelled full circle and are confronted with the problem of the social control of the agencies of control." The question is: "Who will guard the guardians?"

SUMMARY AND CONCLUSION

Two persistent themes of the literature on deviant behaviour are the importance of *socialization* and the importance of *inequality*. The deviant behaviour perspective suggests that deviant motives, attitudes, skills,

etc., are acquired through interaction; deviant behaviour is simply a manifestation of deviant socialization. The labelling perspective, on the other hand, suggests that deviant motives, attitudes, skills, etc., may be acquired as a response to being labelled; people may learn to be deviant *after* their initial act simply because they have been set apart and "forced" to interact with other deviants.

The deviant behaviour perspective emphasizes how unequal access to the legitimate means of success may produce pressures on some groups to engage in certain nonconforming acts. The labelling perspective emphasizes the unequal distribution of power — power to impose definitions of appropriate behaviour, to label and to resist labels. And groups that are labelled deviant will have unequal access to the legitimate means of success. And so we see the "vicious circle" of deviance and control.

We suggested at the outset that some sociologists find in the area of deviance reassurance of human individuality and creativity. Indeed, at least implicit in the work of many labelling theorists is the suggestion that we ought to be more tolerant of deviance and of human diversity. The extreme of this view can be found in the work of R. D. Laing (1967), who describes the mentally ill as the "prophets" in an insane society, psychiatrists as the new police, guardians of the status quo. He decries the conservative ideology and dehumanizing tendency of the social sciences. Our discussion, we hope, demonstrates that sociological discourse can be cast in distinctly human terms, can challenge conventional wisdom and can contribute to our understanding of even what appear to be the most individualistic of acts.

We yet know little of why killers kill, thieves steal and hooligans attack people and property. Some recent attempts to draw social profiles of the archetypal violent criminals, the serial murderers, have raised more controversies than they have provided answers. Controversies continue about how accurately we can predict dangerousness. Confusion persists as to why some within the same family become career criminals and others do not. While we may find that a mass murderer acted out of some intense hatred for the system or some class of people within that system, not all such people act out their hatreds. Why do some act out their hatreds and others not? Why do some insist on becoming high or drunk first?

In this area in which the public desire for understanding and clarity is so great, we have provided little comfort. Those who argue that crime is simply a normal feature of every soci-

ety offer little solace. Those who argue, as described in Chapter 13, that crime is simply another manifestation of the fundamental social cleavages of capitalist society, offer little for social and criminal justice policy. Part 4 of the text looks at the major dimensions of inequality and, in so doing, may suggest future approaches to crime prevention and control. The concept of crime prevention through social development recognizes the root causes of crime in economic inequalities, both real and perceived, and in the fragmentation of family and community.

▌▌▌ SUGGESTIONS FOR FURTHER READING

For a good general overview of earlier approaches to deviance see Howard Becker's *Outsiders* (1963); Albert Cohen's *Deviance and Control* (1966); David Matza's *Becoming Deviant* (1969); Paul Rock's *Deviant Behaviour* (1973); Edmund Vaz's *Aspects of Deviance* (1976); John Lofland's *Deviance and Identity* (1969); and Edmund Lemert's *Human Deviance, Social Problems and Social Control* (1972). Now a classic, Edwin Shur's *Labelling Deviant Behaviour* (1972) shows how the labelling approach draws from conflict theory, functionalism, symbolic interactionism and phenomenology. His *Crimes without Victims* (1965) is a provocative discussion of some of the social policy implications of the labelling approach.

John Hagan's *The Disreputable Pleasures* (1977) is an excellent introduction to deviance in Canada. More recent Canadian texts are Robert Stebbins's *Deviance: Tolerable Differences* (1988) and Desmond Ellis's *The Wrong Stuff: An Introduction to the Sociological Study of Deviance* (1987).

Most of the important theoretical statements and empirical findings are to be found in collections. Some of the more important and interesting of these include Carl Rubington's and Martin Weinberg's *Deviance: The Interactionist Perspective* (1968); Howard Becker's *The Other Side* (1964a); Paul Rock's and Mary McIntosh's *Deviance and Social Control* (1974); and Clifton D. Bryant's *Deviant Behaviour: Occupational and Organizational Bases* (1974). Earlier Canadian collections include Craig Boydell's and others *Deviant Behaviour and Societal Reaction* (1972); Jack Haas's and Bill Shaffir's *Decency and Deviance* (1974); and William E. Mann's *Social Deviance in Canada* (1971).

For an introduction to the work in crime and delinquency see Gwynn Nettler's *Explaining Crime* (1974). Although somewhat dated, David Matza's *Delinquency and Drift* (1964) provides an excellent critical review of the delinquency literature of the time and a useful approach to delinquency research. A now classical work in radical criminology is Ian Taylor's, Paul Walton's and Jock Young's *The New Criminology: For a Social Theory of Deviance* (1973). One of the finest studies of the interpretative process at work in the criminal justice system remains John Hogarth's Canadian study, *Sentencing as a Human Process* (1971). Other useful sources on crime in Canada include:

Craig Boydell's and others *The Administration of Criminal Justice in Canada* (1974); W. T. McGrath's *Crime and Its Treatment in Canada* (1972); Lorne Tepperman's text *Crime Control* (1977); D. J. Baum's *Discount Justice* (1979); E. Vaz's *Crime and Delinquency in Canada* (1979); S. Verdun Jones's and others *The Canadian Criminal Justice System* (1980); and Augustine Brannigan's *Crimes, Courts and Corrections* (1984). Two recent collections of articles are Rick Linden's *Criminology: A Canadian Perspective* (1987) and Silverman's and Teevan's *Crime in Canadian Society* (1987).

A sample of more radical approaches to deviance and criminology in Canada can be found in Brian Maclean's edited collection *The Political Economy of Crime* (1986) and Robert Ratner's and John McMullan's edited collection *State Control: Criminal Justice Politics in Canada* (1988). The edited collection, from a conference organized by The John Howard Society, *Insights into Violence in Contemporary Canadian Society* (1987) provides brief and readable examinations of both perceptions and patterns of violence.

Some of the most controversial work in deviance has raised questions about the meaning of mental illness and the role of psychiatrists. Thomas Szasz, himself a psychiatrist, raises many of the important questions in *The Myth of Mental Illness* (1961) and *Psychiatric Justice* (1965). The Scottish psychiatrist R. D. Laing provides a different kind of challenge to psychiatry in *The Politics of Experience and the Bird of Paradise* (1967). For a vivid and angry rebuke to Laing, see Mark Vonnegut's *The Eden Express* (1975).

PART THREE

PERSPECTIVES ON CANADA

DEMOGRAPHIC PERSPECTIVES

Note: This chapter was prepared with assistance of Dr. Albert Currie.

OVERVIEW

In this chapter we introduce the special discipline of demography—the study of populations, their size, distribution and change. Of course, what demographers do is more complicated than we can convey in this chapter. Our objective is not to teach you the details of this field but, by the end of the chapter, you should have an appreciation of the objectives of demography. And, second, you should have some knowledge of what, generally, is happening to world population and to Canadian population and some of the reasons for the changes in both. More importantly, you should know why these changes matter.

The tools of demography are formulas which try to measure the basic processes which affect population: birth rates, death rates, immigration and emigration rates, life expectancy and infant mortality rates. These formulas, or measures, become important indicators of the values and attitudes of a particular society and of the social and economic conditions of that society. For example, you should not lose sight of the fact that birth rates tell us something about people's decisions and something of the values they attach to having children. Immigration rates tell us not only about the decisions of immigrants but also decisions of governments to limit or invite immigration and to prefer some sources over others for their immigrants. Similarly, death rates, life expectancies and rates of infant mortality provide dramatic indices of the social and economic conditions of a country and inequalities within a country.

This chapter, then, illustrates how demographers can help us demonstrate how societies have changed over time, the persistent differences between developed and developing nations, and, within Canada, between native peoples and the rest of the Canadian population. Put in this context, demography is the study of some of the most dramatic consequences of social, cultural and technological changes.

But, demography is more than this. It also seeks to examine how changes in population act upon and change culture and society. So, for example, just as low birth rates and low population growth seem to be a consequence of industrialization, they may act to change industrial capitalism and even limit the capacity to maintain continued economic growth. Similarly, while improved health care and nutrition may extend life expectancy, the increasingly large cohort of elderly people may create new demands on health care services and may have more profound consequences on the culture and structure of a society such as ours.

Demography is also useful for helping us to understand enduring conflicts and competing interests within and among societies. While some countries, such as Canada, may worry about the possible consequences and impact of declining populations, other countries face more serious problems of how to feed populations which have far outstripped resources. And, on a global level, when we recognize that we all contribute to and share the fate of the planet, we all must make some decisions about what we can do, if anything, to address the dramatically accelerating growth of world population. However remote such issues may seem to Canadians, and however long term to most politicians, the issues of world population are issues for every nation.

INTRODUCTION

In the first parts of this book, we have introduced you to theories and perspectives which, many would argue, have universal validity. That is, what we know about socialization, role playing, deviance and conformity, or the dynamics of small groups, seems to apply if not to all people in all societies, at least to all present-day people in western societies. The chapters that follow focus much more explicitly on Canadian society and, in effect, deal with larger, or macro, issues. As our focus shifts to consider such things as the nature of Canadian capitalism, our class structure, patterns of social mobility, the educational system, ethnic relations and ethnic inequality or social movements, it is less evident that we are now dealing with universal truths. Certainly, many of the theoretical perspectives developed in other societies have relevance to an understanding of Canadian society. But, as sociologists have learned, these must often be modified and rethought in the Canadian context.

THE CANADIAN CONTEXT

One atlas of Canada describes us as a "nation of superlatives." When we think of our geography, our climate and our resources, words such as largest, coldest, longest, even emptiest, spring easily to mind since they can so readily be applied to many aspects of our physical environment. Children, and probably most adults, seem endlessly intrigued by and take immense pride in Canadian trivia: that it is further from Newfoundland to Alberta than to Europe; that virtually all of Europe can be encompassed within our borders; that Japan, with its 115 million people, has less land area than any of the Prairie Provinces; that Ontario has one-quarter of all the available fresh water in the world; that at 7770 km, the Trans-Canada Highway is the world's longest national highway. We could

of course go on. Climate, geology, and geography in both subtle and obvious ways are with us at all times, and have played their part in shaping us and in making us a unique culture, a different society.

In the next chapter we will be looking at some of the attempts to develop theoretical perspectives that recognize the unique characteristics of Canadian society, Canada's history and economic and cultural development. A useful starting point for any analysis of this or any society is an awareness of its demographic characteristics. What is happening to our population not only affects us individually and collectively, it also sets the basic parameters that shape and limit our social and economic development.

DEMOGRAPHIC PERSPECTIVES

Demographers, though often using complicated and sophisticated measures, are essentially concerned with very basic information about a population: births, deaths, movements of people, the distribution of the population, and social characteristics of individuals and families.

Demographic data provide a good starting point for a study of society for several reasons. First, most of the information is collected by governments on a regular basis and comes closer than any other form of data to complete coverage of the population. Because people are legally bound to provide census information, it is probably also the most accurate information that social scientists have at their disposal. Second, demographic data are about "vital" processes, literally life and death matters—birth, marriage and divorce rates, geographical mobility and mortality rates (rates per 100 000 population). In other words, they are about things that affect all of us individually and collectively. Third, what is happening to our population has important social, political, and economic consequences. Figure 8.1

FIGURE 8.1

ISODEMOGRAPHIC MAP OF CANADA

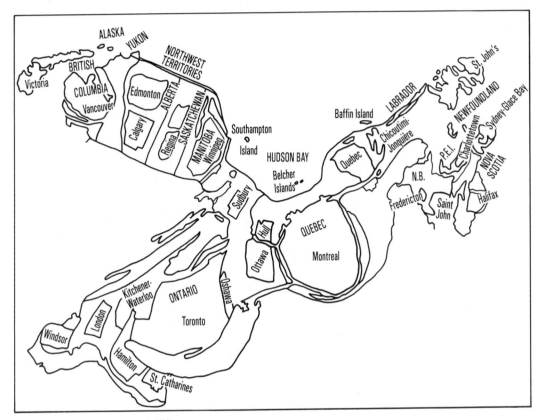

Source: Skoda and Robertson (1972).

provides clues as to why Western and Eastern alienation from Central Canada exists, why regionalism is an issue in Canadian society, why (as we shall see) it has sometimes made sense to talk about conflict between metropolis and hinterland. What one historian, Bercuson, wrote a decade ago still holds true:

The power of Quebec votes and the necessity of the federal government to pay as much heed to Quebec as it does to Ontario reveals the existence of one region—Central Canada—with common characteristics. It is industrialized, populous, part of the St. Lawrence heartland, the holder of an absolute majority of seats in the House of Commons, and the major beneficiary of national, economic, cultural and social policies (1977:2).

The crux of the matter is, of course, population. Nor is the study of population as neutral as it might first appear. For politicians it represents the study of voters; for businesspeople the study of markets; for governments the basis for allocating resources and services. The study of population matters in very real ways. And shifts in population have very real consequences even in our everyday lives.

Ask yourself, for example, what might be the long-run implications for Canadian society of the fact that native people have the highest birth rate or, that at present, Quebecers have the lowest birth rate. At a more personal level, think how you are affected by "steady state stagnation": that as a result of the short-lived "baby boom" of the 1940s and 1950s, the civil service, educational institutions and corporations are, in the 1990s, all administered by people in middle age who are a long way from retirement. And, you might also want to think about what it means to say that Canada has an aging population: that the combination of the baby boom, two decades of a very low birth rate and several decades of long life expectancies mean there are fewer young people to support the pensions and services for growing numbers of old people in our society. We will be considering these and other issues in this chapter and attempting to show how demography provides one kind of perspective on such issues.

POPULATION DYNAMICS

Probably, at some level, we all have at least a dim awareness that the make-up of our society is changing. Demographers quantify these impressions. They seek ways to capture and convey, graphically, these sometimes traumatic changes in population and the best of them go beyond mere reporting of statistics to contemplate what these depictions mean to all of us now and in the future. For example, *population pyramids*, though seemingly rather bland and static depictions of the age and sex structure of a population, contain within them predictions about all of our futures and a chronicle of the past that helps us to understand our history.

A population pyramid is a snapshot of the age and sex structure of a population at a particular time. A succession of such snapshots, taken at regular intervals (as in Figure 8.2), provides a kind of moving picture of changes in the age and sex structure of a population. The horizontal bars show the size of five-year age groups with males on the left and females on the right. Changes in the age-sex structure are a result of the same factors

that cause the overall population to rise or fall. Clearly, population grows as people are added by fertility (births) and by in-migration and declines as a result of mortality (deaths) and out-migration. These components of population that change from one time to another are expressed in the basic **demographic equation**:

Population (time 2) = Population (time 1) + (births—deaths) + (in-migration—out-migration)

As can be seen in Figure 8.2, past events with respect to any of these four components must work their way through the history of a population and have different implications at different times. For example, the 0–4 age group in the 1951 population pyramid is relatively large because the Canadian birth rate was quite high in the 1950s. By 1961, this "birth cohort" was 10–14 years of age and had moved up through the age structure. Notice that the difference between the 0–4 and 5–9 age groups is smaller in 1961 than in 1951. This is because the birth rate dropped quite dramatically during that decade and continued to stay low until the present.

This has had an obvious effect on the structure of the Canadian population. By 1981, the largest age groups in the population were 15 to 24, born during the baby-boom period of 1955 to 1965. The steady decline in fertility between 1961 and 1981 accounts for the smaller age groups between ages 0–4 and 10–14 in 1981. In other words, the pyramid-like shape of these graphs becomes distorted if there are dramatic changes in birth rates, death rates or patterns of migration. If a period of high birth rates is followed by a period of low birth rates, the "pyramid" will no longer be a "pyramid"; it will have shorter bars at the bottom than at the middle.

These population pyramids, then, describe not only demographic changes but also sociological changes, some of which have already happened and others that await us in the near future. Look again at the 1951 Canadian population pyramid in Figure 8.2. When that large group of people in the 0–4 and 5–9 age

FIGURE 8.2
THE AGE-SEX STRUCTURE OF THE CANADIAN POPULATION, 1951–1981

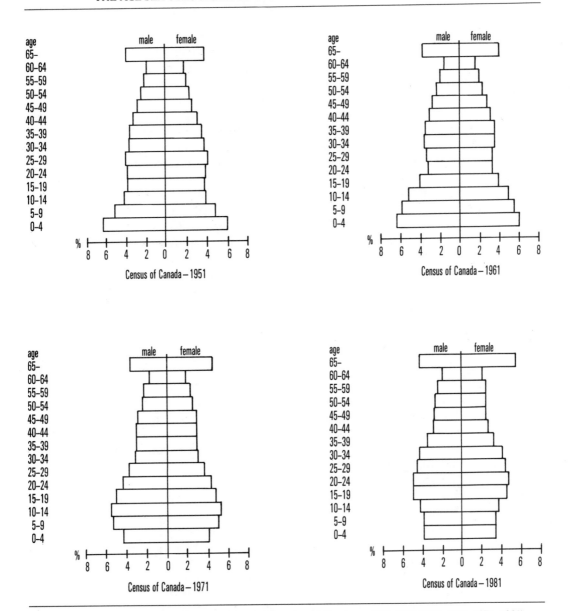

Source: Adapted from *Population by Sex and Age for Canada and Provinces 1951–1981* (1951, 1961, 1971, 1981), Ottawa: Ministry of Supply and Services.

groups were born they created demands on hospitals and the health care system. And, at the same time, they created opportunities for businesses manufacturing and selling products for babies and small children. As these cohorts moved through the population pyramid, schooling became the issue and, as we see in Chapter 12, there was a massive expansion of education, both to meet the current needs of the baby boom children but also in anticipation of their future needs.

Later, many in this generation confronted an increasingly competitive job market, one which was unable to absorb so many young people all at once. Those who followed the baby boom cohort into the work force had even greater difficulty. The best jobs and most senior positions were taken and by relatively young people. The job market was clogged. In the future, this large bulge of people will reach retirement age and will put strains on government pension plans and the health care system. And, because they are followed by smaller cohorts of younger people, there may be intense resentment about the cost of maintaining the baby boomers in their old age.

Perhaps, even more crucial than jobs and the sudden demise of businesses making and selling baby products, is what occurs culturally. In the 1960s and 1970s, the focus was on youth, on their consumer demands, their taste in music and their vision of society. Businesses tried to capture the "youth market"; the cultural industries sought to entertain them. Their power and influence may have helped to change patterns of family life and parenting. To a considerable extent, older generations felt out of place in their own society and often made usually unsuccessful efforts to fit into the youth culture.

As the Doonesbury cartoon has chronicled, the baby boom generation has grown older, and is more affluent and conservative. It remains a dominant force in society but, as this cohort grows older, it forces new changes in our culture. For example, young people today are not growing up in a world in which they are the centre of attention as they were two decades ago.

Or, to take another example, consider what happens when there is a particularly heavy influx of immigrants into a society. Ordinarily, migration, in or out of a society, does not have much impact on the shape of population pyramids. But, as can be seen in Figure 8.2, there are exceptions. During the decade 1901 to 1911, Canada experienced heavy in-migration but most of these immigrants were males, with the result that the male age groups 20–24 and 25–29 are distinctly larger than the corresponding female age groups. This provides, perhaps, some insight into why, during the first decades of this century, there was so much concern about the need for prohibition, about ways to control this large influx of rootless men, destined to life in boarding houses and the bunkhouses of the north.

Finally, Figure 8.3 presents another unusual population pyramid, this time for France in 1959, though we could as easily have used data from other countries in postwar Europe or Japan. Here, we see, graphically, the demographic and sociological impact of two momentous wars on a society. The bars for the age group 15–19 are pinched inward. These people were born between 1940 and 1945, the years of the Second World War, a time when it was difficult for people to marry and to have children. There is an even greater trough in the pyramid at ages 40–44. These people were born between 1915 and 1919, the years of the First World War and also a time of low birth rates. Even more remarkable is that the bars for men between 60–64 and 75–79 are smaller than those for women. This gives some insight into how perilous that war was for men. Not only did trench warfare lead to many more fatalities than later wars but those who were merely wounded or suffering from pneumonia and influenza had a good risk of dying of infection in hospital. Again, contained within these seemingly dry statistical presentations are the structural reasons why those who survived the Great War are often described as the "lost generation."

Clearly, the most important use of demographic techniques such as population pyramids is that they allow us to predict, with a fair degree of certainty, our collective future and the kinds of political and social challenges we face in the decades ahead. But, there is a

---

FIGURE 8.3

AGE-SEX STRUCTURE OF THE POPULATION
OF FRANCE

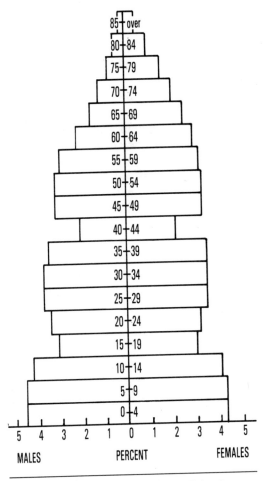

Source: Warren S. Thompson and David T. Lewis,
Population Problems (5th ed.), McGraw-Hill, 1965.

---

degree of irony in all of this precision. Demographers cannot predict whether there will be a sudden upswing in the birth rate and another baby boom. Their predictions do, however, tell us that even if that should not occur, we will for a time at least, inevitably, have a large number of old people being supported by a relatively small group of younger people.

Short of another Holocaust or nuclear war, our immediate demographic future is predestined. And, that means we have the knowledge to begin planning and dealing with the rather predictable problems associated with these progressive changes in the age structure of our population. This, of course, requires commitment to long range thinking, a commitment that is not necessarily consistent with public pressures for immediate solutions to immediate problems. The difficulty of gaining commitment to address long-term problems is nowhere more evident than in the more general issue of population growth.

MALTHUS AND THE PRINCIPLE OF POPULATION

The debate about the advantages and disadvantages of population growth and of a larger or smaller population is not new. Throughout history, there have been arguments both favouring and opposing a growing population. For example, writing in the fifth century B.C., Plato advocated a small and slowly growing population. He wrote that while the population of a city state (a *polis*) must be large enough for military defence, it should not be so large as to place a burden on the food supply. He believed that a population should remain small to allow the more effective functioning of the Athenian democracy. Moreover, he argued that a slowly growing population would allow a more equal inheritance of property and as a consequence would preserve equality among citizens. Aristotle (384–334 BC) held views quite similar to those of Plato. In *Politics* he wrote that uncontrolled population growth "is to bring certain poverty on the citizens, and poverty is the cause of sedition and evil."

However, the more common view has been to advocate a large and growing population. The early Arab social philosopher Ibn

Khaldun (c. 1380) in a book called *Prolegomena* supported the view that a larger population is beneficial for economic growth and military strength. Nico Machiavelli (1469–1527) in *The Prince* also argued that a growing population meant military strength and security, and economic growth; however, he also made the argument in another book, *Discourses*, that the population of a country could become too large, and if it did, poverty and disease would decrease the size of the population to its optimum size.

These were essentially academic arguments because throughout most of human history the population of the world was extremely small and the growth rate was slow compared with the present. Nonetheless, there were many instances of famine when the pressure of population strained available food supplies. As well, some cities were "overpopulated," when too many migrants, from the surrounding countryside, produced pollution from smoke and sewage. The English poet Shelley wrote that "Hell is a city much like London, a populous and smoking city." But none of this became the focus of very much debate until the work of Malthus.

Almost two centuries ago, an English clergyman, Thomas Robert Malthus (1776–1834), published the first of seven editions of his *Essay on the Principles of Population*. Malthus's essay on population gained popularity because he wrote it as an argument against two very prominent schools of thought in 18th century Europe, mercantilism and revolutionary utopianism. Mercantilism was an economic philosophy that held that large national populations were necessary for maintaining economic strength, and for maintaining the military and political power to protect against rival powers.

Revolutionary utopianism, a philosophy current during Malthus's time, embodied a new conception of humanity. According to that philosophy, human betterment and greater equality not only were possible but would be an inevitable product of social evolution. Almost all of the revolutionary utopians also believed that strong population growth was an "indication of the strength of the nation" (Petersen, 1975). Malthus disagreed with both of these ideas and he wrote his *Essay* to address this philosophical debate. Initially, he was not so much concerned about population as challenging the optimistic utopian thinking of his day.

Malthus pointed out that the crux of the population problem was the pressure of a population on resources necessary to sustain it. Writers before Malthus had also made that point. But Malthus succeeded in showing that the problem of population is the balance between population and resources, and that population growth would always reach its limits relative to available resources.

Malthus's argument is basically very simple. If left unchecked, population will increase in a geometric progression, e.g. 1, 2, 4, 8, 16, 32. Malthus thought that the length of time required for each doubling of population was about 25 years, one human "generation." At the same time, Malthus argued that the means of subsistence tend to increase in an arithmetic progression, e.g. 1, 2, 3, 4, 5, 6 in about the same time periods as required for the doubling of population. Even if, at the outset, population were small and resources plentiful, the power of population would soon overtake the growth of the food supply and the availability of other natural resources (see Figure 8.4).

As a population becomes larger, people find it necessary to exploit resources more intensively. Soil becomes less fertile through high intensive farming. Non-renewable resources such as minerals become exhausted. According to Malthus, the population must inevitably decline to reach a balance between numbers of people and the resources available to sustain the population.

Malthus recognized that in human populations, as in animal populations, there are "checks" on population growth. In an animal population, in its natural surroundings, and in the absence of predators to keep the popula-

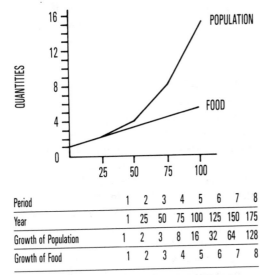

FIGURE 8.4

THE MALTHUSIAN CURVES

Period			1	2	3	4	5	6	7	8
Year			1	25	50	75	100	125	150	175
Growth of Population			1	2	3	8	16	32	64	128
Growth of Food			1	2	3	4	5	6	7	8

Source: Overbeck, J. *History of Population Theories*, (Rotterdam: Rotterdam University Press, 1974), p. 43.

tion in balance with its food supply, the numbers of the species would increase until there were too many of them for the food supply. At that point the population would decline because of lack of food.

In human populations the situation is more complicated because there are checks on population growth which are cultural. Malthus distinguished two types of checks or controls on population increase, ***preventive checks*** and ***positive checks***. The main preventive checks are moral restraint, the postponement of marriage, or sexual abstinence in marriage. The other types of preventive checks he termed vice. These are promiscuity, homosexuality, adultery, and birth control including abortion.

The positive checks were, for Malthus, starvation, famine, disease, and war. Where the preventive checks failed to halt the growth of population, the positive checks would, in his view, eventually come to exert their effect. Starvation, famine and disease result directly from lack of adequate food supplies. War, as a consequence of population pressure, might occur where one nation, experiencing shortages of food and resources because of a growing population, attacks another country in order to expand its territory.

For Malthus, population growth would always be subject to positive and preventive checks. In those countries where the preventive checks were strong (especially moral restraint, because Malthus the clergyman could not condone the "vice of birth control"), positive checks would be less important. However, in countries where preventive checks were weak, the positive checks would eventually prevail.

On the whole, Malthus remained pessimistic about the human condition. He believed that there would always be a tension between population growth and subsistence; however, in the second and subsequent editions of his *Essay*, Malthus modified his "dismal theorem" by extending the types of preventive checks. He argued, for instance, that more education for the poor and higher economic levels would lead to a decrease in the number of children. In other words, economic equality and universal education offered some hope for a way out of the Malthusian trap (Petersen, 1975:155).

Viewed from our vantage point, Malthus's theory contains four basic weaknesses. First, he underestimated how much could be produced from the amount of available land. Advances in agricultural methods, the use of chemical fertilizers and pest controls, animal breeding, and plant genetics have dramatically improved the ability of modern agriculture to produce more food using the same amount of land, though not without costs. Second, Malthus, writing at the turn of the 18th century, could not foresee the possibilities for improvement in standards of living through industrialization and technological advances. Third, the theory did not anticipate the development of new markets and the growth of international trade which took place throughout the nineteenth and twentieth centuries. These factors greatly accelerated economic growth and the wealth of European nations. Finally, perhaps because of his religious beliefs, Malthus ignored the possibility of the development of relatively reliable and safe contraception.

But, on a world scale, Malthus's dismal theory still holds. As is described below, when the traditional checks which had restrained growth of population in many Third World countries were removed, their populations grew in nearly geometric patterns. The populations in many parts of the world have grown so large and so rapidly, that, in the short run, and perhaps the long run, people in these societies face incredible hardships.

Poverty, widespread disease, chronic malnutrition, destruction of the natural environment and momentous urban problems in many Third World countries are vivid reminders that without preventive checks, positive checks will ultimately prevail. Many modern statements of the population problem, such as those in the 1970s by the Club of Rome (Meadows, Meadows, Randers & Behrens, 1972; Mesarvic & Pestel, 1974), are in many ways very similar to Malthus's basic argument. In the next section we consider world population growth and whether the same factors that made Malthus's predictions untrue for Europe and North America will eventually affect population growth in the rest of the world.

THE GROWTH OF WORLD POPULATION

In June, 1987, the world "population clock" in Ottawa "ticked" over the five billion mark. The growth of the world's population over the past century and a half has been so dramatic and the numbers now are so large that demographers have had to resort to metaphors and analogies such as the "population bomb" and the "population explosion" to convey the magnitude of the problem. As Kingsley Davis, a sociologist and demographer, put it some years ago, "viewed in the long run perspective, the growth of the earth's population has been a long, thin powder fuse that burns slowly and haltingly until it finally reaches the charge and then explodes" (Davis, 1949:595).

Figure 8.5 provides a vivid illustration of Davis's depiction. World population grew very slowly during prehistoric times and throughout much of recorded history. After about the year 1000 the population began to rise more steeply than before. After around 1800, the curve representing the growth of the earth's population shot straight upward. Approximately three million years were required to achieve the first billion of world population. The second billion was reached in only 130 years by 1930. Thirty years were required to add the third billion, and 15 years to add the fourth billion. According to population projections, the fifth and sixth billion will be added in 12 years and 11 years, respectively.

Most scientists believe that human beings have existed as a distinct species for about three million years. During 99 percent of this time, humans lived in small hunting and gathering societies. Death rates, as well as birth rates, were very high so that population grew very slowly. As early as 10 000 B.C. there were probably no more than 10 million people on earth (Thomlinson, 1965). By the first year A.D. there were around 300 million human beings, and by 1650 the earth's population probably had reached 500 million. After 1650 it grew a little more rapidly.

One explanation of this growth is the increasing efficiency of agriculture. It appears that with the exception of the African continent, agricultural innovations were occurring independently in many parts of the world and, with a more reliable food supply, the population began to grow more rapidly.

The explosive growth of world population

FIGURE 8.5

WORLD POPULATION THROUGHOUT HISTORY

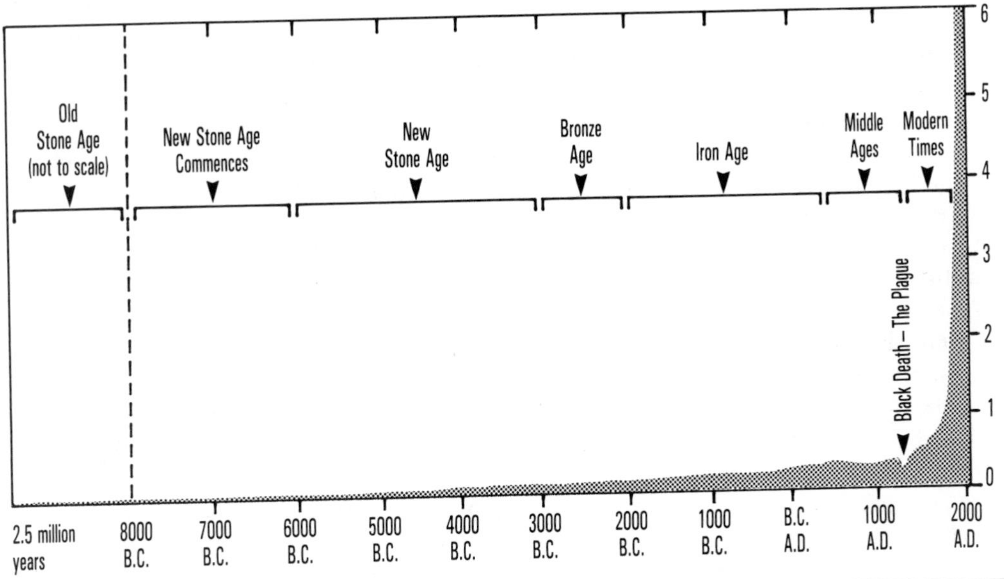

Source: Population Reference Bureau, *World Population: Fundamentals of Growth*, 1984.

in the present century has occurred mainly in Asia, Africa, and Latin America. In these populations, growth rates accelerated very rapidly and in very short periods of time. The numbers of people in the Third World were much larger than in Europe. With a much larger population base, accelerating growth has resulted in the large increases in absolute numbers shown in Figure 8.5 and Table 8.1.

Many people fear that world population growth poses the ultimate threat of destroying the ecological balance of the planet. Some modern counterparts of Malthus emphasize that we live on "spaceship earth." This is an attempt to convey the idea that the earth's life support mechanisms are a closed system. The explosive expansion of one of the interdependent elements of the spaceship earth, the human population, leads to overuse of the environment, to pollution and the ultimate collapse of major segments of the ecosystem

(Ward, 1966). Yet, population growth is uneven. In the highly industrialized societies, there are declining populations; whereas in the rest of the world the opposite is true.

TABLE 8.1

ESTIMATED TIME REQUIRED TO ADD EACH BILLION OF WORLD POPULATION

	TIME REQUIRED	YEAR
First billion	2.5 million years	1800 A.D.
Second billion	130 years	1930
Third billion	30 years	1960
Fourth billion	15 years	1975
Projections		
Fifth billion	12 years	1987
Sixth billion	11 years	1998

Sources: John D. Durand, "Historical Estimates of World Population," *Population and Development Review* 3 (September 1977), and United Nations, *World Population: Trends and Policies*, 1981 Monitoring Report, Vol. 1, Population Trends, United Nations, 1982.

Demographers have attempted to account for the historical pattern of population growth in terms of the **demographic transition theory**. Warren Thompson, writing in the 1920s, developed the theory and identified three types of countries with different combinations of birth and death rates. At that time, all countries we now refer to as Third World countries had what he termed high growth potential (Thompson, 1929). While both birth and death rates were very high, death rates were slightly lower than birth rates so that the population was, in fact, growing very slowly. However, he maintained that these countries had high potential growth because he believed that death rates were about to fall, thus widening the gap between the birth rates and the death rates, and increasing the rate of natural increase.

A second group of countries was undergoing rapid population growth. In Thompson's time, these were the countries of Eastern Europe. These countries have all become slow growth countries now. At that time, however, their birth rates were high and their death rates were low, and their populations were growing rapidly.

Thompson's third group of countries included those in Western Europe. In these countries, both birth rates and death rates were low. The populations of both the first and the third types of countries were growing slowly — the Third World because of high death rates to balance high birth rates and Western Europe because lower birth rates balanced lower death rates.

Later on, other demographers such as Frank Notestein (1944) developed Thompson's observations into the demographic transition theory (see Figure 8.6). It was intended as a highly general theory to explain how populations grew in the past and predict what they will do in the future. The theory states that there are three stages in the demographic history of all populations. These stages correspond to stages of economic development or industrialization.

Stage 1, high birth and death rates, represents the demographic conditions that prevailed among human populations during most of our existence. Women bore large numbers of children, possibly about eight to ten live births. But rates of infant and childhood mortality were also very high; and overall, life expectancy — a measure of the average length of life—was very low. During this stage of the demographic transition, economies were based mainly on hunting and gathering and later on subsistence agriculture. There were, then, often periods of hunger and famine because of unreliable food supplies.

Because basic data from these early periods are almost non-existent or unreliable, estimates of life expectancy vary widely. Life expectancy was probably about 30 years for people living one or two centuries B.C. and may have increased to about 40 years by the eighteenth century (Thomlinson, 1965:77–78). These were the prevailing conditions in Europe prior to the 18th century and in Third World countries up to the middle of the twentieth century.

Stage 2 represents a period in which birth rates and death rates decline but death rates decline much more rapidly. The lag between the decline in death rates and the decline in birth rates leads to larger rates of natural increase and rapid population growth. This stage occurs as agricultural methods become more developed and food supplies become more plentiful and stable. In later phases of the development of Stage 2, improved medical care and sanitation also played a role in the reduction of the death rate. In Europe, sanitation and medical care began to bring down death rates after the middle of the nineteenth century, about a hundred years after noticeable improvements in agriculture.

At the same time, entry into the second stage of the demographic transition by non-western countries was very much related to improved medical care during the 1940s and after. The availability of modern medicine from western countries dramatically lowered

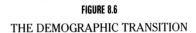

FIGURE 8.6

THE DEMOGRAPHIC TRANSITION

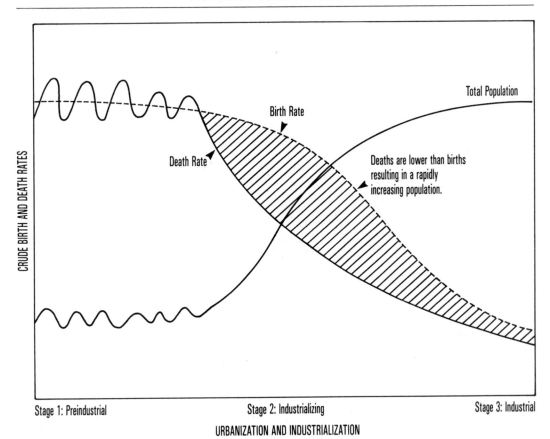

death rates in some areas in very short periods of time. The progress in mortality reduction that took a century or more to occur in Europe, took place in the space of a decade in many Third World countries after World War II. Nutrition was improved as a result of the "green revolution": the introduction and use of fertilizers, insecticides and pesticides, irrigation technology, new disease-resistant varieties of crops, and use of agricultural machinery.

The transition to high rates of natural increase in Europe occurred slowly. Migration to North America, Australia, and South America played an important role in relieving population pressure in Europe. In contrast, the transition to rapid growth in the Third World occurred very quickly. Populations which were much larger than those in Europe, to begin with, grew extremely rapidly in a very short period of time. This accounts for the "explosion" of population shown earlier in Table 8.1.

The European nations, Australia and New Zealand, North America and Japan have all passed into Stage 3 of the demographic

TABLE 8.2
ESTIMATED POPULATION DATA FOR SELECTED EUROPEAN COUNTRIES—1985

COUNTRY	MID-1985 POPULATION ESTIMATE (000 000)	CRUDE BIRTH RATE (PER 1000)	CRUDE DEATH RATE (PER 1000)	ANNUAL NATURAL INCREASE (PER CENT)	POPULATION PROJECTED TO 2000 (000 000)
Denmark	5.1	10	11	−0.1	5.0
Norway	4.2	12	10	0.2	4.2
Sweden	8.3	11	11	0.0	7.9
United Kingdom	56.4	13	12	0.1	57.0
Austria	7.5	12	12	0.0	7.3
Belgium	9.9	12	11	0.1	9.2
West Germany	61.0	10	11	−0.2	49.9
East Germany	16.7	14	13	0.1	16.8
Hungary	10.7	12	14	−0.2	10.5
Italy	57.4	11	10	0.1	54.8

Source: 1985 World Population Data Sheet, Population Reference Bureau, Inc.

transition. As can be seen in Table 8.2, birth rates have declined to about the same level as death rates with the result that there is, in some countries, an actual decline in population, in others "zero population growth" and in still others, a very modest increase. The decline in birth rates is believed to be the result of a variety of factors: changing women's roles, requirements of urban-industrial society, widespread use of contraceptives and, more generally, the fact that in the more advanced stages of capitalism, child labour was abolished; children were now "bread eaters rather than breadwinners," economic liabilities rather than economic assets.

While during the past decade fertility has declined in most Third World countries, it remains questionable whether the Third World will follow a pattern similar to the path of the classic transition theory to low birth and death rates, and slow and stable population growth. This hypothesis nevertheless led population experts to hope that if Third World countries could be transformed from underdeveloped to developed societies, then their

birth rates would also fall. In fact, to some extent, this has occurred. In Latin America, for example, birth rates, though still very high, have fallen slightly. However, in Southern Africa, the Indian subcontinent and Southeast Asia, birth rates remain very high despite the fact that death rates have fallen considerably (Wrong, 1976; Weinstein, 1976). As Table 8.3 suggests, the Third World will, in the future, comprise an even larger proportion of the total world population.

John Caldwell (1973), an American demographer, has developed what he calls a "flow of wealth" theory to account for fertility decline. In those societies where children are economic assets and wealth flows from children to their parents, fertility will remain high. Conversely, in societies where children are economic liabilities, where wealth flows from parents to children, fertility will be low.

In most Third World countries, children are economic assets because, as children, they contribute to the household economy—gathering firewood, working in the fields and caring for younger children—and, as adults, they

TABLE 8.3

POPULATION GROWTH, 1750 TO 2100, WORLD AND FIVE MAJOR REGIONS

(NUMBERS IN MILLIONS)

REGION	TOTAL POPULATION													
	1750		1900		1950		1985		2000		2025		2100	
	N	%	N	%	N	%	N	%	N	%	N	%	N	%
World total	760	100.0	1 630	100.0	2 516	100.0	4 837	100.0	6 122	100.0	8 206	100.0	10 185	100.0
Less developed regions	569	74.9	1 070	65.6	1 681	66.8	3 657	75.6	4 837	79.0	6 799	82.9	8 748	85.9
Africa	100	13.2	133	8.2	224	8.9	555	11.5	872	14.2	1 617	19.7	2 591	25.4
Asia (minus Japan)	455	59.9	867	53.2	1 292	51.4	2 697	55.8	3 419	55.8	4 403	53.7	4 919	48.3
Latin America	14	1.8	70	4.3	165	6.6	405	8.4	546	8.9	779	9.5	1 238	12.2
"European"/ More developed regions	191	25.1	560	34.4	835	33.2	1 181	24.4	1 284	21.0	1 407	17.1	1 437	14.1
Europe, USSR, Japan, Oceania	189	24.9	478	29.3	669	26.6	917	19.0	987	16.1	1 062	12.9	1 055	10.4
North America	2	0.3	82	5.0	166	6.6	264	5.5	297	4.9	345	4.2	382	3.8

Source: Thomas W. Merrick, *World Population in Transition*, Population Bulletin, Population Reference Bureau, 1986, p. 12.

support and care for their now aged parents. In contrast, in highly industrialized societies, children are economic liabilities, in terms of parents' loss of income and career advancement and the cost of supporting and educating them until adulthood. Nor do children ordinarily support their parents in their old age.

The demographic transition theory tells us a good deal about the demographic history of the now developed societies, those which have become highly industrialized. It remains to be seen whether the theory can predict the future of societies where populations continue to grow so dramatically. As we have seen, the situation of Third World countries is quite different from that of the Western societies in the 18th and 19th centuries. Central to the demographic transition theory is that as societies industrialize and urbanize, fertility rates decline. But, while urbanization has certainly occurred in the Third World, indus-

trialization has been uneven and has not been able to follow the Western pattern.

In short, while virtually all Third World countries are industrializing, large segments of the populations of these countries remain within an economy that favours high fertility; for those who in their everyday lives are relatively untouched by industrialization, children remain important economic assets. See Figure 8.7 on the following page.

In sum, during the past decade or more, fertility has declined somewhat in most Third World countries. However, so has the death rate, with the net result that the rate of natural increase in these countries has not fallen appreciably. Given that over the next 100 years demographers estimate a world population of from 7.5 billion to 14.2 billion, whether or not demographic transition theory offers more than an interpretation of a rather unique set of historical events is an extremely critical question.

FIGURE 8.7

THE DEMOGRAPHIC TRANSITION IN THE DEVELOPED AND IN THE DEVELOPING NATIONS

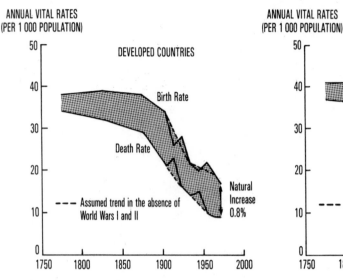

ANNUAL VITAL RATES
(PER 1 000 POPULATION)

DEVELOPED COUNTRIES

Birth Rate

Death Rate

- - - Assumed trend in the absence of
World Wars I and II

Natural
Increase
0.8%

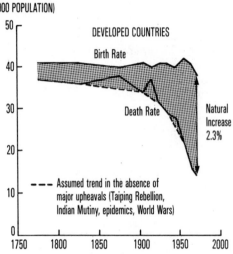

ANNUAL VITAL RATES
(PER 1 000 POPULATION)

DEVELOPED COUNTRIES

Birth Rate

Death Rate

Natural
Increase
2.3%

- - - Assumed trend in the absence of
major upheavals (Taiping Rebellion,
Indian Mutiny, epidemics, World Wars)

In developed countries death rates declined slowly beginning in the late 18th century. Birth rates followed closely. Population growth rates rarely exceeded 1.5% per year.

In developing countries birth and death rates remained high through the first decades of the 20th century. Their death rates began to drop. Birth rates stayed high and populations grew at 2.5, 3.0, and 3.5% or higher a year. Since the mid-1960s some countries' birth rates have begun to decline.

Source: U.S. Department of State, *World Population: Silent Explosion*, 1978.

CONSEQUENCES OF POPULATION GROWTH

The addition of people to the world's population between 1975 and the year 2000 will be almost the equivalent of the total population of the world in 1930. This is the equivalent of adding about twenty-seven new countries with the population of Canada. About 90% of all this growth will occur in Third World countries.

Growing populations in some areas with poor agricultural land are increasing the cultivation of marginal agricultural areas with devastating results for the soil. Soil erosion

and the overuse of marginal agricultural land is in some places creating deserts where plant life once existed. As well, in some countries where firewood is the only fuel available to the vast majority of the population, there is wide scale deforestation. In many countries, for instance in South America and in Southeast Asia, the urgent need for economic development to keep pace with rapidly growing populations has led to large-scale forestry operations in the delicate tropical rain forests. As populations grow, so there is a growing need to cultivate land which, in the past, was seen as marginal or non-usable. The result, in some countries, is deforestation and, in others, the creation of deserts. In South America, delicate rain forests, the source of much of the world's oxygen, are threatened. In North Africa, the Sahara grows each year.

Indeed, there is some evidence from Africa that population growth may be influencing changes in climate (Brown, 1985:4). Overgrazing by domesticated animals, the cutting down of trees for firewood, or the degradation of soil through over-cultivation can all lead to a decrease in the amount of vegetation in an area. Without vegetation to hold water, less moisture evaporates into the air to return again in the form of rain and the result is deserts where once there were forests and arable land.

Another major consequence of rapid population growth is large scale **urbanization**. In countries with rapidly growing populations, rural areas are often overpopulated, and resources and economic opportunities are extremely limited. Cities offer at least the hope of a better life. Massive rural to urban migration swells the slums and barrios daily. Figure 8.8 illustrates the staggering growth of many Third World cities. Huge cities such as these present enormous challenges, not only for providing basic social services and urban amenities to their burgeoning populations,

but also for the economies of those countries. Because of the economic strains imposed by this range of urban social problems, these cities absorb rather than generate wealth. With so much of the national wealth being drawn into one or a few urban areas, there is little left over to distribute to the rest of the country. The non-urban areas remain poor, and the population continues to grow.

Producing enough food to avoid chronic malnutrition and periodic famines on a scale ever greater than what we experience today poses a formidable problem. Currently, most developing nations are capable of producing enough food to feed their populations. However, most do not; partly because large landowners find it more profitable to grow cash crops such as coffee or tea and partly because of inefficient or inappropriate technologies. In many countries of Africa, per capita food production has actually declined.

Present world population is now over five billion and, depending on estimates, will inevitably rise as high as 14.2 billion. However, one demographic prediction is that the population will stabilize at about 10 billion inhabitants by 2100. Bernard Gilland has concluded

---

FIGURE 8.8

TEN LARGEST CITIES IN THE WORLD 1950, 1980, 2000 (POPULATIONS IN MILLIONS)

RANK	1950		1980		2000	
1	New York— N.E. Jersey	12.4	Tokyo-Yokohama	17.0	Mexico City	26.3
			New York— N.E. New Jersey	15.6	Sao Paulo	24.0
2	London	10.4			Tokyo—Yokohama	17.1
3	Shanghai	10.3	Mexico City	15.0	Calcutta	16.6
4	Rhine—Ruhr	6.9	Sao Paulo	12.8	Greater Bombay	16.0
5	Tokyo—Yokohama	6.7	Shanghai	11.8	New York—	
6	Beijing	6.7	Greater Buenos Aires	10.1	N.E. Jersey	15.5
7	Paris	5.5	London	10.0	Seoul	13.5
8	Tianjin	5.4	Calcutta	9.5	Shanghai	13.5
9	Greater Buenos Aires	5.3	Los Angeles— Long Beach	9.5	Rio de Janeiro	13.3
10	Chicago— N.W. Indiana	5.0	Rhine—Rhur	9.3	Delhi	13.3

Source: United Nations, *Estimates and Projections of Urban, Rural and City Populations, 1950–2025: The 1982 Assessment*, United Nations, 1985. pp. 144–147.

that when the population of the world reaches about seven billion, the carrying capacity of the earth will have been stretched to the limit (Gilland, 1983:206) and Malthus's predictions of positive check will come into force.

During the 1960s and the early 1970s the growth of world population was viewed as a major social problem but was supplanted by other issues such as oil shortages and later economic recession. It is perhaps not too surprising that world leaders and the public greeted, with so little enthusiasm, Pierre Trudeau's attempt to define the gap between nations of the North and South as a serious world problem. Trudeau was attempting to "define" a social problem. Other world leaders, however, were more concerned with economic problems such as exchange rates, balance of payments, and trade deficits.

Of course, this does not mean that the problem of world population growth is becoming less serious. While it is true that the fertility rate has diminished in the past several years, world population is still growing and it will inevitably reach a size at least twice as large as at present because of demographic momentum. The populations of countries that have had high levels of fertility in the past have relatively large numbers of younger people. These younger people tend, all other things being equal, to have larger numbers of children. Thus the large populations of countries such as India and China will continue to grow much larger, even though their fertility rates are declining. The high rate of natural increase that prevailed thirty years ago has set in motion an ineluctable pattern of demographic change. Although demographic projections are subject to wide margins of error, especially as we project further into the future, we know what the broad outlines of the future will be, and we can anticipate, though not necessarily act upon, the consequences.

In short, there is no doubt that the world

population is increasing and will continue to do so unless something totally unexpected occurs; inevitably, in the foreseeable future, we must somehow share the same space and limited resources. Nor can we continue in our boundless, no doubt naive, faith in technological solutions. We often seem to treat technology as some kind of mystical force that can act on its own in response to our problems. Sooner or later technological solutions will appear. But is this faith justified? Technology is not some mystical force, however much it may have a life of its own. It is, rather, a force directed by those in pursuit of their best interests and we cannot assume that their best interests and the common good are identical.

THE CANADIAN POPULATION

The estimated population of Canada was 26 223 200 as of June 1989. Our population has grown rapidly since the pre-Confederation era, much more rapidly than the rate of growth of the world's population. For instance, in 1900 the size of the world population was about two billion. By 1980 it had grown to about four billion, roughly a two-fold increase. During the same period, the Canadian population grew from about 5.4 million in 1901 to 24.2 million in 1981 — a 450 percent increase.

Population growth in Canada is beginning to slow down. By about the year 2025, if population trends remain on their present course, population may cease to grow and level off at about 30 million. Canada will have become a zero population growth society, a situation common to most western industrial countries. Most have entered the third stage of the demographic transition.

Table 8.2 showed some demographic data

for several European countries which have come closer to zero population growth societies than Canada. For each country the birth rate is lower and the death rate is higher than the Canadian figures for 1985. However, as the Canadian population ages, and there are fewer women in the child bearing period of 15–45 years of age, the Canadian birth rate may fall. As well, as the population ages, the death rate will increase. If the average number of children born to each woman remains about the same for the coming decades — about 1.7 children per woman — Canada too will approach the status of a zero population growth society.

FERTILITY

In Canada, as well as in other developed nations, *fertility* is by far the most important factor affecting population growth. Mortality, as we shall see in the next section, is not likely to change dramatically in the future. Nor is it likely that the volume of immigration, now at about 100 000 immigrants per year, will change dramatically. Thus fertility remains the crucial variable for the future growth of the Canadian population.

Canadian society has conformed rather closely to the demographic transition theory; the dramatic shift from an agricultural to an industrial and service economy brought in its wake changed attitudes about the value of large families. Except for the rather brief "blip" we described as the baby boom, Canada has had a continuous long-term decline in fertility. For example, the crude birth rate in 1985 was 15.1 live births per 1000 population, a rather momentous decline from the 60 per 1000 estimated at the time of Wolfe's and Montcalm's skirmish on the Plains of Abraham.

THE SOCIOLOGY OF FERTILITY

Predicting future fertility levels is a dangerous business. In the 1930s, the great concern of demographers was the threat of a declining population; while in the 1960s and 1970s, the fear, even in the West, was overpopulation. Now we once more worry about declining fertility rates. Nowhere is this more apparent than in Quebec. Due to the dramatic drop in birth rates, Quebec demographers worry about the progressively fragile demographic situation of the Francophone population. Yet, even as we write, the steadily declining fertility levels of recent decades have, apparently, reversed — perhaps permanently, perhaps only temporarily.

While it is foolhardy to try to predict what people might do in years to come, we can suggest some of the structural and cultural factors that help to explain the downward shift in fertility of the past two and a half decades. For example, the rise in fertility that began during the war years was probably related both to quickly arranged marriages before soldiers left for overseas, and to soldiers returning on furlough. The result was a high rate between 1940 and 1942. And, in turn, the divorce rate rose sharply immediately following World War II, a predictable result of the often hastily arranged wartime marriages.

The rise in the birth rate for a few years following World War II is also easily explained. The marriage rate reached another peak immediately following the war, as many postponed marriages finally took place. The fertility rise after the war, which occurred in many European countries as well, represents postponed fertility by people married during the war and by those who waited and married after. However, the relatively high fertility of the post-war years lasted only

FIGURE 8.9
THE CRUDE BIRTH RATE, CANADA, 1921–1985

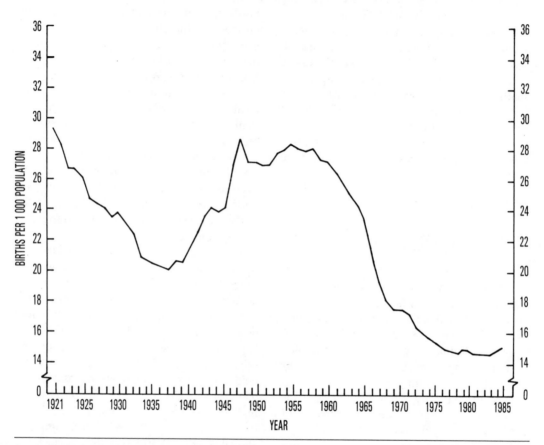

Source: Statistics Canada, 1971 Census of Canada, *Profile Studies, Fertility in Canada*, Vol. V, Part L (Ottawa, 1976), p. 5; and *Vital Statistics*, Vol. L, Fertility, various years 1971 to 1985.

a few years in most European countries, until the delayed fertility had occurred. In Canada, and in the United States, the baby boom continued for a decade after. Figure 8.9 shows the pattern of Canadian fertility since 1921.

FAMILY ROLES

More generally, it may also be that we view children differently than in the past. As described earlier, the economic value of children has diminished with the shift from agri-cultural to industrial-urban society. As this structural change was occurring, and as the average number of children was falling in western societies, children were assuming an affective role in the family rather than an eco-nomic one. Families may have limited the number of children not merely to further their own social and economic mobility, but to assure the future success of mobility oppor-tunities of their children. Families became child-centred in the sense that the number of children was limited in order to maximize advantages for the children.

We no longer need children to ensure our security in old age. Anthony Synnott quotes a father of an earlier time who has just lost his son: "I have lost all I had through the death of my son Raymond. I have no one to work for me." Synnott adds:

A modern father would not speak like this, but, of course, the implications of the death of an only son would be different. The thirteenth-century villager, without a son, was probably condemned to poverty and an early death.

Philip Aries (1980) has written about a more recent shift in the role of the child in modern western culture. He argues that the days of the "child-king" are coming to an end. Couples plan their own lives and limit the number of children they will have in the future; children must fit into the lifestyle preferences and career plans of modern couples. As the child becomes less of a central factor in the lives of couples, not unexpectedly, the number of children people are willing to have has decreased.

Moreover, as demographers have learned, women are, in fact, having fewer births than they had anticipated. This is especially evident in Quebec where a series of surveys have shown declining fertility expectations but even lower birth rates. According to a 1971 survey, women who married between 1966 and 1970 expected, on average, to have 3.2 lifetime births. By 1976 women surveyed expected to have, on average, 2.4 children and by 1980 the number was down to 2.1 (Lapierre-Adamcyk, 1981).

Yet as Caldwell and Fournier (1987:31) point out, actual fertility rates have been considerably below even these declining expectations:

By 1969-70 the total fertility rate fell under the critical 2.1 children per woman level required for replacement. Thereafter, it appeared to stabilize at around 1.8 between 1977 and 1979, which level (well below replacement) provoked much concern at the time. Yet, after 1979 the rate began to decline again, heading for a new floor just under 1.5 (1.454 in 1983 and 1.447 in 1984). Preliminary 1985 figures indicate a stabilization at just under 1.5, a far cry from the 4.0 of 1954.

Not is fertility only declining overall, but the pattern of fertility by age of women is undergoing a shift in Canada. Table 8.4 shows fertility rates per 1000 women for births of all orders and for first births only from 1971 and 1981. Fertility for women in the age groups 15 through 29 has been falling overall. This may be explained by economic factors and by the career and life-style factors discussed previously.

However, the table shows that while the fertility rates for all births to women aged 30–34 and 35–39 have been declining, the rates

TABLE 8.4

AGE-SPECIFIC FERTILITY RATES PER 1000, ALL BIRTHS AND FIRST BIRTHS, CANADA, 1971 AND 1981

AGE	YEAR			
	1971		1981	
	All Births	First Births	All Births	First Births
15–19	39.8	32.9		22.2
20–24	134.4	70.9		56.4
25–29	142.0	43.0		50.9
30–34	77.3	11.5		17.1
35–39	33.6	3.0		3.6
40–44	9.4	0.6		0.5
45–49	0.6	—		—

Source: Statistics Canada, Vital Statistics, Vol. I, Fertility.

for first births among these older mothers have been rising. Women are currently "catching up" for some of the delayed fertility from younger ages but, the fertility of women over age 30 is much smaller than fertility among younger women, and the "catching up" will not likely ever replace the fertility delayed by women at younger ages. The emergence of this fertility pattern suggests the possibility of a long term low fertility level. Canadian women, at present, are not having sufficient babies to maintain or increase our population.

TABLE 8.5

CRUDE DEATH RATES, CANADA, 1921–1984

YEAR	MALE	FEMALE	BOTH SEXES
1921	11.9	11.2	11.6
1931	10.5	9.6	10.2
1941	10.9	9.1	10.1
1951	10.1	7.8	9.0
1961	9.0	6.5	7.7
1971	8.5	6.1	7.3
1981	8.0	6.0	7.0
1984	7.9	6.1	7.0

Source: Statistics Canada, Vital Statistics.

∎ MORTALITY

Compared to fertility, ***mortality*** has ceased to be a very important variable in Canada's demographic equation. This is because while changes in attitudes about having children may cause fluctuations in the fertility rate, mortality rates are, to a greater extent, independent of individual decisions. Mortality differentials between different groups and regions are, however, indicative of inequality and social problems within Canadian society.

Canadian mortality has declined steadily for many decades. As Table 8.5 indicates, we have comprehensive information on crude death rates for Canada only from 1921 onward. This is because the Statistics Canada vital statistics data base only came into existence one year after the 1920 federal-provincial agreement establishing uniform standards for the collection of vital statistics.

In any event, demographers generally prefer the more refined measure of mortality based on the average expectation of life, partly because it is an indicator of the health of a population. Table 8.6 shows the long term trend in life expectancy from the pre-confederation period to the present.

Around 1831 life expectancy in pre-confederation Canada was about 38.3 years for men and about 39.8 years for women. The combined life expectancy was about 39.0 years. This is nearly the same as some African

TABLE 8.6

LIFE EXPECTANCY AT BIRTH BY SEX, CANADA 1831 TO 1981

PERIOD	MALE	FEMALE	BOTH SEXES
Around 1831	38.3	39.8	39.0
Around 1841	39.4	41.3	40.3
Around 1851	40.0	42.1	41.0
Around 1861	40.6	42.7	41.6
Around 1871	41.4	43.8	42.6
Around 1881	43.5	46.0	44.7
Around 1891	43.9	46.5	45.2
Around 1901	47.2	50.2	48.7
Around 1911	50.9	54.2	52.5
Around 1921	55.0	58.4	56.7
1930–32	60.0	62.1	61.0
1940–42	63.0	66.3	64.6
1950–52	66.3	70.8	68.5
1955–57	67.6	72.9	70.2
1960–62	68.4	74.2	71.2
1965–67	68.8	75.2	71.9
1970–72	69.3	76.4	72.8
1975–77	70.2	77.5	73.8
1980–82	71.9	79.0	75.3

Source: Yves Péron and Claude Strohmenger, *Demographic and Health Indicators: Presentation and Interpretation*, Statistics Canada, Ottawa, 1985, Table 28.

countries in the 1980s: Gambia, 35 years; Guinea, 40 years; Mali, 42 years; and Sierra Leone, 34 years. Indeed, there are only a few countries with average life expectancies that are higher than the Canadian figures: Iceland, Switzerland, Norway, Sweden, and the Netherlands.

INDIAN AND INUIT MORTALITY

Within Canada, however, there remain large differences in life expectancy indicative of unequal social and economic conditions. In 1981, one estimate placed life expectancy of Indian men at 62.4 years which was the male life expectancy for the general Canadian population in 1941. Similarly, life expectancy at birth for Indian women was estimated at 68.9 years in 1981, close to the 1951 figure of 70.8 for Canadian women as a whole.

Life expectancy figures present a similar picture for the Inuit populations of Canada. One estimate for the Northern Quebec Inuit placed expectations of life at birth at 62 years for both sexes combined for the period 1971–1981. Life expectancy for both sexes combined was estimated at 66 years for the Inuit of the Northwest Territories.

The infant mortality rate is considered an especially good indicator of the health conditions prevailing in a population. Even in countries with generally low levels of mortality, the infant mortality rates tell us a good deal about group differences in health conditions. Infants up to one year of age are particularly sensitive to health risks from poor conditions; such conditions would not cause increased mortality among older people because they are strong enough to resist diseases and infections. Also health conditions are often very localized, so that some communities will show distinctly higher rates of infant mortality as a result of inadequate health care and poor nutrition.

For example, Tables 8.7 (below) and 8.8 (on page 234) show, respectively, infant mortality rates and estimates of life expectancy for registered Indians and Inuit compared with the general Canadian population. Inadequate levels of services and housing, and lack of access to health care are reflected in the high levels of infant mortality compared with the Canadian population as a whole.

The result is that infant mortality levels of registered Indians lag about twenty years behind the rates for the total Canadian population. For example, the estimate of 37 per 1000 live births for 1976 is about the same as the overall Canadian rate in 1951 of 38.5 per 1000, and the 1981 estimate of 27 per 1000 is about the same as the 1961 Canadian infant mortality rate of 27.2. One estimate of infant mortality among the Inuit of Northern Quebec for the period 1976 to 1982 is 69 per 1000 (Robitaille & Choiniere, 1985:20). This is about the same as the rate for the total Canadian population in 1931. Another estimate places the infant mortality rate in the Northwest Territories in 1981 at 35 per 1000. While this is much higher than the rate of 9.6 for the Canadian population in that year, it is nevertheless a remarkable decline from the 300 infant deaths per 1000 live births in the 1950s (Robitaille & Choiniere, 1985:19).

These figures, which are so much lower than the levels for the Canadian population overall, represent a major improvement over the past thirty years. Life expectancy for the

---

TABLE 8.7

ESTIMATED INFANT MORTALITY RATES FOR THE REGISTERED INDIAN POPULATION, 1976 AND 1981, COMPARED WITH CANADIAN INFANT MORTALITY RATES, AND CLOSEST EQUIVALENT YEAR CANADIAN LEVELS.

YEAR	REGISTERED INDIAN	CANADIAN POPULATION	CLOSEST EQUIVALENT YEAR	CANADIAN INFANT MORTALITY LEVELS
1976	37	13.5	1951	38.5
1981	27	9.6	1961	27.2

Source: G. Rowe and M.J. Norris, *Mortality Projections of Registered Indians, 1982 to 1996*, Demography Division, Statistics Canada, 1985. Table 8.

TABLE 8.8

ESTIMATED EXPECTATION OF LIFE AT BIRTH FOR REGISTERED INDIANS, 1976 AND 1981,
COMPARED WITH CANADIAN EXPECTATION OF LIFE, AND CLOSEST EQUIVALENT YEAR
CANADIAN LEVELS

YEAR	REGISTERED INDIAN	CANADIAN POPULATION	CLOSEST EQUIVALENT YEAR	CANADIAN LIFE EXPECTANCY
		Male		
1976	59.8	70.2	1931	60.0
1981	62.4	71.9	1941	63.0
		Female		
1976	66.3	77.5	1941	66.3
1981	68.9	79.0	1951	70.8

Source: G. Rowe and M.J. Norris, *Mortality Projections of Registered Indians, 1982 to 1996*, Demography Division, Statistics Canada, 1985. Table 7. And Yves Péron and Claude Strohmenger, *Demographic and Health Indicators*, Statistics Canada, 1985. Table 28.

Northern Quebec Inuit for the period 1941–1951 was estimated at 35 years for both sexes combined (Robitaille & Choiniere, 1985:23). For the Inuit of the Northwest Territories, life expectancy for both sexes combined was estimated at 29 years for the period 1941–1950. The improvement is partly attributable to the establishment of a network of health care facilities in the North over the past thirty years. Also, improved transportation in the North has made health care facilities in the South available for treating serious illnesses.

Still the data indicate that the level of health care lags far behind that of most Canadians. While better health care facilities are an important factor in reducing mortality rates, the benefit of these is offset by the various consequences of the extreme poverty of Canada's native peoples: inadequate housing, overcrowding, poor nutrition and functional illiteracy (Robitaille & Choiniere, 1985).

MALE/FEMALE MORTALITY

In the preceding tables, mortality rates are shown separately for males and females, a recognition of one of the universal "facts" of demography: mortality is higher for men than for women. Perhaps to "compensate" for this, more male babies are born. The *sex ratio* at birth is about 105, that is, about 105 male babies for every 100 female babies. However, infant mortality is higher for males, and mortality is higher for males at each age throughout life. The effect of this pattern is that in a normal population there are more elderly women than elderly men.

Demographers have debated the causes of excess male mortality for many years. On the one hand, there is the biological explanation: females for some reason, have an inherent biological advantage over males. In a famous study by two American demographer-sociologists, compared the longevity of Catholic Sisters and Brothers involved in teaching and school administration. The Brothers and Sisters were more closely matched than any other male-female groups in the general population. Mortality differences were less than for the general population, but they still persisted. The Catholic Sisters had significantly lower levels of mortality. Madigan and Vance, the authors of this study, concluded that the female advantage in length of life over men is biological in nature (Vance & Madigan, 1959; Madigan, 1961).

However, the research did not investigate the effects of lifestyle differences between the Brothers and Sisters, such as the consumption of alcohol or smoking cigarettes (a health hazard that was not fully recognized in the 1950s).

Some argue that the explanation for excess male mortality is not in biology but in lifestyle. (Enterline, 1961). This explanation holds that men experience greater occupation-related stress than women and that behaviours related to male lifestyles, such as greater consumption of tobacco and alcohol, contribute to higher mortality.

The biological theory predicts that the gap between male and female expectation of life will persist. The lifestyle theory predicts that the gap will decrease as male and female roles become closer. Table 8.8 compares male and female life expectancy at birth. By subtracting the male from the female figures for each period from, say, 1930-32 we can see that the gap between male and female life expectancy has increased steadily up to 1976. During this period it could be argued that male and female roles were becoming closer and closer; however, life expectancy for women improved at a greater rate than for men. This would seem to indicate that women benefited from the improvements in nutrition and in health care to a greater extent than men. This lends some support to the biological theory.

It is interesting to note, however, that in the 1980s life expectancy appears to have improved more for males than females and the sex mortality differential narrowed very slightly. This is the first time that this has occurred in the Canadian experience, although it has occurred in recent years in other countries such as the United States (whites only) and Great Britain. Because the reversal is not a large one demographers are hesitant to draw conclusions about a trend until subsequent life expectancy data are available from the 1986 census and the full census in 1991.

MARRIAGE AND MORTALITY

There are also systematic differences in levels of mortality for different marital status groups. Table 8.9 shows that regardless of age or of sex, widowed and divorced people have higher rates of mortality than other marital status groups. Single people have the next highest mortality levels and married people have the lowest mortality regardless of age. This suggests that lifestyle related behaviour patterns and possibly psychological states

TABLE 8.9

MORTALITY RATES BY MARITAL STATUS FOR SELECTED AGE GROUPS AND SEX, POPULATION 15 YEARS OF AGE AND OVER, CANADA, 1971.

MARITAL STATUS AND SEX	AGE GROUP				
	15–24	25–44	45–64	65 +	Total
	(rate per 100 000)				
Males:					
Single	165.4	389.0	1 867.9	7 457.6	589.2
Married	114.1	179.7	1 084.4	5 628.4	1 111.8
Widowed & Divorced	268.2	523.8	2 308.5	11 257.3	6 596.0
Females:					
Single	61.9	189.2	783.4	4 525.0	383.0
Married	45.1	103.7	521.6	3 038.2	454.1
Widowed & Divorced	165.4	278.7	931.3	6 022.1	3 735.0

Source: Statistics Canada, Vital Statistics, 1974, Vol. III, Ottawa, 1976, Table 18.

affect life chances with regard to mortality (Grove, 1973). For example, and not surprisingly, young men are more likely than older people to die due to accidents. That widowed and divorced people have much higher rates than those for married people suggests the possibility that the stress associated with marital breakdown may produce higher levels of mortality.

A careful reading of Table 8.9 reveals that the difference in rates of mortality between single and married people is greater for men than for women. Does marriage benefit men to a greater extent than women? As we have seen (Chapter 6) there is considerable evidence that married men are healthier, better off socially and psychologically than are single men, while the opposite tends to be true for married women compared with single women (Bernard, 1973).

IMMIGRATION

Immigration has always played an important role in the growth and composition of the Canadian population. In the first two decades of this century the number of people immigrating to Canada exceeded the number added through natural increase (Table 8.10).

Emigration from Canada was also great during these decades. Many of the emigrants may have been recent immigrants who used Canada as a stepping stone to the United States.

Large volumes of immigration have had an impact on the diversity of the Canadian population. The foreign born component of the Canadian population has been relatively high over the past one hundred years. Historically, British and Northwestern Europeans made up the vast majority of immigrants to Canada. Central and Eastern Europeans, for example the Ukrainians who mostly settled in the Canadian prairies, came to Canada in large numbers earlier in this century. Southern and Southeastern Europeans, for example the Italians who settled in large urban areas such as Toronto and Montreal, came in greater numbers in the 1950s and the 1960s. But, the degree of diversity was limited: between 1926 and 1966, on average only about 3.4 percent of all immigrants were from Asia, Latin America or other parts of the world.

By 1984, however, seven of the top ten source countries were non-European (Table 8.11). This shift in the origins of immigration streams has caused some public debate about the "national character" of Canadian society. Nevertheless, in the face of Canada's contin-

TABLE 8.10

COMPONENTS OF POPULATION CHANGE, CANADA 1891–1981
(POPULATION IN THOUSANDS)

DECADE	NATURAL INCREASE	IMMIGRATION	NATURAL INCREASE PLUS IMMIGRATION	DECADE INCREASE	ESTIMATED EMIGRATION
1891–1901	718 (670)[3]	326(250)[3]	1 044	538	506(380)[3]
1901–11	1 120 (1 030)	1 759(1 550)	2 879	1 836	1 043(740)
1911–21	1 230[1](1 270)	1 612(1 400)	2 842	1 581	1 261(1 090)
1921–31	1 360	1 203	2 563	1 589	974
1931–41	1 222	150	1 372	1 130	242
1941–51	1 971	548	2 520	2 141[2]	379
1951–61	3 148	1 543	4 691	4 229	462
1961–71	2 606[4]	1 429	4 035	3 330	705
1971–81	1 913	1 447	3 360	2 724	636

Source: Adapted from *Perspectives Canada III*, Ottawa: Ministry of Supply and Services, 1982.

TABLE 8.11

TEN MAJOR SOURCE COUNTRIES FOR
IMMIGRANTS TO CANADA 1951–1984

RANK	1951	1984
1	Britain	Vietnam
2	Germany	Hong Kong
3	Italy	United States
4	Netherlands	India
5	Poland	United Kingdom
6	France	Poland
7	United States	Philippines
8	Belgium	El Salvador
9	Yugoslavia	Jamaica
10	Denmark	China

Source: Department of Manpower and Immigration, *The Immigration Program, Vol. 1, A Report of the Canadian Immigration and Population Study*, Ottawa, 1974; Employment and Immigration Canada, *Annual Report to Parliament on Future Immigration Levels*, Ottawa, 1985.

uing low birth rate, the Canadian government has raised immigration levels in order to promote the overall growth of the population.

In the past, immigrants to Canada have possessed attitudes and characteristics that have made it relatively easy for them to become integrated into the economy. Some indication of this can be seen in comparisons between the native-born and the foreign-born based on the 1971 census. At that point, immigrants were better trained than native born Canadians: among the foreign born population in Canada 11.9 percent held a university degree compared with 10.0 percent for the native born. Moreover, immigrant children were more likely to remain in school than the native born. For example, the percentage of persons aged 19–24 living with families remaining in school was 44.3 percent for the foreign born and 37.5 percent for the native born. In 1971 male immigrants had a higher participation rate in the labour force (84.4 percent, compared with 76.2 percent for native born males). Similarly for women, the participation rate for the foreign born was 44.6 percent compared with 39.8 percent for the native born. Immigrants tended to be self-

employed to a greater extent than the native born. In 1971, 11.8 percent of the foreign born were self-employed, compared with 6.9 percent of the native born. A greater percentage of the foreign born, compared with the native born, were employers, 7.6 percent compared with 4.2 percent. Average income of heads of families in 1970 was $8153 for the foreign born and $8009 for the native born. Finally, at all income levels below $20 000, the foreign born were more likely than the native born to own their own homes.

However, as so called visible minorities have become a larger component of immigration to Canada, the relative situation of immigrants has changed. More recent data from the 1981 census show that immigrants from the Caribbean, Africa, and Asia earn between 80 and 90 percent of the income of the Canadian born (Beaujot, Bassavarajappa & Verna, 1986). We do not know how the changing patterns of immigration and the greater diversity of immigrants will affect Canadian population and Canadian society. Perhaps most important is that we do not know how Canadians will react to new sources of immigration and new groups of immigrants. While many Canadians have prided themselves on their tolerance for cultural diversity, this self perception may not have been put to the test because of the selective immigration of the past that brought to Canada people of similar background, religion and colour to the established population.

THE FUTURE OF THE CANADIAN POPULATION

There are at least three social and economic issues that can be directly related to Canadian population trends: the role of elderly people; the response to multiculturalism; and the economic response to a no-growth population. Mortality in Canada has reached a relatively low level. Even with the increasing health consciousness of Canadians, the growing intolerance to smokers, the decline in alcohol consumption and so on, the small improvements in mortality that can be expected during the foreseeable future will have only minor impact on population growth.

As we have seen, fertility levels are also low, currently below replacement level. While some demographers believe that there will be modest upswings in birth rates, most expect fertility to remain at or below replacement level. One demographer has attempted to depict what all of this might mean for Canadian population characteristics in the future.

As can be seen in Table 8.12, without immigration, the average age of Canadians will increase dramatically, the proportion of young people will diminish considerably and there will be an unprecedented number of elderly people in our society. We can, therefore, anticipate that one of the major problems Canadians will have to confront as we approach the twenty-first century is how to reconceptualize the concepts of old and elderly and how to ensure that this growing

segment of the Canadian population remains well-integrated into Canadian social structure. In the past, groups representing interests of elderly people have probably had little influence on social and economic policy; we can expect this to change over the next 20 to 30 years.

If fertility remains constant at about its recent level, immigration will become the critical factor both for the growth of the Canadian population and for slowing down the aging of our population. Between 1976 and 1984 immigration has averaged 114 766 per year (Employment and Immigration Canada, 1985). If immigration is maintained at a level close to 100 000 per year, the population will grow very slowly and possibly will eventually stop growing. If immigration is increased to near 150 000 per year and maintained at that level during the coming years, the Canadian population will, of course, grow somewhat more quickly. These projections are shown in Table 8.13. And, since immigrants tend to be younger people likely to marry and have children, a stepped up rate of immigration would, to some extent, reverse the trends shown in

---

TABLE 8.12

DEMOGRAPHIC CHARACTERISTICS OF A POPULATION WITH A TOTAL FERTILITY RATE OF 1.7 BIRTHS PER WOMAN AND A LIFE EXPECTATION OF 75.2 YEARS, CANADA

DEMOGRAPHIC CHARACTERISTICS	THE FUTURE WITH CONSTANT FERTILITY	END OF THE BABY BOOM PERIOD (1961)
Age Distribution		
0–19	19.91%	41.80%
20–64	55.33%	50.57%
65 +	24.76%	7.63%
Average Age of Population	44.95 years	29.56 years
Birth Rate	9.04 per 1000	26.1 per 1000
Death Rate	18.77 per 1000	7.7 per 1000
Natural Growth Rate	− 9.72 per 1000	18.4 per 1000

Source: A. Romaniuc, *Fertility in Canada: From Baby Boom to Baby Bust*. Ottawa: Statistics Canada, 1984, p. 25.

TABLE 8.13

POPULATION PROJECTIONS, CANADA, 1991 TO 2031

YEAR	PROJECTION A (ASSUMPTIONS: TOTAL FERTILITY = 1.7; IMMIGRATION = 100 000 PER YEAR)	PROJECTION B (ASSUMPTIONS: TOTAL FERTILITY = 1.7; IMMIGRATION – 150 000 PER YEAR)
1991	26 781 100	26 903 900
2001	28 529 200	29 207 800
2011	29 526 500	30 880 600
2021	30 025 400	32 132 300
2031	30 004 100	

Source: Population Projections Section, Demography Division, Statistics Canada, 1985.

Table 8.12. Immigration, in other words, is a key tool for controlling population growth and population characteristics because the level of immigration can be set by the government each year. In contrast, and despite the kinds of incentives recently introduced in Quebec, the level of fertility is much less subject to control.

There is every reason to suppose that the source countries of immigration to Canada will continue to be the developing nations, especially if immigration is maintained at a high level. This will increase the degree of ethnic diversity in Canadian society. Along with the cultural richness and opportunities for economic growth which immigrants will bring to Canada, will come challenges to facilitate the successful integration of the new visible minority groups into the social structure.

Finally there is the question of how our social and economic institutions will adjust to a very slow growth or a no-growth population. Our economy and our institutions are, to a large extent, based on an expectation of continuous growth and expansion. Much of the future challenge will be to reconstruct our thinking and expectations to accommodate too little or no growth and, in turn, different conceptions of success and progress.

 # CONCLUSION

Demographic analysis provides us with objective facts about population — its growth, its structure, its composition and its future. A similar body of facts can be assembled about the history and economy of a society and in the next two chapters we will introduce you to these as they have been perceived by Canadian sociologists. But, as we have argued, the meaning of these facts, which ones we highlight and make into social problems, depends on and is conditioned by our ideological perspective. Undeniably, demographic and economic factors set parameters and are constraints to social action and social change. But, as we have seen, culture and ideology are, in their own way, equally constraining. The dominant ideology sets another constraint to our action, to change, and to our ability to understand existing social structure and above all, to imagine alternatives. Understanding of the major ideologies and counter-ideologies, the political cultures of Canadian society is, then, as important as is knowing its demography. The impact of these ideologies on shaping sociological ideas and perspectives is one of the themes of the next chapter.

III SUGGESTIONS FOR FURTHER READING

The first (1798) edition of *An Essay on the Principle of Population* is available in paperback; the most readily available source for later editions is Malthus (1890). One of the most comprehensive and readable accounts of Malthus and his work is William Petersen's *Malthus* (1979). An excellent discussion of population issues, linguistic balance and regionalism is Roderic Beaujot's and Kevin McQuillan's *Growth and Dualism: The Demographic Development of Canadian Society* (1982). The future characteristics of the Canadian population and the economic implications following from these predictions can be found in David K. Foot's *Canada's Population Outlook: Demographic Futures and Economic Challenges*. You may also want to look at a work we have drawn upon extensively in preparing this chapter, A. Romaniuc's *Fertility in Canada* (1984), published by Statistics Canada.

On a regular basis, Statistics Canada produces reports and pamphlets on both general and specific aspects of Canada's population, its present and future composition. These will be in the Government Documents section of your library and are probably most easily found with the help of a librarian. However, brief summaries of many of these studies can be found in Craig McKie's and Keith Thompson's *Canadian Social Trends* (1990). Finally, the social, economic and political consequences of an older population are explored in two recent works: Maureen Baker's *The Aging Canadian Population* (1987) and Susan McDaniel's *Aging in Canadian Society* (1986).

CHAPTER 9

CANADIAN SOCIOLOGICAL PERSPECTIVES

OVERVIEW

CANADIAN SOCIOLOGY

INTRODUCTION

DEVELOPMENT OF SOCIOLOGY IN CANADA

CANADIANIZATION AND AMERICAN SOCIOLOGY

A CANADIAN SOCIOLOGY

GEOGRAPHY, HISTORY, AND CULTURE

HAROLD INNIS
S. D. CLARK
JOHN PORTER

LIMITATIONS OF EARLY PERSPECTIVES

METROPOLIS HINTERLAND PERSPECTIVE

A CANADIAN EXAMPLE: SINGLE INDUSTRY TOWNS

DEPENDENCY PERSPECTIVES

CANADIAN CULTURE AND IDENTITY

ASSESSMENT OF DEPENDENCY THEORY

FEMINIST PERSPECTIVES

CONCLUSION

SUGGESTIONS FOR FURTHER READING

OVERVIEW

In Chapter I you were introduced to the history of sociology and the fundamental debates that have shaped its development. In this chapter, we introduce you to the more specific debates underlying the development of a distinctive Canadian sociology. As you read this chapter, you may want to look back at the first chapter and, perhaps, as well, the second chapter and the discussion there of the norms of the scientific method. Canadian sociologists have, of course, been influenced by these more general debates about the "goodness" or "badness" of human nature and whether society is essentially subjective or objective. And, certainly, there is the same commitment, among these sociologists, to viewing sociology as a discipline based on a combination of reason and observation, and adherence to the norms of the scientific method. This is the starting point. Canadian sociology differs from other sociologies only in its attempt to develop and use perspectives that help us to understand Canadian society.

In reading this chapter, several things should become obvious to you. First, sociology, a newcomer in the academic and scientific world, has an even shorter history in Canada; to all intents and purposes, the history of Canadian sociology began in the post-war years and mainly after the 1960s.

Second, the sociology we are here calling Canadian is, for the most part, the sociology of English speaking Canada. Unfortunately, but perhaps inevitably, Quebec and English Canadian sociology have been rather separate developments to the extent that the two traditions may be viewed as another example of the "two solitudes" of Canadian society. So, you will learn in this chapter about Anglophone Canadian sociology and only incidentally about what has been happening in Quebec.

Third, it should become apparent to you that those who view themselves as contributing to Canadian sociology have not been bothered very much by the traditional lines between sociology, economics and political science. Rather, most see their work as part of a Marxist-based political economy drawing upon all of these disciplines. In choosing this approach they have made the implicit assumption that the proper subject matter of sociology is the study of the class and the economic structure of our society and how these develop and change.

As you should by now be aware, there are also many Canadian sociologists studying aspects of Canadian society rather than the society as a whole—such as marriage, family and divorce, deviance, criminology, and work who believe that they are contributing both to sociology generally and to our understanding of Canadian society.

Finally, it should become obvious to you that the growth of Canadian nationalism and the development of Canadian sociology have been very much intertwined. This has had both good and bad consequences for a sociological understanding of our society. On the positive side, the growing sense of nationalism in Canada led to the asking of new questions about our society. On the negative side, this intertwining led to parochial approaches that treated Canada as if it were isolated from the world economy and ignored a comparative dimension to what was being learned about Canada.

There are several things you should take away from this first encounter with Canadian sociology. First, you should understand why, in the 1960s, mainstream American sociology — functionalism — came under attack both in Canada and the United States and how part of that attack was political rather than theoretical or empirical in nature. That is, you should leave the chapter with a better appreciation of the changing social, economic and political conditions that led young Canadian academics to reject functionalism and try to develop another perspective that would provide better insight into Canadian society. As you will learn, it was a movement driven by theoretical and empirical concerns certainly, but also by a growing nationalism coupled with growing frustration with a system dominated by American academics and American perspectives of the world.

Second, we hope you will leave the chapter with a better sense of how science progresses through researchers asking new questions, conducting research, publishing their findings and having these challenged through "re-testing" by other researchers. As you will learn in this and following chapters, just as theory and research in the 1960s and 1970s challenged earlier approaches and conclusions about Canadian society, so more recent research has brought about further modifications and sometimes outright rejection of earlier explanations of Canada's particular form of development and the reasons for it. Nor are the debates ended. Should there be a subsequent edition of this text, we expect that this chapter, in particular, would again require considerable revision. Some of these debates are complex and go beyond the scope of an introductory text. At this point, we simply want to leave you with awareness that it is a strength rather than a weakness that theory and research findings in any science, including sociology, are always subject to revision and sometimes outright rejection as new ideas and new research are produced by another generation of scientists.

This chapter cannot do full justice to the development, over the past two decades, of feminist-based sociology. But, you should leave the chapter with a better understanding of how feminist scholarship has challenged and undermined much of what has come to be called "malestream" sociology and how this work is beginning to transform not only Canadian sociology but social science generally. And, you should appreciate how, in bringing about this transformation, feminism has enriched the discipline and expanded our knowledge and understanding of many aspects of our society.

The preceding chapter and the ones that follow are intended to introduce you to various aspects of Canadian society, its structure and its patterns of social inequality. Here, as well as learning about the development of Canadian sociology, you should also know how this sociology has contributed to our understanding of how Canadian culture and Canadians' sense of national identity have, in part, been shaped and influenced by economic domination of a succession of more powerful societies: France, then Britain, then the United States.

One way that you might try to understand this is to move away from the larger picture to the level of everyday life. Consider, for example, how you and your friends react to Canadian music, Canadian films, Canadian novels and Canadian TV programs compared with those you are exposed to from the United States. To what extent are your tastes and choices shaped by remnants of a "colonial mentality"? To what extent, as students of the 1980s, have you transcended this sense of inferiority and become confident that Canadian cultural productions rise or fall on the basis of their own intrinsic quality rather than the fact that they are Canadian?

CANADIAN SOCIOLOGY

INTRODUCTION

In this chapter we describe the development of a distinctive Canadian sociology and the kinds of perspectives sociologists have drawn upon in attempting to understand Canadian society. An enduring and fundamental question has been why, despite initially similar origins and institutions, Canada's economic, cultural and political development differs from the United States. For instance, what factors account for the apparently more conservative nature of Canadian society both politically and culturally? Why, as is often alleged, are Canadians more cautious, less entrepreneurial and achievement oriented than their American counterparts? Why did Canada's economic structure not develop as rapidly and in the same form as that of the United States? Finally, what accounts for the greater emphasis in Canada on ethnic and regional diversity and how do we explain, within Canada, the persistence of regional disparities in wealth and income?

North American sociologists have been particularly drawn to a "scientific" perception of sociology; they have typically looked for the most "objective" bases for an understanding of society and its problems. Demography and population studies, despite their highly technical, often turgid, prose are especially seductive for these very reasons.

We can draw the outlines of Canadian society and the problems it confronts, and make projections of the problems it will confront, with increasingly sophisticated demographic techniques and measures. But nothing in sociology ever moves quite so smoothly. What problems we define as important, how we define them, how we look for solutions, and what we take to be plausible explanations are as much the product of ideology as of science. And, unlike the physical sciences, the social sciences, especially sociology, are profoundly affected by social, economic and political events and changes in society.

As this chapter describes, early explanations of Canada's different cultural and economic development were based on explanations that emphasized our unique geography and the kinds of resources sought by a succession of colonial powers who, themselves, were going through a number of economic and political changes. However, in the 1950s and 1960s American sociology, based on functionalism, dominated the sociological world with the result that, to put it simply, Canada could be seen as a "watered down version of the United States" largely because it had not made the kinds of cultural changes, had not adopted American "liberalism," that had, apparently, made the United States so successful.

In the late 1960s and early 1970s, a new kind of sociology began to emerge in Canada. Much of this sociology has its immediate roots in the rejection of mainstream American functionalist sociology and the image it conveyed of American and Canadian society. But, part of the impetus for a new kind of sociological perspective came also from the emergence in the 1960s of a renewed sense of nationalism within Canada generally. The result was that many sociologists, looking for better ways to understand their society, turned back to the insights of Marx's conflict theory and in the process abandoned and rejected the then dominant ideology of liberalism.

At the same time, the vitality of any science is that the certainties of one generation are inevitably challenged, qualified and sometimes rejected through further research and theoretical thinking. In retrospect, some of the conclusions reached by the first wave of genuinely Canadian sociologists now seem to have been too hasty, overly simplistic, and based on inadequate research. The result is that much of what we described in our earlier texts about Canadian society and Canadian sociology must now be revised or qualified.

Canadian sociology has undergone considerable change and is continuing to develop. While the dominant perspective is still one based on Marxism, or more accurately, "neo-Marxism," the rather simple notion of Canada as a dependent and therefore powerless society has given way to a more complex picture of Canada's position in the world economy and world capitalism. And, at the same time, sociologists in the 1980s have been much more aware that social change is not simply a product of impersonal forces such as the state, or capital, or class relations; people's actions are shaped by these larger forces, but it remains that people also shape social change.

DEVELOPMENT OF SOCIOLOGY IN CANADA

As you progress through university, one of the things you will probably take for granted is that, in most of your courses, a significant proportion of what you are expected to read will be written by Canadians and be about Canada, and that most of the textbooks you are expected to buy for your courses in humanities and social sciences will also be Canadian. This, however, is a relatively recent change. As undergraduate and graduate students, your authors were exposed mainly to American books, texts, and articles for the simple reason that in the 1960s there was very little that was Canadian.

In the late 1970s, when we began to write the first edition of this text, there was still only one introductory textbook in sociology written by Canadians and about Canadian society. By the mid-1980s there were at least a dozen such books, some already in a second edition and there were more in the process of being written. Moreover, in most areas of sociology —family, aging, criminology, ethnic relations, social stratification and so on—there are now competing Canadian textbooks and edited collections available. The explosion in research about Canada now makes it difficult to argue that there is a lack of Canadian materials and empirical examples.

By the beginnings of the twentieth century, sociology was already well-developed in the United States. However, in Canada development of the disciplines was so slow that Robert Brym (1986) has recently depicted the period before 1960 as the "pre-history" of sociology in English Canada. He is referring to the fact that as late as 1958 there were only about 30 sociologists in the whole of Canada: five or six at the University of Toronto, about the same number at McGill and the rest working in a variety of different universities, usually within some other department. In the period between 1925 and 1958 the McGill Department was the only independent sociology department in Canada. In contrast, the University of Toronto department, now the largest in Canada, did not become separated from the Department of Political Economy until the early 1960s. The Canadian Association of Anthropology and Sociology and its journal, *The Canadian Review of Sociology and Anthropology*, were not formed until 1964.

Today, there are more than 1000 sociologists teaching and working in Canada, in universities, community colleges and government. Some 18 universities offer a Ph.D degree and the majority offer M.A. degrees in sociology (Herman, 1986). Sociology shared, perhaps disproportionately, in the massive expansion of higher education in the 1960s. As we discuss in Chapter 12, that growth was the combined result of deliberate government policies to encourage more Canadians to obtain a university education plus the simple fact that those in the first waves of the baby boom were reaching university age. Probably, sociology grew more quickly than the total educational system because of its particular attraction to a generation of students that was politically active, socially conscious and highly critical of virtually all aspects of North American culture and its institutions.

Clearly, given the virtual absence of sociologists in Canada, all of that growth could only come from importing academics from outside of Canada, mainly from the United States. And importing talent from outside the country also meant importing perspectives, approaches, and concerns often not directly relevant to the Canadian situation. As Brym (1986) notes, the lack of an existing sociological tradition in Canada meant that there was little to assimilate to: emigres had to create that tradition and, understandably, they drew upon their own graduate training.

Similarly, the absence of graduate programs in Canada meant that Canadians who wished to teach and to do sociological research were forced to acquire their training outside of Canada, mainly in the United States. Sometimes this has meant a neglect of the unique features of Canadian society, a neglect of how growing up and being educated in Canada might produce a different kind of sociologist than produced elsewhere, a neglect of the dangers of an internationalist perspective in staffing sociology departments and designing courses and programs (Grayson and Magill, 1981).

In its worst forms this meant, at times, that sociologists in their teaching took all their examples and illustrations from the United States so that students in the 1960s and 1970s ended up writing term papers about "our" black problem or the impact of Watergate on "our" political system and so forth. The more subtle and contentious effect of this centres on a question we raised in Chapter 3: What constitutes knowledge? Does a sociological principle found to be true in one society or at one time necessarily have validity in another society or at a later time? Sociologists were, for a time at least, deeply divided about this issue. Some held that scholarship knows no national or temporal boundaries, that like chemistry or biology, sociology will only become a science when its "laws" and generalizations are applicable to any society at any time.

Others, while believing that this may be the ultimate goal of social science, shared C. Wright Mills's contention that sociological theories, to be useful, must also be historically and culturally specific. That is, we must always take into account the historical factors which have led to contemporary society. All of the sociologists whom we now think of as classical sociologists — Marx, Weber, Durkheim, Toennies—were intensely and passionately concerned with the nature and fate of their own societies. They were, in Robert Nisbet's (1965) words, "moral philosophers" who were desperately attempting to interpret and evaluate the changes they felt were occurring around them.

Many of the Canadian sociologists trained elsewhere, have, nevertheless, contributed to our understanding of Canadian society and of more universal human processes. Rex Lucas's *Men in Crisis* (1969), which we described in Chapter 1, remains an insightful contribution to our understanding of small group processes and interpersonal relations. But at the same time, it is probably significant that Lucas never mentions the location of the Canadian maritime mine disaster. That this happened in Canada was not significant for Lucas who, along with many others at the time, were looking only for universal sociological principles that transcended time and place. In his *Minetown, Milltown, Railtown* (1971), the communities are never mentioned; even here Lucas is primarily looking for universals—the consequences of small size, isolation and dependence on a single industry, common to any society. Similarly, Leo Zakuta's (1964) excellent, if somewhat saddening, account of the origins and history of the C.C.F. and its ideology represents a concern with universal processes rather than with the unique social and historical features of Canadian society.

Perhaps even more understandably, some of the American sociologists such as Everett Hughes, who worked for a time in Canada, carried out studies more "in Canada" than "on Canada." So, *French Canada in Transition* (1943), now regarded as a Canadian classic, for Hughes was more likely simply another piece of research and Canada simply a research setting in which to study something more general like a "community in transition." The work of Lucas, Zakuta and Hughes is among the best in this perspective, providing us still with rich descriptions, sensitive insights and often colourful prose and, no doubt, a good deal is gained by their international perspective, by their willingness to take theoretical risks in the search for universals. But, as another generation of sociologists came to realize, something is lost, too.

CANADIANIZATION AND AMERICAN SOCIOLOGY

In Chapter 1 we briefly discussed functionalism and, in Chapter 4, Social Structure, we introduced some of the key concepts that have for the most part developed out of this perspective. We have also discussed some of the weaknesses of this perspective, particularly its failure to take into account how institutions have histories and are shaped by the more powerful members of society to serve and further their interests. Understandably, functionalism came under considerable attack in the 1960s and 1970s. However, as William Goode pointed out at the time, the real villain was not so much functionalism as it was sociology itself — mainstream American sociology.

What sociologists "see" or fail to "see" in their society is shaped by ideology. American sociologists of the time seemed to have internalized the extremely conservative mood of the post-war years and the benign and positive view of their own society and its relationship to other societies. For example, in 1959 one well-known sociologist wrote that the concept of "class" was no longer relevant to an understanding of American society (Wrong, 1959). Somewhat earlier, another equally well-known sociologist argued that commitment to political ideologies is a thing of the past (Bell, 1960).

Yet, a few years later, with the "re-discovery" of poverty and the rise of the Student Movement, both class and ideology loomed rather large in the American consciousness. Terms such as authority gave way to the notion of power. The all encompassing notion of modernization, which had dominated social science for several decades, was translated into discussions of the rise of capitalism, development and underdevelopment, and cultural and economic imperialism. Education, which had been seen as the key to social mobility and equality, was debunked as an institution that served mainly to perpetuate and legitimate class inequality.

One of the ironies is that, in retrospect, it now seems apparent that while committed to the search for universal truths, the actual theories and perspectives of structural functionalism were, in fact, highly specific to American society. An underlying assumption of much of the sociology of that period was that all societies, as they undergo change and development, will go through the same modernization processes as did the United States and will begin to develop similar value systems, similar family and kinship structures and so on. And, implicitly or explicitly, other societies are evaluated against that model. Certainly, part of the conventional wisdom of the early 1960s was the belief that Canada was a much more conservative society than the United States and that this explained its failure to develop as quickly and as dynamically as its southern neighbour. As we shall see later, this depiction of Canada has been sharply criticized in recent years as overly simplistic, as empirically questionable and for ignoring economic and structural aspects of Canada's historical development.

The reasons for the shift away from mainstream American sociology and, in particular, functionalism, are complex. In America, several events coalesced to shake the benign view of American society that had prevailed through the 1950s and early 1960s. The rise of the Black Movement and the fight for civil rights, the growing awareness of poverty in the midst of affluence and, at the end of the 1960s, the intense opposition to the war in Viet Nam could not easily be explained within a functionalist perspective with its emphasis on value consensus and the absence of conflict.

In Canada, equally complex influences were at work. First, during the late 1960s and early 1970s many American academics who came to Canada brought with them their disillusionment with American society and were themselves attempting to develop a more adequate way to understand what was occurring within American society. And, of course, many of those who moved to Canada to evade the draft were especially critical of the society they had just left. Some of these later became academics in Canada.

Beyond these trends was a growing sense of Canadian nationalism. The most eloquent cultural expression of this was, of course, the fervour and euphoria surrounding Expo 67 and the many projects and celebrations marking Canada's first century as a nation. Canadians, generally, but youth in particular, became, perhaps for the first time, proud of their society and smug that Canada did not have the internal and external problems of the United States. And, in the year following Expo 67, the most obvious political expression was "Trudeaumania." Trudeau, with his promise of a "just society" captivated the imagination of both intellectuals and ordinary Canadians.

Another and related factor was the explosive growth of universities in the 1960s. This meant there were now many more young Canadians available to teach in these institutions. Yet, as they came on the job market, new Ph.D.'s in hand, they found the academic market in Canada was dominated by Americans who tended to hire other Americans over Canadians. The early 1970s, then, became a period in which there was a struggle to Canadianize universities. Part of the Canadianization movement was simply a matter of ensuring jobs for Canadians in what was now a shrinking market.

But more was at stake than simply jobs; there were also academic reasons for Canadianization. Students who had experienced the growth of nationalism in Canada and the anti-Americanism of the period were no longer satisfied to learn mainly about the United States; they wanted to be taught about Canada and, in turn, to teach subsequent generations of students about their own society. And, as was later to be demonstrated empirically, those sociologists most likely to do research on Canada were Canadians who had done most of their training in Canada (Grayson and Magill, 1981).

A CANADIAN SOCIOLOGY

In the past two decades, sociology in Canada has been in the throes of a major transformation as it has moved from a basically American and functionalist approach to a nationalistic discipline based on Marxism and the political economy of dependence. And this change has occurred very rapidly. For example, both of your authors were educated in the mid-1960s as were many of your professors. Marxism then was a quiet voice indeed. It would be wrong to say that, during this period, Marxist perspectives were repressed. Rather, they were simply ignored or, if mentioned in class, were treated as irrelevant or wrong.

By 1970, however, younger academics in the United States as well as Canada had begun to react to the apparent conservatism of functionalism. As they rightly pointed out, it failed to deal with the obvious contradictions of the liberal ideology and, in its implicit bias towards the status quo, ignored fundamental questions related to issues such as power and inequality. Furthermore, in Canada, an imported functionalist sociology could not, it was believed, even begin to deal with what is unique about Canadian society and its development (Stolzman and Gamberg, 1975).

By the 1980s, it could be said that mainstream sociology in Canada was predominantly Marxist and informed by and concerned with **political economy**. As Pat Marchak observed at that time, (1981:xi) "a rewriting of Canadian history, political development, sociology and economics is clearly occurring, and the themes go beyond the reinterpretation presented at an official level."

It is not only sociology that has undergone this abrupt transformation. Indeed, the commitment of social scientists to an ideology of the left, to Marxism, has effectively broken down the traditional barriers between political science, economics, sociology/anthropology and social history. Those of the academic left in these various disciplines have more to say to one another than they do to members of their own disciplines who do not share their critical perspective. And this is understandable: political economy provides them with a common vocabulary, common values and a common notion of what are the most pressing issues and questions.

The initial change in Canadian social science is well illustrated by two of the more influential works on Canadian society, John Porter's *The Vertical Mosaic* (1965) and Wallace Clement's *Canadian Corporate Elite* (1975). Porter's analysis of the distribution of power in Canada was perhaps the most important book to be published in this country during the 1960s. He identified the gross inequalities in Canada, the gap between the powerful and powerless, the growing concentration of power and the distance we had to go to reach equality of opportunity, all in a language and liberal optimism that translated easily into the moderate reform ideology of the NDP. And, in concentrating on how we might achieve supposed American standards of equality of opportunity, there was little in his work to threaten American interests in Canada.

His student, Clement, extended his work but at the same time transformed it. In both this and his later book, *Continental Corporate Power* (1977b), Clement drew the relationship between these inequalities and Canada's particular kind of "dependency capitalism." His focus was on inequality of condition rather than inequality of opportunity. Gone was the liberal optimism, replaced now with an analytic, theoretically based indictment of Canadian society and Canadian capitalism.

Clement is part of a "new academic left." Porter, from the "old guard," was concerned primarily with understanding his society, even if from a critical perspective; Clement— and this is what joins left academics whatever their discipline—goes beyond this.

The "new academic left" is also actively engaged in bringing about this change, usually through their commitment to the NDP. In this they are very different from an older generation of academics who tried, we think unsuccessfully, to wear different hats: to be value free in their teaching and research and, at the same time, to be involved citizens. In contrast, the studies we have discussed and will discuss in the chapters that follow make explicit value judgments about capitalism and imperialism and the inequality, exploitation and concentration of power which follow, inevitably, in their wake.

An understanding of capitalism, of ideology, of dependency theory and so on is not, then, merely an academic exercise or, for that matter, simply an attempt to build a theory about what makes societies tick. The intent, rather, is to understand these processes in order to change them and to bring about a socialist revolution. The sociology that emerged in the 1970s explicitly espoused utopian ideals.

The 1970s, then, was a period in which there was a conscious effort to develop a critical Canadian sociology, grounded in Canada's particular historical development, first as a colony and then as a nation in the shadow of a powerful empire. Before examining this more recent sociology, it is useful to look briefly at some of the earlier work that explicitly attempted to understand Canadian society: the geographical and historical perspectives of Harold Innis and S. D. Clark, and the liberal and cultural perspective of John Porter.

GEOGRAPHY, HISTORY, AND CULTURE

HAROLD INNIS

In part because few sociologists practising in Canada were trying to contribute to the development of a general theory, an understanding of the structure and development of Canadian society was largely left to historians, geographers and economists. When, in the 1960s and 1970s sociologists became interested in Canada and its development, they were strongly influenced by the writings and teachings of Harold A. Innis who, until his death in 1952, was head of the Department of Political Economy at the University of Toronto.

In a series of essays and books, Innis (1930; 1940; 1956) developed what is known as the ***staples approach*** to understanding the Canadian economy. Unlike the economies of Britain, the United States and advanced European countries, the Canadian economy, he argued, developed not from manufacturing but from the export of raw materials or staples — fish, fur, lumber, mining products and, more recently, energy — to successive imperialistic empires: France, Britain, and finally the United States.

The consequences of this was that the economic and therefore socio-political development of Canada was shaped and restricted by the interests of empires. We were, in other words, unable to transcend our historical status as "drawers of water," "hewers of wood," dispensers of raw or unfinished products.

While export of these resources enriched and accelerated the economies of Britain and the United States, it did little to transform us into a producer of manufactured goods for the world economy. We could not and cannot (goes this argument) use the profits from selling resources to build an industrial society because we have had little control over where these funds go. As you will see, Innis's work has recently been resurrected and is one of the bases of dependency theory.

The staples approach put great emphasis on the geographical conditions that lead to prosperity and economic development but also to poverty and underdevelopment. But, at the same time, it tended to ignore the role of power in shaping particular societies or regions.

As Brym has shown, New Brunswick is an interesting case in point. From a staples perspective New Brunswick's rise and fall can be described as follows. Because of the Napoleonic Wars, Britain was forced to find a new source of lumber. New Brunswick had abundant forests and lumber could easily be transported down the Saint John River and then across the Atlantic Ocean. Thus, in the early nineteenth century New Brunswick had a flourishing lumber industry accompanied by an equally active shipbuilding industry. Both spawned other kinds of financial and commercial activity.

However, by the mid-1800s steel ships, propelled by steam, were rapidly replacing sail driven wood ships. Regions that both faced the ocean and had access to coal and iron enjoyed a geographical advantage over regions such as New Brunswick that lacked such access. Thus, shipbuilding moved to northern England and the economy of New Brunswick went into rapid decline to the extent that it is now regarded as one of the "have not" provinces.

While it is obvious that geography and availability of natural resources play a crucial role in shaping any society and its economy, Brym points out that the staples approach is too deterministic and underplays the role of human actions and conflict. As is described later, much of the economic demise of New Brunswick and the Maritimes, generally, must be attributed to the power of Central Canada to invoke freight rates and tariffs that worked to its advantage and to the detriment of the Atlantic region.

S. D. CLARK

A somewhat less deterministic approach to understanding Canada was provided in the more cultural and historical approach of S. D. Clark, the first Chair of the newly formed Sociology Department at the University of Toronto. As a student and then as a colleague of Harold Innis at Toronto, Clark was obviously influenced by the "staples approach." But as a sociologist influenced by American sociology, his work complements rather than extends the Innis tradition. That is, he is less concerned with economic factors than with sociological issues such as religious sectarianism, protest movements and urban and rural poverty in Canada.

Clark's theoretical and ideological position is, at best, ambiguous. For the most part, Clark was sympathetic to functionalism but came, eventually, to recognize that in its bias towards order, equilibrium, consensus and integration, it is prone to charges of being conservative and seeming to maintain and uphold the status quo.

Perhaps this sympathy for functionalism reflects the kind of international perspective we have already discussed. Perhaps, at the same time, his reservations about functionalism reflect Clark the historian, who inevitably saw much conflict and inequality in Canada's history. One is never entirely clear just how much he accepts the functional paradigm. For example, up until the 1960s functional theory was, in his view, an important perspective, certainly a satisfactory way for Americans to study their own society. In part this was because functionalism fitted American assumptions about itself as a stable and consensual society. Partly, too, as Clark argues, American sociologists could take for granted their society and put more emphasis on determining how American society "works" rather than explaining its origins (Clark, 1976:4).

According to Clark, Canada was never in this situation and was never a society able to simply take itself for granted; its very survival was and is problematic and this required Canadian sociologists to use different approaches, perspectives and methodologies.

Many students have difficulty with Clark's work, with identifying its main theoretical thrust. We must confess to something of the same difficulty. Sometimes, like Lucas, Zakuta and Hughes, he seems to be taking for granted the dominant American perspectives and to be treating Canada as merely a convenient research setting. It may well be that his commitment to history, to the careful collection and ordering of historical facts, did not allow him easily to ignore or deny features of Canadian history that American perspectives could not capture. So, while he never truly developed an alternative vision for Canadian sociology, he did help us identify some of the unique features of our society. For example, like John Porter and George Grant, Clark also recognizes the conservatism of Canadians, the emphasis on tradition, the lesser concern with progress and individualism, which link English and French Canadians and which set them apart from Americans and the American dream. Clark argues that it is precisely for this reason that we have remained rather "stodgy and backward," reluctant to give up traditional institutions. Conservatism, from the time of the Loyalists onward, represented our main defence against assimilation and absorption into the American empire.

Perhaps the best illustration of Clark's approach is his notion of the Canadian West as a *Hard Frontier*. He argues that the western frontier developed very differently in Canada than in the United States. We have, for instance, no equivalent mythology in Canada to the raw, lawless, anarchic West, the staple of seemingly thousands and thousands of American "Westerns." For Americans, the West was a safety valve, an escape from the confines of civilized society. In contrast, as Clark points out:

The claims to the interior of the (Canadian) continent were staked not by advancing frontiersmen, acting on their own, but by advancing armies and police forces, large corporate economic enterprises and ecclesiastical organizations, supported by the State (1968:24).

In part, of course, this was simply because western Canada, the "North West," was a far less hospitable place in which to escape. One court not, as Huck Finn decided, avoid the confines of civilization by simply "lighting out for the territory." From the fur trade onwards, some rudimentary organization was essential if people were to survive Canadian winters and Canadian wilderness. In other words, compared to the American West, Canada was, for the most part, a hard frontier in which resources, whether fish or furs or lumber, were hard to get at.

What was called for in the opening up of this Northern half of the continent were massive accumulations of capital, large scale forms of economic organization, long lines of communication and transportation, and extensive state support (Clark, 1976:55).

Clark, here, puts considerable weight on geography and in this respect is not too far away from the approach of the staples theorists. But, he was also aware of how social and economic factors determined the development of Canadian society. At various points, both eastern and western Canada, in turn, were regarded not as places to settle, but as places to exploit. As Ralph Matthews (1976:13) observes about Newfoundland, "although tens of thousands of fishermen came annually to fish Newfoundland's waters, almost none chose to settle." Similarly, at times, "settlement interfered with rather than furthered the interests of the fisheries, the fur trade, and later the timber industry" (Clark, 1976:56). So, after 1684, the Hudson Bay Company forbade European women from entering North America because they would have married and had families and created the need for an infrastructure the Company was anxious to avoid (Brown, 1980). Rather than settlers making their way out to western Canada and forming communities, it was the Hudson's Bay Company and what became the Royal Canadian Mounted Police which, as it were, set the scene. Later, it was the CPR and the CNR that shaped the Canadian west.

People, then, were never freed entirely from the bureaucratic and legal controls of eastern Canada; seldom did law and order have to be created on the spot as in the American West. Clark points out that this control extended, though somewhat less effectively, even into the disorderly and disorganized "Gold Rush" societies of the Yukon and Klondike; law and order came about more quickly than in Alaska where there was no equivalent of the federally backed North West Mounted Police (Clark, 1968:97).

When settlement did occur, it was still controlled by political and economic interests in eastern Canada and, to some extent, Britain. Less favoured immigrants to Canada, particularly Ukrainians, were given less favourable land in the northern parts of the prairie provinces; the better land was saved for British and northern European immigrants. As a trip across western Canada will reveal, the stamp of bureaucracy, of central control, is evident even in the placement of towns. Since most were created after the coming of the railroads, they are spaced along the track roughly every nine miles (Robertson, 1973). Roads, too, are set out in grids: every two miles (north and south), every mile (east and west). Also, sections of every township in Alberta, for instance, were initially Hudson's Bay or CPR land, and are still labelled as such by farmers who now own them. And, unlike Texas and Oklahoma, the oil boom in Alberta did not create instant millionaires out of farmers who had oil on their land. Rather, shortly after its creation as a province the Alberta government "bought up" mineral rights from existing farmers and did not give them out later with homesteader land. Particularly in the 1970s Alberta obviously benefited collectively from oil. Individuals who have an oil well on their land, however, receive only a small payment for right of entry and rental of three or four acres of land, enough, perhaps, to pay the taxes for the quarter section of land. We can speculate that these policies had a strong influence on the way capitalism developed in western Canada.

Criticisms of Clark's work came mainly from Marxist sociologists. Without necessarily denying his contribution to Canadian sociology, they argued that despite the influence of Harold Innis, he (and others at the University of Toronto) missed the essential themes of nationality and imperialism, the core of the Innis tradition (Drache, 1976:10). For Clark, the influence of the United States on Canada is a natural and inevitable consequence of the geographic proximity of unequals (Stolzman and Gamberg, 1975). It can also be argued that though espousing an historical perspective, he nevertheless maintained an essentially functionalist perspective. He chose to treat changes as episodic, as a series of events not necessarily tied together, lacking a systematic theory such as Marxist theory would have provided (Watson, 1975:357). And, in his rather ambiguous use of both culture and geography as determining factors shaping Canada's development, he, as with functionalists generally, tended to ignore the role of power in shaping societies and regions.

In sum, while most Marxist sociologists have been critical of Clark's approach and assumptions, there is agreement that he has provided us with a good empirical, perhaps theoretical, starting point on which to build a relevant Canadian sociology (Felt, 1975). In addition to this, Clark made two general contributions. First, he consistently avoided the pitfalls of "abstracted empiricism," the study of particular institutions or social phenomena as if they existed in a social, cultural and economic vacuum. Whatever its specific failings, Clark's sociology is essentially holistic: he showed that to understand a particular aspect of a society, one must also understand the total society and the relationship of the parts to the whole. Clark's second contribution lies in his emphasis on doing historically informed sociology. This, of course, stands in marked contrast to the ahistorical orientation of functionalism that for several decades dominated Canadian as well as American sociology.

JOHN PORTER

Another important figure in the development of Canadian sociology is John Porter, who spent most of his academic career at Carleton University. Porter, though trained in Britain, was also heavily influenced by American sociological perspectives and assumption of the 1950s and 1960s. Although he would have described himself as a socialist, as described earlier, he shared the American liberal views about social change and what is meant by modernization.

We will postpone description of his specific conclusions about Canadian society until our discussion in Chapters 11, 12 and 13 which deal, respectively, with social, educational and ethnic inequality. However, in general and while he was later to revise many of these conclusions, at the time of the writing of the influential *Vertical Mosaic*, Porter accepted the prevailing image of Canada as essentially an inferior and backward society compared to the United States. On the basis of the admittedly limited research available to him in the 1950s and 1960s, he argued that we lagged behind the United States largely because of our failure to provide equality of access to higher education, to assimilate ethnic groups and to open up our elite groups to other than those from advantaged anglo-saxon backgrounds. And he uncritically accepted America's image of itself as a classless society in which anyone with the drive and ability could succeed. For Porter, Canada, in clinging to British culture and institutions, had failed to meet the promise that the New World offered of an open, meritocratic and egalitarian society.

Of course, Porter was not alone in this view. In Chapter 3 we briefly described how one American sociologist, Seymour Lipset (1963b), described Canadian culture and Canadian society as he saw it in the early 1960s. A short term visitor to Canada and to the University of Toronto, Lipset, who was to become a prominent American sociologist, concluded that Canadian society was more conservative, elitist, cautious and, probably, though he did not quite say this, stodgy and boring, compared to the dynamism of American society. And, it is likely that most Canadians, including the few sociologists working in Canada, accepted his rather dismal depiction of Canadian society and the Canadian mentality.

Sir Wilfrid Laurier is reputed to have said that the twentieth century was to belong to Canada. That this did not occur was blamed, by Porter and others, primarily on our failure to change our values and our institutions and become more like the United States. Whereas staples theorists placed most emphasis on

geography as the determining factor in shaping Canadian society, the sociology of the 1950s and 1960s viewed culture as the critical factor in shaping social and economic development.

As noted earlier in this chapter, the power and affluence of American society was attributed largely to its particular value system, which placed greater emphasis on individualism than collectivism, espoused achievement and universalism over ascription and particularism, and which encouraged private over public enterprise. It seemed that societies that wished to modernize would, inevitably, have to embrace these same values and Canada was no exception.

Similarly, it was widely held that to eradicate poverty within particular societies, it is necessary to break down the "culture of poverty" handed down from generation to generation and replace it with a middle-class culture. Such cultural explanations also figured largely in explanations of regional disparities in income and levels of economic development within Canada. As Doug House (1985) has observed, "Newfie jokes" derive, in large part, from the belief that economic inequality, poverty, generally, is the outcome of cultural inferiority. While the jokes seem confined to Newfoundland society, the economic predicament of the whole Atlantic Region is often attributed by Central and Western Canadians to a lack of drive, ambition and entrepreneurialism in Maritimers and it is apparent that many in the region believe this to be true of themselves.

LIMITATIONS OF EARLY PERSPECTIVES

In retrospect, and with further research of a more comparative nature, it has become evident that the image of Canada portrayed in *The Vertical Mosaic* was probably too pessimistic and that of the United States too bright and optimistic. As we describe in later chapters, the United States is not exceptional in in having a high rate of social mobility; comparative studies that all industrial societies, including Canada, have roughly similar and sometimes higher rates of "middle-mass" mobility. And, Canada's elites have been shown to be as open as those of the United States: or to put it the other way, in both societies elite groups are only partially successful in passing on power and privilege to their children and in keeping out others.

Moreover, as you will learn in Chapter 13, most ethnic groups in Canada have experienced considerably more assimilation than was previously believed. Indeed, there is evidence that multiculturalism may have become important to ethnic groups *after* they had achieved a degree of economic and political integration into Canadian society. And, despite the melting pot ideology thought to dominate American approaches to immigration, one of the more studied phenomenon in recent decades has been the rediscovery and resurgence of ethnicity in the United States, what is described in Chapter 13 as the "process of ethnicization."

Finally, more recent research suggests that Canadians have not differed in the past and do not now differ markedly from Americans in entrepreneurial drive and ability, though Canadians have obviously faced greater physical and demographic obstacles than Americans, which prevented them actualizing these drives. This latter point is considered in more detail in the next chapter, which looks at Canadian capitalism and industrialism and the "merchants against industry" thesis which dominated thinking in the early 1970s.

None of this is to deny that Canada's culture, its economy and its social institutions have developed differently from those of the United States. Examples of such differences abound. Until very recently all political parties in Canada were, in various degrees, committed to public enterprise. The C.B.C., Air Canada, the National Film Board, and the many less visible Crown Corporations are examples of how successive governments have sought to do publicly and collectively what, in the United States, was passionately believed to be the province of private enterprise.

For several decades a universal system of medicare has been taken for granted as a basic right of Canadians but has been strenuously resisted in the United States. Our historically lower rates of divorce, of violence, and of gun ownership and other manifestations of social disorganization, provide evidence of a qualitative difference in the culture of the two societies. However, what the later research did suggest is that cultural differences, while they should not be ignored, do not offer a full or adequate explanation of Canada's economic development and its patterns of regional inequality.

In retrospect, it is easy enough to see weaknesses and limitations in both Clark's and Porter's work and to criticize the extent to which both were overly influenced by American sociology of the time. But, it must also be recognized to what extent they were working very much alone. There were very few other Canadian sociologists and it is probably as true for sociology as for anything else that ideas and theories emerge out of dialogue and confrontation. Possibilities opened up as the number of sociologists in Canada expanded and as Canadian universities increasingly trained university professors.

For these emerging Canadian sociologists, the development of a Canadian sociology was not, however, simply a matter of teaching more Canadian content and putting more Canadian illustrations into American models and frameworks. Rather, as many argued, it was necessary to go further than Clark and Porter. As one influential article described, a distinctive Canadian sociology would involve "a thoroughgoing intellectual revolt against imported modes of American sociology, a revolt that would tail, parallel or perhaps even guide the struggle for full national independence" (Stolzman and Gamberg, 1975:99).

In beginning this task, young sociologists in the 1960s and 1970s turned to both the staples approach of Innis and others and

Marx's approach to political economy. And, as the preceding passage should suggest, the new sociology was very much based on the newly discovered sense of nationalism and repugnance for all things American. The result was what came to be called the political economy of dependency theory. In the course of this development, the lines between the various social science disciplines became blurred and, for many, irrelevant.

For those sociologists, intent on carving out a distinctive Canadian sociology, the main issues centred on Canada's uneven and supposedly distorted economic development, its failure to have control of its economic fate and its place in world capitalism. Much of the argument of dependency theory is economic. But, perhaps, some sociological aspects are captured in the part of dependency theory which centres on metropolis-hinterland relationships.

METROPOLIS-HINTERLAND PERSPECTIVE

In the early 1970s Arthur Davis (1971), formerly an American, argued that a more appropriate perspective than functionalism for understanding Canadian society is the *metropolis-hinterland perspective*. As he suggested, the perspective is at least implicit in the work and approach of the earlier staples theorists. Hinterland refers to relatively underdeveloped or colonial areas that provide raw materials or semi-processed goods, and sometimes people, to relatively developed centres of economic and political control such as cities, regions, nations.

Since the metropolis both dominates and exploits its hinterland, conflict is at least inherent in the relationship between the two. Conflict may, for a reasonable time, be latent. Nevertheless, there is "a tendency on the part of hinterland groups and interests to fight back eventually against their metropolitan exploiters in order to gain a larger place in the regional or national or international sun."

Davis, then a sociologist at the University of Alberta, was clearly influenced by the fact that Alberta, long dominated by central Canadian interests, could, because of its oil resources, retaliate. Most of the time the hinterland is powerless but on occasion it can fight back as Alberta was able to do, perhaps for the first time in its history, during the energy crisis of the early 1970s.

Davis suggests that to understand Canadian society both internally and in relationship to the rest of North America and the world, it is necessary to think of a hierarchy of metropolis-hinterland relationships which, like chinese boxes, nestle one inside another. For example, during the fur trade era, the Northwest was a hinterland of Montreal. But Montreal and, in turn, the whole of Canada was a hinterland dominated by Paris and then London. Today, what maritimers still refer to as Upper Canada and Westerners simply as "Down East" — Southern Ontario — is a metropolis for both. Subjective impressions of metropolis-hinterland also vary. For example, though Albertans may view Quebec as part of the metropolis, Quebeckers, in turn had reason, historically, to view their society as a hinterland under the thumb of English Canada. Both objectively and subjectively, when we widen our focus, Canada can be seen as a hinterland of the United States and, in recent decades, Japan. Montreal, Toronto, Calgary and more, recently, Vancouver are intermediaries in this large metropolis-hinterland nexus.

A CANADIAN EXAMPLE: SINGLE INDUSTRY TOWNS

Perhaps the archetypal case of hinterland-metropolis conflict is the one-industry town. While most of us think of social change in Canada in terms of larger and larger urban conglomerations, Canadian industrial expansion has depended, in large part, on the proliferation of small isolated towns created to extract resources. As resources were exploited, corporations had to move increasingly farther away from the metropolis. The towns that have been created share three features: they are small; they are isolated; and they are dependent. They therefore share many features with other communities (regardless of their industrial base) in the north of Canada and in the wilderness areas of Newfoundland and British Columbia. Clearly, many Canadians, in fact about half the population, should be familiar with the features of small-town life in these communities; more Canadians than we typically imagine live in communities of less than 30 000 (Himelfarb, 1977).

A central fact of life, especially in single industry towns, is dependence. The residents are dependent on a sole employer and on the often unrenewable resource being exploited. The community as a whole is dependent on decisions made at corporate headquarters in the metropolis, often a foreign metropolis. Decisions crucial to the life of the community are, then, often made by people far removed from that community. Not surprisingly, the residents can be characterized as resigned and fatalistic; feelings of powerlessness prevail. Nor do the residents know whom to blame; there seems to be little class consciousness and most residents seem to share the feeling that the company, its managers and employees, and the rest of the community are in the same boat, all dependent on vast and impersonal forces over which they have no control. This may, in part, result from the fact that the decision-making processes are remote and invisible. The workers only see the consequences of the decisions, never the decision-making process or even the offices in which decisions are made.

Lucas, in his 1971 book, *Minetown, Milltown, Railtown*, was heavily influenced by functionalism. He portrayed these communities and their culture and structure as an inevitable outcome of Canada's industrialization and unique geography. Indeed, Australia with a similar set of geographical hurdles has similar communities with similar problems (UNESCO, 1974). However, more recent theorists have tended to view the problems of one-industry towns as the inevitable outcome of the exploitation of the hinterland by the metropolis.

From the hinterland-metropolis perspective, there is conflict of interests between the one-industry town and the metropolis-located owners, even when those in the hinterland are unaware of this exploitative relationship and passively acceptant of the situation. Whatever the perceptions, this perspective sensitizes us to the objective vulnerability of the hinterland. Some years ago, in MacAdam, New Brunswick, for example, community residents were forced to confront the reality of their dependence in a way that could no longer be ignored or denied. MacAdam lost the American owned mill that employed the bulk of the workforce and upon which the rest of the community was dependent. This meant more than mass unemployment; it meant, too, that the security that comes from owning a home was rendered meaningless; there is no market for homes in a dying community. It also meant that there were no job alternatives within MacAdam nor any assurance that the workers' skills, which may be obsolete, could easily be traded for jobs elsewhere. MacAdam, the hinterland, has no resources to fight back with. In times of prosperity, dependence may be seen in terms of paternalistic benevolence. MacAdam illustrates the dangers in trusting in such benevolence, the dangers in dependence. Georgia-Pacific, the mill owner, moved back across the border. For some Canadian sociologists, this is a microcosm of the consequences resulting from Canada's dependence on the United States.

DEPENDENCY PERSPECTIVES

In the 1970s, a number of young Marxists built upon and expanded the metropolis-hinterland perspective through development of what came quickly to be known as **dependency theory**. Dependency theory was developed mainly by economists, economic historians and political scientists. For dependency theorists, the critical issues are twofold. First, we live in a liberal democratic society which not only upholds the concept of private property but which enjoins the state to create a climate favourable for capitalism to flourish. Second, dependency enters the picture because Canada, from its conception, has been a colony, a dependent society and economy, first of France, then, of Britain and, since the Second World War, an economic satellite, in effect a colony, of the United States.

In the early 1970s, Robert Laxer (1973:6) described Canada as "a dependency moving towards colonial status in the American empire" thereby echoing Innis's earlier conclusion that we have gone from colony to nation to colony. Therefore, dependency theorists drew upon both Marxist perspectives and the staples approach of Harold Innis and his students.

Dependency theory departed from Clark's historical perspective both in emphasis and in its basic theoretical orientation. In general, Canada's development was not seen simply as the result of a unique geography and climate or of a series of unrelated events or of a particular kind of culture, but as the systematic outcome of imperialism and economic domination and exploitation by a succession of metropolises acting in their own economic interests. While Innis's staples approach was seen as providing valuable clues as to how to go about understanding Canada, dependency theorists increasingly looked to Marxist writers such as Andre Gunder Frank for the appro-

priate analytical tools. Frank's work (1967 and 1969) on Latin America had led him to the conclusion that:

> ... *underdevelopment is not due to the survival of archaic institutions and the existence of capital shortages in regions that have remained isolated from the stream of world history. On the contrary, underdevelopment was and still is generated by the very same historical process which also generated economic development: the development of capitalism itself (1969:9).*

Frank therefore shares with other Marxist thinkers the view that the nature of economic, political, social and cultural institutions in underdeveloped countries (hinterlands) must be as much the outcome of capitalism as are those of developed societies, the metropolises which dominate them. This means that underdevelopment will not simply "go away" and Third World countries will not simply "evolve over time." Nor can they simply incorporate or assimilate into their cultures the skill, knowledge, values and technology that made the imperialist nations economically successful; it is not simply a process of catching up. Rather, according to Frank, policies that will be effective in creating economic development and cultural change will be those that are politically revolutionary, which, in other words, involve the destruction of capitalism in these societies and its replacement with another system—one based on socialism.

Some dependency theorists recognized that Canada is not in the same kind of dependent and underdeveloped situation of most Third World countries; as well as serving as a hinterland for various metropolises, other countries serve as hinterlands for Canada. As Levitt described in her highly influential book, *Silent Surrender* (1970), Canada is in an intermediate situation in which, as a branch plant economy, most of its industries are foreign controlled. At the same time, some Canadian capitalists have been able to control segments of other economies, particularly in the Caribbean.

Although in the context of the world economy Canada is both advantaged and dependent (Carroll, 1986:6), early dependency theorists down played or ignored Canada's intermediate situation and chose rather to see parallels to Third World Countries. For these theorists, the main lines of our economy and social institutions were moulded by the fact that from the outset Canada was a hinterland, a place to extract staples — partially finished raw materials — for manufacturers in Britain and the United States.

We have remained, goes the argument, a branch plant economy, arrested in our development because it was and is in the interest of a succession of metropolises that we should remain so. Early dependency theorists were, then, led to very similar conclusions as others were reaching about the Third World about the kinds of options available to Canadians if they wished to "win back" control of their economy and culture.

CANADIAN CULTURE AND IDENTITY

In Chapter 10 we will consider some of the implications of using the dependency perspective for understanding the nature of Canadian capitalism and its class structure. Here we are concerned with what it tells us about the nature and the development of dominant ideologies and counter-ideologies in Canada.

The dependency perspective provides us with a theoretical explanation of much that is, from other perspectives, puzzling about Canadian society, its dominant ideology and its culture. From this perspective, cultural domination is *cultural imperialism*; in effect, the culture of the mother country, of the metropolis, rides in "on the coat-tails" of economic invasion and take-over. It acts both to legitimate economic domination and to "soften" the hinterland for further rounds of exploitation.

According to dependency theorists, the ideas and the culture of the metropolis take precedence over those of the hinterland and become, in effect, the standards of excellence by which members of the dependent society come to judge themselves. The result is a kind of collective "inferiority complex" in which we debase as second rate our own cultural productions and literally believe that those of the metropolis are inherently superior.

Robin Matthews, an English professor and ardent nationalist, in the early 1970s argued that this process was being hastened by the acceptance in Canada of the American version of the liberal ideology:

It (the liberal ideology) insists that the ideas of mobility put forward by the imperial centre are "progressive." To resist those ideas is "reactionary." It insists that all history is going in one direction, led by the imperial centre, inasmuch as the colonial country is like the imperial country it is "advanced." Inasmuch as it is different, it is "underdeveloped." It insists that ideas created for and propagated from the imperial centre are ideas of universal interests and importance. Inasmuch as the colonial country permits those ideas to be superimposed, and permits them to be superimposed by immigrants from the imperial country, the country is "liberal." Inasmuch as it insists upon the integrity of its own ideas and people, it is, of course, "chauvinistic," "narrowly nationalistic," "navel gazing" and so on (1973:219).

It is in this context, then, that we can best appreciate the late George Grant's concern over the demise of Canadian conservatism. Nationalism, the attempt to recover control of our economy and of our culture, was antithetical to the American liberal ideology. It simply becomes translated as racism or fascism. The reason seems fairly clear. Nationalism, especially when accompanied by socialism, is a significant example of the hinterland fighting back. It threatens, as in Latin America and South America, the continuing freedom of multinationals to do as they like in the hinterland economy. Even cultural concerns, in and of themselves "harmless," may, if left unchecked, become motivating forces, well-springs of social action and conflict in the economic sphere as well.

Dependency theory, then, led to the probably overly pessimistic conclusion that our ability to shape an independent culture and national identity is limited. It is not simply that Canadians are perverse and ambivalent. Rather, fundamental cultural development, it was believed, cannot occur without fundamental change in our economic structure. We cannot, as it were, simply pull ourselves up by our intellectual and cultural bootstraps and create a distinctive national identity while, at the same time, remaining an economic satellite of the United States. It follows, too, that we cannot, as Porter hoped, simply institute policies to end pluralistic conflict and increase equality of educational opportunity — in a word, "catch-up"—unless basic structures of dependency are first eradicated.

ASSESSMENT OF DEPENDENCY THEORY

The Canadian sociology that developed over the 1970s was, then, one which involved a number of issues and objectives. First, along with many other disciplines, there was concern that future academic jobs in the now stagnant market, go to Canadians. Second, was the felt need for Canadian content and Canadian perspectives on our society; Canadian students should be able to know about their society, its structure, its history and its culture and to do so from a different perspective than that offered by American sociology. And, finally, a distinctive Canadian sociology should provide new insights into Canadian society and thereby contribute to the development of a culturally and economically autonomous society.

The first of these concerns, jobs, does, at first glance, seem mainly to reflect the understandable but also self-interested desire of young Canadians for an academic future in their own society and to have little to do with the development of new sociological perspectives. However, nationalists were able to demonstrate that most of the Canadian research was, in fact, being done by Canadian sociologists and especially by those who were trained in Canada. In other words, if students were to have access to Canadian material, the second objective, then it was essential that more Canadians be hired and that Canadian graduate programs be strengthened.

To a large extent, the first and second of these objectives have been achieved. For about a decade, there has been a two-tiered advertising system in place which requires that academic positions in all disciplines must first be advertised to Canadian citizens or equivalents. Only when it can be demonstrated that no suitable Canadian candidate exists can a university advertise outside the country. In sociology this has meant that, in recent years, most new positions have, in fact, been filled by Canadians and that the kinds of concerns expressed in the early 1970s, that Canadianization of our universities was racist and myopic, since social science transcends national boundaries, seems to be a dead issue.

As described earlier in this chapter, the result of this hiring policy and change of attitude has been a massive growth in research on Canadian society and virtually no general sociology courses where it is impossible to draw upon Canadian material. Just as hiring of Canadians is no longer at issue, so, evidently, inclusion of Canadian content and perspectives is taken for granted by most sociologists. For most, use of an American textbook in basic courses is now viewed as inappropriate and as irrelevant as adopting one written for students in Zaire.

It is less clear that the third objective, development of a distinctive Canadian sociology both able to make sense of Canadian society and to point the way to economic and cultural independence, has yet to be achieved. Robert Brym (1986) concludes that part of the problem is that, in so vehemently rejecting American sociology, dependency theorists, in effect, threw the baby out with the bath water: they ignored its many methodological strengths, its emphasis on rigorous testing of hypotheses and its growing use of comparative analyses. As Marchak (1985) puts it, there was a kind of "breathless quality" to the early work in the dependency perspective.

Thus, as we will be describing in subsequent chapters, many of the more specific conclusions reached by this first generation of consciously Canadian sociologists have been challenged by more recent theoretical and empirical work. Subsequent research has shown some of the findings and conclusions of dependency theory to be incorrect or based on dubious use of indicators of distorted or uneven economic development, or to have failed to take into account that what seemed peculiar to Canada was probably true of all western Capitalist societies.

A second problem centres on the ideological commitment of dependency theorists. The liberal ideology had blinded an earlier generation of American and Canadian sociologists to many of the features of their societies. So the more radical ideology of the 1960s and 1970s may have led these theorists, concerned as they were with policy-oriented research, to conclusions which though based on hasty research fitted what was perceived as the political and economic agenda for Canada. As we have seen, sociologists, young academics generally, were highly nationalistic, strongly anti-American and committed to Marxism and socialism. Thus, Kari Levitt's *Silent Surrender* was not simply an academic work: in draft form it was also one of the motivating factors behind the "waffle movement," the unsuccessful attempt to move the NDP to a more radical and nationalistic stance. As we discuss in Chapter 10, dependency theory did offer the solace that, unlike the United States, Canada was not an exploiter of others but a victim of exploitation, but, as we now recognize, this was a too

simplistic picture. The less nationalistic and more sophisticated research of the 1980s has made it more difficult to maintain this kind of innocence: Canadians are part of a world system of capitalism and Canadian capitalists seem to operate much like those in other western societies (Carroll, 1986).

A third problem with dependency theory is that, in its emphasis on the economic determinants shaping Canadian society, it appears to many as overly deterministic and sometimes not too different from the functionalism it was meant to replace. Early on in this book, we criticized both functionalism and conflict perspectives for often failing to take into account how people, through their actions and perceptions, can sometimes modify or, at least, fight back against the constraints of social structure. Marx, in his own writing, was very aware of the role of human agency and action in social change, but, for some varieties of Marxists, this fact is sometimes forgotten.

Many Canadian sociologists, who would call themselves Marxists, as they attempt to understand Canadian society generally, and regionalism particularly, see limitations in a perspective that talks in terms of the "needs" and "goals" of the capitalist system and that attributes social change and social structures solely to impersonal and abstract economic forces; this is the position of some neo-Marxists writing about Canada. As Robert Brym (1989:85) points out, it is people, not socio-economic systems, that have needs and goals. Similarly, in attempting to understand Newfoundland society and its economy, Doug House (1985) has pointed to the need, within the context of dependency, to take the key actors views and behaviour into account. His research and, of course, that of many others, shows, certainly, that materialistic forces shape and constrain us and set parameters to what we can do and be. But it must also be kept in mind that ideas are powerful forces and, as in the rise of Canadian nationalism, may, to some extent have a life of their own.

Perhaps the most fundamental criticism is that the Canadian sociology of the 1970s and

1980s, like that it succeeded, was essentially a distorted sociology because it was written mainly by men and was concerned almost exclusively with male activities and institutions. Paralleling the developing of Canadian sociology has been a massive and sustained attack on what has come to be called "malestream" sociology, a sociology written by and about men.

FEMINIST PERSPECTIVES

In Chapter 6, we described how capitalism and industrialism brought about a separation of the social world into two spheres: the public world of the marketplace and the private world of the family. For the most part, sociology, economics and history have been about the former. Indeed, the sociology of the family has often been regarded as "soft" sociology. Those interested in marriage, family, parenting and divorce, have often had their research viewed as of lesser importance and status than studies of occupational mobility (usually of males), work, economic and political processes, urbanization and bureaucracies.

Use in these studies of "he" was often justified by grammatical convention but it is also apparent that it was mainly men and *their* institutions and activities being studied. Women were "hidden in the household," their activities, projects, perceptions and contributions to society and the economy were ignored or seen as marginal. For example, as we described in Chapter 6, images of the family were typically those of the male sociologists who undertook the research. Similarly, community studies, perhaps because they were largely done by men, ignored women's work, and women's participation in the life of the community being studied. And, studies of social mobility were almost entirely studies of men's mobility opportunities and mobility experiences.

It would be an exaggeration to suggest that all of this has changed. It is still the case that, while the majority of sociology undergraduates are female, only 16 percent of their professors are women and these women are more likely than men to be in the lower ranks of the profession. Feminist scholars have generally faced an uphill battle to have their work taken seriously by male colleagues. In most universities there was initial resistance to women's studies courses and such courses as the sociology and psychology of women were disparaged as non-scientific and parochial. Whereas an earlier generation of sociologists argued that there was no such thing as a "Canadian Sociology," because the principles of sociology must have universal applicability, the more recent argument was that there is no difference between a sociology which examines men and one which examines women.

But, this battle seems to have been largely won: at the beginning of the 1990s, Canadian sociology is a very different discipline than a decade ago. What have been the implications of the growth of the feminist based sociology for Canadian sociology and for our understanding of our society? We would suggest there have been several.

First, this sociology has documented the extent of gender inequality in both the public and private spheres of Canadian society. As will be described in following chapters, women, on average, earn about 65 percent of male earnings, they are under-represented in the more powerful and advantaged positions and face a variety of forms of discrimination within the workplace. In the private sphere, as we have seen, women bear most of the responsibilities for child rearing and do most of the domestic labour and are frequently victims of domestic violence.

Second, recognition of this inequality has led to attempts to explain and to change these patterns of sexual inequality. Those working within a liberal tradition mainly focused on issues of inequality of opportunity and sought to show the subtle and not so subtle ways girls are socialized to anticipate, perhaps even accept as "natural" and inevitable, lower levels of achievement and subordinate roles in the home and the workplace. The emphasis for these sociologists was largely upon finding ways to change attitudes and, in turn, the way in which women and men are socialized.

Without necessarily denying that such changes are desirable, Canadian feminists have, from the outset of the feminist movement, put greater emphasis on structural rather than cultural or psychological explanations of women's oppression and the persistence of patriarchy and patriarchal attitudes. In recent years, the dominant perspective has been that provided by Marxism.

The debate about how to deal with women's oppression within a Marxist framework is one which we think goes beyond what we would expect students to take away from a first year course. It is, in many ways, an abstract and sometimes confusing debate, particularly as we have not, at this point, fully introduced you to the meaning and nature of capitalism and to Marx's analysis of capitalism and class inequality.

For now, we would simply point out that most of the leading feminist social scientists are also Marxists. Yet, it is an uneasy alliance because, as with other classical sociologists we have discussed, Marx did not address many of the questions with which a feminist sociology is concerned. And, as more than one feminist has concluded, the marriage between Marxism and feminism mirrors the marriage between men and women in that, in both cases, the interests of the latter tend to become submerged in those of the former.

Nor are all feminists convinced that the roots of women's oppression are necessarily to be found in the inequalities inherent in capitalism. That is, patriarchy, the political, economic and social control of women by men, quite obviously did not begin with the rise of capitalism. As we have seen in Chapter 6, the situation of women did undergo various changes which most social historians believe led to a worsening of the position of women in society. But, patriarchy goes back much much further in human history.

Still, this Marxist-oriented feminist scholarship has forced a re-evaluation of Canada's early development and regional economies within present-day Canadian society. This research shows the extent to which women's work both within and outside the home contributed to family income and to the economy.

As Bonnie Fox has recently observed, for capitalism and industrialism to occur there generally needs to be a strong agrarian base and women have been important to the survival of family farms. As she points out, while feminist sociology does not necessarily address the key issues of the political economy of dependence, "examining women's role in the development process entails a focus on the *internal* factors important to the development of what is now Canada — and thus promises to counter the emphasis of both Canadian 'dependency theorists' and 'internationalists' on external forces." (Fox, 1989:156). Moreover, as she also observes, the understanding we have of Canada is not simply shaped from the outside. The development of Canada's class structure is incomplete without taking into account how women, through their various roles in the kinship structure and the community, consolidate the class position of families at various levels in the class structure.

The much more explicit focus on women and their position within society has also brought about a re-thinking of the nature and functions of our social institutions. As we have seen in Chapter 6, this has been particularly so with respect to how we conceptualize families and familial relationships. But, it is evident that feminist scholarship has also led to different interpretations of the impact of our laws and legal system and our educational and religious institutions. It has led to a reconceptualization of such acts as rape, incest, sexual harassment, and wife battering, and of the implications of pornography. In other words, the effect of feminism on the discipline is not simply that sociologists now remember to include women in their research but also to bring about a radical transformation of the discipline and of what are considered to be social problems and policy issues.

Perhaps the most fundamental illustration of this transformation is the feminist debate about what constitutes social, but perhaps all, knowledge. As we argued in Chapter 2, what makes a discipline a science is the commitment of researchers to the norms of the scientific method. However, some feminists question whether there is not more than one kind of scientific method, more than one way of knowing. Some argue that science, with its emphasis on categorization, hypothesis testing, quantification and "objectivity" may simply reflect a male bias, how men have typically conceptualized and dealt with the social and physical world. And, since men have dominated science, their reality became *the* reality.

Feminists are divided on this issue. While, as Eichler (1985:631) has pointed out, there is consensus that consciously or unconsciously much present and almost all past sociology is sexist, many feminists are unwilling to abandon, entirely, the norms of the scientific method as we presently know them. These sociologists are concerned that to do so is to take away any means of assessing the goodness or badness of research and the theory both produced by and generated by such research. And, in making that argument, some wonder whether this concern merely indicates the extent to which they were influenced by being trained in a male-dominated educational system (Sydie, 1987).

It may be well, at this point, to stop and consider what images concepts such as "feminism" and "feminist-based research" evoke for you. Many of our students, female as well as male, think of "feminism" as simply another word for "women's lib" and are, in varying degrees, hostile to the whole women's movement or are uneasy with what

it seems to mean both ideologically and to them personally. At the same time, most of our female students feel it unfair that women are, for example, paid less than men for comparable jobs and are unhappy with the fact that women bear the major responsibility for domestic labour and child care. But, in their class discussions and papers, many deny that they would go so far as to label themselves as feminists or "women's libbers," positions that they imply would make them perceived as too extreme or too radical. We know less about what our male students think since most do not enrol in courses where feminist issues are explicitly discussed. Some men, we suspect, though concerned and interested in these issues, believe that only women can be feminists and do feminist research and feel it is not their place to enter into the discussion.

Is there truth in this belief? Can men do feminist-based research? We have not done a poll of our female colleagues who regard themselves as feminists but we suspect that most would, in theory at least, be forced to answer in the affirmative. Men are as capable of learning the lessons of feminism as are women. But, probably most would also note, again in theory, it is possible to put the well-trained cat in with the canary; however, in practice, we will watch it rather closely lest the cat's basic instincts overcome its domestic training. So at this point in the development of Canadian sociology does it appear to the be the case for male sociologists who are interested in the issues and research agenda of feminism.

Certainly, some men, notably social historians, are making important contributions to the growing body of feminist scholarship, but the major dialogue in this area remains between women and women. Ironically, perhaps paradoxically, the 1970s and 1980s have been a time in the development of Canadian sociology where there has been a rather sharp sexual division of scholastic labour. Just as women were, for a very long time, excluded from the "real" and "important" social world which male sociologists defined and studied, so, for a time at least, men are excluded from what, in the past decade, has been the major development in sociology, the growth of a full-fledged feminist sociology. And, perhaps, at this point, this is how it should be.

Margrit Eichler (1985), in her assessment of the contributions of feminism to sociology, concludes that, with the exception of the family, feminist scholarship has, to date, had little impact on mainstream sociology in the sense of making it less sexist and in changing the kinds of questions it address. In the longer run, we would like to believe that the impact of a feminist sociology will be to transform the discipline such that "malestream" sociology and "feminist" sociology will be outdated terms and that sociology will not be about men and women in society but people in society. At the same time, we are sympathetic with the view of some feminists that many aspects of the human condition and the relationship of the individual to her or his society do have a sexual dimension which warrants a sexual division of labour within the discipline. This seems especially so for sociologists who reject quantitative in favour of interpretive approaches and who attempt to ground their theories in the experience of those they study.

Here there are two aspects to consider. First is the respective positions men and women have held within most societies. Just as white sociologists can document empirically but not directly experience what it means to be black in a racist society, so men can quantify but not experience sexual oppression, fear of rape and sexual assault, and the humiliation of sexual harassment in a patriarchal society. Second is biology. While some men have claimed to have experienced post partum symptoms and even more have actively engaged with their new born, we remain sceptical and believe that women's experience of pregnancy, child birth and early nurturing are domains largely inacces-

sible to men. In short, in a variety of ways men and women are different and until very recently have inhabited different social worlds. While we do not for a moment believe that these differences have much relevance in the modern world and the modern economy, they do have relevance in our basic experience of everyday life.

CONCLUSIONS

If you are at all like the students in our classes, you are by now probably fairly confused by all of these perspectives and impatient with debates that perhaps seem to you entirely academic or irrelevant — part of that murky past before you were born. You may also be wishing for someone, anyone, to tell you, once and for all time, what is the "right" perspective, what is the "truth" about Canadian society, what is and is not the subject matter of sociology. And, you may feel some discomfort that so much of this sociology, both feminist and Marxist, points to the need for a radical transformation of the very structures of Canadian society; tinkering may not be enough. Despite the problems of Canadian society, you may feel that you will do alright by the existing system; that in fact you aren't all that keen on participating in a revolution.

About all we can say to that is that the discomfort sociology creates is not all that new. Peter Berger, an American sociologist, writing in the early 1960s, described sociology even then as a discipline devoted to upsetting apple carts, as a *critical* discipline. It is probably safe to say that the revolution is not at hand. It is even safer to say that few, if any, Marxists or feminists, academic or otherwise, have yet drawn the blueprint for the more just and equitable and truly non-sexist society. What they have done, however, is to reinsert a critical perspective into the sociological tradition. They have made us rethink our own history and the explanations we were given for the peculiar development of Canadian society. Moreover, they challenge us to be sceptical of our culture and what it tells us is *the* reality. If nothing else, it may lead you to think harder about what is a private trouble and what may be a public issue and, in the process, may lead you to compassion, if not outrage, at the situation of those not as well-placed as yourself.

However, there is, even among those committed to Marxist and feminist perspectives, a considerable amount of disagreement and controversy about how best to interpret data emerging from their research and what should be the central questions addressed in further research. While confusing to you as a student, you should also recognize that this is a normal part of any healthy and developing science. The internal conflicts that characterize socialist ideology are also present within the academic left and are, in part, the reason that there are these debates and controversies. Canadian sociology has its national socialists and its world socialists, its academic socialists and its engaged activist socialists, its reformers and its revolutionaries. And, within feminism there are equally powerful ideological, theoretical and methodological debates and controversies. None of this makes it easy for us to summarize neatly nor to give you text-book formulations of the present state of the discipline.

As well, we might note that part of the difficulty of trying to work your way through present-day sociology is that a number of sociologists in Canada continue to work with an essentially functionalist perspective. There are, as we have pointed out throughout this book, serious limitations to what this perspective can tell us about our society. But, for many kinds of questions, these sociologists have a considerable amount to teach us: as we have said, the functionalist perspective tells us a good deal about the blueprint and how it is maintained but very little about how it operates within a capitalist framework.

Also, many of those who are teaching you

sociology are drawn to the sorts of problems and everyday life issues that are perhaps most adequately captured by symbolic interaction perspective. For such sociologists, issues of power, class, inequality, exploitation, dependency and underdevelopment are but "distant guns," ultimately important, maybe, but not very germane to what, for example, it means to go through life stuttering, or what it is like to experience a divorce, or how one connects with the gay community, or how, as a provincial court judge, you go about the process of sentencing, of determining when the punishment fits the crime. In other words, not all sociologists, even when committed to a left ideology, necessarily choose to study and think about the sorts of "macro" issues which dominate this and following chapters.

A number of years ago, Robert Lynd, an American sociologist, wrote a book entitled *Knowledge For What.* In the late 1960s, American sociologists wore buttons to their annual meetings with the slogan, *Sociology for Whom.* The first of these questions was a call for less abstract and more relevant theory and for research that dealt with the more pressing problems and questions of the day. The second question had to do with the concern of radical sociologists that sociological knowledge was, seemingly, being produced for the powerful groups in society and the world rather than for those most in need of research that might help them to change their oppressed situation.

We sympathize with the sentiments underlying both of these position and have, in this text, which is meant to give you an overview of the discipline, dealt mainly with these kinds of concerns. Canadian sociologists are involved in developing theory and research that can address the central questions of living in a capitalist and unequal society and how, under these circumstances, change to a more humane, less sexist, and more just society might be realized; we would hardly want it to be otherwise. But, in all of this earnest attention to the problems of our society and in the redirection of sociology towards political economy, we cannot help but feel that something has been lost from the discipline. Perhaps because your authors are of an essentially frivolous nature, or perhaps because we were introduced into sociology just before Marxism and feminism became the dominant perspectives, we do believe that something of the fun of what made us become sociologists in the first place is no longer there.

We miss the kind of thinking that led some sociologists to wonder about "the sociology of the bicycle," or the problem of "being just right," or why children have been seen sometimes as "little devils" and at other times, as "little angels," why "lucre is filthy" or how we engage in "management impression" as we go about presenting ourselves in everyday life or why we need a "sociology of the inept" and so on. All of this is, in the long run inconsequential perhaps, but is also part of what we view as integral to the sociological imagination.

Canada has unique historical, climatic and geographical features that have clearly contributed to the shaping of Canadian society. In its broad outlines, dependency theory did offer us a promising way to understand many aspects of Canadian society, how it has developed, how it has responded to its climate and geography, and to the historic fact of living next to the most powerful nation on earth. And, while the debate is far from over, it has shown us how things might be made better. Indeed, in recognizing the extent and nature of our dependence, we go part way towards the development of a new and stronger national character and identity. So, we believe that the various versions of the conflict perspective, particularly as they have come to be modified by feminist theory and approaches, are the most promising for understanding Canadian society. In the next chapter, we shall use these perspectives for an understanding of Canada as a dependent capitalist but also patriarchal society. The conflict perspective, and particularly a Marxist perspective, offers us a way of perceiving the genesis of Canadian structure and culture.

But, as you read Chapter 10 and those which follow, we do not want you to lose sight of the theme that organized the first half of this text, the link between public and private. Within the larger constraints, people individually and in concert shape and reshape themselves and their society. In our everyday lives, these large structures impinge on us in different ways, depending on our position in the social structure but also depending on whether we are Inuit, French Canadian, or Ukrainian; on whether we are married, divorced or single; on whether we have children or not; on whether we live in Saskatchewan or New Brunswick; on whether we work on an assembly line or in an office; and on whether we are female or male. Only when we can understand these influences, only when we can understand how Canadians experience their everyday lives, can we with confidence draw the link between public and private.

III SUGGESTIONS FOR FURTHER READING

Many of the specific books we might suggest to you, which are relevant to Canadian sociology and its development, we have reserved for inclusion at the end of the chapters that follow. This present chapter has drawn heavily upon Robert Brym's long, insightful and very readable article in *Current Sociology*, entitled "Anglo-Canadian Sociology" (Brym, 1986). This has, with the collaboration of Bonnie Fox, recently been expanded into a book, *From Culture to Power: The Sociology of English Canada*, (Brym and Fox, 1989). It provides an excellent introduction to the history of Canadian sociology, the strengths and weaknesses of dependency, and later perspectives, as well as good introduction to the contributions of feminist sociology.

S. D. Clark's brief *Canadian Society in Historical Perspective* (1976) is a useful introduction to his own contribution to Canadian society and to the development of Canadian sociology more generally. Critical examinations of Clark's contribution can be found in Deborah Harrison's, *The Limits of Liberalism* (1983) and Harry Hiller's, *S. D. Clark and the Development of Canadian Sociology* (1982).

While it is obviously dated, there are still many insights to be gained from reading John Porter's *The Vertical Mosaic* (1965). And, as an indication of how such an influential sociologist was able, near the end of his life, to revise many of his earlier conclusions, we recommend you to Porter's essays in *The Measure of Canadian Society* (1979) and, in particular those dealing with education and the meaning of a just society.

Paul Grayson's and Dennis Magill's update of the 1975 Symons Report: *To Know Ourselves*, and *One Step Forward, Two Steps Sideways: Sociology and Anthropology in Canada* (1981), though itself now dated, is an important illustration of how our dependence has shaped and constrained the development of a Canadian sociology.

Major statements of dependency theory appeared in a succession of edited collections of papers, themselves the outcome of a number of seminars and conferences held over the 1970s. In order of appearance, these are Ian Lumsden's *Close the 49th Parallel, etc: the Americanization of Canada*; Gary Teeple's *Capitalism and the National Question in Canada* (1972); Robert M. Laxer's *Canada Ltd.: The Political Economy of Dependency* (1973); and John Saul's and Craig Heron's *Imperialism, Nationalism and Canada* (1977).

Undoubtedly, one of the more important critiques of these first attempts at developing dependency perspectives is William Carroll's *Corporate Power and Canadian Capitalism* (1986). His opening chapters provide both a very readable but also highly sympathetic critique of this work. Much less sympathetic, but often provocative, are many of the articles in S. D. Berowtiz's edited collection, *Models and Myths in Canadian Sociology* (1984). As an antidote, you might also want to read the articles in the special issue of the *Canadian Review of Sociology and Anthropology* on "The State of the Art and New Directions: Sociology in Anglophone Canada," particularly those by Pat Marchak and Margrit Eichler that deal, respectively, with the contributions of political economy and feminism to Canadian sociology. Much of the flavour of more recent work in Canadian sociology is contained in the two edited works by Robert Brym, *The Structure of the Canadian Capitalist Class* (1985) and *Regionalism in Canada* (1986).

For an introduction into the larger body of literature written from a feminist perspective, we suggest Roberta Hamilton's and Michelle Barrett's edited collection, *The Politics of Diversity: Feminism, Marxism and Nationalism* (1986) as well as many of the articles in the 25th anniversary issue of the *Canadian Review of Sociology and Anthropology*, entitled "Feminist Scholarship" (25:2, 1988).

CHAPTER 10

ECONOMIC PERSPECTIVES

OVERVIEW

INTRODUCTION

INDUSTRIALIZATION

CRITIQUES OF INDUSTRIAL SOCIETY
MODERNIZATION AND CAPITALISM

THE SOCIOLOGY OF CAPITALISM

CAPITALISM: AN ALLEGORY
THE DEVELOPMENT OF CAPITALISM
HISTORICAL MATERIALISM
MARX AND MODERN CAPITALISM
THE SOCIAL PSYCHOLOGY OF CAPITALISM

CANADIAN CAPITALISM

CANADA AS A DEPENDENCY
DEINDUSTRIALIZATION
DILEMMAS OF DEPENDENCY PERSPECTIVES
CHALLENGES TO DEPENDENCY PERSPECTIVES
THE CANADIAN STATE AND CANADIAN CAPITALISM

TRANSFORMATION OF WORK IN CAPITALIST SOCIETY

SHIFT FROM AGRICULTURE
EXPANSION OF THE SERVICE SECTOR
KNOWLEDGE SOCIETY OR HAMBURGER ECONOMY
PROFESSIONALS AND MANAGERS
THE MARGINAL WORKER AND THE UNEMPLOYED
WOMEN IN THE LABOUR FORCE
PRODUCTIVE LABOUR
ALIENATION OF LABOUR

BUREAUCRACY AND CONTROL

SCIENTIFIC MANAGEMENT
BUREAUCRATIZATION
HUMAN RELATIONS
CONTRADICTIONS OF BUREAUCRACY

CONCLUSION

SUGGESTIONS FOR FURTHER READING

OVERVIEW

This chapter we hope will at least make clear to you two ways in which an understanding of Canadian capitalism can help you understand your own actions. First, an understanding of Canadian capitalism can help you understand the nature of the choices you will confront. Living in an industrialized and capitalist society like Canada, with the prospect of a professional career and the affluence and status that brings, you may well have a place in capitalism different from that of traditional labour. Nevertheless, to understand the opportunities and constraints that will face many of you when you leave university or college, you will have to understand something of Canada's particular brand of corporate capitalism.

Second, this chapter illustrates for you the necessity of a historical perspective in coming to understand the larger structures that will frame your actions. It is probably true, too, that through historical perspective, we can learn about the limits to our freedom, what we may have lost in getting where we are and the opportunities for change.

In a sense, this is what we were trying to do in Chapter 3 when we described ideology in Canada. In this chapter, however, we focus on the material base of Canada and how this has changed. At the highest level this means a look at the development of corporate capitalism and of industrialization generally. At a lower level this means a look at Canada's changing labour force. And at the level that will touch most directly on your experience this means a look at the world of work.

As you will learn in this chapter, much of sociology is an attempt to understand the changes in social and economic life which capitalism and industrialism, or more generally, modernization, has brought about. It is difficult to convey these changes because they are, for most of us, so taken for granted. Few, today, have known a world without radio, television, cars, telephones, washing machines, fast food chains and so on. Most of you are barely familiar with the world before computers. At a more fundamental level, none of you has had experience of a world without large corporations, government bureaucracies, and a competitive labour market.

By the end of this chapter you should have an awareness of how theory and research, which focuses on industrialism, differs from that which focuses on the development and consequences of capitalism. And, in considering this theory and research, you should have a better understanding of the basic division in sociology between functionalists and conflict theorists, how the former view these massive changes in our lives in relatively benign terms, and how the latter raise questions about conflicts of interest and about who benefits most from these economic and technological changes.

You should also have some understanding of the meaning of capitalism, how profoundly it differs from other and earlier types of economic organization, its more recent developments and its impact on all of our lives. Third, from this chapter you should derive an understanding of Canadian capitalism and its unique development, and, finally, how, with the growth of capitalism and industrialism, work has been transformed.

INTRODUCTION

It is of some interest that science fiction has, of late, been most successful when it depicts interstellar travel and warfare, space operas far removed from our everyday existence. Science fiction used to be more subtle, based very often on satirical or somber futuristic visions of societies overrun by machines and constrained by bureaucratic rules. One classic example, by Katherine Maclean, depicts a society completely engulfed by a small organization so committed to and effective at growing that it could not be stopped.

Perhaps none of this excites us in quite the same way as in the past because machines and bureaucracies are so much a part of our lives. And it is probably difficult for most of us to imagine a society not driven by the search for profit and growth. This is part of our knowledge of how things work: business-people make profits and they must do this if there are going to be jobs and a good life style for the rest of us; managers make sure things run efficiently; machines and automation have increased our productivity and freed us from the most miserable aspects of work; most of us will work within bureaucracies and, while this will set limits on us, we seem today to feel these limits are necessary and tolerable. The sociology of industrial society looks at these same issues but offers a larger and rather different perspective.

Perhaps you are confused by now about whether one is talking about capitalist or industrial society. This question is not unreasonable but it represents yet another fundamental debate in sociology. For some sociologists, functionalists in particular, the focus has been industrialization. Durkheim, for example, was concerned about the social disorganization arising from industrialization and, as we have seen, he used suicide rates as one way to demonstrate this social disorganization empirically. But, he was optimistic that out of the division of labour would emerge a new form of social solidarity based on the interdependency between various kinds of workers.

To put it simply, what Durkheim was arguing is that in industrial society we are dependent on the skills of others just as they are on us. Accountants need plumbers to fix their leaking toilet and, in turn, plumbers need accountants to do their books. Both may, from time to time, need doctors or lawyers. At another level, while workers are dependent on capitalists for jobs, capitalists are dependent on workers for their production and profit.

In other words, from a functionalist perspective, there must be some level of cooperation between two if the economy is to run at all. In large part, it is this theme of shared interests that has dominated much of organizational and management theory and is, perhaps, why the focus has generally been on the process of industrialization rather than on the development of capitalism. Capitalism, the particular mode of production, has simply been seen as one way systems have adapted to the process of industrialization.

For theorists influenced by Marx, on the other hand, capitalism has been the focus. These theorists have been concerned with how, historically, the development of capitalism has shaped industrialization and how, in turn, industrialization has shaped capitalism. And, as will be described later, the emphasis has been on the ways in which this form of economic organization has generated conflict rather than consensus and has served the interests of one group often at the expense of others. In either case we must look at both industrialization and the rise of capitalism.

INDUSTRIALIZATION

You have all heard about and been taught about the industrial revolution. You probably know this phenomenon as a number of isolated inventions—the steam engine, the cotton gin, the bobbin — and some horrifying depictions of nineteenth century factories and their child labour, as some indication of how far we have progressed. But it is probably true that the dates, the inventions, the descriptions you've been given do not provide you with an intelligible perspective on industrialization or any sense of the profound changes it has meant and which warrant the term *Revolution*.

It is not easy to define **industrialization** because it encompasses so much of our lives. It is the taken-for- granted world in which we live. To say that it is the use of machine technology and energy in the production of goods is correct but fails to convey its human or sociological implications. Daniel Bell captures something of the essence of life before industrialization and the human meaning of the kinds of changes that led us to call what was a very long process: the Industrial Revolution.

Life in preindustrial societies—still the condition of most of the world today—is primarily a game against nature. The labour force is overwhelmingly in the extractive industries: agriculture, mining, fishing, forestry. One works with raw muscle power, in inherited ways, and one's sense of the world is conditioned by the vicissitudes of the elements—the seasons, the storms, the fertility of the soil, the amount of water, the depth of the mine seams, the droughts and the floods. The rhythms of life are shaped by these contingencies. The sense of time is one of duress, and the pace of work varies with the seasons and the weather (1978:147).

This stands in contrast to what Bell views as the impact of the Industrial Revolution, the process of industrialization. In industrial society, as Bell describes it, the game is no longer against nature but against *fabricated nature*. Industrial societies produce goods in a technical and rationalized world. "The machine predominates and the rhythms of life are mechanically paced; time is chronological, mechanical, evenly spaced by the divisions of the clock: (p. 147). Talk of an energy crisis is natural only in an industrial society where energy has replaced muscle power and has fuelled almost unimaginable leaps in productivity. The work world in an industrial society is transformed by machines.

Skills are broken down into simpler components, and the artisan of the past is replaced by two new figures: the engineer, who is responsible for the layout and flow of work, and the semi-skilled worker, who is the cog between machines, until the technical ingenuity of the engineer creates a new machine which replaces him as well (1978:137).

Industrial society is based on organization, the coordination of commodities, including people, markets and products. The hierarchical structure of bureaucracy, an efficiency producing machine, is the embodiment of the industrial society.

CRITIQUES OF INDUSTRIAL SOCIETY

Most depictions of industrialization, of technological change, are mixtures of awe and ambivalence at what we have accomplished in such a short space of time. We congratulate ourselves that, through machines, we have been freed from the drudgeries past generations took for granted. Who, for example, is unimpressed with the benefits of electricity and of running water and the medical advances that have so dramatically reduced infant mortality? Who does not appreciate the fine pleasures that come with a good stereo and the mundane pleasures of watching television? Who would give up their word processor and Xerox machine for a mechanical typewriter and carbon copies?

Yet, there is ambivalence which comes, in part, from a nostalgia for the simpler world which we seem to have lost. There is also considerable guilt as we become increasingly aware that, while we are a diminishing proportion of the world's population, we in the developed world use a disproportionate share of resources and, in doing so, cause irrevocable damage to the environment. Through our use of energy and development of military technology, we threaten the future of the planet and life itself, and we worry about this. Arthur Koestler, for one, shares the concern that we are technologically but not sociologically adept:

The most striking indication of the pathology of our species is the contrast between its unique technological achievements and its equally unique incompetence in the conduct of its social affairs. We can control the motions of satellites orbiting distant planets but cannot control the situation in Northern Ireland. Man can leave the earth and land on the moon, but cannot cross from East to West Berlin. Prometheus reaches out for the stars with an insane grin on his face and a totem symbol in his hand.

At the same time, attached as we are to our technologies and to the latest in gadgets, it is difficult to generate the same moral fervour about industrialization that inspired the classical theorists. In the nineteenth and early twentieth centuries, sociologists and artists were born in one kind of world and died in another. As a result, they were acutely aware of and often condemned the miseries of capitalism, the ravages of industrialism and the mediocracy of mass society. But, many of these same critics were, perhaps naively, also optimistic that through technology and the development of social science, society could be perfected, and utopia would emerge.

Today's critics are caught in something of a dilemma. While few are likely to suggest we do away with technology, many critics are less sanguine than their earlier counterparts that through larger doses of technology we can solve our problems. And, while for some technology is the problem, for most the issue is how technology has developed and how alternative and less damaging technologies have been ignored or repressed because they offer less profit to the capitalists.

MODERNIZATION AND CAPITALISM

All of these kinds of critiques of industrial society, the hopeful and the pessimistic, simply illustrate the preoccupation among social scientists with understanding the phenomenon of ***modernization***. This is word which "contains" many others: the images of complex society we described in Chapter 4, the urbanization we described in Chapter 7, the secularization and the loss of meaning we described in Chapter 3, and the bureaucratization that we shall describe in our discussion of work. And at the level of everyday life it also means the varied roles we play that distance us from ourselves, the games we play, our complex exchange relationships and our attempts to make our lives rational and accountable (Chapter 5).

All of sociology recognizes that the quality of life has changed significantly from the feudal period, and much of its theory has been inspired by a despair for what has been lost or an optimism for what has been gained. Sociologists have sought, in the tradition of positivism, to understand the changes to help us better prepare for the future. Yet most theories of modernization, in particular those of functionalists, serve only to mystify the process. These theories describe modernization as the result of natural evolution; society as an organism becomes increasingly differentiated and complex, much as a cell divides and differentiates to produce a complex organism such as a human being. From this perspective, modernization *happens* at the level of systems.

There are at least three problems with such a view. First, the system is reified, that is, given a life of its own independent of people. Second, and as a result of this, what has happened to us is made mystical rather than an understandable consequence of the actions of people. Finally, such a view limits us by describing processes over which we have no control, which have a necessity of their own and which therefore can never be harnessed for the common good.

Out of a recognition of these limits has emerged a renewed interest in Karl Marx and in what we have throughout referred to as the conflict perspective. Marx and his collaborator Engels provide us with a general theory of modernization which essentially demystifies the process. Whatever it may fail to do, it succeeds in viewing historical change as a result of the actions of people. For Marx, modernization was the impressive creation of a new class of people who emerged out of feudalism and who, in pursuing their own interests, fashioned a new order.

Marx revealed to us that modernization was not a unitary phenomenon but rather was experienced differently by different groups in society and had different consequences for them. His theory, then, could contain both despair and optimism because it was based on the notion that modernization benefited some at the expense of others. As you will see, for Marx, industrialization, as the central aspect of modernization, was the child of capitalism.

The fundamental changes it brought about were new layers of inequality and a relatively new phenomenon, layers of vulnerability. As the constraining but also comforting ties of feudalism gave way to the more precarious relations of the urban-based marketplace, people found themselves confronting the possibility of unemployment and poverty.

Marx provided us with a sociology of capitalism, a way of understanding modernization. He also provided us with an image of a future when we, though ending inequality and vulnerability, would gain control of technology and the whole process of modernization. It would be possible to reshape these processes to suit our human needs and in the process to reshape our natures.

THE SOCIOLOGY OF CAPITALISM

What is the value of a new shirt or a colour television? When you perceive some product to be expensive, you usually don't mean that the cost is excessive against some objective value but rather it is beyond your means or more costly than in the past. We rarely stop to question the value of products except in terms of our own desires and tastes. In our society we simply learn that a product is worth whatever it can command in the marketplace. Take another example of value. How will you determine the value of your work when you enter the job marketplace? Surely, in the end, you'll come to much the same conclusion; that the value of your skills and labour is whatever you can command, that is, how much you can earn.

There are other ways of thinking. We could measure the value of products in terms of their usefulness, the availability of their ingredients and the amount of labour that went into their production. We could measure the value of our labour in terms of the products we produce or the skills and training necessary to produce them. Of course, these kinds of issues do play a part in our thinking. We do get angry that certain kinds of people get paid more than us or that certain products seem inordinately overpriced, given the sloppy workmanship or the lack of usefulness. But we have learned to accept the legitimacy that costs and prices are determined by others and that, inevitably, this means that those who employ us and who own the factories and corporations which produce products, make profits.

This taken-for-granted acceptance of profit is relatively new. It was rather an intriguing phenomenon to many theorists in the nineteenth century. For Marx, it represented the basic contradiction in capitalism. It should not be too surprising that Marx, devoting himself to understanding capitalism as it was developing around him, saw a fundamental contradiction in a system based on taking out more than one puts in. Where did profit come from? What was it about capitalism that set it apart from all previous economic systems?

CAPITALISM: AN ALLEGORY

For many students, the very word capitalism is intimidating with its implications of complex political and economic analyses. Let us for the moment, then, give you a simple handle, a way into what *is* often a complex political and economic analysis of the world in which you live. For now let us just say that **capitalism** is a system based on profits which necessitates capital accumulation. Perhaps you can get a first notion of capitalism and the origins of profit through an allegory.

Potter produces clay bowls which she finds other people in her community would like to own. How much should she price them at? She determines how much money she needs to live comfortably, to pay for her materials and equipment and she determines how many bowls she can make in a day or a week and arrives at a cost equation. If she cannot get her price she must look for other work. If she can get her price she can live comfortably with the thought that she is not really a capitalist but a craftsperson.

But the demand for her bowls outstrips her expectations. Everyone in the community and elsewhere wants one and they are willing to pay. She is able, by increasing the price, to get more money than she needs, perhaps even more than she can spend, but she must work within severe limits. There are only so many bowls she can produce and she can raise the price only so high.

Now she is faced with something of a dilemma: does Potter become a capitalist? Does she take advantage of the potentially larger pottery market? If her answer is no, what does she do when the market dries up, when everyone locally has one of her "pieces"? She can use her accumulated capital to support herself while she learns to make batiks or she can become a capitalist seeking constantly to expand her market.

How does she do this? She is only able to become a capitalist because she has been able to accumulate some capital. She can now buy another kiln and hire a worker or several. To take advantage of or create new markets she must expand. She must continue to hire more workers and perhaps supervise their work in a factory. She now has learned that if she is to grow and expand her markets she will not be able to pay her workers the full value of what they produce. She will have to take part of the proceeds to pay for her equipment and material, what we today call overhead, and she will have to take part of the proceeds as capital reserve, what we call profit. Certainly, as you can well imagine, Potter now lives in a fine house and is clothed in furs, but she cannot spend all the excess money on lifestyle enhancement; she must be able to use some of this excess to expand her enterprise and to make the necessary production changes to deal with the competition.

Things have gone quite well but she confronts a new problem. Despite the fact that she has treated her workers as well as she can afford and still expand the business, they express some concern about the inequities they perceive. She may ruthlessly demonstrate to them their dependence on her; after all she owns the means of production and is, after all, the reason they have jobs. But this, too, is problematic because she is dependent on them and the profit she can extract from their labour. So, more likely, she tries to find some way of managing labour.

But finally, she is anxious about her labour dependence. Added to this is the problem that no matter how mechanized or ordered she makes her factory, there are limits to how much people can produce. And her workers complain of how their skills and training as craftspersons are being wasted, how their craft has been degraded into a series of boring and routine tasks, and what lousy bowls are coming off the "assembly line." In the end, they feel alienated in their work.

Moreover, as we have said, she has competition. There are other potters making inroads in her potential market. She cannot keep raising wages and prices and still survive. She cannot stop growing. She becomes ever more receptive to technological advances, new modes of producing pottery efficiently and cheaply even if she has to borrow money to introduce these advances. Potter, the capitalist, is now in search of the fully automated pottery factory.

This is an allegory. Things really didn't happen this way. But we hope it is useful in helping you make easier sense of the brief history of the development of capitalism that follows.

THE DEVELOPMENT OF CAPITALISM

There is a tendency to think that what characterizes us and motivates us is enduring, that "you can't change human nature," that the changes that have occurred since ancient times are ones of degree not of kind. No doubt there is much about the human condition, about the tension between humans and nature, humans and humans, humans and society, and humans and their gods that is common to all cultures at all times. Otherwise, why would a good liberal education require that we read Thucydides and Plato, Milton and Shakespeare, T.S. Eliot and Shaw? All, it is assumed, have something to tell us about these tensions, about what Lovejoy (1942) called the great chain of being linking us to our past and to all mankind.

At the same time, we should be wary of assuming that the only stable thing in a changing world is human nature. As historians have come to realize, there may have been changes in human consciousness not of degree but of kind, shifts of such magnitude that we would find it perhaps more difficult to communicate with someone in the fifth century than with someone in an underdeveloped backwater today.

The rise of *individualism* seems to many to have been one such important watershed dividing us from our past, as is a secular world view. Similarly, the modern business person, drive by profit, by efficiency and by the desire for expansion is not simply "human nature" now decked out in pin-striped suit instead of robes. He or she appears to be a new species, an outcome of a perhaps unique form of social and economic organization — capitalism.

Most historians are agreed that capitalism can be traced back to about the twelfth century and to developments occurring in towns in northern Italy, Holland and Flanders (Marchak, 1980). The dominant social order was feudalism as it had been since the fall of the Roman Empire. But by the fourteenth century, at the beginning of what is called the Renaissance, the hold of feudalism lost to some extent its monopoly over people's activities.

Ideally, we would like to provide you with a neat and ordered history of progressive stages and easily defined turning points but systems like feudalism died hard and slowly. Nor is it entirely clear where capitalism truly begins. It is the analytical historian who imposes stages to enable us to see the force and direction of history and the watersheds, however difficult to define, which marks the beginning of new social orders.

That capitalism marks a dramatic departure from feudalism is perhaps most clearly evident in our changed attitudes to profit; in feudal society, profit was not considered legitimate. The archaic meaning of the word usuary was simply the lending of money with an interest charge, something we now take for granted, but which in the past carried with it the stigma of getting something for nothing.

How do we account for this change? In the fourteenth century, according to historians, certain basic *material* changes were occurring, changes which, as sociologists, we might describe as providing the *necessary* conditions for capitalism. The expansion of trade, plunder, increasing use of paper currency, for example, made it possible for some to accumulate great wealth. The feudal merchant who was able to accumulate large amounts of wealth could buy armies to protect his trade routes which, in turn, allowed him to expand these routes and his trade. Clearly, the feudal lord could no longer take for granted his power. The success of the merchant, in other words, presaged a change in the dominant mode of production and in the relations of production.

As Marx recognized, the seeds of capitalism were contained in feudalism. Historically, we see this most clearly in the development of medieval towns organized around trade, money and the production of crafts for trade rather than around the production of food. In these towns a new class was consolidating its position in what was to be a new order.

A description of trade in commodities, what you learned in high school history about the importance of spices, the search for new trade routes, may seem far removed from your image of capitalism. But the important point for you to take out of this is that trade and money lending, what is called **mercantilism**, provided the basis for *capital accumulation* and that the relationship between the merchant and the craftperson provided the basis for the relations of production as we know them today, that is, between the capitalists and the working class, what Marx called the bourgeoisie and the proletariat.

As the system of capitalism expanded, the relations of mercantilism, with its financial merchant elite, were gradually displaced by the relations of industrialism and an elite whose profit depended on "exploitation" of labour. In its simplest terms we can understand, if you think back to the Potter allegory, how the merchant's relationship with the craftperson gradually changed from one of a loosely defined exchange relationship to an increasingly ordered hierarchical relationship.

First, we see this in the development of the cottage industry where the producer was relatively removed from the merchant, to the evolution of the factory where the producer was brought under greater control, and where the work was increasingly rationalized, and mechanized, so as to reduce the merchant's dependence on independent craftspeople. This earlier relationship of mutual dependence was gradually transformed into a relationship in which the capitalist could more effectively control the production process and the worker—that is, **industrial capitalism**.

In the continuing struggle to control not only labour but markets of commodities and consumers, the owners have always attempted to limit competition among themselves, even from the times of merchant guilds. Capitalism, as we know it today, emerged out of this world of competing factories and the struggle to grow by reducing competition. **Monopoly capitalism** is a capitalism of ever larger corporations that transcend national boundaries, intrude into every aspect of our lives and limit competition everywhere, except for the competition for jobs among the working class. Figure 10.1 on the following page provides a well-known example of this process in its graphic illustration of the Canadian Pacific Empire.

What we have been describing here may strike you as a rather strange way to deal with the growth of industrialization. For Marx, however, the problem was not the growing rationalization of society, the loss of community and the growth of impersonal cities, or the prospect of a society overrun by machines. These were only problems because of the real villain of the piece, capitalism. It was capitalism that turned technology against workers, dehumanized and alienated both the owners and the workers. Capitalism produced material inequalities and ultimately produced inequalities of power, more striking, pervasive and perhaps more oppressive than any system before. We deal with these issues later in the chapter and more fully in Chapter 11, Social Inequality.

FIGURE 10.1

THE CANADIAN PACIFIC EMPIRE

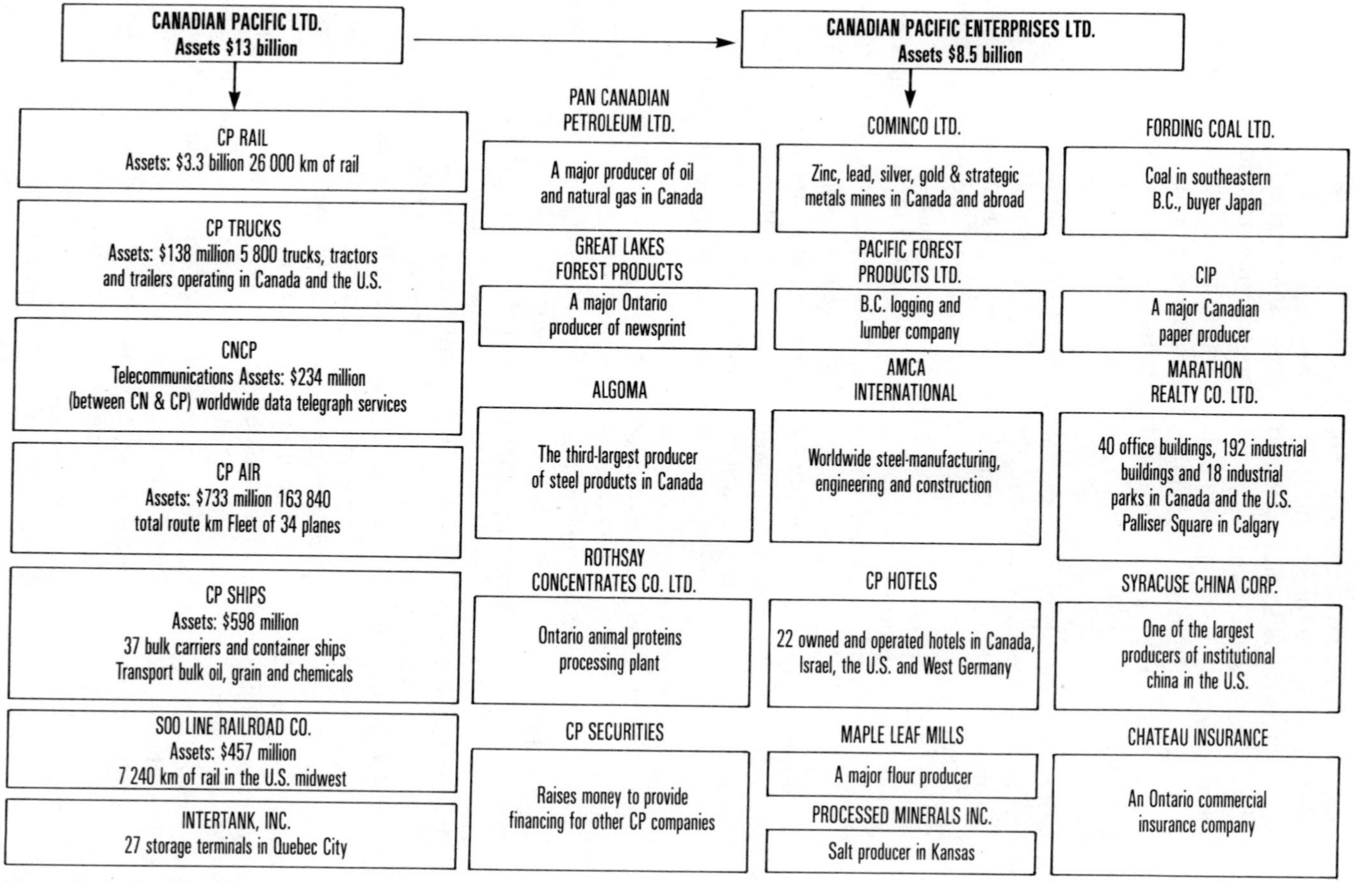

CANADIAN PACIFIC LTD.
Assets $13 billion

CANADIAN PACIFIC ENTERPRISES LTD.
Assets $8.5 billion

CP RAIL
Assets: $3.3 billion 26 000 km of rail

CP TRUCKS
Assets: $138 million 5 800 trucks, tractors and trailers operating in Canada and the U.S.

CNCP
Telecommunications Assets: $234 million (between CN & CP) worldwide data telegraph services

CP AIR
Assets: $733 million 163 840 total route km Fleet of 34 planes

CP SHIPS
Assets: $598 million 37 bulk carriers and container ships Transport bulk oil, grain and chemicals

SOO LINE RAILROAD CO.
Assets: $457 million 7 240 km of rail in the U.S. midwest

INTERTANK, INC.
27 storage terminals in Quebec City

PAN CANADIAN PETROLEUM LTD.
A major producer of oil and natural gas in Canada

GREAT LAKES FOREST PRODUCTS
A major Ontario producer of newsprint

ALGOMA
The third-largest producer of steel products in Canada

ROTHSAY CONCENTRATES CO. LTD.
Ontario animal proteins processing plant

CP SECURITIES
Raises money to provide financing for other CP companies

FORDING COAL LTD.
Coal in southeastern B.C., buyer Japan

CIP
A major Canadian paper producer

MARATHON REALTY CO. LTD.
40 office buildings, 192 industrial buildings and 18 industrial parks in Canada and the U.S. Palliser Square in Calgary

SYRACUSE CHINA CORP.
One of the largest producers of institutional china in the U.S.

CHATEAU INSURANCE
An Ontario commercial insurance company

COMINCO LTD.
Zinc, lead, silver, gold & strategic metals mines in Canada and abroad

PACIFIC FOREST PRODUCTS LTD.
B.C. logging and lumber company

AMCA INTERNATIONAL
Worldwide steel-manufacturing, engineering and construction

CP HOTELS
22 owned and operated hotels in Canada, Israel, the U.S. and West Germany

MAPLE LEAF MILLS
A major flour producer

PROCESSED MINERALS INC.
Salt producer in Kansas

Source: *Maclean's*, August 24, 1981.

HISTORICAL MATERIALISM

A central concern of the sociological tradition is with identifying the driving force, the impetus, behind the growth of capitalism. The classic answer provided by Marx is the dialectic of thesis, antithesis and synthesis. Feudalism (thesis) contains within its contradictions (antithesis), which at some point brings on crisis and a new order, capitalism, the synthesis. Capitalism is both synthesis and thesis since it too contains within it contradictions which, through new crises, create a new synthesis, socialism. This insight into the processes of change is perhaps Marx's most lasting contribution to sociology. His *historical materialism* allows us to view change as more than a series of events. Thesis represents a system's logic of development; antithesis represents a system's illogic; and finally, synthesis the system's new logic. Marx sought to identify for us the logic of feudalism, and the illogic in feudalism, which produced capitalism; and the logic of capitalism, and the illogic of capitalism, which produces socialism.

MARX AND MODERN CAPITALISM

Early Christians lived their lives in anticipation that the second coming was imminent. Only at a later point were they forced to take a somewhat longer view of things. In a similar vein, early Marxists who believed in historical materialism were convinced that capitalism could not sustain itself much longer. The inhumanity it generated, the periodic crises it experienced, and its inherent and ever more obvious contradictions seemed sure portents of its imminent breakdown. And around the time that he and Engels wrote *The Communist Manifesto*, Marx also seemed to believe that the revolution could not be very far off, that the new synthesis, a socialist or communist society, lay in the very near future.

This did not, of course, happen. Critics of Marx have suggested that he underestimated the power of capitalism to provide such affluence, particularly for the working class, the class apparently doomed to absolute and relative impoverishment. They also point out that Marx failed to recognize the importance of the middle classes, the service workers, professionals, managers and small business owners. Rather than "sinking" into the proletariat as Marx anticipated, the middle class has continued to grow, providing what Lopreato and Hazellrigg (1972:236) call a sort of "demilitarized zone," standing formidably between bourgeoisie and proletariat; it is a heterogeneous class with interest which, at times, seem at odds with both of the major classes.

There is obviously a good deal of truth to these arguments. But in defence of Marx's theory and its predictions, Marxists have sometimes argued that we must distinguish between Marx the polemicist and Marx the scientist. The former is perhaps best represented by *The Communist Manifesto*: it captures most of the main themes in Marx's work but it does so at the cost of considerable simplification. Here he painted for us a bold and dramatic picture of pauperization and the polarization of capitalist society into two hostile camps, and all of this is occurring in the midst of economic crisis. There is unbridled optimism that out of the chaos and conflict will emerge a new social order as the now redundant capitalist class (bourgeoisie) is overthrown by the working class (proletariat); the new class, borne out of capitalism, is also its executioner. The message is a powerful one.

Marxists point out, however, that as Marx devoted himself more and more to political economy the message becomes, of necessity, qualified. There are, for example, references throughout his work to the existence of intermediate strata or classes which obscure and confuse the simple and unambiguous dichotomy of oppressor and oppressed. Marx, the scientist, according to some Marxists, is best seen in the works done after further decades of research and study. And, his major work *Capital* was never completed. As Martin Nicolaus (1972:325) puts it, "*Capital* is painfully unfinished, like a mystery novel which ends before the plot is unravelled. But, the *Grundisse* contains the author's plot-outline as a whole." The *Grundisse* is essentially a series of notes not available in the West until it was released from the Moscow Archives in 1939 and was released generally in 1953 (there were no English translations until the 1970s). The discovery of this work, what Martin Nicolaus calls the "unknown Marx," has given new life to Marx's theory and the new ammunition to defend him against his critics.

In the *Grundisse*, Marx argues that "cataclysmic crises rising to a revolutionary crescendo are only one possible variant of the breakdown process" (Nicolaus, 1972:329). Here the breakdown of capitalism is conceived by Marx as a much longer process, the outcome not of economic deprivation but of the abundance and leisure that automation and other advances in technology might produce. At this point in the development of capitalism, the critical class would no longer be the traditional proletariat; it would have all but disappeared and been replaced by an educated and technically competent class of workers. From this perspective, then, some Marxists would argue that it is premature to claim that Marx's basic prediction has turned out to be untrue. Capitalism, it is argued, has not yet exhausted its developmental potential.

This more utopian prognosis has not occurred. While the working class has not been driven into abject poverty, neither have the modes of production so changed as to provide everyone with an abundant and unrestricted leisure. In fact, since Marx's time, it could be argued that capitalism has undergone only a superficial face lifting; in its basic features it is much the same.

The differences are mostly negative ones. With the growth of monopoly capitalism

wealth has become more, not less, concentrated; it is held by an ever tinier minority of the population. And, as will be seen, a large segment of the labour force — the marginal work world — has been separated from the more affluent working class and has not participated fully in the advances made by organized labour.

Also, an ever growing number of people, especially young people, find that modern capitalism and its technology provide no place at all for them; they have no value at all in the marketplace. Rendered superfluous, they have become members of the permanently unemployed.

As we shall see in Chapter 11, a closer look at the incomes of Canadians makes questionable whether there is a growing middle class and whether very many people can afford the package depicted by the media as the middle-class way of life. Inequalities in income and life chances have, in recent decades, not been reduced and have remained very stable. Poverty, rather than disappearing, seems pervasive, perhaps necessary to capitalist society. Factory work may be as tedious and alienating as it was in Marx's time. Finally, we must remember that a good deal of the affluence of capitalist societies has been at the expense of "Third World" countries, which partially explains why Marxism and Communism appeal to these societies; they have grown conscious of their oppressed relationship to the developed world.

It is probable that Marx, even in his later work, underestimated the ability and power of capitalism to justify itself and to give the illusion of change without affecting the basic structure. Legalizing collective bargaining gives workers the semblance of power but actually institutionalizes conflict, contains it and renders it harmless as a potential for revolutionary change. "Progressive taxation" supposedly redistributes income from the rich to the poor but in fact has only a marginal effect on income inequality. The media, by focusing attention on the middle class, present us with images of affluence, not of impoverishment. Credit cards, consumer loans and endless mortgages allow families to appear more middle class, more affluent than they actually are. Many families escape poverty only because of dual incomes. And, the dominant ideologies tell us to view poverty not as a problem of the system but of individuals who will not work and who prefer to live on welfare.

In short, Marx's prophecy of a communist revolution has, in capitalist societies, so far turned out to be a "suicidal prophecy": once people hear about a theory or a prophecy they take steps to avoid what it predicts, thus putting off, perhaps destroying, the prophecy. Threatened with the possibility of revolution, the ruling classes of capitalist societies have acted to reduce and redirect that potential danger. They have done so without removing the underlying problem—class inequality.

At the same time, we should not completely discount the absolute changes that have occurred as capitalism developed. Compared to nineteenth century capitalism, the capitalism of today is, for most workers, a more humane system. And, however inadequate it may be and how much it may "prop up" the system, the welfare system and medicare offer a degree of security unimaginable by 19th century workers living as they were in perpetual fear of the "poor house" or the "work house."

Moreover, countries such as Sweden have through much of this century shown that capitalism and a more just and equitable society can coexist and can provide its citizens with security, affluence, and harmony. After 50 years of this mixture of socialism and capitalism, Sweden's unemployment rate is reputed to be 1.3 percent compared with the 7 to 10 percent rate in Canada, the budget is balanced and regional inequalities have been dramatically reduced. In other words, there is nothing inevitable about how capitalism develops. In Canada, other kinds of social and political decisions might have led to a system

that provided more benefits to everyone and less to the privileged few.

Sweden provides an example of how, perhaps, to do it right. Pat Marchak (1983) who has studied the B.C. forest industry, shows us how we, as Canadians, have done it wrong. The province is (or was) possessed of a valuable and potentially renewable resource — lumber. All of the expectations were that, developed properly, production of lumber could lead to both extraction of a primary resource and a secondary manufacturing industry. Out of both would come other spin offs in the form of service industries of various kinds. On the basis of one resource—lumber — a diversified and stable economy in B.C. could have emerged.

According to Marchak, there were no technological reasons why timber could not be cut and lumber produced in the same locations. But, it was not in the interests of capitalists to do so. Higher profits could be made if trees were cut in B.C. and finished lumber produced elsewhere. One consequence has been the development of an unstable and vulnerable work force.

Unquestionably, Marx has provided us with a powerful analytical tool. But what should be vexing you about this kind of analysis, and what is at the heart of much academic debate over Marx, is the image evoked of history inexorably moving forward independent of the actions of people. Marx was careful to emphasize that people make history but he was most eager to demonstrate how the logic of systems constrains people's actions. In short, his is first an analysis of social structure and only second, of the cultures produced by that structure.

THE SOCIAL PSYCHOLOGY OF CAPITALISM

To make the link between macro and micro, structure and action, we need a social psychology of capitalism. To put this more directly, to say that a system has a logic is not to explain why people behave in terms of that logic. We know that people often do what is "illogical," what may be personally destructive in the long run and so on. Why did the capitalists and labour so faithfully play out their roles?

Perhaps it is here that Max Weber's attempt to contribute to Marx's theory is most relevant. You may recall from Chapter 1 that Weber believed that a particular set of ideas, the Protestant ethic, provided the motivational fuel for capital accumulation and growth. Accumulation, a necessary condition for the development of capitalism, can be viewed as an unintended consequence of commitment to the Protestant creed of ascetism and thrift. Weber uses the somewhat mystical notion of *elective affinity* to capture the fit between the logic of the Puritan ethic and the logic of capitalism. So, just as capitalism demands growth, so too must Puritan capitalists prosper and grow to feel secure in this world or their place in the next. Weber's analysis has tried to show us how capitalism was most likely to flourish where such ideas were available.

Undoubtedly, there is something mystical in Weber's analysis if one takes it to mean a fortuitous coming together of structures and ideas. We are left with the question of where such ideas come from. Are they not simply the productions of a certain time and place in history? We really don't know; this is the question that drives the sociology of knowledge. For this discussion, however, we would answer the question in two ways. First, to understand the rise of capitalism it matters less to understand where these ideas come from than to understand that elites are likely to be more receptive to ideas that make sense of and justify their position and actions. Second, however important such ideas may have been in understanding the rise of capitalism, a Weberian view does not and was not intended to displace a Marxist interpretation. Intentions change in process; the logic of the system will finally make demands upon us

whatever our original intentions. One can think back to the potter allegory as a story of a system that Potter created and that came to engulf her and her workers.

Nor does Weber, by any means, provide us with the whole social psychology. We ask you to return to Chapter 5, to look again at what it is about people that makes them play out their roles; and sometimes not. Perhaps Goffman, for example, will force us to remember that capitalists probably care about how they are seen by others and how they feel about themselves. We do not have to treat cynically, their expressions of concern for employees and their conviction that they are contributing to the larger whole. As Goffman (1959) points out, this may be cynical or sincere. And if the capitalist is sincere, then Goffman may help us to understand how capitalism is alienating for capitalists, who, in "bad faith," do to their workers and the consumers what the system demands.

The symbolic interactionist's understanding of the importance of self and significant others can help us understand the capitalist's desire to succeed in terms of the standards of the culture and, perhaps more significant, to build a growing business that can be passed on to offspring and may, in terms similar to Weber's, ensure a sort of immortality. Finally, the ethnomethodologists allow us to understand how much of what we all do is taken for granted, not held up for inspection. And they make us more aware, as well, of what a relief this is to us.

CANADIAN CAPITALISM

It is established, however, that Marx helped us to identify the material forces that account for the rise of mercantilism, industrialism and, finally, the kind of corporate or monopoly capitalism we know today. He recognized, as well, that old systems did not disappear with the emergence of new systems. Nor, as he was perhaps less aware, was there one consistent pattern of capitalist development in industrializing societies. As we described in the previous chapter, Canadian sociologists have, in recent years, been preoccupied with understanding the development and nature of Canadian society and Canadian culture. And, in large part, this has meant a focus on Canadian capitalism, how it developed and what factors shaped its particular form of development or underdevelopment.

CANADA AS A DEPENDENCY

At issue are such questions as why, despite our vast natural resources, we have, apparently, experienced uneven, retarded and arrested development. Why, in other words, have we remained "hewers of wood, drawers of water"? Or as Kari Levitt (1970:25) put it, we can be described as "the world's richest underdeveloped country."

As we have seen, in the 1970s, the most adequate answer seemed to lie in dependency theory. Economists such as Levitt (1970), historians such as Naylor (1972), and sociologists such as Clement (1977), draw upon dependency theory to argue that capitalism in Canada was never an independent development but was locked into a series of colonial relationships.

This meant, in the nineteenth century, that Canadian businessmen did not, for the most part, become involved in manufacturing or resource extraction but, because it was more profitable, confined themselves to mercantilism and finance. Manufacturing and resource extraction were, from the outset, dominated by powerful interests. As Mel Watkins put it, "the Canadian Capitalist class is a financial bourgeoisie that did not control industrial production in Canada. Hence, bankers are the most powerful section of the Canadian bourgeoisie. They make money financing the foreign takeover of Canada" (Watkins, 1973:257).

Similarly, Wallace Clement (1975), in his study of multinational corporations in Canada suggests that, because so much of our economy is foreign owned and foreign controlled, Canada has two kinds of capitalists, what he calls an *indigenous* elite and a *comprador* elite. The former has, in effect, appropriated a "turf"—finance, transportation and utilities. The dominant comprador elite, on the other hand, is "active in manufacturing and resources, is both national and international, and is located in branch plants of foreign controlled multinationals." Because each has "staked out" different sectors of the economy, Canada is partly foreign controlled, partly Canadian controlled.

As Clement points out, there is interdependence rather than rivalry between the comprador and the indigenous elite. For example, the boards of directors for each are highly interlocked. Financiers serve on the boards of foreign controlled companies involved in manufacturing and resource extraction and vice versa. Moreover, they hold a similar view of Canada as part of the North American economy and, as we have recently seen, therefore favour free trade between Canada and the United States, which they see as inevitable.

DEINDUSTRIALIZATION

One of the more important theses of dependency theory is that Canada, as a hinterland and branch plant economy, is being systematically deindustrialized. In the 1970s, Robert Laxer argued that "deindustrialization is the most important result to Canada of integration in the American Empire" (1973:9). Imperialism, or in the American lexicon, "continentalism," not only keeps the hinterland in a state of underdevelopment, but, it was believed, may at times also result in an absolute decline in manufacturing. Such is likely to be the case when economic conditions in the metropolis begin to deteriorate. To save jobs in the metropolis, branch plants in the hinterland are closed down or allowed to have excess productive capacity. And as Kari Levitt (1970) argued in her influential book, *Silent Surrender*, even at the best of times, research and development that might lead to new industry will be done in the metropolis and not the hinterland.

An illustration of this process of deindustrialization is what has happened to the Maritimes since confederation. According to Acheson (1977), prior to Confederation, Nova Scotia and New Brunswick had a flourishing and growing industrial base. But after the Maritimes joined into Confederation with Upper and Lower Canada, central Canadian businessmen bought out many of these businesses and systematically shut them down in order to reduce competition with their Ontario firms.

As Forbes (1979) describes, this was made possible, perhaps augmented by, policies of the federal government, especially with respect to tariffs and freight rates that favoured central Canada. Gradually, suggests Acheson, the Maritimes have been driven into a condition of dependence and now have an economy reliant upon federal transfer payments.

David Frank, another Maritime historian, has documented a similar transformation of the Cape Breton coal mining industry (1977). Again, as a result of increasing concentration and centralization of capital in central Canada, a once healthy coal and steel industry has been steadily eroded and turned into a lame-duck industry, all, apparently because it serves the interests and needs of the metropolis.

Perhaps we could draw an analogy with interpersonal relations and the ways roles become relatively fixed. For whatever reasons, you develop particular kinds of relationships with other people sometimes only to discover that these relationships serve others better than you, that they may even be destructive of your interests. You will often find that when you attempt to redefine the relationship in light of your new realization, you will encounter resistance. Think of the housewife, for example, who suddenly confronts her husband that she is no longer going to wake up and make his breakfast. His response may very well be something quite like American responses to Canada when it attempts to assert its own interests. So the Americans speak of continentalism and of the greater North American good and of the merits of interdependence and mutual obligation, and perhaps as we recently witnessed, the threat of retributive consequences — legislation in the United States to limit foreign investment, particularly by Canadians if we were not to agree to free trade.

DILEMMAS OF DEPENDENCY PERSPECTIVES

Some of the dilemmas of the dependency view may become apparent if we examine its moral implications. In its extreme version, dependency theory portrays Canada and Canadian capitalism as a product, created by British and American capitalism, as a victim of outside forces that has never been allowed to develop and "grow up" because it goes against these outside interests. What growth and development is "allowed" to occur may be cut off or repressed when things go poorly in the metropolises. Canada does not so much do things as have things done to it.

Perhaps at its worst this makes the rather self-serving suggestion that Canadians may rest easy that the excesses of Canadian capitalism are, after all, produced by the excesses of American capitalism. Like the delinquent boy who is no more than a product of his bad environment, Canada and Canadians cannot be held responsible for their actions. Perhaps part of the reason that so many Canadian socialists have found comfort in dependency theory is that a view of one's society as a capitalist satellite may most easily allow us to reconcile a fervent nationalism with the fervent anti-capitalism of socialism. Perhaps it is easier to love the delinquent who is an unfortunate victim. Of course, a larger part of the attractiveness of dependency theory is that it captures a fundamental fact of Canadian capitalism, in a word, dependence.

CHALLENGES TO DEPENDENCY PERSPECTIVES

But we cannot stop with dependency theory even with all the insights it has offered about Canadian capitalism. As we have seen in Chapter 9, a number of Canadian social scientists have recently challenged some of its basic assumptions, facts, and interpretations. First, early in the debate, Moore and Wells (1975) argued that the thesis of deindustrialization in Canada is largely "myth." They presented statistics that showed that Canada is not unique. Rather, the decline in manufacturing in Canada is part of an international trend, a trend which reduces the relative importance of manufacturing as a percentage of the Gross Domestic Product. While Canada has shown a marked decrease in the percentage of manufacturing, the same can be said of the United States, Britain, France and Sweden.

In absolute terms, manufacturing has increased but not as fast as the super-growth in the public and private service sector. Moreover, with the growth of multinational companies and better transportation and communication, production is moved from the industrialized countries to areas of the world where wages are lower: Mexico, Taiwan, Korea, and so on. This affects all of the more industrialized countries. In short, according to Moore and Wells, Canada compares well with other countries in rate of growth of manufacturing labour productivity.

Second, there has been a more basic criticism that the "Merchants against Industry" thesis simply does not fit the historical facts. Jack Richardson (1982) has argued that this thesis is based on a too broad interpretation of mercantilism and that Canada's early capitalists were very much involved in all spheres of industrialization. This is a view echoed by Robert Laxer (1985) who points out that, at the turn of the century, Canada was the seventh largest industrial nation. It was a leading producer of steel and was at the forefront in a number of technologies, notably farm machinery. And, as MacDonald (1975) has argued, the heavy involvement of nineteenth century capitalists in railroads made them very much industrialists and not simply financial or mercantile capitalists.

Other research (Carroll, Fox and Ornstein, 1982) as well as Richardson (1982) has also questioned whether there is or ever was a separation between the comprador and indigenous elite. This research examines the extent to which the directors of large corporations serve on the boards of other large corporations. They conclude that there is considerable linkage between large financial, merchandising and industrial firms in Canada and that there is no evidence to suggest that Canadian firms are "clustered in disconnected subgroups or cliques based on nationality of ownership or a sphere of economic activity" (Brym, 1985:9).

A third criticism of the dependency theory of Canadian capitalism is that it is based on an inadequate understanding of the complexities of world capitalism and how Canada fits into that system. As we have already seen, within industrial societies, industrial capitalism, based on many small enterprises gave way to monopoly capitalism based on a few large enterprises controlling much of one or more industries. But "capital" knows nothing about borders and flows wherever there is the likelihood of the greatest return on investment. To put that more concretely, capitalism became internationalized as capitalists in one country invested in the economies of others. Writing in the 1970s, Saul and Heron observed that:

. . . the reality of the powerful American grip on the Canadian economy and culture seems to make us look a lot like a dependency. Yet, at the same time, we lack the most obvious attributes of underdevelopment, and possess classes and a state which resemble those of the most advanced capitalist nations and which participate eagerly in various "central" schemes designed to further subordinate the "Third World" (1977:10).

Thus, another image of Canadian capitalism is that it is a kind of "hybrid" or incomplete form of capitalism, what David Drache calls "advanced resource capitalism." This notion of a hybrid is somewhat akin to a view of diminished responsibility. In this version, the delinquent must be held accountable for his actions, even while, at the same time, we recognize the particular circumstances that mitigate his responsibility. Canada may be a satellite but it is not merely a satellite.

More recently, William Carroll (1985) has questioned even this image of ourselves. His work suggests that as capitalism has become internationalized, Canadian capitalists are confined neither to Canada nor to finance and mercantilism. And, throughout most of the century, Canadian capitalists have had considerable control of industry. In his view, the path of development taken in Canada is not unlike that followed by other advanced capitalist countries. While there is considerable foreign investment in Canada and control of many of our industries, Canadian capitalists are, in turn, heavily involved in investments in other countries, particularly the United States.

Partly as a spin-off of the free trade debate, Canadians have become more aware of the extent of the involvement of Canadian capitalists in the economies of other nations, but particularly the United States. The involvement of the Reichman brothers in New York, where they appear to own most of the real estate, is perhaps the most publicized exam-

ple of "Canadian imperialism." And, their subsequent investment and control of Canary Wharf in London is a further reversal of a previous metropolis-hinterland relationship. In general, it is apparent that Canadians are heavily involved in investments beyond their borders to the extent that Canadian investment in the United States will soon equal investments by Americans in Canada.

It has, in other words, become more difficult for Canadians to maintain an image of themselves as victims of outside forces or even as delinquents with diminished responsibility as the notion of hybrid capitalism allowed us. This recent research provides a picture of Canadian capitalism that shows us to be no better (or worse) than any other capitalist society. And, while this undermines our self righteous claim that we're somehow nicer, it may also help to undermine the colonial mentality that Canadians and their accomplishments are somehow inferior relative to those of the American and British.

Clearly, there is much yet to be learned about Canadian capitalism. Many of the basic tenets of the dependency perspective have been undermined by subsequent research in the 1970s and 1980s. No doubt subsequent research will modify many of our present images of what occurred and is occurring.

We have, in this section, given you the gist but not the substance of what is a rather complex, and sometimes arcane, debate about Canada's form of capitalism, its development and the relationship between Canadian and foreign capitalists.

Despite their differences, all of the theorists do agree that in Canada, as in other capitalist societies, wealth and power are heavily concentrated and that a significant portion of our economy is under foreign control (27 percent in 1980). For example, according to Niosi (1985:58), 77 percent of all non-financial institutions were, in the 1970s owned by 1.7 percent of corporations. Most of these 4400 corporations, in turn, are part of conglomerates such as Canadian Pacific, Argus Corporation or Power Corporation. None would dispute that Canadian society and Canadian culture and each of us in our everyday lives are affected by decisions made by these relatively few who own and control Canada's economy.

THE CANADIAN STATE AND CANADIAN CAPITALISM

Perhaps some of you are sufficiently dismayed by the kinds of analyses you have just read that you are promoted to look for ways out, not in some distant Utopian socialism but in the features of Canadian society that are working or could work to restrain capitalists, the elite, and the worst excesses of capitalism. For many, the hopeful answer lies in the state, in its power to intervene and balance interests, in part through constraining the powerful. To understand Canadian capitalism and the limited role of the state, one must understand the contemporary relationship between capitalism and the state.

A major difference between communist and capitalist societies centres on the greater potential power of the state in communist societies to change the course and direction of society. According to Karl Marx, the state under capitalism is "nothing more than the form of organization which the bourgeoisie (capitalist class) necessarily adopt for the mutual guarantee of their property and interests" (Marx and Engels, 1965:78).

Canadian Marxists, such as Panitch (1977) and Clement (1977), draw upon this insight to show that the Canadian state, rather than autonomous and independent, is, to all intents and purposes, controlled by the capitalist class. In situation after situation, they argue the state acts on behalf of, if not necessarily at the behest of, capitalist interests. This is largely because of what is called "interpenetration" between the corporate elite and the state elite, which they maintain has been

increasing in recent years. According to their research, as well as that of John Porter earlier, there is co-optation of capitalists into the top ranks of government and an exit back into business. Such linkages ensure that governments do not take actions that would harm the interests of the capitalist class. Clement concludes that there is

"a confraternity of power" of such dimensions as to permit the clear employment of the term ruling class in the political as well as the economic sense in the Canadian case. It suggests, above all, an ideological hegemony emanating from both the bourgeoisie and the state which is awesome, which is reflected in the sheer pervasiveness of the view that the National interest and business interest are at one, and which certainly ensures the smooth functioning of the relationship between the state and the capitalist class (1977:75).

However, more recent research, again by Marxist sociologists, suggests this may be too strong a depiction of the direct linkage between the state and capitalism. Michael Ornstein (1986), for example, has studied the extent to which, in post-war years, such links between boards of large corporations and the Canadian state do exist. He concludes that while there is considerable interlocking between the two, they are not sufficiently strong to suggest that government is completely dominated by big business. He suggests, rather, that these linkages provide for effective liaison with, though not control of, the government by capitalists. Though linked in many ways, the state and the capitalist class are separate entities that have sometimes similar and sometimes separate concerns and objectives.

This close but sometimes ambivalent relationship between the state and capitalism may also be an outcome of, as Bell (1978:235–37) puts it, "economic growth having become the secular religion of advanced industrial societies: the source of individual motivation, the basis of political solidarity, the ground for the mobilization of society for a common purpose." In peacetime, *the* political issue, the *raison d'être* of government is to promote and maintain economic growth and prosperity. Increasingly, we blame not big business but our elected governments for their failure to regulate, direct, and stimulate the economy.

Against this all other functions of democratic government pale into relative insignificance. In the late 1970s, as inflation reached double digit percentages and unemployment rose, the state was caught in something of a bind. There were pressures from the electorate to develop programs that would offset the consequences of inflation and unemployment. There are, at present, even stronger pressures from capitalists for cutbacks in government expenditures, and to balance the budget or at least reduce the deficit. Such measures are justified as being in the interests not of capitalists but of everybody; they are the outcome of mystical forces: market demands, the international money market, the ups and downs of the business cycle, the greater power of other nations and so forth.

This is not, of course, to suggest that the state has no separate identity from or is completely the servant of capitalism. Capitalists, in many instances, have had to accept state intervention in their affairs, some of which has, it appears, run contrary to their interests, such as the national Energy Plan. And, the fact that the tobacco and gun industries have had to maintain powerful lobbies suggests that the state does not always act in ways that benefit capitalists or does so unpredictably.

In the 1980s, Canada, along with most other industrial societies, entered into what many see as the worst economic crisis since the 1930s. On the basis of pure economic or market forces, the degree of income inequality in Canada should have worsened. Yet, as Banting (1987) finds, distributions of family income have not changed much in 15 years despite changing economic conditions. He concludes that the redistribution role of the state (through the tax system, unemployment insurance and the Canada Assistance Plan) has by and large contributed to social, political and economic stability.

It is probably the case in all capitalist societies that political decisions will seldom run counter to the interests of corporate capitalism and big business. But, there do seem to be reasons to believe that the Canadian state has relative autonomy. Niosi (1985), for example, suggests that because capitalists are divided by region, ethnicity, and nationality, and are often groups with competing interests, it is impossible to speak of a single capitalist class. Brym (1985:14) points out that "the state's relative autonomy derives partly from the mundane fact that state officials want to keep their jobs." While they will normally attempt to produce conditions that benefit both capitalists and workers, this is not always possible. To ensure their re-election, or reappointment, it may be necessary, at times, to introduce changes that are not necessarily beneficial to the capitalist class. As well, Brym suggests a second and more profound source of the state's relative autonomy lies in the fact that progressive laws and institutions may emerge from what are political or legal resolutions of conflicts between different classes and groups.

TRANSFORMATION OF WORK IN CAPITALIST SOCIETY

One of the major consequences of industrialization was the transformation of where and how people did their work. You saw some of this in Chapter 4 where we described the move from simple to complex societies, the transformation of a rural into an urban population and all of the supposedly attendant features — loss of community, a growing depersonalization of relationships. In Chapter 6 we also examined some of the consequences of the way in which industrialism and capitalism separated home and work. All of this reflects the changing nature of work and, as many would argue, new needs of capitalism. As industrial capitalism has changed so too has work.

SHIFT FROM AGRICULTURE

In the first stage of industrial capitalism, the most obvious outcome is the massive shift away from agriculture to urban based occupations. For example, at the turn of the century about 40 percent of the Canadian labour force was engaged in agriculture. By 1981, farmers and farm workers made up only about 5 percent of the labour force. We can easily understand how the mechanization of farming enabled a few people to produce all of the food for the population. However, increased mechanization also meant that it became difficult for small independent farmers to prosper. This resulted in the creation of a large labour force with few options but to sell their labour. Figure 10.2 shows, more generally, the major changes which have taken place in the distribution of the labour force since the beginning of the century.

FIGURE 10.2

PERCENT DISTRIBUTION OF LABOUR FORCE, MAJOR OCCUPATIONAL GROUPS, 1901–1981

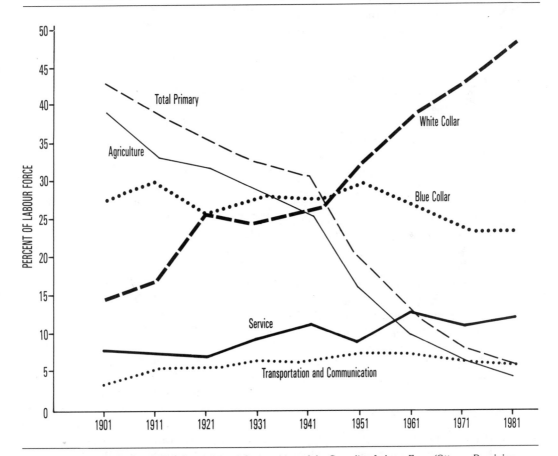

Source: Based on Sylvia Ostry, *The Occupational Composition of the Canadian Labour Force* (Ottawa: Dominion Bureau of Statistics, 1967), Table 2 [for 1901–61]; 1981 Census, *Population: Labour Force—Occupation Trends* (#92-920, Vol. 1) [for 1971–81]. Compiled by H. Krahn and G. Lowe, 1988, p. 43.

EXPANSION OF THE SERVICE SECTOR

As capitalists try to free themselves from labour wage demands through increased mechanization, certain types of work become obsolete and many workers are replaced by machines, but gradually, too, new occupations are created, occupations which revolve around machines — operators, controllers, servicers. As well, with increased capital investment in machinery come increased pressures on the capitalists to minimize risks. They must be sure that commodities are available, that they maintain their technological advantage, that a consumer market whose size and commitment can be accurately predicted exists and, finally, that labour and expertise are successfully educated, recruited, serviced and managed.

As the state is required to play an ever-expanding role in maintaining, developing, and regulating the economy, in responding to the demands of the welfare state, there is a need for what strikes many as an ever-expanding labour force in the public sector. We see, then, a host of new skills: technical expertise, exploration, research and development, marketing, advertising, and management. Professionals of all kinds are required with specialized expertise along with a cadre of lower-level white-collar workers who together make up the service sector.

So, as in all industrial societies, the most significant transformation in Canada's occupation structure is not the shift from agriculture, but the dramatic growth in the white-collar work force. Professionals, managers, clerks and salespeople of various kinds together make up the largest part of the labour force.

KNOWLEDGE SOCIETY OR HAMBURGER ECONOMY

Just as there is controversy about the extent and ultimate direction of our industrialization, so too has there been controversy about how work is transformed under monopoly capitalism. One view is that advanced industrial societies have become **post-industrial societies**. Manufacturing, though a crucial component of the economy, is overshadowed and overwhelmed by the more elusive and invisible industry of "symbol manipulation." According to Daniel Bell (1973), who was one of the first to advance the notion of post-industrial society, we have become a "knowledge society" dependent on specialized skills, expertise, and professionalism.

Whereas, according to Daniel Bell, a pre-industrial society is a game against nature and industrial society is a game against prefabricated nature, post-industrial society, "because it centres on services—human services, professional, and technical services—is a *game* between *persons*" (p.148). For Bell, the distinguishing feature of post-industrial society is that the demands for coordination and authority characteristic of industrial society are replaced by the need for cooperation, reciprocity and negotiation. Post-industrialist theorists view this last transformation of work as involving a transformation of social relations perhaps as great as that which accompanied the shift from pre-industrial to industrial modes of production.

What is meant by post-industrial society can perhaps be seen in Calgary, Alberta. Despite its formidable growth over the past two decades, the "industrial" section of the city seems to have changed very little and may actually have declined. It is in the centre of the city with its many office blocks where most people find employment. For instance, a large proportion of the data processing for the oil industry in Western Canada and the United States is done in Calgary. These and other "hidden industries" account for a large portion of Calgary's growth and prosperity.

The post-industrialist view is a rather positive view of the development of industrialization and the transformation of work. A more gloomy prognosis was that provided by Harry Braverman (1974) in his influential book, *Labor and Monopoly Capitalism*.

Braverman, originally a craftsman himself, argues that, while there has certainly been a growth of managers and professionals, this has been at the expense of workers whose jobs have been progressively deskilled. The reasons for deskilling are outlined later in this chapter when we consider scientific management and bureaucratization. But, the end result, according to Braverman, is a small elite of managers and "knowledge workers" and a mass of unskilled workers, engaged in jobs that require virtually no training or expertise. Moreover, while it is true that there has been impressive growth in the service sector, Braverman argues that much of this is due to expansion of unskilled clerical, sales, and service workers. In other words, expansion of jobs within the "fast food" industry hardly suggests we are becoming a knowledge society.

Which view is correct? John Myles (1988), a Carleton sociologist, has recently examined Canadian census and survey data that are relevant to the post-industrialism-deskilling debate. (See table 10.1). He finds that neither Bell nor Braverman have fully captured what is happening to the Canadian labour force and, in turn, its class structure.

As Bell would have predicted, there has in Canada, been an expansion of middle-class jobs, especially in management. But, this does not seem to have occurred as a result of deskilling the rest of the labour force. Rather than a homogeneously deskilled working class, Myles finds that there is a sharp division between a relatively skilled and an unskilled working class. He concludes that what we now have, in Canada, is, on the one hand, a growth in "knowledge occupations" but, on the other hand, within the working class, a split or dual labour market.

As food and accommodation services continue to expand, we can expect the division, the bifurcation of the working class to become more apparent and more problematic. In the remainder of this chapter, we look, briefly, at these three basic components of the labour force and the role of women in these later stages of industrialization and monopoly capitalism.

PROFESSIONALS AND MANAGERS

There is considerable confusion among Marxists as they try to understand the implications of these changes in the composition of the labour force for class consciousness, and ultimately the socialist revolution, all of which make it impossible to fit everyone neatly into

TABLE 10.1

CHANGES IN OCCUPATIONAL COMPOSITION, EXPERIENCED NON-AGRICULTURAL LABOUR FORCE, 1961–1981[a]

OCCUPATION	1961	1971	1981
Professional and Technical			
1. Professional	7.5	8.3	8.5
2. Semi-professional and Technical	4.2	6.2	7.9
Administration			
3. Managers	3.0	4.2	6.7
4. Supervisors	9.7	9.4	8.2
Mass Occupation			
5. White Collar	29.3	31.5	31.6
6. Blue Collar	46.3	40.4	37.1
Total	100%	100%	100%

a Classification based on Pineo, Porter, and McRoberts (1977)

Source: J. Myles, "The Expanding Middle: Some Canadian Evidence on the Deskilling Debate," *Canadian Review of Sociology and Anthropology*, 1988, 25:3 p. 343.

one or another of Marx's major classes, bourgeoisie or proletariat. In part, the debate springs from Marx's distinction between productive and nonproductive labour. The former produces **surplus value**, i.e., profit for the capitalist; the latter is for the capitalist an expense of doing business, a service which does not produce any value greater than itself.

Some Marxists would argue that, under monopoly capitalism, the distinction between productive and nonproductive labour is not important. Since neither kind of workers own the means of production, both are in the long run part of the proletariat; and almost all are directly or indirectly exploited. And they have been transformed into employees of capital. Others argue that between the proletariat and the bourgeoisie has emerged a new class, the professional-managerial class, a "new middle class" which, as Braverman (1974:407) puts it, takes its characteristics from both sides.

In some ways, in choosing your areas of specialization at university, you may be making a first commitment to one side or another of the struggle. Those of you who have chosen careers in business administration, for example, may well be building careers that serve directly the interests of capitalists. Most of you will take jobs that involve managing labour or consumers. But you will find that you are not a capitalist. You may feel a gratitude to the corporation for the material benefits you receive, for the relative degree of autonomy that your job provides and even for the fact that you have a relative degree of authority over others, whether only over your secretary or a division of workers. But, ultimately, you work in a world that others made and world that sometimes asks you to do things that you consciously abhor. You are in this sense, then, alienated, like the working class.

So, even when you compare yourself favourably to others in terms of income, title, size of staff and privilege, you may from time to time marvel at the compromises you have

learned to make, complain about your bosses and even the irrationality of the organization. Perhaps worst of all, it may be you who receives the brunt of the resentment and antagonism from those who have neither control nor autonomy in their work lives. Your interests and those of the traditional working class will be at odds, perhaps even antagonistic.

Other professional schools and disciplines leave the question more open. Engineers, for example, may often become independent professionals. More often, however, they will be employees in large corporations and in varying degrees will have managerial functions. Similarly, lawyers have in principle the choice of working within the corporation and progressively large law firms or as independent professionals. To some extent, then, the particular career path (independent or corporate) you choose will determine the degree of autonomy you have in your job and the extent to which your work contributes to the exploitation of others.

Moreover, even if you do choose to work within a corporate or government bureaucracy, with all of its objective constraints, at a subjective level you may be better off than other workers. You may feel that, unlike others, you have a choice: you can leave the bureaucracy and become a consultant, a storefront lawyer or even an entrepreneur. And it is apparent that other professions you might choose — doctor, social worker, planner, teacher, researcher — will have career paths that will place you in different relationships with the capitalist class and the working class and will provide different degrees of autonomy. We shall have more to say about the nature of professions in Chapter 12, Education and Inequality.

There is a sense, then, in which the last several generations of parents who have urged their sons, and more recently their daughters, to become doctors, lawyers or engineers, have understood some real features of Canadian social structure. First, we have the appeal of being one's own boss and perhaps these professions, more than those of traditional individual entrepreneurs, can achieve this to some degree even within the constraints of monopoly capitalism. Second, we have the appeal of professions themselves, that they are supposedly based on higher motives: helping, justice, truth and curiosity, rather than on the base motive of profit. Perhaps this is another way of saying that they stand outside the relationship between the exploiter and the exploited and indeed fulfill certain needs of an industrial society however it is organized. Very often this is what professionals believe and argue, a belief buoyed by the degree of autonomy in their work and the subjective sense that even while they work within the confines of a bureaucracy, private or public, they can escape from these confines.

This is not to say that such professionals are in fact free from the constraints of capitalism, nor that they are neither exploiters nor exploited, only that their rather new place in the relations of production means a different experience of work. For sociologists such questions as whether the professional middle class is indeed a new class or simply the old petite bourgeoisè in a new guise, has been an enthusiastic interest in part because it is an area in which Marxists's tools of analysis can be applied creatively. It is a demonstration that a Marxist analysis is not a closed system but rather an open one that provokes new questions in each society, and each historical period.

THE MARGINAL WORKER AND THE UNEMPLOYED

To return for a moment to our discussions of Canada's changing labour force; it would be mistaken to see the expanding service sector as only, or even predominantly, composed of relatively autonomous professionals and managers. The service sector also means a lower occupational level — clerks, typists, waitresses, technicians, drivers and those of the hamburger economy — who cannot claim the same degree of control or autonomy as those better placed in the occupational structure.

While it is technically correct to define these workers as "nonproductive" labour, they are, nevertheless, wage workers. In Marx's time, the service sector was sufficiently small and distinct from the working class as not to be worth separate consideration and analysis. It may even have been the case that nonproductive labour differed qualitatively from productive labour. Harry Braverman (1974) concludes that they have become much alike: "When they were few they were unlike productive labour, and having become many, they are like productive labour . . . . They form a continuous mass of employment which, at present and unlike the situation in Marx's day, has everything in common" (p. 423).

In particular, the service sector shares with blue-collar workers the fact that a significant proportion of its members are at the "bottom" of the occupational hierarchy and in times of economic recession are the most likely to be "shook out" into the underworld of the unemployed. Some of the lowest level service jobs, dishwashers, cleaners, door attendants, distributors of leaflets and brochures and a host of other often hidden occupations that may be characterized as "dirty work," have autonomy only in the sense that the occupants of these roles are forced to drift back and forth from these low-paid and irregular jobs to the ranks of the unemployed. They lack the degree of security enjoyed even by the proletariat or other low-level service jobs. These workers have been portrayed as part of the ***marginal work world***, comprising those who are the most vulnerable in both the service and productive labour forces.

As a context for understanding this marginal work world, one must understand the importance of unemployment to capitalism. Maynard Keynes, the most influential economist of capitalism, argued that for capitalism full employment would be inflationary. To look at this from a Marxist perspective, we might better understand unemployment as the persistent and real threat that constrains the demands of labour, and as the *reserve army of labour* which, even with state intervention, is kept at the poverty level and is thus a readily exploitable army to do the dirty work at low pay.

In both ways, the reserve army of unemployed, through its own vulnerability, accentuates the vulnerability of productive labour. It is from this perspective that we can most readily understand and sympathize with unionized labour's condemnation of nonunion workers who cross picket lines as "scabs" without ourselves condemning the "scabs" out of hand.

But apparently something happens to people when they have been unemployed for a long time and maintained at or near a level of subsistence. Perhaps some of you will know the experience of looking for jobs that do not exist, of the sense of personal failure, defeatism and, ultimately, fatalistic acceptance that unemployment seems to mean. And, finally, unemployment can become a way of life passed on to children, generation after generation. These unemployed may become so distanced from the work world, resigned to a perpetual welfare existence, that they no longer serve the supposed function of a reserve army of labour.

In Chapter 7 we saw something of the extreme vulnerability of this class, as reflected in the frequency with which the poor are arrested, placed before the court and finally incarcerated. Prisons throughout Canada are crowded by the numbers who are there because they hadn't the resources to pay even small fines. And, finally, it is people in this class of the dispossessed who are held up as a symbol of the penalties associated with the failure to commit to values of hard work, acceptance of authority and the like.

It may be that the marginal workers, with no unions to represent them, with no security of employment, with no special skills to trade, disorganized and unstable, provide something of an ongoing reserve army midway between the affluent worker of modern capitalism and those capitalism has fully dispossessed. The marginal work world, then, may be seen as one outcome of the transition from the entrepreneur capitalism of the nineteenth century to monopoly capitalism of today.

As corporations have increased in size, in scope and in bureaucracy, they have also spawned a powerful trade union movement able to provide its members with relative affluence and security. Left in the eddies of the current are smaller enterprises, little businesses whose survival seems to depend on low wages and the exploitation of casual or seasonal labour. The vulnerability of the marginal work world is accentuated, too, by the fact that it is likely to be the job market for those who feel they have no choice but to be docile if they wish to work at all—immigrant groups, ethnic minorities and, in recent years, women.

WOMEN IN THE LABOUR FORCE

An important change in the Canadian labour force is the dramatic increase in female participation. While the number of men in the labour force almost doubled between 1931 and 1971, the number of females increased four and a half times. Over this same period, the participation rate for women, as well as the female percentage of the labour force, doubled. By 1981, more than half (51.6%) of all adult women worked outside of the home (Krahn and Lowe, 1988:126).

The increased participation of women in the labour force either coincides with or is the result of a variety of structural factors described here and in Chapter 8. For example, the low fertility rate of the Canadian population coupled with early marriage means that women are free earlier to enter or reenter the labour force. Urbanization, too, has meant that many women previously in unpaid labour on farms are able to or forced to seek paid jobs outside the home. And most crucial has been the massive increase in the service sector and, in particular, the dramatic growth in clerical occupations.

As can be seen in Table 10.2 women have not entered all occupation divisions equally but have been segregated into sex-typed occupations, jobs which are, in effect, extensions outside the home of what inside the home was traditionally women's work — elementary teaching, nursing, secretarial work, and cleaning — in Marxist terms, *reproductive labour*. Thus, women are under-represented in managerial jobs, in blue-collar jobs in primary industries, and are over-represented or

"ghettoized" in clerical, sales, service and recreation. And if we remove nurses and teachers from the professional and technical category, women are under-represented here as well.

So, as research by Pat Conelly (1979) and particularly by Pat and Hugh Armstrong (1984) documents, rapidly growing numbers of women in the labour force do not signify any fundamental change in attitudes, or in the position or status of women. Rather, because of sexual segregation, there has not been a fundamental alteration in the division of labour by sex or in the nature of women's work.

Using different and more elaborate measures, Lautard (1978) came to similar con-

TABLE 10.2
EMPLOYMENT CONCENTRATION OF WOMEN, CANADA, 1984

OCCUPATION	WOMEN AS A PERCENTAGE OF THE TOTAL LABOUR FORCE IN EACH OCCUPATIONAL CATEGORY
Managerial and administrative	31.9
Natural sciences, engineering, and mathematics	16.9
Social sciences	55.1
Religion	20.6
Teaching	59.3
Medicine and health	78.1
Artistic and recreational occupations	39.2
Clerical	79.1
Sales	43.4
Service	55.8
Agriculture	24.8
Fishing, hunting, and trapping	—
Forestry and logging	5.5
Mining and quarrying	—
Processing	22.0
Machining	7.2
Product fabricating and assembling	23.6
Construction trades	1.8
Transport-equipment operation	7.0
Materials handling	20.4
Other crafts and equipment operating	21.7
Unclassified	63.3
All Occupations	42.2

Source: Labour Canada, *Women in the Labour Force, 1985–86 Edition* (Ottawa: Supply & Services Canada, 1986), p. 19.

clusions. While he found some decline in sexual segregation as Canada becomes a more industrialized society, he also concluded that at the then rate of change, we will have a completely desegregated labour force in about 450 years! While women doubled their representation in the labour force as a whole from 1931 to 1971, their representation in professional and technical occupations had actually declined.

Similarly Fox and Fox (1987) find on the basis of more recent data that while there was some decline in the 1960s and 1970s, *gender segregation* of the labour force remained at a very high level through 1980s. They attribute what decline did occur to women moving into occupations once exclusively male (supervisors, auditors, financial officers) and to the decline or slow growth of some occupations with a high proportion of women (secretaries, stenographers, elementary and kindergarten teachers). Men did not, it seems, move into traditionally female occupations. Still, for there to be no gender segregation, those authors conclude that 60 percent of men or women would have to change their occupational categories.

Segregation of women has also meant that, on average, women's earnings are about 65 percent of male earnings. Here, two factors are at work. First, because these occupations are extensions of work done in the home, they have been regarded as less important or requiring less training and therefore not as deserving of higher pay.

Second, where women and men are employed in the same occupations, various kinds of sexual discrimination — refusal to promote women as supervisors of men; penalizing them for "taking time off" to have children or for conflicts between their work and their domestic duties; and sexual harassment — have meant that women end up earning less than their male counterparts.

The latter source of inequality has led to calls for legislation ensuring "equal pay for equal work" and for greater recognition that

while both women and men have family and domestic responsibilities, these fall more heavily on women. The former source of inequality, ghettoization, has led to the more difficult concept of equal pay for work of equal value. This is more difficult to implement because, as we have seen, under capitalism, the value of anything, including labour, is elusive and subject to the market.

Women have not only been segregated into certain jobs, but married women in particular, have also formed a pool of cheap labour, a reserve army. "Women," observes Harry Braverman (1974:315), "form the ideal reservoir of labour for the new mass occupations. The barrier which confines women to much lower pay scales is reinforced by the vast numbers in which they are available to capital."

Part of women's vulnerability, then, comes from the pressure on those in ill-paid jobs from the many not yet part of the labour force. The unemployed would "gladly" replace them however ill-paid and irregular the work. Also, the growing numbers of women who, through separation, divorce or desertion find themselves single parents—sole supporters of their families — contribute further to the vulnerability of female workers, often forcing them to be docile members of the marginal work world. And, as Dorothy Smith (1981) describes, unionized male workers in the central work world have, on the issue of women's equality, generally sided with the ruling class. Both in the United States and Canada, trade and labour union policies have typically contributed to rather than resisted sexual (and ethnic) stratification in the labour force.

PRODUCTIVE LABOUR

In North America, a typical response to the theories of Karl Marx has been that Marx underestimated the ability of capitalism to provide affluence for its workers. Marx was blinded, the argument goes, by his moral outrage at the extremes of poverty in the capitalism of his day. In contrast, workers are better off today and some could be described as affluent. However, the poverty, insecurity and vulnerability of those in the marginal work world and in the "reserve army" should represent one major rebuttal to this kind of optimism.

Unquestionably, labour in the central work world has achieved a significant level of affluence. Of course, this was achieved through a long and often violent struggle to unionize. Unions, through the threat of withholding labour and thereby temporarily shutting down expensive technology, have been able to achieve for at least some male workers substantial material benefits.

However, the role of unions in Canada has always been limited. First, only a minority of Canadian workers are unionized, even today. Second, about one-half of Canadian unions are "branch plants" of large American unions that have been extremely conservative and that have, not surprisingly, traded off the interests of Canadian workers for the benefit of the American majority. And finally, Canadian unions are not formally affiliated with a political party which can directly express their interests but have, rather, a loose, often uncomfortable alliance with the NDP.

Another major damper to the optimism of those who feel capitalism can create a broadly based affluent society is the unwillingness or inability of unions to make autonomy and control a central issue in collective bargaining. Rather, in their struggle to obtain higher wages and shorter hours, unions have acted, intentionally or unintentionally, to integrate workers into the corporate capitalist system rather than to react against it. As James Rinehart concludes:

They (unions) do not face the issue of who is to govern the means and ends of production. Instead, unions have resigned themselves to the structure if not the logic of the existing system of power and authority at the workplace as well as outside it . . . Rather than trying to resolve the

conflict between capital and labour, unions institutionalize it. This means that unions are defensive and accommodative organizations. They seek a "better deal" (defined primarily in economic terms) within the limits of capitalist enterprise (1975:155).

Work, however well-paid, however much it is compensated by time off, is, in capitalist society, alienating.

ALIENATION OF LABOUR

For Marx, work was the central realm, a world of necessity which brought people together with other people and where, by satisfying their wants, they express themselves and reproduce themselves in both unexpected and novel ways. Marx's history of capitalism is in many ways the history of the progressive **alienation of labour**. As he puts it:

*What constitutes the alienation of labour? First, that the work is **external** to the worker, that it is not part of his nature; and that, consequently, he does not fulfill himself in his work but denies himself, has a feeling of misery rather than well being, does not develop freely his mental and physical energies but is physically exhausted and mentally debased. The worker therefore feels himself at home only during his leisure time, whereas at work he feels homeless. His work is not voluntary but imposed, forced labour. It is not the satisfaction of a need, but only a **means** for satisfying other needs. Its alien character is clearly shown by the fact that as soon as there is no physical or other compulsion it is avoided like the plague.*

External labour, labour in which man alienates himself, is a labour of self-sacrifice, of mortification. Finally, the external character of work for the worker is shown by the fact that it is not his own work but work for someone else, that in work he does not belong to himself but to another person (Fromm, 1961:98-99).

Intuitively, we understand alienation to mean that most work is routine, boring, monotonous and unsatisfying. The philosophical Marx left us with a variety of meanings of alienation. Workers need be less cooperative in their labour in an assembly line, for example, and the hierarchies and distinctions based on skill in which they work distance the workers from one another. Rex Lucas's (1969) study of miners, for instance, describes the many fine distinctions of work the miners use to distinguish and separate themselves from their fellow workers.

Marx also understood that when production was broken down into its component parts and each worker performed his or her small component activity, the workers would be alienated from the products of their labour. Imagine devoting your life to working with a technology that you do not understand to produce one small part or aspect of a final product which is not of your creation. Imagine that you may not even be able to afford one. Most important, imagine working towards a final product for which you can feel no pride, no sense of personal accomplishment. In the words of Kyo, a Malraux character, "there is no possible dignity, no real life for a man who works twelve hours a day without knowing why he works." It is not clear that paying someone more to work fewer hours solves the basic problem.

We can all fairly easily relate to these meanings of alienation. Nor are these forms of alienation restricted to productive labour. The housewife surrounded by the technology of her work, which she does not fully understand, and cut off from her fellow workers, has often discovered the meanings of her alienation through consciousness-raising groups which, at the very least, allowed the expression of discontent. And your own pleas for relevant courses and your sense of isolation from fellow students may yet be other reflections of a kind of alienation.

Often we react to these feelings of alienation in a superficial way, assuming that these feelings can be wiped away by making work more fun, more cooperative and by involving workers more fully in the entire production process. While there is obvious merit in these

assumptions, they miss what is the most fundamental meaning of alienation.

Marx and others have understood that work in capitalism meant a diminishing or denial of self. We are, after all, working in a world created by others and for the interests of others. Without doubt capitalism has provided great scope for creativity in work but increasingly this is so only for the capitalists and, to a lesser extent, the experts and technicians who serve them. For labour, on the other hand, even in the face of relative affluence, there has been a progressive degradation of work and, as symbolic interactionists have understood it, this has meant, for many, a loss of respect for self, a loss of the sense of one's own power and, often, a resignation to one's diminished status, with episodic bursts of inarticulate protest — malingering, absenteeism, pilfering, goldbricking, and even industrial sabotage (Rinehart, 1987).

And even yet, we miss what Marx tried to capture by alienation because it is hidden or buried under the very language of capitalism, a language which allows us to view others as means. In viewing others as means, we come together in social ties of exploitation rather than cooperation. Finally, the individual himself or herself is "split up," a means, a part of a larger machine. People no longer use tools but become tools and, therefore, lose all freedom.

BUREAUCRACY AND CONTROL

If you have trouble accepting such a depiction of work, if you feel it is an unnecessarily one-sided, even a melodramatic characterization, perhaps you are reflecting the success of capitalism in appeasing labour through the various techniques of management that have culminated in experiments to produce a happier and more satisfied work force. In many ways, the history of bureaucracy is the history of the management of labour.

SCIENTIFIC MANAGEMENT

When Marx wrote of capitalism, capitalists routinely controlled their workers through repression and force. In part this was because the workers were readily accessible; capitalists and workers were housed in the same factories. With the increasing rationalization and mechanization of work, workers were directly controlled not by force, but by the operations, pace and requirements of the machines they served. The archetypal example is the assembly line which is premised on the notion that workers must be made to work to the pace of the machines. This may strike you as self-evident and not very significant but just think of how much easier it is to dupe a foreman into thinking you are pulling your load than to dupe a conveyor which delivers sixty cars an hour, whatever the worker's mood or energy level.

But the assembly line is only one technology of production even if in a sense it has provided the model for how all production might be done. However much work had begun to revolve about machines, a variety of industries still required the same worker to perform many and varied tasks. The attempt to reproduce machine-like control in all industries was the impetus for the development of the most influential school of management, *scientific management*.

What started as a social movement in the late nineteenth century, was very much the child of Frederick W. Taylor, scientific management or the application of "scientific principles" to the organization of labour is now an institutionalized feature of capitalist society. We think of it as a refreshingly unhypocritical acceptance of capitalism and its need to create effective control of workers to maximize production. To Taylor, general orders, supervision and discipline were not enough because the workers retained their hold on the productive process. Harry Braverman summarizes Taylor's position:

So long as they (workers) control the labour process itself, they will thwart efforts to realize to the full the potential inherent in their labour power. To change the situation, control over the labour process must pass into the hands of management . . . by the control and dictation of each step of the process, including its mode of performance (Braverman, 1974:100).

The exponents of Taylorism asked such questions as "what is the most efficient division of labour and mode of specialization?" or "what kind of and how much reward is necessary to induce workers to produce at maximum efficiency?" Another way of putting it is to say that scientific management sought explicitly to remove the human element from work. It is an approach that ignored the subjectives of work, the fears and insecurities of workers, their boredom and the like, in part because it was premised on the belief that workers who produced efficiently and effectively would inevitably be happy workers.

BUREAUCRATIZATION

In many sociology texts, scientific management is described as part of the larger, more general social process Max Weber calls *bureaucratization*. Weber's view takes us back to the question of the relationship between industrialism and capitalism. For Weber, bureaucratization, based on the principles of rationalization and efficiency, threatened to dominate modern society in all spheres. The link of bureaucracy to capitalism was fortuitous. For Marxists, on the other hand, bureaucratization is intimately tied to the rise of capitalism and the need to control labour. In any case, bureaucracy represents another and perhaps the dominant mode in modern society for the control of labour, productive and nonproductive, as well as for the control of professionals and managers.

The starting point for any analysis of bureaucracy is Max Weber's distinctive formulation of it as a *rational-legal model*. Weber tried to define the *essence* of how social arrangements, social organization, were changing in his society (the early twentieth century). For Weber, many of these changes were captured by the notion of the growth of bureaucracy. Weber did not so much define bureaucracy as provide a blueprint, what he called an *ideal type*. He constructed this ideal type of bureaucracy by accentuating and exaggerating what he perceived to be happening in his society. By magnifying these elements he hoped to make them more apparent and comprehensible. Although Weber did not mean ideal types as an indication of the desirability of bureaucracy, it is probably fair to say that he never fully understood how bureaucracy was created by some to control others.

Weber saw bureaucracy as a rational-legal model. He saw the basis of authority — the legitimation of power — as shifting from traditional to rational-legal. By this he meant that rules or the right to create rules could no longer be justified by some statement such as "things are so because they've always been so," but instead in terms of formally stated principals which are thought to contribute to efficiency. Authority, then, derives out of technical competence.

This shift in the basis of authority is reflected in the characteristics Weber attributes to bureaucracy. This ideal type of bureaucracy is organized into hierarchical positions, each with its own area of jurisdiction and guided by a general set of rules. These rules are formal, that is, written, and specify the precise amount of authority in each office. Authority is attached to the position, not the person. The various positions demand different kinds of skills and areas of technical competence and therefore require "thorough and expert training." The coordination and management of the bureaucracy is guided by relatively stable and exhaustive rules which everyone within the organization can learn. For Weber, the bureaucracy is an efficiency-producing machine:

The fully developed bureaucratic mechanism compares with other organizations exactly as does the machine with the non-mechanical modes of production. Precision, speed, unambiguity, knowledge of the files, continuity, discretion, unity, strict subordination, reduction of friction and of material and personal costs — these are raised to the optimum point in the strictly bureaucratic administration . . . . (Gerth and Mills, 1958:214).

In addition to machine-like efficiency, Weber suggests that the bureaucracy may also produce machine-like predictability:

Its specific nature, which is welcomed by capitalism, develops the more perfectly the more the bureaucracy is "de-humanized," the more completely it succeeds in eliminating from official business, love, hatred, and all purely personal, irrational, and emotional elements which escape calculation (Gerth and Mills, 1958:216).

Weber did, however, recognize that bureaucracy is Janus-faced, that when people occupy the system of positions they also bring with them nonrational factors which inevitably affect the organization. In Weber's terms, they bring with them their loves, hatreds and "purely personal, emotional, and irrational elements." Communication, for example, does not always flow along formal lines as specified in the organization chart; informal networks are inevitably part of any bureaucracy.

What is perhaps most significant and most revealing about Weber's position is his notion of the nonrational or irrational impediments to bureaucratic efficiency. What are we saying when we describe an employee's hatred of his or her boss as nonrational? Or when we so describe a worker's desire to make friendly contact with fellow workers or to innovate his or her own procedures? What all of this implies, quite clearly, is that the overriding rationality is the efficiency of production and this swallows up, takes precedence over, all other interests.

Increasingly, those working within this Weberian perspective came to realize that the bureaucracy would never be able perfectly to reduce humans to machines. People persisted in doing "irrational" things like refusing to turn out more "widgets" for extra wages and bonuses. The notion of bureaucracy has in fact expanded since Weber to include the human side of work.

A turning point for how bureaucracies are perceived and organized was the now classic Hawthorne studies. In a series of experiments and observational studies, the researchers tried to find out how such physical factors as amount of lighting and work-breaks affected production at the Hawthorne plant of Western Electric. Their conclusions redirected future studies of bureaucracy.

▌ HUMAN RELATIONS

Although their findings have been challenged in terms of poor research design and in terms of the influence of the investigator's values, these investigations do provide a rather interesting case of serendipity in sociological research.

In one of the Hawthorne experiments, a number of female workers were segregated and, as they worked, the experimenters adjusted the amount of light in their room. They then observed their production, comparing it with the production of a "control" group, who worked under constant light conditions. What the investigators purportedly found was that, when segregated, both the experimental and control groups increased their production. The experimental group produced more regardless of changes in the lighting, even when the lighting was as dim as moonlight.

The conclusion of the study was that "human factors" accounted for the increased production. Apparently, because these workers had been selected for the experiment and had by implication been singled out for special attention, they felt better about themselves and their work and therefore worked better. These finds were influential in creating a somewhat new approach to organizational studies—the *human relations* approach.

This new approach held that to understand bureaucracies one must take into account the nonrational factors inherent in work rela-

tions. Somehow theorists must include in their analyses that, for example, the coffee break is more than simply a way to reduce physical fatigue but may also be the forum in which workers gain self-esteem, social support, the emotional satisfactions of sociability. The friendships that arise may provide important informal networks of communication.

Still, this approach represents only a modification of scientific management. The goal is still the most efficient machine possible, now with the added recognition that the human factor must also be considered.

This approach has brought with it some profound changes in how work is organized. Out of human relations there emerged participatory leadership, encounter groups, suggestion boxes, work teams, a concern for recreation within the corporation. More fundamental has been the empirical search for more humane modes of organizing work. Researchers have compared worker satisfaction in industries organized around craft production (printing), industries organized around continuous process production, where workers tend machines (chemical plants), and have found, consistently, a more satisfied, less alienated work force than on the assembly line. There have been experiments in increasing worker autonomy in setting their pace and hours of work. There have been experiments involving workers in the entire process of production so that they gain pride in newly acquired skills, an understanding of the process and a closer relationship to the final product.

We cannot help but view these experiments positively, as perhaps the basis or direction of the future society in which the definitive criterion for organizing work is the satisfaction that comes from autonomous creativity. But within contemporary capitalism, the defining criterion is not human relations but rather productive efficiency, and human relations is another mechanism of control to achieve this end. This means that experiments in new organizations of work "succeed" or "fail" based not on their humanitarianism but rather on their profitability.

CONTRADICTIONS OF BUREAUCRACY

As long as human relations is a mechanism, bureaucracy will remain a contradiction, an organization based on an image of people as machines but which must be populated by people who are not machines. Bureaucracy will always have dramatic human costs and these human costs will always interrupt the flow of the machine. For example, Michael Crozier (1968:178) suggests that there is a contradiction, of which Weber was well aware, involving a "double belief in the superiority of bureaucratic rationality—in the domain of efficiency and its threatening implications in the domain of human values." Robert Michels (1915), in proposing his "iron law of oligarchy," argued that those with authority will always be willing to sacrifice the values of the organization as their prime concern becomes the preservation of their position within the organization.

In the 1950s, William Whyte wrote what became a very popular book, *The Organization Man* (1957), in which he tries to capture some of the dehumanizing effects of life in complex organizations, where "organization men" come to lose their individuality, their capacity for creative work and are encouraged to be mediocre.

In Robert Merton's terms, bureaucracies unintentionally produce inflexible bureaucrats who typically lose sight of the goals of the organization; the rules and regulations become ends in themselves; bureaucratic performance becomes a matter of ritual. It is no doubt this aspect of bureaucracy — red tape and impersonal treatment — that most of us typically think of.

Since functionaries minimize personal relations and resort to categorization, the peculiarities of individual cases are often ignored. But the client who, quite understandably, is convinced of the special features of his own problem often objects to such categorical treatment. Stereotyped behaviour is not adapted to the exigencies of individual problems. The impersonal treatment of affairs which are at times of great personal significance to the client gives rise to the charge of "arrogance" and "haughtiness" of the bureaucrat (Merton, 1968:256).

On the other hand, in contemporary highly complex bureaucracies only those who can handle and manipulate the new technology and who are flexible in the face of changing circumstances may survive. The new bureaucrat, then, may affect our lives not through bumbling and rigidity but through competence with a technology unavailable to us.

The computer, a seemingly natural adjunct to bureaucracy, has provided the bureaucrat with what is to many of us an intimidating resource but nonetheless a resource which allows the collection and storage of information which can be translated into power. These issues raise perhaps the most fundamental question about Weber's ideal type. What are some of the unanticipated consequences? Is the ideal type in fact the most efficient system?

Elliot Leyton has examined the workings of one bureaucracy, the Workmen's Compensation Board, and its effects on workers in St. Lawrence, a mining community in Newfoundland (Handelman and Leyton, 1978). Leyton argues that this bureaucracy, by acting "rationally," ends up acting inhumanely, and without any regard for suffering and anguish.

Since the early 1960s, it has been recognized that fluorspar mining leads to lung cancer. Miners have about an 80 percent chance of contracting one of several work-related diseases. At some point, company doctors declare a man unfit for mining and therefore unemployable, at which point he must apply for workmen's compensation benefits. Some men declared unemployable receive full compensation; some receive only a portion; some receive nothing and must go on welfare.

When these men die, often prematurely, their widows are subject to the same bureaucratic rules that applied to their husbands. Some continue to have full pension; others are cut off the day their husbands die. Members of the community all "know" that their disability is a result of working in the mine and they expect the Board to compensate them. The Board, however, demands scientific (medical) proof of the link between the disease and the mine.

This proof is not easy to provide so the rulings of the Board, apparently based on some attempted objectivity, are viewed by the local people as capricious and arbitrary. In this case the bureaucratic rules ignore the needs and unique circumstances of the community which the Board is supposedly serving. What Leyton is describing, then, is the classic confrontation between the traditional values based on kinship and community and the "modern" values of the impersonal bureaucratic society.

CONCLUSION

Throughout this chapter, as throughout this book, we have asked you to keep in mind that while we are products of society, we are also producers of society. As we have argued, a weakness of theories that focus on industrialization and modernization is that these processes are seen as inevitable consequences of technological and economic change. People and their actions and conflicts are left out of the picture.

An important contribution of Marx was to reintroduce the human action into the process of history and social change. Yet, Marxists who focus on "the logic of capitalism" or who enter into abstract discussions of "capital," rather than of decisions by capitalists, introduce another kind of functionalist explanation of the development of Canadian capitalism, one which also denies people a role in human history.

What we want to leave you with is an understanding that, while capitalism and industrialism do create pressures towards one kind of society, one kind of world, these are not inevitable consequences. For example, comparative research suggests that deskilling and segmentation of the labour force, alienation of work and creation of a class of working poor may be peculiar to American and Canadian capitalism and not solely an outcome of the logic of capitalism at all. And, as we have seen, the extremes of inequality and vulnerability experienced in many capitalist societies have, in others, been mitigated through government policies and legislation.

This brings us back to the beginning, to our discussion of modernization and our critiques of industrial society. The questions remaining are largely questions for the future. In our Utopia how will we organize work so that it is creative and fulfilling? Do the liberal reforms of the human relations approach provide us a basis for the future? Perhaps we are talking about degrees of alienation. Perhaps a technical- bureaucratic society can only be made more, not perfectly, humane.

Marx understood that there were costs as well as rewards in living in society, that there was a tension between the individual and the collective, that people's precarious harmony with nature, with others and with themselves, would always mean a continuing and only partially successful history of accomplishment. More than anything else, we have tried to convey to you the liberating hopefulness of Marx, not that people would ever be totally freed from these tensions but that they would be freed from their one-dimensional acquisitive, greedy natures—the result of capitalism—to remake not only society but human nature.

III SUGGESTIONS FOR FURTHER READING

Many of the readings that followed the preceding chapter will also be the starting place for an understanding of Canadian capitalism and capitalism more generally. Again, we would urge you to go to the source, the work of Karl Marx. His most thorough analysis of capitalism is, of course, to be found in the three volumes of *Capital* but, at this point, there are easier places to start. A sample of his work can be found in Lewis Feuer's *Marx and Engels* (1959); Robert Tucker's *The Marx-Engels Reader* (1978); and Tom Bottomore's and M. Rubel's *Karl Marx* (1973). We would particularly urge you to try Erich Fromm's *Marx's Concept of Man* (1966) which contains Marx's most eloquent statements on work and alienation. In a number of these collections you will find, and should read, *The Communist Manifesto*.

An extensive examination of the professional-managerial class can be found in Pat Walker's collection, *Between Labour and Capital* (1980). These articles help illustrate the power of analytical Marxism. In this respect you should also find useful Harry Braverman's *Labor and Monopoly Capital* (1974). This highly readable book draws heavily on the classic analysis of capitalism, Baran's and Sweezy's *Monopoly Capital* (1966). Another classic is E. P. Thompson's *The Making of the English Working Class* (1963).

There is an incredibly large literature on capitalism which these few references should open up to you. For some sense of what we have called the social psychology of capitalism, you should start with Max Weber's classic *Protestant Ethic and the Spirit of Capitalism* (1958 ed.) A contemporary, sometimes confusing, often brilliant portrayal of people living in capitalist society is Richard Sennett's *The Fall of Public Man: The Social Psychology of Capitalism* (1978).

Recently, a large number of books and articles have appeared on capitalism in Canada, its development and the state and capitalism. A controversial account of the development of Canadian capitalism is R.T. Naylor's *The History of Canadian Business, 1867-1914* (1975). However, first year students might find particularly helpful Pat Marchak's *In Whose Interest?* (1979). This deals with many of the issues also considered earlier by W. Clement in his *Continental Corporate Power* (1977) and Kari Levitt in her influential *Silent Surrender* (1970).

These works are among the best in the dependency perspective. Criticisms of this perspective are found mainly in journal articles but many of these authors have restated their arguments in R. Brym's edited collection *The Structure of the Canadian Capitalist* (1985), which also contains a useful summary of this debate. Also useful for understanding this debate is the first chapter of William Carroll's excellent study, *Corporate Power and Canadian Capitalism* (1986). Another influential book is J. Niosi, *Canadian Capitalism* (1981).

In addition to the various collections listed at the end of Chapter 8, the role of the state in capitalist society is examined in Leo Panitch (ed.) *The Canadian State: Political Economy and Political Power* (1977). Panitch draws much of his perspective from his former teacher, Ralph Miliband. See for example Miliband's *The State in Capitalist Society* (1969). Another more recent collection is by Paul and Linda Grayson, *Class, State, Ideology and Change* (1980) and A. Moscovitch and G. Drover, *Inequality: Essays on the Political Economy of Social Welfare* (1981).

Other non-Marxist visions of industrialization and capitalism are nowhere better captured than in Daniel Bell's *The Coming of Post-Industrial Society* (1973) and his *The Cultural Contradictions of Capitalism* (1978). Textbooks which draw upon a variety of approaches are J. Smucker's *Industrialization in Canada* (1980); H. Krahn's and Graham Lowe's *Work, Industry and Canadian Society* (1988); and Mervin Chen's and Thomas Regan's *Work in the Changing Canadian Society* (1985).

There is a large body of writing on bureaucracy. A sample of early literature can be found in Robert Merton et al., *Reader in Bureaucracy* (1967). Review of some of the classic bureaucratic and organizational literature can be found in N.P. Mouselis's *Organization and Bureaucracy* (1967), David Silverman's *The Theory of Organizations* (1970), Charles Perrow's *Complex Organizations: A Critical Essay* (1972) and Rosabeth Moss Kanter's *Men and Women of the Corporation* (1977). Don Handelman and Elliott Leyton provide a particularly insightful Canadian example in their *Bureaucracy and World View: Studies in the Logic of Official Interpretation* (1981). A Marxist analysis of these changes in ideologies of management is Richard Edwards's *Contested Terrain* (1980).

Canadian examples of discussions of work and the workplace are James Rinehart's *The Tyranny of Work*, 2nd ed. (1987), Graham Lowe's and Harvey Krahn's edited collection, *Working Canadians: Readings in the Sociology of Work and Industry* (1988), R. Argue's, C. Gannage's and D.W. Livingstone's edited collection, *Working People and Hard Times* (1987) and K. Lundy's and B. Warme's *Work in the Canadian Context* (1981).

Studies of specific jobs and industries include Pat Marchak's *Green Gold* (1983); Graham Lowe's *Women in the Administration Revolution: The Feminization of Clerical Work* (1987); Graham Lowe's and Herbert Northcott's *Under Pressure: A Study of Job Stress* (1986), Wallace Clement's *Hard Rock Mining* (1981) and *The Struggle to Organize: Resistance in Canada's Fisheries* (1986) and Charlene Gannage's *Double Day, Double Bind: Women Garment Workers* (1986).

As in other areas of Women's Studies, there is a growing body of literature on women and work. While much of this is in article form, Paul and Erin Phillips's *Women and Work* (1983), introduces you to many of the issues as does Pat and Hugh Armstrong's *A Working Majority: What Women Must Do For Pay* (1983) and *The Double Ghetto: Canadian Women and their Segregated Work* (2nd ed.) (1984) and Pat Armstrong's *Labour Pains: Women's Work in Crisis* (1983). Finally, what has become something of a classic is Meg Luxton's *More Than a Labour of Love* (1981).

INEQUALITY IN CANADA

CHAPTER 11

SOCIAL INEQUALITY

OVERVIEW

SOCIOLOGY AND SOCIAL INEQUALITY

THE ISSUE OF SOCIAL INEQUALITY

IDEOLOGY AND INEQUALITY
EQUALITY OF CONDITION
EQUALITY OF OPPORTUNITY

SOCIAL STRATIFICATION

THE FAMILY AND SOCIAL STRATIFICATION
OPEN AND CLOSED SOCIETIES
CASTE, ESTATE, AND CLASS
CASTE
ESTATE
CLASS

THEORIES OF CLASS INEQUALITY

KARL MARX
MAX WEBER
CLASS, STATUS GROUP, AND PARTY
THE FUNCTIONAL THEORY OF STRATIFICATION
ISSUES AND DEBATES

CLASS INEQUALITY IN CANADA

INEQUALITY OF CONDITION: THE MIDDLE MASS
OCCUPATION
WOMEN AND SOCIAL CLASS
INCOME INEQUALTIY
POVERTY IN CANADA

SOCIAL MOBILITY IN CANADA

SOCIAL MOBILITY IN INDUSTRIAL SOCIETY
ELITE MOBILITY

CONCLUSION

SUGGESTIONS FOR FURTHER READING

OVERVIEW

This chapter is about social inequality. However, when you have read it you will still not have the answer to one of the most intriguing and perplexing questions to philosophers and social scientists: what are the origins of inequality? Why, for example, in virtually all societies beyond mere subsistence level do some manage to obtain more of scarce resources — wealth, power, prestige — than others? Why, in apparently all societies, do men have more power than women? Why do some religious or ethnic groups find themselves at the bottom of the social structure and others at the top? Sociology, and for that matter, social philosophy, has not provided very convincing answers to these questions.

Sociologists have, however, been more successful in answering other kinds of questions about social inequality. What this chapter does do is help you, first of all, to understand the various forms that social inequality takes, what sociologists refer to as patterns of social stratification. Second, it shows you the various ways people have learned to justify social inequality and to make it seem legitimate that some have more than others. Third, you should understand the ways in which inequalities are passed on from generation to generation and become fundamental structures of a society. Finally, by the end of this chapter you should have an appreciation of the social and personal consequences of inequality, why it is that social inequality is viewed by most as a social problem. These are the issues that define the field of social stratification.

In this chapter, you will be exposed to the major theories of social stratification, those of Marx, Weber and the functionalists. You should come to understand that all of these theories are based on the appreciation that industrial societies are characterized by sharp inequalities but you should also understand how they differ in terms of the degree of inequality they perceive as tolerable or necessary, the complexity of inequality and the consequences of inequality for societies and for individuals. In reading about these theorists, you should be aware of how much their work is infused with ideology and you should be able to place the work in terms of our discussions of conservatism, liberalism, and socialism.

From this chapter you should derive at least four key conceptual distinctions: 1) social inequality versus social stratification, the social inequality passed on through the family; 2) equality of opportunity, the liberal hope that everyone has an equal chance to achieve success, versus equality of condition, the socialist hope that "success" can be relatively equally shared; 3) open (or class) systems of stratification that allow and encourage social mobility versus closed (or caste) systems that do not; 4) power elites made up of those who shape the destiny of their societies versus veto groups, made up of those whose power is constrained.

Perhaps most importantly you should be able to use the material in this chapter to examine your own views about inequality, to think about your own ambitions and aspirations. When you learn about how social inequality is justified or legitimated, you are also learning about how problematic these justifications are. It is important, at the same time, that you do not confuse what is intended in the chapter by concluding that the rich and powerful are bad and the poor somehow noble. The sociological study of inequality is the study of how social structure and culture shape people, their lifestyles and life chances, often in ways of which they, themselves, are unaware.

The final part of the chapter, which examines social inequality in Canada, should make it easier for you to understand the implications of the ideologies, theories and concepts of social stratification not only for your own society but for your own family and your everyday interactions.

SOCIOLOGY AND SOCIAL INEQUALITY

In the preceding chapter we examined Canada as a dependent society subject to imperialism. But we also pointed out that Canada is internally stratified, an unequal society perhaps not very different from other industrial societies. This chapter is mainly concerned with various general theories about the legitimization and maintenance of structured inequality and of social stratification. For most sociologists, to understand the system of stratification of any society is to understand its social structure, and when sociologists classify societies they often do so on the basis of their particular form of stratification, their system of patterned inequality.

More generally, sociology is, to a very large extent, the study of social inequalities—their origins, their inevitability, the ways they are justified and their consequences. As Alfred Hunter points out:

. . . concern with 'who gets what, when, and how' as Lasswell and Kaplan frame the issue, or with 'the question of classes and class conflict', as Giddens characterizes it, was an important impetus to the initial development of sociology and it continues to provide the motivation behind much modern theory and research (1981:1).

The problem of inequality, then, is inextricably part of the sociological, indeed the intellectual tradition of Western thought. It is at the core of the work of virtually all of the classic sociologists we have mentioned. Stanley Ryerson observes that:

Although the concept of equality is respectably ancient, going back to and beyond the Politics of Aristotle and the Ethics, the actual ways in which people have been bothered about the question of equality and inequality, the urgent issues around which people have grouped themselves, and organized and fought and died, and sometimes won, make up in large part the tissue of history (1981:373).

Moreover, inequality is not something we can make go away simply by not thinking about it. It affects all of us in our everyday lives regardless of whether we are on the receiving or delivering end of an unequal relationship. Indeed, of the various aspects of social structure which shape and constrain us, those based on relationships of inequality are by far the most powerful.

The personal and social consequences of poverty and racial and sexual discrimination are vivid reminders of what we have already seen in earlier chapters: that while social reality is built up by people and can, in principle, be "reconstructed" or changed, society often confronts us in ways that make it seem objective and unchangeable. Inequalities are key "facts" of social life. They set out the parameters to our structures of opportunities; they constrain us and limit what we might be and do.

For Native people, for example, "racial" inequality means to be born poor and to face limited opportunities to improve that condition. It may also mean that relative to white

Canadians, life for Canada's native peoples is shorter and unhealthier.

To grow up in poverty, whatever one's ethnic or racial background, may be to face narrowed horizons and to have one's imagination, curiosity, and talents systematically blunted. It is also to know, at first hand, powerlessness and humiliation, the price paid by those who must deal with and depend upon the welfare system of our country.

To be a woman is to learn that some jobs are officially or unofficially male jobs; that men often receive more pay for the same work, that women are "not taken seriously" or are regarded as inherently incompetent to do "man's" work.

Even those "lucky enough" to be born male, white, with the proverbial silver spoon in mouth are constrained by the social fact of inequality. To maintain our advantageous position we may have to believe and behave in *bad faith*; that is, to "pretend something is necessary that in fact is voluntary" (Berger, 1963:143). Bad faith is to believe in our own ideologies, the "film of lies" by which we maintain and rationalize our secure or privileged positions.

To accept the privilege and power of being white in a racist society, then, may be to believe in racial superiority — to hold, in effect, beliefs that fly in the face of scientific evidence and humanistic values. To be male and to conform to the norms of a sexist society is another example of bad faith. It is also to deny oneself the pleasures and pains of child rearing and the range of emotional responses humanly possible but forbidden by traditional stereotypes of masculinity.

While the injustices that flow from being labelled or defined as "inferior" are fairly obvious ones, it should be remembered that there are also costs attached to advantaged positions. Here, we are in effect returning to our discussion, in Chapter 5, of role. Positions in society demand things from us and can, if we let them, dominate us. And in the process, our "humanness" is diminished. It is, of course, in this sense that Marx argued that it is not only the worker who is alienated; so is the capitalist who, like the Potter of our allegory in Chapter 10, acts in terms of the dictates of the logic of capitalism rather than from a sense of humanity.

THE ISSUE OF SOCIAL INEQUALITY

IDEOLOGY AND INEQUALITY

As we have seen, sociology emerged out of the tumult and unrest of eighteenth century France. Sociologists and social philosophers had to come to grips with the fact that the two revolutions, the French Revolution and the Industrial Revolution, were undermining what had for centuries been taken for granted: that some people, by virtue of birth, were entitled to power, wealth and deference while others, again solely on the basis of which family they were born into, were destined to powerlessness, poverty and subservience.

Sociology emerged at the point in history when hereditary aristocracies could no longer be tolerated. But what, asked these thinkers, was to replace them? If the mere fact of being born to wealth and privilege was no longer viewed as just, what then would be social justice? Should all people be forced to be equal whatever their talents? Should those lucky enough to be born with ability be the ones to rule, to be accorded prestige, to become rich? These questions continue to plague us and remain central to the sociological tradition.

In the nineteenth century, in France, Britain, the United States, indeed anywhere that capitalism took root, the dominant answer was that provided by *liberalism*.

Liberals argued that traditional forms of inequality could no longer be tolerated, not because there was so much disparity between lord and serf, but because hereditary aristocracies impeded progress and allowed no place at the top for the new class of industrialists or capitalists. In the eighteenth and nineteenth centuries, America was viewed as a utopia, not because everyone was happy or affluent — of course they were not — but because it was a new society which had no aristocracy to impede the upward movement of the ambitious and ruthless "Robber Barons," the new aristocracy produced by capitalism.

Conservatism and socialism provide a kind of counterpoint to liberalism and its emphasis on equality of opportunity. Indeed, it is in how these ideologies approach the question of inequality that the fundamentally contrasting images of human nature and our relationship to society emerge most clearly. To repeat what we said in Chapter 1, the liberal ideology is based on and starts from the premise contained in Rousseau's contention that "man is born free but everywhere is in chains." The overriding concern of liberalism is therefore the individual, his or her autonomy and civil, political and social rights. It seeks the advancement not of society but of the individual and is critical of those institutions and forms of inequality which stand in the way of that advancement.

At the same time, liberalism offers optimism that without radical restructuring of society, these institutions can be made better. They can be changed so that they no longer corrupt or fetter people in their quest for self-fulfillment and self-actualization. The liberal answer to the problem of inequality is not to do away with it but to change its basis. Liberals wished to replace socially created and imposed inequalities with natural inequalities, those that allegedly derive from individual differences in ability and talent. And many liberals, uncomfortable with the notion that there must be winners and losers, looked to a kind of utopian pluralism where everyone can win at something; one must simply find what one is best at and be given equal opportunity to use those talents in the marketplace.

The *conservative ideology* is rooted in exactly opposite premises. For conservatives, people, if they are to be healthy and to survive, have a fundamental need for the sort of security which comes from living within a well-ordered and predictable social structure. Society rather than the individual must be strengthened because it is from society that we gain our strength; for the conservative, the autonomous individual is an alienated, or perhaps an anomic, individual. For conservatives, maintenance and preservation of traditional systems of hierarchy, of inequality, give people a sense of "place," limits to their aspirations and the security that comes from continuity of culture.

The second counterpoint to liberalism is, of course, *socialism*, especially, though not exclusively, as embodied in the work of Karl Marx. Socialism shares with liberalism the same basic optimism in human nature and the same faith that if society is improved, so people will be. But unlike liberalism, the concern is with advancement not of the individual but of the common good and in particular of those who are oppressed and exploited. Socialists also differ from liberals in their belief that to improve society you must fundamentally restructure it. The creation of an entirely new social order is necessary if people and their institutions are to be rehabilitated and freed. Socialists, Marxists more specifically, are seen as radical because of their belief that the problem of social inequality cannot be resolved through changing its basis, but by doing away with it entirely.

What we have just described is a debate about social inequality which, in its purest forms, can be found only in the writings of 18th and 19th century social thinkers. As we have described in Chapter 3, over time, as they have been imported to new societies such as Canada and the United States and as the nature of capitalism, itself, has changed, liberalism, conservatism and socialism have borrowed from one another and undergone other kinds of transformations. But, however murky these political labels may have become, it is out of them that we continue to debate what constitutes social justice: ***equality of condition*** or ***equality of opportunity***.

EQUALITY OF CONDITION

Sociologists, such as Marx, in advocating equality of condition question whether there should be social inequalities between people at all. Why, it is asked, should some receive more than others? What does this mean in practice? Kurt Vonnegut, satirist, writer of science fiction, or however one labels him, has written more than one parody of what it would be like to live in a society in which "everyone was the same." In his imaginative future, the beautiful would wear masks, the strong, the graceful, and the athletic would wear weights, the highly intelligent would have implanted in their heads devices which, just as a thought or idea was forming, would give off sounds — symbols clashing, bells ringing, jack hammers working and the like — all handicaps to ensure that no one had an "unfair" advantage in life. Others, more grimly, have envisaged grey bleak cities filled with robot-like people, distinguishable from one another only by numbers. For these writers, the socialist's vision of an equal society means facelessness and bureaucratic repression and the end of individualism; in short, dystopia, not utopia.

In contrast to what has often been said of him, Marx did not think that communist society, his vision of utopia, meant levelling of everyone to the lowest common denominator or, we assume, creating the kind of world George Orwell depicted in his dystopian novel, *1984*. In fact he regarded this as *crude* communism, the culmination not of humanism but of envy. For Marx, at issue is not whether A makes more money than B or has

a finer house than C or can afford a more expensive car than D. No doubt these things matter, especially if you are B, C or D, but the more critical issue is that ownership of private property, the means of production of a society, necessarily involves relationships of exploitation.

Recall our potter analogy in Chapter 9. Potter, through her efforts, creativity and entrepreneurial skills and the decision she makes to become a capitalist, ends up possessing furs, diamonds, the nice house on the hill and a healthy stock portfolio. But, Potter, now turned capitalist, has achieved this through entering into an exploitative relationship with her workers. As a capitalist, she has no choice. She must pay her workers a wage which, while perhaps providing them with a decent standard of living, still leaves her with a profit at the end of the year. Socialism, for Marx, did not mean that the "natural" differences between people would disappear but only those that are social, arbitrary, and exploitative would disappear because they are based on class privileges, class distinctions and alienating class relationships.

In criticizing the program of one socialist party of his time, he argued that in a just society, a worker who is physically or mentally superior to another should receive more than one less endowed. Similarly, if one worker has many children and another none, even "with an equal performance of labour, and hence an equal share in the social consumption fund, one will in fact receive more than another, one will be richer than another, and so on" (Feuer, 1963:119). Only in a higher phase of communist society, when abundance has been achieved, can "society inscribe on its banners: From each according to his ability, to each according to his needs" (Feuer, 1963:119).

At the same time, it is this latter slogan that has driven some of the critique of inequality of condition in capitalist societies. Socialists, most of whom would label themselves as

Marxists, certainly believe that a better society would be one in which everyone rather than the few benefited from industrialism. But there is also moral outrage at the wide discrepancies in income, and in turn, life chances, experienced by working Canadians who are not part of the capitalist class.

Later in this chapter we describe some aspects and implications of income inequality in Canada. But, at this point we would simply note that most of the working poor, those working in the marginal work world at the minimum wage, have little knowledge of just how much more managers, doctors, professors and so on earn than themselves. It is perhaps because the gap is so large that those with high incomes, who in interviews will easily and sometimes at great length talk about their sex life or their marital situation, become silent and apprehensive, when asked to state their income. The size of the gap, perhaps, explains why financial matters are kept so confidential. Evidently, those who work in satisfying and lucrative occupations fear the resentment of those who work in boring and repetitive jobs and who earn very low incomes for their efforts.

Some, particularly functionalists, have argued that without some differentials in income, nobody would be motivated to take on the more difficult and responsible occupational positions within industrial society. They may be right that there has to be some difference in rewards to motivate people. But, as socialists ask, how much? Industrial societies differ considerably in the amount of inequality they are prepared to tolerate. Communist and socialist states, such as China and Sweden, for instance, believe that equality of condition is both a desirable and ultimately achievable goal. In Canada and the United States, the much less successful attempts to redistribute income through progressive taxation and guaranteed annual income programs nevertheless do reflect social and political pressures for a more egalitarian and, in socialist terms, a more just society.

EQUALITY OF OPPORTUNITY

For the most part, the debate about inequality has not been about equality of condition but about what constitutes the best basis (justification) for inequality. What is sometimes called the "meritocratic" critique of inequality assumes that social inequality is inevitable. Those who hold this view, essentially the view of the liberal ideology, are concerned with how people are *recruited* to favourable positions and with the *process* and *justifications* by which inequalities are transmitted from one generation to another.

At least since the beginnings of sociology in the eighteenth century, the main concern has been not with equal rewards but with equal opportunities to compete for those rewards (Parkin, 1971:13). Traditionally, the battle has been between merit on the one hand and hereditary privilege on the other, between liberal and conservative, respectively.

According to the liberal ideology the just and equal society is one in which there is equality of opportunity: regardless of their social origins, people should be able to achieve their positions in society. Canadians are, paradoxically, sympathetic to both conservatism and socialism. But most also share the liberal *ideal* that *ascribed* statuses, such as sex, race, ethnicity and family background, should not be relevant in assigning people to various positions in the social hierarchy.

People who advocate the ideal of equality of opportunity are therefore not challenging the existence of a social hierarchy. Rather, their concern is with the extent to which these unequal positions are open to everyone in the society, to what extent they are reserved for the children of those who already hold these positions. In other words, to what extent are societies likely to be characterized by *social stratification*?

SOCIAL STRATIFICATION

To say that a society is stratified is to say that it can be divided into unequal or hierarchical categories or social strata that persist for a long period of time. The study of social stratification is about both *structure* and *process*. An interest in structure leads to questions about the nature and type of social stratification in a particular society and to comparisons between present societies and those of the past.

The concept of process, on the other hand, directs us to look at how wealth, power and prestige (and their opposites, poverty, powerlessness and low status) are passed from one generation to the next and how this is justified or legitimated. Social stratification, then, is in large part, about how inequalities become crystallized into social classes. It is the element of continuity of particular forms and patterns of social inequality that distinguishes a stratified society from one in which there is simply social inequality.

THE FAMILY AND SOCIAL STRATIFICATION

Normally, inequalities become crystallized into specific social strata because of the existence of the family and the kinship structure. Peter Newman notes that for the Canadian establishment:

The "Family" is a kind of sacred institution in these circles, not as a result of any unusual filial feelings but because it is the vessel that passes on the money (1979:306).

And, of the Eaton family:

One of the great mysteries about the Eaton empire is how the family manages to pass it on from generation to generation without paying the succession duties that cripple enterprises many times smaller. The secret is a process called "estate freezing," which involves hiving off assets to a holding company, which controls all the common stock, placed in the hands of each succeeding generation after payment of a relatively modest gift tax (p. 328–329).

Families, whether as powerful as the Eatons or more ordinary, do not create inequality; rather they respond and adapt to it, attempting to pass on to their children the same positions and privileges they have enjoyed. As we have seen in Chapter 6, the new layers of vulnerability brought about by the rise of capitalism mean that, in different ways, people, families, will use the resources of kinship whenever it is to their advantage to do so.

It is because of this connection between the family and structured inequality that those who have wanted to create utopias have usually begun by abolishing the family as we know it. Only by turning over to the state the responsibility for child rearing, it has been argued, could privilege and influence be eliminated and "natural" talents be allowed to emerge.

OPEN AND CLOSED SOCIETIES

Almost all known societies have been stratified. Nevertheless, there are important differences in the degree to which social positions are likely to be determined by particularistic-ascribed (family-type) relationships. In industrialized societies there has been a marked transition from **closed** to **open systems** of stratification.

In closed systems it is difficult, sometimes illegal, to leave the social stratum in which one is born. Social position is fixed at birth so that one does not expect to rise or to fall in the social hierarchy. Open systems, on the other hand, permit a good deal of movement from lower social strata to higher social strata and vice versa. In open systems there is both a greater chance to "rise" and a greater risk of "falling." In a completely closed system of social stratification all members of each stratum would be recruited from that stratum, usually by inheriting their parents' status and occupation. There would therefore be "perfect" social stratification. At the other extreme we can conceive of a society in which there is "perfect" equality of opportunity. This would mean that the family has no influence on the individual's eventual social position. In this case there could still be social inequality but, because it is renewed in each generation, there would be no social stratification.

To clarify this somewhat, it may be helpful to think of a very simple hypothetical society in which there are exactly 1000 fathers who have exactly one son each and one daughter. Let us suppose, too, that like most other societies, past and present, our imaginary society is also a sexist society; women are allowed to hold no other positions in society besides that of wife and mother. Women's status, their social and economic fate, is totally dependent on what happens to their husbands. Finally, imagine that this is a two-class society; an elite of 100 families and a nonelite of 900 families.

Figure 11.1 presents three hypothetical situations with respect to social movement. In Case A, a totally closed society, there is no social mobility; every elite son would inherit his father's position; every nonelite son would remain a member of the nonelite. Now, let us suppose that in this hypothetical society a law is passed which forbids any sons of elite fathers from inheriting an elite position (Case B). Because of the law, *all* sons of elite fathers are downwardly mobile and are replaced by 100 sons of nonelite fathers. Note, however, that even with "complete mobility," 800 sons will have to settle for a nonelite position. There is not enough room in the elite for everyone.

Finally, Case C shows what would happen if there were full equality of opportunity, that is, if family background had no influence on what happens to people in terms of their social position. As we can see, ten sons of elite fathers could be expected to "inherit" an elite status and ninety sons would be downwardly

FIGURE 11.1

CASE A
A TOTALLY CLOSED SOCIETY

FATHER'S GENERATION	SON'S GENERATION		
	Elite	Non-Elite	Total
Elite	(1) 100	(2) 0	100
Non-Elite	(3) 0	(4) 900	900
Total	100	900	1000

CASE B
TOTAL CIRCULATION OF ELITES

FATHER'S GENERATION	SON'S GENERATION		
	Elite	Non-Elite	Total
Elite	(1) 0	(2) 100	100
Non-Elite	(3) 100	(4) 800	900
Total	100	900	1000

CASE C
FULL EQUALITY OF OPPORTUNITY

FATHER'S GENERATION	SON'S GENERATION		
	Elite	Non-Elite	Total
Elite	(1) 10	(2) 90	100
Non-Elite	(3) 90	(4) 810	900
Total	100	900	1000

mobile. At the same time, ninety nonelite sons would be expected to move upward and 810 would remain nonelite. Simply, the elite comprises 10 percent of the population and therefore full equality of opportunity leads us to expect that the elite in the next generation would consist of the same proportion — 10 percent of elite sons.

Obviously no society is as simple or as neat as to fit any of these cases. Not all fathers will have a son while others will have several. Generations do not split quite this easily either. Further, as various things happen, the size of the elite may change. A war may create a need for more leaders and for a larger elite. Or, at the same time as there is a decrease in positions for nonelite members, there is an increase in need for people to manage the society.

Both the failure of the elite to reproduce itself and changes in the composition of the labour force create a demand for *structural mobility*. But even if conditions remain pretty much the same, some nonelite sons will have sufficient ability and drive to "push" their way upwards. Similarly, some elite sons are likely to be incompetent or lack the desire to assume an elite position and will "fall" to a nonelite position.

Our hypothetical examples illustrate two important points. First, even as in Case B where no one is allowed to inherit a favoured position, we do not have equality of condition but what Pareto called a *circulation of elites*. Second, even with full equality of opportunity, the liberal ideal, not everyone can be upwardly mobile. There is, in other words, only so much room at the top. Only a minority can expect to rise and unless the structural conditions are changing, a number of those born in advantaged positions must expect to lose that advantage.

Some structural changes in the Canadian labour force—more white collar workers and fewer factory workers and farmers — were outlined in Chapter 10. These changes clearly have produced a good deal of the social mobility in industrial societies. This illustration will also have further relevance when we consider the nature of the Canadian elite later in this chapter and when we look at education in the next chapter.

CASTE, ESTATE, AND CLASS

No society has ever been either perfectly closed or perfectly open. It is usual, however, to consider **caste** and **estate** as examples of relatively closed systems, and **class** systems of modern society as examples of relatively open systems. All these are unequal societies, ones in which some have control of resources and others do not. It makes more sense to think of caste, estate and class not as different types of stratification, but as different *systems of justification* for inequality.

To repeat what we have said before, no system of inequality can be maintained for very long by force alone. Force works of course, but it is always precarious. At some point the bully must sleep and is then defenseless. Nor can he rely on his police or the military. Both are notorious for deciding, eventually, that it is better to give than to receive orders. So, on the basis of force alone, those who "have" find themselves in constant danger from those who "have not." To have the biggest piece of the cake, and to eat it, requires an ideology of justification. And there are perhaps as many variations of these as there are unequal societies.

Undoubtedly the favourite justification has been that God or the gods ordained it; the fact that some have and some have not is god given—simply the universe unfolding according to some divine plan. And, of course, some "haves" have made the stronger claim that they *are* gods, are descended from gods or are in communication with the relevant deities.

In recent decades the most powerful justifications have revolved around the concepts of "merit" and "functional importance." The first derives from Herbert Spencer's notion of survival of the fittest: those who rise to the top of society do so because they have the most ability, talent and drive; as the "fittest" members of society they deserve the most.

The second often goes hand in hand with the first: the economy, if it is to prosper, requires that there be E. P. Taylors, K. C. Irvings and Conrad Blacks with the ability to amass and organize vast industrial empires and million-dollar a year executive officers to run these enterprises. In this context, then, caste, estate and class systems of stratification also represent the main ways privileged groups have sought to justify their favoured positions.

CASTE

The main, and perhaps only, example of the caste system is found in the ancient system of stratification of India. Castes are hereditary ranked divisions of Hindu society that are religiously and traditionally sanctioned. Membership is based on the fact that one is born into a particular caste so that movement into or out of a caste is prohibited. Since castes are also endogamous (marriage occurs only within the caste), they have, in their broad outlines, been able to exist unchanged for several thousand years. The distinguishing feature of caste systems as opposed to other systems of stratification is their systematic reliance upon religious, philosophical and genetic explanations to maintain and justify inequality and to do so without much challenge for a very long time.

ESTATE

The estate system of stratification stands somewhere between a caste system and a class system. Historically the feudal system of medieval Europe provides the most specific example of this form of stratification. Like the caste system, estates were essentially closed social strata in which intermarriage and social movement were virtually impossible. Estate systems were based on an agrarian economy in which one's social position was intimately tied to the ownership or nonownership of land.

At the top was a hereditary aristocracy or nobility, followed by merchants and craftsmen. At the bottom were free peasants and then serfs who were tied to the land. The clergy, though most closely associated with the aristocracy, was itself arranged into a hierarchy interacting with the secular hierarchy at various levels.

CLASS

The distinctive feature of class systems of stratification is that *social mobility* becomes institutionalized and expected. Instead of rigid boundaries of castes and estates, classes, by definition, allow for movement into and out of them. In a class system, wealth rather than birth becomes the main basis for stratification. As well, in theory at least, class position does not confer any legal or political rights not available to all citizens within the society.

THEORIES OF CLASS INEQUALITY

The replacement of the estate systems of stratification by a class system had profound implications for the social order. The human implications, the new layers of vulnerability that this transition brought about, are perhaps most vividly depicted by novelists such as Charles Dickens. But, as we have seen, all of the classic sociologists were attempting to understand both the personal and social implications of this transition from feudalism to capitalism. Of these various thinkers, present-day sociologists continue to draw upon the insights of Karl Marx and his major, though very sympathetic, critic, Max Weber, to understand both the genesis and nature of capitalism and the particular forms of inequality it produces.

Their work comprises the two major conflict theories of social stratification. Both are rooted in the assumption that inequality, particularly economic inequality, engenders conflict and that this conflict is an important source of social change. As we describe below, their differences seem to centre around their degree of optimism that replacing capitalism with socialism would bring an end to conflict and the rise of a more just and cooperative society.

A third theory, what is usually referred to as the functional theory of stratification, has also had considerable influence on American and Canadian sociology, in part perhaps because it is compatible with the liberal argument that inequality is necessary and inevitable and need not lead to conflict.

KARL MARX

As we have seen, "class," "class formation," "class struggle" and "class conflict" are at the very core of Marx's sociology and of his analysis of capitalism. It is in the struggle between bourgeoisie and aristocracy that capitalism is born out of feudalism. And, it is with the proletariat — the product of capitalism — and its possibly violent confrontation with the bourgeoisie that Marx locates the impetus for the new society, the classless and nonantagonistic communist or socialist society.

A class analysis forces us, as it were, to cut through the double-talk and thereby ask whose definition of social reality dominates and why. We begin to ask how, in the interest of maintaining the existing system, ruling class control of the major institutions shapes, directs, and limits our thinking, our definitions of what is just, our values about what ought to be, and our perceptions of what in the human condition is universal, and what is specific to a particular form of social organization. And in asking these questions we come to understand not only how society is organized but how it changes.

Marx's work, then, as theory and as political doctrine, makes class, class analysis, and class point of view central and overriding. Some who followed him have built on his work, some have tried to refute it, but none can ignore him. But having said all of this, we must at once add a somewhat paradoxical

qualification: nowhere in his voluminous writing do we find an explicit definition of class.

We search in vain for a well-worked out and consistent theory of classes and their formation; rather than a clear picture of the class structure of capitalist societies we are at times given a picture of two major antagonistic classes locked in battle and, at other times, an image of many intermediate classes whose permanence or impermanence, importance or unimportance, is ultimately unresolved.

One reason for this apparent oversight is that he simply ran out of time. The third volume of *Capital*, Marx's final and perhaps most important work, breaks off dramatically just as he is about to address the question of what constitutes a class; he died before the question, let alone the answer, could be properly formulated.

This is not, of course, to suggest that Marx had nothing to say about class in earlier writings. In fact he said a good deal and it is possible to pull together a definition. Here is one:

A class is a group of people holding a common relationship to the means of production, to the political-power structure, and to the ideas of the time, a relationship which necessarily brings it into conflict with some other group having divergent ideas and different interests with respect to the economic and political structures (Lopreato and Hazellrigg, 1972:19).

The key to social change for Marx lies in the inherent conflict between the class which has and the class which has not. Marx contended that in every period of history, society breaks down into two basic and inherently hostile classes — a ruling class that owns the means of production and a class that is ruled or oppressed.

Within capitalist societies, the two main and opposed classes are the *bourgeoisie* — capitalists and the large landowners who had survived — and the *proletariat* — the class of modern wage earners who, having no means of production of their own, are reduced to selling their labour power in order to live. According to Marx, the material condition of the proletariat could only worsen, what is often referred to as the "law of increasing misery."

At first, this "pauperization" leads only to misdirected conflict and struggle. Unaware yet of their revolutionary potential, the working class is distracted from direct confrontation with the capitalist class. Workers compete among themselves for better conditions; they attack the factories rather than the factory owners; they fight the remnants of the aristocracy, "the enemies of their enemies" rather than the capitalists. In time, Marx anticipated, these distractions are set aside. Workers become conscious of their class interests, their shared predicament. The proletariat becomes a revolutionary class and it is with this class that he pinned his hopes for revolutionary change.

There are problems with Marx's analysis of the class structure of capitalist societies and there is perhaps much in his work which is polemical. But, as we have stressed throughout the book, he has provided us with theory and concepts that in our view most adequately allow us to analyze our society—capitalist society—in its entirety. And in the more philosophical parts of his writing we are constantly reminded that sociology is and should be a humanistic discipline.

Marx's philosophy, his concept of humankind, is a strong counter to the conservative argument that there is something inherent in human nature that makes class inequality, injustice, and oppression inevitable aspects of human societies. In contrast, we find in his work optimism that through our own efforts and intellect we can both imagine and fashion a new social order.

MAX WEBER

It is sometimes argued that Weber's theory of social stratification represents a refutation of Marx's theory. It is more accurate, however, to view Weber's work as an academic "rounding out" of Marx's obviously more political and largely unfinished contribution.

Marx put great emphasis on the importance of economic factors in determining the fundamental basis of social stratification. Weber shared with Marx the view that ownership and nonownership of property are crucial determinants of class formation and position. He agreed, also, that under some circumstances groups of people sharing similar economic interests might form into a coherent and conscious class. But, he argued, economic interests do not form the sole basis for social stratification, for class formation, and for social conflict. Ideas and attitudes held by people are also important determinants of how society is organized and stratified. While ideas are likely to be conditioned by economic institutions, ideas and ideologies are themselves social forces that must be taken into account.

Weber's theory of stratification centres around the notion that social stratification derives from an unequal distribution of power or *life chances*, that is, everything from the chance to stay alive during the first year after birth to the chance to view fine art, the chance to remain healthy and grow tall, and if sick to get well again quickly, and the chance to avoid becoming a juvenile delinquent (Gerth and Mills, 1953:13). While a family's economic power is an extremely important determinant of these life chances, Weber argued that power can be expressed in more ways than simply the economic dimension. This becomes especially the case as new groups of classes — professionals, managers and government bureaucrats — emerge which are neither capitalist or proletariat but something in between.

CLASS, STATUS GROUP, AND PARTY

Weber contended that individuals and their families are, at once, members of three different orders of stratification — class, status and party (or power as it is usually translated). *Class* or class situation refers essentially to economic stratification and is fairly close to

Marx's use of the term. **Status** or status situation refers to the way in which social honour or prestige is distributed. Status situation comes not only from wealth but from *lifestyle*, how one spends money and how one thinks and behaves, and from ascribed factors, in particular, family background. Status is based not so much on what we possess as upon how others treat us. By *party*, Weber seemed to mean the distribution of "pure" political power in a society. As with status, political power may arise independently of economic power and be valued for its own sake.

Ordinarily, people are likely to be located at roughly the same place in each of these three hierarchies. In that case, the distinction between the three is *analytical* rather than *empirical*. But it is also easy to find examples where the three are incongruent so that individuals are quite differently ranked on each dimension. Ministers and priests, for instance, enjoy considerable prestige within a community and may have considerable power. But generally they have little or no wealth. Politicians may gain considerable political power but be neither rich nor accepted members of the Canadian establishment. Extremely rich men, such as the late Howard Hughes, may seek anonymity and therefore be almost unknown among those who determine social standing. Wayne Gretzky has become very wealthy and enjoys considerable esteem and prestige, but possesses little or no political power.

Classes, for Weber, are essentially economic groups. People can be placed objectively in terms of whether they are owners or nonowners of the means of production, whether they possess wealth or not. Status, on the other hand, is more subjective: how do individuals see themselves; how do others define them? As Weber showed, under ordinary circumstances, *status situation* rather than *class situation* is likely to create in people a sense of class consciousness.

Nor is money, in and of itself, sufficient to give a person access to certain status groups. Winning a million dollars in Loto 649 for example, will not necessarily mean that one is invited to join an exclusive golf and country club. Similarly, a substantial loss in income does not necessarily mean an equivalent loss of social status. Often, old established families may possess higher social status than the *nouveaux riche* even when the latter are in fact richer. And because the economic base is so secure, the most important issues for some may centre on what for most of us seem quite irrelevant. Peter Newman, in his contrast between the "old rich" and "new rich" segments of the Canadian establishment, nicely captures these irrelevancies:

These strange paladins of wealth obviously don't enjoy simple lives. One problem is that having exceptional fortunes no longer guarantees much personal distinction. That's why the rich are so zealously class conscious. No other class has the time or money to uphold such rigid common standards; at no other level are class distinctions so minutely observed. Established money is obsessed with the notion of keeping the parvenus at bay—those cigar chompers and haunch grabbers in their silk suits and pomaded haircuts, whose status just hangs out like a dirty shirt tail.

The difference that counts is between being Old Rich and New Rich. Adherents of both groups give themselves away in all sorts of subtle ways—where they summer or winter, how they decorate their houses and offices, what they wear, drive, and eat, whom they marry and sleep with. What the New Rich can never quite grasp is that the surest way of being excluded is to compare possessions. By specifying the exact length of their Chris-Craft, boasting about their latest car, gadget, mistress, or French Impressionist painting, they betray a gauche insecurity the true Establishmentarian never feels (1979:303).

Weber's third dimension, **party**, refers to the fact that people do not necessarily require high status or great wealth in order to wield considerable political power. Hitler would seem to be such an example as are the "Mandarins," the higher civil servants in the federal government. For Weber, then, class, status and party are the three basic resources people have available to them to control their own and other people's life chances.

In most cases, however, it is difficult to

think of Weber's major concepts separately. Indeed, Weber was clearly aware that class, status and party usually come together, but he was arguing that the degree to which they intersect is an empirical question. It is this issue which C. Wright Mills addresses in *The Power Elite* (1956) when he tries to demonstrate the interlocking of the political, military and economic elites in America.

John Porter (1965) tried to put these ideas to the test in Canada in his examination of the relationships among the economic elite, labour elite, political elite, bureaucratic elite and what he calls the ideological elites who dominate the media, higher education and organized religion. More recently, as described in Chapter 10, many theorists and researchers on power have concentrated almost exclusively on the economic (corporate) elite, presumably because economic power underlies any other form of power; indeed economic power is seen as the only power.

Power is one of the trickiest notions in sociology because it has been used to describe so many different things. We are all likely to understand the notion at the level of everyday life. Children know the power of their parents; employees the power of their bosses; students the power of their teachers, and so on. We know that there are people who have more influence over our actions than we have over theirs. We also know that there are a number of people who, because of their status, can influence us to do even what we do not wish to do. And, as we have described, probably all of us have encountered the power of bureaucrats who can make recourse to official practice to justify their cavalier treatment of us. All of these examples have in common the ability of the "powerful" to mobilize resources, as Weber described them, economic resources, status resources and political resources (practices). At the same time, this kind of power is situation specific and depends in large part on our own volition. Such power is not absolute and it is exerted within the existing social structure.

At another level, and as our discussion of the state and capitalism in Chapter 10 suggests, power has been used to describe the ability of some groups actually to shape the structure and direction of society. More precisely, power in this usage refers to the ability of some groups to shape society in their own best interests. Some American sociologists have argued that there is no single "power elite", but rather a plurality of "veto groups," each with its own sphere of interests and whose power is highly constrained by the competition of elites and by the need of these elites to enlist the support of the public. David Reissman calls these elites veto groups because they act only when their particular interests are challenged.

Against this, Marxist and neo-Marxist theorists argue that there is a single unified elite that can at times act in concert to promote and defend its shared interests. While it may at times appear that there are a number of elite groups and that they are in conflict with one another, these theorists argue that this may only be true for relatively trivial issues, those which do not represent a fundamental threat to the existing social structure. As the research in this tradition shows, there cannot be very serious conflict between these elites because to a large extent they are indistinguishable from one another; there is a high degree of interpenetration between elites, what Leo Panitch (1977) calls a "confraternity of power." In other words, powerful people in one sphere either sit on the governing bodies of other spheres or they have relatives who do so.

Because of the very nature of power itself, this debate is far from resolved. We have seen something of this debate in Chapter 10 where we considered recent research on the relationship between the corporate elite and the state. The debate goes on because power is the least known aspect of stratification. As Mills (1956) has shown, it is hidden in at least partial secrecy. People who seem to be part of the power elite may deny it. Some, perhaps believing their own propaganda and the prevailing ideology, fail to recognize how much power they do in fact possess.

Moreover, the most that researchers such as Porter, Clement and Panitch and their critics, such as Ornstein, can do is locate those who they *think* have power by virtue of their position. But because they have only limited access to these "higher circles" (the boardrooms of large corporations, the inner group around a prime minister), we generally obtain only glimpses, only circumstantial evidence, of how power is distributed and employed. In short, it is relatively easy to determine people's class situation and status situation; it is less easy to determine how much power goes with these positions.

Marx and Weber were both in somewhat different ways emphasizing how inequality and conflict are closely related. Marx concentrated on the inherent conflict existing between those who own private property and capital and those who do not. And, he was optimistic that with the end of private property would come the end of conflict and the beginnings of a cooperative society.

Weber, though a very sympathetic critic of Marx, did not share his optimism that the end of capitalism and its basic forms of inequality would bring about utopia. Perhaps because he lived and wrote at a later time than Marx, Weber saw socialism as likely to create a "dictatorship of officials" rather than a "dictatorship of the proletariat" and in this, he anticipated the growth of monopoly capitalism, the welfare state and the "knowledge society."

Marx offers us the optimistic vision that with the end of class inequality will come the end of alienation and conflict. Weber provides us with the bleak picture that under any form of society, people are in a constant and inevitable struggle, not only for wealth, but also for status and power and, in his view, this could not be changed simply by abolishing private property. Weber's perspective on stratification suggests that status is not a passive characteristic of groups. Rather, status groups attempt to appropriate or have a monopoly over certain symbols, lifestyles, occupations, and kinds of education both to protect and expand their own special interests (Grabb, 1984).

THE FUNCTIONAL THEORY OF STRATIFICATION

An alternative and more benign view of social stratification was first expressed by two American sociologists, Kingsley Davis and Wilbert Moore, in the 1940s (Davis and Moore, 1945). The functional theory of stratification begins with an argument that many people might make if they wished to defend inequality.

All societies, they argue, must have a way of assigning people to the various positions or occupations in a society. Once allocated to a position, people must be motivated to perform their roles adequately. If all positions were equally important or if everyone were equally talented, then it would not matter much who did which job. But, say Davis and Moore, this is not the case. Talent is scarce. Some positions are more important or functional for the survival of a society. Some jobs which must be done are more demanding, requiring more skills and more training.

In short, the functional theory holds that a society must offer differential rewards as incentives to get people to take on these jobs and to carry them our properly. Davis and Moore suggest that these rewards will consist of money, prestige and leisure. These rewards go with the position itself and are viewed as independent of particular individuals. Moreover, there is, in most societies, a high degree of consensus about the appropriateness of these inequalities in rewards. In contrast to the Marxist perspective, inequality from a functionalist perspective is viewed not only as inevitable but as necessary or *functional* for the survival of any society:

Social inequality is thus an unconsciously evolved device by which societies insure that the most important positions are conscientiously filled by the most qualified persons. Hence every society, no matter how simple or complex, must differentiate persons in terms of both prestige and esteem and must therefore possess a certain amount of institutionalized inequality (Davis, 1948:367–38).

Most sociologists now regard the Davis-Moore argument as a "rationalization" for inequality more than it is a theory of inequality and have levelled a number of criticisms at it. The first is that it is difficult, if not impossible, to say for certain which are the more important positions in society. Are lawyers more important than farmers? Are accountants more valuable than coal miners? Can we make the functionalist assumption that values and norms are so widely shared and that there is a good deal of consensus about what constitutes the grounds for inequality and what positions are most important? From the functionalist perspective, these judgements are assumed to be part of most people's socialization; people will have internalized values which hold that, for instance, a doctor is entitled to more social honour and more income than a factory worker. To hold a different view is therefore to be inadequately or improperly socialized.

Conflict theorists do not necessarily deny that these values or moral judgements are widely shared by members of a society. They ask, however, *whose* value judgements are likely to dominate? Where do these values come from? Whose definition of the situation determines what is thought to be an important or valuable position? In short, institutionalization of inequality simply shows how successful the more powerful may be in justifying their privileged positions.

A second criticism is that even if the importance of a position could somehow be established, there is no guarantee that the "best" people are in fact recruited to these positions. As we have already seen, high status families will want to pass advantages on to their children, thus creating social stratification rather than social inequality based around meritocracy. As a result, "important" positions may, and until recently, certainly, be reserved for those born into high status positions and be closed to talented members of lower social strata. Davis and Moore, then, neglected to consider the dysfunctions—the negative consequences — that may accompany the supposed positive functions of inequality. And, as with most functionalists they, therefore, ignore or downplay the importance of structured inequality, of social classes and their relationship to one another.

Finally, many critics have posed the question of how unequal the rewards need to be in order to motivate people to carry out society's tasks. The answer is that we don't know. Some occupational groups, because they have earned more in the past, expect to do so in the future and are dissatisfied if they don't. Some, such as the medical profession, have secured a monopoly on the services they provide and therefore have a great deal of control over what they are paid. What does seem clear is that functionalism cannot provide us with an adequate explanation of the extremes in income or for the increasing concentration of wealth in capitalist societies. Except in satirical terms, it is difficult to imagine why poverty is functional in any society.

We include this brief description of the functionalist theory of stratification not because we believe it to be a strong rebuttal to either Marx's or Weber's analyses but because it is so central to the ideology of capitalism, to the liberal and conservative ideology. And, while it may, by now, seem to you that sociological theories are rather abstract and have little to do with everyday life, the functional theory of stratification, or at least its basic assumptions about inequality, has shaped our thinking about poverty, what we think should be the functions of education and how, in general, we define a just society.

ISSUES AND DEBATES

These theories of stratification we have just described fall on different sides of the debate that introduced the chapter, and each theory points to different kinds of research. Marxist theories direct us to the types of questions that emerge from an examination of inequality of condition. Some researchers influenced by Marx have focused on *power*; who has it and how much do they have? Others have studied poverty, emphasizing the sharp economic disparities in capitalist societies and the social and social-psychological consequences of inequality. And, all have sought to understand present-day capitalist societies in terms of class and class relations.

Functionalism has been the most important influence on liberal sociologists. Their concern has been to establish the degree of *inequality of opportunity* in any society and the social and social-psychological consequences of blocked mobility. These functionalist, particularly American sociologists, have chosen largely to ignore the very top and bottom of the stratification system. They have often ignored questions of poverty by defining it away. And, attached as they were to the functionalist view of inequality, they were uncomfortable with concepts such as power and class inequality and, for a time, denied that there were social classes in American or Canadian society. Rather, they focused on the status and income differences, the cultures and lifestyles, of the large middle mass of "classless" individuals and viewed poverty as a temporary problem. They drew upon Weber's discussion of status but largely ignored his conception of society as one of struggle and of conflict between competing groups or classes.

Many sociologists, John Porter, for example, have been influenced by both Marx, Weber and the functionalists. And, more recent theories about social inequality have, while usually rejecting the functionalist perspective, attempted to use the insights and perspective of both Marx and Weber to understand the class structure of advanced capitalist societies. There are all sorts of problems and no easy solutions since it appears that both Marx and Weber were, in different ways, correct in their analyses. Monopoly capitalism has brought about the existence of a bourgeoisie, a capitalist class, which, through its decisions and its power over the state and the economy has consequences for all of us in our everyday life and in our precarious hold on the life and future of this planet. But, monopoly capitalism has also brought about groups of workers who do not fit neatly into any Marxist category. And, it is here that Weber makes his contribution because he recognized that many of the struggles, the conflict, would not be between capitalists and labour but between the intermediate groups—managers and professionals—who owe allegiance to neither.

To confuse things further, we live in an era of monopoly capitalism but much of our wealth comes from small-scale entrepreneurs —farmers, fishers, small business people—all of whom enter into relationships of exploitation but none of whom can, individually, perhaps even collectively, exert much power over the direction of our society. In present day Canadian society we have both big capitalists and little capitalists.

Where, for example, do we place farmers in the class structure? What, as a class, are their interests? On the one hand, farmers have generally been exploited and their recognition of this has made them, collectively, an important source of populist movements. On the other hand, as "independent" businesspeople, they have tended to see their interests as divergent from and antagonistic to those of labour. Moreover, the different organization of farming from urban businesses and professions means that they can't be treated like other middle-class groups. And we should keep in mind that the relationship of various groups to the class structure is a changing one; what was true of farmers, or professionals, or small business owners under industrial capitalism, may be quite different with the growth of monopoly capitalism. And, we could make a similar argument about fishers, who are sometimes capitalists and sometimes labour and sometimes in between.

We have already discussed some of the complexities of the professional and managerial class and how to fit them into a class system of stratification. As Weber foresaw, we have a large part of the labour force engaged in activities that do not fit neatly into either the capitalist class or the working class. One of your authors, for example, is a university professor and the other is a government bureaucrat. Where do we fit into the Marxist class structure?

To answer these kinds of questions, modern theorists have had to draw upon both Marx and Weber. Marx has provided them with a means to understand the larger picture, how concentration of wealth, the ownership of the means of production, shapes our society, its particular ideology and its relationship with other societies. But, Weber has allowed us to see how, within that big framework, we carve out our advantaged or disadvantaged position. And, as we see in the following chapters, how ascribed factors such as ethnicity and supposedly achieved factors such as education, are ways in which groups use these resources to maintain or improve their position within this capitalist framework.

CLASS INEQUALITY IN CANADA

What we believe is the nature of class in Canada depends, partly, on what questions we ask, on which portion of the stratification system we are focusing upon and whether our interest is in social status, wealth and power, or poverty. Figure 11.2 provides a rough picture of the stratification profile of capitalist

societies, including Canada. At the top are the rich and the tiny minority that comprises the Canadian economic and social elite. At the other extreme are the 10 percent to 35 percent of the population who, depending where we draw the line, find themselves living below or at the "poverty line."

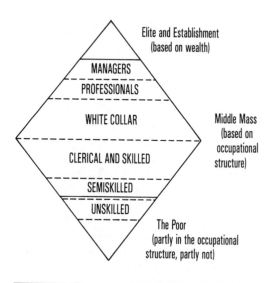

FIGURE 11.2

STRATIFICATION IN CAPITALIST SOCIETIES

We find Figure 11.2 a useful way to show you how sociologists have asked questions about social stratification. But we hope that our discussions in this and the previous chapter will have made you aware that this is not, nor is it intended to be, an accurate or comprehensive depiction of the class structure of capitalist society. Indeed, as we have mentioned, there remains considerable debate about what such a depiction would and should look like. Certainly, this figure leaves out some of the most interesting but as yet unresolved questions about the relationship between sexual, ethnic and class inequality and the way all three have changed as capitalism has changed.

When we look at the top of Figure 11.2, we are asking questions about power: the concentration of wealth and the ownership of the means of production in Canadian society. When we look at the bottom of the diamond we are asking questions about powerlessness: the inability of the poor, individually or collectively, to create change and to improve their own and their children's life chances. Many sociologists, however, have ignored top and bottom, treating their society as one large middle class. Just as Canadians generally may often be blinded to the top and bottom of the stratification system, so too may sociologists be blinded to the issues of power and poverty by the perspective that they have adopted and their background assumptions. Nevertheless, although sociologists who concentrate on questions of status and income difference do not capture the structure of stratification, they do tell us a good deal about the middle mass and about inequality as it is expressed in our everyday lives.

INEQUALITY OF CONDITION: THE MIDDLE MASS

OCCUPATION

One of the first questions we are likely to ask of a stranger is what he does for a living. Occupation tells us generally what to expect from a person, how much a *man* earns, how well he is educated, where he is likely to live and what his standing is likely to be in the community. To learn that a man has been given a large promotion is to assume that he will also move up a step or two in the social hierarchy. Unemployment may mean downward mobility. Occupations are perhaps the best single indicator of status or power within the middle mass (Runciman, 1968).

Note, however, only recently have we learned to ask a woman the same question.

We have been more hesitant to assume that her occupation provides us with the full story. We have been more likely to ask her marital status. If married, we may have wanted to know, as well, what her husband does for a living. If single we wondered about her father's occupation before deciding where she fits in the class structure. **Occupational prestige**, it seems, has worked differently for women than it has for men.

The tradition that the man is the head of the household and the woman is the dependent dies hard. The result is that women who do work and have careers are still categorized on the basis of their husband or father; they are not accorded status in terms of their own achievements. As Margrit Eichler (1973) has shown, women are subject to a kind of double ranking. When they participate in the labour force they derive, as do men, an independent status from their occupation but with an additional factor, "femaleness," included. At the same time, they also have a derived or dependent status based on the male to whom they are attached.

The dependent status of women emerges most clearly when we consider the unpaid position of housewife. A later study by Eichler (1977) finds that while people on average rank housewife at about the same level as stenographer and typist, there is considerable discrepancy in responses. Table 11.1 (on the following page), taken from this study, shows that people by and large regard housewives as deriving their status from their husbands. The prestige of a housewife married to a physician (81.5) is almost comparable to that of a female university professor (82.9). In short, our measures of social class apply mostly to men and to the family. The problem of how to measure the position women hold independently in the class structure is as yet unresolved, and perhaps will remain so until women are accorded full equality with men.

More generally, it seems people mean several things when they talk about the "prestige" of an occupation. Some, certainly use

TABLE 11.1

MEAN PRESTIGE SCORES OF HOUSEWIVES WITH HUSBANDS' OCCUPATIONS SPECIFIED

Housewife whose husband is a physician	81.5	170
Housewife whose husband is a social worker	62.5	170
Housewife whose husband is a plumber	57.2	171
Housewife whose husband is a commercial farmer	56.4	171
Housewife whose husband is an elevator operator	37.1	172

Source: Eichler (1973:162).

the Davis-Moore argument and give high prestige to the jobs they think of as most useful to the community or which they think require the most skills and training. Others put more emphasis on the income the jobs earn. For still others, the main criterion is how pleasant and interesting the job is or how much autonomy it offers. As it happens, the specific criteria do not seem to matter very much; in the end people come up with what on average are similar rankings of the prestige of occupations.

For example, Pineo's and Porter's Canadian study of occupational prestige yielded a scale fairly similar to what researchers have found in the United States, Britain, and elsewhere (Pineo and Porter, 1967). Blishen, in 1967, again in 1976 and in 1986, has measured the socio-economic status of occupations by adding an average income and educational level to prestige. There is close agreement between his scale and the Pineo-Porter scale. Table 11.2 gives Blishen scores for some selected occupations as of 1986.

We should stop here, for a moment to consider what all this means. At first glance, these scales do seem to be providing straight facts, apparently straightforward, objective data about people's values and preferences. There should be no debate about what they tell us. But what do they tell us? Once again, ideology affects how we answer. Functionalists, for example, have usually taken these scales as empirical evidence of what they have assumed all along: there is a considerable degree of value consensus in society gener-

ally and in particular about the grounds for and appropriateness of social inequality.

TABLE 11.2

BLISHEN SCORES FOR SELECTED OCCUPATIONS

OCCUPATION	SCORE
Dentists	101.74%
Physicians and Surgeons	101.32
Judges and Magistrates	93.27
University Teachers	75.87
Managers	71.6
Architects	68.12
Elementary School Teachers	63.44
Police Officers	58.77
Real Estate Salespersons	49.99
Carpenters	34.86
Cashiers and Tellers	28.31
Farmers	27.92

Source: Blishen, Carroll and Moore (1987)

From the conflict perspective, however, these scales are simply an illustration of how the powerful are able to impose their values on the rest of us. This perspective suggests that we should not be too surprised by the "fact" that people are in general agreement about occupational prestige. Canadians, like their counterparts in other capitalist societies, have since childhood been told what are the appropriate or relevant criteria for evaluating occupations (Baldus and Tribe, 1978). We have learned that professions are "superior," more "functional," more "necessary" than trade; that white-collar work is "better" than blue-collar work and so on. We do not need to know much about a specific occupation in order to rank it. Pineo and Porter found, for example, that many people could rank fictitious occupations such as "biologer" and "archaeopotrist".

However, researchers find important differences when people are first asked to rank occupations the way they think most people would and then as they personally feel. Many manual workers feel lawyers and accountants are overrated and coal miners and farmers are not given their just due. Some would turn the whole status hierarchy on its head. Others would like to do away with it entirely. It seems that while people know what the ideology tells them they should think — what are the relevant criteria — those in the lower classes have not always internalized the values of the upper classes. They know the ideology but they haven't necessarily bought it.

▌ WOMEN AND SOCIAL CLASS

As we have seen in previous chapters, one of the main changes in the occupational structure is the dramatic increase in participation of women in the Canadian labour force: from about 22 percent in 1931 to just over 56 percent in 1986. By contrast, over this same period, male participation rates declined from 87 percent to about 77 percent (Krahn and Lowe, 1988:40). It is fairly obvious, however, that women do not earn as much from their work as do men. Women who work full time in Canada in 1988 earned, on the average, about 65 percent as much as male full time workers, a figure which has remained fairly constant over the last 15 to 20 years. And, while more women have entered higher paying occupations the same and often larger gaps between women and men's earnings persist. Krahn and Lowe conclude "that in even the most lucrative occupations, being a female increases the probability of receiving a lower salary" (1988:137).

Traditionally these discrepancies have been rationalized by employers, males and often sociologists, by arguing that women may justifiably be paid less because theirs is a second income. This, of course, ignores the many women who choose not to marry, have not yet married, have divorced or have been widowed or deserted—any of whom may suffer economic hardship because of this second income assumption. More generally, and more fundamentally, the notion of "second income" reflects the lower status of women in our society, that so many of us will virtually automatically think of the husband as the breadwinner and the wife as one who works for the pleasure, the diversion or the extra frills. On the contrary, the ongoing research by Pat and Hugh Armstrong (1983 and 1984) and Pat Connelly (1979) shows quite conclusively that women work for the same reasons as men; not to "fulfill themselves" but because they must.

So pervasive is sexual inequality that some sociologists argue that along with the other dimensions of stratification we also need to think in terms of sexual stratification. They point to such facts as that two-fifths (38.7 percent in 1986) of female single parents have family incomes that put them and their children below the poverty line as evidence that women form a kind of underclass in Canadian society.

However, as we have suggested, these are issues of inequality, not issues of stratification. That is, while women at all levels of the class structure are worse off than men at equivalent levels, there is almost as much inequality among women as there is among men. Moreover, as the Family History Survey finds, the status of lone parent is on average of relatively short duration, ranging from 4.4 years on average to 5.3 years, depending on what brought about lone parenting: women enter into new unions or the children leave home (Moore, 1988). Women, in our view, do not form a class in any sociologically meaningful sense. And to talk of sexual stratification is to ignore, also, the element of continuity — the ability of the dominant class to pass on wealth, power and privilege through the family.

If we forget, for the moment, the discrepancies between male and female incomes, we can view the problem in structural terms, as an outcome of our particular form of stratification. Most jobs in capitalist society are "low-class" jobs. Most men, as well as most women, in the labour force hold jobs of low income and low prestige. As more women enter the labour force, it is these jobs they will be taking; equality with men in the labour force means that most women will be getting the same kinds of "bad" jobs as most men.

Clearly, income discrepancies between men and women in the same occupation are a social injustice that cannot be tolerated. But we are asking whether there is not a much larger question facing the women's movement and all others who seek greater equality: Is equality between males and females the primary issue or is it, as we believe, more important to ask about capitalism more generally?

To say this is not to imply, as does much of the recent work on sexual inequality and discrimination, that nothing short of a social revolution will end sexism. To link Marxism and feminism, to assume that patriarchy is a necessary component of capitalism, is perhaps to introduce an unwarranted degree of pessimism. It is apparent that patriarchy has obvious benefits (positive functions) for capitalism. Within the home, women's domestic labour — maintenance, nurturing children, looking after husbands — indirectly produces surplus value for the capitalist. And as women increasingly find it necessary to work outside the home, patriarchy adds to their vulnerability; as we have seen, they find themselves, more often than not, part of the marginal work world — a segment of the reserve army of labour of capitalist society.

But a sexist ideology cannot be explained by capitalism alone. For one thing, sexism seems to be much older than capitalism and may even have its roots in the now fairly irrelevant differences in biological functions of men and women. So, rather than "inventing" patriarchy, capitalists appropriated it both because it continued to legitimate male domination and because it was apparently good for profits. For another, we have only faith to support the assumption that socialism would mean an end to sexism.

Child labour, long working hours, laws against collective bargaining and other unpleasant features of nineteenth century capitalism were also profitable. But these were changed largely through piecemeal reforms. To repeat, it is wrong to underestimate the flexibility of capitalism to incorporate a wide variety of changes within the system as long as these do not affect the basic structure of private property and concentration of wealth and power. In other words, equal pay for equal work, better day care facilities, greater equality within families and between men and women generally are goals that need not wait for a socialist revolution.

INCOME INEQUALITY

The structural approach becomes even more relevant when we consider the extent of income inequality in Canada. Again, we should emphasize that income studies do not directly tell us about the concentration of wealth, the ownership of the means of production or capital or, for that matter, about discrete social classes. Nor are such data easily come by; although wages and salaries are almost completely reported, investment income may be unreported by as much as 50 percent.

Nevertheless, even from these more narrowly defined studies, it is evident that there are marked inequalities in Canadian society. This is most effectively seen when we divide the population up into quintiles, equal fifths of the population. If everyone earned roughly the same in Canadian society, each quintile would receive roughly 20 percent (one-fifth) of the total income. This is most emphatically not the case in Canada. Table 11.3 and Figures 11.3 (below) and 11.4 (on the next page) show that the bottom one-fifth of the Canadian population receives only 6 percent of the total income; the bottom 40 percent receives only about 19 percent. At the top end, 20 percent of the population earns nearly 40 percent (38.0 percent) of the total income. There are even larger gaps for unattached individuals. Nor have these distributions changed much over the years, although there has been some improvement for low income groups since the 1960s and 1970s.

The main response to this persistent inequality in income distribution and growing impoverishment has been a large increase in the number of wives in lower income families working outside the home. Pat and Hugh Armstrong (1984:174) show that over the last thirty years, there has been steadily increasing inequality in income distribution between individual wage earners. Those in the bottom three quintiles received decreasing shares of the total income while, at the same time, those in the top two quintiles increased their shares.

TABLE 11.3

SHARES OF TOTAL INCOME BY INCOME QUINTILE, 1951 AND 1986

	FAMILIES		UNATTACHED INDIVIDUALS	
	1951	1986	1951	1986
lowest quintile	6.1%	6.3%	2.7%	5.3%
second quintile	12.9	12.3	8.9	10.4
middle quintile	17.4	17.9	16.1	15.3
fourth quintile	22.4	24.1	25.8	24.2
highest quintile	41.1	39.4	46.6	44.7
top/bottom	6.7	6.3	17.3	8.4

Source: Table B.C., National Council of Welfare (1989:106).

FIGURE 11.4

SHARE OF TOTAL INCOME, UNATTACHED INDIVIDUALS, BY INCOME QUINTILE, 1951 AND 1986

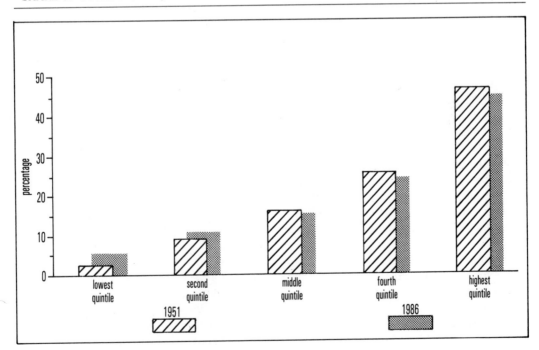

Source: National Council of Welfare (1989: 104).

FIGURE 11.3

SHARE OF TOTAL INCOME, FAMILIES, BY INCOME QUINTILE, 1951 AND 1986

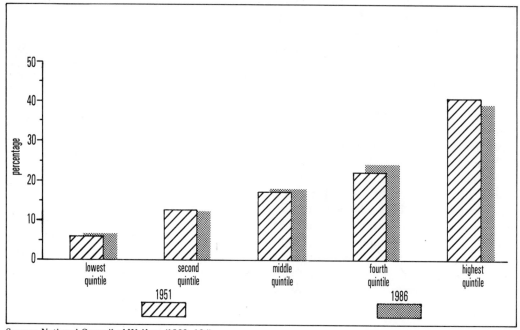

Source: National Council of Welfare (1989: 104).

But, the distribution of family income has changed very little between 1971 and 1986. The two lowest quintiles have held their own and experienced little or no change in their share of total income while the middle groups increased their share. The top quintile had, by 1981, experienced a slight decline in its share of total income. The Armstrongs argue that the reason for the slightly different pattern for families is that wives work in order to help the family maintain its financial position. The steadily increasing proportions of dual income families camouflages the increasing impoverishment and income inequality occurring among individuals, whether male or female.

Of course, quintiles are a sociologist's device for making income comparisons. Nevertheless, it is safe to say that at least the bottom quintile does constitute a unique category. This quintile is below the poverty line. There are various definitions of the poverty line and it is evident that the definition we choose will determine whether we believe there to be a great deal or very little poverty in Canada. In turn, the definition we feel most comfortable with is linked to our ideology.

POVERTY IN CANADA

Conservatives are likely to conceive of poverty in **absolute** terms and, in their more extremist positions, to argue that, compared to the situation of many in the Third World, there is no poverty in Canada. In its more modest, and perhaps, common-sense terms, an absolute definition of poverty leads us to ask whether people have enough money for "essentials" such as food, clothing and shelter. The difficulty, of course, is in determining what is a necessity and what is a luxury. In the absence of good public transportation, should we view a car as luxury or necessity?

Liberals, for the most part, have also conceived of poverty in absolute terms. But, once having established a poverty line, they have argued that with economic growth everyone can be pulled above that line, that poverty can be eradicated.

Socialists, while certainly concerned about absolute poverty, have generally conceived of poverty in *relative* terms and, as we have just seen, made as their focus how unequally income is distributed in Canadian society. From this perspective, estimates of the cost of basic necessities of food, clothing and shelter and how many cannot afford these, tell us only part of the picture if, with increasing affluence, necessities for more affluent Canadians include a car, a television, a VCR, vacations, and a university education for their children.

Even though we can take comfort that few Canadians live in the abject poverty of the Third World, relative definitions of poverty remind us that as long as there is inequality in incomes, people may face both absolute poverty and, more often, perhaps, the relative deprivation of living in an affluent society where there remain such large differences in discretionary income.

But, for those focusing on relative poverty, there is also the value question of how much inequality of income distribution we are willing to tolerate. And, whereas economic growth in principle could mean the "end of absolute poverty," unless there is equality of income distribution, the proportion of people living in relative poverty won't change whether there is growth or recession.

Statistics Canada and, in turn, the National Council of Welfare have, through establishing poverty lines (absolute poverty) and patterns of income distribution (relative poverty), attempted to take into account both of these definitions of poverty though, clearly, the focus is mainly on determining the number of Canadians in absolute poverty. The poverty line (low income line) is defined as the point where 58.5 percent of incomes goes to food, clothing and shelter. This figure comes from the finding that Canadian families spend, on average, 38.5 percent of their income on these basic necessities. The poverty line is set where 58.5 (20 percentage points above the average) goes to the essentials of life (National Council of Welfare, 1988:1). These estimated poverty lines differ both by family size and community size. They are adjusted annually to take into account changes in the cost of living.

As Table 11.4 shows, at the end of the 1960s, 23 percent of Canadians were below the poverty line. By 1986, and after some

TABLE 11.4
POVERTY TRENDS, 1969–1986

	FAMILIES		UNATTACHED INDIVIDUALS		ALL PERSONS	
	POVERTY RATE	NUMBER	POVERTY RATE	NUMBER	POVERTY RATE	NUMBER
1969	20.8%	1 002 000	42.8%	693 000	23.1%	4 851 000
1979	13.1	788 000	40.3	1 011 000	15.7	3 728 000
1980	12.2	745 000	39.6	1 041 000	15.1	3 475 000
1981	12.0	768 000	37.8	962 000	14.7	3 495 000
1982	13.2	869 000	37.4	998 000	16.1	3 897 000
1983	14.0	924 000	41.3	1 091 000	17.1	4 155 000
1984	14.5	972 000	37.8	1 026 000	17.3	4 214 000
1985	13.3	908 000	36.8	1 009 000	16.0	3 951 000
1986	**12.2**	**851 000**	**34.3**	**982 000**	**14.9**	**3 689 000**
Percentage Change:						
1969/86	−40.9%	−15.1%	−19.9%	41.7%	−35.5%	−24.0%
1980/86	0.8	14.2	−13.4	−5.7	−1.3	6.2
1985/86	−7.5	−6.3	−6.8	−2.7	−6.9	−6.6

Source: National Council of Welfare (1989:7).

increases during the recession of the 1980s, the poverty rate for families had fallen to 14.9 percent. While over three and a half million Canadians are still living below the poverty line, the incidence of poverty, using this arbitrary definition, was cut by one-third from 1969 to 1986.

These average figures mask the considerable differences by region and sex. Poverty rates, for families in 1986, ranged from 21.2 percent in Newfoundland to 8.7 percent in Ontario. And, approximately four in ten families (38.7 percent) headed by women live in poverty compared to about one in ten (9.0 percent) led by men. Similarly, more than half, some 56 percent of female single parents, compared to 23 percent of male single parents, lived in poverty in 1986 (National Council of Welfare, 1988).

As those in these government agencies who produce these estimates are quick to acknowledge, their statistics do not capture fully the extent of poverty in Canada and are highly conservative estimates of the poverty rate. First, they do not tell us just how far below these poverty lines many Canadians are located and, instead, tell us only the upper limit of the lower income population. For example, a single mother on income assistance with one child is estimated to have a total family income, which depending on province and size of community, is 59 to 84 percent of the 1986 poverty line. Similarly, those working for minimum wage are, by definition part of the working poor. After deductions, a minimum wage worker in, say, Halifax, would have take home pay that is only 68 percent of the poverty line for that size of city. If he is "supporting" a family he or she will fare even worse.

Second, before we congratulate ourselves on the apparent reduction in poverty in Canada, we must also ask how much have expectations changed since 1969. To take what may be a trivial example, Canadians, on average, eat about one-third of their meals outside of the home. Obviously, they do so in establishments that range from fast food out-lets to the dimly lit and expensive. The poor family, subsisting for part of each month on Kraft Dinner and what the food banks offer, seldom can afford the occasional convenience of a McDonald's or Pizza Delite and never the quality and ambience of a Hy's Steak House.

Finally, a relative definition of poverty suggests that the region or context in which poor people find themselves will affect how they feel about their poverty. As we have just seen, Ontario has the lowest poverty rate, Newfoundland the highest. One of your authors lives in Fredericton, by New Brunswick standards, an affluent city, travels frequently to St. John's also relatively affluent compared to the rest of Newfoundland and recently spent a year in Toronto, one of the most affluent cities in Canada. In the first context, he feels average, in the second, relatively privileged and, in the third (where the Mercedes, BMWs and other cars all costing about the same as his Fredericton house seemed to be everywhere) impoverished. How much more acute and real must these feelings be for those living in Toronto who must cope with a much lower wage than enjoyed by professors?

Are there solutions to poverty? Can poverty be eradicated. In principle, if not practice, it is possible that economic growth and increasing affluence might lift everyone above some arbitrarily defined level of basic subsistence. But, the fact that the media have had to invent the notion of the "yuppie culture" and the more cynical notion of "DINK's" (Double Income, No Kids) it is apparent that the standards of what constitutes middle class life do not remain at some constant level. So, we should not expect that, in the minds of most Canadians who are poor, an acceptable poverty line is one established 20 years ago and changed only to reflect changes in the cost of living which, in any event, only partially reflect their everyday costs of subsistence. As a *Globe and Mail Report on Business* pointed out, while costs of things purchased mainly by the affluent have risen modestly during the 1980s, everyday things from popsicles to pizzas, to disposable diapers to a case of beer, have risen much more dramatically and it's these costs rather than airline fares or holidays in Bermuda or ski lift tickets that affect the poor the most.

But, even if we could produce the economic growth to provide everyone with what we, today, conceive of as the middle class standard of living, there remains the problem that, as we have seen in Chapter 8, such unprecedented economic expansion carries with it greater devastation to our fragile environment. And, there are few who would question that, at the present population level of the world, raising of the "have-not nations" to the level of affluence of the advanced industrial nations would severely overtax the carrying capacity of the world and probably mean the end of planet earth.

Logically there is a need within societies and between societies to bring about greater equality of condition. Within societies this means a drastic redistribution of income through taxation or, more generally, greater equality in incomes to begin with. Between societies this means a massive increase in foreign aid and, at the same time—at least until such time as we have reduced world population—an also drastic lowering of expectations among the richer nations as to what constitutes an adequate standard of living.

But, understandably, these are not "solutions" that sit at all well with most who can count themselves among the "haves," including, if the truth be known, your present authors, both of whom would, in the interests of social justice, find it difficult to give up their relatively comfortable life styles. As with most in the academic community who view themselves as socialists, we are like alcoholics who know and are afraid of what drinking is doing to their health but are just as afraid of what we see as the rather bleak and boring life without booze. We know, in other words, what constitutes social justice and a more utopian society but we are, like most Canadians, reluctant to suffer the personal consequences —the changes in our lifestyles—of bringing about the better society.

And, of course, most Canadians are not socialists and are not even vexed by these issues of personal sacrifice to improve the lot of everyone. An increase in taxes, if it affects the better off, or corporations is rarely welcomed. Pressures for greater equality in incomes of Canadians is simply viewed as envy and "ressentiment" that some should earn so much more than others and as undermining the work ethic. At the same time, it is worth noting that even those who are unabashedly capitalists question whether anyone is worth the kind of income paid to some executives (often of failing enterprises) and to sports figures and so on. Even capitalists, at times, wonder about how much inequality of income is tolerable and just.

Whether defined in absolute or relative terms or something in between, it is apparent that the welfare system and "progressive" taxation have done little to alter inequalities in the distribution of income in Canada. This is not to suggest that the policies that do exist have not mattered. The Canadian poor would be much worse off without the existing programs, particularly during the economic crisis of the early 1980s. But, as we described in Chapter 10, the most that the state has been able to do is to maintain some degree of stability through the various ups and downs of capitalism, of the business cycle.

In any case, none of these "solutions" come to grips with the real meaning of poverty. While at the common-sense level poverty obviously means lack of money, it is more useful to view the poor as those unable to mobilize resources, those who are not heard. Few studies in Canada have explored the social-psychological consequences of poverty; nevertheless, the army of unemployed and those in the "marginal work world" must face material deprivation and instability and the widespread belief that poverty is an individual problem, the result of individual inadequacy. The poor must also live with a future that promises no improvement and with the probably realistic picture that they will die poor and pass on their poverty to their children.

SOCIAL MOBILITY IN CANADA

The conventional answer in North America to poverty and inequality has been to try to ensure the opportunity for upward social mobility. There have been two streams in this liberal solution. The first is based in the "rags to riches myth," the Horatio Alger stories, the notion that "anyone can make a million." If people work hard, have the right values and perhaps a bit of luck, they can rise to the top. Sociologists have called movement up or down the stratification system within one's lifetime *intragenerational* or *career* mobility.

A second, somewhat contradictory theme is that everyone should start out the race on an equal basis. This is the *meritocratic* principle that those who win are the best. Social and economic advantages should not be passed on to children. The measure of the extent to which children are able to rise above or fall below the level of their parent is referred to, by sociologists, as *intergenerational* social mobility.

Strictly speaking, people can be mobile upwards or downwards in any one of Max Weber's three dimensions of social stratification—class, status, or power. In fact the third dimension, power, has not received very much attention for the same reasons outlined earlier in the chapter — it is difficult to pin down and measure. Rather, most sociological interest in mobility has centred on changes in "class" situation (economic mobility) and status situation (changes in prestige) in the middle mass of society.

Indeed, in its fullest sense, social mobility seems to mean that people have experienced both economic mobility and status mobility. They have experienced a change in lifestyle, attitudes, and most crucially, patterns of social relationships. For example, first prize in Super Loto is obviously economic mobility and will certainly affect the winner's life chances, lifestyle, and social life. But will winning a million

dollars make him or her a "millionaire"? Will it give him or her entry into establishment circles?

Peter Newman's *The Canadian Establishment* suggests that in most cases the answer is probably no. Money, it seems, is not enough. On the one hand, it is almost impossible as an adult to shed the habits, viewpoints, tastes and speech patterns of a lifetime for those of another perhaps higher social class. On the other hand, there is the apparently intense desire of those at the top to maintain their exclusivity. Higher status groups may, as they have often done, refuse to accept the *nouveaux riches* on the grounds that their family background is "questionable" or that they went to the "wrong" schools or that they lack "refinement."

Of course, few people come into sudden wealth or, for that matter, have large fortunes to lose. For most, changes in occupation are the result of promotion or demotion or through starting out their work life in a "better" occupational position than their parents. In deciding whether a society is "open" or "closed," the amount of intergenerational mobility is of greatest interest and relevance. However, it is probably intragenerational or career mobility which most people have in mind when they think of "moving up in the world." Generally it seems we base success not so much on how we have fared relative to our parents but on how we have fared over our own lifetime. We look for jobs with a career ladder and with built-in mobility rather than dead-end jobs, those we describe as having "no future."

SOCIAL MOBILITY IN INDUSTRIAL SOCIETY

During the past twenty years a number of countries have carried out mobility studies to determine just how open or closed their society is. The Canadian National Mobility Study by a team of sociologists at Carleton, McMaster, and the University of Waterloo was the first national study of social mobility in Canada. In most cases what these studies actually measure is intergenerational occupational mobility. Since many occupations have a very similar social standing, it is common to think in terms of occupational categories or divisions.

Previous mobility studies have provided us with a remarkably consistent set of findings about trends and rates of social mobility in industrial society. The Canadian Mobility Study contains few surprises and provides a picture for Canada very similar to that found in Britain, the United States, and other industrial societies. (Jones and McRoberts, 1977).

First, most mobility is short distance mobility. It appears that the changes in occupational status which people experience are usually quite modest. Few rise from the very bottom to the very top of the social hierarchy, even fewer make long falls downward. Second, there is less social mobility that there would be if there was complete equality of opportunity. To put that another way, parents' status still influences what happens to sons and daughters. This is especially so at the top (professional, managerial) and at the bottom (unskilled). Both tend to be more "closed," more subject to ascription than are categories towards the middle of the occupational hierarchy.

As the authors of the Canadian Mobility Study point out, with the exception of farmers and small business owners, in industrial societies such as Canada, fathers can seldom directly pass on their occupational positions to their sons. But, they can determine the extent and quality of their son's education and this, in turn, has profound impact on occupational achievement (McRoberts, 1982).

But, while family matters, it seems to do so much less and more indirectly than was perviously believed. Another Canadian mobility study by John Goyder and James Curtis (1977) was able to collect occupational information not only on respondents to the survey and their fathers but also on respondents' grandfathers and sons. This study shows that while fathers' status and sons' status is certainly linked, the relationship is not a strong one, with the result that knowing a father's status, we would be right in predicting the son's status only about 25 percent of the time. Over the four generations, there is a declining relationship between statuses so that by the fourth generation (great grandfathers and great grandsons), there is virtually no relationship between these generations.

Most of what we know about social or occupational mobility has been about men. This is because national mobility studies have usually neglected the mobility patterns of women in the labour force. Monica Boyd (1977a), however, has analysed the data on women interviewed for the Canadian National Mobility Study. She finds that although the gross patterns of female mobility seem to parallel those of males, there are important differences. Because fathers have less influence on the occupational attainment of their daughters than of their sons, it seems that women neither suffer the worst consequences nor reap the greatest benefits of occupational inheritance. That is, women continue to be under represented at the very top and bottom of the occupational structure; they get neither the best jobs nor the worst jobs that Canadian society has to offer.

ELITE MOBILITY

Discussions of mobility are not about the very poor nor are they about the elite, what Peter Newman calls the "Canadian Establishment." The Canadian Mobility Study, for instance, is based on a survey which, for the most part, fails to capture adequately either the top or the bottom of the class structure; the elite because it is so small and inaccessible, the poor because its members are not part of the occupational structure or are difficult to locate and are therefore usually under represented in sample surveys.

Information that we do have on mobility into and out of the elite comes, then, from more specific studies, notably from Porter's *The Vertical Mosaic* (1965) and Wallace Clement's *The Canadian Corporate Elite* (1975). In updating and extending Porter's work, Clement found that, if there is any change, it is towards greater closure, a greater tendency for the Canadian corporate elite to be self-perpetuating. That is, there is a greater chance today that sons, and in more complex ways daughters, will inherit a position in the elite than for the period Porter was examining. Lorne Tepperman (1977a), examined Toronto's elite, historically, and came to similar conclusions. It has apparently been possible for all members of the elite to pass on a similar position to their children. Upward mobility into the elite has occurred. But this is because, with economic growth, there are more elite positions than in the past and not because the top has become more open. People are also able to move upwards into the elite because elite families do not always reproduce themselves or, at least, not at a high enough rate to match the structural changes taking place.

However, more recent research challenges this accepted view of the Canadian elite as so closed and exclusive as these influential studies suggest. Campbell and Szablowski (1979), in their study of "superbureaucrats," conclude that this elite is remarkably open in the sense that there has been considerable mobility into the elite from working class origins. For example, some 44 percent of those studied had fathers who had not completed high school. Part of the difference in the conclusions is that the earlier studies assumed that middle origin can be inferred from a father having a university education. Their interview data suggest that this is not always the case and suggests that if this section of the elite is typical of other sectors, there may be at least twice as much upward mobility as previously believed (Ogmundson, 1982).

These studies, then, simply demonstrate what we have already said about class systems of stratification. In the middle mass of society, social classes are quite open and there is considerable movement in and out of them generationally. Structural changes in the labour force, notably the decline in the numbers engaged in agriculture and manufacturing, have meant considerable mobility, most of which is upward from an economic point of view. To experience that upward mobility, both men and women must usually do so through educational achievements; they must become better educated than their parents rather than simply inherit a position. There seems little doubt that the very rich and powerful have greater resources that allow them to pass on their wealth, power and position to their children. But, apparently, many through entrepreneurship or educational and professional achievements are able to reach these positions starting from relatively humble, though probably not seriously disadvantaged, origins.

CONCLUSION

Previous chapters should have given you the context for understanding the issues of inequality. Inequality and an understanding of it are shaped by the kind of society in which we live. By looking at systems of inequality, we are describing the most important of the human consequences of living in different kinds of societies. We have also tried to show you here that much of what you "know" about class and inequality in Canada is ideological rather than descriptive. It is part of our culture, our common stock of knowledge, to believe that inequality is inevitable, that anyone can make it and that poverty is a sign of personal failure, laziness and ineptitude. It is part of our political culture to translate our vulnerability and alienation into mobility aspirations or, more recently, fatalistic resignation.

If nothing else, then, this chapter should help remind you that social inequality remains a central and important feature of Canadian life and that much of what you believe about inequality in Canada and your own achievements and goals is conditioned by your own class background and by the fact that you live in a dependent capitalist society. At the same time, we remind you that soci- ology is very much premised on the belief that the kinds of analyses we have presented, the kinds of radical critiques and empirical find- ings, can help you transcend the constraints to your perceptions and understandings.

The importance of social inequality should become more evident as you read the remain- ing chapters, all of which focus on some dimension of inequality and responses to it.

III SUGGESTIONS FOR FURTHER READING

Because the issue of inequality is so central to the sociological tradition, there are an enormous number of texts, books and articles which deal directly or indirectly with inequality and social stratification. Most of the suggested readings at the end of Chapters 9 and 10, for example, could as easily have appeared here. Probably the most readable account of the classical theories is Edward Grabb's *Social Inequality: Classic and Contemporary Theorists* (1984). While somewhat dated, we also recommend Frank Parkin's *Class Inequality and Political Order* (1971) and Charles Anderson's *The Political Economy of Social Class* (1974). Dennis Forcese's text, *The Canadian Class Structure* (1980), addresses specifically Canadian issues as does Alfred Hunter's *Class Tells* (1986) and James Curtis's and Sid Gilbert's *Social Inequality in Canada: Patterns, Problems, Policies* (1988). Some of the difficulties of applying a Marxist perspective to stratification in modern Canadian society can be seen in Henry Veltmyer's *The Canadian Class Structure* (1986) and Wallace Clement's *The Challenge of Class Analysis* (1988). A sample of Canadian research on social stratification can be found in James Curtis's and William Scott's *Social Stratification: Canada* (1980), John Harp's and John Hofley's *Structured Social Inequality* (1980) and Allan Moscovitch's and Glenn Drover's *Inequality: Essays on the Political Economy of Social Welfare* (1981). You might also want to look at John Porter's classic study, *The Vertical Mosaic* and the further work in this area done by Wallace Clement in his *The Canadian Corporate Elite* (1975) and by Dennis Olsen in his *The State Elite* (1980). Pat and Hugh Armstrong's *The Double Ghetto* (1984) is a highly readable account of their research on sexual segregation and inequality in the Canadian labour force. See also Pat Connelly's *Last Hired, First Fired* (1979). Detailed findings from the Canadian Mobility Study, including an analysis of female mobility patterns, can be found in Monica Boyd and others' *Ascription and Achievement* (1985).

Tables and statistics give one perspective on class inequality and social mobility. The human side, the personal and social consequences of inequality are caught in a number of works: Ian Adams's *The Poverty Wall* (1971); Terry Copp's historical account of working-class conditions in Montreal, *The Anatomy of Poverty* (1974); Richard Sennett's and Jonathan Cobb's *The Hidden Injuries of Class* (1972). At the other extreme, Peter Newman's *The Canadian Establishment* (1975) gives lively accounts of the personal lives of the Canadian elite.

Anselm L. Strauss's *The Contexts of Social Mobility* (1971) provides a nonstatistical and provocative enquiry into the meaning and nature of social mobility.

EDUCATIONAL INEQUALITY

OVERVIEW

In Chapter 6, we suggested that among the institutions you might study in a sociology course, the family is the one that most directly affects you in everyday life. Clearly, at this point in your life, a close runner up is education. This chapter introduces you to the kinds of questions sociologists of various theoretical persuasions have asked about this institution. Again, as with the family, you will learn that changes within education are intimately linked to changes in industrial and capitalist society. And, in turn, educational change, at times, has an impact on culture and society, on the structure of opportunities and the way in which we think about ourselves as Canadians.

You will not have had to read this chapter to be aware that opportunity and success are, in all modern societies, closely linked to educational achievement. Sociologists who have studied education have mostly been concerned with the extent to which this avenue is open to all. As you will learn, the concern is with how education either breaks down the kinds of barriers to equality discussed in Chapter 11, or perpetuates them.

It follows, then, that most of what you will read in this chapter reflects and describes these kinds of preoccupations. But you should also recognize that, to some extent, relating education to inequality is to emphasize the unintended, perhaps unanticipated consequences of education and, in the process, to tell only part of the story. In reading this chapter you should keep in mind the deeper controversy about what education is all about. Is it a means to an end, a place where we acquire the skills, values, and credentials necessary for a good job? Or is it an end in itself, a place where nonconventional ideas may be preserved, where alternative futures may be imagined and even tried out, where people can develop and learn critical perspectives on society, where people learn to think? In other words, ought education to be vocational or humanistic?

Perhaps the most important issue for you to come to grips with in this chapter is the link between education and social class. There are three questions you should be able to answer at the end of the chapter. First, what have been the implications for education, educators, and students of the liberal functional view of education as job training and a route to upward mobility? Second, what is the impact of the social class background of students on their educational success and experience? And, third, is education, in fact, contributing to making an open class system characterized by more upward and downward social mobility or is the liberal functional model simply a way of justifying and perpetuating the class structure?

We would also remind you, as many students remind us, that education is not simply what happens in schools, colleges and universities. You should be thinking about the implications for you and society of removing from the church, the family, and the community, much of the responsibility for socialization and education.

INTRODUCTION

A few decades ago, a chapter on religion would have seemed more appropriate than one on education. Then, religion (and the family) rather than education was in many ways and at many levels *the* crucial institution, the taken-for-granted aspect of most people's lives. Religion permeated and dominated life from birth to death. For most, exposure to education, if it occurred at all, was short lived. And those who did receive an education would also have found that the two, religion and education, were closely linked; for much of history, religion and education were seen as largely inseparable.

While the financial success of TV Evangelism and the publicity accorded the "sinful behaviour" of some of its "stars" suggests a large following, the fact is that most Canadians are, if not antagonistic, at least indifferent to organized religion. The real "priests" of today's Canadian society are those who have access to "new gods"—those who understand and can pass on secrets of computer science, cost accounting, thermodynamics or system design.

We focus on education, then, because it has to such an extent replaced religion as one of the key institutions of Canadian society. While we can, if we desire, opt out of religion and its influences this is no longer true for education; its impact is too pervasive for us not to be affected, positively or negatively. Much that was previously done by the family — passing on the culture to the next generation, teaching adult skills — is now almost exclusively the province of the educational system.

Education also plays a very central role in what might be called the "total selection process," sifting and sorting people into various roles in the social hierarchy and, more important perhaps, making people accept as just and proper their position in that hierarchy.

The bond between education and occupation grows ever tighter. We have become a "credentials society," one in which knowledge and ability seem not to exist unless there is a degree attached. The main way to move upwards or to avoid downward mobility is through formal education.

A university degree may not any longer mean automatic and immediate employment or guarantee that those with such a degree will not, for a while at least, experience impoverishment. In the preceding chapter we presented some statistics on the extent of poverty in Canada. About 4 percent of families "headed" by a university graduate have incomes below the poverty line. But just under 17 percent (four times as many) families headed by someone with an elementary education fall below this line.

It is understandable, then, that we all have a personal stake in what happens to education. But another reason that it is so central in our thinking and debates is the persistent faith and optimism that educational change and reform can bring about social change and reform. Education may be about jobs but it is also about knowledge, about values, about shaping and developing human nature.

From Plato's time to the present, utopian and social reformers have seen in education a panacea for personal, social and economic ills. They have argued that to create a better society we must first create "better" people and that schooling can potentially put right what parents at times do so badly.

It is at least partly in terms of these goals that we can best understand and evaluate the episodic experiments with open classrooms and non-graded elementary schools, with a myriad of evaluative and teaching devices, with "cafeteria-type" curricula and with "multimedia" approaches. And it is within this context of optimism that education is about more than jobs that we must view the also episodic counter-movements back to a greater emphasis on the "basics," to more structure, to more rigorous standards, the very things seen previously as "restrictive," "repressive" and "discriminatory."

The debate is a complex one with more than two sides. For example, many who oppose the increasing emphasis on job-specific education are simply arguing that to train people to be good citizens and integrated members of society requires that they be provided with more general skills and with the ability to think. Conservatives often worry that these more general skills can be assimilated by only a select few and may be "misused" in a dangerous way by the "masses." A little knowledge, they tell us, is a dangerous thing. They advocate two educational systems: one for the elite and one for the "masses." Educational critics worry, on the other hand, that present day education provides few ideas that could be dangerous to the *status quo*, that there is no such thing as the free marketplace of ideas or the community of scholars who pursue knowledge for its own sake. Instead, many argue, education produces unreflective conformists.

The more radical of these critics castigate educational institutions because of their ideological functions. They point out the role of education in justifying and preserving the *status quo*, the institutionalized inequalities in society. And in making these arguments against education, the more humanistic critics imply that things could be different. Underlying their criticisms is a commitment to the liberating potential of education and knowledge, a potential as yet largely unrealized.

Most people—educators, parents, and students — are, however, increasingly viewing education as a means to an end, specifically a good job, a better job than one's parents. Educators experience pressure to make their courses "relevant" not in political but in occupational terms. And they may succumb to these pressures as they are increasingly called upon to play the numbers game. Students demand that courses be justified in terms of their employment potential as they are increasingly called upon to play the credentials game. Parents worry about whether their children's educational choices are "sound" and "practical" as they have come increasingly to recognize that their children's life chances are determined by their educational achievement.

EDUCATION AND RELEVANCE

One aspect of this relevancy debate, then, centres on what is and ought to be taught in our schools and universities, and the issues are largely at the personal or individualistic level. Another, and more recent aspect of the debate centres on the relevancy of university research. In a book entitled *The University Means Business*, Janice Newson and Howard Buchbinder have considered some of the implications of the increasingly close link between corporations and universities. Simply, there is growing pressure on universities to become what one government report refers to as "service universities." In a variety of direct and indirect ways, industry, with the collusion of government agencies, attempts to "energize universities in the direction of being better servants to corporate research and development needs" (Newson and Buchbinder, 1988:84).

In the past, educational expansion was seen as necessary because of the need to build "human capital." The more recent argument is that expenditure on universities can only be justified if universities are contributing to the growth of capitalism itself.

In part, this means that the research done by your professors increasingly is judged in terms of its marketability, its direct usefulness to the corporate sector, and not in terms of its importance to science or to an understanding of the social world and the human condition. As one senior business executive has argued, "a professor's ability to generate funds should be one of the conditions of tenure" (Cochrane,

1986). While his wish has yet to be granted, it is apparent that those who can bring in large research grants and contracts from corporations often enjoy more prestige and power within their university and, probably, earlier promotion than those whose research is not of direct interest to the private sector.

To promote this vision of the "service university," the federal government as well as some provincial governments have developed "matching grants" programs: up to certain levels, dollars raised for research from the private sector will be matched with government funding. Clearly, the kinds of research that corporations are likely to support are those they believe have direct benefit to them; the work of medieval scholars, critical sociologists, astronomers and those doing very basic research in medicine or physics is not likely to attract much in the way of corporate funding. It is, for example, highly unlikely that John Polanyi would have won Canada's first Nobel Prize in chemistry had he been forced to tailor his research program to the short run interests of the corporate world.

More generally, engineers in particular talk approvingly of "transfer of technology" and by this they mean that a major function of the university should be to assist business to learn about and use technologies created within the universities that could make them more competitive, more efficient and more profitable. As one government report argues, "Most university and industry spokesmen (sic) agree that the encouragement of increased interaction is in the public and national interest and will become part of the goals of all publicly funded universities in the next decade" (Enros and Farley, 1986:12).

So, what we begin to see developing are university-industry research centres and university "spin-off firms." For example, universities develop CAD/CAM (Computer Assisted Design; Computer Assisted Manufacturing) units which have, as their major goal, to help businesses automate their work places fur-

ther, and in the process bring about another transformation of work and, perhaps, yet another layer of alienation in the work place. Left out are social and psychological considerations about what this new technology may mean to people. And, in its most extreme forms, we are beginning to hear threats that if universities do not become "indus-versities," industry may by-pass them altogether and set up its own equivalent of higher-education institutions.

Probably, universities have always been under attack for not upholding or contributing to various groups' goals and beliefs. In both the nineteenth and twentieth centuries, religious groups, for example, have often worried about what might be taught to their young people in the public universities and have set up their own colleges and sometimes universities. And, there are numerous examples of academics who, critical of some aspects of their society, have been denied a tenured position or who could not find a position at all.

But, one of the hard fought battles has been for the right of scientists and academics to pursue unfashionable and what often seems at the time to be irrelevant research and to be effective social critics without fearing for their jobs. As Pat Marchak notes, the problem with tying tenure (and promotion) to the ability to generate funds is that:

. . . entrepreneurial talent is but one dimension of human beings; to oblige everyone to be a salesperson above all else would be to deny society the aesthetic, intellectual, scientific, athletic and numerous other gifts that its members possess. It would also deprive society of internal sources of dissent, and thus of visions of alternatives. This yardstick turns every talent into a commodity and values nothing which is not marketable (Marchak: 1988:189).

Another concern is that even where the findings of researchers do have immediate relevance — and we are not suggesting that the only good research is that which is removed from the real world — the concept of the "service university" poses problems for the development of science itself.

In Chapter 2, we outlined what we believe most scientists think are the norms of the scientific method. One of the norms we mentioned centred on the notion of publicity: the findings of research, whatever the science, must, through publication, be, in principle, made available to all. We say, in principle, because the common language of those who study the physical world is mathematics and most of us are so mathematically illiterate that only simplistic popular presentations of relativity theory, small particle physics, the "big bang" and black holes makes even remote sense. And equally, those who study the social world invoke the language of jargon, which nobody can understand including many social scientists.

But the knowledge is available. And, as we pointed out in Chapter 2, there are two reasons why publicity of research findings is important. First, it is important to science in that it allows others who are not mathematically illiterate, or who can break through the jargon of social science, to challenge the findings through finding errors in the reasoning or their inability to replicate the experiment or study. And, when the findings do seem sound, it spurs further theory and research by those reading the findings. This is at the heart of science and how it progresses, and why the attempts of governments to declare certain kinds of research as classified, because of military importance, is often counterproductive. And, second, as we described, briefly in Chapter 2 and again in Chapter 9, knowledge, especially social knowledge, should not be a resource available only to the powerful — those who can pay for it. For example, while the federal government can afford and does carry out research on various aspects of Canada's native people, those studied should have the right to know about what was said of them, to comment on the accuracy of the research, and to use the research in pursuit of their particular concerns and goals.

The concept of the "indus-versity," the Service University, then, threatens the norms of the scientific method and the idea of a university as a place of free and open thought. Much of what is involved in transfer of technology, for example, will, almost by definition, involve secrecy. Corporations, which contract for research in the hope of new products, or for consulting on their method of production, or which ask to have something tested in a laboratory, will hardly want the findings publicized and available to their competitors. Managers, having hired a consultant from a business administration faculty to do research on their work force will not, generally, feel the findings should be made available to workers and the union. And, finally, corporations which fund a chair in, say, nuclear physics, will not be happy about the faculty of that university taking a stand against nuclear power.

┃ SOCIOLOGICAL PERSPECTIVES ON EDUCATION

As we might expect, these controversies are very much part of the sociology of education. Predictably the main debate has been between functional and conflict theorists. However, sociologists working out of an interactionist perspective — as well as ethnomethodologists — have contributed to our understanding of what education is all about and what it does to people and to society.

The functionalist view of education, its purpose and how it must change has been the dominant perspective. Functionalism provides a view of education that is both optimistic and familiar to most Canadians. Education is seen as a good thing for the individual and for society. From this perspective, education is, for the individual, the key to success and opportunity. The goal, one shared by most sociologists, has been to remove the barriers standing in the way of equality of educational opportunity and to create equal access at all levels of education for those who want to or can benefit from it. And, most functionalist sociologists have explicitly or implicitly believed that economic growth and expansion is linked to educational expansion. Reducing family and class influence over people's life chances not only benefits the individual, but also contributes to the development of human capital; counteracting these influences meant for most functionalists a more open, meritocratic and efficient society, one better able to cope with the post-industrial or knowledge society.

However, in the 1970s, with the resurgence of Marxism in sociology, those interested in education and inequality began to ask rather different questions. Through their theory and research, Marxists challenged many of the taken-for-granted assumptions we had learned from functionalists. These sociologists pointed out that although we have spent a great deal of money on educational expansion and put a lot of effort into educational reform, not much has changed. The basic patterns of inequality of condition and inequality of opportunity are largely unaffected by what happens to the educational system.

Indeed, from this Marxist or conflict perspective, education is seen as reproducing, not altering, existing patterns of social inequality and social stratification. You cannot change society by changing education, say these theorists, because the problem does not lie with education but with capitalist society, with class and status inequalities. Unlike liberal-functional sociologists, who view educational systems as at least partly an independent variable, able to effect social change, Marxists view education as dependent on what is happening economically and culturally in the wider society outside the school.

At the same time, the approach and method of interpretive sociology — what we have referred to as the interactionist perspec-tive — for a while at least, forced attention back to what goes on inside the school and to what has come to be called the **hidden curriculum**. Researchers working within the interactionist perspective examined assumptions and goals that lie behind what is taught in school, who is defined as "bright," who is "dull" and so on. Some began to look more carefully at how student and teacher definitions of situations and rules vary and are worked out through "negotiation" (Martin, 1976).

There was, especially in the 1970s, a good deal of rethinking and reevaluation of the functionalists' assumptions about the role and function of education in society. Most of this came from Marxists and led one of your authors to conclude in the late 1970s that the sociology of education was at something of a watershed (Richardson, 1977). He expected that a new sociology of education would emerge, one which would draw more on Marx and Weber than on the functionalists and produce a quite different research program. This hasn't happened with the result that we have been forced to put much of this discussion in the past tense.

In previous chapters, particularly Chapters 9, 10 and 11, we have described how some theory and research about Canadian society and its patterns of inequality, which seemed to everyone the final word have, in the 1980s, been subject to challenge and qualification. But, a decade after our first book, we have little to report about the sociology of education that wasn't true then. While the issues have not gone away, the energy to pursue them seems to have been transitory, the concern by both educators and sociologists with how things could be understood and maybe changed seems, in retrospect, a mere blip in the history and sociological analysis of educational systems.

In previous editions, we called this chapter "Educational Inequality" and we continue to do so because, however dated they may be, all of these sociological perspectives on education ultimately reflect sides of the debate considered in Chapter 10: equality of opportunity versus equality of condition. In this chapter we will consider theories about the relationship of education to social mobility, social stratification, and industrial capitalist society. As we shall see, education is like other institutions in that it cannot be studied in a cultural, economic or historical vacuum. It, too, must be viewed in the context of power and inequality and must be seen as the outcome of people's actions and decisions.

EDUCATION IN INDUSTRIAL SOCIETY

GROWTH OF EDUCATION: THE CONTEXT

Education is such a pervasive and taken-for-granted part of our lives and a degree seems so obviously the path to a good job, that we forget how rapidly this has occurred. We forget that what was the general rule, illiteracy, has become a relatively rare phenomenon and a social problem. Most of us are shocked at the persistently high rate of functional illiteracy in Canada (perhaps as high as one in thirteen adults), but not long ago, *most* Canadians were completely illiterate.

Until nearly the end of the nineteenth century, education at even an elementary level was reserved almost exclusively for the rich. The majority of children simply stayed at home until they were old enough to work on the farm, in the factory or down a mine. Even when legislation on compulsory education was introduced, in 1870 and again in 1900, most left at the minimum age of fourteen or fifteen since it was easy to circumvent the laws. Many parents took their children out of school early on various pretexts or allowed them to attend only a few weeks a year. Later, when resistance to compulsory attendance

had abated somewhat, World War I, then the Depression intervened. So it was not until the end of World War II that compulsory education until fourteen, fifteen, or sixteen was firmly entrenched in Canada (Philips, 1957).

Secondary schooling for those other than the rich was even slower to develop. The Depression of the 1930s and World War II meant that a high school diploma was a rarity, perhaps equivalent to a B.A. in the 1970s, perhaps even an M.A. degree in the 1980s. As late as the 1950s we lagged far behind the United States in secondary enrollments and despite great increases we have not yet caught up.

The decade of the 1960s saw massive and unprecedented growth in the Canadian educational system. Elementary and secondary systems were swelled by the "baby boom" of the postwar years. In response new schools, especially for vocational training, were constructed and existing facilities were upgraded. The then existing universities embarked on large scale building programs and faculty recruitment. New universities and community colleges sprung up across Canada. The 1960s, then, were indeed an exciting time to be a student, teacher or administrator. By the early 1970s, the "party" seemed to have come to an end. And like all "good binges," the morning after was a time for sober recriminations and for facing the inevitable mess.

THE TECHNICAL-FUNCTION MODEL OF EDUCATION

Why this rapid growth in education? One answer came from functionalists who argued that the expansion was in response to changing demands of industrial society. Collins (1971), an American sociologist, labelled this approach to education a *technical-functional explanation* of education and educational expansion.

Functionalists argued that education

became important in industrial society because the skill requirements of jobs are constantly rising due to technological change. Formal education is necessary so that the more highly skilled occupations can be filled adequately. This means that educational requirements for employment must also constantly rise, causing larger numbers of people to stay in school for ever longer periods of time. As status came more and more to be based on what we achieve rather than what we inherit, education became the key to mobility and to maintenance of a high family status.

In other words, expansion of education has typically been seen as serving a dual role. On the one hand, key occupational roles could be filled more adequately and performed more efficiently; on the other, extending and expanding the educational system increases mobility by making education more accessible to all members of society.

In Canada, the most influential and persuasive argument for the technical-functional perspective was John Porter's *The Vertical Mosaic*. Although this important book was not published until 1965, various findings from Porter's lengthy and ambitious research emerged in the early 1960s and no doubt provided considerable impetus and rationale for the expansion that followed. His message was clear. In retaining essentially British elitist attitudes and practices, Canada had failed to develop an educational system capable of producing the skills required in an industrial society.

Rather than train Canadians for skilled positions, Porter argued that we had become an affluent and industrial society by bringing in skilled people from elsewhere, notably Britain, the United States and Europe. This created an illusion that we were somehow coping with industrialization. Canadian society emerged, then, as one characterized by considerable inequality of opportunity and a much lower level of economic productivity than in the United States.

Porter concluded that the educational system would have to be drastically expanded and reformed. We would have to abandon the British *elitist* model for the *egalitarian* model of the United States. As he pointed out:

Modern education should be examined against the kind of model which is here being suggested —that is, a society in which the allocation of individuals to social tasks and access to educational resources is determined by ability. Thus two ends are served: the occupational structure will reflect a more rational allocation of ability; and individuals will have the greatest opportunity to develop their talents and make their contributions to the social good . . . . The principle of equality and the principle of the rational use of economic resources thus have a mutually reinforcing function. Now, more than ever, education means opportunity. A system which does not provide equal opportunity is also inefficient (1965:167).

However, by the 1970s, it was becoming more and more apparent that the image of America as the land of opportunity was ideology rather than reality. The United States had not been any more successful in achieving the model Porter had in mind than other Western societies and, in certain respects, was further away from the goal of equality of opportunity. What the research showed was that the United States was not much different from other capitalist societies. American society is also characterized by considerable inequality of income, by a growing concentration of wealth and power and, at the same time, an underclass consisting of those who live in persistent poverty.

While the United States is certainly an open society, there does not appear to be greater equality of opportunity than is found in Britain or Canada where higher education was, until recently, less available to any but the elite. John Porter was too good a sociologist and scholar not to be willing to revise what were, after all, conclusions based on 1950s research and in his later work he presented a quite different view of Canadian education.

CRITICISMS OF THE TECHNICAL-FUNCTIONAL MODEL

In the 1970s, social scientists interested in education and equality began to point out some anomalies that called into question the basic and underlying assumptions of the technical-functional model of education. First, as students have increasingly become aware, higher education does not automatically guarantee a high status job. Education, like most other things it seems, is subject to "inflation." That is, the occupational status one could "buy" twenty years ago with a high school degree now requires a university degree, perhaps a second degree.

Studies of graduates from Ontario universities provide impressive evidence of this process (Harvey and Charner, 1975 and Harvey, 1988). The study compares the occupational success of 1960, 1964 and 1968 graduates. Those who graduated in 1964 were in the most advantageous position whatever their degree or academic record. By 1968, graduates needed a second degree to get an equivalent job to what a 1964 graduate could obtain with only one degree. The authors of these studies suggest, then, that "rates of return" have fallen because of an oversupply of graduates and a changing labour market.

Second, and more generally, there is the paradox that educational requirements have risen more quickly than the skill or technical requirements of most jobs. While he was concerned mainly with the demise of crafts, of skilled labour, Harry Braverman, in his work, *Labor and Monopoly Capital* (1974), is critical of the assumption that modern industrial and office work require better trained and better educated workers. According to his research, much of the "upgrading" of workers is more apparent than real; it is an artifact of the way we classify workers as "skilled," "semi-skilled" and "unskilled." Workers in none of these categories require more than a few days or weeks training, and compared to craft and farm workers are all unskilled and have seen their work progressively degraded. He cites evidence that in the United States approximately two-thirds of *all* jobs "involve such simple skills that they can be — and are — learned in a few days, weeks, or at most months of on-the-job training" (Braverman, 1974:433).

If you think back to our discussion in Chapter 10 of the development of capitalism and industrialism and our pottery analogy, it is easier to understand how skills, crafts and trades have in general been downgraded, not upgraded. It is obviously more efficient and profitable to hire workers who can prepare the clay, others who can turn a pot, others who do nothing but mix glazes, others who apply glazes and still others who do nothing but tend the kilns, rather than hiring craftspersons who have years of training, apprenticeship, and experience which allows them to carry out the whole operation of making a finished bowl. The Potter retains control of the production process and calls upon a limited number of specialists when glazes don't fire properly or pottery cracks on firing. As Braverman points out, a capitalist mode of production progressively destroys traditional crafts and skills.

What emerged from the 1970s debate about the functionalist explanation of educational expansion was that there was a very close link between education and jobs. A highly influential book by Ivor Berg, entitled *Education and Jobs* (1970), did much to undermine the functionalist argument. The book is subtitled "The Great Training Robbery" which nicely sums up its central message. Berg concludes that education makes very little contribution to individual productivity and performance. In fact, in a number of occupations, he finds that highly educated employees are not more productive and may be less productive than those with less education.

Other research suggests, too, that educational qualifications are not very closely connected to the actual demands of the job. For example, large organizations generally require more education than small organizations for exactly the same work. Also, educational requirements for jobs are higher in the spring (when there are a lot of graduates in the market) than they are in the autumn. In short, educational requirements do not seem to be based on fixed demands of the job. Rather they are worked out through "bargaining" between employee and employer, the outcome depending on the balance of power between the two (Collins, 1971).

PROFESSIONALIZATION AND EDUCATION

The dramatic growth of the professional managerial class may perhaps cause you to feel somewhat skeptical of these arguments. Managers, technicians and above all, the rise of professions, surely vindicates the technical-functional explanation of education expansion. None of the critics of this explanation is denying that some occupations involve skills, expertise and knowledge that require considerable training and experience. In present day capitalism, there is a growing split in the labour force. Some jobs do, apparently, require high levels of education but many do not. Both the highly skilled and the very unskilled jobs are increasing in numbers (Myles, 1988). The questions that critics like Randall Collins are asking are how do we decide when education is needed for the job or when educational credentials are simply a resource that allows occupational groups to monopolize opportunities?

It is in the context of this question that *professionalization* —the tendency of various occupational groups to try to emulate medicine — must be understood. Medicine, and law are what most of us first think about when we use the word professional. Both have managed to convince us that the work

doctors and lawyers do requires an expertise and knowledge too specialized and complex for us, the patients and clients, to understand. Nor, supposedly, can we judge good work from bad; only those who are the peers of these practitioners can make that kind of assessment. It is on the basis of these assumptions that professions are, by definition, self-regulating bodies. The state gives the medical and legal professions exclusive power to set standards, to train new members, to decide on the criteria for admitting new members, to decide on the number to be trained and admitted, to judge the conduct and performance of its members and, to a considerable extent, to set tariffs or fees.

What all of this means, of course, is that those occupational groups, successful in being defined as professions, are in effect monopolies, able to set prices, keep out competition, and control supply. And in many instances, this is backed up by the state and, ultimately, the police. It is, for example, illegal to practice medicine without a licence or to work as a lawyer until admitted to the Bar. While professions are formed partly for altruistic reasons — i.e., to protect the patient or client — professionalization is also another way in which groups, in a stratified society, seek to consolidate and maintain their position.

Obviously, other occupational groups, teachers, social workers, accountants, real estate salespersons and so on, want to achieve the same degree of invulnerability to market demands and competition as doctors and lawyers. Inevitably, the shortest route to professional status is to make the knowledge hard to get, to require that new members are "accredited" — they have gone through a training program and have the credentials to prove it. For example, to sell houses one must have a real estate certificate — in the United States, probably a degree in real estate — before being admitted to the real estate "profession."

In sum, while a few occupations demand a considerable amount of education, there are too few to explain the massive expansion of education, especially post-secondary education. It is not that most jobs have become more complex. Rather, occupational groups use education — educational credentials and all the trappings, mystifying jargon and ritual — as a status resource, because they hope that it will provide them with "professional" status and therefore some measure of security and will allow them to exclude those who challenge their position. The outcome is educational inflation. As those who aspire to higher positions begin to get the credentials, they find these are not enough. The rules have changed; now a second degree is needed, or the only degree that counts is from an elite university beyond most people's financial reach.

The argument that educational growth is an outcome of more general conflicts about class, status, and power implies that what is at stake is not what is learned in the classroom, but the credentials which come at the end. Some sociologists, however, have argued that while education may not be specifically about job training, we should not assume it to be a purposeless institution or that nothing is learned in school. And it is in this analysis that we see again how functionalist and conflict perspectives force us to ask different questions and to develop different answers to what is the function of education.

SCHOOLS AND SCHOOLING

WHAT HAPPENS IN THE SCHOOL?

One answer, essentially a functional explanation, is that schools teach the norms of industrial society. An American sociologist, Robert Dreeben (1968a and b), suggested that we should focus not on what children are taught — the formal curriculum — but on the nature of their experiences as they face the particular organization of schooling—the hidden curriculum. He starts with what we have already considered in Chapter 4, that norms appropriate within the family are inappropriate in an industrial and bureaucratic society. As education becomes separated from the family, children, in going off to school every day, move from primary group norms to secondary group norms. They are in the process of learning the difference between the private world of the home and household and the public world of work and of the marketplace.

In common-sense terms, we are expected to act one way at work, another way at home. Marital and family relationships are expected to be primary relationships. They are, ideally, warm, personal, and diffuse. Spouses and children are seen as unique and irreplaceable, i.e., particularistic. At home the good parent is one who continues to love and accept children whether they are successful or unsuccessful, high achievers or low achievers. In other words, the role of son or daughter is ascribed, not achieved. Finally, family members are expected to act collectively, not independently, helping one another and sharing equally with other members.

In contrast to the world of the family is the world of the school. Even in the early grades children learn not to invest too much emotional involvement in one adult. Unlike parents who are more or less fixed for all time, teachers change each year, only in rare cases following children up through the grades. Later, instead of classroom teachers, students begin to go to various teachers, who perform highly specific roles, teaching art or mathematics or physical education. Similarly, students normally move in age cohorts through the grades so that "Johnny" is not a unique son but a category; he is now in grade four and aged nine. Certain universal things are expected of him. Test results, for instance, suggest whether he is "normal," "above average," "slow for his age" and so on.

Children, then, are encouraged to view themselves not as a "special case," as in the family, but as member of a category. Streaming—ability grouping—probably contributes to this since it reduces the need of teachers to treat certain students as "special cases," for example the child with emotional problems or a reading disability. Gradually, too, children are not expected to help one another but to work on their own, to be independent and individualistic. Finally, the child's performance begins to be judged in the concrete language of grades. Status in school, then, comes to be achieved rather than ascribed as it is in the home.

While Dreeben was, we think, critical of the way schooling is organized and of the hidden curriculum it conveys, his work is, nevertheless, a good example of functionalist thinking. Functionalist theorists view the growth of education, the way it is organized and the socialization experiences it produces, intentionally and unintentionally, as more or less inevitable outcomes of other charges. As one part of the system changes this causes other parts to change and adapt. Industrialization "creates" an elaborate and complex division of labour, new kinds of specialized expertise and bureaucratic control.

From a functionalist perspective, educational systems expand because education is a mechanism. It teaches the skills and norms of industrial society. Since stratification—structured inequality—is also seen as functional in complex societies, education is important because it creates in students consensus about the rightness and justice of inequalities. And finally, education is bureaucratic because in complex societies there appears to be no alternative; bureaucracy is a social fact, a necessity and people should learn, as early as possible, to live within and cope with bureaucratic institutions. And from a system perspective, all this happens because of changing system needs. Left out are people and their actions.

Throughout the book we have argued that one of the strengths of a conflict or Marxist perspective is that it doesn't simply describe the blueprint, it forces us to recognize that despite their seeming inevitability and objectivity, institutions have histories. Institutions are human constructions, the outcomes of actions and decisions of real and powerful people trying to work out what they thought was best or more often, what arrangements were most suited to their interests.

In analyzing most institutions, this is more a perspective than something we can actually demonstrate empirically. Religion, family, marriage, patriarchy are certainly humanly constructed institutions. But they are also institutions whose origins are, as we say, "buried in the mists of time"—they are prehistorical rather than historical. One of the reasons we have chosen to write a chapter on education is that, in its modern form, it is unequivocally an institution with a documented history. As we have seen, the present educational system is an outcome, not of decisions made in the dim and inaccessible past, but in the late nineteenth century, a time when people put their ideas to paper and had their words taken down verbatim by legislative records and newspaper reports.

The documented history of the development of education in the United States and Canada allows us, in a way not true of other institutions, to put people back into the process, to test empirically the functional explanation of how and why education developed as it did. The best work we know on the subject has been done by an American social historian, Michael Katz, who, while teaching in Canada, stimulated a number of Canadian students to do research that reached similar conclusions to those he reports in *Class, Bureaucracy and Schools* (1970).

Here and in other writings, Katz shows that a number of motives — including the desire for greater efficiency and altruism — lie behind the development and expansion of the educational system. However, the one factor most convincing to decision makers was that educated workers were more compliant and easier to control — more cooperative, conservative and, what is most crucial, more likely to be "company men" than "union men." And while education did become organized as a bureaucracy, this was not seen as the only and the inevitable way to proceed. According to Katz, there were debates and controversy about how education should be organized; people were fully aware of alternatives.

What emerged was a system that reflected the class bias and, perhaps, the class interests of decision makers. Sociologists, Marxists as well as functionalists, are concerned with the consequences that flow from people's actions and decisions. But, as Robert Merton taught us many years ago, it is dangerous to infer motives from consequences, since they may or may not be related. In promoting compulsory education, people were doing so for many and probably mixed motives. These ranged from a belief in the benefits that would flow from a more enlightened citizenry to unhypocritical expectations that educating the masses would result in a more compliant and subservient labour force. What Katz is arguing is that consciously or unconsciously, the educational system that developed was one that "resonated" with conceptions of how the powerful believed society, generally, should be organized.

From a conflict perspective, a major function of education is to legitimize existing patterns of inequality. As Herbert Gintis (1972:57), a Harvard economist, puts it, "The social relations of education produce and reinforce those values, attitudes and affective capacities which allow individuals to move smoothly into an alienated and class-stratified society." From this viewpoint, then, schooling is mostly about producing compliant and docile workers who will respect authority and accept the fact that society is hierarchical. Ivan Illich (1971), author of the much quoted book *Deschooling Society*, went further and maintained that education schools people "down to size," robs them of their creativity and forces them to discount their own experience and to believe that the only valuable knowledge is that which is certified by degrees and diplomas.

The extent to which education does do all of the things attributed to it remains controversial and, in large part, untestable. Because we do not have a comparison group of people not exposed to education, it is difficult to know how much of the "hidden curriculum" is not simply part of our more general socialization. What does seem apparent is that schools, education, generally, does little to challenge the dominant ideology or to make us more critical of our society and more aware of how it might be changed.

VALUES EDUCATION

Whatever their starting point, all of these analyses have in common that they are focusing on the latent functions or consequences of education. The hidden curriculum is "hidden" because its content — the values, the uncritical acceptance of and compliance with existing structures, the conformity if teaches — is largely unintended and until pointed out by sociologists, unrecognized. Partly in response to the fact that, intentionally and unintentionally, schools convey values and value positions, educators have in recent years developed curricula that are explicitly intended to "teach values" in the classroom. Known as "moral values education," these programs attempt to go beyond merely reciting lists of virtues and rule giving, to provide students with an opportunity to reason out, clarify and reflect upon their values through discussions of and confrontations with "real life" situations, many of which involve moral dilemmas and conflicts.

For example, ten-year-olds are asked to discuss stealing. Is there any difference between stealing from Woolworth's and stealing from another child's locker? Would it make any difference if the other child was popular, unpopular, rich or poor? Is it acceptable for a parent to steal bread for a starving child? What about stealing from a blind man and so forth. As Kathleen Gow describes:

Now follows free discussion of all opinions offered by the class with no point of view treated as more "right" or "wrong" than any other. The teacher accepts every child's response as equally valid. The teacher has been told that his or her role is not to examine stealing in terms of right and wrong, but rather to provide a forum within which each student may clarify or create his or her own values (1980:17).

In other situations, students are asked to consider the situations under which cannibalism might be justified, to decide who should and should not be allowed on a life raft or in a fallout shelter which cannot hold all of the survivors, to determine under what circumstances swapping of marital partners would or would not be moral and so on.

While sympathetic to the motives and goals of moral values education, Gow correctly points out that the old hidden curriculum has been replaced by a new hidden curriculum, one based on values of individualism and moral relativism. What is being taught is a new value, the doctrine of value neutrality and individualism. Moral values education is premised on the notion that values are not autonomous, absolute or universal, but are situational and, in the final analysis, a matter of opinion. And all opinions, including the teacher's, are equally valid. There is no right or wrong; "what is good is what is good for me."

Gow's concern is that in failing to teach values, this approach leaves small children confused, perhaps frightened, and older children in a moral vacuum, in a world with no absolutes or universals, where "everyone does his own thing." In its consequences it is the ideology of corporatism. At the level of everyday life, this means a preoccupation with self at the expense of community.

But in an unequal society, people, and in turn corporations, have unequal resources, unequal opportunities to "do their own thing." In effect, the rich and powerful are "naturally" entitled to do as they please. At the social

structural level, moral relativism, the absence of absolute standards of morality, means that there is infinite flexibility for the powerful to justify their actions and the social arrangements that serve their interests.

EDUCATION AND MOBILITY

SELECTION FUNCTION

It seems evident, and could hardly be otherwise, that in an unequal society people enter the educational system from different levels in the social hierarchy. Just as clear is that if inequality in the wider society is to persist, the outcomes of education will also have to be unequal. That is, educational systems are at least partially responsible for deciding who is likely to make it to the top, who will be at the bottom of the social hierarchy, who will be motivated to achieve, and who will be "cooled-out" of mobility striving.

These are not, of course, problems unique to industrial society. Indeed, all societies must somehow solve the problems of selection, allocation, training and regulation of ambition. In previous eras, however, these were largely resolved through inheritance and ascription. It was expected that men would generally follow in their fathers' footsteps and take up an occupation, if not identical, then very similar to theirs. Women were expected to become wives and mothers. Perhaps because they are more complex and because of the liberal tradition in Western society, these problems, in industrial societies, are mainly resolved by the educational system.

Of course, family background is still important. Those who enter professions such as medicine and law often come from families where one or both parents are, themselves, part of the professional-managerial class. But, as we described in Chapter 11, few in industrial societies inherit their parents' favorable position. Rather, the most families can usually do for their children is to ensure that they get a good education. Family matters because those in more advantaged positions in society can afford to send their children to university and, much more crucially, provide the role models and encouragement that ensures that the children will take for granted that they will complete their education. "Credentials" have in part replaced moral, religious or legal justifications of the past. Similarly, even for those who take over smaller family businesses, an engineering degree, perhaps a Master's degree in business administration, becomes increasingly essential if not to their work directly, in legitimating their right to the position.

Industrial societies, in other words, are increasingly becoming **meritocracies** in which one of the main ways of legitimating or justifying inequality is by the possession of educational credentials. Michael Young (1958), who coined the term "meritocracy," meant by it that those who form the elite and fill the most important roles in society would be those who are most intelligent. But he also pointed out that meritocratic rule would be one of the hardest justifications to counter. If people did in fact rise and fall on the basis of talent and ability, as proponents of equality of opportunity have always desired, how would those at the bottom cope with their "failure"? No longer could they put the blame on the "system" and claim that they did not have the opportunity or that they were discriminated against. "Failure" becomes a "private" trouble rather than a "public" issue.

Part of Ivan Illich's condemnation of education came from a similar recognition:

The hidden curriculum of schools . . . teaches all children that economically valuable knowledge is the result of professional teaching and that social entitlements depend on the rank achieved in a bureaucratic process. The curriculum transforms the explicit curriculum into a commodity and makes its acquisition the severest form of wealth. Knowledge certificates — unlike property rights, corporate stock, or family inheritance — are free from challenge (1971:46).

SPONSORED AND CONTEST MOBILITY

While educational systems are intimately related to the selection process, they do not necessarily operate in exactly the same manner in every society. One problem is when should selection occur? Are people to be "sorted" at the end of elementary school or high school or perhaps in university? Whatever point is chosen is likely to be controversial. It may be seen as unfair or premature to "stream" children at age eleven or twelve because it does not leave room for "late bloomers." At the same time, late selection is likely to be criticized as inefficient, as creating "lower standards" and as "holding back" the bright students.

Norms and values about social mobility and assumptions about the nature and source of ability, then, shape what happens within the educational system. Ralph Turner, an American sociologist, labelled American norms about mobility as "contest" norms, those of Britain, "sponsorship" norms. He suggested that mobility in the United States corresponds to a race or contest in which elite status goes to those who have, as it were, run the hardest or shown the greatest perseverance:

Contest mobility is like a sporting event in which many compete for a few recognized prizes. The contest is judged to be fair only if all the players compete on an equal footing. The most satisfactory outcome is not necessarily a victory of the most able, but of the most deserving. Applied to mobility the contest norm means that victory by a person of moderate intelligence accomplished through the use of common sense, craft, enterprise, daring and successful risk-taking is more appreciated than victory by the most intelligent or the best educated (1960:857).

In contrast, sponsorship mobility as found in England favours a controlled selection process:

Elite recruits are chosen by the established elite or their agents and elite status is given on the basis of some criterion of supposed merit and cannot be taken by any amount of effort or strategy. Upward mobility is like entry into a private club, where each candidate must be sponsored by one or more members (1960:865).

Although the orthodox way to move upward in the United States is through education, innovative or irregular ways of achieving success are also admired. In the United States, those who are self-made, who, through their own efforts, ingenuity, and drive reach the top, such as the inventors of the Apple Computer, become modern day folk heroes. And as we suggested in Chapter 7, the mobility ethos in its extreme form may lead to such "innovations" as robbing a bank. For example, the film *The Godfather* is ultimately about upward social mobility of those prohibited from rising through legitimate channels.

Under sponsorship norms, ambition is not legitimate until selection occurs. This does not, of course, mean that people in Britain do not do things such as starting a business unless they are selected by the educational system. But it does mean that their success will not smell so sweet. They may not be accepted by members of the higher classes who view them as "pushy" or perhaps as "uncultured" or "uncouth." Thus the path upwards for those who are sponsored is likely to be an easier one than for those who move upwards without education (Richardson, 1977).

THE NURTURE-NATURE DEBATE

Underlying these mobility norms are different assumptions about the amount and source of talent and ability in society. In fact, these norms reflect different sides of what has come to be known as the **nurture-nature** or environment-heredity debate. Contest mobility implies that differences in ability are the result of differences in the social and physical environment. People, according to this view, are very much alike at birth. Later differences can be explained by inequalities in life chances

which work to the detriment of some and to the advantage of others. Those who hold this view have argued that it should be possible to offset the consequences of poverty through providing disadvantaged children with various kinds of "head start" programs. Similarly, it is argued that there should not be early streaming of children because some may be "late bloomers"; they need more time than others to develop their abilities.

Sponsored mobility starts from opposite premises. It is based on the assumption that there is a limited pool of talent in society and that heredity rather than environment explains differences in ability. For this last reason, it makes no sense to try to educate everyone exactly the same. Rather, higher education should be reserved for those who have the ability to benefit from it. Others in the society, the majority, should have a different education, one suited to their lower abilities — a terminal vocational or commercial program. Finally, where contest mobility tries to equalize opportunities for everyone, sponsored mobility is more concerned with "wasted talent" — those who have ability but are held back by social and economic factors.

CANADIAN EDUCATION

Where does Canada fit in Turner's scheme? Sponsorship and contest mobility mean approximately the same thing as *elitist* and *egalitarian* ideologies, respectively. Until very recently, Canadians were most influenced by British elitism: we, too, believed that children should be sorted early and educated according to their abilities. Streaming of children, then, has always been part of the Canadian educational system. While in recent years, academic, commercial, and technical students have usually been housed in the same building, the programs seldom overlap. Channels across exist in theory but in practice few students move from the commercial and technical streams to the academic stream.

Nevertheless, we have also been influenced by the United States with the result that enrollments in universities and colleges rose steadily in recent decades (from 91 000 in 1951 to 796 000 in 1986). But, there does not seem to have been the same pressure for open admissions as there has been in the United States. And, when community colleges were established in the 1960s and 1970s, their structure and organization were shaped more by an elitist ideology than an egalitarian ideology. For example, Ontario community colleges (colleges of applied arts and technology) might have been modelled on the California system of junior colleges, which offer two-year programs, some of which lead to university. Instead, the deliberate decision was made in Ontario to make these terminal diploma programs and not "back-door" entries into university. This has recently been a matter of renewed debate.

INEQUALITY OF EDUCATIONAL OPPORTUNITY

Nevertheless, it remains the case that in both elitist and egalitarian societies, and mixtures of the two such as Canada, there has been an expansion in education. But, the goal of equal access to higher education is still distant and unfulfilled. In Canada, although universities are not solely the preserve of an elite, class of origin, ethnicity, sex, and even the region of Canada where one grows up remain important determinants of who does and does not complete high school and go on to post-secondary education. So pervasive and persistent are these ascribed factors that Breton (1972) concluded that any study that did not find them at work would be suspect (Breton, 1972).

We are, of course, some way from being able to predict educational and occupational achievement. Studies that use more complicated statistical techniques show that there are still many factors we have been unable to measure. The most readable account of these techniques is probably by Christopher Jencks and his associates (Jencks, 1972). In the end they conclude that a good deal of what happens to people is due to "luck" rather than systematic factors like class or ethnicity.

Still the most important influence on educational aspirations and actual achievement is the social class background of students. Generally, those from higher-class backgrounds have higher aspirations. This remains true even among those who have the same level of measured intelligence (Breton, 1972; Porter and others, 1973). Of course, the higher the income of parents, the more likely are their children to attend university (Macdonnel, 1987). And, it appears that students from lower social classes who do go on to post secondary education are more likely to attend a community college.

As we might expect, educational opportunities follow quite closely the pattern of economic inequality between provinces. For instance, Martin and Macdonell (1978) have shown that educational expenditures, teacher qualifications and retention of students are lowest in the Atlantic Provinces and Quebec, highest in Ontario, Alberta and British Columbia.

Until very recently, sex was also an important determinant of aspirations and of who goes on to university. While girls often do better than boys in school, girls were less likely than boys to go on to university. At the undergraduate level this has now changed. By the 1980s about 51 percent of undergraduate students were female. However, women are less likely than men to do graduate work: some 41 percent of Master's degrees and 24 percent of doctorates were awarded to women.

Further, while women are equally represented in the undergraduate university population, they are segregated into fields of study that lead to employment in traditional female occupations: nursing, home economics and education. The most recent study of undergraduates finds that, in general, those most likely to train for the higher paid occupations such as law and medicine tend to come mainly from high socio-economic backgrounds. But, this is particularly so for women. Women who choose non-traditional fields — law, medicine and engineering come mainly from backgrounds where both the father and mother are well educated and have relatively high incomes (Macdonnell, 1987). Finally, some 61 percent of part-time students are women (Education, Culture and Tourism Division, 1985:33).

CLASS AND EDUCATION

In the first decades of this century, the major barrier to equal educational opportunity was sheer poverty. This seemed to overwhelm any other kinds of explanations of why some children do not get very far in school. Obviously, extreme poverty, whether due to unemployment, poor wages, a large family or a single parent family, is bound to have an important effect on the child's ability to learn and to concentrate. For example, as a British study found, overcrowding and bad living conditions are strongly related to academic performance and measured intelligence; children who scored low on these tests did much better after their families had been moved by the government to larger and more modern homes (Douglas, 1964).

Compulsory education, of course, has kept both rich and poor children in school until age fifteen. It is at the secondary and postsecondary levels that economic factors have had their most dramatic impact. In the past, few low income families could afford to forego the earnings of young people. Often, then, there were parental pressures to leave school and get a job whatever the ability of the child.

This may still be true for those children in families below the poverty line. Certainly, as more than one study has shown, "money still matters," in determining whether children go on to university (Porter and others, 1973). But, the economic situation of the family does not fully explain why children of disadvantaged families drop out of school as soon as they can or end up in programs that destine them to the bottom of the occupational structure.

INTELLIGENCE AND EDUCATION

Some have explained the differences in educational achievements between those in the upper and middle and the lower classes as being simply a result of differences in intelligence. In a society in which educational credentials are our most marketable commodity, the poor are those who lack the ability to achieve or acquire these commodities. People, goes this argument, are poor because they are stupid rather than stupid because they are poor. Sad though it may be for these people, the fact remains that in a meritocracy, the bright will rise and the dull will fall.

At least one problem with this argument is that, while various studies have shown some differences in measured intelligence between social classes, the difference is not all that great (possibly no more than fifteen points from top to bottom). There is, in fact, nearly as much variation within social classes as between them. While upper classes will have some people of higher measured intelligence than found in lower classes, a large proportion of people at the bottom of the social hierarchy will have higher measured intelligence than some of those at the top. The difference in IQ between classes is not large enough to account for differences in educational aspirations or performance.

The long and recently heated controversy about what IQ scores measure and where intelligence comes from provides a good illustration of how ideology influences the kinds of questions sociologists ask. Whatever IQ means, these scores have been increasingly used as the justification for selection decisions in education. Most liberal social scientists have held for some time now that differences in measured intelligence among social categories can be explained in terms of differences in physical and cultural backgrounds. Educational discrimination on the basis of IQ, they argue, is unjust because it simply reinforces and perpetuates the disadvantaged position of some groups. These sociologists were given rather a shock (to which they responded with extreme hostility) when Arthur Jensen (1969) took what was to many a backward step by arguing that IQ differences by "race" and "class" were mainly the result of genetic differences. It is probably safe to say that neither camp has succeeded in making its case empirically.

Nor do we wish to enter this destructive debate that is essentially among psychologists, except perhaps to suggest that the attempt by Jensen and his followers to "prove" that these genetic differences exist *and* the reaction to this work are misdirected. First, it is not entirely clear why we would compare the abilities of racial groups at all. We return to this issue in the next chapter. In any case, whichever is "right," inequality justified on the basis of intelligence remains inequality. That is, whether intelligence is the result of environment or heredity, it is in either case beyond the control of the individual to do much about. It is at least in part an ascribed, rather than an achieved, characteristic.

Preoccupation with the meritocratic ideology has led, as well, to a preoccupation with how to measure who is "best"; the persistence of inequality is taken for granted. But as Jensen himself admits, job allocation decisions based on IQ do not truly reflect job demands; there are probably few jobs that demand the "highest level of intelligence." And there seems to be little correlation between intelligence and job performance (Jensen, 1969:16; Gintis, 1973:58).

In any case, studies in a number of countries have shown that there are large class differences in educational achievement, even among those of high ability. For example, when people of the same measured intelligence but different class background are compared, those from higher social backgrounds are more likely to be in an academic stream. At the same time, children of lower ability but from middle or upper-class backgrounds will also be in the academic stream in large proportions.

In other words, while IQ is an important factor, class background may be even more important in determining who goes on to university (Porter et al., 1973). Other studies, particularly in the United States, suggest that while class influences diminish among those who go on to college or university, they do not disappear entirely. Even at this stage, social class still has a direct effect on graduation rates (Corwin, 1974).

COGNITIVE POVERTY

A better answer than intelligence differences is that students from different class backgrounds bring with them to the school different kinds of resources. It has become obvious that children raised in families where there are good books, conversation, discussion, stimulating toys, and so on are likely to have a "head start" over those raised in a more impoverished environment. There is increasing recognition that poverty is not simply lack of money. It is also, at times, a world-view or a subculture that leads to a kind of cognitive poverty — a world with narrowed horizons, limited aspirations, and inadequate knowledge and social skills.

The lower-class subculture may, perhaps, be best seen as an adaptive response to poverty, uncertain employment and low status. But it is also likely to be in conflict with the middle-class culture of schools. Parents who do not themselves have good memories of school, for example, may feel ill at ease in talking to teachers and principals who treat them in a "professional" manner. Lower-class children, too, may find the cool and impersonal world of school with its regulations and norms about social order very different from what happens in their home and community (Willmott, 1969).

VALUE DIFFERENCES

Probably, too, we should not assume that all lower-class people share middle-class values about the goodness of education and are simply repressed. One of John Porter's concerns, for example, was that the problem industrial societies face is not how to increase opportunities, but how to induce people to take advantage of those that already exist (Porter, 1968). For example, as we have seen in the previous chapter, people at lower levels in the occupational hierarchy do not always agree about which jobs are most important. Many manual workers have a very low opinion of "office jobs" compared to skilled trades and are less likely to encourage children to stay on in school if the result will be "an unproductive desk job." Some parents, too, may be concerned that too much education will change the child's attitudes and in effect cause him or her to move psychologically and physically away from the family.

Finally, working-class parents may be more willing to accept teachers' evaluations of their children than are middle-class parents. When they learn that their child is not doing well in school they may encourage him or her in different directions in an effort not to put too much "pressure" on the child. In contrast, middle-class parents may consult with the teacher, try a different school, hire tutors, and as a last resort perhaps put the child in a private school.

In short, what may seem like indifference, even antagonism about education may, from the parents' perspective, be an attempt to be tactful and accepting of the child whatever his or her level of achievement (Richardson, 1977).

In sum, creating complete equality of educational opportunity is not an easy task. While it is true that the school has taken over many of the socialization functions of the family, the first five or six years of life remain very crucial in the formation of attitudes, values, and behaviour. And of course, most children continue to live with their parents throughout their school years. Family influences as well as the class influences of peer groups and the community are formidable barriers overwhelming what is often the very limited involvement in the classroom.

EDUCATION AND INEQUALITY OF OPPORTUNITY AND CONDITION

Nevertheless, *educational* opportunities have obviously improved dramatically since World War II. Certainly, university students still come disproportionately from relatively affluent families, but no longer is university exclusively the preserve of the rich. Large numbers of young people from lower-class backgrounds do make it either to university or to a community college. But as many sociologists have begun to realize, education expansion and reform do not appear to make much difference as far as equality of opportunity or equality of condition is concerned. To understand why this should be the case requires that we widen the focus beyond simply the educational system. We need to look again at the nature of social mobility and its relationship to education.

As we have seen in Chapter 11, rates of social mobility are not very different between Western industrial societies. What differences there are do not appear to be related to social and educational policy or the kinds of ideologies we described earlier as contest and sponsored norms about mobility and education. For example, despite the fact that there are nearly four times as many people in higher education in the United States than in Britain, rates of social mobility for the two countries are pretty much the same. Although Canada falls somewhere between, it has a very similar rate of social mobility.

In terms of equality of opportunity, it does not seem to matter very much whether a society is elitist or egalitarian, or whether it tends towards sponsored or contest norms about social mobility. Nor, despite expansion of the educational system, have rates of social mobility changed much over this century. People were about as likely to move up or down in the social hierarchy in 1900 as in the 1980s. For those who felt that education is the key to mobility and to the creation of a meritocratic society these were puzzling and shocking findings.

Part of the reason that mobility rates do not change very much should have been obvious but was not. It is simply that not everyone can be upwardly mobile. In an unequal society some will rise to the top; most will end up in less favoured positions. In short, no matter what happens in terms of social and educational policy, the majority cannot expect to be socially mobile.

There is no doubt that educational opportunities for lower-class children have improved dramatically in recent decades. But they have also improved for everyone; as those at the bottom begin to get more education so do those at the top. In fact most policies designed to help out the disadvantaged — head start programs, kindergartens, scholarships and bursaries, counselling and so on—probably do help. It is just that other classes benefit from them even more. As far as social mobility is concerned, the end result is a static situation and "educational inflation": the educational system expands without narrowing relative differences between groups or changing the underlying structure of opportunities (Karabel, 1972).

In sum, education seems relatively impotent to bring about changes in social mobility.

Those most likely to benefit from a "good education are those who had a head start in the first place. This means two things: (1) we have not achieved equality of educational opportunity; lower-class students do not do as well or go as far, and (2) equality of educational opportunity, even if it were a reality, is not the same thing as equality of opportunity. A good education does not guarantee a good job. Although education has come to be seen as a resource for improving one's social and economic position, it is better viewed as a resource of the powerful for assuring their position and the position of their children.

CONCLUSIONS: EDUCATION AND CHANGE

There is now, we think, consensus that educational change is fairly impotent to bring about changes in class structure, the kinds of inequalities we described in Chapter 11. Educational systems are shaped by, but do not shape, social arrangements; they respond to social and economic forces in the wider society. Educational reform and expansion cannot create equality of condition or produce a more efficient society. Rather, the main function of education seems to be to reproduce and legitimize inequality. Change and innovation within the educational system therefore must probably wait for more fundamental changes in the wide society.

This partly explains the demise and failure of the free school movement and of experimental university programs of the 1960s and 1970s. Like most utopian solutions, they failed to confront the fundamental issues of capitalism and bureaucracy; they ignored "structure" and acted as if they were in a social and economic vacuum.

Few today would disagree with the ideals of a "liberated education": freedom from the constraints and repression of the hidden curriculum with its grades and rules and structures and, instead, learning as an end in itself, not a means to other ends. But free schools were often little more than "isolated havens for the over-privileged" — escapist enclaves for those who could afford to ignore for a while the demands of the credentials society. Probably wisely, lower class parents and children saw them as irrelevant, maybe even harmful, in a society that puts so much emphasis on marketable educational qualifications.

The first edition of this text was written in the late 1970s and, at the time, your authors could still remember vividly the excitement about educational reform that pervaded the period between about 1967 and 1975. We had shared that optimism. But, as educators and sociologists we were emotionally and intellectually torn by the criticism that emerged in the 1970s. At one level, we found it difficult to argue against the critics of educational reform and innovation; fundamental restructuring of education is probably impossible as long as it is an institution constrained by and serving the interests of capitalism. But, at another level, we found it difficult to accept that educational reform and social reform could not be interrelated.

By the time of our second edition of this book, the early 1980s, we found nothing in the literature to suggest that our assessment of the critics of educational reform had been incorrect. But, we asked students to recall the discussion in the chapter on deviance of diversion programs and other attempts to make Canada's criminal justice system more humane.

Like diversion, educational innovations and experiments are only "band-aid" solutions. They are within-system changes that do not and cannot address the larger issues of power and inequality in capitalist society. For this and other reasons, most will fall short of achieving their objectives. But, as we argued, like diversion programs, educational change offers the possibility of a better deal for those who must spend such a major part of their lives in educational institutions. However formidable the obstacles to "real" reform, we have an obligation to work within these constraints to improve things now and not simply to wait until the wider structures have changed.

So, as bleak as the prospects for fundamental change may seem to be, our sympathies are with those who have been unwilling to abandon reforming education and educational systems. After all, as a visit to any Canadian school will show, despite the large structural limitations, many things have changed and in ways that are relevant. Compared to the past, most schools and universities are freer, less regimented, less authoritarian and less repressive and all of this has occurred without any discernible undermining of capitalism.

At the beginning of the present decade, we find ourselves unwilling to abandon either the hopes and aspirations which drove both students and teachers in the 1960s or our more limited vision of educational reform outlined in the previous edition of this book. The 1980s was a decade in which debate about education, its objectives and functions, was rather muted. At the same time, as present participation rates in post-secondary education indicate, education has, if anything, become a more important determinant of who succeeds and who fails in Canadian society.

The sociological study of education is, in the end, a vivid example of what we mean in this book by humanistic sociology and of the paradox that people are both products and producers of social structure. In this chapter we have emphasized the intimate and complex relationship between the educational system and the inequality of the wider society, what might be called the *latent consequences* of education. But we have also tried to show that these emerge more or less clearly, are interpreted differently, and seem more or less inevitable and taken for granted as we move from one value position to another.

In the process we have largely ignored what education is manifestly about — the teaching of skills, values and ideas. We have done so because the main contribution of the sociological perspective is to make us aware of what can be changed and what cannot. Thus in education, as in social life generally, we cannot simply will social change into being — the mistake of the free school movement. We must first come to understand the limits to freedom of action that economic and social structures impose and eventually the choices open to us. Only at this point can education be liberating instead of repressive.

III SUGGESTIONS FOR FURTHER READING

As we have described in this chapter, the major debates about education took place in the 1960s and 1970s and there has been relative silence in the 1980s. This does not mean that the debates have gone away or that much that was written in this earlier period has become irrelevant. The issue of education and inequality has been addressed in a number of works. We especially recommend that you look at the articles in Jerome Karabel's and A. H. Halsey's edited collection, *Power and Ideology in Education* (1977). Two other collections that will give you some sense of the debate about education are Michael F. D. Young's *Knowledge and Control* (1971) and Earl Hopper's *Readings in the Theory of Education Systems* (1971).

Some basic textbooks that provide considerable Canadian data are Wilf Martin's and Allan Macdonnell's *Canadian Education* (1982) and Raymond Murphy's *Sociological Theories of Education* (1979). And, we would recommend that you look at Jane Gaskell's and Arlene Tigar McLaren's edited collection, *Women and Education: A Canadian Perspective* which provides both a Canadian and a feminist perspective on education.

During the 1960s a number of social scientists and educators were experimenting with and writing about educational reform. Drawing explicitly on the socialization theories of Jean Piaget, a number of educators tried to find ways of giving students greater autonomy in their own education. A sample of these efforts can be found in a collection compiled by E. B. Nyquist and G. R. Hawes, *Open Education* (1972). Other reformers and critics drew their inspiration from philosophers and theorists ranging from Plato to Montessori, and this is reflected in the varieties of reform proposals. One of the most controversial experiments remains the English school, Summerhill, founded by A. S. Neill (1960). A representative sampling of what were then seen as new and radical approaches to school reform is R. Gross's and B. Gross's *Radical School Reform* (1969). Two important works out of this period are Neil Postman's and Charles Weingartner's *Teaching as a Subversive Activity* (1969) and Charles E. Silberman's *Crisis in the Classroom* (1970). Perhaps even more controversial are the works by Ivan Illich cited in this chapter.

Counterpoints to these critiques emerged in a number of books and articles. A sample of these "counterideologies" can be found in Cornelius J. Troost's *Radical School Reform: Critiques and Alternatives* (1973). Samuel Bowles's and Herbert Gintis's *Schooling in Capitalist America* (1976) remains a powerful Marxian critique of existing education and attempts, at that point, to bring about educational reform. Michael B. Katz's *Class, Bureaucracy and Schools* (1970), an historical account of the development of education, takes a similar position to Bowles and Gintis.

The issue of inequality of opportunity stimulated a great deal of research. A landmark study in this area is what is usually called the *Coleman Report*, James S. Coleman and others, *Equality of Educational Opportunity* (1966). A very readable and important book is Christopher Jencks et al., *Inequality: A Reassessment of the Effects of Family and Schooling in America* (1972).

British researchers have, it seems, been more successful in capturing the subtle relationships between the home, the community and the school. In particular, we recommend Brian Jackson's and Dennis Marsden's *Education and the Working Class* (1962); Brian Jackson's *Streaming: An Educational System in Miniature* (1964); and Peter Willmott's *Adolescent Boys of East London* (1969). However, Bell Kaufman's *Up the Down Staircase* (1964); Jonathan Kozol's *Death at an Early Age* (1967); and David Roger's *110 Livingston Street* (1968) are important American examples of this more humanistic and non-quantitative tradition in educational research.

There have been a number of important Canadian studies that have attempted to depict the extent of inequality of educational opportunity in Canadian society. One influential study was Raymond Breton's (in collaboration with John McDonald and Stephen Richer) *Social and Academic Factors in the Career Decisions of Canadian Youth* (1972). Studies that focus on post-secondary education in Canada include Edward Harvey's *Educational Systems and the Labour Market* (1974); Marion Porter and others, *Does Money Matter? Prospects for Higher Education* (1973); and Robert M. Pike's *Who Doesn't Get to University—and Why: A Study on Accessibility to Higher Education in Canada* (1970). These and other studies are reviewed in Paul Anisef's *Accessibility to Post Secondary Education in Canada: A Review of the Findings* (1985).

In a different vein, Heather Robertson's *Reservations Are for Indians* (1970) is a powerful indictment of the effects of "white man's" schooling on native peoples. Various articles in Elia Zureik's and Robert M. Pike's *Socialization and Values in Canadian Society* (1975) develop this and other themes about the effects of schooling. Alison Prentice and Susan Houston have put together an interesting and useful collection of their research on the history of Canadian education, *Family, School and Society in Nineteenth-Century Canada* (1975). See also Prentice's book *The School Promoters* (1977). Randle Nelson's and David Nock's edited collection, *Reading, Writing and Riches: Education and the Socioeconomic Order in Canada* (1978) is, a decade later, still worth reading. A recent collection of articles on feminism and education is Jane Gaskell's and others *Claiming an Education* (1989).

Finally, while we have in earlier chapters suggested that you look at John Porter's *The Vertical Mosaic* (1965), we urge you to do so now. For his later thinking, we strongly recommend that you read his essay entitled "Education, Equality, and the Just Society" in his *The Measure of Canadian Society: Education, Equality and Opportunity* (1979), a series of essays put together by Porter but published just after his untimely death in 1979.

CHAPTER 13

ETHNIC INEQUALITY

OVERVIEW

This chapter completes our discussion of various dimensions of social inequality in Canadian society. In Chapter 10, you were introduced to how capitalism brings about new forms of inequality and vulnerability and a new form of social stratification based ultimately on ownership and non-ownership of the means of production. In Chapter 11, you were presented with the major theories about class inequality and how this form of inequality is passed on from generation to generation, and is legitimated and becomes structured inequality. And, in Chapter 12, our discussion of education was, in large part, a discussion of educational inequality, of how this institution is both shaped by, but also shapes, social inequality and social stratification in capitalist society.

Historically, differences based on ethnic origins have been an important dimension of social inequality in Canadian society. In understanding why ethnic difference has often also meant ethnic inequality, you may want to look back to our discussion in Chapter 11, of Max Weber's perspective on social stratification. He pointed out that debates and conflict over who gets what from society and why they are entitled to whatever they get, does not, as Karl Marx implied, occur only in the economic sphere. Weber recognized that, in an unequal society, people will use whatever resources are available to maintain or consolidate their position. As you have learned in the preceding chapter, one such resource is educational credentials and, as you will learn in this chapter, another such resource is ethnicity.

With the exception of Canada's native peoples, Canadian society is a "society of immigrants" in the sense that virtually all of us can trace our roots to some other society and culture outside of North America. This has meant that social scientists, and governments, have given particular attention to ethnicity, to ethnic relations and to policies related to multi-culturalism. After reading this chapter, you will know something about this large body of research and writing but, more importantly, you should understand why we view much of it from the standpoint of understanding ethnicity as a resource for both the powerful and the powerless.

Dominant groups, through nepotism and subtle and not so subtle discrimination, have used ethnicity to assure their privilege and as another form of closure to exclude others from privileged positions. As you will learn, the *Charter Groups*, the French and English, but especially the latter, were, for a considerable time, successful in imposing an *entrance status* on later groups of immigrants, one that destined them to a subordinate status in Canadian society. But, these subordinated groups also found in ethnicity a resource which, like kinship, offers some protection from the vulnerabilities and uncertainties of capitalism and an impersonal labour market and which, from time to time, became a focal point for collective action. And, finally, in everyday life, at the interpersonal level, ethnicity may also be a resource that we all use as a way of creating a sense of identity for ourselves, a sense of continuity with the past and a bond with some others in our community.

You should, by the end of this chapter, know several specific and more general things about ethnicity, ethnic relations and ethnic inequality. First, you should know and appreciate why "race" is unscientific, meaningless and, ultimately, a dangerous concept and why "ethnic group" is preferable. Second, you should understand the distinction between "structural assimilation" and "behavioural assimilation" and why there is debate as to whether the former is possible without the latter. Third, when you finish reading this chapter you should recognize that, while ethnicity obviously is an objective phenomenon in the sense that one either is or is not a Scot, a Greek, an Italian, or a Sikh, the concept of "situational ethnicity" leads to an understanding that ethnicity is also subjective, a symbolic resource that we use or do not use as our definition of situation changes.

You should also leave our discussion of ethnicity, ethnic relations, and ethnic inequality skeptical that conflict, prejudice, and discrimination are inevitable outcomes when two or more ethnic groups are present in the same society. Rather, conflicts which seem, at first glance to be based on ethnicity, and sometimes religion, usually originate in economically based inequalities within that particular society.

Finally, while the future of "visible minorities" in Canada and the eventual fate of Canada's native peoples are, at this point, unknown, you should leave this chapter with some degree of optimism: there is unmistakable evidence that today Canada's ethnic mosaic is less vertical than John Porter found to be the case only a few decades ago.

INTRODUCTION

If one substantive area has captured the interest of Canadian sociologists, it is the study of ethnic groups and ethnic relations. Certainly, most Canadians experience Canada as a multi-ethnic nation. They hear different languages, eat in ethnic restaurants and attend ethnic folk festivals. They are also preoccupied by language conflicts, questions of the rights of native peoples, fear of accusations of prejudice and discrimination and, in turn, fear of suffering the consequences of prejudice and discrimination.

Part of the consciousness of being Canadian is to realize that Canada is a society of immigrants. Canada, rather than a "colony of conquest," was essentially a "colony of settlement." Harold Innis (1956) points out that "fundamentally the civilization of North America is the civilization of Europe" and that

"Canada has remained fundamentally a product of Europe." In the process, native people, the indigenous population of North America, were not so much conquered as swept aside. Except during the short-lived fur trade, and perhaps in the provision of place names, Indians and their culture were to all intents and purposes made irrelevant.

For our forebears, Canada, like the United States, Australia and New Zealand, could be described as "new countries" or "empty lands" or "areas of recent settlement" or "undeveloped areas," or simply "the frontier" (Watkins, 1980:380). The continuous failure to recognize that Canada was a populated territory no doubt contributed to the failure of the Meech Lake Accord.

Those who settled in Canada came for different reasons, with different skills and resources, at strategic and less strategic times and with different levels of commitment to the "new land." Some came as refugees, driven here by religious and political persecution. For many others, the stay in Canada was meant to be temporary. Perhaps they anticipated moving on to the United States or eventually returning home once their "fortune" was made or economic conditions in the homeland improved.

For many, of course, this never happened. Rather, they and in turn their children became Canadians and North Americans. In various degrees they became integrated economically, politically, and perhaps culturally. Yet it seems that for many immigrant groups, integration does not mean a total loss of ethnic commitment. Ethnic diversity, rather than ethnic assimilation, seems to characterize Canadian society.

For sociologists, one of the key issues has been whether this apparent ethnic diversity is "real," that is, more than the superficial remnants of ethnic groups which no longer exist in Canada. Is Canada an ethnic mosaic? If the differences are real, why do they persist? Whose interests do they serve? And what are the social consequences of these differences? If these differences are only apparent, perhaps even trivial, then why have so many attached such importance to them?

Some would argue that the trivial differences became important because real differences, ethnic diversity, are impossible in the face of the intrusions of the dominant culture. Others have argued that because Canada was settled by two dominant cultures, there has been more tolerance of ethnic diversity than in countries such as the United States.

Most liberal sociologists, however, have understood the question as a matter of degree. They frame the question in terms of a dilemma faced by all immigrant groups. Do they assimilate or do they preserve their cultural heritage? In part, then, this is seen as a dilemma of choice. If immigrants are to compete equally with other Canadians for the scarce resources, that is, if they are to be structurally assimilated, how much of their cultural heritage can they preserve? To what extent does structural assimilation require

behavioural assimilation? In other words the liberal is again asking questions about equality of opportunity. To what extent do ethnic differences impede opportunities for social mobility?

Do social scientists view ethnic diversity as good or bad? For the most part the conventional answer is that ethnic diversity is to be valued. When Canadians speak of their country as a mosaic rather than as a melting pot, they often do so with pride. Canada, in these terms, is described as having a particularly rich and diverse culture, possible only in the placid Canadian context of tolerance. Canadians "do not have a race problem," for example. Indeed, the promotion and encouragement of ethnic diversity and ethnic pluralism — multi-culturalism — has for a long time been a deliberate policy of federal governments.

Many social scientists would agree with such a policy but for somewhat different reasons. For many, ethnic groups serve at least in part to fill the gap created by secularization, the breakdown of traditional authority and the loss of community. They may even celebrate the fact that within the homogenizing confines of mass society, ethnicity—the clinging to and perhaps rediscovery of one's "primordial ties" — flourishes. Even if this diversity creates conflict, they argue, it is a small price to pay if the rediscovery of ethnicity serves as a bulwark against the dullness and predictability of Howard Johnson's, McDonald's and Holiday Inns. Perhaps ethnicity provides one way we can do battle against the impersonality of a technological and bureaucratic society.

On the other hand, many sociologists, arguing from a conflict perspective, find the preoccupation with ethnicity repugnant. In this view, to talk about human diversity is simply to rekindle the flame of racism and racial conflict. Encouraging ethnicity is to invite the continuation of ethnic inequality. Stephen Steinberg (1981) has suggested that an unquestioned assumption among social scientists is the existence of a kind of "iron law of ethnicity." Where there are ethnic differences, there will be ethnic conflict.

But, Steinberg is skeptical that, in and of themselves, ethnic differences lead automatically and inevitably to conflict. If we look closer at such conflicts, in Northern Ireland, in Lebanon, in Africa, in Quebec and the Soviet Union, we see that underlying these often deeply entrenched and persistent hatreds and disputes are class-based and regional inequalities.

This is not to suggest that religious and ethnic differences are not important influences on attitudes and behaviour. Quite clearly, ethnicity and religion do matter, do act somewhat independently to shape and constrain our actions and our consciousness. But these same factors may also obscure the more basic cleavages in society: those which derive from class or regional inequality.

From a Marxist perspective ethnicity, like religion, is a superstructure, another mechanism for maintaining the status quo. Ethnic conflicts inhibit class consciousness by making cultural (and racial) what is most often, at base, economic. The promotion of and pre-occupation with issues of ethnicity is, for Marxists, a misdirection of efforts.

Nevertheless, there has been a growing recognition that ethnicity may be a valuable *resource* for the rallying and expression of collective interests. Indeed, many would argue that more people will initially perceive shared interests in terms of ethnicity rather than in purely class terms. Ethnic conflicts might be viewed as a kind of primitive political expression of what are ultimately class conflicts. Whatever the initial issues, some people at least, in the experience of confrontation and an interaction with others who share their grievances, will come to recognize not only the troubles of personal *milieu* but also the larger structural problems. Hence questions of ethnic identify and national character may become transformed into questions of political economy.

A conflict perspective also allows us to see that ethnicity as a resource is double-edged.

Just as ethnicity may be a useful resource in expressing the collective discontent of disadvantaged groups, so too is it a resource available to the powerful to minimize and channel social discontent. From this perspective, then, ethnic conflict is resource management; ethnicity is a resource which can be used either to organize dissent or to divide and rule.

We find the resource conception of ethnicity a particularly useful device for viewing the diverse theoretical and empirical work on ethnic relations. We can view ethnicity as a resource used by "those who have" to block the mobility of "those who have not." We can view it as a resource used by the disadvantaged to protect themselves from the effects of discrimination and as a lever for individual and collective mobility. And on the level of personal identity in everyday life, ethnicity is a cultural resource, part of the common stock of knowledge we can call on in particular situations.

Indeed, by this point in the book, there is not a great deal we can say about ethnic relations that is "new." Ethnicity serves as another illustration of how power and inequality shape interaction, of how people make sense of their world, give meaning to their experiences and come to act back on the structures which constrain them. Viewing ethnicity as a resource keeps in the fore-front that people create and maintain social structures. This chapter, then, examines how, in Canada, this resource is managed by the powerful, the less powerful, and all of us in everyday life.

RACE AND RACIAL THINKING

IS RACE A CONCEPT?

Race, ethnicity, and minority group are often used rather loosely and interchangeably. And as with most sociological concepts, there is often a discrepancy between the technical definition and what people mean by the term in everyday life. Leaving aside for the moment sociological definitions, common-sense definitions of race and ethnicity and how people use these terms have a profound influence on how the various groups interact.

Particularly in the nineteenth century, race became an unquestioned means of classifying people. Not only could people be put in one of several racial categories but it was also assumed that mental and social characteristics were closely associated with certain physical characteristics. A very easy, perhaps inevitable, step was to assume that races could be ranked from superior to inferior.

As the recent controversy over the work of Phillip Rushton suggest, we have yet to escape fully the effects of the myth of racial differences and racial superiority. We are, for instance, still living with, trying to cope with and understand the kind of madness that lay behind the Holocaust — the deliberate and systematic murder of twelve million Jews, Slavs and Gypsies. This was a program of genocide without precedence and which was based on a totally erroneous belief in the superiority of the so-called Aryan race. That many people believed that Aryans constituted a race at all was clearly powerfully influential even though no technical definitions, not even in nineteenth century thinking, would have accepted or condoned Aryan as a racial category.

Understandably, since World War II, the concept of race has been subjected to very close scrutiny. Despite the view of some psychologists, the overwhelming conclusion is that race is a meaningless, unscientific, and ultimately dangerous notion, whether considered in terms of biology or anthropology.

RACIAL THINKING

Many sociologists and anthropologists believe it is one of the tasks of their disciplines to "re-educate" people away from erroneous and,

as in this case, dangerous beliefs about race. While we certainly agree that this should be the goal, we would also remind you that people do not act on the basis of objective data but on their interpretation of the situation.

We must also view *racial thinking* in this way, as a set of unscientific and erroneous beliefs which, because people believed in them, have had real consequences. We have to cope with the fact that people do think in terms of races and that, at a minimum, most people would say there are three, perhaps four, basic races — yellow, black, red and white — even though we know that on the basis of skin colour or any other characteristic, they would often be unable to place an individual into one of these categories.

Furthermore, we have to cope with the equally incorrect belief that appearance and behaviour are somehow both hereditary, and these characteristics are likely to be evaluated. As well, those labelled as "inferior" may come to accept as true the negative (sometimes positive) stereotypes placed on them by the dominant group. Some Indians, for example, come to believe the white stereotype which lies behind the Indian Act. They accept as "truth" that there is some genetic or biological reason why they cannot "handle liquor" and must be controlled (De'Ath and Padbury, 1977).

As a result of racial thinking, people are likely to have characteristics or attributes imputed to them that may or may not be accurate. This is what is meant by *stereotyping*: the assumption that what we have observed or only heard about some members of a group — whether racial or ethnic — applies to all members of that group.

Racial thinking also leads to discrimination, the selecting or rejecting of people on the basis of some physical characteristic associated in people's minds with some stereotype. Rather than taking people on their individual merits, they are treated favourably or unfavourably on the basis of skin colour, religion, or presumed ethnic background. The end result is the vicious circle of segregation, an attempt by one group to maintain social distance from another.

In other words, the processes of stereotyping and labelling we discussed in the chapter on deviance are also the essence of racial thinking. Race, like deviance, is a matter of social definition. People are categorized in terms of some racial designation with implicit and often explicit stereotypes and moral evaluations. Individuals are labelled as belonging to one of these categories and are then treated in terms of the label. And some people will have the power to make their labels and stereotypes "stick."

When a teacher assumes that Indian students are inferior to white students, however subtly, this assumption influences not only how the teacher responds to the Indian but also perhaps how he or she evaluates the student's work. Where a white student's failure may indicate the need for special attention, the Indian student's failure may be taken as evidence for the appropriateness of the stereotype. Indian students may be edged out of the school, may come to view the white educational system with antagonism or, perhaps what is more serious, may come to accept the label and stereotype imposed upon them by the teacher.

This suggests that there are a number of responses to racial thinking, just as there are to any negative labelling. Some may accept and even welcome the racial designation, the imputation that they are different, but deny the conventional stereotypes and moral evaluation. So black, or red, is beautiful. Others may deny the label and dissociate themselves from the racial category. So blacks may straighten their hair; Jews may get a "nose job." And if they think that they are able, some may try to "pass" as members of the dominant group. As will become evident in our discussions of ethnic assimilation and ethnic diversity, whatever the rewards, there are substantial costs in any of these adaptations to racism.

PERSPECTIVES ON PREJUDICE

Perhaps inspired by the ideal of ethnic diversity without conflict, many liberal social scientists have tried to discover the sources of prejudice and discrimination. There are at least three positions, each with its own prognosis. The psychological viewpoint looks for the source of prejudice in individual personality. Prejudice is irrational and there must be something wrong with the person who could hold such a belief. Either that, or prejudice is a "defence mechanism" and ethnic groups the "scapegoats" for the failure of others. The prognosis, at least implicitly, is pessimistic.

A second position, a somewhat more optimistic perspective, is that prejudice is one of the earliest learned attitudes. Children may learn in the home to view as inferior and to hate groups they may never have encountered. This line of argument usually holds that just as people learn prejudice, they can learn tolerance. Changing people's beliefs and attitudes, "resocialization," will probably be more difficult, but it is possible.

A now famous and much debated illustration is the Hilltown study of a biracial housing project (Merton, 1968:488–490). Prior to moving into the project, most people expected a good deal of friction in a community made up of equal numbers of blacks and whites. However, fewer than one-fifth of the whites and one-third of the blacks reported friction along racial lines. Many have concluded from this that continued peer interaction breaks down stereotypes. Others, even more optimistic, have argued that as our knowledge increases and as we become more aware that race is a meaningless concept, prejudice will diminish.

Certainly, not all "experiments" such as this have succeeded and from the evidence it seems premature to be optimistic. In any case it is difficult to assess such studies except in the context of larger social conditions. For example, how much unemployment is there in the community under-going "integration"? Or, to put it another way, to what extent is the "inferior" group seen as an economic threat? Similarly, "busing" in the United States may actually have increased interracial conflict, not so much because of prejudice but because it threatens people's notions of individuals' rights and freedoms.

A third position holds that prejudice is not a result of personal pathology but of social pathology. For example, this position would hold that dominant group members are more likely to hold prejudicial attitudes in times of economic instability. In this case prejudice reflects their economic and status interests, which may appear to them to be threatened. According to this argument, they begin to look for a reason, a scapegoat, to explain their deteriorating position. One might understand the British response to immigrant groups, at least in part, in terms of Britain's economic problems.

e of this is to suggest that prejudice is a fabrication, a resource people use to t their interests. Certainly, ideas reflect rests but they also become the definitions reality that guide people's conduct, and as definitions of reality they may become self-perpetuating. From a sociological point of view, it is the latter two perspectives which offer the most promise.

We agree with Schermerhorn that it is somewhat unproductive to try to prove that prejudice is a personality trait, some flaw in people or in their socialization that has made them hold and sometimes act upon beliefs that look from the outside to be irrational. As he points out:

If research has confirmed anything in this area, it is that prejudice is a product of situations, historical situations, economic situations; it is not a little demon that emerges in people simply because they are depraved (1970:6).

From a sociological perspective, we might begin by looking at the *structural conditions* which intensify and may actually create prejudiced attitudes and sentiments. From this viewpoint, prejudice and racism are not the monopoly of any one type of individual or any one group. Blacks as well as whites may act and feel the same if they find themselves in similar situations.

Peter Carstens (1971), for example, has suggested that the reservation system for Indians in Canada is structurally very similar to apartheid in South Africa and leads to very similar results, a view corroborated by Arch Bishop Desmond Tutu during a visit to Canada in 1990. Both systems segregate members of the indigenous population from the mainstream culture, create a sense of paternalism in whites and tend to perpetuate a system of inequality and a sense of powerlessness on the part of those living on reserves.

Similarly, David Stymeist (1975) used some of Carsten's insights to show how, in a small Ontario town, hostility to native people is a product of historical and economic factors which on a day-to-day basis formally and informally exclude Indians from town and informally exclude Indians from town life. Dominant groups will always try to justify exclusion and inequality. As Stymeist shows, segregation reinforces and perpetuates the various stereotypes whites have about Indians and Indians have about whites.

Racial thinking, then, is best viewed as an ideology to justify structural conditions. Once this ideology becomes part of the common stock of knowledge it will be passed on to future generations through the process of socialization. And, as many of us are "cultural dopes," we will accept the labels, the stereotypes, and the evaluations and act in terms of them.

When racial thinking is part of the culture, even those who reject it must come to grips with it. We might take as an analogy Fred Davis's (1964) study of the interaction between "normals" and the visibly handicapped. In this study, Davis points out the double bind of the normal. Imagine, for example, that you are interacting with someone with a severely scarred face. You believe, or wish to believe, that this makes no difference to you. You wish, as well, to convey this to the other. You know that you should not stare at the scar because not only is it rude, it also makes it appear that you think the scar important. Of course, it is just as bad to avoid self-consciously looking at it. Does one talk about it or self-consciously avoid any mention of this scar or scars in general? This is, of course, only an analogy but it does convey how a racist culture must inevitably influence us all at the level of everyday life. When we have learned the racial categories, that racial distinctions are important whether we like them or not, we are also likely to wonder often how to avoid seeming to be prejudiced when interacting with others.

An illustration of the double bind of prejudice and discrimination is provided by Donald Dutton's (1972) study. Dutton performed an experiment involving a number of the more expensive restaurants in Toronto and Vancouver. He selected restaurants that required men to wear ties. Each restaurant was then visited by two couples. Both members of one couple were black, the other white. Sometimes the black couple would enter first and sometimes the white. The males were not wearing ties. Dutton found the restaurateurs were more lenient with the black couples; that is, few of the black couples were refused service. The restaurateurs, then, treated whites and blacks differently — discriminated—perhaps to avoid seeming prejudiced. Ironically, the restaurateurs acted in terms of the racial distinction apparently to show that the distinction was not important to them.

So, for example, prejudicial attitudes and beliefs about Indians may well have arisen to justify the power relationships and structural arrangements of the reserve system. But these ideas of Indian inferiority do in a sense take on a life of their own and are passed on from generation to generation as though they are *the* reality rather than a human-made reality.

PREJUDICE IN CANADA

Canadians, for the most part, have prided themselves on not being prejudiced. Most would say that racial thinking is not part of our culture. The simple fact is that up until recently we have not, as a nation, really been put to the test. Racist policies in the nineteenth and early twentieth centuries meant that most immigrants were white Northern European. While there have been blacks (sometimes slaves) in Canada since long before the conquest, they have been largely "invisible" because they became structurally segregated into pockets of poverty in much the same way as Indians (see: Clairmont and Magill, 1974; Spray, 1972).

But as a number of studies have shown, we have little reason for smugness. Whenever there is contact between white and non-white in Canada, Canadians do not turn out to be much different from Americans or anyone else for that matter. This seems to be true whether we consider the treatment given Japanese Canadians in World War II (Adachi, 1976), native peoples throughout Canada (Frideres, 1981), Sikhs in the Vancouver area (Ferguson, 1975; Ames and Inglis, 1975), Blacks in Nova Scotia (Henry, 1971), or the Chinese who came in the 19th century to work building the "National Dream" (Berton, 1970).

While discussion and research on race have tended to be heated, this has been less the case when sociologists use what they hope will be the more neutral terms, ethnic group and ethnic relations. Indeed, these terms have led many sociologists to emphasize cultural differences often perhaps at the expense of ignoring material and power differences. As we shall see, however, ethnic relations must be understood within the larger structural conditions; they must be understood in terms of the distribution of power, prestige and wealth.

ETHNIC GROUP AND ETHNIC INEQUALITY

ETHNIC GROUP OR MINORITY GROUP?

There is almost as much ambiguity and confusion about the meaning of ethnic groups as there is about the now discredited concept of race. While Isajiw (1974), a University of Toronto sociologist, was able to ferret out some seventy definitions of ethnicity and ethnic group, there is probably agreement that at least three ideas have usually been involved when we talk about ethnicity: (1) reference to common origins; (2) a conception of distinctiveness; and (3) the necessity that ethnicity is relevant only when two or more categories of people are involved in the same society or community (Hicks, 1977).

Thus, for an earlier generation of sociologists, ethnic group had no meaning in a culturally homogeneous society. Nor, for that matter, did Europeans think of themselves as ethnics until they became immigrants and found themselves treated as distinct from the host or mainstream culture. Very often they also discovered that they were part of a **minority group**, a group of people who, because of physical and/or cultural characteristics, are singled out for differential and unequal treatment.

Besides ethnic minorities, the concept of minority group has been used to include women, homosexuals, and people who are disabled, collectivities which numerically may or may not be a minority. The concept of minority group, in fact, has nothing to do with numbers but with the way in which a collectivity may be disadvantaged with respect to the power it has to control its own destiny (Elliott, 1971:3). In terms of ethnicity, it clearly puts the focus on the inequality of conditions and opportunity an ethnic group may face relative to others in the mainstream culture.

Minority group and ethnic group are so intertwined that at times it seems they have meant the same thing. Indeed, for Anglo-Saxon Canadians, ethnic group has often only had a meaning when one was talking about immigrant groups who spoke a different language and who were at the bottom of the occupational hierarchy. Cabbage rolls and lasagna were regarded as "ethnic" foods; roast beef and Yorkshire pudding apparently were not. But in recent years ethnicity has been a term applied not only to minority ethnic groups but also to dominant and mainstream groups as well.

In recent decades, Anglo-Saxon Canadians have been labelled "Wasps" by European and Asian ethnic groups and as *les anglais* by *les québécois* and we can conjecture that, as various immigrant groups become second and third generation Canadians, who is and is not regarded as "ethnic" will undergo further transformation.

ETHNICITY AND INEQUALITY

What happens when groups of people with different languages, contradicting religions, unique tastes in food, disparate manners, dress and customs, and a variety of skin colours find themselves occupying the same territory? Some, sold on the "iron law of ethnicity," think conflict, prejudice, discrimination and ultimately inequality are the inevitable outcome of trying to put together such a mixture.

In the United States, the image of America as a melting pot was, historically, the preferred way to try to avoid the anticipated outcomes of the waves of immigration. Through resocialization and indoctrination, immigrant groups could, it was hoped, be processed into a homogeneous mass. Over time, it was anticipated, people would lose their ethnic identities and simply become Americans. However, there is considerable debate about whether the melting pot analogy captures adequately the American ethnic experience or is mainly an ideology which, however optimistic and idealistic, does more to confuse than explain.

Perhaps the dominant image in Canada is of an ethnic mosaic rather than a melting pot. As we shall see, this image is also in many ways ideological, in part because, for many ethnic groups, it tells more about the ideal than the real. The mosaic ideology upholds the ideal that people should be encouraged to perpetuate the language, religion, and culture of their forebears. The ideal is that there should be social differentiation but not ethnic stratification; ideally ethnicity as an ascribed attribute should not enter into the ways in which people are allocated to various positions in the society.

The expectation is that a multicultural society is one in which there is **structural assimilation** without **behavioural assimilation**. People do not have to submerge or renounce their ethnic identity and lifestyles and completely adopt those of English Canadians or French Canadians in order to participate equally in the economic, political, and social life of Canadian society.

Structural assimilation means that, if a particular ethnic group comprises say 10 percent of the population, then we would expect that over time about 10 percent of university students, doctors, lawyers, members of parliament, members of the corporate elite, skilled and unskilled workers and so on would be members of that ethnic group. This is essentially what the contentious quota systems in the United States — reverse discrimination as some call it — sought to achieve.

Of course, some ethnic groups have been able to change their initial entrance status. As in the case of social mobility generally, we have to distinguish between individual and group mobility. Studies that focus on ethnic *groups* are obviously concerned mainly with group mobility. Studies that use census data, on the other hand, are dealing with both group mobility and mobility of individuals who at the time of the census enumeration may be "pressured" to declare an *ethnic*

affiliation, even though they may no longer think of themselves as "Greek" or "Italian" or "Ukrainian."

Some members of ethnic groups move upwards simply by disappearing from the group, perhaps by Anglicizing their names and moving away from areas where there is a concentration of immigrants. Probably this is a relatively common practice for those who make it to university since it is often possible for graduates to change their names for their diplomas. More generally, it has been noted that, in Manitoba alone, more than 2000 Slavs made name changes from Slavic to Anglo-Saxon in the years 1937–1957 (Radecki and Heydenkorn, 1977).

This is not an easy decision to make. Herbert Gans (1962), for instance, has drawn a neat parallel between the problems of upward mobility from an Italian community and those of moving out of a traditional working-class community as is found in Britain. In both cases, the general view is that it is acceptable to improve economically but one should not start to adopt middle-class and non-ethnic ways. Those who do so are criticized and eventually ostracized for having gone "high society." Attempts at upward mobility are likely to be interpreted as a repudiation of traditional values. Unrealistically, young people are encouraged to get an education and a better job but at the same time are told they should not change in the process.

Studies of specific ethnic groups have generally concentrated on how the group as a whole has fared. For example, a study of Polish Canadians by Radecki and Heydenkorn concluded that between 1951 and 1961 many moved from being agricultural or unskilled workers to becoming professionals, managers and business owners.

Isajiw and Hartmann (1970) came to a similar conclusion about Ukrainians in Canada. They suggest that three steps are involved in ethnic mobility. First is cultural assimilation. In moving off the farms, Ukrainians begin to take over values and behavioural patterns of the Canadian Anglo-Saxon society. The second pattern is related to the process of structural assimilation, "a reach for equality of opportunities through participation in what popularly is defined as 'decent' jobs" (p. 105). In the third stage, what they call "a process of structural modification," the ethnic group comes to be part of the establishment, having power and influence meaningful in the society as a whole.

But while Ukrainians may have advanced through two of these stages, the authors of this study point out that they have not reached this third level of occupational change. Similarly, Radecki and Heydenkorn temper their optimism about Polish structural integration by noting that "the doors to the corporate elite remain at present closed to them, as they are largely closed to many other immigrant groups . . . " (P. 182).

This was shown more systematically by Wallace Clement in his book *The Canadian Corporate Elite* (1975). He found that until the 1970s the elite was still mainly composed of people of British descent; other ethnic groups and the French were under-represented.

Similar conclusions emerge from Kelner's (1970) study of the Toronto elite. Though non-Anglo-Saxons had made important steps upwards in Toronto's social structure, she found that the core or nucleus of the elite was almost entirely Anglo-Saxon.

Richmond's work on postwar immigration shows that both British and non-British immigrants experienced some downward mobility on coming to Canada, though about half of those who fell were eventually able to recover or improve on their former position. However, his data show that British immigrants are far more likely than non-British immigrants to experience upward mobility after spending some time in Canada. "English speaking immigrants added to the existing association between British ethnic origin and high social status in Canada" (Richmond, 1970:90). Nevertheless, his overall conclusions about ethnic mobility share the same optimism Radecki and Heydenkorn express about the changing situation of Polish Canadians.

ETHNICITY AND SOCIAL CLASS

As we look over Canada's history, it has made sense to think of ethnic relations as meaning ethnic inequality. In Canada, this connection was made most forcibly by John Porter. The title of his most influential work, *The Vertical Mosaic* (1965), tells most of the story. On the basis of his research, it seemed clear that ethnic or immigrant groups in Canada did not disappear or simply become part of a pluralistic mosaic. Rather, ethnic differentiation led to ethnic stratification — the ordering of ethnic groups into a more or less permanent hierarchy of inequality.

Porter viewed ethnicity as an important cause of class inequality: "immigration and ethnic affiliation (or membership in a cultural group) have been important factors in the formation of social classes in Canada" (Porter, 1965:73). There is, in his view, "a reciprocal relationship between ethnicity and social class" that Porter views as arising out of the relative power of some groups to appropriate the top positions and to assign later immigrant groups to lower positions.

It may be that the vertical mosaic is an historic rather than an enduring feature of Canadian society. In the late 1970s, Gordon Darroch (1979), a York University professor, took what he called "another look" at the supposed relationship between class and ethnicity. While the Canadian corporate elite has been slow to admit other than Anglo-Saxons, the picture in the middle-mass of Canadian society is quite different. Darroch finds that while ethnicity may have been a central feature of the system of stratification in Canada, it ceased to be such by 1961. Since then, only Italians, Jews and native peoples are significantly over or under-represented in various levels of the occupational hierarchy.

Tables 12.1 and 12.2, taken from his study, provide the basis for this conclusion. The first table uses data from *The Vertical Mosaic*. The second, from Dennis Forceses's (1975) book on social stratification in Canada, examines data up to 1971. Both use a measure called an "index of dissimilarity." The indices for each ethnic group and for each decade show the proportion of people who would have to change their occupation to match the distribution of the total labour force. So, for example, looking at Table 12.1 we see that, in 1961, only 4.7 percent of the British group would have to move occupational levels for it to be completely structurally integrated. In contrast, 42.9 percent of Indians and Inuit, 23.1 percent of Jews, 20.8 percent of Asians, and 17.9 percent of Italians would have to be in a higher or lower occupational category for us to say that these groups are structurally assimilated. Also, the means — averages — over these four decades show that the occupational segregation of ethnic groups has progressively declined.

Darroch suggests that instead of maintaining a kind of blanket allegiance to ethnic stratification, "we should focus on the bases of the continued importance of ethnicity for *specific* ethnic populations in the context of the broader tendencies toward integration" (Darroch, 1979:212). In other words, what are the historical and structural factors that have resulted in native peoples and Italians being so *under-represented*, and Asians and Jews being so *over-represented*, in the upper levels of the occupational structure?

Rather than looking at these kinds of factors, the tendency among sociologists has been to explain the different achievement levels of ethnic groups in terms of cultural—i.e., ethnic — factors. Supposedly, it is because Jews have had strong commitment to family and education that they have been successful. Apparently Italians, as a group, lack these characteristics. Left out of the analysis are such important questions as when various immigrant groups came to Canada, the class position they left behind and the skills and resources they brought with them to North America.

Stephen Steinberg makes a strong case that, in the United States, cultural factors do not explain the relative success of various ethnic groups. His research shows that if Jews

TABLE 12.1

OCCUPATIONAL DISSIMILARITY OF ETHNIC GROUPS FROM TOTAL MALE LABOUR FORCE FOR 1931, 1951 AND 1961 (FROM PORTER, 1965: TABLE 1)

	DISSIMILARITY INDEXES		
ETHNIC GROUP	1931	1951	1961
Total British	7.9	5.7	4.7
French	3.4	3.0	3.7
German	21.0	19.1	8.8
Italian	33.4	19.5	17.9
Jew	48.1	31.6	23.1
Dutch	18.5	17.3	10.3
Scandinavian	21.2	14.7	10.6
East European	26.9	14.1	7.8
Other European	35.8	11.1	6.9
Asian	38.0	23.9	20.8
Indian and Inuit	45.3	47.0	42.9
Mean (X)	27.23	18.82	14.32
Mean excluding Asian and Native groups (comparable to Lieberson's groups for American cities)	24.02	16.64	10.01

Source: Darroch (1980:211).

TABLE 12.2

OCCUPATIONAL DISSIMILARITY OF ETHNIC GROUPS FROM TOTAL LABOUR FORCE, 1971 (FROM FORCESE, 1975: TABLE 2-3)

ETHNIC GROUP	DISSIMILARITY INDEX
British Isles	5.9
French	5.5
German	8.8
Hungarian	12.9
Italian	26.4
Jewish	29.8
Netherlands	10.9
Polish	9.6
Russian	8.2
Scandinavian	9.8
Ukrainain	8.0
Asiatic	16.3
Native Indian	29.0
Other	13.0
Mean (X)	13.9

Source: Darroch (1980:213).

were successful (and many were not) it is because they came at the right time with the right skills for that stage in the development of capitalism and not, initially, as a result of the special value they placed on education or of other features of their family and cultural life.

Because of religious persecution, most Russian and European Jews were not allowed to own land and therefore could not be farmers. Through force of necessity they were mainly urban dwellers who had learned trades and other industrial and urban skills, all of which were immediately useful in North America. It appears that Jews in the United States were first upwardly mobile and only then translated their cultural bias towards knowledge and education into a desire to give their children a formal education.

In contrast, Swedes, Poles, Ukrainians, Italians and others who came to North America were usually peasants and farmers. Since they were often illiterate and had few skills, they were poorly equipped to deal with or to profit from the burgeoning industrial capitalist society in which they found themselves and were, rather, more likely to be exploited.

Similarly, Irish men gravitated to labouring jobs and Irish women became domestic servants. Does this say something about Irish culture, of the greater tolerance of the Irish for domestic work? Steinberg suggests not. As the old saying goes, the main export of Ireland has been people. Between 1850 and 1900 the population of Ireland halved itself, in part because of emigration. Moreover, unlike other immigrant groups in which either intact families moved or men came ahead, there was economic pressure and incentive for single women to move on their own. In the late nineteenth and early twentieth century, these women were highly vulnerable; there were few options but to remain in domestic service until something better could be found. By the second generation, most were able to move out of domestic service. By then, "Irish were not much more likely than other groups to work as domestics" (Steinberg, 1981:164).

Steinberg makes a similar argument about the success of Asians, particularly Japanese, in North American society. Again, those who emigrated came with resources and skills that were marketable in the capitalist society in which they found themselves, and as a result they have become structurally assimilated.

Steinberg is writing about the United States. But except for the historical details of when various ethnic groups migrated to Canada, we think his findings and argument have equal relevance to Canada. At this stage in Canada's history, we do not believe that, except for entry into the elite, ethnicity is a very crucial factor in determining who "has" and who "has not."

The Vertical Mosaic thesis implies that those of British origin are at the top and everyone else is below. While this is true in one sense, it ignores the fact that the British are fairly evenly distributed throughout the occupational and class structure. As S. D. Clark has pointed out, the British Charter group was admittedly very much on the top but they were on the very bottom as well.

What all of this tells us is that ethnicity may not any longer be a very good determinant of what will happen to most people. In Canada, now, there is probably as much difference *within* various ethnic groups in occupational status as between them (Darroch, 1979:222). Most ethnic groups may not be so far away from structural assimilation as previously supposed.

ASSIMILATION AND ETHNIC IDENTITY

Does this mean that people must shed their ethnic identity in order to be successful in North America; is behavioural assimilation inevitably related to structural assimilation? Conventional sociological wisdom suggests the answer is yes: ethnic group members are faced with a choice — participate equally in the competition for resources and give up ethnic group identification, or maintain the commitment to the ethnic group at the risk of blocked mobility. In more technical language, equal participation in opportunity structures seems to require *acculturation*, acquiring the culture of the dominant ethnic group, and acculturation seems to lead to *assimilation*, absorption into the dominant group (Shibutani and Kwan, 1965).

An earlier generation of Canadian sociologists believed first, that structural assimilation was not possible without cultural assimilation and, second, that there were powerful forces undermining ethnicity and replacing it with cultural differences based in class and education (Clark, 1976).

John Porter took this position in his discussions of ethnicity. Both in *The Vertical Mosaic* and later work, he maintained a consistent argument against the mosaic ideology. In his view the revival of ethnicity creates a high risk of ethnic stratification and the perpetuation of ethnic inequality (Porter, 1975:289). Moreover, the depiction of Canada as a multiethnic society is, he argues, partly an artifact of Statistics Canada's insistence that at census time we must pin an ethnic label on ourselves since until recently "Canadian" was not a valid answer to questions on ethnicity; for census purposes both those born in Canada and immigrants had to have a non-North American ethnicity (Porter, 1975:279). He suggests, then, that a large number of people may no longer think of themselves as Polish, Hungarian, Italian, Irish and so on, but as simply Canadians. If so, cultural assimilation of Canada's immigrants has proceeded much further than the mosaic ideology implies.

This is also essentially the conclusion of another influential Canadian sociologist, S. D. Clark. He has argued that since the Second World War, behavioural assimilation to a "middle-class culture" has occurred very rapidly in Canada. The result is that cultural differences are no longer based on ethnic origin, but social class, education and religion (Clark, 1976a:2).

Others such as Vallee (1960) argued that minority groups cannot, on the one hand,

strive to maintain an ethnic language and culture and, on the other, successfully prepare their members for competition in the larger or mainstream culture of which they are a part; they are caught in a kind of "mobility trap" (Wiley, 1967). Vallee is referring to what Breton (1960) calls the degree of **institutional completeness** of an ethnic group: the extent to which the ethnic community can perform all the services required by its members.

For example, one of your authors, an Anglo-Saxon, spent his sabbatical year living in an area of Toronto which the street signs label as "Little Italy," though "Little Portugal" would be as accurate. Those who live in this area are able to carry out virtually all aspects of their lives — shopping, banking, legal advice, real estate and often employment — without speaking English or interacting with other than Italians or Portuguese. Not far away, the signs, the language, the food, change dramatically: in what was once a Jewish area the Chinese of Toronto have also created this same kind of institutional completeness.

Sociologists, such as Vallee and Breton, argued that institutional completeness limits interaction with those "outside" the ethnic community and acts as a barrier to structural assimilation. Many, such as Breton, were confident that with time ethnic organizations and services will disappear as the children of immigrants, if not the immigrants themselves, are drawn into the social and cultural mainstream. But, as these sociologists readily admitted, the paradox was that at the very time when many of the most obvious differences between ethnic groups were disappearing, a new and sometimes very self-conscious sense of ethnicity emerged in Canada and the United States. Glazer and Moynihan suggest that we have to change our thinking about ethnic groups.

Formerly seen as survivals from an earlier age, to be treated variously with annoyance, toleration, or mild celebration, we now have a growing sense that they may be forms of social life that are capable of renewing and transforming themselves (1975:4).

Several things seem to be happening at once. As we have suggested, even while cultural differences based on ethnicity may be disappearing, ethnicity is becoming an important resource both to dominant and dominated groups.

ETHNICITY AS RESOURCE

DOMINANT GROUPS

As we have stressed, structural assimilation is mainly a middle-class phenomenon. Non-Anglo-Saxon ethnic groups have not been as successful in achieving access to the most powerful positions in Canadian society. And we should not over-estimate the degree of structural assimilation or assume that it is uniform in all sectors of the society. No doubt, people will use kinship influences—nepotism —when it is to their advantage to do so. As with nepotism, so it is with ethnicity, whether we are talking about succession to elite status or who gets the better jobs in communities of single industry.

As Lucas (1971:135–136) described, ethnicity and nepotism were so closely intertwined on the railroad that after some sixty years of hiring, the "British represented 100 percent of the managerial group, 91 percent of the train crews, but only 15 percent of the labourers" (p. 136). News of an upcoming vacancy circulates informally among the running trades group which is almost entirely British. A son or a friend is told to drop in and see the "super" and others put in a good word for him. Nepotism becomes ethnic sponsorship. *If a man of French or "other" ethnic background applies for a job, the superintendent tells him with perfect honesty and sincerity: I'm sorry but there are no openings in the crews. . . . When the job is posted formally, it has already been filled informally (1971:136).*

Also, from a Marxist perspective, the resurgence of ethnicity might be interpreted as evidence of the success of capitalism, or of the ruling class, in diffusing the underlying conflict inherent in class inequality. From this perspective ethnicity is a kind of false consciousness diverting attention away from the objective interests that lower classes, whether of Italian, Indian or Portuguese ancestry, have in common.

Ethnicity may, then, have important functions for the dominant or mainstream culture as well as for minority groups. It may take some pressure off the system. As we have said, class and ethnicity are not exactly synonymous but they are intimately related. Focusing on ethnicity rather than poverty, as in the case of Indians, provides a neat rationalization of why some people are poor or without power. The problem, we are able to say, is that they will not assimilate or change their ways. It is a process akin to castigating those on welfare or those who are unemployed because "they won't work." It makes it the individual's fault, his or her problem, rather than a weakness of society.

When we blame ethnicity we are saying, if only people would assimilate then their troubles would be over. Marcel Rioux (1971:17) points out that it is a common explanation of Quebec's problems: Quebeckers are "the authors of their own misfortunes." The church held them back; they have outmoded attitudes about work and business; they elect reactionary and corrupt politicians and so on. But what is seldom asked is why these values and traditions developed and are maintained. As Quebeckers have come to recognize, these are in part adaptations and responses to 200 years of political and economic domination and exploitation.

Perhaps the clearest illustration of the use of ethnicity can be seen in both the early and present attempts by charter groups to control immigration. John Porter based his analysis around two key concepts, ***charter group status*** and ***entrance status***. A charter group as the first ethnic group to enter a previously unpopulated territory has the most say about who else may later enter and what jobs they are allowed to have. In Porter's words:

A given ethnic group appropriates particular roles and designates other ethnic groups for the less preferred ones. Often the low status group accepts its inferior position. Through time the relative status positions, reinforced by stereotypes and social [types]—the Irish policeman and the Irish maid, for example—harden and become perpetuated over a very long time. In the general scheme of class and status that evolves with economic growth and immigration there exists an "entrance status" to be assumed by the less preferred ethnic groups. Entrance status implies lower level occupational roles and subjection to processes of assimilation laid down and judged by the charter group. Over time the position of entrance status may be improved or it may be a permanent caste-like status as it has been, for example, with Chinese in Canada. Thus most of Canada's minority groups have at some time had this entrance status. Some, but not all, have moved out of it (1965:63–64).

As Porter suggests, it was easy enough in the nineteenth century for the two charter groups, and particularly for the English, to justify immigration policies that were explicitly racist and discriminatory. The seeming complexity and high level of social and economic development of Britain, France and Germany were taken as clear evidence of innate superiority over nationalities in the east and south of Europe. More generally, the reports of anthropologists and others who visited and studied tribal societies seemed to confirm the idea that societies *evolve* from the "savage" and "primitive" to the "civilized" and "complex." Thus, what we now refer to as preliterate societies were of interest mainly for the clues they seemed to provide about our own prehistoric past.

As another generation of anthropologists with different views about how to do research went out into the field, this simple evolutionary model began to look more and more implausible. What mainly shattered it was that unlike their predecessors, who had been content simply to observe, later anthropolo-

gists held that one could not stand outside of social action; it was necessary to participate, to attempt to understand the culture on its own terms, not those of the researcher. The first step in that process is, of course, learning the language. This in turn led to an awareness of just how complex all cultures are whatever their form of economic development.

While genetic or racial explanations have been more or less discarded, nineteenth century views and beliefs about racial and cultural inferiority still haunt us, often only thinly disguised beneath the now more acceptable emphasis on cultural factors. The result is that despite occasional reversals, Canadian immigration policy has been implicitly, sometimes explicitly, racist. Earlier in this century there was an outright preference for northern European immigrants and a rejection of "too many" southern Europeans. And, racist and anti-semitic attitudes were the underlying reason few Jewish refugees were admitted to Canada during the Second World War (Abella, 1982).

Until very recently, Asians and Africans were inconceivable as regular immigrants and potential Canadians. By the time the Green Paper on immigration emerged in 1975, only the language had changed — to vague references to the "resilience" of Canadians in accommodating so many "foreign migrants." Since all migrants are by definition foreign, this was obviously a euphemism for non-white immigrants or "visible minorities" as some prefer to call Asian and Caribbean immigrants.

SUBORDINATE GROUPS

Ethnic groups may, over time, give up many aspects of their culture, but in the process of living and working in North America they may sometimes invent new attributes that bear only vague resemblance to what the original immigrants brought with them. This is nicely illustrated by what has happened to the Italian language in Toronto. Rather than give up speaking Italian entirely, immigrants have created "Italiese, a brand-new hybrid tongue somewhere between Italian and Inglese." Basically, English words are given Italian pronunciation and spelling: hurry up —*arriapa*; backyard—*bacchi-iarda*; city hall —*sitialla*; report card—*reportacarta* and so on (Clivio, 1977). Apparently, Portuguese has been undergoing a very similar transformation as Azorean and mainland immigrants cope with the Canadian environment: people *usam o snowshovel* and *pogam os bills* (pay the bills), for example (Anderson and Higgs, 1977:179).

Some members of an immigrant group may have vested interests in maintaining ethnic differences. They may find in ethnicity a resource for individual mobility. Breton (1964) points out that when immigrant groups come to Canada with limited skills and resources, there is an important gap to be filled by the social entrepreneur. "His rewards would be either monetary profit, prestige in the community, more members for his church, or more buyers for his newspapers" (p. 93). Similarly, Beiler Brettel (1977:179) argues that "ethnicity is partially sustained in urban areas as a good business venture." She is referring to the profusion of Portuguese travel agents in some areas of Toronto, examples of what she calls "ethnic entrepreneurs." As well as selling travel, these agents read mail, write letters, place phone calls, fill out forms for people, thereby assuring themselves of a steady flow of Portuguese clients. Such entrepreneurs act simultaneously as a communication link between the ethnic group and the wider society. In this way, the boundary between the two is sustained and sometimes created (Nagata, 1974). In some senses, then, "ethnic entrepreneurs" or "brokers" are seen as contributing to the isolation of the ethnic group (De'Ath and Padbury, 1977).

This, we might add, has long been the situation of English Canadians in Quebec. Vested interests—the media, the educational system and business—often operated so as to keep their English-speaking constituency ignorant of what is happening politically and socially in Quebec society and incapable of participating fully in the society. There is, for instance, evidence that Montreal's two English newspapers, *The Gazette* and the late *Montreal Star*, often misled their English readership with biased, sometimes downright incorrect, reporting of facts about such political developments as Bill 22 and Bill 101 (Elkin, 1970; Caldwell, 1975).

This, however, does not explain why there may be a continuing market for ethnic entrepreneurs and ethnic associations. Ethnic entrepreneurs and institutions are, no doubt, supported because people feel that they have something to gain by ethnic affiliation. They may feel that complete assimilation in private life as well as public life undermines values that seem worth sustaining. In other words, people may want to have the best of both worlds; they want the material advantages of Canadian society but not at the cost of giving up the important and positive things about, say, family life.

What Kurt Danziger (1974) describes about Toronto Italians illustrates the problems and tensions involved in acculturation. As he shows, it is not simply that Italians do not want to mix with others or that they prefer to "stick together." Just the contrary. Like just about everyone else in Canada, they want to enjoy the material advantages this society offers. But such conformity also poses a threat to traditional core values about family, about the place of women, courtship and so on. The solution, he suggests, is to let men "bear the brunt of the acculturation process and to take steps to protect the girls, in the hope that they will become the guardians of the core values of the traditional culture" (p. 134).

Italian girls, for example, are encouraged to retain traditional expectations about domestic and mothering roles. Efforts are made to supervise whom they see, where they go, and to insulate them from the "winds of change" such as feminism. In varying degrees this is probably true of many ethnic groups. In public life, immigrant groups may appear to be highly assimilated and accultur-ated. In the privacy of family relationships, however, ethnicity remains of considerable symbolic importance (McCready, 1975; Nagata, 1974).

People may maintain and revive their eth-nicity in part as a way of adapting to and coping with the marginal and highly vulner-able status at least temporarily accorded them in Canadian society. And in part, they may feel they have no choice; ethnicity is often imposed upon them from "above." But this does not fully explain the continuing signifi-cance of ethnicity. After all, the experience is that most disadvantaged groups have tried to shed their ethnic identity at least publicly. Consciously or unconsciously they have rec-ognized how little they stand to gain from multiculturalism — the mosaic ideology — as long as it derives from past and present layers of ethnic inequality.

In any event, the most powerful pressures for ***ethnicization*** do not come from the least privileged economically, but from those groups that have achieved some degree of economic success. In part, the salience of eth-nicity may simply be a carryover from past indignities and experiences of vulnerability. The work of Jeffrey Reitz on survival of ethnic groups in Toronto suggests that "middle-class ethnicity is more prevalent in those ethnic groups that have a history of the most severe inequality, economic segregation and dis-crimination" (Reitz, 1980:233). Whatever the past, there is agreement that the "rediscovery of ethnicity" and the attachment to and pro-motion of policies of ethnic pluralism is a mid-dle-class interest.

On looking back on their own famous study, *Beyond the Melting Pot* (1963), Glazer and Moynihan conclude that ethnicity, as well as class, becomes a resource to focus on and mobilize for the pursuit of group or individual interests.

One of the striking characteristics of the present situation is, indeed, the extent to which we find the ethnic group defined in terms of interest, as an interest group. Thus, whereas in the past a religious conflict, such as that which is tearing Northern Ireland apart, was based on such issues as the free and public practice of a religion, today it is based on the issue of which group shall gain benefits or hold power of a wholly secular sort (1975:7).

But why should groups that have achieved relative affluence want to maintain, rediscov-er and even invent their ethnicity? What are the group interests served by ethnicity?

By now you should have some sense of the subjective side of capitalism, of the alienation and layers of vulnerability. In Chapter 5 and in a different way in Chapter 10 we have tried to show how much of our activity can be char-acterized as our attempts to deal with our alienation and somehow reduce our vulner-ability. For those at the very bottom, the char-acteristic response has been fatalistic submission. But for most Canadians, those who have achieved some degree of affluence, the response has been one of shoring up against attacks from the rear and reducing resources. Of course, for most of us real wealth and the power it brings are beyond our reach. We are competing for small prizes — social honour, prestige, some small mea-sure of autonomy and power. Here we find useful Max Weber's understanding of the var-ious forms of inequality that matter most to us most of the time. He understood that for most of us the competition was not for real power but for more money, more prestige, and more power over our life chances. And it is in this competition for these limited prizes that ethnicity becomes a resource.

Immigrant groups are a particularly apt illustration of Weber's notion of inequality as multidimensional. Clearly the first battle a new immigrant group must fight is for a big-ger share of the economic pie. For first-gen-eration immigrants, economic advancement may be enough even if the cost is a loss of language and ethnicity in the second and third generations. But will their children be content by simply having "made it" economically? Probably not. For succeeding generations, structural assimilation will not be enough.

They will also want to participate more fully in the political, social, and cultural as well as economic institutions of Canadian society and will in turn see this as necessary for their continued economic well-being. They seek, in other words, at least full "middle-class standing."

As Weber's thesis implies, middle-mass conflicts which emerge out of these efforts to consolidate and make congruent class, status, and power, though seldom violent, are intense and ongoing. One aspect is that the more established groups keep changing the rules. We have already seen one example of this in the previous chapter: as various groups begin to achieve the educational credentials traditionally held by the elite, new definitions of what is a "good" education are invented. Similarly, as ethnics finally break down the social and economic barriers that kept them out of a "fashionable" neighbourhood, they find it has become unfashionable; the dominant groups have moved on to a new area of the city where once more barriers can be erected to maintain exclusiveness.

Quite apart from the imposition of ethnicity, it may be that under certain circumstances ethnicity, however that comes to be interpreted, provides a focal point for collective action and the formation of interest groups. One set of interests, then, is to achieve structural assimilation. Paradoxically, the rediscovery of ethnicity is seen as one way to avoid and eventually overcome ethnic discrimination. But as we have seen, ethnicity can also be a resource of the more powerful groups, a useful way to keep others out and "in their place." It is equally useful to not so dominant groups, fighting their way up and threatened by those one step below.

It is in this sense that we see clearly that discrimination is not the exclusive property of any one group, any one culture. Certainly there is something rather pure—even heroic — in accounts of immigrants making it economically and eventually breaking down some of the barriers which kept their children out of the better schools and themselves out of the better neighbourhoods. However, there is a good deal of irony in seeing their children and grandchildren erecting barriers to keep out the latest immigrants and justifying it on the grounds of the need to defend and preserve the ethnic character of their schools and neighbourhoods, perhaps the very ones their parents fought so hard to "de-ethnicize."

The revival of ethnicity must be viewed, then, with a good deal of skepticism. Steinberg points out that "just as ethnic groups have class reasons for tearing down ethnic barriers ahead of them, they also have class reasons for raising ethnic barriers behind them" (1981:285). Attachment to ethnic pluralism, as long as it implies ethnic stratification in terms of class, status and power, involves a kind of "doublethink": "negative discrimination is when 'we' are the ones to be excluded; positive discrimination is when we are excluding someone else" (Steinberg, 1981:259). Which definition of the situation will prevail? A question answered by a question: who has the most power to transform their definition into social policy?

All of this may strike you as unduly cynical. The survival and saliency of ethnicity cannot be explained wholly in structural terms. Some of the attachment to ethnic pluralism undoubtedly derives from an "irrational" and "non-calculating" desire to preserve particular traditions and values and to ensure that, as well as those of main stream cultures, these become part of the Canadian identity. Moreover, whatever its implications for Canadian social structure, ethnicity may also, at the level of everyday life, provide us with a sense of tradition, continuity and identity.

INTERPERSONAL RELATIONS

Some anthropologists and sociologists focus on the meanings of ethnicity in everyday life. They suggest that we should concentrate on *ethnicity* as an interpersonal resource, rather than as a fixed or objective status; ethnic identity is a *processual* and *subjective* status. Ethnicity is seen as one of a number of symbolic "props" with which we present ourselves and, like other roles we play, it is **situational**. Our use of the prop depends on the context in which we find ourselves. While one's objective cultural or ethnic background may be important in how we view the world and how others treat us, Frederik Barth (1969) argues that it is by no means crucial in how, ethnically, we choose to present ourselves to others. Hicks suggests that

people often have a repertoire of ethnic attributes from which they can select the ones most suitable to a given situation. The possibility is opened for people, as it were, to leap back and forth across several ethnic boundaries (1977:17).

This is also Judith Nagata's experience from doing research of Greek immigrants in Toronto. She finds that there is considerable discrepancy in ethnic behaviour between public performances and those in the privacy of the family. As she points out:

What apparently emerges is not so much a "unilinear" model of acculturation, whereby individuals become progressively "less Greek" or more "Canadian," and from which no reversal is possible, but a "situational" process in which sometimes Greekness prevails, sometimes Canadianness. The norms and behaviours that prevail on any particular occasion depend as much on expediency as on loyalties to either culture (1969:53).

Situational ethnicity reaches some sort of extreme in David Stymeist's (1975) study, *Ethnics and Indians*. Stymeist went to "Crow Lake" expecting to find different ethnic groups arranged in some sort of order. Rather, what he found was that ethnicity was not very pervasive, nor was it very closely connected to position in the community. He found that sometimes people would state they were perhaps Scottish or Ukrainian, even Indian. But on other occasions and in different situations they would deny these labels and attach another ethnicity to themselves. How is this possible? They key seemed to be that under, say, the general heading of Ukrainian and Polish, someone who referred to himself and

was considered "Ukrainian" would, on being pressed, admit that in fact both his parents were born in Poland; it was just more convenient — more meaningful in the community — to call himself Ukrainian. It was also more convenient for others in the community to be able to lump him in with Ukrainians. Moreover, in relationship to Indians in the community, people tended to downplay and ignore their ethnic differences, identities which in other contexts could be fairly important and divisive.

Probably many of us have practised situational ethnicity at one time or another. When we travel to Europe, for instance, our various ancestries may give way to the label "Canadian" as we seek to distinguish ourselves from Americans by sticking Maple Leaf flags on back packs and suitcases. At other times, when we are travelling through the country of origin of our parents or their parents, we may become more conscious of our ethnic roots. People who ordinarily do not think of themselves as Jewish may, in talking to some people, want to make it known that they have Jewish ancestry. In still another setting, the fact that they are also of Hungarian descent may overwhelm their identification with Jews.

The idea of situational ethnicity, then, moves the concept of ethnicity from a highly objective category of people who have a common cultural heritage to a more subjective emphasis on identification, or self-labelling. Barth (1969:13–14), for example, holds that "to the extent that actors use ethnic identities to categorize themselves and others for purposes of interaction, they form ethnic groups."

The notion of situational ethnicity emphasizes that people are not determined by their ethnic origins and are not passive recipients of an ethnic culture, but rather they use ethnicity as a resource to achieve a number of purposes. It may be a private resource to maintain the solidarity in the family, as a source of familial rules and ritual. Similarly, it may be a resource for maintaining a sense of community. And as we have seen, it may be a resource in the public sphere, a rallying point for collective interests.

Viewing ethnicity as resource allows us to capture more clearly some of the complexity of ethnic relations. For example, it allows us to recognize that ethnic conflict may be only nominally ethnic, in fact a reflection of deeper structural cleavage. As well, someone who seems to be holding fast to an ethnic identity or apparently rejecting it is acting in a situation and in terms of the perceived demands of that situation. Such a perspective seems particularly apt for the Canadian case.

ETHNICIZATION

Compared to some societies, ethnic diversity and processes of assimilation are, in Canada, especially complex. It makes sense in the United Kingdom, for instance, to talk about a host population and an immigrant group, but much less so in Canada. Here, it is not at all clear who is doing the assimilating. Who for instance constitutes the host population in Canadian society? Those who claim British decent? Both French and English? Francophone and Anglophone Canadians? In either case, how do we deal with relationships between French and English? Furthermore, how do we deal with native peoples, since they are neither an immigrant population nor part of the mainstream culture, French or English?

All of this suggests the need for new terms to replace the static and deterministic concept of ethnic group. Ironically, these issues have been most effectively addressed by an American sociologist, Andrew Greeley, who developed the concept of **ethnicization**. He describes the concept as follows:

Implicit in this perspective is the notion that ethnicity is not a residual social force that is slowly and gradually disappearing; it is, rather, a dynamic, flexible social mechanism that can be called into being rather quickly and transformed and transmuted to meet changing situations and circumstances (1974:301).

The approach recognizes that ethnic boundaries are permeable, that the bases of ethnic-

ity are not fixed and that over time and through interaction with one another, both the dominant and subordinate ethnic collectivities change. In these terms, as in ours, ethnicity is a resource, ethnicization the process of resource management. The utility of such an approach for bringing together apparently conflicting accounts of assimilation and the rediscovery of ethnicity can be illustrated in the Quebec case.

QUEBEC SOCIETY

The mobilization of ethnicity as a resource will depend on the availability of other resources, both human and material. In this context, Quebec is in rather a unique position, simultaneously the host culture to immigrant groups, and, historically, a subordinate culture compared to English Canada; even within its own boundaries, power rested in the hands of the Anglo "minority." Québécois until recently have had limited experience with the absorption and assimilation of immigrant populations since typically, immigrants who settled in Quebec moved towards Anglophone rather than Francophone culture (Caldwell, 1974:112).

Until the 1960s this did not matter since the "battle of the cradle" was obviously being won by French Canadians. The dramatic fall in the Quebec birth rate changed all that; whether as a separate state or a province with special status in confederation, Quebec society has for two decades been demographically threatened. The shortfall in births can only be made up through immigration. Part of the motivation for introducing language legislation was to ensure that immigrants become part of French rather than English culture in Quebec.

Official policy has been to encourage assimilation of immigrants into Quebec society. But this is difficult to do in practice. Compared to the concept of "Canadian," *Canadien* or Québécois is unambiguous; it means that one can trace his or her roots back to what Jones (1972:40) calls the "primordial event of the conquest." The result is that Quebec society views itself not only as a charter group but also as a *nation*, a community of people who see themselves as linked together by a common culture, history, and language (Ryerson, 1972).

When we consider the relationship of Quebec to the rest of Canada, an "ethnic group" perspective seems no longer useful or applicable. Marcel Rioux (1971:78) argues that French Canadians in Quebec ceased in the 1960s to think of themselves as an ethnic community and began, rather, to see themselves simply as an industrial society of the twentieth century. Assertions of collective equality, self-determination and sovereignty became taken for granted and are no longer questioned by most Quebeckers.

It seems, too, that English Canadians, however reluctantly, also came to accept Quebec as a distinct society. They no longer assumed that with time and economic development Quebeckers will simply become neutral Canadians and North Americans. To use Lower's phrase, the people of Quebec have gone from *Colony to Nation*. In the process they no longer find it necessary to take refuge in the past, to call upon ethnicity as a resource. Like other industrial societies, Quebec seeks its utopia in the future rather than in some bygone era in its own history. This has been forcibly illustrated by the high level of support shown by Quebeckers toward free trade. Clearly, there is less fear in Quebec than in English Canada of what the free trade agreement might do to its cultural identity.

This argument perhaps ignores the extent to which ethnicity has been a powerful resource in mobilizing people towards nationhood. Ethnicity, as we have said, is a powerful means to focus interests, pull people together, and bring them to an awareness of their shared economic or class position. According to Milner and Milner:

. . . the presence of a different ethnic and cultural group at the top of the social structure facilitates the recognition of power relationships and class distinctions on the part of the lower classes within the population. Added to this are cases of outright discrimination and expressed attitudes of disdain towards the French Canadians and their culture which aggravate and expose the social class distinctions (1973:230).

Rioux's wish to underplay the role of ethnicity was understandable. He took the radical position that the focus on ethnicity obscures the real bases of conflict which are always economic. So, for Rioux, ethnic consciousness and class consciousness developed along parallel lines, an argument which does not share Milner's optimism that ethnic consciousness is a mechanism which may lead to class consciousness.

However, Rioux does capture the other side of the coin, that dominant groups may use ethnicity in different ways. Certainly, as we have shown, it may be used to obscure class differences and inhibit class consciousness, At the same time, it may provide a mechanism for exploitation. It is, for example, no accident that during the Quiet Revolution companies like Labatt's Breweries were able to multiply their sales by tying their products to the historical heritage of the province, or that countless *brasseries* throughout Quebec have adopted a *"Habitant"* decor and menu; it made good economic sense to tap what was latent and unfulfilled in the culture.

At the time the first edition of this book was published (1978), it was taken for granted by many Quebeckers, particularly intellectuals, that separation from Canada was both desirable and inevitable. The ethic and rhetoric of the Quiet Revolution of the 1960s emphasized the need, particularly in education, to "catch up" with the rest of Canada. Through educational reform Quebeckers would be able to compete and be mobile individually in North American Society. And, to a large extent, this happened: social mobility research provides unmistakable evidence that by the 1970s the mobility experiences of anglophones and francophones were not very different and that it no longer made sense to speak of "linguistic stratification" (McRoberts et al., 1976:78).

But, this structural assimilation did not, as anticipated, result in behavioural assimilation. Instead, with growing affluence came a renewed, revitalized and, sometimes, violent quest for ethnic identity, self-realization and sovereignty within Quebec society. And all of this reached some sort of climax with the election of a Parti Quebecois government, a party committed to separation. November 15, 1976 seemed to most to be an historical watershed after which things would never be quite the same in Quebec or in Canada.

Current events make liars of us all. A decade later, the Parti Quebecois seemed a spent political force and separation had become a dead issue in the minds of most Quebeckers. The "no" to sovereignty association in the 1983 referendum seemed a clear signal that most preferred the precarious status of being an ethnic group, admittedly a special ethnic group, to the uncertainties of being a separate nation within the North American continent. Yet, the failure to ratify the Meech Lake Accord and its recognition of Quebec as a distinct society may, perhaps, have renewed separatist aspirations and made the future of Quebec within Canadian society problematic and uncertain.

Where does all of this leave French Canadians in the rest of Canada? Traditionally, federal policy has been to give these groups a special status denied other ethnic groups in Canada. When separation was alive, the concern was that, should Quebec go its own way, these groups might eventually lose their constitutional rights. The Meech Lake Accord was seen by many as posing another threat to Francophones outside of Quebec. This is because, as with women and native peoples, these groups were not singled out for special consideration. The provinces could, conceivably, undermine constitutional rights and those provided under the Charter of Rights and Freedoms. As with the fears about what the Free Trade Agreement might do to our social programs and, ultimately, our sovereignty as a nation, we do not know what would have been the long-term consequences

of the Meech Lake Accord. It is apparent, in undermining the concept of federalism, the Accord might have led to a kind of "balkanization" and, potentially, an end to francophone rights outside of the province of Quebec.

But all of this may be both too objective and too premature. It ignores the concept of situational ethnicity, the fact that individuals may construct or reconstruct an ethnic identity, may use this identity as the basis for group formation, and may exert sufficient political force so as to maintain their special status within Canadian society.

The alienation of Quebec from the rest of Canada and its threat to separate had the ironic effect of forcing these groups to reevaluate what they had taken for granted—their continuing existence as a cultural group in Canada. This seems to be as true for the French in Alberta, Manitoba and New Brunswick as it is for Acadians in New Brunswick and Nova Scotia, who have in recent years also talked of separation. As recent developments in Saskatchewan and to some extent, Alberta, suggest, with or without federal policies designed to further bilingualism and biculturalism, French Canadians will remain an important ethnic force in the Canadian mosaic.

NATIVE PEOPLES

What we know about ethnicization applies mainly to European immigrant groups. While, as we have seen, ethnic diversity is still a major factor in Canada and the United States, it is conceivable that individuals, even collectivities, could "disappear" into the mainstream culture. Indeed, as immigrants come to this country, it is easy enough to make the case that "these people" have some sort of obligation to become "Canadian" and to learn the language, be it French or English. However, no such case can be made for Canada's native peoples. They did not contract to become Canadians, they did not choose to cut ties with their original culture, they did not emigrate to a new land.

The nineteenth century justifications for segregating native people and assigning them an inferior status no longer hold up for most Canadians. There is undoubtedly developing among Canadians a collective guilt about the history of abuse and the contemporary situation for native peoples. In any case, as we learn more about the history of white/native relations, it is less and less clear that native peoples owe any allegiance to Canadian legal and political institutions. It is conceivable that treaties signed a century or more ago are between native peoples and the British monarchy and legally have nothing to do with Canada at all. Wherever they are settled, we are likely to be in for a long and protracted period of legal, political and violent conflict.

Virtually all of the ethnic groups who make up the Canadian mosaic have benefited from the general growth and prosperity of Canadian society. Again, the exception is Canada's native peoples who from all accounts and measures experience poverty, hardship and mortality rates which in many ways surpass what is typical of the poorest Third World countries. Writing more than a decade ago, Alan Borovoy described the plight of Indians:

The poverty of Indians staggers the imagination of white men. It simply drains our mental resources to conceive of how in the technological Canada of 1966 over 80% of Indian homes are devoid of such elementary facilities as sewers, septic tanks, flush toilets, running water, and telephones . . . The suffering occasioned by their poverty is intensified by temperatures of 40 and 50 degrees below zero. Being so far removed, we cannot feel the horror which lies behind the fact that Indian pre-school mortality is eight times the national average and school age mortality, three times the national average (1966:13).

Unfortunately there is no evidence that the situation of Indians and Inuit has changed much in the last two decades. Frideres (1974), writing in the 1970s, showed that on virtually any measure we might choose, Indians are severely disadvantaged compared to the rest of Canadian society (see also Stanbury, 1975). Similarly, Inuit find themselves caught in the vicious circle that now they require guns and snowmobiles to make a living, houses and convenience foods to be part of the Canadian culture. But they also find the traditional occupations fail to provide sufficient income to pay for these things.

What is the solution? Some, including the federal government, have from time to time advocated that the Reserve System be terminated. It seems that the situation of native peoples offends the liberal ideology. On the one hand, education should be the panacea for Indian and Inuit problems in the same way as it should be for everyone else. On the other hand, the special status of native peoples is also offensive to this ideology because it sets them apart from the rest of Canadians and seems somehow to give them an advantage denied to others in the society. The result is lip service to the cultural autonomy of native peoples and also impatience that they have not simply done like everyone else and become part of the mainstream culture. In practice, this has generally meant resocializing Indians and Inuit to Canadian culture and in the process denigrating native cultures, traditions, and economies. For example, until recently there has been little provision for teaching children in their own language. Nor have there been many native people trained as teachers and other professionals to service their own people on their own terms.

It is evident that Indians and Inuit have been put in a particularly tense version of the assimilationist dilemma all ethnic groups face. To participate equally in the wider society means that members cannot expend scarce energies and resources in order to maintain a traditional culture. Thus education is two-edged. It is offered as the only hope of freeing native people from the wretched circumstances in which so many of them live. But as McElroy (1974) points out, education and change are solutions from a white society perspective; the message is that if native people want jobs and houses and cars then they will have to change their ways and become North American.

However, Indian students who do well in

school and achieve high status roles must do so on white people's terms and must move wholly into white society. Mobility in white society deprives Indian and Inuit communities of leadership, and this makes mobilization of collective interests unlikely. The most able members are gone, unable to act as role models for following generations of young people who begin to ask themselves the recurring question of youth: "What do I want to be?"

It is not even clear that if native people are willing to pay the costs of "surrendering" their heritage, they will then be allowed to do so, that is, to assimilate. Numbers of Indians, for instance, have left the reserves, usually for economic reasons, and moved to Canadian cities. Most, however, find themselves in low-paid casual and seasonal jobs, subject to indifference and sometimes racism by urban society. Those who do "make it," what Edgar Dosman (1972) referred to as "affluents," have done so by becoming bureaucrats in the Department of Indian Affairs. They have in effect become ethnic brokers or mediators between Indian and white society. Alternatively, Frideres (1974:88) points out that "successful" Indians in the city are those who are able to "pass" as something else — whites, French, and in some instances, Hawaiian. They cannot be simply Indians if they want decent jobs and housing.

So, leaving the reserve has not been the answer for most Indians. Like other rural people they lack occupational and urban skills and an effective social network or ethnic enclave in the city (see Clark, 1978). Thus they quickly find themselves caught up in a cycle of poverty from which the only escape is to return to the reserve. It is, for instance, no accident that in doing research on urban Indians, Nagler (1970) found many of his interviewees in hotels and hostels bordering on "prerestoration" Cabbage-town, when it was a slum area of Toronto almost totally lacking formal or informal neighbourhood or community networks.

Racism, though having an individualistic or

psychological component, arises out of structural conditions and arrangements, which are both ultimately the result of differences in power between two groups of people. At the outset of their contact with Europeans, Indians were in a powerful position. They were in the majority and it was they who had knowledge of how to survive in Canada and how to trap the valued furs (Trigger, 1985). But, they could hardly have estimated how much power lay behind those first tiny ships and probably lonely men who had braved the Atlantic in search of the wealth of the North American continent. Powerful in the beginning, Indians rapidly moved into a powerless position and found themselves faced with the choice of annihilation or segregation. Frideres argues that Indians became a *colonized* people subject to exploitation and social control and it is as colonized people that they must assert, collectively, opposition to the dominant group. Thus Frideres resolves the individual and collective dilemma facing Indians by proposing that:

. . . Natives must reject the notion of individual entrepreneurship or individual capitalism. Instead of seeking personal economic development they should aim at "native community development" which entails community ownership and control of the economy (1974:162).

Frideres agrees with most Indians that the clock cannot be turned back. But Canadians can, for humane reasons and at the same time for sound sociological reasons, hand back to Indians control of their own lands, resources and educational, bureaucratic and political institutions. They must, in other words, be given power over their own life chances and lifestyles.

Conflict is inherent in attempts at community control, conflict which will no doubt have additional teeth as Indians and Inuit collectively benefit from land claim and resource settlement and compensation. But, as recent developments suggest, it is not clear that the future development of native peoples will be in directions compatible with the "goals" of the rest of Canadian society or that it will always be in the best interests of all native peoples. Certainly, it is far better that native peoples suffer from their own collective mistakes and blunders than from those imposed from outside and above, by social scientists, bureaucrats or the elite.

This is not to say that social scientists who study native peoples, those who live among them, can have no role in facilitating change. The question of just what the sociologist's role is, as we have seen, is highly controversial within the discipline. At this point, it is enough to say that the sociologists can play an instrumental role in helping native peoples achieve their collective interests, not by imposing their own version of what this collective interest is, but rather by coming to understand the subjective life of the communities they are studying and by helping these communities link their private dissatisfactions to problems in the social structure.

In other words, the sociologist must learn from the community its collective interest and return to that community this knowledge in a way that they may call upon it as a resource. Nor will Canadians, even those unsympathetic to native claims, be able for very much longer to ignore the issue. With very high native birth rates, and increasing migration of Indians to cities, Indian poverty is coming out from hiding in reservations, and is becoming more plainly visible to us all; it will unquestionably lead to a louder and angrier voice for change.

CONCLUSION

Ethnicity, historically and in the present, is very central to an understanding of Canadian society. As it happens it is also a very interesting and vital part of Canadian sociology. What we have tried to do in this chapter is to understand ethnic groups and ethnicization within the context of inequality of power, wealth and status. Obviously in a capitalist society these inequalities would not disappear if we were to become an ethnically homogenized society. But often, because of nepotism, ethnic sponsorship, prejudice and discrimination, and perhaps because an ethnic group has not yet learned how to compete successfully in Canadian society, structured inequality cannot wholly be reduced to class inequality.

As our patterns of immigration change, we are faced with new and, as yet, little understood or researched questions. On the one hand is that, as with many immigrant groups of the past, some of our recent immigrants come with few resources but, unlike these earlier groups, they also face the additional burden of being a visible minority in Canadian society because of their skin colour. Individual mobility through passing as a member of the dominant culture is more difficult. On the other hand is the unmistakable fact that at least a minority of our new immigrants come with considerable resources and may, in fact, have bought their way into Canada because of the wealth they promise to bring into the country. Both those who lack resources, and who are therefore exploitable, and those with resources, who promise to be exploiters, capitalists in Canada instead of Hong Kong, will have an impact on the fabric of Canadian society the nature of which we cannot, at this point, fully predict.

We have concentrated on ethnicization because, whether we are speaking of Quebec society, native peoples, or recent immigrant groups in Canada, it seems to us that ethnic awareness and ethnic identity, rather than disappearing, have become more pervasive. Ethnicity persists even though an outsider may be unable to detect any differences between the ethnic group and the mainstream culture.

Indeed, from an objective viewpoint, it may appear that everyone is assimilating towards a rather neutral middle-class society, a sort of watered-down version of the United States. Some would argue, then, that the much talked-about tolerance in Canada for ethnic diversity is illusory, that while the so called Anglo-Saxon majority may encourage ethnic folk festivals, arts and restaurants, it does not tolerate values, modes of thought and interpersonal behaviour that are different or alien.

Is ethnicity, then, simply "all in the mind," something which may once have existed but does so no longer? The concept of ethniciza-tion implies that the answer is yes and no. It seems that we are subject to two simultaneous forces. One is the simple reality of living in North America. No one, for example, is immune to the influences of television and of mass marketing of everything from movies, hamburgers, and children's toys—what Isajiw (1978) refers to as the technological culture.

There are at the same time strong diversi-fying forces. For various reasons, we also have strong identifications with the regions in which we live, with our ethnic groups and probably with our nation. Difficult as it may be for out-siders to tell the difference, Canadians — Eng-lish or French — do see themselves as somehow unique, set apart from Europeans certainly, but also from Americans.

As in the United States, Canadians make further distinctions, in some situations mak-ing regional identities salient and in other sit-uations emphasizing ethnic differences. These have not disappeared and as sociolo-gists we must accept this as a social fact. Eth-nic groups are not static but are shaped and reshaped through the interaction within and with the larger society. At the same time, as Greeks in Canada rapidly lose sufficient "Greekness" almost to be foreigners in Greece, present-day English and French Canadians become unrecognizable to their grandparents' generation. Nor, of course, are they English or French. Both host and immi-grant groups change and in effect become ethnic groups and, at the same time Canadians.

In short, as long as some ethnic groups find that, because of nepotism and/or outright dis-crimination, they are excluded or under rep-resented in the places where political and economic decisions are made, we can expect ethnicity to remain an important focus for social conflict. Rather than a survival from a previous age, ethnicity turns out to be a dynamic and flexible resource, capable of being called into action when needed and capable also of being transformed and rein-vented as the situation demands.

III SUGGESTIONS FOR FURTHER READING

In the previous chapter we noted that, while a number of important works about education were published in the 1970s, we could not find much of significance which had been published in the 1980s. To a large extent, this is also true of ethnic relations; most of the theoretical work, the books and articles that influenced our thinking, were published before the last edition went to press. It seems that ethnicity and ethnic relations have not loomed so large in the thinking of Canadian sociologists during the 1980s. However, to get a sense of the recent work on ethnicity, check the journal *Canadian Ethnic Studies*.

We have been able to make only passing reference to the many ethnographic studies of the various ethnic groups that make up the Canadian ethnic mosaic. In the 1970s, a project sponsored by the Secretary of State resulted in a number of studies of various ethnic groups in Canada such as Japanese Canadians (Adachi, 1976); Portuguese Cana-dians (Anderson and Higgs, 1977); Polish Canadians (Radecki and Heydenkorn, 1977); and Scottish Canadians (Reid, 1977). More recent works, in this same tradition, include

Peter Ward's *The Japanese in Canada* (1982); J. Tan's and P. Roy's *The Chinese in Canada* (1985), Peter Li's *The Chinese in Canada* (1988) and O. W. Gerus's and J. E. Rea's *The Ukrainians in Canada* (1985). There are many other studies of ethnic groups in Canada which examine such diverse groups as Hutterites, Doukhobors, Mennonites, Canadian Jews, Slavic Canadians, Italian Canadians and Dutch Canadians. Of particular interest within the perspective we have presented is the study of Nova Scotia blacks by Don Clairmont and Dennis Magill, *Africville: The Life and Death of a Canadian Black Community*, originally published in 1974 and updated and expanded in 1986.

There is understandably a large body of research on Canada's native peoples. Mark Nagler's *Perspectives on the North American Indians* (1972) remains something of a landmark study of the plight of those who leave the reserve for the city as does Edgar Dosman's *Indians: The Urban Dilemma* (1972). Some important works on Indians in Canada are James Frideres's *Canada's Indians: Contemporary Conflicts* (1974), Michael Asch's *Home and Native Land: Aboriginal Rights and the Canadian Constitution* (1984) and Anastasia Shkolnyk's powerful book, *A Poison Stronger Than Love* (1985). A provocative account of the destructive processes of colonialism on the Inuit is Hugh Brody's *The People's Land* (1975). Conventional wisdom has it that Canada's native peoples were both naive and easily impressed by the apparent sophistication of the Europeans who first came to these shores and that they were easy prey to the fur traders and to the missionaries. Bruce Trigger, in a number of books and articles, has provided a very effective argument that the initial economic relationships between Indians and the French were not so one-sided. His *Natives and Newcomers: Canada's "Heroic Age" Reconsidered* (1985), which won the John Porter Award, is perhaps his most thorough statement of this thesis.

The best general introduction to the processes of ethnicization are Andrew Greeley's *Ethnicity in the United States* (1974), Nathan Glazer's and Daniel P. Moynihan's edited collection *Ethnicity* (1975), and Stephen Steinberg's *The Ethnic Myth* (1981). Some Canadian collections also reflect what Greeley called the "rediscovery of ethnicity": Leo Driedger's *The Canadian Ethnic Mosaic: A Quest for Identity* (1978), W. W. Isajiw's *Identities: The Impact of Ethnicity on Canadian Society* (1976), J. Goldstein's and R. M. Bienvenue's *Ethnicity and Ethnic Relations in Canada* (1981), and J. Dahlie's and T. Fernando's *Ethnicity, Power and Politics in Canada* (1981). Two important Canadian books on ethnicity are A. Anderson's and J. Frideres's *Ethnicity in Canada: Theoretical Perspectives* (1981) and J. Reitz's *The Survival of Ethnic Groups* (1980). John Young's edited collection, *Breaking the Mosaic: Ethnic Identities in Canadian Schooling* (1987), presents articles which deal with many of the themes of this and the previous chapter. Also useful is Peter Li's edited collection, *Ethnic Inequality in a Class Society* (1988). An important historical work, which documents the depth of anti-semitism in Canada during the years of the Second World War, is Irving Abella's *None Is Too Many* (1982).

As we have tried to show in this chapter, ethnicity and ethnic relations permeate many aspects of Canadian society and its patterns of inequality. A book we recommended that you read in connection with industrialism and capitalism, Charlene Gannage's *Double Day, Double Bind: Women Garment Workers* (1986), will also give you important insights into the plight of immigrant women in Canadian society. This is also true of Roberta Hamilton's and Michele Barrett's edited collection, *The Politics of Diversity: Feminism, Marxism and Nationalism* (1986), which contains a number of articles relevant to the relationship in Canada between sexual and ethnic inequality.

PART
FIVE

CONCLUSION

DIMENSIONS OF SOCIAL CHANGE

OVERVIEW

In a sense the entire text has been about social change. This chapter should help you see that social change does not simply happen to people. Many theories of change bypass people. Thus, progress or decline or some sort of pendulum or cycle is characterized as inevitable. People are simply drawn into these inexorable processes.

This chapter, on the other hand, is about people as agents of change, about how people acting collectively can, to some degree, shape the future. To be sure, you will learn some of the key factors, the social conditions, which favour or inhibit social action. But above all, this chapter should help you understand change as the outcome of human decisions, not simply structural conflicts.

By the end of the chapter you should know something of why inequality does not inevitably lead to social action and protest. You should understand the role of ideology in both inhibiting and fuelling conflict and the complex relationship between social organization and social change. You should be able to specify the conditions that foster and mobilize collective action.

Finally, you should understand something of the "career" of social action, why collective protests may sometimes die quickly, sometimes escalate to violence, sometimes become part of the very society under attack—and almost always change society in some way.

INTRODUCTION

The past decade has been a significant one for Canada. We have seen changes in the fortunes of Canada's political parties and their leaders, changes in our international relations, particularly our relations with the United States, changes in the relationships between our levels of government, and perhaps too, changes in our perceptions of the role of government. Free Trade, Meech Lake, Bill 178, the selling of Air Canada, the changes in Canada Post, the Supreme Court decision on abortion and the compromise legislation which followed are all indicators, whatever one's position, of a new Canada.

Canadians probably do agree that major shifts are occurring, that something big is happening. In the midst of all of this, the conflicts among Canadians are emerging more clearly, regional conflicts, linguistic conflicts, moral conflicts and labour/management conflicts. Conflicts are not new, but they may be crystallizing as Canadians are trying to understand, inhibit, promote or adapt to social and cultural change.

Some people, sociologists included, characterize social change as something outside of the actions of humans. In this view, what people, even politicians, want is irrelevant; change just happens. Optimists like to think of such changes as part of the inexorable force to progress. Societies *evolve* and even if the fearful resist, the evolution is inevitably leading to higher states of social development.

Pessimists tend to think of most changes as part of the inevitable decline of human civilization. Each major shift is examined for how it will contribute to the decay of morality and quality of life.

The more practical-minded view changes as part of some recurrent cycle, a shift of a pendulum that will invariably, sooner or later, swing back. In this view people have seen it all before, and survived.

In current Canadian debates one can find all of these broad models of social change.

Some are promising the coming of a new and better order, others are predicting doom, and the end of Canada as a sovereign nation, and yet others are saying that after all the heat, we'll go on much as before.

All of these models treat humans as victims of these forces or cycles. Humans may resist or adapt—but they do not create the changes. This chapter, on the other hand, looks at change as a human process, viewing humans as not only products but producers of their societies.

CONFLICT GROUPS AND SOCIAL MOVEMENTS

CONFLICT AND CHANGE

Throughout this book we have emphasized that social conflict is inherent in the very fact of social organization. Social structure implies conflict. Anthony Oberschall summarizes this:

At any given moment, there exists a certain distribution of scarce resources and of rewards— the good things desired and sought after by most, such as wealth, power and prestige—among the individuals, groups and classes in a society. Some are better off, and others are worse off. Those who are favoured have a vested interest in conserving and consolidating their existing shares; those who are negatively privileged seek to increase theirs, individually or collectively. Social conflict results from this clash of opposing interests (1973:33).

The structures that create impoverishment and oppression for some people provide privilege and pleasure for others. It is not surprising that people are unwilling to give up their privileges and will resist the attempts of others to snatch them away. Disadvantaged groups, then, must take considerable risks and sacrifices when they collectively attempt to gain a greater share of the valued resources.

Overt conflict is not, of course, inevitable. After all, as we have seen, dominant groups are such because they have control of the resources of the society; they have at their disposal several lines of defence against structural changes which threaten their privilege.

Frequently, because they control media and educational institutions, they are successful with their first and most subtle line of defence, ideology, the rationalization and justification of inequality. Poor people, may, for a time at least, believe they are better off spiritually than the rich, or that they are poor because they are stupid, or that by being poor they are freed of the "burdens" of power. They may also be diverted by popular media, fads and crazes — the contemporary equivalent of Roman circuses. At other times, subordinate groups may reject the ideology but still feel powerless to act. People know that there are other lines of defence — economic reprisals, arrest and ultimately soldiers, guns and tanks.

Between these extremes there are, of course, two other possibilities that make conflict less likely. First, people may strive *individually* rather than *collectively* to improve their position through the legitimate channels for upward mobility. Second, when these channels are blocked, they may, in Merton's terms, innovate, attempt "illegitimately" to get a share of what the privileged groups possess. Though viewed inevitably as a social problem by those in power, crime may also act as a "safety valve" that reduces some of the pressure which might otherwise be directed towards collective conflict.

If these defences of the dominant group were totally successful there would be no revolutions, uprisings and riots; collective action would emanate only from immediate circumstances, never from long-standing structural grievances. History, of course, reveals that this is far from the case, that the lack of open conflict, the accommodative relationship which may be established between conflict groups, is always fragile, unstable and never permanent. And as the fortunes of groups in society rise and fall, the accommodative structures are regularly challenged.

The relationships among collectives are continually shifting in our century of rapid and widespread change. Changes in the size and distribution of population, changes in the technology of production and communication, and the changes we have been talking about throughout this book also find their counterpart in changes in our everyday lives. Some will feel threatened, some will be given hope, some will entrench against these changes, some will try to speed them along. Aspects of the culture long held sacred, perhaps taken for granted, may come to appear obsolete or at least open to challenge; new ideas may gain currency. As Barrington Moore (1972:56) points out, we are living in an age when people are more willing to "reject *in toto* the social system under which they live, the goals of their community and its moral standards."

Clearly social change and social conflict are intertwined; the relationship, however, is a complex one. In the following section, we shall examine more closely some of the economic and political factors which may create widespread discontent, but there is no mechanical relationship between this discontent and collective action. Groups characterized by widespread discontent might best be viewed as "publics," which *may* be mobilized to collective action. In this sense a public is an amorphous and as yet unorganized collectivity (Mauss, 1975:12). The study of collection action, then, is the study of the mobilization of discontent.

STRUCTURAL SOURCES OF DISCONTENT

Understandably, most social scientists have focused on economic change; how economic trends are directly or indirectly related to grievance and protest. Karl Marx, as you will recall, argued that the increasing misery of the worker — deepening economic crises, lower wages, increasing impoverishment and so on — would produce a potential for revolution. On the other hand, Tocqueville long ago argued that immediately preceding the French Revolution was a period of economic prosperity and it was this prosperity that promoted unrest.

Some have looked at economic changes in absolute terms while others have focused on relative gains and losses, how some groups have fared relative to others. Some theorists have focused on long-term trends and others on the short term. As Shorter and Tilly (1974:4–11) rightly point out, it will make quite a difference whether we look at economic changes over a ten-year period or a hundred-year period. Long-term deprivation and short-term deprivation, for example, are likely to have different consequences. And the controversies continue.

One influential approach focuses on *relative deprivation*, a perceived gap between what people feel they should get and what they actually get, that is, between expectations and achievements. James Davies (1962), for example, argues that revolutions and rebellions are most likely in societies in which a period of economic improvements is followed by a sharp reversal. People's hopes and expectations will have been raised during the time of prosperity and then frustrated during the decline. For example, it was not until French Canadians had experienced some degree of economic prosperity that the Quiet Revolution began and demands for social change became more vociferous.

Relative deprivation occurs, then, if expectations outstrip achievements whether because expectations have risen, achievement has fallen or both. Subordinate groups may also feel deprived relative to the superordinate groups in society. For example, while it is no doubt true that the objective economic conditions of American blacks have improved, particularly over the last fifty years, these improvements have been even greater for whites; the gap between the groups has increased.

Terence White (1975) has used a similar argument to explain the opposition to international unions among Canadian workers who apparently feel that American workers have often been benefiting at the expense of their Canadian counterparts. White explains the decisions of Canadian locals to break away from the international unions in terms of the pervasive "feelings of relative deprivation in regard to union services (that is, bread and butter issues), rather than by nationalism alone" (p. 302).

Aggregate or overall economic trends will affect various groups in society in different ways. General economic prosperity may increase the gaps between rich and poor; prices may rise faster than wages; some regions may remain underdeveloped; some occupations may no longer be in demand; some industries may be caught with obsolescent technology. In short, even in times of economic growth, some groups will suffer relative or even absolute deprivation.

Furthermore, different kinds of changes will be important to different groups: those living a marginal or subsistence existence will be affected by food shortages and rising food prices; peasants will be affected by land shortages; commercial farmers will be affected by changes in world food prices; wage workers will be affected by wage cuts, declining purchasing power and unemployment; and so on.

The intensely conflicting views of Canadians about the impact of free trade reflects, in part, the reality that the impact will be felt differently among the various occupational groups and regions. In sum, however complex the relationship, it is obvious that real or perceived change in the distribution of resources will make some groups feel deprived. Nor are economic changes the only threat to accommodative structures.

Political discontent may also arise from changes in the distribution and use of power. One example is provided by imperialism. As we indicated earlier in the text, the history of imperialism and colonialism is a history of violence and conflict. The attempt to impose external authority on a previously autonomous people will always meet discontent and resistance.

Similarly, Charles Tilly (1964), in a most influential study, explains the Vendée counterrevolution of 1793 in terms of the increasing interference by the revolutionary government in Paris in the affairs of the Vendée population. Grievances built up as the Paris government imposed military conscription, land reforms and other changes which unsurped the authority of local influentials, and these grievances led eventually to the attempted counterrevolution.

Political discontent may also arise "from the demands for greater authority, rights, and recognition by those who are excluded from the polity and from full citizenship rights" (Oberschall, 1973:44). Allen Grimshaw (1970) points out that as these excluded groups gain in number, become organized and recognize their strength, they will increasingly participate in the struggle for power. Attempts of the ruling group to block them will only serve to increase their discontent. Political turmoil and collective violence are most likely to result if the ruling groups are perceived to be abusing their power—rigging elections, the continued use of force—in their attempts to block the excluded groups' demands.

The sources of political and economic discontent are too numerous and varied to be catalogued here. The important point to be taken from this discussion, is that times of social turmoil and upheaval are likely to be characterized by some combination of economic and political discontent spread widely throughout the society, while at the same time more concentrated in particular social strata. But such discontent, in itself, is a not sufficient condition for **collective action**. It is not enough that people know that something is wrong. Somehow, and this remains the most pressing question, they must be **mobilized** into crowds, interest groups, pressure groups, or social movements if they are to participate in the active pursuit of collective goals.

MOBILIZATION

There is nothing automatic in the transformation of collectivities, which share grievances and discontent and which objectively share common interests, into interest groups pursuing common goals. At the very least, the collectivity must develop common definitions of villains and victims, oppressors and oppressed, if they are to engage in collective action. Even if only these minimal conditions are present, however, collective action is likely to be episodic and uncoordinated, much as Hobsbawn (1963) describes the "primitive rebels" in preindustrial society. It is in this kind of collective action that it is perhaps hardest to distinguish between "social banditry" and "criminality."

In his discussion of the soaring crime rates during Canada's Depression, Barry Broadfoot (1975) suggests that at least part of the reason for these inflated rates was just this kind of primitive protest, what he terms "rough justice." This protest was not guided by a full-blown counterideology or what Mannheim calls a "utopia." Rather, it was much more spontaneous, directed at little more than meting out punishment to those thought responsible for destroying the old order.

If protest is to be more sustained and coordinated, other conditions are necessary: (1) an ideology which can unify potential members; (2) willing and able leadership to articulate this ideology and to organize activities; and (3) channels for communication and a network of cooperative relationship (Clark et al., 1975:12–18).

IDEOLOGY

There has been a good deal of debate about the precise role of ideology in collective action. In part, at least, the controversy stems from the fact that few of the participants in collective behaviour will ever hold a well-developed ideology (see Mueller, 1970). Ideologies are always *emergent* in collective behaviour but are rarely full-blown. Nevertheless, counterideologies, always readily available in any society, are what give meaning to collective discontent.

Of course this is *not* to say, as conventional wisdom would have it, that "outside agitators" spread ideas which create grievances and collective outbursts. Such an image is often fostered by the powerful groups as a means of challenging the legitimacy of the grievances of those less powerful. For example, in his description of the Estevan Strike of 1931, S. D. Hanson (1974) indicates that the authority's decision to blame "the troubles" on outside agitators allowed them to break the strike.

Ideologies do not create grievances; the grievances simply reflect structured inequalities. Ideologies help define and explain the grievances, identify the heroes and the villains, define collective goals and strategies for achieving these goals and provide moral justification for the pursuit of these goals. The ideology serves to translate private troubles into public issues and describe what must, practically and morally, be done. Such ideas do more than coordinate activities; they also promote commitment to the collective and to the cause. Although obviously not all participants in collective action will accept all aspects of the proffered ideology, *conversion* to this ideology is an important predictor of commitment to and support for the protest group.

LEADERSHIP

Sustained protest also requires leaders who are sufficiently motivated and skillful to articulate the ideology and to coordinate collective activities. Obviously such leadership is not always available and, because of this, much collective behaviour may not move beyond the primitive stage. Sometimes lead-

ership comes from outside the strata which generated the collective protest; leadership may even come from men and women who have belonged to the social strata of the dominators. But such leadership may often encounter "a certain aloofness and mistrust" which inhibits mobilization (Freire, 1970:162–165). Leadership is most likely to be successful if it emerges from within the collectivity but even then it will encounter problems. Leaders of conflict groups are constantly open to challenge. Their positions are obviously less clearly defined than are conventional authority positions; they cannot so easily call upon shared norms of obedience or institutionalized sanctions to implement their decisions. There are, however, at least two conditions under which these problems may be minimized.

First, leadership may be drawn from an already existing organizational base. In fact, a good deal of evidence suggests that protest leaders typically already have a legitimate authority base. This was the case, for example, for the leadership during the development of the CCF in western Canada.

Though it was a new radical party, the CCF did not have to build up an organization from scratch. It was organized from the start by the "local" class and community leaders of rural Saskatchewan. The fact that the province was so well organized on an occupational basis enabled the new party leaders to obtain the support of the politically conscious community leaders. By the early 1940s, the CCF communities, composed in the main of the same people who were the officials of the other rural organizations, were operating in almost every district in the province (Lipset, 1950:252).

Second, protest groups may develop special kinds of leaders, what Weber has called **charismatic leaders**, whose authority rests on their personal characteristics, indefinable qualities which seem to endow them with exceptional powers. While we know little about charisma, it appears that the availability of such leaders can greatly facilitate mobilization.

J. S. Woodsworth, the first leader of the CCF, has often been described in these terms (Zakuta, 1964). Perhaps the most obvious example in Canadian political life is William Aberhart, the founder of the Social Credit movement in Alberta. Much of the early success of this movement has been attributed to Aberhart himself, his physical presence, his oratorical skills, even his hypnotic powers (Clark and others, 1975:15).

COMMUNICATION NETWORKS

Aberhart also serves as a good illustration of the importance of developing channels for communication and a network of cooperative relationships among the potential participants in collective action. Aberhart first gained prominence as a religious figure. In the years between 1910 and the early 1920s he had developed such a large following that the audience for his weekly Bible lectures numbered about 2200.

Owing to the enthusiasm of his followers he was persuaded, in 1925, to broadcast his Sunday services over CFCN, known as "The Voice of the Prairies" and (for years) the most powerful radio station in Canada. In addition to his Bible Conference, he organized a Radio Sunday School which continued to function throughout the worst years of the Depression. By his use of radio, he built up a personal following that, according to certain estimates, numbered between two and three hundred thousand persons. In 1927 his organization was put on a more permanent basis when he and his followers constructed in the heart of Calgary, at a cost of $65 000, the large Prophetic Bible Institute which thenceforth became the centre of all his religious activities (Irving, 1975:131–132).

In other words, Aberhart did not have to depend only on charisma. He already had access to communication media through which he could propagate his version of Social Credit ideology and he had created a network of cooperative relationships which enhanced communication and which provided a base

for block recruitment to the movement. Aberhart's followers were therefore able to support and encourage one another in their decisions to participate in the movement.

A THEORY OF MOBILIZATION

Implicit in the preceding discussion is that the conditions for successful mobilization — ideology, leadership, and communication networks — are most likely if the collectivity already has an **organizational base.** Anthony Oberschall (1973), in particular, has contributed to the development of a sociological theory of mobilization which emphasizes principles of social organization. He focuses on two aspects of social organization: the organizational base is the horizontal dimension describing the links within a collectivity; **segmentation** is the vertical dimension describing the links between the collectivity and other collectivities, particularly those higher up in the system of stratification (Oberschall, 1973:119).

ORGANIZATIONAL BASE

A collectivity's organizational base may be rooted in either of two social structures. First, the collectivity may be held together by **communal ties:** traditional lines based on, for example, kinship or ethnicity. It is in this sense, as we argued in the previous chapter, that ethnicity can be seen as an effective rallying point for collective action. Second, the collectivity may be tied together through **associational ties:** secondary relationships, associations based on occupational, religious, economic and other interests. The CCF in Saskatchewan, for example, could draw on an organizational base provided by the many already existent farmers' cooperatives, civic associations and agrarian social movements.

In general, "political protest in the west was greatly facilitated by the pre-existing dense network of ties which bound western farmers together" (Brym, 1978:6). Robert Brym and Barbara Neis (1978) make a similar argument in their examination of regional variation in support for the Fishermen's Protective Union of Newfoundland, a populist movement of the 1910s and 1920s. They show that mobilization of support for the FPU was most likely in those regions of Newfoundland where fishermen already had the "proper organizational foundations."

This, of course, turns upside down "mass society theory," which argues both that collective action is most likely in societies that lack organizational structures and that participants in collective action are typically those people least integrated into these structures, usually the desperately poor who are alienated from conventional society. On the contrary, communal or associational ties provide the horizontal links, social solidarity and established leadership necessary for the effective mobilization of collective behaviour. And most studies agree that "misfits," "outcasts," the socially isolated and atomized, are unlikely to participate in *any* political activity —not in the ordinary political process nor in the formation of protest groups. They may sometimes jump on the bandwagon of a movement already well underway and established, but they will play little role in the formation and early stages of conflict groups or political activism generally (Oberschall, 1973:135–137).

It was precisely in these terms that Karl Marx (1971) explained the conservatism and political impotence of the nineteenth century French peasantry. Marx compared the peasantry to so many potatoes in a sack. Nothing held the peasants together; there was little need for them to enter into mutual intercourse as each small isolated peasant holding was more or less self-suficient. Their mode of production, then, involved them in an exchange with nature rather than with others

in society. Robert Brym offers a similar explanation for the of agrarian radicalism in New Brunswick. He argues that because most farmers were involved in subsistence rather than commercial farming, they were socially atomized.

The preponderance of subsistence farming meant that there was no need in New Brunswick for the kinds of co-operative ventures which blossomed in the west, and therefore no social mechanisms within which a collective spirit could be generated. Why form an organization to market crops when there are no crops to be sold on the market? For that matter, why come into contact with other farmers at all? Already in 1924 Louis Aubrey Wood noted that the "cooperative movements in the Maritime Provinces are now in a dormant state except in certain localities." He was certainly overly optimistic to add that they "undoubtedly will flourish again" (1978:9).

SEGMENTATION

A theory of mobilization, however, requires us to consider not only the links within a collectivity but also the links between the collectivity and other collectivities, especially those higher up in the stratification system. The mobilization of a collectivity into some kind of protest group is most likely when the society is not only highly stratified but also highly segmented. This simply means that the collectivity has few bonds or links with the powerful groups in society. This will be the case, for example, when the powerful groups:

no longer exercise protective, political, judicial, administrative, and diffuse social leadership functions among the lower orders, yet still derive their economic livelihood from the subordinate collectivity as landlords or employers, often in an absentee capacity, and the lower orders are cut off from the upper- status groups (Obserschall, 1973:119).

A particularly important example from Canadian political life is the rise of class consciousness as expressed through militant unionism in western Canada early in the century. The last decade of the nineteenth century was a time of economic boom, a time when all Canadians seemed to prosper — all Canadians, that is, except the Canadian worker.

To him the twentieth century ushered in no new changes — or at least, no changes for the better. His conditions of work were still appalling, and his wages — though somewhat higher — could not keep up with spiralling living costs. Indeed, the influx of hundreds of thousands of hungry, penniless immigrants even made it difficult to hold a job. And what jobs! Stuffy, unventilated factories; sixty hours a week; back-breaking work; all for a dollar a day. These were the conditions of work for the men, women and children of Canada. And a dollar a day was considered excellent pay for the thousands of boys and girls, some not yet in their teens, who were forced to find jobs (Abella, 1975:3).

Irving Abella, a professor of history at York University, describes how a hostile government-employer alliance fought most legislation that might have protected the worker. The western worker was forcibly made aware that he or she was going to make no headway in the face of this powerful and hostile alliance, and out of this awareness emerged a new radicalism, a new commitment to industrial unionism and independent working-class politics. By 1920, the hostility, the class antagonism, had erupted into countless bloody battles akin to class warfare (Abella, 1975:7–14).

When the bonds between the dominated and dominant are strong, the mobilization of collective protest is unlikely. If, for example, the most ambitious people in the collectivity are able to rise in the stratification system and become coopted by the dominant groups, the collectivity is deprived of leadership. It will look to the dominant group to solve its problems and provide leadership. For example, Raymond Hebert and Jean-Guy Vaillancourt (1971) speculate that a major reason for the failure of French Canadians in Manitoba to sustain their protest was the cooptation of much of their leadership by the elite. According to Hebert and Vaillancourt, this "circulation of elites" not only deprived French

Canadians of protest leaders but also provided the traditional elite with new blood and therefore new vigor. Paulo Friere explains how the dominant groups, as part of their program of divide and rule, use the "promotion of individuals who reveal leadership capacity and could signify a threat if they were 'not softened' up in this way" (1970:140–141).

MOBILIZATION: SUMMARY

Figure 14.1 summarizes the relationship between social structure and collective protest. Collectivities that are highly organized and have weak links to the power structure (Cell D) will be most rapidly and intensely mobilized to collective action. This is the basis, for example, for the history of agrarian radicalism in western Canada. Collectivities that are weakly organized and have an integrated relationship to the structures of power (Cell A) are unlikely to be mobilized for collective protest. This is probably true for the very poor, who are socially atomized and who may be so badly off that they fear any change because it may mean things will become even worse.

FIGURE 14.1

COLLECTIVITIES CLASSIFIED ALONG VERTICAL AND HORIZONTAL DIMENSIONS OF INTEGRATION

HORIZONTAL DIMENSION: LINKS WITHIN THE COLLECTIVITY		
	Un- or Weakly Organized	Organized
Vertical Dimension: Links Between Collectivities		
Integrated	A	B
Segmented	C	D

Source: Adapted and simplified from Obserschall (1973:120).

Saul Alinsky (1971), writing about how to organize the poor, argues that it simply is not true that the poor have nothing to lose. Rather, they have everything to lose, with the result that they may be afraid to protest at all. Alinsky goes on to suggest that if mobilization is to be successful and if the poor are to be organized, protest cannot be directed at abstract rights such as equality or political representation but must focus on concrete issues like bad landlords, dishonest merchants and so on. What we are suggesting, then, is that the very poor do not provide the basis for radical protests, and perhaps because they are objectively or subjectively dependent on a "protective" state, any protest generated is likely to seek change *within* the system rather than *of* the system.

If the collectivity is organized but has strong links to the power structure (Cell B), collective opposition is likely to be expressed through routine, institutionalized channels such as established lobby groups, political parties and trade unions. This describes, for example, much of the English-speaking political activity of middle-class Canadians fighting for their own special interest groups—against or for liberalized abortion laws, against the Spadina Expressway in Toronto, against spruce budworm spray programs, planned parenthood groups, and so on. In fact, many of these movements seem to have been brought to Canada and may be sustained by Americans in what might be seen as another example of cultural imperialism.

Finally, if the collectivity is segmented from the rest of society, particularly the power structures, but is at the same time relatively unorganized (Cell C), collective protest, when it does occur, is likely to be itself unorganized, short-lived and often violent (Rudé, 1964). Charles Tilly (1969) has pointed out that this kind of collective behaviour and violence is being replaced by "modern" collective conflict. His research points to the fact that the relatively unorganized and backward-looking rebellions of the past, protests in search of "rough justice," are being replaced by more

complexly organized and forward-looking movements based on associational rather than communal ties and unified through already developed ideologies. Such conflict groups are perhaps best illustrated by Canada's political movements and its labour movement. In sum, collective behaviour is most likely in highly segmented societies, but whether this collective behaviour is sustained and organized will depend on whether the collectivity is internally organized.

Social segmentation, however, refers not only to the relationships of a collectivity to the structures of power, but also to the relationships among collectivities more generally. Segmentation, in other words, refers to any social cleavages in society, cleavages that inhibit communication and cooperation between groups. Such cleavages often serve to divide the working class and inhibit the formation of broadly based working-class movements.

The questions here are obviously highly complex. While we have suggested that the recognition of common interests in terms of ethnicity may eventually lead, for some, to class consciousness, ethnic identification may also serve to inhibit the development of class consciousness and cooperative relationships among the working class. Such internal divisions may often lead to competition and suspicion within the dominated class.

We must also examine, then, the conflicts and coalitions among the various dominated segments of society. For example, Brym (1979) argues that to understand the emergence of left-wing populism in Saskatchewan and right-wing populism in Alberta, we must consider the "inter-class coalitions" in these two provinces. He suggests that part of the explanation rests on the fact that the Saskatchewan farmers had strong ties to the Saskatchewan working class, whereas the farmers of Alberta were most strongly tied to the urban *petit bourgeoisie*. Clearly, sharp divisions among the dominated make it less likely that they will be able, collectively, to organize for substantial structural change.

Once a collectivity has been mobilized to form a conflict group of some kind, the course or direction of collective behaviour still remains in doubt. Earlier we described how labelling theory emphasized the role of lawmakers, police and other powerful "labellers" in creating and shaping deviant behaviour. A number of theorists have also pointed out that we must examine how outsiders, especially authorities, react to initial attempts at collective behaviour and thereby help shape its course. Dick Gregory (1978:119), the comedian and political activist, for example, describes how in the sixties the government's too willing response of force often transformed nonviolent demonstrations into angry "mob violence."

SOCIETAL RESPONSE AND CONFRONTATION

It seems evident that incipient conflict groups, crowds, for example, will be influenced by how onlookers and the general public react. The consequences will be different, depending, for example, on whether onlookers try to fight the crowd, ignore it or actively encourage it.

In an influential article, Ralph Turner (1969) describes the dilemma faced by those participating in collective protest activities. Their actions must be sufficiently provocative to attract the attention of the general public (and the elite) but not so provocative that they are seen as threatening to the point that their message is "blocked out." In other words, while a minority group will be trying to call attention to some shared grievances, the general public, if it feels threatened, may not even interpret their actions as protest. So urban race riots and student demonstrations are very often defined by outsiders as criminal rather than political activities.

Similarly, those who feel most personally threatened by the prospect of Quebec separatism are most likely to oppose it, even to see it as absurd. For example, a study of students at McGill University and the University of Toronto found that those who thought they would be most adversely affected by Quebec separation were least likely to see it as a real possibility, that is, to see it as credible, and were also likely to see it as an expression of real economic grievances, perhaps *because* they felt more personally threatened by the prospect. It is interesting to note, however, that this "head in the sand" tendency was less likely if the students were aware of the history of Quebec and separatism (Archibald, 1978:261).

According to Turner, protest activities are likely to receive the most sympathetic response from people who have themselves had similar experiences and who have participated in related activities. It is probably in this sense that the student movement of the 1960s has had its greatest impact. Now that we have witnessed the widespread participation of middle-class youth in protest activities, we can never view these activities in quite the same light. Most of your teachers, for instance, and probably your parents, were involved in "sixties protest," either directly through their own participation or indirectly through the participation of those close to them.

Because of this we are probably far less able to dismiss collective protest as the actions of extreme fringe groups, outside agitators or criminals. On the other hand, it is well to remember at the same time that most Canadians supported the invocation of the War Measures Act and the severe treatment of the FLQ members and sympathizers after the kidnapping of Pierre Laport and James Cross. Clearly, most Canadians saw the FLQ actions as more threatening than the government response.

STATE RESPONSE

The most important response to consider is that of the state. As we have indicated, the state may often simply ignore some instances of collective protest if they are seen as posing no threat to the social order.

On the other hand, the state may enter into negotiations with the protest group. This will most likely be the case if the state feels that the demands of the protesters are credible and can be met within the system and if it fears that the protest could grow to threatening proportions. This may well be the case, for example, in the past willingness by officials to enter into negotiations with Indians concerning land claims.

Finally, the state may attempt to obstruct the collective behaviour through cooptation and manipulation or through the use of force. Ted Gurr (1969), for example, has shown that nations with a large and loyal coercive police force are able to keep political disturbances to a minimum. Most Canadians were probably surprised by what we have learned about the role played by Canadian police, particularly the RCMP, in controlling strikers, political protesters, and radicals (see, for example, Brown and Brown, 1973).

One of the clearest examples of the importance of the response of the state in shaping collective action is provided by Irving Abella (1974) in his discussion of labour struggles in Canada. He points out that most Canadians would be very surprised to learn that labour disputes in Canada were much more likely to be violent than those in Europe. Canada has a history of violent strikes, but to understand this violence we must appreciate the "heavy hand of government" in attempts to thwart the growing Canadian labour movement.

Abella discusses six key strikes in the history of Canadian labour between 1919 and 1949:

In each of (these) strikes . . . the heavy hand of government . . . grinds down upon labour. In each of these conflicts, the state comes down forcefully and aggressively on the side of capital. Labour was left to fend for itself against both business and government. Workers were to be crushed and unions destroyed whenever they posed a serious threat to the industry. And to support business, the full resources of the state were always available. The army, police, legislation—all were at the disposal of industry in its efforts to keep labour weak and divided . . . this is a major theme of the history of the Canadian labour movement during those years. In each of the strikes . . . violence, or the threat of violence, is a key factor. And usually, the violence is a direct result of the intervention of the state at the behest of industry to crush a strike (1974:xv).

The climax of the Winnipeg General Strike of 1919, for instance, occurred on June 21 when the police response to the strikers created a panicking crowd very much like that described long ago by Gustave LeBon. Twice the Mounted Police charged through the crowd and then were ordered to draw their pistols and fire a volley at the strikers. Their shooting continued for several minutes during which time one striker was killed and others were wounded. Not surprisingly, the crowd "panicked," a panic no doubt fed as well by the fact that the police were making mass arrests of the fleeing strikers. The monolithic response to the Winnipeg General Strike was to sap much of the energy and vigour of what was by then a powerful Canadian labour movement (Bercusen, 1974).

We cannot hope to understand collective violence or protest more generally without considering the consequences of official attempts at controlling the crowd, without considering the *confrontation* between the crowd and representatives of the state—the police and the army.

Much work remains to be done in this area; the relationship between crowd behaviour and social control is difficult to sort out. On the one hand, the government's use of the police or military to disband a crowd may serve to prevent the crowd from developing into something more permanent and organized. On the other hand, it may also serve to politicize and even radicalize members of the crowd and sympathetic onlookers, thus planting the seeds of a more radical social movement.

VARIETIES OF SOCIAL MOVEMENTS

Social movements differ from crowds simply in degree: social movements are more enduring and are at least somewhat more organized. One can classify social movements in terms of their orientation to social change. **Revolutionary movements** seek wholesale and immediate change in the social order. Such movements will often use violent means in their attempt to dislodge the established authorities from their positions of power. The FLQ in Canada illustrated well the impact that such movements can have even when there are few active members. As we have mentioned, the fact that Canada (or the U.S.) has never known a broadly based, sustained revolutionary movement is often taken as a refutation of Marx and sometimes as an indication of the vitality of Canadian capitalism.

More often, however, social movements seek to change some specific aspects of society. Richard Allen (1975), for example, describes the Canadian **reform movements** which arose between 1890 and 1928 as largely a response to the social problems created by slums and immigration. The goals of reform movements generally involve specific legal reforms that they hope to achieve through influencing the power groups by some combination of manipulation and threat. While such movements as the black civil rights movement, youth movements of the 1960s, and Women's Liberation are often successful in achieving certain limited objectives, they are unlikely to fundamentally alter the power structure. Often one aspect of these movements is the attempt to create, through consciousness-raising groups and the like, a subjective revolution, or what Reich (1971) described as "Consciousness III."

In his highly popular book *The Greening of America,* Reich tried to argue that a structural revolution would be the natural and inevitable consequence of a subjective revolution; that is, fundamental structural change would be achieved through the massive changes in people's perceptions and definitions. But as Peter Archibald (1978) suggests, however valuable change in consciousness may be, people will encounter the weight of the structures of power when they try to realize their ideals.

However, it is not always easy to draw the line between reform and revolutionary movements. Clearly, many movements have elements of both and may even be divided internally on the issue of how much change is necessary.

Such a split is nicely illustrated in Zakuta's (1964) discussion of the "right and left wings" of the CCF. Perhaps this split reached a climax with the emergence and "near success" of the Waffle group within the NDP. This group of nationalists and socialists surprised the party "old guard" by their show of strength at the 1969 federal convention in Winnipeg. Many of the established leaders within the "right" wing of the party tried, with a good deal of success, to crush the Waffle group, expressing their concern that these radical politics would tarnish the public image of the NDP. And despite the growing activism of radical academics trying to push the NDP to the left, the party remains one essentially of reform.

Reactionary movements, on the other hand, seek to stop the changes they think are occurring in society and even to recapture a past way of life. For example, Women's Liberation, later feminism, seems to have spawned a number of countermovements which hark back to the days when a woman "knew her place" and stayed home to raise and care for her family.

The most powerful movement in Canada today may be just this kind of reactionary populism. As J. Richards (1981) describes it, in the absence in Canada of left-wing populism, there is a growing right-wing populist reaction, evidenced in western separatism and backlash against homosexuals, abortion, feminists and all things liberal. We have recently seen, in the U.S., how early "liberal" could become a term of disparagement. We wonder what this movement augurs for Canada's future.

Whatever their differences, however, social movements are a major source of social change, of new values, of new ways of looking at the world. The Quebec separatist movement has obviously shown its influence in concrete ways but it has also demanded that we all consider the position in Canada of French Canadians and reexamine our old definitions and values. Surely most of us, men and women, have been changed by feminism.

Of course not all movements are so successful. Most die a quick death; others barely persist in the face of fierce public resistance. Few conflict groups are able to muster the organizational base and continuous leadership necessary for sustained protest. Dependent as they are on the commitment of their members and the support of the public, most social movements eventually "water down" their ideology so that the public finds their ideas more palatable and the members see the goals of the movement as more readily attainable.

Even movements that are successful in getting some of their goals accepted tend to become similarly watered down, more pragmatic and less idealistic. During this state of *routinization*, a movement may evolve into a specialized association, for example, a political party or a union, and become an institutionalized part of the society it started out to change.

It will typically have a formalized leadership and administrative staff, holding clearly defined positions of authority and operating under explicit rules and regulations. Supporters of the association will usually be less enthusiastic than were supporters of the movement, but often more reliable because their participation will follow certain stable norms that obligate them to give a specific amount of time and money to the association (Clark et al., 1975:32).

This is the main thrust of Zakuta's *A Protest Movement Becalmed* (1964) in which he traces the change in the CCF as it evolved from a loosely organized social movement to a political party. We can also trace Canadian labour unions to their origins in a weak but radical social movement "whose members lived in constant fear of losing not only their jobs but perhaps even their lives" (Abella, 1974:xv). The NDP, contemporary unions and the like are in a sense remnants of social movements. But they are much more. They serve as reminders of people who tried to change their society and to some extent succeeded.

CONCLUSION

Collective action may be the concerted and deliberate attempt of a number of people to change their social environment. Many of the characteristics typically associated with collective action and protest, the confusion, the emotionalism, the violence, may simply reflect the fact that trying to change one's social world is difficult and risky and is often met with strong resistance. And as William Gamson (1975:143) asks, "If it costs so much to succeed, how can we be confident that there are not countless would-be challengers who are deterred by the mere prospect?" The study of protest and collective action reminds us that change does not happen independently of the actions of people. It is in large part the study of people actively shaping history and as such it must have a central place in sociology.

Of all the concerns in sociology, none is more important nor more problematic than social change. Sociologist are not prophets; they cannot foretell the future. At most, sociologists have hoped to be able to predict a change in one variable when some other variable has also changed — for example, a change in family roles with increasing female participation in the labour force. But just what will this mean? How might such a change *within* the system influence change *of* the system? In an earlier chapter we rejected the notion that massive subjective change — a subjective revolution — could produce fundamental, structural change, that is, change of the system. Indeed, Harris (1973) calls this emphasis on a subjective revolution the "new witchcraft," dangerous because our attention is deflected from the issues of power and inequality. But what is the relationship between changes in definition or lifestyle and structural changes?

As David Lockwood reminds us, values and ideologies must be taken into account because of what they tell us about how people orient and respond to objective inequalities (Lockwood, 1970). And just when do we decide that fundamental structural change has occurred? What criteria do we use to establish that the old order has become the new order? Or how do we distinguish precisely between change within the system and change of the system, or even between change that is real and change that is only apparent? There is much we simply do not know about the relationship between order and change, reform, and revolution.

What should be clear is that change does not just happen. People make decisions, take actions (or not) and through these collective decisions and actions shape the future.

Sociologists are, or can be, part of this equation. One thing sociologists can do and have done is to imagine alternative futures, not to predict but to offer possibilities. This means more than simply drawing "scenarios" of what might occur; it is also asking questions about what ought to occur, raising questions about values.

For example, can we tolerate the environmental and human costs of increasing technology and even economic growth? Fear that there will be a continuing deterioration in the quality of our lives and of our relationships and that the pursuit of economic growth will aggravate inequalities and further curtail our freedom, have led a number of social scientists and philosophers to a critique of our values, to the search for alternative technologies and to the advocacy of a no-growth economy. What these thinkers share in common is the conviction that social forces do not operate independently of the actions of people and that a critical perspective encourages people to try to harness these forces for the deliberate pursuit of consciously chosen futures.

The 1960s were a time of protest, however chaotic and piecemeal. Cherished values — material success, Canadian unity, the authority of husbands, parents, teachers and governments — could no longer be taken for granted. The 1970s might be described as a time of confusion and, for many, disappointed expectations. The 1980s, in the face of economic uncertainty and restraint, has been a period of retrenchment and conservatism. It may well be a conceit of most people that the time that they are living through is somehow a crucial point in history. Nevertheless, it seems inescapable that Canada is at such a point and that it is now a time when sociologists or, better, Canadians must address themselves to social issues. Sociologists cannot afford to sit on the sidelines. Meech Lake, Free Trade, cultural sovereignty, the environment and the role of government do matter. The task now facing sociology is not simply to sit back and describe the changes but to help in creating a particular kind of Canada.

BIBLIOGRAPHY

Abella, Irving, ed.
1974　*On Strike: Six Key Labour Struggles in Canada 1919–1949.* Toronto: James Lewis and Samuel.
1975　*The Canadian Labour Movement, 1902–1960.* Ottawa: Canadian Historical Society. Historical Booklet No. 28.

Abler, T.
1973　*A Canadian Indian Bibliography 1960–1970.* Toronto: University of Toronto Press.

Abrahamson, Mark
1983　*Social Research Methods.* Englewood Cliffs N.J.: Prentice-Hall.

Acheson, T. W.
1972　"The Social Origins of the Canadian Industrial Elite, 1880–1885," in *Canadian Business History, Selected Studies, 1947–1971,* edited by D. S. Macmillan, Toronto: McClelland and Stewart.
1973　"Changing Social Origins of the Canadian Industrial Elite, 1880–1910." *Business History Review* XLVII (2) Summer.
1977　"The Maritimes and 'Empire Canada'," in Bercuson (1977:87–114).

Adachi, K.
1976　*The Enemy that Never Was: A History of the Japanese Canadians.* Toronto: McClelland and Stewart.

Adams, Bert N.
1975　*The Family: A Sociological Interpretation.* Chicago: Rand McNally College Publishing Company.

Adams, Ian.
1971　*The Poverty Wall.* Toronto: McClelland and Stewart.

Adams, Ian, W. Cameron, B. Hill, and P. Penz.
1971　*The Real Poverty Report.* Edmonton: M. G. Hurtig.

Adorno, T. W.
1950　*The Authoritarian Personality.* New York: Harper & Brothers.

Alexander, David
1977　*The Decay of Trade: An Economic History of the Newfoundland Saltfish Trade, 1935–1965.* No. 19. St. John's: Institute for Social and Economic Research, Memorial University of Newfoundland.

Allen, Richard.
1975　"The Social Gospel and Reform Tradition in Canada, 1890–1928," in Clark et al. (1975:45–61).

Alinski, Saul.
1971　*Rules for Radicals.* New York: Random House.

Ambert, Ann-Marie.
1976　*Sex Structure.* Toronto: Longman Canada.
1980　*Divorce in Canada.* Toronto: Academic Press Canada.

Ames, Michael M., and Joy Inglis.
1975　"Tradition and Change in British Columbia Sikh Family Life," in Ishwaran (1975:77–91).

Andersen, Allen, and James Frideres.
1981　*Ethnicity in Canada: Theoretical Perspectives.* Toronto: Butterworths.

Anderson, Charles.
1974　*The Political Economy of Social Class.* Englewood Cliffs, N.J.: Prentice-Hall.

Anderson, G. M., and D. Higgs.
1977　*A Future to Inherit: The Portuguese Communities of Canada.* Toronto: McClelland and Stewart.

Anderson K., and others.
1987　*Family Matters: Sociology and Contemporary Canadian Families.* Toronto: Methuen.

Anderson, Michael.
1971　*Family Structure in Nineteenth Century Lancashire.* Cambridge: Cambridge University Press.

Andreski, Stanislav.
1974　*Social Sciences as Sorcery.* London: Penguin Books.

Archibald, W. Peter.
1978　*Social Psychology as Political Economy.* Toronto: McGraw-Hill Ryerson.

Argue, R., C. Gannage and D. W. Livingstone (eds).
1987   *Working People and Hard Times: Canadian Perspectives.* Toronto: Garamond Press.

Ariès, Philippe.
1962   *Centuries of Childhood: A Social History of Family Life.* New York, Random House.
1980   "Two Successive Motivations for the Declining Birth Rate in the West." *Population and Development Review* Vol. 6 (4).

Armstrong, Pat, and Hugh Armstrong.
1975   "The Segmented Participation of Women in the Canadian Labour Force." *Canadian Review of Sociology and Anthropology* 12 (4) November: 370–384.
1978   *The Double Ghetto.* Toronto: McClelland and Stewart.
1983   *A Working Majority: What Women Must Do For Pay.* Ottawa: Canadian Advisory Council on the Status of Women.

Aron, Raymond.
1965   *Main Currents in Sociological Thought.* Vol. I and II. London: Weidenfeld and Nicolson.

Atkinson, J. W., and D. C. McClelland.
1948   "The Protective Expression of Needs." *Journal of Experimental Psychology 38.*

Atwood, Margaret.
1972   *Survival: A Thematic Guide to Canadian Literature.* Toronto: House of Anansi Press.

Babbie, Earl.
1989   *The Practice of Social Research*, Belmont Calif: Wadsworth.

Baker, Maureen.
1984   *The Family: Changing Trends in Canada.* Toronto: McGraw-Hill Ryerson.
1988   *Aging in Canadian Society: A Survey.* Toronto: McGraw-Hill Ryerson.

Bala, Nicholas, and Kenneth Clarke.
1981   *The Child and the Law.* Toronto: McGraw-Hill Ryerson.

Baldus, Bernd, and Verna Tribe.
1978   "The Development of Perceptions and Evaluations of Social Inequality Among Public School Children." *Canadian Review of Sociology and Anthropology* 15(1): 50–60.

Baldwin, Elizabeth.
1977a "The Mass Media and the Corporate Elite: A Re-analysis of the Overlap between the Media and Economic Elites." *Canadian Journal of Sociology* 2 (1) Winter: 1–28.
1977b "On Methodological and Theoretical Muddles in Clement's Media Study." *Canadian Journal of Sociology* (2) Spring: 215–222.

Banting, Keith G.
1987   "The Welfare State and Inequality in the 1980's." *Canadian Review of Sociology and Anthropology* 24 (3) 309–338.

Banton, Michael.
1965   *Roles.* London: Tavistock Publications.

Baran, Paul, and Paul Sweezey.
1966   *Monopoly Capital.* New York: Monthly Review Press.

Barber, Bernard.
1957   *Social Stratification.* New York: Harcourt, Brace and World.

Barth, Fredrik.
1969   "Introduction," in *Ethnic Groups and Ethnic Boundaries.* Boston: Little Brown: 3–98.

Baum, David J.
1979   *Discount Justice.* Don Mills: Burns and MacEachern.

Beaujot, Roderic.
1988   "The Family in Crisis?" *Canadian Journal of Sociology* 13 (3) 305–311.

Beaujot, R., K. G. Bassavarajappa and R. Verna.
1986   "The Relative Income of Immigrants: Are the New Immigrant Groups at a Disadvantage." *CSAA Meetings, Winnipeg.*

Beaujot, R., and K. McQuillan.
1982   *Growth and Dualism.* Toronto: Gage Publishing.

Becker, Howard S.
1958   "Problems of Inference and Proof in Participant Observation." *American Sociological Review* 23 (3): 652–660.

1963 *Outsiders.* New York: Free Press.
1964a "Social Interaction," in *A Dictionary of the Social Sciences,* edited by J. Gould and W. L. Kolb. London: Tavistock.
1964b *The Other Side: Perspectives on Deviance.* Glencoe: Free Press.
1967 "Whose Side Are We On?" *Social Problems* 14:239–247.

Beigel, Hugo.
1951 "Romantic Love." *American Sociological Review* 15 (1951): 326–334.

Bell, Colin.
1968 *Middle-Class Families.* London: Routledge and Kegan Paul.

Bell, Daniel.
1960 *The End of Ideology.* New York: The Free Press.
1973 *The Coming of Post-Industrial Society.* New York: Basic Books.
1978 *The Cultural Contradictions of Capitalism.* New York: Basic Books.

Bell, David, and Lorne Tepperman.
1979 *The Roots of Disunity.* Toronto: McClelland and Stewart.

Bendix, Reinhard.
1963 *Work and Authority in Industry.* New York: Harper Torchbook.

Benedict, Ruth.
1934 *Patterns of Culture.* New York: Mentor Books.

Bercuson, David.
1974 "The Winnipeg General Strike," in Abella (1974:1–32).

Bercuson, David. ed.
1977 *Canada and the Burden of Unity.* Toronto: Macmillan.

Bercuson, David, and L. A. Knafla.
1979 *Law and Society in Canada: in Historical Perspective.* Calgary: University of Calgary. Studies in History, No. 2.

Berg, Ivor.
1970 *Education and Jobs: The Great Training Robbery.* New York: Beacon Press.

Berger, Brigitte, and Peter Berger.
1983 *The War Over the Family: The Search for A Middle Ground.* New York: Basic Books.

Berger, Peter L.
1963 *Invitation to Sociology: A Humanistic Perspective.* New York: Doubleday Anchor.
1971 "Sociology and Freedom." *American Sociologist* 6:1–6.

Berger, Peter, and Hansfried Kellner.
1964 "Marriage and the Construction of Reality." *Diogenes,* Summer: 1–24.

Berger, Peter, and Thomas Luckmann.
1966 *The Social Construction of Reality: A Treatise in the Sociology of Knowledge.* New York: Doubleday.

Berger, Peter, and Richard Neuhaus.
1970 *Movement and Revolution: On American Radicalism.* Garden City, New York: Doubleday.

Berk, Richard A.
1974 *Collective Behavior.* Dubuque, Iowa: William C. Brown.

Berkowitz, S. D., ed.
1984 *Models and Myths in Canadian Sociology.* Toronto: Butterworths Canada.

Bernard, Jessie.
1972 *The Future of Marriage.* New York: World Publishing Co.

Berne, Eric.
1964 *Games People Play.* New York: Grove Press.

Bernstein, Basil
1961 "Social Class and Linguistic Development: A Theory of Social Learning," in *Education, Economy, and Society,* edited by A. H. Halsey, Jan Floud, and C. Arnold. New York: Free Press: 288–314.

Berry, J. W., and G. J. S. Wilde.
1972 *Social Psychology: The Canadian Context.* Toronto: McClelland and Stewart.

Berton, Pierre.
1975 *Hollywood's Canada.* Toronto: McClelland and Stewart.

Beyer Gammon, Mary Alice.
1978 *Violence in Canada.* Toronto: Methuen Publications.

Bieler Brettel, Carol.
1977   "Ethnicity and Entrepreneurs: Portuguese
        Immigrants in a Canadian City," in Hicks
        and Leis (1977: 169–180).

Bigo, Pierre.
1977   *The Church and Third World Revolution.*
        New York: Orbis Books.

Birnbaum, Norman.
1971   *Toward a Critical Sociology.* New York:
        Oxford University Press.

Blau, P. M.
1955   *The Dynamics of Bureaucracy.* Chicago:
        University of Chicago Press.
1956   "Social Mobility and Interpersonal
        Relations." *American Sociological Review*
        21(3) June: 290–295.
1964   *Exchange and Power,* New York: Wiley.

Blau, P. M., and O. D. Duncan.
1967   *The American Occupational Structure.*
        New York: Wiley.

Bleier, Ruth.
1984   *Science and Gender: A Critique of Biology
        and Its Theories on Women.* New York:
        Pergamon Press.

**Blishen, Bernard, William Carroll and
Catherine Moore.**
1987   "The 1981 Socio-Economic Index for
        Occupations in Canada." *Canadian
        Review of Sociology and Anthropology*
        46: 1–53.

Blum, Alan F., and Peter McHugh.
1971   "The Social Ascription of Motives."
        American Sociological Review 36 (1): 98–
        109.

Blumer, Herbert.
1957   "Collective Behavior." In *Review of
        Sociology: Analysis of a Decade,* edited
        by J. B. Gittler. New York: Wiley.
1969   *Symbolic Interactionism: Perspective and
        Method.* Englewood Cliffs, N.J.: Prentice-
        Hall.

Bodemann, Michael Y.
1978   "A Problem of Sociological Praxis: The
        Case for Inventive Observation in Field
        Work." *Theory and Society* 5: 387–420.

Boissevain, J.
1970   *Italians of Montreal.* Ottawa: Queen's
        Printer.

Borovoy, A. A.
1966   "Indian Poverty in Canada." *Canadian
        Labour* 12, December: 13–15.

Bott, Elizabeth.
1971   *Family and Social Network.* London:
(1975) Tavistock.

Bottomore, T. B.
1965   *Classes in Modern Society.* London:
        George Allen and Unwin.

Bottomore, T. B., and Maximilien Rubel, eds.
1963   *Karl Marx: Selected Writings in Sociology
        and Social Philosophy.* London: Pelican
        Books.
1966   *Elites and Society.* London: Pelican
        Books.
1979   *Karl Marx.* London: Basil Blackwell.

Bowen, Elenore Smith.
1964   *Return to Laughter.* Garden City, New
        York: Anchor Books.

Bowles, Samuel, and Herbert Gintis.
1976   *Schooling in Capitalist America.* New
        York: Basic Books.

Boyd, Monica.
1977a   "The Forgotten Minority: The Socio-
        Economic Status of Divorced and
        Separated Women," in Marchak (1977:
        46–71).
1977b   "Occupational Attainments of Native-
        Born Canadian Women: Results from the
        1973 Canadian National Mobility Study."
        Paper presented at the CSAA meetings,
        Fredericton, N.B.

**Boyd, Monica, John Goyder, F. E. Jones,
H. A. McRoberts, P. C. Pineo and John Porter.**
1985   *Ascription and Achievement: Studies in
        Mobility and Status Attainment in
        Canada.* Ottawa: Carleton University
        Press.

Boydell, Craig, and others, eds.
1972   *Deviant Behaviour and Societal Reaction.*
        Toronto: Holt, Rinehart and Winston.
1974   *The Administration of Criminal Justice in
        Canada,* Toronto: Holt, Rinehart and
        Winston.

Braverman, Harry.
1974   *Labor and Monopoly Capital.* New York:
        Monthly Review Press.

Breton, Raymond.
1964 "Institutional Completeness and Ethnic Communities and Personal Relations to Immigrants." *American Journal of Sociology* 70 (2): 193–205.
1972 *Social and Academic Factors in the Career Decisions of Canadian Youth* (with J. McDonald and S. Richer). Ottawa: Information Canada.

Brim, O. G., Jr., and S. Wheeler.
1966 *Socialization After Childhood: Two Essays.* New York: Wiley.

Brittan, A.
1973 *Meanings and Situations.* London: Routledge and Kegan Paul.

Broadfoot, Barry.
1975 *Ten Lost Years, 1929–1939.* Don Mills, Ontario: General Publishing Company (Paperjacks).

Brody, Hugh.
1975 *The People's Land.* London: Penguin Books.

Bronfenbenner, Urie.
1970 *Two Worlds of Childhood.* New York: Russell Sage.

Brown, Lester.
1985 "A False Sense of Security," in *State of the World.*
1986 "Anglo-Canadian Sociology." *Current Sociology* 34 (1) 1–152.

Brown, Lorne, and Caroline Brown.
1973 *An Unauthorized History of the RCMP.* Toronto: James Lewis and Samuel.

Brown, Roger.
1965 *Social Psychology.* New York: Free Press.

Bryant, Clifton D.
1974 *Deviant Behavior: Occupational and Organizational Bases.* Chicago: Rand McNally.

Brym, Robert.
1978 "Regional Social Structure and Agrarian Radicalism in Canada: Alberta, Saskatchewan and New Brunswick." *Canadian Review of Sociology and Anthropology.*

Brym, Robert (ed.)
1985 *The Structure of the Canadian Capitalist Class.* Toronto: Garamond Press.

1986 *Regionalism in Canada.* Toronto: Irwin.

Brym, Robert (with Bonnie Fox).
1989 *From Culture to Power: The Sociology of English Canada.* Toronto: Oxford University Press.

Brym, Robert, and Barbara Neis.
1978 "Regional Factors in the Formation of the Fishermen's Protective Union of Newfoundland." *Canadian Journal of Sociology* (3).

Brym, Robert, and R. James Sacouman.
1979 *Underdevelopment and Social Movements in Atlantic Canada.* Toronto: New Hogtown Press.

Burke, Edmund.
1955 *Reflections on the Revolution in*
(1790) *France,* Indianapolis: Bobbs-Merrill.

Burke, Kenneth.
1965 *Permanence and Change.* 2nd rev. ed. Indianapolis: Bobbs-Merrill.
1969 *A Grammar of Motives.* Berkeley:
(1945) University of California Press.

Caldwell, Gary.
1974 *A Demographic Profile of the English-Speaking Population of Quebec 1921–1971.* Québec: Centre International de Recherches sur le Bilinguisme.
1978 *Out-Migration of English Mother-Tongue High School Leavers from Quebec 1971–76.* Lennoxville: Bishop's University.

Caldwell, G., and D. Czarnocki.
1975 "Interpreting Social Change in Post-War Quebec in a Quebec-Ontario Comparative Perspective." Paper presented at the CSAA meetings, Edmonton.

Caldwell, G., and Daniel Fournier.
1987 "The Quebec Question: A Matter of Population," *Canadian Journal of Sociology* (12: 1–2).

Caldwell, John.
1973 "The World Fertility Survey: Problems and Possibilities." *World Fertility Survey.* Occasional Papers (No. 2).

Campbell, Colin, and George J. Szablowski.
1979 *The Superbureaucrats: Structure and Behaviour in Central Agencies.* Toronto: Gage Publishing.

Caplow, T.
1956   "A Theory of Coalitions in the Triad."
       American Sociological Review 21,
       August: 489–493.

Carnoy, Martin.
1974   *Education as Cultural Imperialism.* New
       York: David McKay.

Carstens, Peter.
1971   "Coercion and Change," in Ossenberg
       (1971: 126–145).

Carroll, William K.
1986   *Corporate Power and Canadian
       Capitalism.* Vancouver: University of
       British Columbia Press.

**Carroll, William K., John Fox and Michael D.
Ornstein.**
1982   "The Network of Directorate Interlocks
       Among the Largest Canadian Firms."
       *Canadian Review of Sociology and
       Anthropology* 19 (3): 44–69.

Castaneda, Carlos.
1968   *The Teachings of Don Juan: A Yaqui Way
       of Knowledge.* New York: Ballantine
       Books.

Castellano, Marlene Brant.
1970   "Vocation of Identity: The Dilemma of
       Indian Youth," in *The Only Good Indian*,
       edited by Waubageshig. Toronto: New
       Press.

Chen, M., and Thomas Regan.
1985   *Work in the Changing Canadian Society.*
       Toronto: Butterworths.

Cherlin, Andrew.
1981   *Marriage, Divorce, Remarriage.*
       Cambridge: Mass: Harvard University
       Press.

Chomsky, Noam.
1957   *Syntactic Structure.* The Hague: Mouton.

Cicourel, Aaron V.
1964   *Method and Measurement in Sociology.*
       New York: Free Press.
1970   "Basic and Normative Rules in the
       Negotiation of Status and Role," in *Recent
       Sociology, No. 2.*, edited by Hans P.
       Dreitzel. New York: Macmillan, 4–45.

Clairmont, Don, and Dennis Magill.
1974   *Africville: The Life and Death of a
       Canadian Black Community.* Toronto:
       McClelland and Stewart.

Clairmont, Don, and Fred Wien.
1974   "Segmentation, Disadvantage and
       Development: An Analysis of the
       Marginal Work World, Its Linkages with
       the Central Work World and Its Role in
       the Maritime Provinces." Halifax:
       Institute of Public Affairs, Marginal Work
       World Program.

Clark, Burton R.
1960   "The Cooling-Out Function in Higher
       Education." *American Journal of
       Sociology.* 65, May: 569–576.
1962   *Educating the Expert Society.* San
       Francisco: Chandler.

Clark, Lorenne, and Debra Lewis.
1977   *Rape: The Price of Coercive Sexuality.*
       Toronto: The Women's Press.

Clark, S. D.
1948   *Church and Sect in Canada.* Toronto:
       University of Toronto Press.
1959   *Movements of Political Protest in Canada,
       1640–1840.* Toronto: University of
       Toronto Press.
1968   *The Developing Canadian Community*,
       2nd ed. Toronto: University of Toronto
       Press.
1976a *Canadian Society in Historical
       Perspective.* Toronto: McGraw-Hill
       Ryerson.
1976b The Issue of Canadian Identity." Paper
       presented at St. Thomas University,
       Fredericton, N.B.

**Clark, Samuel D., J. Paul Grayson, and Linda
M. Grayson.**
1975   *Prophesy and Protest: Social Movements
       in Twentieth-Century Canada.* Toronto:
       Gage Educational.

Clark, Susan, and A. S. Harvey.
1976   "The Sexual Division of Labour: The Use
       of Time." *Atlantis* 2 (1): 46–66.

Clement, Wallace.
1974   "Inequality of Access." *Canadian Review
       of Sociology and Anthropology* 12 (L):
       33–52.

1975 *The Canadian Corporate Elite*. Toronto: Macmillan Co. of Canada.

1977a "The Canadian Bourgeoisie: Merely Comprador?" in Saul and Heron (1977:71–84).
Continental Corporate Power. Toronto: McClelland and Stewart.

1977c "Overlap of the Media and Economic Elites." *Canadian Journal of Sociology* 2 (2) Spring: 205–214.

1981 *Hard Rock Mining*. Toronto: McClelland and Stewart.

1986 *The Struggle to Organize: Resistance in Canada's Fisheries*. Toronto: McLelland and Stewart.

Clivio, Gianfenzo.
1977 "Italiese Glossary." Report of research in *University of Toronto Graduate* V (2) Winter: 1, 7.

Cloward, R. A., and L. E. Ohlin.
1960 *Delinquency and Opportunity*. New York: Free Press.

Cochrane, W.
1986 "Symbiosis with a Silver Lining." Toronto Area Higher Education Seminar, October.

Cohen, Albert F.
1966 *Deviance and Control*. Englewood Cliffs, N.J.: Prentice-Hall.

Cohen, Percy S.
1968 *Modern Social Theory*. London: Heinemann.

Cohen, Stanley, ed.
1971 *Images of Deviance*. London: Penguin.

Cohen, Stanley.
1973 "Protest, Unrest and Delinquency: Convergences in Labels and Behaviour." *International Journal of Criminology and Penology* 1: 117–128.

Coleman, James, and others.
1966 *Equality of Educational Opportunity*. Washington, D.C.: U.S. Government Printing Office.

Colfax, J. David, and Jack L. Roach, eds.
1971 *Radical Sociology*. New York: Basic Books.

Collins, Randall.
1971a "Functional and Conflict Theories of Educational Stratification." *American Sociological Review* 36 (6) December: 1002–1019.

1971b "A Conflict Theory of Sexual Stratification." *Social Problems* 19 (1): 3–21.

1974 "Where are Educational Requirements for Employment Highest?" *Sociology of Education* 47 (4) Fall: 419–442.

1979 *The Credentials Society*. New York: Academic Press.

Collins, R., and M. Makowsky.
1978 *The Discovery of Society*. New York: Random House.

Comte, Auguste.
1893 *The Positive Philosophy of Auguste Comte*. Translated by Harriet Martineau. London: Bell.

Connelly, M. Patricia.
1977 "The Economic Content of Women's Labour Force Participation in Canada," in Marchak (1977: 10–27).

1979 *Last Hired, First Fired: Women and the Canadian Labour Force*. Toronto: Women's Educational Press.

Connelly, M. Patricia, and Linda Christiansen-Ruffman.
1977 "Women's Problems: Private Troubles or Public Issues." *Canadian Journal of Sociology* 2 (3): 167–178.

Cook, Gail, ed.
1976 *Opportunity for Choice*. Ottawa: Statistics Canada and C. D. Howe.

Cook, Shirley J.
1969 "Canadian Narcotics Legislation, 1908–1923: A Conflict Model Interpretation." *Canadian Review of Sociology and Anthropology* 6: 36–46.

Cooley, Charles H.
1902 *Human Nature and the Social Order*. New York: Scribner.

1909 *Social Organization*. New York: Scribner.

1926 "The Roots of Social Knowledge." *American Journal of Sociology* XXXII, July: 59–79.

Cooper, David.
1970   *The Death of the Family*. London: Penguin Books.

Copp, Terry.
1974   *The Anatomy of Poverty*. Toronto: McClelland and Stewart.

Coser, Lewis A.
1956   *The Functions of Social Conflict*. London: Free Press.
1971   *Masters of Sociological Thought: Ideas in Historical and Social Context*. New York: Harcourt Brace Jovanovich.

Cottle, Thomas J.
1980   "Goodbye Kids, Mother's Leaving Home." *The Atlantic Monthly:* 43–38.

Coxon, Anthony, and Charles Jones.
1978   *The Images of Occupational Prestige: A Study in Social Cognition*. London: Macmillan.

Crawford, Elizabeth, and Stein Rokkan.
1976   *Sociological Praxis: Current Roles and Setting*. London: Sage.

Crean, S. M.
1976   *Who's Afraid of Canadian Culture?* Don Mills: General Publishing Co.

Crozier, Michel.
1964   *The Bureaucratic Phenomenon*. Chicago: University of Chicago Press.

Cruikshank, J.
1971   "Matrifocal Families in the Canadian North," in Ishwaran (1971: 39–53).

Curtis, J., and Sid Gilbert.
1988   *Social Inequality in Canada: Patterns, Problems, Policies*. Toronto: Prentice-Hall.

Curtis, J., and Lorne Tepperman.
1990   *Images of Canada: The Sociological Tradition*. Toronto: Prentice-Hall.

Dahlie, Jorgen, and Tissa Fernando.
1981   *Ethnicity, Power and Politics*. Toronto: Methuen.

Dahrendorf, Ralf.
1958   "Out of Utopia: Toward a Reorientation of Sociologal Analysis." *American Journal of Sociology* 64, September.
1959   *Class and Class Conflict in Industrial Society*. Stanford: Stanford University Press.
1969   "On the Origin of Inequality between Men," in *Social Inequality*, edited by A. Beteille. London: Penguin: 16–44.

Danziger, Kurt.
1974   "The Acculturation of Italian Immigrant Girls in Canada," in *Sociology Canada: Readings*, edited by Christopher Beattie and Stewart Crysdale. Toronto: Butterworths.

Darroch, Gordon A.
1980   "Another Look at Ethnicity, Stratification and Social Mobility in Canada," in Goldstein and Bienvenue (1980: 203–230)

Davies, James C.
1962   "Toward a Theory of Revolution." *American Sociological Review 27*, February: 5–19.

Davis, A. K.
1971   "Canadian Society as Hinterland Versus Metropolis," in Ossenberg (1971: 6–32).

Davis, Fred.
1964   "Deviance Disavowal: The Management of Strained Interaction by the Visibly Handicapped," in Becker (1964b).

Davis, John.
1975   "Learning the Norm of Universalism: The Effect of School Attendance," in Pike and Zureik (1975: 84–98).

Davis, Kingsley
1948   *Human Society*. New York: Maxmillan.

Davis, Kingsley, and W. E. Moore.
1945   "Some Principles of Stratification." *American Sociological Review* 10 (2): 242–249.

Dawe, Alan.
1970   "The Two Sociologies." *British Journal of Sociology* 21 (2) June: 207–218.

De'Ath, Colin E., and Peter Bradbury.
1977   "Brokers and the Social Ecology of Minority Groups," in Hicks and Leis (1977: 181–200).

Denis, Ann B.
1975   "CEGEP Students: Varieties in Socialization Experience," in Pike and Zureik (1975: 209–238).

Denzin, Norman K.
1969 "Symbolic Interactionism and Ethnomethodology: A Proposed Synthesis." *American Sociological Review* 34, December.
1970 *The Research Act.* Chicago: Aldine.

Dickinson, James, and Bob Russell, eds.
1986 *Family Economy and State: The Social Reproduction Process Under Capitalism.* Toronto: Garamond Press.

Djilas, Milovan.
1959 *The New Class: An Analysis of the Communist Systems.* New York: Praeger.

Dosman, Edgar.
1972 *Indians: The Urban Dilemma.* Toronto: McClelland and Stewart.

Douglas, Jack D.
1967 *The Social Meaning of Suicide.* Princeton: Princeton University Press.

Douglas, Jack D., ed.
1970 *Understanding Everyday Life.* Chicago: Aldine.

Douglas, J. W. B.
1964 *The Home and School.* London: Granada.

Drache, Daniel.
1976 "Rediscovering Canadian Political Economy." *Journal of Canadian Studies* XI (3) August: 3–17.
1977 "Staple-ization: A Theory of Canadian Capitalist Development," in Saul and Heron (1977: 34–47).

Dreeben, Robert.
1968a "The Contribution of Schooling to the Learning of Norms." *Harvard Educational Review* 37 (2) Spring 1967: 211–237. Reprinted in *Socialization and Schools.* Harvard Educational Review, Reprint Series No. 1.
1968b *What Is Learned in School.* Reading, Mass.: Addison-Wesley.

Dreitzel, Hans Peter, ed.
1970 *Recent Sociology, No. 2: Patterns of Communicative Behavior.* New York: Macmillan.
1972 *Marriage, Family and the Struggle of the Sexes.* New York: Collier-Macmillan.

Driedger, Leo, ed.
1978 *The Canadian Ethnic Mosaic: A Quest for Identity.* Toronto: McClelland and Stewart.

Dumont, Louis.
1970 *Homo Hierarchicus: The Caste System and Its Implications.* Chicago: University of Chicago Press.

Durkheim, Emile.
1960 *The Division of Labor in Society.* Glencoe,
(1893) Ill.: Free Press.
1938 *The Rules of the Sociological Method.*
(1895) Chicago: University of Chicago Press.
1951 *Suicide.* Glencoe, Ill.: Free Press.
(1897)
1915 *The Elementary Forms of the Religious*
(1912) *Life.* London: Allen and Unwin.

Dutton, Donald G.
1972 "Reactions of Restaurateurs to Blacks and Whites Violating Dress Requirements," in Berry and Wilde, eds. 1972; 320–324).

Easterline, R. A.
1976 "The Conflict Between Aspirations and Resources." *Population and Development Review* 2 (3 and 4).
1978 "What Will 1984 Be Like? Socioeconomic Implications of Recent Trends in Age Structure." *Demography* 15 (4).

Easto, Patrick C., and Marcello Truzzi.
1974 "The Carnival as a Marginally Legal Work Activity: A Typological Approach to Work Systems," in Bryant (1974).

Edwards, Richards.
1979 *Contested Terrain.* New York: Basic Books.

Ehrlich, Paul R.
1968 *The Population Bomb.* New York: Ballantine Books.

Eichler, Margrit.
1973 "Women as Personal Dependents: A Critique of Theories of the Stratification of the Sexes and an Alternative Approach," in Stephenson (1933: 36–55).
1977 "The Prestige of the Occupation Housewife," in Marchak (1977).
1985 "And the Work Never Ends: Feminist Contributions." *The Canadian Review of Sociology and Anthropology* 22 (5) 619–644.
1988 *Families in Canada Today.* 2nd ed. Toronto: Gage Publishing.

Elkin, Frederick.
1971 "Mass Media, Advertising and the Quiet Revolution," in Ossenberg (1971:184–206).

Elkin, Frederick, and Gerald Handel.
1973   *The Child and Society: The Process of Socialization.* 2nd ed. New York: Random House.

Elliot, Jean, ed.
1971   *Immigrant Groups.* Toronto: Prentice-Hall.

Ellul, Jacques.
1967   *The Technological Society.* New York: Vintage Books.

Enros, P., and M. Farley.
1986   *University Offices for Technology Transfer: Toward the Service University.* Ottawa: Science Council of Canada.

Enterline, P. E.
1961   "Causes of Death Responsible for Recent Increases in Sex Mortalities Differentials in the United States." *Millbank Memorial Fund Quarterly*, Vol. 39.

Erikson, Eric.
1963   *Childhood and Society.* New York: Norton.

Evans, Robert, ed.
1969   *Readings in Collective Behaviour.* Chicago: Rand-McNally.

Eysenck, H. J.
1971   *Race, Intelligence and Education.* London: Temple Smith.

Fanon, Franz.
1968   *The Wretched of the Earth.* New York: Grove.

Farberman, H. A., and G. P. Stone.
1970   "On the Edge of Rapprochement: Was Durkheim Moving Toward the Perspective of Symbolic Interaction?" in *Social Psychology Through Symbolic Interaction*, edited by Farberman and Stone. Wattham, Mass.: Ginn-Blaisdell.

Felt, Lawrence E.
1975   "Nationalism and the Possibility of a Relevant Anglo-Canadian Sociology." *Canadian Journal of Sociology* 1 (3) Fall: 377–386.

Ferguson, T.
1975   *A White Man's Country: An Exercise in Canadian Prejudice.* Toronto: Doubleday.

Festinger, L., and others.
1956   *When Prophesy Fails.* Minneapolis: University of Minnesota Press.

Feuer, Lewis A., ed.
1959   *Marx and Engels: Basic Writings on Politics and Philosophy.* Garden City, New York: Anchor.

Firestone, Shulamith.
1973   *The Dialectic of Sex.* New York: Morrow.

Firth, R., J. Hubert, and A. Forge.
1969   *Families and Their Relatives.* London: Routledge and Kegan Paul.

Foot, R. N.
1951   "Identification as the Basis for a Theory of Motivation." *American Sociological Review* 16, February: 14–21.

Forbes, E.
1977   "Misguided Symmetry: the Destruction of Regional Transportation Policy for the Maritimes," in Bercuson (1977: 60–86).
1979   *The Maritime Rights Movement, 1919–1927: A Study in Canadian Regionalism.* Montreal: McGill-Queen's University Press.

Forcese, Dennis.
1980   *The Canadian Class Structure.* Toronto: McGraw-Hill Ryerson.

Forcese, Dennis, and Stephen Richer.
1975   *Issues in Canadian Society: An Introduction to Sociology.* Toronto: Prentice-Hall.

Fox, Bonnie.
1980   *Hidden in the Household: Women's Domestic Labour Under Capitalism.* Toronto: Women's Press.

Fox, Bonnie, and John Fox.
1987   "Occupational Gender Segregation in the Canadian Labour Force, 1931–1981." *The Canadian Review of Sociology and Anthropology* 24 (2) 374–397.

Frank, André Gunder.
1969   *Latin America: Underdevelopment or Revolution.* New York: Monthly Review Press.

Freire, Paulo.
1970   *Pedagogy of the Oppressed.* New York: Seabury.

Frideres, James.

1974   *Canada's Indians: Contemporary Conflicts*. Toronto: Prentice-Hall.

Fromm, Erich.

1963   *Escape from Freedom*. New York: Holt, Rinehart and Winston.

1966   *Marx's Concept of Man*. New York: Frederich Ungar.

Fry, John A.

1979   *Economy, Class and Social Reality*. Toronto: Butterworths.

Frye, Northrop.

1977   "A Summary of the Conference," in Conference on the Future of the Canadian Federation. *Options*. Toronto: University of Toronto Press: 435–448.

Fullan, Michael.

1972   "Overview of the Innovative Process and the User." *Interchange* 3 (2/3): 1–46.

Gaffield, Chad.

1984   "Wage Labour, Industrialization and the Origins of the Modern Family," in Baker (1984: 21–34).

Gamson. William A.

1961   "A Theory of Coalition Formation." *American Sociological Review* 26, June: 565–573.

1975   *The Strategy of Social Protest*. Homewood, Ill.: Dorsey.

Gannage, Charlotte.

1986   *Double Day, Double Bind: Women Garment Workers*. Toronto: Women's Press.

Gans, Herbert J.

1962   *The Urban Villagers*. New York: Free Press.

1968   "The 'Equality' Revolution." *New York Times Magazine* November 3: 36–39.

1972   "The Positive Functions of Poverty." *American Journal of Sociology* 78, September: 275–289.

Garfinkel, Harold.

1956   "Conditions of Successful Degradation Ceremonies." *American Journal of Sociology* 61, March: 420–424.

1967   *Studies in Ethnomethodology*. Englewood Cliffs, N.J.: Prentice-Hall.

Garigue, P.

1956   "French-Canadian Kinship and Urban Life." *American Anthropologist* 58, December: 1090–1101.

Gartner, Alan, Colin Greer, and Frann Rieshan, eds.

1974   *The New Assault on Equality, I.Q. and Social Stratification*. Toronto: Harper and Row.

Gaskell, Jane, and Arlene Tigar McLaren, eds.

1987   *Women and Education: A Canadian Perspective*. Calgary: Detselig Enterprises.

Gavron, Hannah.

1966   *The Captive Wife: Conflicts of Housebound Mothers*. Middlesex, England: Penguin Books.

Geertz, Clifford.

1963   "The Integrated Revolution," in *Old Societies and New Societies*, edited by Clifford Geertz. Glencoe, Ill.: Free Press.

Gerth, Hans H., and C. Wright Mills.

1953   *Character and Social Structure*. New York: Harcourt, Brace and World.

1958   *From Max Weber: Essays in Sociology*. New York: Oxford University Press.

Gertler, Len, and Ron Crowley.

1977   *Changing Canadian Cities: The Next 25 Years*. Toronto: McClelland and Stewart.

Gerus, O. W., and J. E. Rea

1988   *The Ukrainians in Canada*. Ottawa: Canadian Historical Association.

Giddens, Anthony.

1971   *Capitalism and Modern Social Theory: An Analysis of the Writings of Marx, Durkheim and Max Weber*. Cambridge: Cambridge University Press.

Giffen, P. J.

1966   "The Revolving Door: A Functional Interpretation." *Canadian Review of Sociology and Anthropology* 3 (2): 154–166.

Gigeroff, Alex K.

1968   *Sexual Deviations in the Criminal Law*. Toronto: University of Toronto Press.

Gilder, George.

1974   "In Defense of Monogamy." *Commentary* 58 (5) November: 31–36.

Gilland, Bernard.
1983   "Considerations on World Population and Food Supply." *Population and Development Review* 9 (2).

Glaser, Barney G., and Anselm Strauss.
1976   *The Discovery of Grounded Theory: Strategies for Qualitative Research.* Chicago: Aldine.
1971   *Status Passage.* Chicago: Aldine.

Glazer, Nathan, and Daniel P. Moynihan.
1963   *Beyond the Melting Pot.* Cambridge, Mass.: M.I.T. Press and Harvard University Press.

Glazer, Nathan, and Daniel P. Moynihan, eds.
1975   *Ethnicity.* Cambridge, Mass.: Harvard University Press.

Goffman, Erving.
1959   *The Presentation of Self in Everyday Life,* New York: Doubleday Anchor.
1961a   *Asylums.* Garden City, New York: Doubleday Anchor.
1961b   *Encounters.* Indianapolis: Bobbs-Merrill.
1963a   *Behavior in Public Places.* New York: Free Press.
1963b   *Stigma: Notes on the Management of Spoiled Identity.* Englewood Cliffs, N.J.: Prentice-Hall.
1974   *Frame Analysis.* New York: Harper and Row.

Goldstein, Jay, and Rita Bienvenue.
1981   *Ethnicity and Ethnic Relations in Canada.* Toronto: Butterworths.

Goldthorpe, John.
1980   *Social Mobility and Class Structure in Modern Britain.* Oxford: Clarendon Press.

Goode, W. J.
1959   "The Theoretical Importance of Love." *American Sociological Review* 24 (1) February: 38–47.
1960   "Norm Commitment and Conformity to Role-Status Obligations." *American Journal of Sociology* 66, November: 248–261.
1963   *World Revolution and Family Patterns.* Glencoe, Ill.: Free Press.
1964   *The Family.* Englewood Cliffs, N.J.: Prentice-Hall.
1973   *Explorations in Social Theory.* New York: Oxford University Press.

Gorer, Geoffrey.
1967   *Sex and Marriage in Britain Today.* London: Heinemann.

Goslin, David A.
1969   *Handbook of Socialization: Theory and Research.* Chicago: Rand McNally.

Gouldner, Alvin W., and Richard A. Peterson.
1962   *Technology and the Moral Order.* Indianapolis: Bobbs-Merrill.
1970   *The Coming Crisis in Western Sociology.* New York: Basic Books.

Gow, Kathleen.
1980   *Yes, Virginia, There is a Right and Wrong.* Toronto: John Wiley.

Goyder, J. C., and J. E. Curtis.
1977   "Occupational Mobility in Canada Over Four Generations." *Canadian Review of Sociology and Anthropology* 14 (3): 303–319.

Grabb, Edward.
1984   *Social Inequality: Classical and Contemporary Theorists.* Toronto: Holt, Rinehart and Winston.

Graham, Hugh D., and Ted R. Gurr, eds.
1969   *Violence in America.* New York: Bantam Books.

Grant, George.
1970   *Lament for a Nation.* Toronto: McClelland
(1965)   and Stewart.
1969   *Technology and Empire.* Toronto: House of Anansi.

Gray, James.
1972   *Booze.* Toronto: Macmillan.

Grayson, Paul, and Linda Grayson.
1980   *Class, State, Ideology and Change.* Toronto: Holt, Rinehart and Winston.

Grayson, Paul, and Dennis Magill.
1981   *One Step Forward, Two Steps Sideways: Anthropology and Sociology in Canada.* Montreal: Canadian Sociology and Anthropology Association.

Greeley, Andrew M.
1974   *Ethnicity in the United States.* New York: Wiley.

Greer, Scott.
1969   *The Logic of Social Inquiry.* Chicago: Aldine Press.

Gregorovich, A.
1972   *Canadian Ethnic Groups Bibliography.*
Ottawa: Queen's Printer.

Gregory, Dick.
1968   *The Shadow That Scares Me.* New York:
Doubleday.

Griffiths, C. J., J. F. Klein and S. W. Verdun-Jones.
1980   *Criminal Justice in Canada.* Toronto:
Butterworths.

Grimshaw, Allen D.
1970   "Interpreting Collective Violence: An Argument for the Importance of Social Structure," in Short and Wolfgang (1970: 9–20).

Gross, Edward, and Gregory, P. Stone.
1970   "Embarrassment and the Analysis of Role Requirements," in Stone and Farberman (1970: 174–190).

Gross, R., and B. Gross, eds.
1969   *Radical School Reform.* New York: Simon and Schuster.

Grove, W. R.
1973   "Sex, Marital Status and Mortality."
American Journal of Sociology, 79 (1).

Gurr, Ted Robert.
1969   "A Comparative Study of Civil Strife," in
Violence in America: Historical and Comparative Perspectives, edited by Hugh David Graham and Ted Robert Gurr. Report submitted to the National Commission on the Causes and Prevention of Violence. New York: Bantam Books: 572–632.

Gusfield, Joseph R.
1962   "Mass Society and Extremist Politics."
American Sociological Review 27, February: 19–30.
1972   "Moral Passage: The Symbolic Process in Public Designation of Deviance," in *An Introduction to Deviance: Readings in the Process of Making Deviants,* edited by W. J. Filstead. Chicago: Markham.

Guyatt, D.
1971   *One-Parent Family in Canada.* Ottawa:
Vanier Institute of the Family.

Haas, Jack, and William Shaffir.
1974   *Decency and Deviance.* Toronto:
McClelland and Stewart.

1978   *Shaping Identity in Canadian Society.*
Toronto: Prentice-Hall.

Hagan, John.
1977   *The Disreputable Pleasures.* Toronto:
McGraw-Hill Ryerson.

Hagan, John, and Jeffrey Leon.
1977   "Rediscovering Delinquency: Social History, Political Ideology, and the Sociology of Law." *American Sociological Review* 42. August: 587–598.

Hall, Edward T.
1959   *The Silent Language.* Greenwich, Conn.:
Fawcett.
1966   *The Hidden Dimension.* Garden City, N.Y.
Doubleday.

Hamilton, Richard, and Maurice Pinard.
1977   "Poverty in Canada: Illusion and Reality."
Canadian Review of Sociology and Anthropology 14 (2): 247–252.

Hamilton, Richard, and James Wright.
1975   *New Directions in Political Sociology.*
Indianapolis: Bobbs-Merrill.

Hamilton, Roberta, and Michele Barrett, eds.
1986   *The Politics of Diversity: Feminism, Marxism and Nationalism.* London:
Verso.

Handelman, Don, and Elliott Leyton.
1978   *Bureaucracy and World View: Studies in the Logic of Official Interpretation.* St.
John's: Institute of Social and Economic Research.

Hanson, S. D.
1974   "Estevan 1931," in Abella (1974: 33–46).

Hardin, Herschel.
1974   *A Nation Unaware: The Canadian Economic Culture.* Vancouver:
J. J. Douglas.

Hareven, Tamara.
1982   "American Families in Transition: Historical Perspectives on Change," in Skolnick and Skolnick (1983: 73–91).

Harrington, Michael.
1965   *The Accidental Century.* Baltimore:
Penguin Books.

Harris, Marvin.
1968   *The Rise of Anthropological Theory,* New York: Thomas Y. Crowell.

1974 *Cows, Pigs, Wars and Witches: The Riddles of Culture*. New York: Random House.

1980 *Cultural Materialism: The Struggle for a Science of Culture*. New York: Random House.

Harrison, Deborah.
1983 *The Limits of Liberalism*. Montreal: Black Rose Books.

Hartz, Louis, ed.
1964 *The Founding of New Societies*. New York: Harcourt, Brace and World.

Harvard Educational Review.
1969 *Environment, Heredity and Intelligence*. Reprint Series No. 2. Cambridge, Mass.: *Harvard Educational Review*.

Harvey, Edward.
1974 *Educational Systems and the Labour Market*. Toronto: Longman.

Harvey, Edward, and Ivan Charner.
1975 "Social Mobility and Occupational Attainments of University Graduates." *Canadian Review of Sociology and Anthropology* 12 (2): 134–149.

Hawthorn, Geoffrey.
1970 *The Sociology of Fertility*. London: Collier-Macmillan.

Heberle, Rudolph.
1951 *Social Movements: An Introduction to Political Sociology*. New York: Appleton-Century-Crofts.

Hébert, Raymond, and Jean-Guy Vaillancourt.
1971 "French-Canadians in Manitoba: Elites and Ideologies," in Elliott (1971: 175–190).

Henry, Frances.
1971 *Forgotten Canadians: The Blacks of Nova Scotia*. Toronto: Longman.

Henshel, Anne-Marie.
1973 "Swinging: A Study of Decision Making in Marriage." *American Journal of Sociology* 78 (4): 885–891.

Herrnstein, R.
1971 "I.Q." *Atlantic Monthly*, December.

Hicks, George L.
1977 "Introduction: Problems in the Study of Ethnicity," in Hicks and Leiss (1977: 1–20).

Hicks, George L., and Philip E. Leiss, eds.
1977 *Ethnic Encounters: Identities and Contexts*. Belmont, Calif.: Wadeworth.

Hiller, Harry.
1976 *Canadian Society: A Sociological Analysis*. Toronto: Prentice-Hall.

1982 *Society and Changes: S. D. Clark and the Development of Canadian Sociology*. Toronto: University of Toronto Press.

1986 *Canadian Society: A Macro-Analysis*. Toronto: Prentice-Hall.

Himelfarb, Alex.
1975 "Fat Man, Thin World: A Participant Observation Study of Weight Watchers." Ph.D. Dissertation, University of Toronto.

1977 *The Social Characteristics of One-Industry Towns in Canada*. Ottawa: Supply and Services.

Himelfarb, A., and J. Evans.
1974 "Deviance Disavowal and Stigma Management: A Study of Obesity," in Haas and Shaffir (1974: 221–232).

Himelfarb, Alex, and Aurim Lazar.
1981 *Legal Aid for Mental Patients*. Ottawa: Department of Justice, Canada.

Himelfarb, Alex, Avrim Lazar and James Richardson.
1980 "Reconciliation or Conciliation and Changing Conceptions of the Family," in *Helping Networks and the Welfare State*. Toronto: Faculty of Social Work.

Himelfarb, Alex, and James Richardson.
1980 *People, Power and Process: A Reader*. Toronto: McGraw-Hill Ryerson.

Himelfarb, Frum.
1981 "Towards a Model of Values Education." Ottawa: University of Ottawa (Mimeo).

Hobsbawn, E. J.
1965 *Primitive Rebels*. New York: W. W. Norton.

Hoffer, Eric.
1931 *The True Believer: Thoughts on the*

Nature of Mass Movements. New York: Harper and Row.

Hoffman, Lois.
1972   "Early Childhood Experiences and Women's Achievement Motives." *Journal of Social Issues* 28 (2).

Hofley, John.
1971   "Problems and Perspectives in the Study of Poverty," in *Poverty in Canada*, edited by J. Harp and J. R. Hofley. Toronto: Prentice-Hall: 101–116.

Hogarth, John.
1971   *Sentencing as a Human Process.* Toronto: University of Toronto Press.

Hollander, Edwin, and Raymond Hunt.
1971   *Current Perspectives in Social Psychology.* New York: Oxford University Press.

Holt, John.
1964   *How Children Fail.* New York: Pitman.
1967   *How Children Learn.* New York: Pitman.
1969   *The Underachieving School.* New York: Pitman.

Holzner, Burkhart.
1968   *Reality Construction in Society.* Cambridge, Mass.: Schenkman.

Homans, George C.
1950   *The Human Group.* New York: Harcourt, Brace and World.
1958   "Social Behavior as Exchange." *American Journal of Sociology* 62, May: 597–606.
1961   *Social Behavior: Its Elementary Forms.* New York: Harcourt, Brace and World. (Revised 1974)

Hopper, Earl.
1971   "Educational Systems and Selected Consequences of Patterns of Mobility in Industrial Societies: A Theoretical Discussion," in *Readings in the Theory of Educational Systems*, edited by E. Hopper. London: Hutchinson.

Horowitz, Gad.
1965a   "Creative Politics." *Canadian Dimension* 3 (1): 14–15, 28.
1965b   "Tories, Socialists and the Demise of Canada." *Canadian Dimensions*, May-June: 12–15.

1966   "Conservatism, Liberalism and Socialism in Canada: An Interpretation." *Canadian Journal of Economics and Political Science* 32, May.

Horowitz, Irving Louis.
1973   "The Hemispheric Connection: A Critique and Corrective to the Enterpreneurial Thesis of Development with Special Emphasis on the Canadian Case." *Queen's Quarterly* 80: 327–359.

Horowitz, I. L., and M. Liebowitz.
1968   "Social Deviance and Political Marginality: Toward a Redefinition of the Relation Between Sociology and Politics." *Social Problems* 15, Winter: 280–296.

House, Doug.
1985   "The Mouse that Roars: New Directions in Canadian Political Economy—The Case of Newfoundland," in Brym (1986: 161–196).

Huber, Jean, ed.
1973   "Changing Women in a Changing Society." Special Issue of *American Journal of Sociology* 78 (4) January.

Hughes, D., and E. Kallen.
1974   *The Anatomy of Racism: Canadian Dimensions.* Toronto: Harvest House.

Hughes, Everett.
1943   *French Canada in Transition.* Chicago: University of Chicago Press.

Humphreys, Laud.
1970   *The Tearoom Trade.* Chicago: Aldine.

Hunter, Alfred.
1981   *Class Tells: On Social Inequality in Canada.* Toronto: Butterworths.

Hyman, H. H., and E. Singer, eds.
1968   *Readings in Reference Group Theory and Research.* New York: Free Press.

Illich, Ivan.
1970   *The Celebration of Awareness.* Garden City. New York: Doubleday.
1971   *Deschooling Society.* New York: Perennial Library (Harper Row).

Inkeles, Alex.
1964   *What Is Sociology?* Englewood Cliffs, N.J.: Prentice-Hall.

Innis, Harold A.
1930 *The Fur Trade in Canada: An Introduction to Canadian Economic History.* New Haven: Yale University Press.
1940 *The Cod Fisheries: The History of an International Economy.* New Haven: Yale University Press.
1956 *Essays in Canadian Economic History.* Toronto: University of Toronto Press.

Irving, Howard K.
1972 *The Family Myth.* Toronto: Copp Clark.
1980 *Divorce Mediation: The Rational Alternative.* Toronto: Personnel Library Publishers.

Irving, Howard K., ed.
1981 *Family Law: An Interdisciplinary Perspective.* Toronto: The Carswell Company.

Irving, John A.
1960 *The Social Credit Movement in Alberta.* Toronto: University of Toronto Press.
1975 The Evolution of the Social Credit Movement," in Clark et al. (1975: 130–152).

Isajiw, W. W.
1974 "Definitions of Ethnicity." *Ethnicity* 1: 111–124.
1976 *Identities: The Impact of Ethnicity on Canadian Society.* Toronto: Peter Martin.

Isajiw, W. W., and Norbert Hartmann.
1970 "Changes in the Occupational Structure of Ukrainians in Canada," in *Social and Cultural Change in Canada*, Vol. 2., edited by W. E. Mann. Toronto: Copp Clark.

Ishwaran, K.
1976 *The Canadian Family.* Toronto: Holt, Rinehart and Winston.
(1971)
1980 *Canadian Families: Ethnic Variations.* Toronto: McGraw-Hill Ryerson.
1983 *Marriage and Divorce in Canada,* Toronto: Methuen.

Jackson, Brian.
1964 *Streaming: An Educational System in Miniature.* London: Routledge and Kegan Paul.

Jackson, Brian, and Dennis Marsden.
1962 *Education and the Working Class.* London: Routledge and Kegan Paul.

Jackson, John D.
1975 *Community and Conflict: A Study of French-English Relations in Ontario.* Toronto: Holt, Rinehart and Winston.

Jackson, Winston.
1988 *Research Methods: Rules for Survey Design and Analysis.* Toronto: Prentice-Hall.

Jencks, Christopher.
1972 *Inequality: A Reassessment of Family and Schooling in America.* New York: Harper and Row.

Jensen, Arthur R.
1969 "How Much Can We Boost I.Q. and Scholastic Achievement?" *Harvard Educational Review* 39 (1): 1–123.

Johnson, Leo A.
1973 *Disparity and Impoverishment in Canada since W.W. II.* Toronto: New Bytown Press.

Johnson, Terrence.
1977 "The Professions in the Class Structure," in *Industrial Society: Class, Cleavage and Control*, edited by Richard Scase. London: Ruskin House.

Jones, Frank E., and Hugh A. McRoberts.
1977 "Social Origins, Education and Occupational Attainment: Some Preliminary Findings." Paper presented at CSAA meetings, Fredericton, N.B.

Kalbach, Warren E., and Wayne W. McVey.
1979 *The Demographic Bases of Canadian*
(1971) *Society.* Toronto: McGraw-Hill Ryerson.

Kaplan, Abraham.
1964 *The Conduct of Inquiry: Methodology for Behavioral Science.* San Francisco: Chandler.

Karabel, Jerome.
1972 "Community Colleges and Social Stratification." *Harvard Educational Review* 42 (4): 521–563.

Karabel, Jerome, and A. H. Halsey.
1977 *Power and Ideology in Education.* New York: Oxford University Press.

Katz, Michael B.
1971 *Class, Bureaucracy and Schools.* New York: Praeger.
1975 *The People of Hamilton Canada West:*

Family and Class in a Mid-Nineteenth-Century City. Cambridge, Mass: Harvard University Press.

Kaufman, Bel.
1964   *Up the Down Staircase*. Englewood Cliffs, N.J.: Prentice-Hall.

Kelner, Merrijoy.
1970   "Ethnic Penetration into Toronto's Elite Structure." *Canadian Review of Sociology and Anthropology* 7, May: 26-35.

Kirby, Sandra, and Kate McKenna.
1989   *Experience Research, Social Change: Methods from the Margins*. Toronto: Garamond Press.

Kirk, Russell.
1961   "Is Social Science Scientific?" *New York Times Magazine*, June 25. Reprinted in *Social Realities*, edited by George Ritzer, Boston: Allyn and Bacon, 1964.

Kluckhohn, Clyde.
1949   *Mirror for Man*. New York: McGraw-Hill.

Kohl, S., and J. W. Bennett.
1965   "Kinship, Succession and the Migration of Young People in a Canadian Agricultural Community." *International Journal of Comparative Sociology* 6, March: 95–116.

Kohlberg, Lawrence.
1963   "The Development of Children's Orientations toward a Moral Order: A Sequence in the Development of Moral Thought." *Human Development*.
1964   "The Development of Children's Orientations toward a Moral Order: Social Experience, Social Conduct, and the Development of Moral Thought." *Human Development*.
1970   "Moral Development," in *Adolescents and the American High School*, edited by R. F. Purnell. Toronto: Holt, Rinehart and Winston.

Kornhauser, William.
1959   *The Politics of Mass Society*. New York: Free Press.

Kozol, Jonathan.
1967   *Death at an Early Age*. Boston: Houghton-Mifflin.

Krahn, Harvey, and Graham Lowe.
1988   *Work, Industry and Canadian Society*. Toronto: Nelson.

Kressel, Kenneth.
1985   *The Process of Divorce*. New York: Basic Books.

Kroeber, A. L., and Talcott Parsons.
1958   "The Concept of Culture and of Social System." *American Sociological Review* 23, October.

Kubat, D., and David Thornton.
1974   *A Statistical Profile of Canadian Society*. Toronto: McGraw-Hill Ryerson.

Kuhn, Thomas.
1962   *The Structure of Scientific Revolutions*. Chicago: University of Chicago Press.

Laing, R. D.
1967   *The Politics of Exprience and the Bird of Paradise*. London: Penguin.

Lang, Kurt, and Gladys E. Lang.
1961   *Collective Dynamics*. New York: Thomas Y. Crowell.

Lapierre-Adamcyk, E.
1981   "Les aspirations des Québécois en matière de fécondité." *Cahiers québécoise de démographie* 10(2).

Larson, Lyle E.
1976   *The Canadian Family in Comparative Perspective*. Toronto: Prentice-Hall.

Lasch, Christopher.
1977   *Haven in a Heartless World*. New York: Basic Books.

Laslett, Peter.
1965   *The World We Have Lost*. New York: Scribner.

Laslett, Peter, and Richard Wall.
1972   *Household and Family in Past Time*. Cambridge: Cambridge University Press.

Lasswell, Harold D.
1950   *Politics: Who Gets What, When, How*. New York: Peter Smith.

Lautard, Hugh, and Neil Guppy.
1990   "The Vertical Mosaic Revisited: Occupational Differentials among Canadian Ethnic Groups," in Li (1990: 189–208).

Laxer, Robert, ed.
1973   *Canada Ltd: The Political Economy of Dependency*. Toronto: McClelland and Stewart.

1985   "Foreign Ownership and Myths About Canadian Development." *The Canadian Review of Sociology and Anthropology* 22 (2) 311–345.

Lazarsfeld, Paul F., and others, eds.
1972   *Continuities in the Language of Social Research.* New York: Free Press.

Le Bon, Gustave.
1960   *The Crowd: A Study of the Popular Mind.*
(1895) New York: Viking Press.

Lemert, E. M.
1951   *Social Pathology.* New York: McGraw-Hill.
1972   *Human Deviance, Social Problems, and Social Control.* Englewood Cliffs, N.Y.: Prentice-Hall.

Lenski, G. E.
1966   *Power and Privilege.* New York: McGraw-Hill.

Lenton, Rhonda.
1990   "Techniques of Child Discipline and Abuse by Parents." *The Canadian Review of Sociology and Anthropology* 27 (2) 157–185.

Lévesque, René.
1968   *An Option for Quebec.* Toronto: McClelland and Stewart.

Lévi-Strauss, Claude.
1956   "The Family," in *Man, Culture, and Society*, edited by Harry L. Shapiro. New York: Oxford University Press, 142–170.
1963   *Totemism.* Translated by R. Needham. Boston: Beacon Press.
1969   *The Elementary Structures of Kinship.* Boston: Beacon Press.

Levitt, Kari.
1970   *Silent Surrender: The Multinational Corporation in Canada.* Toronto: Macmillan.

Levy, Marion J., Jr.
1965   "Aspects of the Analysis of Family Structure," in Coale and others (1965: 1–63).

Leyton, Elliott.
1975   *Dying Hard.* Toronto: McClelland and Stewart.

Libby, Roger W., and Robert N. Whitehurst.
1973   *Renovating Marriage: Toward New Sexual Life Styles.* Danville, Calif.: Consensus.
1977   *Marriage and Alternatives: Exploring Intimate Relationships.* Glenview, Ill.: Scott, Foresman.

Li, Peter.
1981   *Social Research Methods: An Introduction* Toronto: Butterworths.

Li, Peter, ed.
1990   *Race and Ethnic Relations in Canada.* Toronto: Oxford University Press.

Lieberson, Stanley.
1970   *Language and Ethnic Relations in Canada.* New York: Wiley.
1985   *Making It Count.* Berkeley: University of California Press.

Lindesmith, A. R.
1965   *The Addict and the Law.* Bloomington, Ind.: Indiana University Press.

Lindesmith, A. R., and A. L. Strauss.
1968   *Social Psychology.* New York: Holt, Rinehart and Winston.

Linton, Ralph.
1936   *The Study of Man.* New York: Appleton-Century-Crofts.
1963   *The First New Nation: The United States in Historical Perspective.* New York: Basic Books.

Lipset, Seymour M.
1963a   *Political Man.* New York: Doubleday Anchor.
1963b   "The Value Patterns of Democracy: A Case Study in Comparative Analysis." *American Sociological Review* 28, August.
1966   *Agrarian Socialism: The Cooperative Commonwealth Federation in Sasktchewan, A Study in Political Sociology.* Revised 1968. Berkeley: University of California Press.

Litwak, E.
1960a   "Occupational Mobility and Extended Family Cohesion." *American Sociological Review* 25: 9–21.
1960b   "Geographic Mobility and Extended Family Cohesion." *American Sociological Review* 25: 386–394.

Lockwood, David.
1970   "Social Integration and System Integration," in *Modern Sociology*, Edited by P. Worsley, London: Penguin, Chapter 66.

Lofland, J.
1969   *Deviance and Identity.* Englewood Cliffs, N.J.: Prentice-Hall.

Lofland, Lyn H.
1975   "The 'Thereness' of Women: A Selective Review of Urban Sociology," in Millman and Kanter (1975: 144–170).

Lopata, H. A.
1971   *Occupation Housewife.* New York: Oxford University Press.

Lopreato, J., and E. Hazelrigg.
1972   *Class Conflict and Mobility.* San Francisco: Chandler.

Lorimer, James, and Myfanwy Phillips.
1971   *Working People.* Toronto: James Lewis and Samuel.

Lowe, Graham.
1987   *Women in the Administrative Revolution.* Toronto: University of Toronto Press.

Lowe, Graham, and Harvey Krahn, eds.
1984   *Working Canadians: Readings in the Sociology of Work and Industry.* Toronto: Methuen.

Lowe, Graham, and Herbert Northcott.
1986   *Under Pressure: A Study of Job Stress.* Toronto: Garamond Press.

Lower, A.
1964   *Colony to Nation.* Toronto: Longman.

Lucas, Rex A.
1969   *Men in Crisis: A Study of a Mine Disaster.* New York: Basic Books.
1971   *Minetown, Milltown, Railtown: Life in Canadian Communities of a Single Industry.* Toronto: University of Toronto Press.

Luce, R. D., and H. Raiffa.
1957   *Games and Decisions.* New York: Wiley.

Lukes, Steven.
1967   "Alienation and Anomie," in *Philosophy, Politics and Society*, Edited by Peter Laslett and H. G. Runciman. Oxford: Oxford University Press.

Lumsden, Ian.
1970   *Close the 49th Parallel Etc.* Toronto: University of Toronto Press.

Lundy, Katherine, and Barbara Warme, eds.
1986   *Work in the Canadian Context: Continuity Despite Change.* Toronto: Butterworths.

Lurie, Alison.
1967   *Imaginary Friends.* London: Pan Books.

Luxton, Meg.
1980   *More Than a Labour of Love.* Toronto: Women's Press.

Luxton, Meg, and Harriet Rosenberg.
1986   *Through the Kitchen Window: the Politics of Home and Family.* Toronto: Garamond Press.

MacDonald, L. R.
1975   "Merchants Against Industry: An Idea and Its Origins." *Canadian Historical Review* LVI.

Macdonell, Allan.
1987   *Canadian Degree Undergraduates and Their Study Preferences.* Ottawa: Statistics Canada.

Macpherson, C. B.
1962   *The Political Theory of Possessive Individualism: Hobbes to Locke.* Oxford: Clarendon.

Malinowski, B.
1945   *The Dynamics of Cultural Change.* New Haven: Yale University Press.

Malthus, Thomas.
1970   *An Essay on the Principle of Population*
(1798)   *as It Affects the Future Improvements of Society.* London: Penguin Books.
1890   *An Essay on the Principle of Population of a View of Its Past and Present Effects on Human Happiness.* London: Ward, Lock and Co.

Mann, W. E., ed.
1970a *The Underside of Toronto.* Toronto: McClelland and Stewart.
1970b *Social and Cultural Change in Canada.* Toronto: Copp Clark.
1971   *Social Deviance in Canada.* Toronto: Copp Clark.

Manis, Jerome, and Bernard Meltzer.
1972   *Symbolic Interactionism: A Reader in*
(1967)   *Social Psychology.* Boston: Allyn and
Bacon.

Manzer, Ronald.
1974   *Canada: A Socio-Political Report.*
Toronto: McGraw-Hill Ryerson.

Marchak, Pat.
1979   *In Whose Interests?* Toronto: McClelland
and Stewart.
1981   *Ideological Perspectives in Canada.*
Toronto: McGraw-Hill Ryerson.

Marchak, Pat, ed.
1977   *The Working Sexes.* Vancouver: The
Institute of Industrial Relations.
1983   *Green Gold: The Forest Industry in British
Columbia.* Vancouver: UBC Press.
1985   "Canadian Political Economy." *The
Canadian Review of Sociology and
Anthropology* 22 (5) 673–709.

Marris, Peter.
1973   *Loss and Change.* London: Routledge and
Kegan Paul.

Marsden, Lorna.
1972   *Population Probe: Canada.* Toronto:
Copp Clark.
1975   "Population Issues in the Immigration
Debate." *Canadian Ethnic Studies* VII (5):
22–29.

Marsden, Lorna, and E. B. Harvey.
1979   *Social Change in Canada.* Toronto:
McGraw-Hill Ryerson.

Martel, George, ed.
1974   *The Politics of the Canadian Public
School.* Toronto: James Lewis and
Samuel.

Martin, F. M.
1954   "Some Subjective Aspects of Social
Stratification," in *Social Mobility in
Britain*, edited by David Glass. London:
Routledge and Kegan Paul, 51–78.

Martin, Wilfred B. W.
1976   *The Negotiated Order of the School.*
Toronto: Macmillan.

Martin, Wilfred B. W., and A. J. Macdonnel.
1976   "Aspects of Educational Opportunity in
the Atlantic Provinces." Paper presented
at the 11th annual meeting of the
Atlantic Association of Sociologists and
Anthropologists, Fredericton, N.B.
1978   *Canadian Education: A Sociological
Analysis.* Toronto: Prentice-Hall.

Martin-Matthews, Ann.
1977   "The Newfoundland Migrant Wife: A
Power Versus Powerless Theory of
Adjustment." *Atlantis* 2 (2): 152–166.

Marx, Gary T.
1970   "Issueless Riots," in Short and Wolfgang
(1970: 21–23).

Marx, Karl.
1971   "Peasantry as a Class," in *Peasants and
Peasant Societies: Selected Readings,*
edited by Teodor Shanin.
Harmondsworth: Penguin: 229–237.
1973   *The Grundrisse.* New York: International
(1859)   Publishers.

Marx, Karl, and Frederich Engels.
1967   *The Communist Manifesto.* London
(1848)   Penguin Books.
1970   *The German Ideology.* New York:
International.

Masters, D. C.
1950   *The Winnipeg General Strike.* Toronto:
University of Toronto Press.

Mathews, Robin.
1973   "Canadian Culture and the Liberal
Ideology," in Laxer (1973: 213–231).

Matthews, Ralph.
1976   *There's No Better Place Than Here: Social
Change in Three Newfoundland Communities.* Toronto: Peter Martin Associates.

Matza, D.
1964   *Delinquency and Drift.* New York: Wiley.
1969   *Becoming Deviant.* Englewood Cliffs, N.J.:
Prentice-Hall.

Mauss, Armand L.
1975   *Social Problems as Social Movements.*
Philadelphia: Lippincott.

McCall, G. J., and J. L. Simmons.
1978   *Identities and Interactions: An
Examination of Human Associations in
Everyday Life.* New York: Free Press.
1969   Issues in Participant Observation.
Reading: Addison-Wesley.

McCrorie, James N.
1964 *In Union is Strength.* Saskatoon: Saskatchewan Farmers Union.

McDaniel, Susan.
1986 *Canada's Aging Population.* Toronto: Butterworths.

McDonald, Lyn.
1975 "Wages of Work: A Widening Gap Between Women and Men." *Canadian Forum.* April-May, 4–7.

McElroy, Ann.
1975 "Ethnic Identity and Modernization: The Biculturation of Baffin Island Inuit Children," in Pike and Zureik (1975: 262–290).

McGrath, W. T., ed.
1975 *Crime and Its Treatment in Canada.* 2nd ed. Toronto: Macmillan.

McHugh, Peter.
1968 *Defining the Situation.* Indianapolis: Bobbs-Merrill.

McLuhan, Marshall.
1965 *Understanding Media: The Extensions of Man.* New York: McGraw-Hill.

Mead, George Herbert.
1934 *Mind, Self, and Society.* Chicago: University of Chicago Press.

Mead, Margaret.
1928 *Coming of Age in Samoa.* New York: Morrow.
1955 *Cultural Patterns and Technical Change.* New York: Mentor.

Meadows, D. H., D. L. Meadows, J. Randers, and W. W. Bahrens.
1972 *The Limits to Growth.* New York: New American Libary.

Meisel, John.
1977 "Who Are We? Who Are They? Perceptions in English Canada," in Conference on the Future of the Canadian Federation, *Options.* Toronto, University of Toronto; 13–34.

Meissner, Martin, and others.
1975 "No Exit for Wives: Sexual Division of Labour." *Canadian Review of Sociology and Anthropology* 12: 4 (1): 424–439.

Merton, Robert K.
1939 "Social Structure and Anomie." *American Sociological Review* 3: 672–687.
1961 "Now the Case for Sociology." *New York Times Magazine*, July 16. Reprinted in *Social Realities*, edited by George Ritzer. Boston: Allyn and Bacon.
1968 *Social Theory and Social Structure.* Chicago: Free Press.

Merton, Robert K., Ailsa P. Gray, Barbara Hockey, and Hanan C. Selvin.
1952 *Reader in Bureaucracy.* New York: Free Press.

Metzger, L. Paul.
1971 "American Sociology and Black Assimilation: Conflicting Perspectives." *American Journal of Sociology* 74 (4) January: 643–644.

Michels, Robert.
1959 *Political Parties*, New York: Dover.
(1915)

Miliband, Ralph.
1969 *The State in Capitalist Society.* London: Hunt Barnard Printing Ltd.

Miller, S. M.
1960 "Comparative Social Mobility." *Current Sociology* 9 (1): 1–80.

Millman, Marcia, and Rosabeth Moss Kanter, eds.
1975 *Another Voice: Feminist Perspectives on Social Life and Social Science.* Garden City, New York: Anchor.

Mills, C. Wright.
1942 "The Professional Ideology of Social Pathologists." *American Journal of Sociology* 6: 165–180.
1949 "Situated Actions and Vocabularies of Motive." *American Sociological Review* 5. December.
1951 *White Collar.* New York: Oxford University Press.
1967 *Power, Politics and People: The Collected Essays of C. Wright Mills.* Edited by Irving Louis Horowitz. London: Oxford University Press.

Milner, Sheilagh, H., and Henry Milner.
1973 *The Decolonization of Quebec.* Toronto: McClelland and Stewart.

Miner, Horace.
1939   *St. Denis: A French-Canadian Parish.* Chicago: University of Chicago Press.
1956   "Body Ritual among the Nacirema." *American Anthropologist* 58 (3): 503–507.

Minifie, James M.
1971   "Mass Media and their Control," in Ossenberg (1971: 169–183).

Mitford, Jessica.
1977   *The American Way of Death.* New York: Fawcett World Library.

Montagu, Ashley.
1969   "The Concept of Race in the Human Species in the Light of Genetics," in *The Concept of Race,* edited by A. Montagu, London: Collier-Macmillan, 1–11.

Moore, Barrington, Jr.
1972   *Reflections on the Causes of Human Misery and Upon Certain Proposals to Eliminate Them.* Boston: Beacon.

Moore, Maureen.
1989   *"Female Lone Parenting Over the Life Course,"* Canadian Journal of Sociology 14 (3) 335–352.

Moore, Steve, and Debi Wells.
1975   *Imperialism and the National Question in Canada.* Toronto: S. Moore.

Moreux, Colette.
1971   "The French-Canadian Family," in K. Ishwaran, ed. (1971): 126–147).

Morgan, D. H.
1975   *The Family and Social Theory.* London: Routledge and Kegan Paul.

Morris, R. N., and C. M. Lanphier.
1977   *The Three Scales of Inequality: Perspectives on French-English Relations.* Toronto: Longman.

Morton, M. E., and W. G. West.
1977   "The Myth of Community and the Ideology Surrounding Diversion." Paper presented, Canadian Conference on Diversion, Quebec, P.Q.

Mossman, Mary Jane.
1985   "Family Law and Social Welfare in Canada," in I. Bernier and A. Lajoie (eds.), *Family Law and Social Welfare Legislation in Canada.* Toronto: University of Toronto Press.

Mount, Ferdinand.
1982   *The Subversive Family: An Alternative History of Love and Marriage.* London: Jonathan Cape.

Mouzelis, Nicos.
1967   *Organisation and Bureaucracy.* London: Routledge and Kegan Paul.

Mueller, Claus.
1970   "Notes on the Repression of Communicative Behaviour," in Dreitzel (1970).
1973   *The Politics of Communication.* New York: Oxford University Press.

Mumford, Lewis.
1934   *Technics and Civilization.* New York: Harcourt, Brace and World.

Murdock, G. P.
1949   *Social Structure.* New York: Free Press.

Murphy, Raymond.
1980   *Sociological Perspectives on Education.* Toronto: McGraw-Hill Ryerson.

Muscovitch, Alan, and Glen Drover, eds.
1981   *Inequality: Essays on the Political Economy of Social Welfare.* Toronto: University of Toronto Press.

Myles, John.
1988   "The Expanding Middle: Some Canadian Evidence on the Deskilling Debate." *The Canadian Review of Sociology and Anthropology* 25 (3) 335–364.

Nagata, Judith A.
1969   "Adaptation and Integration of Greek
(1977)   Working Class Immigrants in Toronto: A Situational Approach." *International Migration Review 4 (10) Fall. Reprinted in Sociology Canada: Reading,* 2nd edition, edited by Christopher Beattie and Stewart Crysdale. Toronto: Butterworths, 148–157.

Nagler, Mark.
1970   *Indians in the City.* Ottawa: Canadian Research Centre for Anthropology, University of Saint Paul.

Nagler, Mark, ed.
1972 *Perspectives on the North American Indians*. Toronto: McClelland and Stewart.

National Council of Welfare.
1988 Poverty Profile: 1988.
1989 Poverty Lines. Ottawa: Ministry of Supply and Services.

Naylor, R. T.
1972 "The Rise and Fall of the Third Commercial Empire of the St. Lawrence," in Teeple, ed. (1972: 1–42).

Nicalous, Martin.
1972 "The Unknown Marx," in R. Blackburn, (ed). *Ideology in Social Science*. London: The Chaucer Press.

Neill, A. S.
1960 *Summerhill: A Radical Approach to Child Rearing*. New York: Hart.

Nelsen, Randle W., and David A. Nock.
1978 *Reading, Writing and Riches: Education and the Socio-Economic Order in North America*. Kitchener, Ont.: Between the Lines.

Nett, Emily.
1981 "Canadian Families in Social-Historical Perspective." *Canadian Journal of Sociology*, 6(3) 239–260.
1988 *Canadian Families: Past and Present*. Toronto: Butterworths.

Nettler, Gwynn.
1974 *Explaining Crime*. New York: McGraw-Hill.

Newman, Peter C.
1975 *The Canadian Establishment*. Vol. 1. Toronto: McClelland and Stewart.

Newson, Janice, and Howard Buchbinder.
1988 *The University Means Business*. Toronto: Garamond Press.

Nie, Norman H., and others.
1975 *Statistical Package for the Social Sciences*. New York: McGraw-Hill.

Niosi, Jorge.
1981 *Canadian Capitalism: A Study of Power in the Canadian Business Establishment*. Toronto: James Lorimer.

Nisbet, Robert A.
1967 *The Sociological Tradition*. London: Heinemann.
1969 *Social Change and History*. London: Oxford University Press.

Notestein, Frank.
1944 *The Future Population of Europe and the Soviet Union*. New York: League of Nations.

Novak, Mark W.
1975 *Living and Learning in the Free School*. Toronto: McClelland and Stewart.

Nyquist, E. B., and G. R. Hawes, eds.
1972 *Open Education*. New York: Bantam.

Oakley, Ann.
1974 *The Sociology of Housework*. New York: Pantheon.

Oberschall, Anthony.
1973 *Social Conflict and Social Movements*. Englewood Cliffs, N.J.: Prentice-Hall.

Ogburn, William F.
1950 *Social Change with Respect to Culture*
(1922) *and Original Nature*. New York: Viking.

Olmstead, Michael S.
1959 *The Small Group*. New York: Random House.

O'Neill, John.
1972 *Sociology as a Skin Trade: Essays Towards a Reflexive Sociology*. New York: Harper Torchbooks.

O'Neill, Nena, and George O'Neill.
1972 *Open Marriage*. New York: Avon Books.

Ontario, Province of.
1972 *The Learning Society*. Toronto: Commission on Post-Secondary Education.

Opie, I., and P. Opie.
1959 *The Lore and Language of School Children*. London: Oxford University Press.

Ornstein, Michael.
1986 "The Political Ideology of the Canadian Capitalist Class." *The Canadian Review of Sociology and Anthropology* 23 (3) 182–209.

Ortega y Gasset, José.
1932   *The Revolt of the Masses.* London:
(1961) Unwin.

Osberg, Lars.
1981   *Economic Inequality in Canada.* Toronto:
Butterworths.

Ossenberg, R. J., ed.
1971   *Canadian Society: Pluralism, Change and
Conflict.* Toronto: Prentice-Hall.

Ostry, Sylvia.
1967   *The Occupational Composition of the
Canadian Labour Force.* Ottawa:
Dominion Bureau of Statistics.

Packard, Vance.
1957   *The Hidden Persuaders.* New York:
D. McKay.

Pahl, J. M., and R. E. Pahl.
1971   *Managers and their Wives.* London: Allen
Lane, Penguin.

Panitch, Leo, ed.
1977   *The Canadian State: Political Economy
and Political Power.* Toronto: University
of Toronto Press.

Parkin, Frank.
1971   *Class Inequality and Political Order.*
London: Paladin.
1976   "Ethnic Conflict and Social Theory."
Paper presented at the annual meeting of
the Canadian Sociology and Anthropology Association, Fredericton, N.B.

Parkinson, C. Northcote.
1957   *Parkinson's Law.* New York: Ballantine.

Parsons, Talcott.
1951   *The Social System.* Glencoe, Ill.: Free
Press.
1954   "The Kinship System of the
Contemporary United States," in *Essays
in Sociological Theory,* by Talcott
Parsons, New York: Free Press.

Parsons, Talcott, and R. F. Bales.
1955   *Family, Socialization and Interaction
Process.* Glencoe, Ill.: Free Press.

Paul, Gurbachan.
1975   "The Green Paper and Third World
Immigrants: A Subjective Analysis."
Canadian Ethnic Studies VII (1): 40–49.

Pearson, Geoffrey.
1975   *The Deviant Imagination: Psychiatry,
Social Work and Social Change.* London:
Macmillan.

Peers, Frank.
"Oh Say Can You See?" in Lumsden
(1970: 135–156).

Pelletier, Gérard.
1971   *The October Crisis.* Toronto: McClelland
and Stewart.

Penner, Norman.
1977   *The Canadian Left.* Toronto: Prentice-
Hall.

Perrow, Charles.
1972   *Complex Organization: A Critical Essay.*
Glenview, Ill.: Scott, Foresman, and Co.

Persig, Robert M.
1975   *Zen and the Art of Motorcycle
Maintenance.* New York: Bantam.

Peter, Karl.
1976   "The Dialectic of Family and Community
in the Social History of the Hutterites," in
*The Canadian Family in Comparative
Perspective,* edited by Lyle E. Larson.
Toronto: Prentice-Hall.

Peter, Lawrence J., and Raymond Hull.
1969   *The Peter Principle.* New York: Morrow.

Petersen, William.
1975   *Population.* New York: MacMillan
Publishing Co. Inc.
1979   *Malthus.* Cambridge: Harvard University
Press.

Phillips, Paul, and Erin Phillips.
1983   *Women and Work: Inequality in the
Labour Market.* Toronto: James Lorimer.

Piaget, Jean.
1948   *The Moral Judgement of the Child.* New
York: Free Press.
1952   *Judgement and Reasoning in the Child.*
New York: Humanities Press.
1954   *The Construction of Reality in the Child.*
Basic Books.

Piddington, Ralph.
1961   "A Study of French-Canadian Kinship."
*International Journal of Comparative
Sociology* 2, March: 3–22.

Pike, Robert M.

1970 *Who Doesn't Get to University—and Why: A Study of Accessibility to Higher Education in Canada*. Ottawa: Association of Universities and Colleges of Canada.

1975 "Legal Access and the Incidence of Divorce in Canada: A Sociological Analysis." *Canadian Review of Sociology and Anthropology* 12 (2) May: 115–133.

Pilisuk, Marc, and Thomas Hayder.

1965 "Is There a Military Industrial Complex Which Prevents Peace?" *Journal of Social Issues* 21, July: 67–117.

Pinard, M.

1971 *The Rise of a Third Party: A Study in Crisis Politics*. Englewood Cliffs, N.J.: Prentice-Hall.

Pineo, Peter.

1961 "Disenchantment in the Later Years of Marriage." *Marriage and Family Living* 23 (1) February: 1–11.

1969 "The Extended Family in a Working-Class Area of Hamilton," in *Canadian Society*, edited by Blishen and others. Toronto: Macmillan.

1977 "The Social Standings of Ethnic and Racial Groupings." *Canadian Review of Sociology and Anthropology* 14 (2): 147–157.

Pineo, P. C., and John Porter.

1967 "Occupational Prestige in Canada." *Canadian Review of Sociology and Anthropology* 4: 24–40.

Platt, Anthony M.

1969 *The Child Savers: The Invention of Delinquency*. Chicago: University of Chicago Press.

Polsky, Ned.

1969 *Hustlers, Beats, and Others*. New York: Anchor.

Pomfret, Alan.

1976 "Conceptual Issues in the Study of Planned School Change." Paper presented at the annual meetings of the Canadian Sociology and Anthropology Association, Laval, Quebec.

Porter, John.

1965 *The Vertical Mosaic: An Analysis of Social Class and Power in Canada*. Toronto: University of Toronto Press.

1967 "Canadian Character in the Twentieth Century." *Annals of the American Academy of Political and Social Science* 370, March: 48–56.

1968 "The Future of Upward Mobility." *American Sociological Review* 33 (1) February: 5–19.

1975 "Ethnic Pluralism in Canadian Perspective," in Glazer and Moynihan, eds. (1975: Chapter 9).

1979 *The Measure of Canadian Society: Education, Equality and Opportunity*. Toronto: Gage Publishing.

Porter, Marion R., John Porter, and Bernard Blishen.

1973 *Does Money Matter? Prospects for Higher Education*. Toronto: Institute for Behavioural Research.

Portes, Alejandro.

1971 "Political Primitivism, Differential Socialization, and Lower-Class Leftist Radicalism." *American Sociological Review* 36, October: 820–835.

Posgate, Dale, and Kenneth McRoberts.

1976 *Quebec: Social Change and Political Crisis*. Toronto: McClelland and Stewart.

Postman, Neil, and Charles Weingartner.

1969 *Teaching as a Subversive Activity*. New York: Dell.

Potter, Joan.

1981 "The Pitfalls of Pre-trial Diversion." *Corrections Magazine*, February.

Pozsonyi, Judith.

1973 "A Longitudinal Study of Unmarried Mothers Who Kept Their First-Born Children." London, Ontario: Family and Children's Services of London and Middlesex.

Prentice, Alison.

1977 *The School Promoters: Education and Social Class in Mid-Nineteenth Century Upper Canada*. Toronto: McClelland and Stewart.

Prentice, Alison, and Susan Houston, eds.
1975 *Family, School and Society in Nineteenth Century Canada.* Toronto: Oxford University Press.

Queen, Stuart A., and Robert W. Habenstein.
1974 *The Family in Various Cultures.* 4th ed. Philadelphia: Lippincott.

Radcliffe-Brown, A. R.
1952 *Structure and Function in Primitive Society.* New York: Macmillan.

Radecki, H., and B. Heydenkorn.
1977 *A Member of a Distinguished Family: The Polish Group in Canada.* Toronto: McClelland and Stewart.

Radzinowski, L.
1948 *A History of English Criminal Law.* Vol. 1. London: Stevens.

Ramu, G. N. (ed).
1979 *Courtship, Marriage and the Family.* Toronto: Macmillan of Canada.

Ramu, G. N., and Stuart D. Johnson.
1976 *Introduction to Canadian Society: Sociological Analysis.* Toronto: Macmillan.

Rapoport, R., and R. Rapoport.
1971 *Dual Career Families.* Middlesex: Penguin.

Ray, M. B.
1961 "The Cycle of Abstinence and Relapse among Heroin Addicts." *Social Problems* 9, Fall: 132–140.

Reich, Charles A.
1971 *The Greening of America.* New York: Bantam.

Reid, S., ed.
1977 *The Scottish Tradition in Canada.* Toronto: McClelland and Stewart.

Reiss, Albert.
1961 "The Social Integration of Peers and Queers." *Social Problems* 9: 102–119.

Reitz, Jeffrey G.
1974 "Language and Ethnic Community Survival." *Canadian Review of Sociology and Anthropology.* A special publication on the occasion of the VIIIth World Congress of Sociology: 104–122.

Renner, K. E.
1979 "The Two Faces of Diversion: Reform Versus a Conceptual Alternative as the Choice Between Broadening the Net and Avoiding the System." Paper presented, Canadian Association for Prevention of Crime, Halifax, Nova Scotia.

Reusch, Hans.
1951 *Top of the World.* Richmond Hill, Ont.: Simon and Schuster.

Richards, J.
1981 "Populism: A Qualified Defence." *Studies in Political Economy* Spring, No. 5.

Richardson, C. James.
1977a *Contemporary Social Mobility.* London: Frances Printer Publishing.
1977b "Education and Social Mobility: Changing Conceptions of the Role of Educational Systems." *Canadian Journal of Sociology* 2 (4) Fall: 417–433.
1977c "The Problem of Downward Mobility." *British Journal of Sociology* 28 (3) September: 303–320.
1987 "Children in Divorce," in K. Anderson et al. (1987).
1988 *Divorce and Family Mediation Research Study in Three Canadian Cities.* Ottawa: Ministry of Supply and Services.
1988 *Court-Based Divorce Mediation in Four Canadian Cities: An Overview of Research Results.* Ottawa: Ministry of Supply and Services.
1989 *Evaluation of the Divorce Act, 1985: Monitoring and Evaluation.* Ottawa: Department of Justice, Canada.

Richardson, R. Jack.
1982 "Merchants Against Industry: an Empirical Study of the Canadian Debate." *Canadian Journal of Sociology.*

Richer, Stephen, and Pierre Laporte.
1971 "Culture, Cognition and English-French Competition," in Elliot (1971: 141–150).

Richert, Jean Pierre.
1974 "The Impact of Ethnicity on the Perception of Heroes and Historical Symbols." *Canadian Review of Sociology and Anthropology* 11 (2) May: 156–163.

Richmond, Anthony H.
1967a *Post-War Immigration in Canada.*

Toronto: University of Toronto Press.

1967b *Immigrants and Ethnic Groups in Metropolitan Toronto*. Toronto: Institute for Behavioural Research, York University.

1970 "Immigration and Pluralism in Canada," in Mann (1970: 81–95).

1975 "The Green Paper: Reflections on the Canadian Immigration and Population Study." *Canadian Ethnic Studies* XII (1): 5–21.

Riesman, David, and others.

1950 *The Lonely Crowd*. New Haven: Yale University Press.

Rinehart, James.

1987 *The Tyranny of Work: Alienation and the Labour Process*. Toronto: Harcourt Brace Jovanovich.

Rioux, Marcel.

1971 *Quebec in Question*. Toronto: James, Lewis and Samuel.

1973 "The Development of Ideologies in Quebec," in *Communities and Culture in French Canada*, edited by G. A. Gold and M. A. Tremblay, Toronto: Holt, Rinehart and Winston: 260–278.

Rioux, Marcel, and Yves Martin.

1964 *French-Canadian Society*. Vol. 1. Toronto: McClelland and Stewart.

Ritzer, George.

1972 "Sources of Controversy in Sociology," in *Issues, Debates and Controversies*, edited by G. Ritzer. Boston: Allyn and Bacon.

Roberts, Wayne.

1976 *Honest Womanhood*. Toronto: New Hogtown Press.

Robertson, Heather.

1970 *Reservations Are for Indians*. Toronto: James, Lewis and Samuel.

1973 *Grass Roots*. Toronto: James, Lewis and Samuel.

Robitaille, Norbert and Robert Choinière.

1985 *An Overview of Demographic and Socio-economic Conditions of the Inuit in Canada*. Ottawa: Indian and Northern Affairs.

Rocher, Guy.

1970 "L'Avenir de la Sociologie au Canada," in *The Future of Sociology in Canada*, edited by Jan J. Loubser. Montreal: Canadian Sociology and Anthropology Association.

1972 *A General Introduction to Sociology*. Translated by Peta Sheriff. Toronto: Macmillan.

1975 "Formal Education: The Issue of Opportunity," in Forcese and Richer (1975: 137–161).

Rock, Paul.

1973 *Deviant Behaviour*. London: Hutchinson.

Rock, Paul, and Mary McIntosh.

1974 *Deviance and Social Control*. London: Tavistock.

Rogers, David.

1968 *110 Livingston Street*, New York: Random House.

Romaniuc, A.

1984 *Current Demographic Analysis, Fertility in Canada: From Baby Boom to Baby Bust*. Ottawa: Statistics Canada.

Roth, Julius.

1971 "Hired Hand Research," in *Sociological Methods*, by Norman K. Denzin, Chicago: Aldine: 531-539.

Roussopoulos, Dimitrios I.

1973 *Quebec and Radical Social Change*. Montreal: Black Rose Books.

Rousseau, Jean-Jacques.

1973 *The Social Contract*. London: J. M. Dent.
(1762)

Royal Commission on Bilingualism and Biculturalism.

1968 *Report*. Vol. 2. Ottawa: Queen's Printer.

Rubington, E., and M. S. Weinberg.

1968 *Deviance: The Interactionist Perspective*. London: Macmillan.

Rudé, G.

1964 *The Crowd in History*. London: Wiley.

1970 *Paris and London and the Eighteenth Century: Studies in Protest*. London: Fontana.

Runciman, W. G.

1966 *Relative Deprivation and Social Justice*. London: Routledge and Kegan Paul.

1968 "Class, Status and Power?" in *Social*

Stratification, edited by J. A. Jackson. Cambridge: Cambridge University Press, 25–61.

Ryerson, Stanley.
1972 "Quebec: Concepts of Class and Nation," in Teeple (ed.) (1972).
1981 "A Future for Equality in Canada?" in Muscovitch and Drover (1981: 373–384).

Safilios-Rothschild, Constantina.
1977 *Love, Sex and Sex Roles.* Englewood Cliffs, N.J.: Prentice-Hall.

Saturday Review of Education.
1973 "How Will We Raise Our Children in the Year 2000?" Symposium. *Saturday Review of Education*, March. Reprinted in *Social Realities*, edited by George Ritzer. Boston: Allyn and Bacon.

Saul, John, and Craig Heron.
1977 *Imperialism, Nationalism, and Canada.* Toronto: New Hogtown Press.

Saunders, Iwan.
1975 "Canadian Law and Marriage," in Wakil (1975: 43–58).

Sawchuk, P.
1974 "Becoming a Homosexual," in *Decency and Deviance*, edited by J. Haas and B. Shaffir. Toronto: McClelland and Stewart: 233–245.

Scanzoni, J. H.
1972 *Sexual Bargaining: Power Politics in the American Marriage.* Englewood Cliffs, N.J.: Prentice-Hall.

Schermerhorn, Richard A.
1970 *Comparative Ethnic Relations: A Framework for Theory and Research.* New York: Random House.

Schlesinger, Benjamin E.
1971 "Remarriage as Family Reorganization for Divorced Persons," in K. Ishwaran, ed. (1971: 377–395).

Schlesinger, Benjamin, ed.
1977 *Sexual Behaviour in Canada: Patterns and Problems.* Toronto: University of Toronto Press.

Schur, Edwin.
1965 *Crimes Without Victims.* Englewood Cliffs, N.J.: Prentice-Hall.

1971 *Labeling Deviant Behaviour: Its Sociological Implications.* New York: Random House.

Schutz, Alfred.
1964a *Collected Papers.* Edited by M. Natanson. The Hague: Nijhoff.
1964b "The Stranger," in Schutz (1964: 91–105).

Scott, M. B., and S. M. Lyman.
1968 "Accounts." *American Sociological Review* 33, February: 46–62.

Seeley, John R., and others.
1963 *Crestwood Heights: A Study of the Culture*
(1956) *of Suburban Life.* New York: Wiley.

Sennett, Richard.
1970 "The Brutality of Modern Families." *Transaction: Social Science and Modern Society* 7 (4): 29–37.
1978 *The Fall of Public Man: On the Social Psychology of Capitalism.* New York: Vintage Books.

Sennett, Richard, and Jonathan Cobb.
1972 *The Hidden Injuries of Class.* New York: Random House.

Shackleton, Doris.
1977 *Power Town: Democracy Discarded.* Toronto: McCelland and Stewart.

Shaw, Martin.
1972 "The Coming Crisis of Radical Sociology," in *Ideology in Social Science*, Robin Blackburn (ed.), London: Fontana: 32–44.

Shibutani, Tamotsu,
1955 "Reference Groups as Perspectives." *American Journal of Sociology* 60: 560–569.
1966 *Improvised News: A Sociological Study of Rumor.* Indianapolis: Bobbs-Merrill.

Shibutani, Tamotsu, and Kian M. Kwan.
1965 *Ethnic Stratification: A Comparative Approach.* New York: The Macmillan Company.

Short, James F., Jr., and Marvin E. Wolfgang.
1970 *Collective Violence.* Special Edition of The Annals of The American Academy of Political and Social Science, 391 September.

Shorter, Edward, and Charles Tilly.
1974 *Strikes in France, 1830–1968.* London: Cambridge University Press.

Silberman, Charles E.
1970   *Crisis in the Classroom*. New York: Random House.

Silverman, David.
1970   *The Theory of Organizations*. London: Heinemann.

Silverman, R., and J. Teevan, eds.
1975   *Crime in Canadian Society*. Toronto: Butterworths.

Simmel, Georg.
1964   *The Sociology of Georg Simmel.* Translation and introduction by K. H. Wolff. New York: Free Press.

Singelmann, P.
1972   "Exchange as Symbolic Interaction: Convergences between Two Theoretical Perspectives." *American Sociological Review* 37 (4) Skidmore, William.
1975   *Theoretical Thinking in Sociology.* Cambridge: Cambridge University Press.

Skoda, L., and J. C. Robertson.
1972   *Isodemographic Map of Canada.* Ottawa: Information Canada.

Skolnick, Arlene S.
1987   *The Intimate Environment.* Boston: Little Brown.

Skolnick, Arlene, and Jerome H. Skolnick.
1988   *Families in Transition.* Boston: Little Brown.

Skolnick, Jerome H., ed.
1969   *The Politics of Protest.* New York: Simon and Shuster.

Smelser, Neil J.
1959   *Social Change in the Industrial Revolution.* Chicago: University of Chicago Press.
1962   *The Theory of Collective Behavior.* New York: Free Press.

Smith, Dorothy.
1973   "Women, the Family and Corporate Capitalism," in M. Stephenson, ed. (1973: 5–35).
1981   "Women's Inequality and the Family," in Musovitch and Drover (1981: 156–198).
1987   *The Everyday World as Problematic: A Feminist Sociology.* Toronto: University of Toronto Press.

Smucker, Joseph.
1980   *Industrialization in Canada.* Toronto: Prentice-Hall.

Sorokin, Pitirim.
1959   *Social and Cultural Mobility.* New York:
(1927) Free Press.

Sperling, Gerald.
1979   "Confessions of a TV Addict," in Fey (1979: 316–349).

Spiro, Milford E.
1956   *Kibbutz: Venture in Utopia.* Cambridge: Harvard University Press.
1958   *Children of the Kibbutz.* Cambridge: Harvard University Press.

Spray, W. A.
1972   *The Blacks in New Brunswick.* Fredericton: New Brunswick.

Sprott, W. J. H.
1958   *Human Groups.* London: Penguin Books.

Stanbury, William T.
1975   *Success and Failure: Indians in Urban Society.* Vancouver: University of British Columbia.

Stebbins, R. A.
1967   "A Theory of the Definition of the Situation." *Canadian Review of Sociology and Anthropology* 4 (3): 148–164.

Steele, Brandt F., and Carl B. Pollock.
1971   "The Battered Child's Parents," in Skolnick and Skolnick, eds. (1971: 356–365).

Steinberg, Stephen.
1981   *The Ethnic Myth.* Toronto: McClelland and Stewart.

Steinmetz, S. K., and M. A. Strauss.
1974   *Violence in the Family.* New York: Dodd Mead.

Stephenson, Marylee, ed.
1977   *Women in Canada.* Don Mills: General Publishing.

Stolzman, James, and Herbert Gamberg.
1975   "The National Question and Canadian Sociology." *Canadian Journal of Sociology* 1 (1) Spring: 91–106.

Stone, G. P.
1962   "Appearance and the Self," in *Human*

Behavior and Social Processes, edited by A. M. Rose. Boston: Houghton-Mifflin: 86–118.

Stone, G. P., and H. A. Farberman.
1970   *Social Psychology Through Symbolic Interaction*. Waltham, Mass.: Ginn-Blaisdell.

Stone, Lawrence.
1979   *The Family, Sex and Marriage in England 1500–1800*. London: Penguin Books.

Stone, Leroy O.
1967   *Urban Development in Canada*. Ottawa: Dominion Bureau of Statistics (Statistics Canada).

Stone, Leroy O., and Claude Marceau.
1977   *Canadian Population Trends and Public Policy Through the 1980's*. Montreal: McGill-Queen's University Press.

Strauss, Anselm L.
1971   *The Contexts of Social Mobility: Ideology and Theory*. Chicago: Aldine.

Stub, Holger R., and Robert R. Bell.
1968   *The Sociology of Education: A Sourcebook*. Homewood, Ill.: Dorsey.

Stymeist, David H.
1975   *Ethnics and Indians*. Toronto: Peter Martin.

Sudnow, David, ed.
1972   *Studies in Social Interaction*. New York: Free Press.

Susskind, M. B.
1953   "The Help Pattern in the Middle-class Family." *American Sociological Review* 18, February: 22–28.

Sutherland, Edwin H.
1961   *Principles of Criminology*. Philadelphia:
(1939)   Lippincott.
(1949)   *White Collar Crime*. New York: Dryden.

Sydie, Rosalind.
1987   *Natural Women, Cultured Men: A Feminist Perspective on Sociological Theory*. Toronto: Methuen.

Symons, T. H. B.
1975   *To Know Ourselves: The Report of the Commission on Canadian Studies*. Ottawa: Association of Universities and Colleges of Canada.

Synge, Jane.
1977   "The Sex Factor in Social Selection Processes in Canadian Education," in Carlton and others (1977: 298–310).

Szasz, Thomas.
1960   "The Myth of Mental Illness." *American Psychologist* 15: 5–12.
1961   *The Myth of Mental Illness*. New York: Harper.
1965   *Psychiatric Justice*. New York: Macmillan.

Szymanski, Al.
1980   "A Critique and Extension of the PMC," in Walker (1980: 49–66).

Talmon, Yonina.
1972   *Family and Community in The Kibbutz*. Cambridge, Mass.: Harvard University Press.

Tan, J. and Patricia Roy.
1988   *The Chinese in Canada*. Ottawa: Canadian Historical Association.

Taylor, Ian.
1971   "Soccer Consciousness and Soccer Hooliganism," in Cohen (1971: 134–164).

Taylor, Ian, Paul Wilson, and Jock Young.
1973   *The New Criminology: For a Social Theory of Deviance*. London: Routledge and Kegan Paul.

Teeple, G., ed.
1972   *Capitalism and the National Question in Canada*. Toronto: University of Toronto Press.

Tepperman, Lorne.
1975   *Social Mobility in Canada*. Toronto: McGraw-Hill Ryerson.
1977a   *Crime Control: The Urge Toward Authority*. Toronto: McGraw-Hill Ryerson.
1977b   "Effects of the Demographic Transition upon Access to the Toronto Elite." *Canadian Review of Sociology and Anthropology* 14 (3): 285–293.

Thomlinson, Ralph
1965   *Population Dynamics: Causes and Consequences of World Demographic Change*. New York: Random House.

Thompson, D. C.
1973   *Quebec Society and Politics*. Toronto: McClelland and Stewart.

Thompson, E. P.
1963   *The Making of the English Working Class.*
        London: Pelican.

Thompson, Warren S.
1929   "Recent Trends in World Population."
        American Journal of Sociology, 34 (6)
        969–975.

Thompson, Warren, and David Lewis.
1965   *Population Problems.* New York:
        McGraw-Hill.

Thorne, Barrie, and Marilyn Yalom, eds.
1982   *Rethinking the Family: Some Feminist
        Questions.* New York: Longman.

Thornton, Leonard M.
1975   "People and the Police: An Analysis of
        Factors Associated with Police Evaluation
        and Support." *Canadian Journal of
        Sociology* 1 (3): 325–342.

Tilly, Charles.
1964   *The Vendée.* Cambridge, Mass.: Harvard
        University Press.
1967   "Migration to American Cities," in *The
        American City*, edited by Daniel P.
        Moynihan, New York: Basic Books.
1969   "Collective Violence in European
        Perspective," in Graham and Gurr (1969:
        12–24).

Tocqueville, Alexis De.
1955   *The Old Regime and the French
        Revolution.* New York: Doubleday.

Toffler, Alvin.
1971   *Future Shock.* New York: Bantam.

Trigger, Bruce.
1985   *Natives and Newcomers: Canada's Heroic
        Age Reconsidered.* Montreal: McGill-
        Queen's Press.

Troost, Cornelius J., ed.
1973   *Radical School Reform: Critique and
        Alternatives.* Boston: Little, Brown.

Trudeau, Pierre E.
1968   *Federalism and the French-Canadians.*
        Toronto: Macmillan.

Trudeau, Pierre E., ed.
1974   *The Asbestos Strike.* Toronto, James,
        Lewis and Samuel.

Truman, Tom.
1971   "A Critique of Seymour M. Lipset's
        Article, 'Value Differences, Absolute or
        Relative: The English-Speaking
        Democracies'." *Canadian Journal of
        Political Science* 4 (4) December.

Tucker, Robert C., ed.
1978   *The Marx-Engels Reader.* 2nd ed. New
        York: Norton.

Touraine, Alain.
1971   *The Post-Industrial Society.* New York:
        Random House.

Tumin, Melvin.
1967   "Some Principles of Stratification: A
(1953) Critical Analysis," in Bendix and Lipset
        (1967: 53–58).

Tumin, Melvin, ed.
1967   *Comparative Perspectives on Race
        Relations.* Boston: Little, Brown.

Turk, J. L., and N. W. Bell.
1972   "Measuring Power in Families." *Journal
        of Marriage and the Family* 24, May:
        215–222.

Turner, Jonathan H.
1977   *The Structure of Sociological Theory.*
        Homewood, Ill.: Dorsey.

Turner, Ralph H.
1960   "Sponsored and Contest Mobility and the
        School System." *American Sociological
        Review* 25 (6) December: 855–867.
1964   "New Theoretical Frameworks."
        Sociological Quarterly 12, April: 122–132.

Turner, Ralph B.
1969   "The Public Perception of Protest."
        American Sociological Review 34,
        December: 815–831.

Turner, Ralph, and Lewis M. Killian.
1972   *Collective Behavior.* 2nd ed. Englewood
        Cliffs, N.J.: Prentice-Hall.

Tylor, E. B.
1958   *Primitive Culture.* New York: Harper
        Torchbooks.

Udry, J. R.
1974   *The Social Context of Marriage.* 2nd ed.
        Philadelphia: Lippincott.

UNESCO.
1974   *Man and the Environment: New Towns in
        Isolated Settings.* Kambalda, Australia.

University of Toronto.
1977 *Options: Proceedings of the Conference on the Future of the Canadian Federation.* Toronto: University of Toronto Press.

Vallee, Frank, and Norman Shulman.
1969 "The Viability of French Groupings Outside Quebec," in *Regionalism in the Canadian Community 1867–1967.* Toronto: University of Toronto Press.

Vallieres, Pierre
1971 *White Niggers of America.* Toronto: McClelland and Stewart.

Van den Berghe, Pierre L.
1974 "Introduction" to *Class and Ethnicity in Peru*, by Pierre L. Van den Berghe. Leiden: E. J. Brill.

Van Den Haag, Ernest.
1974 "Love or Marriage," in *The Family: Its Structure and Functions*, edited by Rose Laub Coser. 2nd ed. York: St. Martins Press: 141–142.

Van Stolk, Mary.
1972 *The Battered Child In Canada.* Toronto: McClelland and Stewart.

Vaz, Edmund W.
1965 "Middle-Class Adolescents: Self-Reported Delinquency and Youth Culture Activities." *Canadian Review of Sociology and Anthropology* 2.
1976 *Aspects of Deviance.* Toronto: Prentice-Hall.

Veltmyer, Henry.
1986 *The Canadian Class Structure.* Toronto: Garamond Press.

Veevers, Jean.
1973 "Voluntary Childlessness: A Neglected Area of Family Study." *The Family Coordinator* 23: 199–205.
1977 "The Child-Free Alternative: Rejection of the Motherhood Mystique," in Marylee Stephenson (1977).

Vercors.
1953 *You Shall Know Them.* Translated by Rita Barisse. Toronto: McClelland and Stewart.

Vinacke, E. W.
1969 "Variables in Experimental Games: Toward a Field Theory." *Psychological Bulletin* 71: 293–318.

Vonnegut, Mark.
1975 *The Eden Express.* New York: Praeger.

Wakil, S. Parvez, ed.
1975 *Marriage, Family and Society: Canadian Perspectives.* Toronto: Butterworths.
1976 *Marriage and the Family in Canada.* Calgary: *Journal of Comparative Family Studies.*

Wallerstein, Judith, and Joan Kelly.
1980 *Surviving the Breakup: How Children and Parents Cope with Divorce.* New York: Basic Books.

Walker, Pat, ed.
1980 *Between Labor and Capital.* Montreal: Black Rose Books.

Wangenheim, Elizabeth.
1968 "The Ukranians: A Case Study of the Third Force," in *Canada: A Sociological Profile*, 1st ed., edited by W. E. Mann. Toronto: Copp Clark: 178–189.

Ward, Barbara.
1966 *Spaceship Earth.* New York: Columbia University Press.

Wargon, Sylvia.
1972 "Using Census Data for Research on the Family in Canada," *Journal of Comparative Family Studies*, 3 150–158.

Warner, Lloyd.
1963 *Yankee City.* New Haven: Yale University Press.

Warnock, John W.
1970 "All the News It Pays to Print," in Lumsden (1970: 117–134).
1974 "Metropolis/Hinterland: The Lost Theme in Canadian Letters." *Canadian Dimension* 10 (2) June: 42–47.

Warriner, C. K.
1970 *The Emergence of Society.* Homewood, Ill.: Dorsey.

Watkins, Mel.
1973   "Contradictions and Alternatives in Canada's Future," in Laxer, ed. (1973: 250–269).

Watson, G. Llewellyn.
1975   "The Poverty of Sociology in a Changing Canadian Society." *Canadian Journal of Sociology* 1 (3) Fall: 345–362.

Webb, Eugene J., and others.
1966   *Unobtrusive Measures: Nonreactive Research in the Social Sciences.* Chicago: Rand McNally.

Weber, Max.
1958   *The Protestant Ethic and the Spirit of Capitalism.* New York: Scribner.

Weinstein, Jay A.
1976   *Demographic Transition and Social Change.* Morristown, N.J.: General Learning Press.

Weiss, Carhol H.
1972   *Evaluation Research: Methods for Assessing Program Effectiveness.* Englewood Cliffs, N.J.: Prentice-Hall.

Weitzman, Lenore.
1985   *The Divorce Revolution: The Unexpected Social and Economic Consequences for Women and Children in America.* New York: The Free Press.

Werthman, Carl, and I. Piliavin.
1967   "Gang Members and the Police," in *The Police*, edited by D. J. Bordua, New York: Wiley.

Westergaard, John.
1974   *Class in Capitalist Society.* London: Heinemann.

Westhues, Kenneth.
1975   "Inter-Generational Conflict in the Sixties," in Clark et al. (1975: 387–408).

White, T. H.
1975   "Canadian Labour and International Unions in the Seventies," in Clark et al. (1975: 288–305).

Whyte, William F.
1943   *Street Corner Society.* Chicago: University
(1955) of Chicago Press.

Whyte, William H., Jr.
1956   *The Organization Man.* New York: Doubleday Anchor.

Whorf, Benjamin L.
1956   *Language, Thought, and Reality.* Cambridge, Mass.: M.I.T. Press.

Willey, Basil.
1962   *The Eighteenth Century Background.* London: Penguin.

Willmott, Peter.
1969   *Adolescent Boys of East London.* London: Pelican.

Willmott, Peter, and Michael Young.
1960   *Family and Class in a London Suburb.* London: Routledge and Kegan Paul.

Wilson, Susan J.
1986   *Women, the Family and the Economy.* Toronto: McGraw-Hill Ryerson.

Wilson, Thomas P.
1970   "Normative and Interpretive Paradigms in Sociology." In Douglas (1970: 57–79).

Winch, R. F.
1971   *The Modern Family.* 3rd ed. New York: Holt, Rinehart and Winston.

Wirth, Louis.
1938   "Urbanism as a Way of Life." *American Journal of Sociology* 44, July: 1–24.

Wise, S. F., and Robert Craig Brown.
1967   *Canada Views the United States, Nineteenth Century Political Attitudes.* Toronto: Macmillan.

Woods, John.
1976   "Repatriating the Canadian University." *Journal of Canadian Studies* XI (4): 56–66.

Wrong, Dennis.
1959   "The Decline and Fall of Social Class." *Pacific Sociological Review*, 2 (Spring) 11–17.

1961   "The Over-Socialized Conception of Man in Modern Sociology." *American Sociological Review* 26, April.

1964   "Social Inequality without Social Stratification." *Canadian Review of Sociology and Anthropology* I (1): 5–16.

1977   *Population and Society.* 4th ed. New York: Random House.

Young, Jock.

1971   "The Police as Amplifiers of Deviance," in Cohen (1971).

Young, John, ed.

1987   *Breaking the Mosaic: Ethnic Identities in Canadian Schooling.* Toronto: Garamond Press.

Young, Michael.

1958   *The Rise of the Meritocracy.* London: Penguin.

Young, Michael F. D.

1971   *Knowledge and Control.* London: Heinemann.

Young, M., and P. Willmott.

1957   *Family and Kinship in East London.*
Baltimore: Penguin.

1973   *The Symmetrical Family.* London: Routledge and Kegan Paul.

Zakuta, L.

1963   "Equality in North American Marriages." *Social Research* 30, Summer: 157–170.

1964   *A Protest Movement Becalmed.* Toronto: University of Toronto Press.

1970   "On 'Filthy Lucre'," in *Human Nature and Collective Behavior*, edited by T. Shibutani. Englewood Cliffs, N.J.: Prentice-Hall: 260–270.

Zaretsky, Eli.

1973   *Capitalism, the Family and Personal Life.* New York: Harper and Row.

Zeitlin, Irving.

1968   *Ideology and the Development of Sociological Theory.* New York: Prentice-Hall.

Zureik, Elia, and Robert M. Pike, eds.

1975   *Socialization and Values in Canadian Society.* Vols. I and II. Toronto: McClelland and Stewart.

KEY CONCEPTS

CHAPTER 1

Altruistic Suicide: the type of suicide identified by Emile Durkheim which can be attributed or explained by people's identification with their social group or society.

Anomie: this concept is most closely associated with the work of Emile Durkheim and literally means "normlessness." Durkheim used the term to depict what he saw as the lack of social integration or consensus about values and norms that characterized the society of his time. Rates of certain kinds of suicide were, for him, one empirical indicator of the degree of anomie or social disorganization in a particular society.

Anomic Suicide: the type of suicide identified by Emile Durkheim which can be attributed to or explained by a perceived or actual loss of clear and meaningful goals and rules.

Bourgeoisie: the term used by Karl Marx to describe the class that owns the means of production in capitalist society. We would, today, call this the capitalist class.

Conflict Perspective: a view of society that stresses how social structure consists of layers of social inequality and that society is held together by force and manipulation by those on the top layer. This perspective is most closely associated with the work of Karl Marx.

Definition of the Situation: a central concept of the sociological perspective is that people generally do not act on the basis of objective factors in their physical and social environment but on the basis of their interpretation of these phenomena (their *definition of the situation*). This notion is given particular importance by those working within the symbolic interaction perspective.

Egoistic Suicide: the type of suicide identified by Emile Durkheim which can be attributed to or explained by people's lack of identification with their group or society.

Idea of Progress: the belief that because people are essentially good and are shaped by social structure, society can be improved through the use of the scientific method.

Manifest and Latent Functions: terms coined by Robert K. Merton, an important American structural-functionalist, to distinguish between those consequences of purposive behaviour which are intended and recognized by people (manifest functions) and those which are unintended and/or unrecognized by these same people but which may be discovered by sociologists (latent consequences).

Mechanical Solidarity: the term used by Emile Durkheim to depict societies characterized by a simple division of labour based in age and sex which results in commonly shared beliefs and values and a high degree of social solidarity.

Order Perspective: a view of society that stresses how the parts of society form an integrated system based on common values. This perspective is more specifically known as structural functionalism.

Organic Solidarity: the term used by Emile Durkheim to depict the future state of industrial society in which, despite an elaborate division of labour and a lack of common beliefs and values, there will be a high degree of social solidarity because of the need for interdependence.

Positivism: the philosophy of science that argues that science should be based on empirical data, that is, things that can be observed.

Private Troubles and Public Issues: the distinction made by C. Wright Mills between the private sphere and the public sphere. He argued that central to the *sociological imagination* is the ability to recognize and distinguish between what are individual problems and what are those which, though having a private dimension, are generated by how society is structured or organized.

Proletariat: the class identified by Karl Marx as being forced by the rise of capitalism to sell their labour to the bourgeoisie or capitalist class. We would, today, refer to this segment of society as the working class.

Role-Taking: the notion, developed by George Herbert Mead that before we can interact successfully with another, we must put ourselves in his or her shoes. The person we are interacting with must do the same with us.

Scientific Method: the combination of reason and observation by which we look for patterns in observations and test the theory we have built with further observations.

Secularization: the shift from explanations based on religion or superstition to ones based on the use of the scientific method. Institutions such as the family come to be seen as human rather than divine constructions.

Social Structure: the patterns of social relationships and institutional arrangements which, to a large extent, shape and constrain our thinking and behaviour.

Structural Functionalism: this version of the order perspective is most closely associated with Talcott Parsons and was, for a time, the dominant approach of American sociology. It is an approach that focuses specifically on the contribution or functions of parts of the system in maintaining the whole system and how changes in one part of the system may bring about changes in other parts of the system.

Symbolic Interaction Perspective: a view of society that stresses how people, through social interaction create, maintain, and modify social structure and social institutions. This perspective is most closely associated with George Herbert Mead and other American sociologists who sought to develop a more subjective and interpretive approach to understanding society and human behaviour.

Value-Free Sociology: Max Weber's notion that while social scientists can study people's values and these values influence their behaviour, science does not provide us with a way to judge or evaluate these values, to determine what is good and bad.

Verstehen: Max Weber's term for subjective interpretation of behaviour. The term literally means "understanding" and is similar to the later notion of "taking the role of the other" advanced by American sociologists such as George Herbert Mead.

▌ CHAPTER 2

Applied Sociology: the use of sociological theory and research methods to answer questions of immediate relevance to various decision makers in both government and industry.

Classical Experimental Design: a research design that compares two similar groups both before and after some test factor has been introduced to the experimental group but not the control group.

Deductive Reasoning: the development of testable hypotheses from an existing theory or set of hunches about how things may be related.

Descriptive Statistics: measures such as percentages, averages, medians and frequency distributions and measures of association that summarize and standardize large amounts of information for both comprehension and comparison.

Ethnomethodology: the term literally means a "methodology of people." It is an approach to understanding society and interaction which makes as its focus how both people who are being studied and social scientists who are studying them construct social structure and give meaning to behaviour.

Inferential Statistics: a variety of statistical techniques which tell us the probability that what was found in a random sample is true for the population from which the sample was drawn or is due to chance. The probability is expressed as a level of statistical significance.

Hypothetico-Deductive Model: the development of hypotheses deduced from theory and the testing of these through empirical data. On the basis of observations, the theory may be strengthened, modified or rejected.

Inductive Reasoning: research approaches that begin by observations that lead to theory and hypotheses.

Inferential Statistics: a variety of statistical techniques that tell us the probability that what was found in a random sample is true for the population from which the sample was drawn or is due to chance. The probability is expressed as a level of statistical significance.

Measures of Association: a statistical relationship between two or more variables. There is, for example, a strong relationship between age and height in children.

Norms of Scientific Method: in their attempt to combine reason and observation, scientists are also bound by rules of honesty, objectivity, and openness in interpreting and reporting their research findings.

Objective Approaches: research methods based on the assumption that the key concepts are those developed by the researcher and may or may not be perceived by those being studied. Observation and measurement is generally highly precise and quantitative in nature. Most studies based on survey research or use of census data are using objective approaches.

Participant Observation: research methods used by researchers who believe it essential to capture the process of interpretation through which people construct and rationalize their actions. They do so through observing and interacting with those being studied. The role of the researcher ranges from openness to covertness (infiltration) and from low to high commitment to the goals and interests of the groups being studied.

Prior Randomization: the attempt in the classical experimental design to make the experimental and control groups the same, except for the test factor, by randomly assigning subjects to the two groups.

Quasi-Experimental Design: a research design commonly used when it is impossible, randomly, to assign subjects to an experimental and control group. The researcher "controls" important variables (factors) in order to make the groups being composed as similar as possible on all things besides the test factor.

Random Sample: a sample drawn in such a way that all members of the population have an equal probability of being in the sample.

Subjective Approaches: research approach methods based on the belief that the most relevant information for sociologists comes from learning how people define situations and, through social interaction, construct social reality. Most studies based on participant observation use a subjective approach.

Survey Research: a systematic study of a population or, more commonly, a sample of a population of individuals based on the use of a questionnaire or an interview.

Unobtrusive Measures: research approaches that attempt to minimize the observer's influence on those being studied.

Variable: a concept, such as age or education, that can take a number of values. Changes in what are called independent variables are seen as bringing about changes in what are called dependent variables.

▌ CHAPTER 3

Common Stock of Knowledge: the taken-for-granted knowledge of our society and culture, past and present, which we are all assumed to possess as a result of formal and informal processes of socialization and education.

Counter Culture: the notion that in relatively complex societies groups may under some circumstances develop an ideology and culture that challenges the values and standards of the dominant culture or ideology.

Cultural Relativism: the view that since people have developed diverse ways to organize themselves into societies and to deal with their environment, we should not judge other cultures using the standards of our own. Cultural relativism is, therefore, a counter to extreme ethnocentrism.

Culture Shock: the feeling of unreality and disorientation when one's taken for granted ways of thinking and acting are challenged or no longer found appropriate. This is most likely to occur when one is exposed to a new and different society or culture.

Dominant Ideology: the view that cultural ideas will be shaped by those with the power and resources to make their values, and their standards *the* values and standards.

Ethnocentrism: the concept literally means "people centred" but more generally refers to the tendency for people to view their own culture as *the* culture and to judge all others against this standard.

Ideal Culture: the system of beliefs, values and ways of thinking and the plans or recipes for behaving in any group, specifically those passed on from generation to generation.

Ideology: while used in a variety of ways, the concept most often means the beliefs or values either created or upheld by dominant groups in society to justify and legitimate existing patterns of social inequality and which also limit or prevent understanding of our society, its arrangements and the possibility of change.

Material Culture: the artifacts and technology produced by human societies as a result of particular systems of ideal culture or systems of thought.

Subculture: the notion that in relatively complex societies, groups with less power and resources will, without necessarily challenging the dominant culture or ideology, develop a different and adaptive culture or ideology.

Symbols: any object to which people have attached some shared value and meaning. The most important system of symbols is language.

Value-Committed Sociology: the view that sociologists should both be aware of and make explicit their own values and also develop standards to evaluate not only their own but other cultures.

Values: beliefs about what ought to be and, therefore, the standards by which we judge our own and others' ways of thinking and acting as good or evil, correct or wrong.

▌ CHAPTER 4

Aggregates: categories of people, such as income groups, developed for descriptive or research purposes.

Collectivities: a relatively large number of people with some values, norms and goals in common but whose interaction with one another is not patterned or sustained as in social groups.

Complex Societies: societies characterized by an elaborate division of labour, specialization of knowledge and differentiation of institutional orders. As well as the primary relationships of kin and family, there is found in complex societies secondary relationships and associations of urban, industrial, and bureaucratic society.

Conflict Perspective: one of the three major perspectives on society most closely associated with the work of Karl Marx. Conflict theories emphasize how inequalities become structured or created as a result of the mode of production and how these structures generate conflict and, in turn, social change.

Functional Needs: these are sometimes referred to as functional prerequisites, the notion that societies must meet basic biological, economic and social needs if they are to survive.

Institution: the regular and patterned behaviour to achieve some goal. Institutions can be considered the human equivalent of instincts in that they guide and channel behaviour in fairly predictable ways. It is in this sense that we think of marriage and family as institutions.

Institutional Orders: the various parts of a society that, because of their particular function, contribute to the integration of the society.

Pattern Variables: a series of dichotomous issues or dilemmas of choice that, according to Talcott Parsons, must be addressed differently as we interact with others in different situations in complex societies and between simple and complex societies.

Primary Groups: small groups such as the nuclear family that are characterized by intimate ties and spontaneous and diffuse or all encompassing interpersonal relations and that are typically viewed by members as ends in themselves rather than means to other ends.

Secondary Groups: groups, or more usually relationships, that are roughly the opposite of primary groups, primary relationships. Relationships are expected to be cool, impersonal and sometimes contractual and are likely to be seen as means to other ends rather than ends in themselves.

Secularization: as well as the definition in Chapter 1, this concept also refers to the shift from relationships based on sacred bonds to relationships based on contractual or secular ties.

Simple Societies: societies characterized by primary relationships based on kinship ties in which the division of labour is limited to considerations of age and sex and institutional orders are embedded in the kinship structure.

Social Groups: two or more people who are in contact with one another, who take one another into account and are aware of one another.

Structural Functionalism: one of the three main perspectives on society most closely associated with American sociology and in particular Talcott Parsons. Functionalists view society as a system and explain the parts or institutional orders of society in terms of their functions in maintaining the system.

Symbolic Interactionism: one of the three major perspectives on society most closely associated with the work of George Herbert Mead. Its proponents emphasize how self, society and culture are created, maintained and modified through social interaction and our attempts to fit our lines of action with those of others.

❚ CHAPTER 5

Anticipatory Socialization: the process of learning and internalizing values and norms associated with various roles the child will be expected to play in later life.

Dramaturgical Model: an approach to understanding social interaction most closely associated with Erving Goffman. This approach views social life as analogous to improvised theatre and is concerned with how, in everyday life, we are often engaged in impression management as we attempt, through our actions and behaviour, to convey who and what we are.

Ethnomethodological Model: an approach to understanding social interaction that begins with the question of how people plan and explain their behaviour to themselves and others in the process of interacting and thereby act as if the social world is real and orderly.

Exchange Model: an approach to social interaction that focuses on the assumption that in all interaction people act in such a way as to maximize rewards and minimize costs.

Game Model: an approach to understanding social interaction that views much of social life as analogous to game playing bounded by rules and in which, "to win," we must be able to imagine the others' likely action in given situations.

Generalized Other: the third stage of socialization identified by George Herbert Mead in which the child learns to take on several roles simultaneously and to judge himself or herself from a generalized standpoint.

"I" and the "Me": George Herbert Mead argued that the self consists of a spontaneous and creative component, the "I," and a socialized component, the "Me," that is, the rule-following and conforming aspect of the personality.

Primary Socialization: the initial process of socialization by which children develop a sense of self as they are, through social interaction, learning their language and culture.

Reference Groups: groups, real or imaginary, in which we may or may not be a member, that provide us with standards and a perspective to view and evaluate our own and others' behaviour and situation.

Role: the set of obligations and expectations as well as behaviour associated with positions (status) in society.

Secondary Socialization: the notion that socialization is an ongoing process over one's lifetime. For example, an important part of professional education is learning and perhaps internalizing the values and norms of the profession.

Socialization: the interactive process whereby people acquire and internalize the culture of a group and, in the process, develop a concept of self.

Stages of Socialization: the process identified by George Herbert Mead whereby children gradually come to acquire a sense of self as they acquire language and learn to take the role of the other, first through imitation and later through role playing and interpretation.

Status: the positions in a group or society. These may be hierarchical, ascribed or achieved and involve rights and obligations that may be formal or emergent through interaction and negotiation.

Symbolic Interaction Model: an approach to understanding social interaction that emphasizes that we are symbol users and that communication involves interpretation of behaviour and symbols. Thus we do not act on the basis of stimuli but on the basis of meanings as we handle, interpret, and modify these through an interpretive process in interaction.

▌ CHAPTER 6

Census Family: the definition of family used by Statistics Canada for census purposes. It includes husband and wife with or without never married children, one-parent families and common-law relationships.

Child Custody: the legal right, on separation or divorce, of one or more people to make decisions about the education and welfare of the children of the marriage. Sole custody may be granted to one parent (or a third party) or both parents may be granted joint legal custody, in which case both have a say in how the children are raised. In either sole or joint custody arrangements, parents may share in the parenting.

Domestic Labour: the notion that with the rise of industrial capitalism, work within the home and child care, which had been economic activity, became defined as unproductive and unpaid labour carried out mainly by women. Hidden in the household, such labour both lacks prestige but also makes women more dependent on men's earnings in the labour market.

Endogamy: formal or informal rules about which "out-groups" into which one cannot marry. In Canada, such rules are largely informal and are maintained largely through the pressures of religious groups, one's parents and wider patterns of ethnic and racial prejudice.

Exogamy: rules that all societies seem to have as to who in the "in-group" is not an acceptable marriage partner. Rules about exogamy are, essentially, rules about what constitutes incest.

Family Functions: the argument that there are universal functions served by the family that include reproduction, economic maintenance, status placement and socialization. These are more correctly viewed as variables that have more or less importance depending on the nature of the society and its level of development.

Homogamy: the tendency for most people, in most societies, to marry people with roughly the same social background, religion, ethnicity and education as themselves.

Industrial Family: the family form that emerged with the development and the rise of industrial capitalism in the 19th and 20th century whereby there became a greater separation between the private space of the home and the public space of the work world; women's domestic labour became "unproductive labour" and the family gradually moved from production unit to consumption unit as more and more goods were produced in factories.

Kinship: the patterns of relationships, obligations, expectations and loyalties extended to those defined as relatives who are outside of the nuclear family.

Kinship as Resource: the notion that under some economic conditions and circumstances, people will use kinship ties and connections whenever it is to their advantage to do so in an effort to maintain or improve their position in society.

Nuclear Family: the family form consisting of husband, wife and children which, when resources permit, maintains a separate household. Some anthropologists and sociologists believe that this family form comes close to being the universal family form.

Patriarchy: the economic, social and political dominance of men over women and children. In Western societies as well as most others, the family has, historically, been patriarchal.

Pre-Industrial Family: the family form prior to the rise of industrial capitalism that was essentially a production unit and in which both men's and women's work in the home contributed to the family economy and the economy generally and there was not a clear separation between the private space of the home and the public space of the market place.

Privatization: the gradual process by which there comes to be a separation between the closed world of the family and the larger world of work and of bureaucracy. It is in this sense that women's work within the home can be seen as "hidden in the household."

Romantic Love Complex: a concept which attempts to capture how our choice of marriage partner is both based on and legitimated in terms of romantic love. It is called a "complex" because the empirical evidence is that most people make fairly rational decisions as to who is a desirable mate before deciding to fall into love.

Symmetrical Family: the modern family in which there is a tendency for there to be less traditional segregation of the roles of men and women.

▌ CHAPTER 7

Corporate Crime: crimes such as pollution, price fixing, tax evasion etc., committed by individuals on behalf of the business organization.

Crimes Against Person: those acts such as murder and sexual and physical assault that bring about death or injury to others.

Crimes Against Property: the largest category of crime in Canada which ranges from shop lifting and vandalism to burglary and robbery. A considerable portion of the *Criminal Code of Canada* is concerned with property crimes.

Deviant Behaviour Perspective: the sociological view that behaviour viewed as deviant is not inherently wrong or necessarily the product of biological or psychological defects, but is deviant only in relationship to given norms in particular statuses and situations and may be viewed differently in different times and from place to place.

Deviant Careers: the sometimes irreversible and self-fulfilling process by which those labelled as deviant may be rejected by conventional society and forced to associate with others similarly labelled, thus reinforcing and confirming the initial label.

Differential Association Theory: most closely associated with the work of Edwin Sutherland, this approach to understanding deviance emphasizes the differences in norms and values among various groups in society and the different socialization experiences to which various members of society are exposed. Deviant behaviour is, in this view, learned in the same way as non-deviant behaviour.

Diversion: the attempt in sentencing to minimize or eliminate the contact offenders, particularly juveniles, have with the courts and prisons in order to counteract the labelling process.

Individualized Justice: the view that in sentencing offenders, particularly juveniles, judges should have discretion in order to give sentences that will be rehabilitative or treatment oriented rather than retributive or punishment oriented.

Labelling Theory: an approach to understanding deviance that focuses on the process whereby powerful groups within society generate deviance by creating and enforcing rules. The labelling approach draws on both conflict and symbolic interaction perspectives for insights into how deviance is created, but also the interaction between the labellers and those labelled as deviant.

Master Status: the notion that labelling individuals as deviant may mean that they now see themselves and are so seen by others primarily in terms of the label, thereby ignoring the extent to which they may be conforming in other facets of their lives.

Theory of Anomie: an approach to understanding deviance most closely associated with the work of Robert Merton, which emphasizes the role of social structure in pressuring some groups to commit deviant acts. The emphasis is particularly on the disjuncture between cultural success goals and the lack of access of some groups to the legitimate means to achieve these goals.

Victimless Crimes: forms of deviance where the participants are willing and no one is directly injured but which powerful groups in society are able to have criminalized because they do not approve of the behaviour or there are interests served by making these behaviours illegal.

White-Collar Crime: crimes against property, committed by the more powerful members of society, such as embezzlement, computer theft, inside trading, etc., which are both more difficult to detect and less likely than street crimes to be processed as criminal offenses.

❘ CHAPTER 8

Canadian Census: the attempt by the Government of Canada both to count the number of people in Canada but also to collect information on a variety of characteristics of Canadians such as age, occupation, ethnicity, sex, place and type of residence etc. A complete census is conducted every ten years and a sample census is conducted half way through the decade.

Demographic Equation: for the world population, changes in population are simply the result of an excess of births over deaths or vice versa. In any society or region, the differences between in-migration and out-migration (immigration and emigration) must be added into the equation.

Demographic Transition Theory: a theory that explains the tendency in Western societies for birth rates to fall in response to declining death rates in terms of industrialization and urbanization. The expectation was that Third World societies, as they developed, would undergo a similar transition.

Demography: the concept literally means "study of people" and is concerned with factors related to changes in the size and structure of population as a result of birth rates, death rates and the movements of people within and between countries.

Emigration: the movement of people out of a society or region.

Exponential Growth: the tendency, first identified by Thomas Malthus, for populations, if unchecked, to grow in geometrical rather than arithmetical progression (2, 4, 8, 16, 32 etc).

Fertility: the rate of reproduction of a society, generally expressed as the number of births per 1000 population (*the crude birth rate*) or the number of births per 1000 women in various age groups (*the age-specific birth rate*) in a given period.

Immigration: the movement of people into a society or region.

Mortality: the rate of death in a society, generally expressed as the number of deaths per 1000 population (*the crude death rate*) in a given period or as life expectancy.

Population Pyramids: a graphical presentation of the age and sex structure of a population. In an aging population these may look more like a Christmas tree than a pyramid.

Positive Checks: controls on population growth identified by Thomas Malthus as those over which people have little or no control, such as famine, plague and war.

Preventive Checks: controls on population identified by Thomas Malthus as those over which people have control, such as delaying marriage, abstinence and, more recently, contraception.

Urbanization: literally, the movement of people from rural areas to cities. The concept is also meant to capture the shift in values from rural to urban—those living in rural areas will have taken on many of the same values as their urban counterparts.

▍ CHAPTER 9

Canadianization: in the most general sense this concept refers to the attempt to gain control of Canada's economy and culture. In the specific context of sociology it refers to the development of theory and research explicitly focused on the development of a distinctive Canadian sociology.

Cultural Explanation: an attempt to explain societies and their development in terms of values and ideas.

Cultural Imperialism: the notion that economic domination of one society over another leads to cultural domination.

Dependency Theory: the approach to understanding Canada's social and economic development in terms of our history of being a dependent hinterland of more powerful and economically advanced nations: France, then Britain and in the 20th century, the United States.

Feminist Perspectives: the development of theory and research that both takes into account women's roles and experiences and attempts to explain women's inequality. The exact meaning of feminist theory remains under debate.

Hard Frontier: a concept used by S. D. Clark in his attempt to explain, in terms of differences in geography, differences in the culture and social structure of the Canadian and American West.

Metropolis-Hinterland: a perspective that focuses on the inherent conflict between underdeveloped regions or societies that provide resources to economically developed cities, regions or societies.

Staples Approach: a theory most closely associated with Harold Innis that sought to explain Canada's social and economic development in terms of the resources various colonial powers extracted from Canada.

Single Industry Communities: relatively isolated and dependent communities created explicitly to extract a particular resource. Such communities provide a vivid illustration of the consequences of metropolis-hinterland relationships.

Historical Perspective: the explicit attempt by sociologists such as S. D. Clark to draw upon the insights of American sociology to understand Canadian society but to do so in the context of concrete historical research and analysis.

Malestream Sociology: the dominance of American functionalist sociology in the 1950s and 1960s led to it being called "mainstream sociology." The notion of "malestream" recognizes that until recently virtually all sociology was done by males about males and excluded women and their perspectives.

Political Economy Perspective: the attempt to explain patterns of culture and social structure in terms of economic relationships. It is an approach based on Marxism or what, more generally, is referred to throughout the text as a conflict perspective.

▌ CHAPTER 10

Alienation of Labour: Karl Marx's depiction of conditions within capitalism in which, among other things, the worker does not receive the full psychological, sociological, and economic benefits of his or her labour.

Bureaucratization: the form of social organization identified by Max Weber as accompanying the rise of capitalism which is based on rationality and efficiency.

Capitalism: at its most basic, an economic system based on the notions of profit, accumulation of wealth, and private property.

Gender Segregation: a term used to describe how the labour force is divided into "female" and "male" occupations with the result that women in female-dominated occupations generally earn about 65 percent of average earnings in male-dominated occupations.

Human Relations: an approach to management that followed that of scientific management and which attempts to control and motivate workers through recognition that social and emotional needs may be as important as economic needs.

Industrial Capitalism: the transition from work done within the household to its centralization in factories and under the direct control of capitalists who also generally manage the enterprise.

Industrialization: at the simplest level, the use of machine technology and energy in the production of goods. At a more general level, the term means a change to a more complex division of labour and a different way of organizing work.

Marginal Work World: the segment of the labour force characterized by low pay, lack of benefits, and lack of employment security. Many jobs in the service industry are part of the marginal work world.

Mercantilism: the form of capitalism based in trade and money lending rather than the production of goods.

Modernization: a complex term which embodies the various changes in values, sources of knowledge, and social relationships which accompanied the shift from feudalism to capitalism and industrialism.

Monopoly capitalism: the development of larger and often multinational capitalist enterprises which dominate the industry and in which there is generally a split between ownership and management.

Post-Industrial Societies: concept based on the notion that in modern industrial societies the major product is not goods but services, particularly those connected with management and communication of specialized knowledge.

Rational-Legal Model: the type of decision making identified by Max Weber as being based on scientific or economic considerations rather than tradition.

Scientific Management: an approach to organizing and controlling workers which breaks jobs down into unskilled tasks and gives management control of the work process.

Surplus Value: a concept developed by Karl Marx to describe how, with the combination of machine technology and the division of labour, workers are able to produce more in a given time than they require for their subsistence. The proceeds of this extra production are expropriated by the capitalist to pay for the costs of production and as profits.

▌ CHAPTER 11

Absolute Poverty: the measurement and estimate of the level of poverty on the basis of assessments as to the minimum income required to provide the basic essentials of life.

Caste: a very closed system of social stratification based on inheritance in which social mobility and intermarriage across caste lines is not permitted and for which the main legitimation for social inequality is religious.

Class: a relatively open system of social stratification based on wealth and ownership of the means of production. Classes are not legal entities and permit considerable upward and downward social mobility in part on the basis of merit and achievement.

Class, Status and Party: the analytical and sometimes empirical distinction made by Max Weber with respect to the economic, prestige and power dimensions of social inequality.

Conservative Ideology: a political philosophy that emphasizes the benefits for the society and individual of relatively stable patterns of social inequality based on tradition.

Estate: a relatively closed system of social stratification based primarily on ownership of land and in which membership in various strata—peasantry or aristocracy—is largely hereditary. Religion upholds, but is not the sole legitimation for, social inequality.

Equality of Opportunity: the goal of creating a more just society by making it possible for people to move into various social classes and statuses on the basis of merit and achievement rather than tradition and inheritance. Such a society is generally referred to as a *meritocracy*.

Equality of Condition: the goal of creating a more just society by reducing the amount of economic inequality, and thereby the differences in power and status through redistribution of the wealth of the society, and by abolishing private property in the form of ownership of the means of production.

Functional Theory of Social Stratification: a conservative explanation of social inequality first advanced by Kingsley Davis and Wilbert Moore that focuses on the notion that some statuses or occupations are more functional than others with respect to the survival of a society, that talent is scarce and that inequalities in economic and social rewards both motivate people to fill these positions but also to perform the roles adequately.

Income Quintiles: the division of all incomes into five ranked groups in order to determine how equally or unequally income is distributed in a society.

Liberal Ideology: a political philosophy that emphasizes equality of opportunity and an open society in which people are free to move upwards and downwards in the social or class hierarchy.

Occupational Prestige: the social standing people are willing to accord to various occupations based in part on the income and education required for the occupation, its functional importance in society and the cultural values we have learned and perhaps internalized. The uniformity and consistency of these rankings is what has led sociologists to view occupation as the single best indicator of social class.

Open and Closed Societies: refers to the relative amount of upward and downward social mobility there is in a society. In open societies, social mobility is both legitimate and encouraged. In closed societies, social mobility may be both discouraged and illegal.

Relative Poverty: the measurement and assessment of the level of poverty through comparisons of the distribution of income levels in a society and through determination of what proportion of individuals and families have incomes below some proportion of the average income. The focus is on the relative as well as the absolute deprivation of living on a low income.

Social Mobility: the movement of individuals and groups from one social strata to another which generally involves a change economically, relationally and attitudinally. For most of us, the main kind of social mobility is occupational mobility in comparison both with our parents' occupation (*intergenerational mobility*) and our initial occupational status (*intragenerational or career mobility*).

Socialist Ideology: a politial and social philosophy that emphasizes the constraints and injustices of social inequality and the desirability of equality of condition in the sense of the abolition of private property.

Social Stratification: the division of society into unequal and hierarchical categories which through family, kinship, race and ethnicity may persist for a long period of time. Caste and estate are relatively closed systems of social stratification; class is a relatively open system of social stratification.

❙ CHAPTER 12

Conflict Theory of Education: an explanation of the expansion of mass education that focuses on the ways in which this development served the interests of the capitalist class through both teaching basic skills but also respect for the ruling class and its dominant culture. This perspective also emphasizes the role educational credentials play in maintaining and enhancing the position of various status groups in society.

Contest Mobility: a concept of social mobility most closely associated with the American sociologist, Ralph Turner. He argued that the relevant analogy to describe American views about social mobility was that of a race in which selection must come late because it is never certain who will be the winner (he is contrasting this pattern to what he depicted as the sponsored mobility characterizing British patterns of social mobility and education).

Credentialism: the notion that as various occupational groups attempt to maintain and enhance their position in capitalist society, academic credentials, aside from whatever else they may convey in terms of skills and training, are, in and of themselves, important economic and status resources.

Deskilling of Work: a view of work most closely associated with Harry Braverman who argued that rather than skills increasing with industrialization, they were declining as the work of craftspeople became *degraded* as a result of capitalism (see: Scientific Management in Chapter 10). The deskilling argument offers a powerful critique to the technical-functional explanation of the development of mass education.

Egalitarian Model: the organization of education is, from this perspective, based on the assumption that talent and intelligence are more or less equally distributed and that everyone can benefit from education beyond the basic minimum with the result that streaming into academic and vocational programs will occur very late or be done very subtly. This is essentially an American view, one which has, in recent decades, had considerable impact on Canadian views about education.

Elitist Model of Education: the organization of education is, from this perspective, based on the assumption that talent and intelligence are unequally distributed in society and that only a few can benefit from education beyond the very basic and minimum. The result is that students are likely to be streamed early into academic and vocational programs. This is essentially a British view which, historically, has also permeated Canadian thinking about education.

Hidden Curriculum: the notion that as well as teaching basic skills, educational curriculums, in more subtle ways, socialize us to be accepting rather than critical of the dominant culture and existing arrangements in society.

Meritocracy: a term coined by Michael Young in 1958. He was focusing, somewhat satirically and critically, on the tendency in Britain to move from an aristocracy based on birth to one based on talent. The term has come to refer to societies in which position or status in society is based on merit and achievement rather than traditional patterns of heredity or, more generally, ascribed status.

Nurture-Nature Debate: in the context of this chapter, the ongoing debate whether intelligence is the result of social and physical environment or genetic inheritance. In broader terms, the debate is whether human nature is the result of environment or heredity.

Professionalization: the process by which various occupational groups attempt to emulate the medical and legal professions and control entry into their occupation through setting educational credentials and standards.

Selection Function: this concept simply refers to the fact that however educational systems are organized, one of their principal functions in capitalist society is to allocate people to various positions in the society and to do so largely on the basis of their having acquired or failed to acquire educational credentials and the associated status training.

Sponsored Mobility: a concept most closely associated with Ralph Turner, who argued that British (and, for a time, Canadian) patterns of upward social mobility, if they were to be successful, involved the kind of sponsorship required to get into an exclusive country club (the opposite of contest mobility).

Technical-Functional Model: until the 1970s, the prevailing view that educational systems expand in response to the functional and technical demands of industrial society and that economic development was best met through producing human capital rather than technology.

▎ CHAPTER 13

Behavioral Assimilation: the extent to which various ethnic groups have taken on the values, norms and lifestyle of the dominant culture and ethnic group and in the process given up much of their ethnic identity.

Charter Groups: a concept introduced by John Porter who argued that as the first Europeans to settle North America, the English and French had considerable power in deciding who else should come to Canada and where they should fit in the social structure.

Entrance Status: a concept introduced by John Porter who argued that French and English, because of their dominance in Canada, were able to assign later immigrants to a lower and more specialized status in Canadian society.

Ethnic Group: groups that claim common origins, view themselves as distinct in terms of culture and language and that, in particular societies, view themselves as different and apart from other groups, especially the dominant or host groups.

Ethnicization: the process whereby various groups construct or reconstruct an ethnic identity. Such an identity will be called into being when ethnicity can be used as a resource to maintain or enhance the group's position in society or for individuals to establish a role and identity.

Ethnic Stratification: the ordering of ethnic groups into a relatively stable hierarchy of social inequality. Such ordering is likely to be based on the economic, occupational, educational and political achievements of the particular ethnic group relative to other ethnic groups.

Institutional Completeness: the extent to which an ethnic group can perform all of the services required by its members.

Minority Group: this concept refers to groups within a society that are singled out for differential and unequal treatment. Such groups may or may not comprise a minority of the population as in the case of women in Canadian society or Quebecois prior to the Silent Revolution.

Multiculturalism: the policy in Canada whereby ethnic groups are encouraged to maintain their separate identity but to participate fully in Canadian society. This policy, then, attempts to promote structural assimilation without behavioral assimilation.

Racial Thinking: the assumption that, as a result of their "race," people possess particular levels of intelligence, talent and kinds of personality. While the concept of race has not disappeared from our vocabulary, it is a concept with no scientific meaning or validity and racial thinking is best viewed as the attempt of some groups to legitimate the oppression of other groups.

Situational Ethnicity: a concept introduced by anthropologist Fredrik Barth who argues that ethnic background may be used in interaction in a number of ways and that it is best viewed as a symbolic prop to present ourselves rather than a fixed and objective attribute of individuals or groups.

Stereotyping: generalizing to all of a group characteristics or behaviour observed after having interacted with one or more members of the group.

Structural Assimilation: the extent to which various ethnic groups are proportionally represented in the various occupational and elite categories in society.

▌ CHAPTER 14

Associational Ties: the situation in which the major ties between members of the collectivity, the potential protest group or social movement, are based on secondary relationships such as those provided by occupation, religious or economic concerns.

Charismatic Leadership: a term used by Max Weber to describe a type of leader whose right to lead derives not from traditional or legal authority but from personal characteristics, from his or her "charisma."

Collective Action: the process whereby individuals and groups come together as a larger collective to protest some objective or perceived injustice or to seek some political or economic end.

Communal Ties: the situation in which the major ties between members of the collectivity, the potential protest group or social movement, are based in traditional ties of kinship and ethnicity.

Mobilization: the process by which discontent of groups is transformed into social or collective action in the form of interest groups, pressure groups or social and revolutionary movements.

Organizational Base: the social links or ties within a collectivity that hold it together and which have impact on the likelihood of collective action.

Segmentation: the extent to which potential protest groups or collectivities are set apart from the mainstream society and are, themselves, internally divided into factions. Both will have implications for how readily such groups enter into collective action.

Reactionary Movements: social movements that seek to stop the changes they think are happening in the society. In other words, they want change *within* the system or change *of* the system often to a past way of life which may or may not have ever existed.

Reform Movements: social movements that seek change of some specific aspects of the social order. In other words, they want change *within* but not *of* the system.

Relative Deprivation: the perceived gap between what people receive and what they feel they should receive as they compare themselves with some reference group.

Revolutionary Movements: social movements that seek wholesale and immediate change in the social order. In other words, they want change *of* the system as compared to change *within* the system.

NAME INDEX

SUBJECT INDEX

STUDENT REPLY CARD

In order to improve future editions, we are seeking your comments on *Sociology for Canadians: Images of Society*, Second Edition, by Himelfarb/Richardson.

After you have read this text, please answer the following questions and return this form via Business Reply Mail. *Thanks in advance for your feedback!*

1. Name of your college or university: _____

2. Major program of study: _____

3. Your instructor for this course: _____

4. Are there any sections of this text which were not assigned as course reading? _____
   If so, please specify those chapters or portions:

5. How would you rate the overall accessibility of the content? Please feel free to
   comment on reading level, writing style, terminology, layout and design features,
   and such learning aids as chapter objectives, summaries, and appendices.

— — — — — — — — — — — — *FOLD HERE* — — — — — — — — — — — — —

6. What did you like *best* about this book?

7. What did you like *least?*

If you would like to say more, we'd love to hear from you. Please write to us at the
address shown on the reverse of this card.